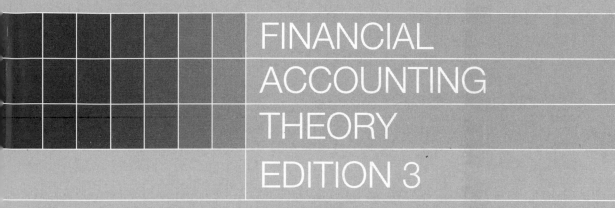

FINANCIAL
ACCOUNTING
THEORY
EDITION 3

To my daughter Cassie for all her love and support

FINANCIAL ACCOUNTING THEORY

CRAIG DEEGAN

EDITION 3
www.mhhe.com/au/deegantheory3e

The **McGraw·Hill** Companies

Boston   Burr Ridge, IL   Dubuque, IA   Madison, WI   New York
San Francisco   St. Louis   Bangkok   Bogotá   Caracas   Kuala Lumpur
Lisbon   London   Madrid   Mexico City   Milan   Montreal   New Delhi
Santiago   Seoul   Singapore   Sydney   Taipei   Toronto

National Library of Australia Cataloguing-in-Publication Data
Deegan, Craig Michael.
Financial accounting theory / Craig Deegan.

3rd ed.
Includes index.
ISBN 978 0 070 27726 7 (pbk.)

Target Audience: For tertiary students.
Accounting.
Accounting—Study and teaching.

657.48

Published in Australia by
McGraw-Hill Australia Pty Ltd
Level 2, 82 Waterloo Road, North Ryde NSW 2113
Publisher: Paula Harris
Production Editor: Emma Mullenger
Copy Editor: Felicity McKenzie
Proofreader: Terry Townsend
Indexer: Mary Coe, Potomac Indexing
Cover and internal design: Peta Nugent
Art Director: Astred Hicks
Typeset in India by diacriTech
Printed in China on 70 gsm matt art by iBOOK printing Ltd

BRIEF CONTENTS

CONTENTS

CHAPTER 1

▪▪▪▪▪▪▪▪▪▪▪▪▪▪

INTRODUCTION TO FINANCIAL ACCOUNTING THEORY

CHAPTER 2

▪▪▪▪▪▪▪▪▪▪▪▪▪▪

THE FINANCIAL REPORTING ENVIRONMENT

CHAPTER 3

▪▪▪▪▪▪▪▪▪▪▪▪▪▪

THE REGULATION OF FINANCIAL ACCOUNTING

CHAPTER 4

INTERNATIONAL ACCOUNTING 104

CHAPTER 5

NORMATIVE THEORIES OF ACCOUNTING—THE CASE OF ACCOUNTING FOR CHANGING PRICES 162

CHAPTER 6

NORMATIVE THEORIES OF ACCOUNTING—THE CASE OF CONCEPTUAL FRAMEWORK PROJECTS 208

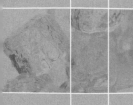

CHAPTER 7

CHAPTER 8

CHAPTER 9

CHAPTER 10

REACTIONS OF CAPITAL MARKETS TO FINANCIAL REPORTING 458

CHAPTER 11

REACTIONS OF INDIVIDUALS TO FINANCIAL REPORTING: AN EXAMINATION OF BEHAVIOURAL RESEARCH 500

CHAPTER 12

CRITICAL PERSPECTIVES OF ACCOUNTING 526

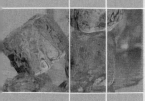

ABOUT THE AUTHOR

CRAIG DEEGAN, BCom (University of NSW), MCom (Hons) (University of NSW), PhD (University of Queensland), FCA, is Professor of Accounting in the School of Accounting & Law at RMIT University in Melbourne. Craig has taught at both undergraduate and postgraduate level in Australia for more than two decades and has presented lectures internationally, including in the United States, France, England, Wales, Scotland, New Zealand, Malaysia, Singapore, South Africa, South Korea, Hong Kong and China.

Prior to working in the university sector, Craig worked as a chartered accountant. His research has tended to focus on various social and environmental accountability and financial accounting issues and has been published in a number of leading international accounting journals, including *Accounting, Organizations and Society*, *Accounting and Business Research*, *Accounting, Accountability and Auditing Journal*, *Accounting and Finance*, *British Accounting Review* and the *International Journal of Accounting*. Craig's primary teaching interests are in the area of financial accounting, financial accounting theory, and research methods. He has successfully supervised more than ten PhD students to completion who have subsequently taken academic positions in Australia and overseas and he continues to supervise many research students. He also serves on the editorial boards of several international accounting journals.

Craig regularly provides consulting services to corporations, government and industry bodies on issues pertaining to financial accounting and corporate social and environmental accountability. He also works closely with the Australian accounting profession and has authored a number of research papers and monographs issued by the profession, as well as being a former chairperson of the Triple Bottom Line Issues Group of the Institute of Chartered Accountants in Australia and board member of the National Institute of Accountants. He has been the recipient of various teaching and research awards, including teaching prizes sponsored by KPMG and the Institute of Chartered Accountants in Australia. In July 1998 he was the recipient of the Peter Brownell Manuscript Award, an annual research award presented by the Accounting and Finance Association of Australia and New Zealand. In 1998 he was also awarded the University of Southern Queensland Individual Award for Research Excellence.

Craig is also the author of the leading financial accounting textbook *Australian Financial Accounting*, now in its sixth edition, and (with Grant Samkin) its adaptation *New Zealand Financial Accounting* (now in its fourth edition). *Financial Accounting Theory* is widely used throughout Australia as well as a number of other countries. With the assistance of Jeffrey Unerman, it has also been adapted for the European market.

PREFACE

This book has been written to provide readers with a balanced discussion of different theories of financial accounting. Various theories for and against regulation of financial accounting are critically discussed and various theoretical perspectives, including those provided by Positive Accounting Theory, Political Economy Theory, Stakeholder Theory, Institutional Theory and Legitimacy Theory, are introduced to explain different types of voluntary reporting decisions. The book also describes and evaluates the development of various normative theories of accounting, including various approaches developed to account for changing prices, different normative perspectives about the accountability of business entities, as well as various conceptual framework projects. It also emphasises the role of a number of factors in explaining both international differences in accounting and recent efforts towards the globalisation of international financial reporting standards.

Apart from providing explanations for why or how organisations should disclose particular items of financial information, the book investigates research that explores how or whether people at an aggregate and individual level demand or react to particular disclosures. Reflecting the growing relevance of social and environmental reporting issues to students, government, industry and the accounting profession, social and environmental reporting issues are discussed in depth. The book also provides an insight into the role of financial accounting from the perspective of a group of researchers who are often described as working from a 'critical' perspective.

Divided into twelve chapters sequenced in a logical order, this book provides the basis for subjects or units that investigate financial accounting theory. Alternatively, the book can be used as a key text for more general courses that include coverage of aspects of financial accounting theory. The entire book could realistically be used in the average eleven- to thirteen-week university term, with chapters being studied in the sequence in which they are presented. Because it presents a balanced perspective on alternative and sometimes conflicting theories of financial accounting, it also provides a sound basis for readers contemplating further research in different areas of financial accounting.

In writing this book, a style has been adopted that enables students at both the undergraduate and the postgraduate level to gain a sound understanding of financial accounting theory. As each chapter incorporates research from around the world, the book is of relevance to financial accounting theory students internationally. To assist in the learning process, each chapter provides learning objectives, chapter summaries and end-of-chapter discussion questions. Throughout the book readers are encouraged to critically evaluate and challenge the various views presented. To give the different perspectives a 'real world' feel, many chapters use recent articles from newspapers, directly related to the issues under consideration.

In the nine years since the first edition of this book was published, it has proved very popular with students and lecturers in Australia and internationally. This new edition retains and builds on the features of the first and second editions that students and lecturers found so appealing and distinctive, such as the use of straightforward explanations, the assessable nature of the language, frequent practical examples, and illustrations using newspaper articles. I have taken the opportunity of updating the text to reflect the sometimes significant developments in accounting theory over the past nine years.

I hope readers continue to find this book interesting, informative and enjoyable to read and I welcome constructive feedback.

Craig Deegan
RMIT University

ACKNOWLEDGMENTS

Many people helped me write this book. I would like to thank all those who generously provided some very useful ideas in the early stages of developing the first edition, including Professor Rob Gray from the University of St Andrews in Scotland, Professor David Owen from the University of Nottingham in England, Professor Reg Mathews who is now Adjunct Professor at RMIT University, Professor Julie Cotter and Mark Vallely from the University of Southern Queensland, and Michaela Rankin from Monash University.

In relation to this edition, I would first like to thank Jeffrey Unerman from the University of London. Jeffrey was my co-author for the European edition of *Financial Accounting Theory*, which was released in London in 2006. Some of the material provided by Jeffrey has been used in writing this third Australian edition. I also thank Professor David Owen for his helpful comments. Appreciation is also extended to the staff at McGraw Hill Australia for providing great support throughout the various writing and publication phases.

I would also like to join McGraw-Hill in thanking the following people, who very kindly provided feedback on various chapters, including Stacey Cowan at Central Queensland University; Xu Dong Ji at La Trobe University; Ron Day at Macquarie University; Dianne English at Griffith University; Don Geyer at Charles Sturt University; Jinghui Liu at Adelaide University; Anja Morton at Central Queensland University; Colleen Puttee at University of Western Sydney; Kay Plummer at Charles Sturt University; Bernadette Smith at University of Tasmania; Carol Tilt at University of South Australia; Peter Tedfor, formerly at University of Southern Queensland; Mark Wilson at Australian National University and Michael White at the University of the South Pacific.

My thanks also go to a number of colleagues at RMIT for providing great friendship and encouragement for my various projects. I would also like to thank my various PhD students for the insights and challenges they have given me at various times. Thanks also to Mary Exton for her support, and lastly, but certainly not leastly, appreciation goes to my daughter and best friend, Cassie.

SOLUTIONS MANUAL AND POWERPOINTS

Craig Deegan BCom, MCom, PhD, FCA

The solutions manual and PowerPoints accompanying this edition have been prepared by the author, Craig Deegan.

TEST BANK

Parmod Chand BA, MA, PhD

A new test bank has been prepared by Parmod Chand of Macquarie University.

Parmod Chand has substantial experience in teaching financial accounting courses, at both undergraduate and postgraduate levels. Dr Chand's research on accounting convergence is prominent both nationally and internationally. His most significant contributions to the field of international accounting research have been his publications in leading international accounting journals on issues relating to convergence of accounting standards. In addition, he has a number of publications on issues confronting accountants.

Dr Chand also has substantial experience in serving professional accounting institutes. He is currently serving as Senior Lecturer in the Department of Accounting and Finance at Macquarie University.

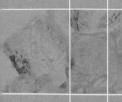

HIGHLIGHTS IN THIS EDITION

OVERALL

Various theories for and against the regulation of financial accounting are critically discussed, including different types of voluntary reporting decisions. The development of various normative theories of accounting is evaluated. The role of a number of factors in explaining the differences in international accounting and recent efforts towards the globalization of international financial reporting standards are discussed. The growing relevance of social and environmental reporting issues is discussed in depth in various chapters. The end-of-chapter questions have been increased and strengthened with additional questions.

CHAPTER 1: INTRODUCTION TO FINANCIAL ACCOUNTING THEORY

- *Why it is important for accounting students to study accounting theory.*
- *Can we prove a theory?*
- *A brief overview of theories of accounting.*
- *Evaluating theories* – considerations of logic and evidence.

CHAPTER 2: THE FINANCIAL REPORTING ENVIRONMENT

- *An overview of the development and regulation of accounting practice.*
- Minor changes and updating to allow for recent changes in the profession and legislation.

CHAPTER 3: THE REGULATION OF FINANCIAL ACCOUNTING

- An overview of the 'free-market' perspective, including discussion about market-related incentives.
- New section, *What is regulation?*
- Additional material on the desirable effects of regulation and the effects of excessive regulation.
- *Capture theory*: expanded section.
- *Pro-regulation perspective*.

- *Economic and social impacts of accounting regulation:* discussion on impact of AASB2 – Share-based Payment and AASB 138 – Intangibles.
- *Lobbying and the economic interest group theory of regulation.*
- *Accounting regulation as an output of a political process.*

CHAPTER 4: INTERNATIONAL ACCOUNTING

- This chapter has been extensively revised.
  - *Evidence of international differences in accounting prior to recent standardisation initiatives –* updated section.
  - New section discussing the pros and cons of countries using different accounting methods.
  - *Brief overview of IASB and its globalisation activities*: new section.
  - New section, *The United States role in the international standardisation of financial accounting.*
  - New discussion, *Does the internationalisation of accounting standards necessarily lead to the international standardisation of accounting practice?*
  - *Reasons for harmonisation and standardisation.*
  - *Obstacles to harmonisation and standardisation of accounting*: additional discussion.

CHAPTER 5: NORMATIVE THEORIES OF ACCOUNTING – THE CASE OF ACCOUNTING FOR CHANGING PRICES

- Minor updates.
  - Discussion of cost accounting from both historical and contemporary perspectives.
  - Explanation of various theories of accounting for changing prices.

CHAPTER 6: NORMATIVE THEORIES OF ACCOUNTING – THE CASE OF CONCEPTUAL FRAMEWORK PROJECTS

- Enhanced discussion throughout on the pros and cons of the IASB Framework versus the former Australian conceptual framework.

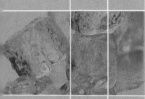

CHAPTER 7: POSITIVE ACCOUNTING THEORY

- Additional discussion and research on:
  - *Positive Account Theory defined*: origins and development discussed
  - agency theory
  - efficiency or opportunistic perspectives, with new media extract
  - accounting-based bonus schemes
  - R&D spending in relation to market-based bonus schemes
  - impact of IAS 38/AASB 138: intangibles
  - senior executive incentives and shareholder interests
  - equity based incentives/propensity to disclose information
  - incoming CEOs 'taking a bath' in relation to expenses
  - political costs
  - criticisms of PAT on perceived lack of development.
- *Debt contracting*: updated discussion.

CHAPTER 8: UNREGORATE CORPORATE REPORTING DECISIONS: CONSIDERATION OF SYSTEMS-ORIENTED THEORIES

- *Institutional Theory:* major section.
- Substantial research and discussion:
  - legitimacy, legitimacy gaps and the legitimating process with examples from the business world
  - disclosures of company annual reports on social and environmental issues
  - managerial attitudes towards the role of corporate reporting in legitimation strategies
  - overlapping areas of stakeholder theory and legitimacy theory.
- Media extracts illustrating:
  - negative impact on companies who fail to fulfil social obligations
  - relationships between media, corporate legitimacy and corporate disclosure policies
  - differing expectations of various stakeholder groups
  - social contracts.

CHAPTER 9: EXTENDED SYSTEMS OF ACCOUNTING – THE INCORPORATION OF SOCIAL AND ENVIRONMENTAL FACTORS WITHIN EXTERNAL REPORTING

- Expanded discussion reflecting the growing acceptance of corporate social responsibility reporting, incorporating new industry examples, media extracts and significant new research.

- Significant sections include:
  - developing notions of sustainability
  - objectives of the social and environmental reporting process – the *why* stage
  - identifying stakeholders – the *who* stage
  - identifying stakeholder information needs and expectations – the *what do we report* stage
  - theoretical perspectives on some social and environmental procedures – the *how* stage
  - the role for the Global Reporting Initiative (GRI) in reporting procedures for sustainability
  - accounting for externalities
  - social auditing.

CHAPTER 10: REACTIONS OF CAPITAL MARKETS TO FINANCIAL REPORTING

- *Relaxing assumptions about market efficiency*: discussion of new research.
- New media extracts and commentary illustrating recent events within capital markets.

CHAPTER 11: REACTIONS OF INDIVIDUALS TO FINANCIAL REPORTING: AN EXAMINATION OF BEHAVIOURAL RESEARCH

- Expanded information on the definition of, and schools of, behavioural research as it applies to accounting theory.
- Discussion of the Brunswik Lens model.
- *The relevance of differences in culture*: expanded section.

CHAPTER 12: CRITICAL PERSPECTIVES OF ACCOUNTING

Major sections include:
- *Critical perspective defined.*
- *Critical accounting research versus social and environmental accounting research.*
- *Possible impact of critical accounting research on social practice.*
- *Role of the state versus role of accounting in supporting existing social structures.*
- The subjectivity of accounting reports.
- Literary and legitimacy theory research.

LEARNING OBJECTIVES

Each chapter starts with a list of learning objectives that flag what you should know when you have worked through the chapter. Checking through them to confirm your knowledge is an excellent way of preparing for exams. For example, do you understand the key factors which are leading to greater international harmonisation of accounting? See Chapter 1, page 2.

OPENING ISSUES

At the beginning of each chapter, a number of issues or questions are raised that relate to the material covered. You should be able to answer these on completing the chapter. You might like to try providing an answer to the opening issues before reading the chapters, and then revisiting the *Opening Issue* to see whether you might change your opinions as a result of being exposed to particular points of view covered in the chapter. See Chapter 2, page 33.

INTRODUCTION

An *Introduction* to each chapter highlights the material to be covered and shows how it builds on topics introduced in previous chapters. See Chapter 3, page 58.

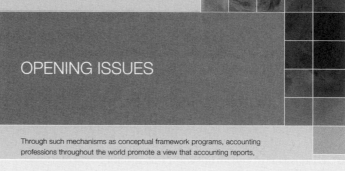

LEARNING OBJECTIVES

On completing this chapter readers should:

- understand that there are many theories of financial accounting;
- understand how knowledge of different accounting theories increases our ability to understand and evaluate various alternative financial accounting practices;
- understand that the different theories of financial accounting are often developed to perform different functions, such as to *describe* accounting practice, or to *prescribe* particular accounting practices;
- understand that theories, including theories of accounting, are

OPENING ISSUES

Through such mechanisms as conceptual framework programs, accounting professions throughout the world promote a view that accounting reports,

INTRODUCTION

Chapter 2 briefly considered a number of theories to explain the existence of accounting regulation. This chapter extends that discussion. While financial accounting is quite heavily regulated in many countries, with the level of regulation generally increasing in the aftermath of the high-profile accounting failures at Enron, Worldcom, HIH Insurance, Parmalat and other

Accounting Headline 4.4 A European company departs from an IASB standard

New York Times, 7 March 2008, p. C1

Loophole lets bank rewrite the calendar

FLOYD NORRIS

It is not often that a major international bank admits it is violating well-established international organization with the power to enforce them and assure that companies are in compliance. 'It is inappropriate,' said Anthony T. Cope, a retired member of both the I.A.S.B. and its American

ACCOUNTING HEADLINES

Media extracts highlight the relevance of the chapter content to the business world and often present thought-provoking or opposing viewpoints. Most are recent, but some older ones are included to illustrate defining moments. See the many *Accounting Headlines* in Chapter 4, from page 131 onwards.

FROM THIS BOOK

Exhibit 9.2 Environmental Financial Statement as shown in the *2007 Environmental, Health and Safety Performance Report* of Baxter International

Baxter 2007 Environmental Financial Statement
Estimated Environmental Costs, Income, and Savings and Cost Avoidance Worldwide (dollars in millions)[1]

Environmental Costs	2007	2006	2005
Basic Program			
Corporate Environmental—General and Shared Business Unit Costs[2]	1.6	1.4	1.5
Auditors' and Attorneys' Fees	0.4	0.4	0.4
Energy Professionals and Energy Reduction Programs	1.0	1.0	1.0
Corporate Environmental—Information Technology	0.3	0.3	0.3

CHAPTER SUMMARY

This chapter considered various arguments that either supported or opposed the regulation of financial accounting. Advocates of the 'free-market' (anti-regulation) approach argue that there are private economic incentives for organisations to produce accounting information voluntarily, and imposing accounting regulation leads to costly inefficiencies. To support their argument for a reduction in financial accounting regulation, the 'free-market' advocates rely on such

REFERENCES

Bebbington, J., R. Gray & R. Laughlin (2001), *Financial Accounting: Practice and Principles*, London: International Thomson Business Press.

FASB (1976), *Scope and Implications of the Conceptual Framework Project*, Financial Accounting Standards Board.

Feyerabend, P. (1975), *Against Method:*

QUESTIONS

1.1 What is the difference between a positive theory of accounting and a normative theory of accounting?

1.2 If you developed a theory to explain how a person's cultural background influences how they prepare financial statements, would you have developed a positive theory or a normative theory?

1.3 What is a conceptual framework, and would it be considered to be a positive or a normative theory of accounting?

26 • FINANCIAL ACCOUNTING THEORY

1   For example, some researchers operating within the Positive Accounting Theory paradigm (for example, Ness & Mirza, 1991) argue that the voluntary disclosure of social responsibility information can be explained as a strategy to reduce political costs. Social responsibility reporting has also been explained from a Legitimacy Theory perspective (for example, Deegan, Rankin & Tobin, 2002), and from a Stakeholder Theory perspective (for example, Swift, 2001).

320 • FINANCIAL ACCOUNTING THEORY

EXHIBITS

Exhibits generally contain extracts from company documents, annual reports or websites to help show the relevance of the theory to business life. See Chapter 9, page 431.

SUMMARY

Each chapter concludes with a summary of the key topics and viewpoints that have been covered.

REFERENCES

Each chapter is extensively referenced, allowing students wishing to undertake further studies to explore topics in greater depth.

QUESTIONS

A variety of thought-provoking questions are provided at the conclusion of each chapter.

FOOTNOTES

Extensive footnotes add insights and information, as well as linking to additional coverage of topics elsewhere in the text. See footnotes in Chapter 8, commencing page 320

E-STUDENT

PowerPoint® slides

PowerPoint® slides, prepared by Craig Deegan, summarise the key points of each chapter. They can be downloaded as a valuable revision aid and printed either in colour or black and white.

Have your say!

The online learning centre also provides email links to our webmaster and editorial department. We would welcome your feedback on any aspect of the text or on the supplementary material.

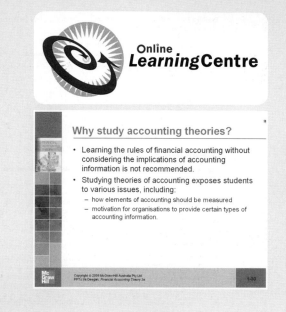

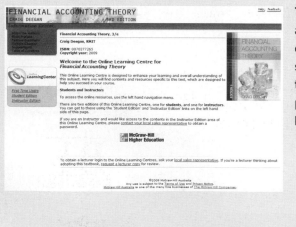

The Online Learning Centre which accompanies this text, is an integrated online product designed to assist students and lecturers alike in getting the most from their subject. This text provides a powerful learning experience beyond the printed page.

E-INSTRUCTOR

Solutions manual
Prepared by the author, the Solutions manual features comprehensive answers and discussion points to the end-of-chapter questions.

PowerPoint® slides
PowerPoints® prepared by Craig Deegan, summarise the key points of each chapter. They can be downloaded and adapted to suit individual lecturer's requirements, or distributed to students as lecture notes. PowerPoints® are also provided on the student website.

Test bank
Written by Parmod Chand the comprehensive test bank contains approximately 50 multiple-choice questions and true/false questions for each chapter. It is formatted for delivery in WebCT or Blackboard formats.

Course Management System (CMS)
Course Management Systems allow you to deliver and manage your course via the internet. McGraw-Hill can provide online material to accompany this text, formatted for your chosen CMS. See your McGraw-Hill representative for details.

Contact the author
Craig Deegan welcomes your feedback and comments on the text. An email link is provided for instructors.

INTRODUCTION TO FINANCIAL ACCOUNTING THEORY

LEARNING OBJECTIVES

On completing this chapter readers should:

- understand that there are many theories of financial accounting;
- understand how knowledge of different accounting theories increases our ability to understand and evaluate various alternative financial accounting practices;
- understand that the different theories of financial accounting are often developed to perform different functions, such as to *describe* accounting practice, or to *prescribe* particular accounting practices;
- understand that theories, including theories of accounting, are developed as a result of applying various value judgements and that acceptance of one theory in preference to others will in part be tied to one's own value judgements;
- be aware that we should critically evaluate theories (in terms of such things as the underlying logic, assumptions made and evidence produced) before accepting them;
- understand why students of accounting should study accounting theories as part of their broader accounting education.

OPENING ISSUES

At the beginning of each chapter a number of issues or problems are raised that relate to the material covered. On completion of the chapter you should be able to supply answers to the problems. In this introductory chapter, some of the issues that are considered are as follows:

1. Why do students of financial accounting need to bother with the study of 'theories'? Why not just study some more of the numerous accounting standards (and there are certainly plenty of them!) or other pronouncements of the accounting profession?

2. Why would (or perhaps 'should') accounting practitioners and accounting regulators consider various theories of accounting?

3. Do all 'theories of accounting' seek to fulfil the same role, and, if there are alternative theories to explain or guide particular practice, how does somebody select one theory in preference to another?

No specific answers are provided for each chapter's opening issues. Rather, as a result of reading the respective chapters, readers should be able to provide their own answers to the particular issues. You might like to consider providing an answer to the opening issues before reading the material provided in the chapters, and then, on completing the chapter, revisit the opening issues and see whether your opinions have changed as a result of being exposed to particular points of view.

WHAT IS A THEORY?

In this book we consider various theories of financial accounting. Perhaps, therefore, we should start by considering what we mean by a 'theory'. There are various perspectives of what constitutes a theory. The *Oxford English Dictionary* provides various definitions, including:

> A scheme or system of ideas or statements held as an explanation or account of a group of facts or phenomena.

The *Macquarie Dictionary* provides the following definition of a theory:

> A coherent group of general propositions used as principles of explanation for a class of phenomena.

The accounting researcher Hendriksen (1970, p. 1) defines a theory as:

> A coherent set of hypothetical, conceptual and pragmatic principles forming the general framework of reference for a field of inquiry.

The definition provided by Hendriksen is very similar to the US Financial Accounting Standards Board's definition of its Conceptual Framework Project (which in itself is deemed to be a *normative* theory of accounting), which is defined as 'a coherent system of interrelated objectives and fundamentals that can lead to consistent standards' (FASB, 1976). The use of the word 'coherent' in three of the above four definitions of theory is interesting and reflects a view that the components of a theory (perhaps including assumptions about human behaviour) should logically combine together to provide an explanation or guidance in respect of certain phenomena. The definitions are consistent with a perspective that theories are not *ad hoc* in nature and should be based on logical (systematic and coherent) reasoning. Therefore, when we talk about a 'theory' we are talking about much more than simply an idea or a 'hunch', which we acknowledge is different from how the term 'theory' is used in some contexts (for instance, we often hear people say they have a 'theory' about why something might have occurred when they really mean they have a 'hunch'). As will be seen in this book, some accounting theories are developed on the basis of past observations (empirically based) of which some are further developed to make predictions about likely occurrences (and sometimes also to provide explanations of why the events occur). That is, particular theories may be generated and subsequently supported by undertaking numerous observations of the actual phenomena in question. Such empirically based theories are said to be based on inductive reasoning and are often labelled 'scientific', as, like many theories in the 'sciences', they are based on observation. Alternatively, other accounting theories that we also consider do not seek to provide explanations or predictions of particular phenomena but, rather, *prescribe* what *should* be done (as opposed to describing or predicting what is done) in particular circumstances. Llewelyn (2003) points out that the term 'theory' in accounting not only applies to 'grand theories' that seek to tell us about broad generalisable issues (like the theory of gravity in physics) but also applies to any framework that helps us make sense of aspects of the (social) world in which we live, and that helps provide a structure to understand our (social) experiences. We stress that different theories of accounting often have different objectives. Llewelyn provides some interesting views about what constitutes theory. She states (2003, p. 665) that:

> Theories impose cohesion and stability (Czarniawska, 1997, p. 71). So that whenever 'life' is ambiguous (which is most of the time!) people will work at confronting this ambiguity through 'theorizing'. Also, because 'life' and situations commonly have multiple meanings and give rise to different assessments of significance, everyone has a need for 'theory' to go about their everyday affairs. 'Theories' do not just reside in libraries, waiting for academics to 'dust them down'; they are used whenever people address ambiguity, contradiction or paradox so that they can decide what to do (and think) next. Theories generate expectations about the world.

Because accounting is a human activity (you cannot have 'accounting' without accountants), theories of financial accounting (and there are many) will consider such things as people's behaviour and/or people's needs as regards financial accounting information, or the reasons why people within organisations might elect to supply particular information to particular stakeholder groups. For example, this book considers, among others, theories that:

- *prescribe* how, based on a particular perspective of the role of accounting, assets should be valued for external reporting purposes (such prescriptive or normative theories are considered in Chapters 5 and 6);
- *predict* that managers paid bonuses on the basis of measures such as profits will seek to adopt those accounting methods that lead to an increase in reported profits (such descriptive or positive theories are considered in Chapter 7);
- seek to *explain* how an individual's cultural background will impact on the types of accounting information that the individual seeks to provide to people outside the organisation (such a theory is considered in Chapter 4);
- *prescribe* the accounting information that should be provided to particular classes of stakeholders on the basis of their perceived information needs (such theories are often referred to as decision usefulness theories, and are discussed in Chapter 5);
- *predict* that the relative power of a particular stakeholder group (with 'power' often being defined in terms of the group's control over scarce resources) will determine whether that group receives the accounting information it desires (which derives from a branch of Stakeholder Theory, which is discussed in Chapter 8);
- predict that organisations seek to be perceived by the community as legitimate and that accounting information can be used by the organisation as a means of gaining, maintaining or regaining legitimacy (which derives from Legitimacy Theory, considered in Chapter 8).

WHY IT IS IMPORTANT FOR ACCOUNTING STUDENTS TO STUDY ACCOUNTING THEORY

As a student of financial accounting you will be required to learn how to construct and read financial statements prepared in conformity with various accounting standards and other professional and statutory requirements. In your working life (whether or not you choose to specialise in accounting) you could be involved in such activities as analysing financial statements for the purposes of making particular decisions, compiling financial statements for others to read, or generating accounting guidance or rules for others to follow. The better you understand the accounting practices underlying these various activities, the more effective you are likely to be in performing these activities—and therefore the better equipped you are likely to be to succeed in your chosen career.

Given that accounting theories aim to provide a coherent and systematic framework for investigating, understanding and/or developing various accounting practices, the evaluation of individual accounting practices is likely to be much more effective if the person evaluating these practices has a thorough grasp of accounting theory. Although all students of accounting (like students in any subject) should be interested in critically evaluating the phenomena they are studying, we recognise that, in the past, many students have been content with simply learning how to apply various accounting practices without questioning the basis of these practices.

However, in the wake of a growing number of high-profile accounting failures (such as Enron and WorldCom in the United States, and ABC Learning, Fincorp, HIH Insurance, One.Tel and Harris Scarf within Australia), it has arguably never been more important for accountants to understand thoroughly and be able to critique the accounting practices that they use. Without such a theoretically informed understanding, it is difficult to evaluate the suitability of current accounting practices, to develop improved accounting practices where current practices are unsuitable for changed business situations, and to defend the reputation of accounting where accounting practices are wrongly blamed for causing companies to fail. This is a key reason why it is important for you to study and understand accounting theories.

As a result of studying various theories of financial accounting in this book, you will be exposed to various issues, including:

- how the various elements of accounting should be measured;
- what motivates managers to provide certain types of accounting information;
- what motivates managers to select particular accounting methods in preference to others;
- what motivates individuals to support and perhaps lobby regulators for some accounting methods in preference to others;
- what the implications for particular types of organisations and their stakeholders are if one method of accounting is chosen or mandated in preference to other methods;
- how and why the capital markets react to particular accounting information;
- whether there is a 'true measure' of income.

Accounting plays a very important and pervasive role within society. Simply to learn the various rules of financial accounting (as embodied within accounting standards, conceptual frameworks and the like) without considering the implications that accounting information can have would seem illogical and, following the high-profile accounting failures at Enron and other organisations, potentially dangerous. Many significant decisions are made on the basis of information that accountants provide (or in some circumstances, elect not to provide), so accountants are often regarded as being very powerful and influential people. The information generated by accountants enables others to make important decisions. For example: Should they support the organisation? Is the organisation earning sufficient 'profits'? Is it earning excessive 'profits'? Is the organisation fulfilling its social responsibilities by investing in community support programs and environmentally responsible production technologies and, if so, how much?

In considering profits, is profitability a valid measure of organisational success? Further, if the accountant/accounting profession emphasises particular attributes of organisational performance (for example, profitability) does this in turn impact on what society perceives as being the legitimate goals of business?[1] As a result of considering various theories of financial accounting, this book provides some answers to these important issues.

At a broader level, an understanding of accounting theories can be crucial to the reputation and future of the accounting profession. Unerman and O'Dwyer (2004) have argued that the recent rise in high-profile accounting failures has raised the level of awareness among non-accountants of some of the significant impacts that accounting has on their lives. These events have also led to a substantial reduction in the level of trust that many non-accountants place in financial accounts and in accountants. If this trust is to be rebuilt, along with the reputation of accountants, it is now more crucial than ever that we develop the capacity to critically evaluate accounting practices and to refine these practices as the business environment rapidly changes. The insights from a varied range of accounting theories are essential to this process of continual improvement in financial accounting practices.

A BRIEF OVERVIEW OF THEORIES OF ACCOUNTING

There are many theories of financial accounting. That is, there is no universally accepted theory of financial accounting or, indeed, any universally agreed perspective of how accounting theories should be developed. In part this is because different researchers have different perspectives of the role of accounting theory and/or what the central objective, role and scope of financial accounting should be. For example, some researchers believe that the principal role of accounting theory should be to *explain* and *predict* particular accounting-related phenomena (for example, to explain why some accountants adopt one particular accounting method while others elect to adopt an alternative approach), whereas other researchers believe that the role of accounting theory is to *prescribe* (as opposed to *describe*) particular approaches to accounting (for example, based on a perspective of the role of accounting, there is a theory that prescribes that assets *should* be valued on the basis of market values rather than historical costs).

Early development of accounting theory relied on the process of induction, that is, the development of ideas or theories through observation. According to Chalmers (1982, p. 4), there are three general conditions that would ideally exist before theory could be developed through observation:

1. The number of observations forming the basis of a generalisation must be large.
2. The observations must be repeated under a wide variety of conditions.
3. No accepted observation should conflict with the derived universal law.

---

1   Chapters 2 and 3 consider some research (for example, Hines, 1988) that suggests that accountants and accounting do not necessarily provide an unbiased account of reality, but rather create reality. If the accounting profession emphasises a measure (such as profitability) as being a measure of success and legitimacy, then, in turn, profitable companies will be considered successful and legitimate. If something other than profitability had been supported as a valid measure, then this may not have been the case.

From approximately the 1920s to the 1960s, theories of accounting were predominantly developed on the basis of observation of what accountants actually did in practice. That is, they were developed by the process referred to as 'induction'. This can be contrasted with a process wherein theories are developed by deductive reasoning, which is based more on the use of logic rather than observation.[2]

Returning to the use of observation to develop generalisable theories (inductive reasoning), after observing what accountants did in practice, common practices were then codified in the form of doctrines or conventions of accounting (for example, the doctrine of conservatism). Notable theorists at this time included Paton (1922), Hatfield (1927), Paton and Littleton (1940) and Canning (1929). Henderson, Peirson and Harris (2004, p. 54) describe the approaches adopted by these theorists as follows:

> Careful observation of accounting practice revealed patterns of consistent behaviour. For example, it could be observed that accountants tended to be very prudent in measuring both revenues and expenses. Where judgement was necessary it was observed that accountants usually underestimated revenues and overstated expenses. The result was a conservative measure of profit. Similarly, it could be observed that accountants behaved as if the value of money, which was the unit of account, remained constant. These observations of accounting practice led to the formulation of a number of hypotheses such as 'that where judgement is needed, a conservative procedure is adopted' and 'that it is assumed that the value of money remains constant'. These hypotheses were confirmed by many observations of the behaviour of accountants.

While there was a general shift towards prescriptive research in the 1960s, some research of an inductive nature still occurs. Research based on the inductive approach (that is, research based on observing particular phenomena) has been subject to many criticisms. For example, Gray, Owen and Maunders (1987, p. 66) state:

> Studying extant practice is a study of 'what is' and, by definition, does not study 'what is not' or 'what should be'. It therefore concentrates on the status quo, is reactionary in attitude, and cannot provide a basis upon which current practice may be evaluated or from which future improvements may be deduced.

In generating theories of accounting based on what accountants actually do, it is assumed (often implicitly) that what is done by the majority of accountants is the most appropriate practice. In adopting such a perspective there is, in a sense, a perspective of *accounting Darwinism*—a view that accounting practice has evolved, and the fittest, or perhaps 'best', practices have survived. Prescriptions or advice are provided to others on the basis of what most accountants do, the 'logic' being that the majority of accountants must be doing the most appropriate thing. What do you think of the logic of such an argument?

---

2   Chapter 5 considers various theories of accounting that were developed to deal with problems that arise in times of rising prices—for example, when there is inflation. Such theories include one developed by a famous accounting researcher named Raymond Chambers. His theory of accounting, known as Continuously Contemporary Accounting, was developed on the basis of a number of logical assumptions about what types of information the readers of financial accounting reports needed. His theory was not based on observing what accountants do (which would be inductive reasoning); rather, his theory was based on what he thought they *should* do. Using various key assumptions about people's information needs, he derived his theory through deductive (logical) reasoning. His proposals for accounting represented radical departures from what accountants were actually doing in practice.

As a specific example of this inductive approach to theory development we can consider the work of Grady (1965). His research was commissioned by the American Institute of Certified Public Accountants (AICPA) and was undertaken at a time when there was a great deal of prescriptive (as opposed to descriptive) research being undertaken. Interestingly, in 1961 and 1962 the Accounting Research Division of the AICPA had already commissioned prescriptive studies by Moonitz (1961) and Sprouse and Moonitz (1962) which proposed that accounting measurement systems be changed from historical cost to a system based on current values. However, before the release of these research works, the AICPA released a statement saying that 'while these studies are a valuable contribution to accounting principles, they are too radically different from generally accepted principles for acceptance at this time' (Statement by the Accounting Principles Board, AICPA, April 1962).

History shows that rarely have regulatory bodies accepted suggestions (or, as some people call them, *prescriptions*) for significant changes to accounting practice. This is an interesting issue which is considered more fully in Chapter 6 when conceptual framework projects are discussed. However, it is useful to consider at this point a statement made in the United States by Miller and Reading (1986, p. 64):

> The mere discovery of a problem is not sufficient to assure that the FASB will undertake its solution … There must be a suitably high likelihood that the Board can resolve the issues in a manner that will be acceptable to the constituency—without some prior sense of the likelihood that the Board members will be able to reach a consensus, it is generally not advisable to undertake a formal project.

Grady's (1965) work formed the basis of APB Statement No. 4, 'Basic Concepts and Accounting Principles Underlying the Financial Statements of Business Enterprises'. In effect, APB Statement No. 4 simply reflected the generally accepted accounting principles of the time. That is, the research was inductive in nature (as it was based on observation) and did not seek to evaluate the logic or merit of the accounting practices being used. It was therefore not controversial and had a high probability of being acceptable to the AICPA's constituency (Miller & Reading, 1986).

While some accounting researchers continued to adopt an inductive approach, a different approach became popular in the 1960s and 1970s. This approach sought to *prescribe* particular accounting procedures, and as such was not driven by existing practices. The period of the 1960s and 1970s is commonly referred to as the 'normative period' of accounting research. That is, in this period the financial accounting theories were not developed by observing what accountants were doing; many of the theories being developed at this time were based on the development of arguments about what the researchers considered accountants *should* do. Rather than being developed on the basis of inductive reasoning, these theories were being developed on the basis of deductive reasoning. At this time there tended to be widespread inflation throughout various countries of the world and much of the research and the related theories sought to explain the limitations of historical cost accounting and to provide improved approaches (based on particular value judgements held by the researchers) for asset measurement in times of rapidly rising prices. However, while a number of highly respected researchers were arguing that measuring assets on the basis of historical cost was inappropriate and tended to provide misleading information, particularly in times of rising prices, there was a lack of agreement between the various researchers about what particular asset measurement basis should be used.

For example, some argued that assets should be valued at replacement costs, some argued that assets should be valued at net realisable value, and others argued for measurements based on present values. Throughout this debate there was no clear choice in terms of which approach was best, and, perhaps because it was difficult to resolve the differences in opinions provided by the various normative researchers, the historical cost approach to accounting continued to be used.

In the mid to late 1970s there were further changes in the focus of accounting research and theory development. At this time a great deal of accounting research had the major aim of *explaining* and *predicting* accounting practice, rather than *prescribing* particular approaches. This was another movement by many accounting researchers away from descriptive research—this time towards predictive research. Nevertheless, there are many researchers who still undertake descriptive research. What is being emphasised is that a variety of accounting theories have been developed across time; for example, some are descriptive in nature, some attempt to explain and predict particular aspects of financial accounting practice, and others generate guidance about what accountants should do. Different theories serve different purposes.

In reading accounting research you will see that much research is labelled either *positive research* or *normative research*. Research that seeks to predict and explain particular phenomena (as opposed to prescribing particular activity) is classified as positive research and the associated theories are referred to as *positive theories*. Henderson, Peirson and Harris (2004, p. 414) provide a useful description of positive theories. They state:

> A positive theory begins with some assumption(s) and, through logical deduction, enables some prediction(s) to be made about the way things will be. If the prediction is sufficiently accurate when tested against observations of reality, then the story is regarded as having provided an explanation of why things are as they are. For example, in climatology, a positive theory of rainfall may yield a prediction that, if certain conditions are met, then heavy rainfall will be observed. In economics, a positive theory of prices may yield a prediction that, if certain conditions are met, then rapidly rising prices will be observed. Similarly, a positive theory of accounting may yield a prediction that, if certain conditions are met, then particular accounting practices will be observed.

As noted above, positive theories can initially be developed through some form of deductive (logical) reasoning. Their success in explaining or predicting particular phenomena will then typically be assessed based on observation—that is, observing how the theory's predictions corresponded with the observed facts.[3] Empirically (observation) based theories can continue to be tested and perhaps refined through further observation, perhaps in different institutional or geographical settings, and a great deal of published research is undertaken to see if particular results can be replicated in different settings, thereby increasing the generalisability of the theory in question. Apart from providing the basis for predicting future actions or effects, positive accounting research often goes to the next step of attempting to provide explanations for the phenomena in question.

---

3   Again, it is stressed that not all theories will be assessed in terms of how the theory's predictions match actual behaviour. Normative theories, for example, might provide prescriptions about how accounting should be undertaken, and such prescriptions might represent significant departures from current practice. These theories, which may be developed through logical deduction, should not be evaluated by observing the theories' correspondence with current behaviours of accountants.

Chapter 7 considers a positive theory of accounting principally developed by Watts and Zimmerman (relying on the works of other researchers, such as Jensen and Meckling (1976) and Gordon (1964)). Their positive theory of accounting, which they called *Positive Accounting Theory*, seeks to predict and explain why managers (and/or accountants) elect to adopt particular accounting methods in preference to others.[4]

Chapter 7 demonstrates that the development of Positive Accounting Theory relied in great part on work undertaken in the field of economics, and central to the development of the theory was the acceptance of the economics-based 'rational economic person assumption'. That is, an assumption was made that accountants (and, in fact, all individuals) are primarily motivated by self-interest (tied to wealth maximisation), and that the particular accounting method selected (where alternatives are available) will be dependent on certain considerations, such as:

■ whether the person supporting the use of a particular accounting method, for example a manager or an accountant, is rewarded in terms of accounting-based bonus systems (for example, whether they receive a bonus tied to reported profits);

■ whether the organisation they work for is close to breaching negotiated accounting-based debt covenants (such as a debt-to-asset constraint);

■ whether the organisation that employs them is subject to political scrutiny from various external groups, such as government, employee groups or environmental groups (with that scrutiny being focused on the organisation's reported profits).

The assumption of self-interest, as embraced by researchers that use Positive Accounting Theory, challenges the view that accountants will predominantly be objective when determining which accounting methods should be used to record particular transactions and events (objectivity is a qualitative characteristic promoted within various conceptual frameworks of accounting, as will be seen in Chapter 6).[5]

Positive theories of accounting do not seek to tell us that what is being done in practice is the most efficient or equitable process. For example, while we have a (positive) theory of accounting, developed to predict which accounting methods most accountants will use in particular circumstances (Positive Accounting Theory), this theory will not tell us what we should do (it is not a 'prescriptive' theory), nor will it tell us anything about the efficiency of what is being done. As Watts and Zimmerman (1986, p. 7) state:

> It [Positive Accounting Theory] is concerned with explaining [accounting] practice. It is designed to explain and predict which firms will and which firms will not use a particular [accounting method] ... but it says nothing as to which method a firm should use.

---

4   It should be noted at this point that Positive Accounting Theory is one of several positive theories of accounting (other positive theories that relate to accounting include Legitimacy Theory, Institutional Theory and certain branches of Stakeholder Theory). This book uses lower case when referring to the general class of theories that attempt to explain and predict accounting practice (that is, 'positive theories of accounting') and refers to Watts and Zimmerman's positive theory of accounting as 'Positive Accounting Theory' (that is, it uses upper case).

5   As emphasised throughout this book, researchers make a choice between the theories they will apply in particular circumstances. In part, the choice of theory will be influenced by the researcher's own beliefs and values. For example, many accounting researchers will not use Positive Accounting Theory to explain particular phenomena because they reject the central assumption made within the theory that all individual action is best described on the basis that individuals are driven by self-interest. For example, Gray, Owen and Adams (1996, p. 75) reject Positive Accounting Theory because it portrays 'a morally bankrupt view of the world'. We will return to Gray, Owen and Adams' dismissal of this theory later in the chapter.

As will be seen shortly, the practice of electing not to advise others as to what should be done in particular circumstances has been the subject of criticism of positive accounting research.

While positive theories tend to be based on empirical observation, there are other theories that are based not on observation but on what the researcher believes *should* occur in particular circumstances. For example, Chapter 5 discusses a theory of accounting developed by Raymond Chambers. His theory of accounting, called *Continuously Contemporary Accounting*, describes how financial accounting *should* be undertaken. That is, his theory is prescriptive. Central to his theory is a view that the most useful information about an organisation's assets for the purposes of economic decision making is information about their 'current cash equivalents'—a measure tied to their current net market values. As such, it prescribes that assets should be valued on the basis of their net market values. Theories that prescribe (as opposed to describe) particular actions are called 'normative theories', as they are based on the norms (or values or beliefs) held by the researchers proposing the theories (they are also often referred to as 'prescriptive theories'). The dichotomy of positive and normative theories is one often used to categorise accounting theories and this dichotomy is adopted throughout this book.

As noted above, normative theories of accounting are not necessarily based on observation and therefore cannot (or should not) be evaluated on the basis of whether the theories reflect actual accounting practice. In fact they may suggest radical changes to current practice. For example, for a number of decades Chambers had been advocating the valuation of assets on a basis related to their net market values—a prescription that challenged the widespread use of historical cost accounting (it is interesting to note, however, that in recent years the use of market values for asset valuation has gained popularity with the International Accounting Standards Board). Other researchers concerned about the social and environmental implications of business (see, for example, Gray and Bebbington, 2001; Gray, Owen and Adams, 1996; Mathews, 1993) have developed theories that prescribe significant changes to traditional financial accounting practice (Chapters 9 and 10 of this book consider such theories). The conceptual framework of accounting that is discussed in Chapter 6 is an example of a normative theory of accounting. Relying on various assumptions about the types or attributes of information useful for decision making, the conceptual framework of accounting (within Australia, this is referred to as the *Framework for the Preparation and Presentation of Financial Statements*, which is based on the conceptual framework developed by the International Accounting Standards Board) provides guidance on how assets, liabilities, expenses, income and equity should be defined, when they should be recognised, and ultimately how they should be measured. As will be seen in later chapters, normative theories can be further subdivided. For example, some normative theories can be classified as 'true income theories' and other theories as 'decision usefulness theories'. The true income theories make certain assumptions about the role of accounting and then seek to provide a single 'best measure' of profits (for example, see Lee, 1974).[6]

Decision usefulness theories ascribe a particular type of information for particular classes of users on the basis of assumed decision-making needs. According to Bebbington, Gray and Laughlin (2001, p. 418), the decision usefulness approach can be considered to have two branches, the *decision-makers emphasis* and the *decision-models emphasis*. The decision-makers

---

6　Much of the work undertaken in developing 'true income theories' relies on the work of Hicks (1946). Hicks defined 'income' as the maximum amount that can be consumed by a person or an organisation in a particular period without depleting the wealth that existed for that person or organisation at the start of the period.

emphasis relies on undertaking research that seeks to ask the users of the information what information they want.[7] Once that is determined, this knowledge is used to prescribe what information should be supplied to the users of financial statements. Much of this research is questionnaire-based. This branch of research tends to be fairly disjointed, as different studies typically address different types of information, with limited linkages between them.

Another variant of the decision-makers emphasis, which is explored in Chapter 11, is security price research. Briefly, security price research works on the assumption that if the capital market responds to information (as evidenced through share price changes that occur around the time of the release of particular information) the information must be useful.[8] This forms the basis for subsequent prescriptions about the types of information that should be provided to users of financial statements. It also has been used to determine whether particular mandatory reporting requirements (such as the introduction of new accounting standards) were necessary or effective, the rationale being that, if a new accounting standard does not evoke a market reaction, it is questionable whether the new requirement is useful or necessary in providing information to the stock market or investors. Research that evaluates information on the basis of whether it evokes a market reaction, or whether stakeholders indicate that it is useful to them, ignores the possibility that there could be information that is 'better' than that provided or sought. There is also the broader philosophical issue of whether the information they 'want' is actually what they 'need'. These broader issues are explored throughout this book.

On the other hand, proponents of the decision-models emphasis develop models based on the researchers' perceptions of what is necessary for efficient decision making. Information prescriptions follow (for example that information should be provided about the market value of the reporting entity's assets). This branch of research typically assumes that classes of stakeholders have identical information needs. Unlike the decision-makers emphasis, the decision-models emphasis does not ask the decision makers what information they want; instead, it concentrates on the types of information considered useful for decision making. As Wolk and Tearney (1997, p. 39) indicate, a premise underlying this research is that decision makers may need to be taught how to use this information if they are unfamiliar with it.

EVALUATING THEORIES OF ACCOUNTING

In the process of studying accounting, students will typically be exposed to numerous theories of accounting, and the accompanying research and argument that attempts to either support or reject the particular theories in question. In undertaking this study, students should consider the merit of the argument and the research methods employed by respective researchers. What students often find interesting is that many researchers seem to adopt one theory of accounting and thereafter adopt various strategies (including overt condemnation of alternative theories) in

---

7   For example, in recent years a number of research studies have asked a number of different stakeholder groups what types of social and environmental performance information the stakeholders considered to be useful for their various decision-making processes.

8   Based on the Efficient Markets Hypothesis, which predicts that the stock market instantaneously reacts, through price adjustments (changes), to all relevant publicly available information.

an endeavour to support their own research and theoretical perspective. In some respects, the attitudes of some researchers are akin to those of the disciples of particular religions. (In fact, Chambers (1993) refers to advocates of Positive Accounting Theory as belonging to the 'PA Cult'.) Deegan (1997) provides a series of quotes from the works of various high-profile researchers who are opposed to Watts and Zimmerman's Positive Accounting Theory. In providing arguments against the contribution or validity of Positive Accounting Theory, the opponents used such terms and descriptions as:

- It is a dead philosophical movement (Christenson, 1983, p. 7).
- It has provided no accomplishments (Sterling, 1990, p. 97).
- It is marred by oversights, inconsistencies and paradoxes (Chambers, 1993, p. 1).
- It is imperiously dictatorial (Sterling, 1990, p. 121).
- It is empty and commonplace (Sterling, 1990, p. 130).
- It is akin to a cottage industry (Sterling, 1990, p. 132).
- It is responsible for turning back the clock of research 1000 years (Chambers, 1993, p. 22).
- It suffers from logical incoherence (Williams, 1989, p. 459).
- It is a wasted effort (Sterling, 1990, p. 132).

These criticisms indicate the degree of emotion that a particular theory has stimulated among its critics, particularly those accounting researchers who see the role of accounting theory as providing prescription rather than description. Students of financial accounting theory will find it interesting to ponder why some people are so angered by such a theory—after all, it is just a theory (isn't it?). Many proponents of Positive Accounting Theory have also tended to be very critical of normative theorists.

The Positive Accounting theorists and the normative theorists would be considered to be working from different 'paradigms'—paradigms that provided greatly different perspectives about the role of accounting research. According to Hussey and Hussey (1997, p. 47):

> The term paradigm refers to the progress of scientific practice based on people's philosophies and assumptions about the world and the nature of knowledge; in this context, about how research should be conducted. Paradigms are universally recognised scientific achievements that for a time provide model problems and solutions to a community of practitioners. They offer a framework comprising an accepted set of theories, methods and ways of defining data ... Your basic beliefs about the world will be reflected in the way you design your research, how you collect and analyse your data, and even the way in which you write your thesis.

Hussey and Hussey's discussion about 'paradigms' is consistent with Kuhn (1962), who states that a paradigm can be defined as an approach to knowledge advancement that adopts particular theoretical assumptions, research goals and research methods.[9]

In explaining or describing why a certain 'camp' of researchers might try to denigrate the credibility of alternative research paradigms, it is relevant to consider one of the various views about how knowledge advances. Kuhn (1962) explained how knowledge, or science,

---

9   A similar definition of a paradigm is provided by Wolk and Tearney (1997, p. 47). They define a paradigm as a shared problem-solving view among members of a science or discipline.

develops: scientific progress is not evolutionary but revolutionary. His view is that knowledge advances when one theory is replaced by another as particular researchers attack the credibility of an existing paradigm and advance an alternative, promoted as being superior, thereby potentially bringing the existing paradigm into 'crisis'. As knowledge develops, the new paradigm may be replaced by a further research perspective, or a prior paradigm may be resurrected. In discussing the process of how researchers switch from one research perspective (or paradigm) to another, Kuhn likens it to one of 'religious conversion'.[10] While the perspective provided by Kuhn does appear to have some relevance to explaining developments in the advancement of accounting theory, so far no accounting theory has ever been successful in overthrowing all other alternatives. There have been, and no doubt will continue to be, advocates of various alternative theories of accounting, many of which are discussed in this book.

Returning to our brief review of financial accounting theories, we have stated previously that positive theories of accounting do not seek to prescribe particular accounting practices (that is, they do not tell us which accounting practices we should adopt). Some critics of this positive theoretical perspective have argued that the decision not to prescribe could alienate academic accountants from their counterparts within the profession. As Howieson (1996, p. 31) states:

> ... an unwillingness to tackle policy issues is arguably an abrogation of academics' duty to serve the community which supports them. Among other activities, practitioners are concerned on a day-to-day basis with the question of which accounting policies they should choose. Traditionally, academics have acted as commentators and reformers on such normative issues. By concentrating on positive questions, they risk neglecting one of their important roles in the community.

Counter to this view, many proponents of Positive Accounting Theory have, at different times, tried to undermine normative research because it was not based on observation but on personal opinion about what *should* happen. (Observation-based research was deemed by them to be 'scientific', and 'scientific research' was considered to be akin to 'good research'.) Positive Accounting theorists often argue that in undertaking research they do not want to impose their own views on others as this is 'unscientific'; rather, they prefer to provide information about the expected implications of particular actions (for example the selection of a particular accounting method) and thereafter let people decide for themselves what they should do (for example, they may provide evidence to support a prediction that organisations that are close to breaching accounting-based debt covenants will adopt accounting methods that increase the firm's reported profits and assets thereby 'loosening' the effects of the accounting-based debt covenants).

However, as a number of accounting academics have quite rightly pointed out, and as should be remembered when reading this book, selecting a theory to adopt for research (such as Public Interest Theory, Capture Theory, Legitimacy Theory, Stakeholder Theory or Positive Accounting Theory) is based on a value judgement; what to research is based on a value judgement; believing that all individual action is driven by self-interest (as the Positive Accounting Theorists do) is a

---

10   Kuhn's 'revolutionary' perspective about the development of knowledge is in itself a theory and, as with financial accounting theories, there are alternative views of how knowledge develops and advances. Although a review of the various perspectives of the development of science is beyond the scope of this book, interested readers are referred to Popper (1959), Lakatos and Musgrove (1974), Feyerabend (1975) and Chalmers (1982).

value judgement; and so on. Hence, no research, whether using Positive Accounting Theory or otherwise, is value free and it would arguably be quite wrong to assert that it is value free. As Gray, Owen and Maunders (1987, p. 66) state:

> In common with all forms of empirical investigation we must recognise that all perception is theory-laden. That is, our preconceptions about the world significantly colour what we observe and which aspects of particular events we focus upon. Thus accountants are more likely to view the world through accounting frameworks and conventions.

Watts and Zimmerman (1990, p. 146) did modify their original stance in relation to the objectivity of their research and conceded that value judgements do play a part in positive research just as they do in normative research. They stated:

> Positive theories are value laden. Tinker et al. (1982, p. 167) argue that all research is value laden and not socially neutral. Specifically, 'Realism operating in the clothes of positive theory claims theoretical supremacy because it is born of fact, not values' (p. 172). We concede the importance of values in determining research: both the researcher's and user's preferences affect the process.
>
> Competition among theories to meet users' demand constrains the extent to which researcher values influence research design. Positive theories are 'If ... then' propositions that are both predictive and explanatory. Researchers choose the topics to investigate, the methods to use, and the assumptions to make. Researchers' preferences and expected pay-offs (publications and citations) affect the choice of topics, methods and assumptions. In this sense, all research, including positive research, is 'value laden'.

The position taken in this book is that theories of accounting, of necessity, are abstractions of reality, and the choice of one theory in preference to another is based on particular value judgements. Some of us may prefer particular theories in preference to others because they more closely reflect how we believe people do, or should, act. We cannot really expect to provide perfect explanations or predictions of human behaviour, nor can we expect to assess perfectly what types of information the users of financial statements actually need—my perceptions of information needs will probably be different from your views about information needs. There is a role for prescription if it is based on logical argument, and there is a role for research that provides predictions if the research methods employed to provide the predictions are assessed as valid.

CAN WE PROVE A THEORY?

This book does not intend to provide an in-depth insight into the development of scientific thought, but one interesting issue that often arises with students is whether a theory can actually be 'proved'. In this book various theories are considered, a number of which provide alternative explanations for the same events. The next section of this chapter considers how to evaluate a theory in terms of logic and evidence, but before this we should perhaps look at the issue of whether we can prove a theory.

One's view about whether we can prove a theory as correct depends on how one views the development of scientific thought. When it comes to accounting theories—which might, for example, consider how people react to particular accounting numbers, or might consider why accountants would choose particular accounting methods in preference to others—we need again to appreciate that financial accounting is a human activity (we cannot have accounting without accountants) and that common sense would dictate that not all people will react in a similar way to accounting numbers. Hence, logic might indicate that a theory of financial accounting (and therefore a theory that describes human behaviour in relation to accounting numbers) would not provide perfect predictions of behaviour in all cases (and in this explanation we are talking about positive theories—theories that seek to explain and predict particular phenomena).

If the theories of financial accounting were developed to explain and predict people's actions and reactions to financial accounting information (that is, they are positive theories), we might consider that if a theory provides sound predictions the majority of the time then the theory is still of use, albeit that its predictions are not 'perfect'. That is, we would evaluate it on the basis of the correspondence between the prediction of behaviours provided by the theory and the subsequent behaviour, and we might accept that a theory is useful even though it does not provide accurate predictions in all cases. That is, an 'acceptable' theory might admit exceptions.[11] It should also be appreciated that, while we might use observations to 'support' a theory, it would generally be inadvisable to state that we have proved a theory on the basis of observations. There is always the possibility that one further observation might be made that is inconsistent with our theory's predictions.

In relation to the issue of whether we can 'prove' a theory (or not), it is useful to refer to insights provided by a group of theorists known as 'falsificationists', the major leader of which is considered to be Karl Popper.[12]

Popper and the falsificationists consider that knowledge develops through trial and error. For example, a researcher might develop hypotheses from a theory.[13] To develop scientific knowledge, the falsificationists believe that these hypotheses must be of a form that allows them to be rejected if the evidence is not supportive of the hypotheses. For example, a hypothesis of the following form would be deemed to be falsifiable:

Hypothesis 1: Managers who receive bonuses based on accounting profits will adopt income-increasing accounting methods.

According to Popper and other falsificationists, knowledge develops as a result of continual refinement of a theory. When particular hypotheses are deemed to be false through lack of empirical support, the pre-existing theories will be refined (or abandoned). The refined

---

11 The degree to which we might consider a theory to be acceptable will perhaps depend on the costs or implications associated with the theory 'getting it wrong' in a particular circumstance. For example, if the theory related to medicine and the theory was wrong only 10 per cent of the time—thereby causing deaths in 10 per cent of the patients—such a theory might not be acceptable. In accounting we might tolerate higher levels of inconsistency between theory predictions and related outcomes.

12 One of the first detailed descriptions of falsificationism appeared in Karl Popper, *The Logic of Scientific Discovery*, Hutchinson, London, 1968.

13 Simply stated, a hypothesis can be defined as a proposition typically derived from theory which can be tested for causality or association using empirical data. For example, a hypothesis might be: the greater the negative media attention given to a particular social issue the greater the amount of annual report disclosures addressing the issue.

theories will be accepted until a related hypothesis is deemed to be false (falsified), at which time the theory will be further refined. Chalmers (1982, p. 38) provides a useful overview of falsificationism. He states:

> The falsificationist freely admits that observation is guided by and presupposes theory. He is also happy to abandon any claims implying that theories can be established as true or probably true in the light of observational evidence. Theories are construed as speculative and tentative conjectures or guesses freely created by the human intellect in an attempt to overcome problems encountered by previous theories and to give an adequate account of the behaviour of some aspects of the world or universe. Once proposed, speculative theories are to be rigorously and ruthlessly tested by observation and experiment. Theories that fail to stand up to observational and experimental tests must be eliminated and replaced by further speculative conjectures. Science progresses by trial and error, by conjectures and refutations. Only the fittest theories survive. While it can never be legitimately said of a theory that it is true, it can hopefully be said that it is the best available, that it is better than anything that has come before.

Popper's view regarding how theories are developed can be contrasted with the views adopted by the inductivists considered earlier in the chapter. The inductivists construct theories based on typically long periods of careful observation. This discussion will not be pursued any further in terms of how theories develop, but consistent with some of the above discussion we would caution readers about making any claims to 'proving' a theory. It is always safer to say that our evidence 'supports' a theory but that it is also possible that we might embrace an alternative theoretical perspective at a future time should better explanations for a particular phenomenon become available.

EVALUATING THEORIES—CONSIDERATIONS OF LOGIC AND EVIDENCE

Throughout this book various theories of financial accounting are discussed. Where appropriate, an evaluation of the theories is also undertaken. The book considers such issues as whether the argument supporting the theories is (or at least appears to be) logical and/or plausible in terms of the central assumptions (if any) that are being made. If possible, the argument or theory should be broken down into its main premises to see if the argument, in simplified form, appears logical. What is emphasised is that we/you must question the theories that we/you are exposed to—not simply accept them. Acceptance of a theory and its associated hypotheses must be tied to whether we accept the logic of the argument, the underlying assumptions and any supporting evidence provided. (As indicated previously, hypotheses can be described as predictions typically expressed in the form of a relationship between one or more variables.)

As an example of logical deduction, consider the following simplistic non-accounting-related argument (reflecting the bias of the author—it refers to surfing). It shows that, although the argument may be logical (if we accept the premises), if it can be shown that one of the premises is untrue or in doubt, then the conclusions or predictions may be rejected. Where there are a number of premises and a conclusion, it is often referred to as a 'syllogism'.

- All surfers over the age of 35 ride longboards.
- Jack is a surfer over the age of 35.
- Jack therefore rides a longboard.

If we accept the above premises, we might accept the conclusion. It is logical. To determine the logic of the argument, we do not need to understand what a 'surfer' is or what a 'longboard' is. That is, we do not need to refer to 'real world' observations. We could have deconstructed the argument to the form:

- All As ride a B.
- C is an A.
- Therefore C rides a B.

An argument is logical to the extent that *if* the premises on which it is based are true *then* the conclusion will be true. That is, the argument (even if logical) will only provide a true account of the real world if the premises on which it is based are true. Referring to the above syllogism, evidence gathered through observation will show that the first premise does not always hold. There are surfers over 35 who do not ride longboards. Hence we reject the conclusion on the basis of observation, not on the basis of logic. Therefore, we had two considerations. If the argument seeks to provide an account of real-world phenomena, we must consider the logic of the premises and the correspondence between the premises and actual observation. This simplistic example can be extended to a review of theories. We might try to break the theory down into a series of premises. When the central premises are considered, do they lead to a logical conclusion? Further, if the premises are based on 'real world' observation, do they seem to be true? However, it should be remembered that not all theories or arguments seek to correspond with real-world phenomena—for example, some normative theories of accounting promote radical changes to existing practices. For many normative theories we might consider only the logic of the argument and whether we are prepared to accept the premises on which the argument is based.

Returning to the subject of the syllogism provided above, we could have argued alternatively that:

- A lot of surfers over 35 ride longboards.
- Jack is a surfer over 35.
- Therefore Jack rides a longboard.

The above is not a logical argument. The first premise has admitted alternatives and hence the conclusion, which does not admit alternatives, does not follow. We can dismiss the argument on the basis of a logical flaw without actually seeking any evidence to support the premises.

Chapter 7 reviews in greater depth Positive Accounting Theory as developed by such researchers as Jensen and Meckling (1976) and Watts and Zimmerman (1978). As noted earlier, their positive theory of accounting has a number of central assumptions, including an assumption that all people are *opportunistic* and will adopt particular strategies to the extent that such strategies lead to an increase in the personal wealth of those parties making the decisions. That is, self-interest is a core belief about what motivates individual action. Wealth accumulation is assumed to be at the centre of all decisions. The theory does not incorporate considerations of morality, loyalty, social responsibility and the like.

If we were to accept the economics-based assumption or premise of researchers such as Watts and Zimmerman that:

■ self-interest tied to wealth maximisation motivates *all* decisions by individuals, and *if* we accept the following premises (which we might confirm through direct observation or through research undertaken by others) that:

■ manager X is paid on the basis of reported profits (for example, he/she is given a bonus of 5 per cent of accounting profits), and

■ accounting method Y is an available method of accounting that will increase reported profits relative to other methods, *then* we might accept a prediction that, all other things being equal,

■ manager X will adopt accounting method Y.

This argument appears logical. Whether manager X is paid on the basis of reported profits and whether accounting method Y will increase reported profits are matters that can be confirmed though observation. But if the premises are both logical and true, then the conclusion will be true.

The argument may be logical but we might accept it only if we accept the critical assumption that the actions of individuals are motivated by the desire to maximise personal wealth. If we do not accept the central assumption, then we may reject the prediction. What is being emphasised here is that you need to consider whether you are prepared to accept the logic *and* the assumptions on which the arguments are based. If not, then we may reject the theory and the associated predictions. For example, in Gray, Owen and Adams (1996) the authors explicitly state that they reject the central assumptions of Positive Accounting Theory (although by their own admission it has 'some useful insights') and that they will not use it as a means of explaining or describing the practice of corporate social responsibility reporting. (The topic of corporate social reporting is covered in Chapter 9 of this book.) As Gray, Owen and Adams state (p. 75):

> There is little doubt that these theories have provided some useful insights into the way in which they model the world. There is equally little doubt that some company management and many gambling investors may act in line with these theories. It is also the case that some authors have found the form of analysis employed in these theories useful for explaining corporate social reporting; but apart from the limitations which must arise from a pristine liberal economic perspective on the world and the profound philosophical limitations of the approach, the approach cannot offer any justification why we might accept the description of the world as a desirable one. It is a morally bankrupt view of the world in general and accounting in particular. Its (usual) exclusion of corporate social reporting is therefore actually attractive as an argument for corporate social reporting.

Chapter 6 discusses the Conceptual Framework Project, which is considered to be a normative theory of accounting (applying a decision usefulness perspective). This framework provides a view about the objective of general purpose financial reporting (to provide information that is useful for economics-based decisions) and the qualitative characteristics that financial information should possess. It also provides definitions of the elements of accounting (assets, liabilities, income, expenses, equity) and prescribes recognition criteria for each of the elements. As discussed in Chapter 6, in recent years the US Financial Accounting Standards Board (FASB) and the International Accounting Standards Board (IASB) have been undertaking an initiative to develop, on a joint basis, an improved conceptual framework for financial reporting. In May 2008 the IASB and the FASB jointly released an exposure draft entitled *Exposure Draft of an Improved Conceptual Framework for Financial Reporting*, which provided a definition of the revised conceptual framework as:

> a coherent system of concepts that flow from an objective. The objective of financial reporting is the foundation of the framework. The other concepts provide guidance on identifying the boundaries of financial reporting; selecting the transactions, other events and circumstances to be represented; how they should be recognised and measured (or disclosed); and how they should be summarised and communicated in financial reports.

Hence, if we were to decide whether we agreed with the guidance provided within the revised conceptual framework, which is an example of a normative theory (as already indicated, a normative theory prescribes how we should undertake a particular activity—in this case, how we should do financial accounting), then we clearly would need to evaluate the assumed objective identified in the framework. As everything else is constructed around this objective (as the quote shows, it is deemed to be the 'foundation of the framework'), then, logically, if we disagree with the stated objective, we would have to disagree with the balance of the prescriptions provided in the revised conceptual framework. The *Exposure Draft* states:

> The objective of general purpose financial reporting is to provide financial information about the reporting entity that is useful to present and potential equity investors, lenders and other creditors in making decisions in their capacity as capital providers.

Therefore, if we believed that the central objective of financial accounting was to provide information to a broad cross-section of stakeholders, inclusive of employees, local communities and other groups that are not directly involved as capital providers, then we would reject the conceptual framework being developed by the IASB and FASB, despite the fact that it might be considered to be logically structured.

While the in-depth study of logic and a critique of argument are beyond the scope of this book, interested readers should consider studying books or articles that concentrate on the development of logical argument.[14] Thouless (1974) describes various approaches to identifying logical flaws in arguments and he also identifies thirty-eight 'dishonest tricks in argument' that some writers use to support their arguments. Some of the 'tricks' he refers to, and which are often used to distract readers from limitations in the logic of an argument or theory, are:

- the use of emotionally toned words;
- making a statement in which 'all' is implied but 'some' is true;
- evasion of a sound refutation of an argument by use of a sophisticated formula;
- diversion to another question, to a side issue, or by irrelevant objection;
- the use of an argument of logically unsound form;
- change in the meaning of a term during the course of an argument;
- suggestion by repeated affirmation;

---

14 A good book in this regard is *Straight and Crooked Thinking* by Robert H. Thouless (1974). Sterling (1970) is also useful.

- prestige by false credentials;
- the appeal to mere authority;
- argument by mere analogy.

When reading documents written to support particular ideas or theories, we must also be vigilant to ensure that our acceptance of a theory has not, in a sense, been coerced through the use of colourful or emotive language, or an incorrect appeal to authority. Earlier, reference was made to terms and descriptions used by critics of Positive Accounting Theory, some of which were very emotive. Quite often (but not always) emotive or colourful language is introduced to support an otherwise weak argument. Where emotive or colourful language has been used, we should perhaps consider whether we would take the same position in terms of accepting the author's arguments if the author had used relatively neutral language. Thouless (1974, p. 24) provides some advice in this regard:

> The practical exercise which I recommend is one that I have already performed on some passages in which truth seemed to be obscured by emotional thinking. I suggest that readers should copy out controversial passages from newspapers, books, or speeches which contain emotionally coloured words. They should then underline all the emotional words, afterwards rewriting the passages with the emotional words replaced by neutral ones. Examine the passage then in its new form in which it merely states facts without indicating the writer's emotional attitude towards them, and see whether it is still good evidence for the proposition it is trying to prove. If it is, the passage is a piece of straight thinking in which emotionally coloured words have been introduced merely as an ornament. If not, it is crooked thinking, because the conclusion depends not on the factual meaning of the passage but on the emotions roused by the words.

While we must always consider the logic of an argument and the various assumptions that have been made, what we also must remember is that theories, particularly those in the social sciences, are by nature abstractions of reality. We cannot really expect particular theories about human behaviour to apply all the time. People (thankfully) are different and to expect theories or models of human behaviour (and remember, accounting theories relate to the action of accountants and the users of accounting information) to have perfect predictive ability would be naive. If a number of theories are available to describe a particular phenomenon, then considering more than one theory may provide a more rounded perspective. Difficulties will arise if the theories provide diametrically opposite predictions or explanations, and in such cases a choice of theory must generally be made.

For those theories that attempt to predict and explain accounting practice (positive theories of accounting) it is common practice to test the theories empirically in various settings and across various types of decisions. But what if the particular theories do not seem to hold in all settings? Should the theories be abandoned? Returning to an issue considered previously in this chapter, can we accept a theory that admits exceptions? Certainly, readings of various accounting research journals will show that many studies that adopt Positive Accounting Theory as the theoretical basis of the argument fail to generate findings consistent with the theory (however, many do). According to Christenson (1983, p. 18), an outspoken critic of Positive Accounting Theory:

> We are told, for example, that 'we can only expect a positive theory to hold on average' [Watts and Zimmerman, 1978, p. 127, n. 37]. We are also advised 'to remember that as

in all empirical theories we are concerned with general trends' [Watts and Zimmerman, 1978, pp. 288–289], where 'general' is used in the weak sense of 'true or applicable in most instances but not all' rather than in the strong sense of 'relating to, concerned with, or applicable to every member of a class' [American Heritage Dictionary, 1969, p. 548] … A law that admits exceptions has no significance, and knowledge of it is not of the slightest use. By arguing that their theories admit exceptions, Watts and Zimmerman condemn them as insignificant and useless.

Christenson uses the fact that Positive Accounting Theory is not always supported in practice to reject it.[15] However, as stressed previously, as a study of people (accountants, not 'accounting'), it is very hard to see how any model or theory could ever fully explain human action. In fact, ability to do so would constitute a very dehumanising view of people. Hence, the failure of a particular study to support a theory might not in itself provide a basis for rejecting a theory as 'useless and insignificant'. From another perspective, the failure to support the theory may have been due to the data being inappropriately collected or the data not providing a sound correspondence with the theoretical variables involved. However, if the theory in question continuously fails to be supported, then its acceptance will obviously be threatened. At this point we could speculate whether in fact there are any theories pertaining to human activities that always hold.

In developing and testing accounting theories, many accounting researchers use methods borrowed from the pure sciences (such as physics and chemistry) which assume that the phenomena being studied will behave in the same way in all similar situations. As we will see when reading accounting (and other) research, these researchers believe that it is possible to develop generalisable accounting theories and therefore that the results they derive from particular samples of observations can be generalised to the broader population of the phenomenon in question. Other researchers hold the opposite view—that it is not possible to make any valid generalisations in the social sciences as we are dealing with human activity, and human behaviour varies from person to person. These researchers will develop theories of a fundamentally different nature from those developed by researchers who believe that it is possible to generalise in accounting theory, and these theories will tend to deal with specific localised situations. Between these two extremes, there are other researchers (such as Laughlin, 1995, 2004) who believe that it is possible to make some very broad generalisations in developing social science theories, but the way these broad generalisations apply to specific situations will vary according to the specific individual factors applicable to each situation. Researchers holding this view regarding the way the world works may use some very broad theories to help understand some aspects of the phenomena they are studying, but are ready to amend and adapt these broad generalisations in light of specific evidence from each individual study.

While a comprehensive review of research methods is beyond the scope of this book, if researchers are attempting to generalise the findings of their studies (based on particular samples)

---

15 Where a proposition is not supported in a particular instance, many of us have probably heard the phrase 'the exception proves the rule' being applied. Such a statement implies that we cannot accept a rule or proposition unless we find some evidence that appears to refute it. This clearly is an illogical argument. As emphasised above, we must always guard against accepting arguments that are not logically sound.

to a larger population, we need to consider the data on which the generalisation is based.[16] For example, if we are going to generalise our findings from a sample (we typically cannot test the whole population), then we must consider how the original sample was chosen. For instance, if we have a prediction that all companies will adopt a particular accounting method in times of inflation and we test this prediction against the ten largest companies listed on the stock exchange in a period of inflation, then common sense should dictate that the findings really should not be considered generalisable. Can we really be confident about what small companies will do given that our sample included only large listed companies? Hence, throughout your readings of various research studies you should consider not only how the argument is developed, but also how it is tested. If there are flaws in how the testing has been done, we may question or reject the significance of the findings. We must evaluate whether the data collected really represent valid measures of the theoretical variables in question.

As noted previously, for normative theories it is usually not appropriate to test them empirically. If researchers are arguing that accountants should provide particular types of accounting information, or if other researchers are providing a view that organisations have a social responsibility to consider the needs of all stakeholders, then this does not mean that what they are prescribing actually exists in practice. For example, if Chambers' model of accounting prescribes that all assets should be valued at their net market value, and we go out and find that accountants predominantly value their assets on the basis of historical cost, we should not reject Chambers' theory, as he was *prescribing*, not *predicting* or *describing*. We should always keep in mind what the researchers are attempting to achieve. Our acceptance of Chambers' theory is dependent on whether we accept the logic of the argument as well as the assumptions made by Chambers, including the assumption that the central role of accounting should be to provide information about an entity's ability to adapt to changing circumstances (which he argues is best reflected by measures of assets that are tied to their net market values), and the assumption that firms should exist primarily to increase the wealth of the owners.

OUTLINE OF THIS BOOK

A book of this size cannot be expected to cover all the theories of financial accounting. Nevertheless, it covers those theories that have gained widespread acceptance by various sectors of the accounting community.

Chapter 2 provides an overview of various financial reporting decisions that entities typically face, emphasising that some reporting pertaining to particular transactions and events is regulated, and some is unregulated. The chapter emphasises that financial accountants typically make many professional judgements throughout the accounting process, and discusses the qualitative attribute of objectivity, but it emphasises that considerations (other than the

---

16 Entire books are dedicated to research methods. Interested readers may refer to: C. Humphrey & B. Lee (eds) (2004), *The Real Life Guide to Accounting Research: A Behind-the-Scenes View of Using Qualitative Research Methods*, Kidlington, Oxford: Elsevier; J. Collis & R. Hussey (2003), *Business Research*, London: Palgrave Macmillan; A. Bryman (2004), *Social Research Methods*, 2nd edn, Oxford: Oxford University Press; P. Ghauri & K. Gronhaug (2002), *Research Methods in Business Studies: A Practical Guide*, Harlow: FT Prentice Hall.

pursuit of objectivity) may sometimes influence accounting method selection and disclosure practices.

Chapter 3 provides an overview of various arguments for and against the regulation of financial reporting, with an overview of various perspectives on the costs and benefits of regulating financial reporting. The chapter explores why some accounting approaches and/or methods are adopted by regulators and/or the profession while others are not. The political process involved in the setting of accounting standards is highlighted.

Chapter 4 explores the international harmonisation of accounting requirements. Recently, moves have been made to standardise accounting practices internationally. Australia and the European Union were at the forefront of such moves. This chapter considers some potential costs and benefits of this process. Particular consideration is given to issues of *culture* and how *cultural differences* have typically been proposed as a reason to explain international differences in accounting requirements. International standardisation ignores this research and assumes that all countries (with different cultures) can and should simply adopt the same accounting practices.

Chapter 5 gives an overview of various normative (or prescriptive) theories of accounting that have been advanced to deal with various accounting issues associated with periods of rising prices (inflation). The chapter considers such issues as whether there is a 'true' measure of income. Conceptual frameworks as normative theories of accounting are considered in Chapter 6. Applying material covered in Chapter 3, Chapters 5 and 6 also consider why various normative theories of accounting did not gain favour with the accounting profession or the accounting standard-setters.

Chapters 7 and 8 show that, while much financial reporting is regulated, organisations still have some scope for voluntarily selecting between alternative accounting methods for particular types of transactions. The treatment of many transactions and the disclosure of many/most issues associated with various social and environmental events relating to an organisation are unregulated. Chapters 7 and 8 consider some theoretical perspectives (including Positive Accounting Theory, Legitimacy Theory, Stakeholder Theory, Political Economy Theory and Institutional Theory) that explain what drives the various unregulated/voluntary reporting decisions.

Chapter 9 considers the development and use of new systems of accounting that incorporate the economic, social and environmental performance of an organisation. The relationship between accounting and sustainable development is explored. This chapter includes a consideration of the limitations of traditional financial accounting, with particular focus on its inability to incorporate social and environmental issues.

Chapters 10 and 11 consider how individuals and capital markets react to various corporate disclosures. The chapters consider the various theories that have been used to test whether the market is actually using particular types of disclosures, as well as theories that indicate how individuals use accounting information. The chapters also consider who should be deemed to be the users of various types of disclosures. Issues associated with stakeholder *rights to know* are also explored.

The concluding chapter, Chapter 12, provides an overview of various critical perspectives of accounting—perspectives that tend to criticise the entire system of accounting as it stands (accounting practice is anthropocentric, masculine and so on)—arguing that accounting tends to support current social systems, which favour those with economic power but marginalise the interests of parties that lack control of necessary resources.

In summary, the balance of this book can be presented diagrammatically, as in Figure 1.1.

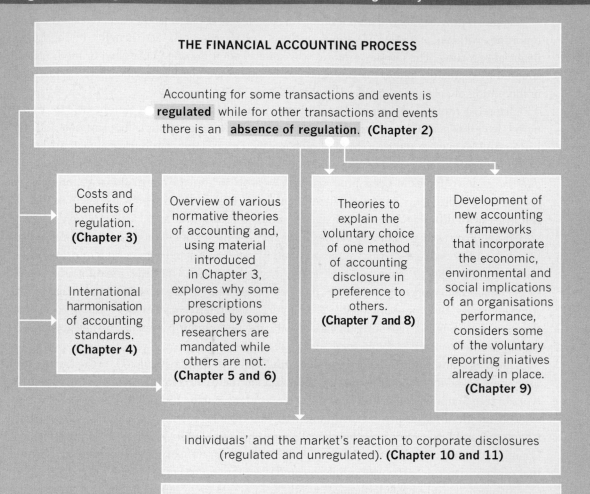

Figure 1.1 Diagrammatic overview of *Financial Accounting Theory*

THE FINANCIAL ACCOUNTING PROCESS

Accounting for some transactions and events is **regulated** while for other transactions and events there is an **absence of regulation**. **(Chapter 2)**

Costs and benefits of regulation. **(Chapter 3)**

International harmonisation of accounting standards. **(Chapter 4)**

Overview of various normative theories of accounting and, using material introduced in Chapter 3, explores why some prescriptions proposed by some researchers are mandated while others are not. **(Chapter 5 and 6)**

Theories to explain the voluntary choice of one method of accounting disclosure in preference to others. **(Chapter 7 and 8)**

Development of new accounting frameworks that incorporate the economic, environmental and social implications of an organisations performance, considers some of the voluntary reporting iniatives already in place. **(Chapter 9)**

Individuals' and the market's reaction to corporate disclosures (regulated and unregulated). **(Chapter 10 and 11)**

Critical perspectives of accounting—tend to be critical of all existing systems, hence they are subject of their own stand-alone chapter. **(Chapter 12)**

QUESTIONS

1.1 What is the difference between a positive theory of accounting and a normative theory of accounting?

1.2 If you developed a theory to explain how a person's cultural background influences how they prepare financial statements, would you have developed a positive theory or a normative theory?

1.3 What is a conceptual framework, and would it be considered to be a positive or a normative theory of accounting?

1.4 In an article that appeared in the *Age* ('Way cleared for Turnbull to challenge', by Michelle Grattan, 12 September 2008), Peter Costello, former federal treasurer, is quoted as saying, 'I have a theory that every government wins one more term than it should.' Do you believe he really has a 'theory' in terms of the way a 'theory' is defined in this chapter?

1.5 Why would it not be appropriate to reject a normative theory of accounting because its prescriptions could not be confirmed through empirical observation?

1.6 The IASB and the FASB are currently developing a revised conceptual framework of financial reporting. If you have been asked to review the framework—which is an example of a normative theory of accounting—why would it be important for you to pay particular attention to how the objective of financial reporting is defined within the framework?

1.7 If a normative theory of financial accounting has been developed to prescribe how we should do financial accounting, is it possible that we can decide to reject the theory because we do not agree with a central assumption of the theory (such as an assumption about the objective of financial reporting), but at the same time decide that the theory is nevertheless logical? Explain your answer.

1.8 What is the difference between developing a theory by induction and developing a theory by deduction?

1.9 Is the study of financial accounting theory a waste of time for accounting students? Explain your answer.

1.10 In the 1960s a number of accounting researchers concentrated on developing theories of accounting based on observing and documenting the behaviour of practising accountants. Do you think that such research is useful in improving the practice of financial accounting? Explain your answer.

1.11 Gray, Owen and Maunders (1987, p. 66) make the following statement in relation to research based on the inductive approach (that is, research based on observing particular phenomena):

> Studying extant practice is a study of 'what is' and by definition does not study 'what is not' or 'what should be'. It therefore concentrates on the status quo, is reactionary in attitude, and cannot provide a basis upon which current practice may be evaluated or from which future improvements may be deduced.

With this comment in mind, do you consider that research based on induction is useful for improving the practice of financial accounting? Explain your answer.

1.12 Explain the meaning of the following paragraph and evaluate the logic of the perspective described:

> In generating theories of accounting that are based upon what accountants actually do, it is assumed (often implicitly) that what is done by the majority of accountants is the most appropriate practice. In adopting such a perspective there is, in a sense, a perspective of accounting Darwinism—a view that accounting practice has evolved, and the fittest, or perhaps 'best', practices have survived. Prescriptions or advice are provided to others on the basis of what most accountants do, the logic being that the majority of accountants must be doing the most appropriate thing.

1.13 In 1961 and 1962 the Accounting Research Division of the American Institute of Certified Public Accountants (AICPA) commissioned studies by Moonitz and by Sprouse and Moonitz. These studies proposed that accounting measurement systems be changed from historical cost to a system based on current values. However, before the release of these studies, the AICPA released a statement saying that 'while these studies are a valuable contribution to accounting principles, they are too radically different from generally accepted principles for acceptance at this time' (Statement by the Accounting Principles Board, AICPA, April 1962). Explain why if something is 'radically different' (though it might be logically sound) this difference in itself might be enough to stop regulators embracing a particular approach to accounting.

1.14 Read the following quotation from Miller and Reading (1986, p. 64). If constituency support is necessary before particular accounting approaches become embodied in accounting standards, does this have implications for the 'neutrality' and 'representational faithfulness' (qualitative characteristics that exist in various conceptual framework projects around the world) of reports generated in accordance with accounting standards?

> The mere discovery of a problem is not sufficient to assure that the Financial Accounting Standards Board will undertake its solution ... There must be a suitably high likelihood that the Board can resolve the issues in a manner that will be acceptable to the constituency—without some prior sense of the likelihood that the Board members will be able to reach a consensus, it is generally not advisable to undertake a formal project.

1.15 As Watts and Zimmerman (1986, p. 7) state, Positive Accounting Theory 'is concerned with explaining [accounting] practice. It is designed to explain and predict which firms will and which firms will not use a particular accounting method ... but it says nothing as to which method a firm should use'. Do you think that this represents an 'abrogation' of the academics' duty to serve the community that supports them?

1.16 Briefly identify the two branches of 'decision usefulness' theories described in this chapter and explain what they are.

1.17 Briefly explain the revolutionary perspective of knowledge advancement proposed by Kuhn (1962).

1.18 What is a 'paradigm' and would you expect accounting researchers to embrace more than one paradigm when undertaking research? Explain your answer.

1.19 In your opinion, can accounting research be 'value free'? Explain your answer.

1.20 What role do value judgements have in determining what particular accounting theory a researcher might elect to adopt to explain or predict particular accounting phenomena?

1.21 If an accounting researcher adopts a particular accounting theory to predict which firms will make particular accounting disclosures, how much supporting evidence must the researcher gather before he or she can claim that the theory is 'proved'? Explain your answer.

1.22 Assume that you have been asked to evaluate a particular theory of accounting. What factors would you consider before making a judgement that the theory appears 'sound'?

1.23 If you were trying to convince another party to support your theory about a particular facet of financial accounting, would you be inclined to use emotive or colourful language? Why, or why not?

1.24 What do we mean when we say that 'theories are abstractions of reality'? Do you agree that theories of accounting are necessarily abstractions of reality?

1.25 What is a 'hypothesis' and do you consider that accounting research should necessarily involve the development of empirically testable hypotheses?

1.26 Would you reject as 'insignificant and useless' a positive theory of accounting on the basis that in a particular research study the results derived failed to support the hypotheses and the related theory? Explain your answer.

1.27 If a researcher tested a theory on a particular sample of companies, what considerations would you examine before you would agree with the researcher that the results can be generalised to the larger population of companies?

REFERENCES

Bebbington, J., R. Gray & R. Laughlin (2001), *Financial Accounting: Practice and Principles,* London: International Thomson Business Press.

Bryman, A. (2004), *Social Research Methods,* 2nd edn, Oxford: Oxford University Press.

Canning, J. B. (1929), *The Economics of Accountancy: A Critical Analysis of Accounting Theory,* New York: Ronald Press.

Chalmers, A. F. (1982), *What Is This Thing Called Science?,* 2nd edn, St Lucia: University of Queensland Press.

Chambers, R. J. (1993), 'Positive accounting theory and the PA cult', *ABACUS,* 29(1), pp. 1–26.

Christenson, C. (1983), 'The methodology of positive accounting', *The Accounting Review,* 58 (January), pp. 1–22.

Collis, J. & R. Hussey (2003), *Business Research,* London: Palgrave Macmillan.

Deegan, C. (1997), 'Varied perceptions of positive accounting theory: a useful tool for explanation and prediction, or a body of vacuous, insidious and discredited thoughts?', *Accounting Forum,* 20(5), pp. 63–73.

FASB (1976), *Scope and Implications of the Conceptual Framework Project,* Financial Accounting Standards Board.

Feyerabend, P. (1975), *Against Method: Outline of an Anarchic Theory of Knowledge,* London: New Left Books.

Ghauri, P. & K. Gronhaug (2002), *Research Methods in Business Studies: A Practical Guide,* Harlow: FT Prentice Hall.

Gordon, M. J. (1964), 'Postulates, principles, and research in accounting', *The Accounting Review,* 39 (April), pp. 251–63.

Grady, P. (1965), *An Inventory of Generally Accepted Accounting Principles for Business Enterprises, Accounting Research Study No. 7,* New York: AICPA.

Gray, R. & J. Bebbington (2001), *Accounting for the Environment,* London: Sage Publications Ltd.

Gray, R., D. Owen & C. Adams (1996), *Accounting and Accountability: Changes and Challenges in Corporate Social and Environmental Reporting,* London: Prentice Hall.

Gray, R., D. Owen & K. T. Maunders (1987), *Corporate Social Reporting: Accounting and Accountability,* Hemel Hempstead: Prentice Hall.

Hatfield, H. R. (1927), *Accounting, Its Principles and Problems,* New York: D. Appleton & Co.

Henderson, S., G. Peirson & K. Harris (2004), *Financial Accounting Theory,* Sydney: Pearson Education Australia.

Hendriksen, E. (1970), *Accounting Theory,* Illinois: Richard D. Irwin.

Hicks, J. R. (1946), *Value and Capital,* Oxford: Oxford University Press.

Hines, R. (1988), 'Financial accounting: in communicating reality, we construct reality', *Accounting, Organizations and Society,* 13(3), pp. 251–62.

Howieson, B. (1996), 'Whither financial accounting research: a modern-day Bo-peep?', *Australian Accounting Review,* 6(1), pp. 29–36.

Humphrey, C. & B. Lee (eds) (2004), *The Real Life Guide to Accounting Research: A Behind-the-Scenes View of Using Qualitative Research Methods,* Kidlington, Oxford: Elsevier.

Hussey, J. & R. Hussey (1997), *Business Research: A Practical Guide for Undergraduate and Postgraduate Students,* London: Macmillan Business.

International Accounting Standards Board (2008), *Exposure Draft of an Improved Conceptual Framework for Financial Reporting,* IASB, London.

Jensen, M. C. & W. H. Meckling (1976), 'Theory of the firm: managerial behavior, agency costs and ownership structure', *Journal of Financial Economics,* 3 (October), pp. 305–60.

Kuhn, T. S. (1962), *The Structure of Scientific Revolutions,* Illinois: University of Chicago Press.

Lakatos, I. & A. Musgrove (1974), *Criticism and the Growth of Knowledge,* Cambridge: Cambridge University Press.

Laughlin, R. (1995), 'Empirical research in accounting: alternative approaches and a case for "middle-range" thinking', *Accounting, Auditing and Accountability Journal,* 8(1), pp. 63–87.

Laughlin, R. (2004), 'Putting the record straight: a critique of "Methodology choices and the construction of facts: some implications from the sociology of knowledge"', *Critical Perspectives on Accounting,* 15(2), pp. 261–77.

Lee, T. A. (1974), 'Enterprise income—survival or decline and fall', *Accounting and Business Research,* 15, pp. 178–92.

Llewelyn, S. (2003), 'What counts as "theory" in qualitative management and accounting research?', *Accounting, Auditing and Accountability Journal,* 16(4), pp. 662–708.

Mathews, M. R. (1993), *Socially Responsible Accounting,* London: Chapman & Hall.

Miller, P. B. W. & R. Reading (1986), *The FASB: The People, the Process, and the Politics,* Illinois: Irwin.

Moonitz, M. (1961), *The Basic Postulates of Accounting, Accounting Research Study No. 1,* New York: AICPA.

Paton, W. A. (1922), *Accounting Theory,* Kansas: Scholars Book Co., reprinted 1973.

Paton, W. A. & A. C. Littleton (1940), *An Introduction to Corporate Accounting Standards,* USA: American Accounting Association.

Popper, K. R. (1959), *The Logic of Scientific Discovery,* London: Hutchinson.

Popper, K. (1968), *The Logic of Scientific Discovery,* 2nd edn, London: Hutchinson.

Sprouse, R. & M. Moonitz (1962), *A Tentative Set of Broad Accounting Principles for Business Enterprises, Accounting Research Study No. 3,* New York: AICPA.

Sterling, R. R. (1970), *Theory of the Measurement of Enterprise Income,* USA: University of Kansas Press.

Sterling, R. R. (1990), 'Positive accounting: an assessment', *ABACUS,* 26(2), pp. 97–135.

Thouless, R. H. (1974), *Straight and Crooked Thinking,* London: Pan Books.

Tinker, A. M., & B. D. Merino & M. D. Neimark (1982), 'The normative origins of positive theories: ideology and accounting thought', *Accounting Organizations and Society*, 7(2), pp. 167–200.

Unerman, J. & B. O'Dwyer (2004), 'Enron, WorldCom, Andersen et al: a challenge to modernity', *Critical Perspectives on Accounting*, 15(6–7), pp. 971–93.

Watts, R. & J. Zimmerman (1978), 'Towards a positive theory of the determination of accounting standards', *The Accounting Review*, 53(1), pp. 112–34.

Watts, R. L. & J. L. Zimmerman (1986), *Positive Accounting Theory*, Englewood Cliffs, New Jersey: Prentice Hall.

Watts, R. L. & J. L. Zimmerman (1990), 'Positive accounting theory: a ten year perspective', *The Accounting Review*, 65(1), pp. 259–85.

Williams, P. F. (1989), 'The logic of positive accounting research', *Accounting, Organizations and Society*, 14(5/6), pp. 455–68.

Wolk, H. I. & M. G. Tearney (1997), *Accounting Theory: A Conceptual and Institutional Approach*, International Thomson Publishing.

CHAPTER 2

THE FINANCIAL REPORTING ENVIRONMENT

LEARNING OBJECTIVES

On completing this chapter readers should:

- have a broad understanding of the history of the accounting profession and of accounting regulation;
- be aware of some of the arguments for and against the existence of accounting regulation;
- be aware of some of the theoretical perspectives used to explain the existence of regulation;
- be aware of how and why various groups within society try to influence the accounting standard-setting process;
- acknowledge that many accounting decisions are based on professional opinions and have an awareness of some of the theories used to explain what influences the accountant to choose one accounting method in preference to another;
- be aware of some of the arguments advanced to support a view that the accountant can be considered to be a powerful member of society.

OPENING ISSUES

Through such mechanisms as conceptual framework programs, accounting professions throughout the world promote a view that accounting reports, when prepared properly, will be objective and will faithfully represent the underlying transactions and events of the reporting entity. Is it in the interests of the accounting profession to promote this view of objectivity and neutrality, and if so, why? Further, because of the economic and social impacts of many accounting decisions (for example, decisions that involve choosing one method of accounting in preference to another), and because accounting standard-setters take such economic and social impacts into account when developing new accounting standards, standard-setters themselves are not developing accounting standards that can subsequently enable a reliable account of organisational performance to be provided. Do you agree or disagree with this view, and why?

INTRODUCTION

Financial accounting is a process involving the collection and processing of financial information to assist in the making of various decisions by many parties internal and external to the organisation. These parties are diverse and include present and potential investors, lenders, suppliers, employees, customers, governments, the local community, parties performing a review or oversight function, and the media. Financial accounting deals with the provision of information to parties not necessarily involved in the day-to-day running of the organisation. As there are many parties external to the firm, with potentially vastly different information demands and needs, it is not possible to generate a single report that will satisfy the specific needs of all parties (reports that meet specific information needs are often referred to as 'special purpose reports'). As such, the process of financial accounting leads to the generation of reports deemed to be general purpose financial statements.[1]

Financial accounting tends to be heavily regulated in most countries, with many accounting standards and other regulations governing how particular transactions and events are to be recognised, measured and presented. The reports generated, such as the balance sheet (or, as it is now to be called, the 'statement of financial position'), the profit and loss account (or, as the revised statement is now to be called, the 'statement of comprehensive income'), the statement of cash flows, the statement of changes in equity and the supporting notes, are directly affected by the various accounting regulations in place.[2] When existing accounting regulations change, or new accounting regulations are implemented, this will typically have an impact on the various accounting numbers (such as particular revenues, expenses, assets and liabilities) included in the statements provided to the public.

Ideally, users of financial statements should have a sound working knowledge of the various accounting standards and other regulations, because without such a knowledge it can be difficult (or perhaps near impossible) to interpret what the statements are actually reflecting. For example, 'profit' is the outcome of applying particular accounting rules and conventions, many of which are contained within accounting standards. As these rules change (as they frequently do), the same series of transactions will lead to different measures of 'profits' and net assets. Such a situation leads to an obvious question: should readers of financial statements be expected to understand financial accounting? The answer is 'yes', even though many users of financial

---

1   In its *Preface to International Financial Reporting Standards* (IASB, 2002, paragraph 10), the International Accounting Standards Board defines 'general purpose financial statements' as financial statements 'directed towards the common information needs of a wide range of users'. Paragraph 6 of *The Framework for the Preparation and Presentation of Financial Statements* (issued by the AASB in July 2004) states that the framework 'is concerned with general purpose financial statements including consolidated financial statements. Such financial statements are prepared and presented at least annually and are directed toward the common information needs of a wide range of users. Some of these users may require, and have the power to obtain, information in addition to that contained in the general purpose financial statement. Many users, however, have to rely on the financial report as their major source of financial information and such financial reports should, therefore, be prepared and presented with their needs in view'.

2   As a result of the release of the revised AASB 101 'Presentation of Financial Statements' in September 2007 (its international equivalent being IAS 1), which is effective from 1 January 2009, important terminology will change. For example, a balance sheet will now be referred to as a 'statement of financial position', and an income statement will now be replaced by a 'statement of comprehensive income'. There is no clear theory to explain how changing the names or formats of these financial statements will provide benefits for the users or preparers of them.

statements (including many company directors and financial analysts) have a very poor working knowledge of accounting.

Throughout the world, various professional accounting bodies have stated specifically that users of financial statements do need to have some level of knowledge of financial accounting if they are to understand financial statements properly. For example, *The Framework for the Preparation and Presentation of Financial Statements* (released by the Australian Accounting Standards Board in July 2004, and equivalent to the IASB Framework) states that:

> ... users are assumed to have a reasonable knowledge of business and economic activities and accounting and a willingness to study the information with reasonable diligence.[3]

A review of an annual report of a company listed on a stock exchange will soon reveal just how confusing such a document would be to readers with a limited knowledge of accounting (and, as became clear in the aftermath of the collapse of Enron, HIH Insurance and other entities, many people with formal qualifications in accounting also have trouble interpreting the accounting reports of companies that have complex financial structures and engage in complex financial transactions). Unfortunately, many readers of financial statements have tended to consider figures such as 'profits' or 'assets' as being 'hard' objective numbers that are not subject to various professional judgements. Hence, although such users may not understand some of the descriptions of accounting methods used, they may believe that they understand what 'profits' and 'net assets' mean. As we know, however, the accounting results (or numbers) will be heavily dependent on the particular accounting methods chosen, as well as on various professional judgements made. Depending on who compiles the accounting reports, the measures of profits and net assets can vary greatly.[4]

Many companies provide summary 'highlight' statements at the beginning of their annual reports. Often, multi-year summaries are given of such figures as profits, return on assets, earnings per share, dividend yield and net asset backing per share. By highlighting particular information, management could be deemed to be helping the less accounting-literate readers to focus on the important results. However, a downside of this is that management itself is selecting the information to be highlighted (that is, such disclosures are voluntary) and, as a result, a large amount of otherwise important information may be overlooked.

Financial accounting can be contrasted with management accounting. Management accounting focuses on providing information for decision making by parties who work within an organisation (that is, for internal as opposed to external users) and it is largely unregulated. Whereas most countries have a multitude of financial accounting standards that are often given the force of law, the same cannot be said for management accounting. Because management accounting relates to the provision of information for parties within the organisation, the view taken is that there is no

---

3   Within the United States Conceptual Framework Project, reference is made to the 'informed reader' who should have sufficient knowledge of accounting to be able to appropriately interpret financial statements compiled in accordance with generally accepted accounting principles. As indicated in Chapter 6, there is currently a joint project being undertaken between the International Accounting Standards Board (IASB) and the Financial Accounting Standards Board (US) to develop a revised conceptual project. In an exposure draft released by the IASB in May 2008 (entitled *Exposure Draft of an Improved Conceptual Framework for Financial Reporting*), it was noted that users 'should have a reasonable degree of financial knowledge and a willingness to study the information with reasonable diligence'.

4   Yet the various financial statements prepared by the different teams of accountants for the same organisation may be deemed to be true and fair despite the differences in net assets or reported profits—which implies that different teams of accountants are able to provide different versions of the 'truth'.

need to protect their information needs or rights. It is the information rights of outsiders who are not involved in the day-to-day management of an entity that must be protected. Because financial statements are often used as a source of information for parties contemplating transferring resources to an organisation, it is arguably important that certain rules be put in place to govern how the information should be compiled. That is (adopting a pro-regulation perspective), to protect the interests of parties external to a firm, some regulation relating to financial accounting information is required. We now briefly consider the history of accounting practice and its associated regulation.[5]

AN OVERVIEW OF THE DEVELOPMENT AND REGULATION OF ACCOUNTING PRACTICE

While the practice of financial accounting can be traced back many hundreds of years, the regulation of financial accounting in most capital-market-dominated economies (such as the United States, the United Kingdom, Ireland, Australia and Canada) generally commenced in the twentieth century. In part this lack of regulation in the early days may have been due to the fact that there was limited separation between the ownership and management of business entities, and, as such, most systems of accounting were designed to provide information to the owner/manager. In the twentieth century there was an increase in the degree of separation between ownership and management in many countries, and with this increased separation came an increased tendency to regulate accounting disclosures.

RELIANCE ON DOUBLE-ENTRY ACCOUNTING

Early systems of double-entry bookkeeping and accounting, similar to the system we use today, have been traced back to thirteenth- and fourteenth-century northern Italy. One of the earliest surviving descriptions of a system of double-entry accounting is by the Franciscan monk Luca Pacioli as part of his most famous work, *Summa de Arithmetica, Geometrica, Proportioni et Proportionalita*, published in Venice in 1494. A review of this work (there are translated versions) indicates that our current system of double-entry accounting is very similar to that developed many hundreds of years ago. Even in the days of Pacioli there were debits and credits, with debits going on the left and credits on the right.[6] There were also journals and ledgers. Reflecting on the origins of double-entry accounting, Hendriksen and Van Breda (1992, p. 36) state:

> Debits, credits, journal entries, ledgers, accounts, trial balances, balance sheets and income statements all date back to the Renaissance. Accounting, therefore, can claim as

---

5   Although this text focuses on financial accounting, a similar argument can be made in favour of the regulation of social and environmental reporting. Corporations generate many social and environmental impacts that can affect a variety of stakeholders. Such stakeholders arguably have a right to know about the social and environmental implications of an organisation's operations. Such information could then provide the basis for decisions about whether to support the organisation's operations.

6   According to Hendriksen and Van Breda (1992, p. 36), our use of the word 'debit' can be traced back to the word *debere* (shortened to 'dr'), which is the Latin word for an obligation and can be interpreted as meaning to owe. The word 'credit' (abbreviated to 'cr') can be linked to the Latin word *credere*, which means to believe or trust in someone.

noble a lineage as many of the liberal arts.[7] Accounting students can take pride in their heritage. Part of this heritage is a rich vocabulary, almost all of which dates back to this period and much of which is fascinating in its origin.

Debits and credits have, over the ages, proved to be the bane of many an accounting student. So, did we really need them? Why couldn't we have simply used positive and negative numbers? For example, if we were to pay wages, why couldn't we have simply put a positive number under the wages column and a negative number under the cash column? The simple answer to this question appears to be that negative numbers were not really used in mathematics until the seventeenth century. Hence, the t-account was devised to solve this problem, with increases being on one side and decreases on the other. But why keep the t-account, now that we accept the existence of negative numbers? Pondering this issue, Hendriksen and Van Breda (1992, p. 51) comment:

> Textbook writers still explain how debits are found on the left and credits on the right and teach students the subtraction-by-opposition technique that was made obsolete in arithmetic three centuries ago. Programmers then faithfully seek to reflect these medieval ideas on the modern computer screen.

As will be seen in subsequent chapters, there are many criticisms of our financial accounting systems. For example, there is an increasing trend towards the view that financial accounting should reflect the various social and environmental consequences of a reporting entity's existence. Unfortunately, however, our 'dated' double-entry system has a general inability to take such consequences into account—but more of this is covered in later chapters, particularly Chapter 9.

doesn't reflect consequences of entities

EARLY DEVELOPMENT OF PROFESSIONAL ACCOUNTING BODIES

While accounting and accountants have existed for hundreds of years, it was not until the nineteenth century that accountants within the United Kingdom and the United States banded together to form professional associations. According to Goldberg (1949), a Society of Accountants was formed in Edinburgh in 1854, later to be followed by a number of other bodies, including the Institute of Chartered Accountants in England and Wales (ICAEW), which was established in 1880. According to Mathews and Perera (1996, p. 16), from the early years the ICAEW was very concerned about the reputation of its members and as a result set conditions for admission, including general education examinations, five years of articles served with a member of the institute, and intermediate and final examinations in a range of subjects.

In the United States the American Association of Public Accountants was formed in 1887 (Goldberg, 1949). This association went on to form the basis of the American Institute of Certified Public Accountants (AICPA). While members of these bodies were often called upon to perform audits in particular circumstances, and while companies were generally required to

---

7   Hatfield (1924) points out that Luca Pacioli (who was a prominent academic of his day) was a close friend of Leonardo da Vinci, and that da Vinci was one of the first people to buy a copy of *Summa de Arithmetica* and drew the illustrations for one of Pacioli's later books.

early issue of not knowing what to include

prepare accounting reports subject to various company laws and stock exchange requirements,[8] there was a general absence of regulation about what the reports should disclose or how the accounting numbers should be compiled (that is, there was effectively a 'free-market' approach to accounting regulation)[9].

EARLY CODIFICATION OF ACCOUNTING RULES

REGULATION lack made comparison hard

In the early part of the twentieth century there was limited work undertaken to codify particular accounting principles or rules. Basically, accountants used those rules of which they were aware and which they (hopefully) believed were most appropriate to the particular circumstances. There was very limited uniformity between the accounting methods adopted by different organisations, thereby creating obvious comparability problems. Around the 1920s a number of people undertook research that sought to observe practice and to identify commonly accepted accounting conventions. That is, they sought to describe 'what was', rather than assuming a normative position with regards to 'what should be'. By simply describing current practice, the researchers gave themselves limited possibilities of actually improving accounting procedures. As Mathews and Perera (1996, p. 20) state:

set specific rules rather than freedom to judge situations

> This led to a practice–theory–practice cycle and tended to retard the progress of accounting, because there was no value judgement exercised in respect of the practices which were observed. In other words, there was no opportunity to examine critically what was being practised before the next generation of accountants were prepared in the same manner.

Early researchers who provided detailed descriptions of existing conventions of accounting included Paton (1922), Paton and Littleton (1940), Sanders, Hatfield and Moore (1938) and Gilman (1939). These studies described such things as the doctrines of conservatism, concepts of materiality, consistency, the entity assumption and the matching principle.

A great deal of the early work undertaken to establish particular accounting rules and doctrines was undertaken in the United States. In 1930 the accounting profession within the United States cooperated with the New York Stock Exchange (NYSE) to develop a list of broadly used accounting principles. According to Zeff (1972), this publication is one of the most important documents in the history of accounting regulation and set the foundation for the codification and acceptance of generally accepted accounting principles. The NYSE asked the accounting profession to compile the document as it was concerned that many companies were using a variety of (typically undisclosed) accounting methods.[10]

---

8   For example, within the United Kingdom the *Joint Stock Companies Act* of 1844 required that companies produce a balance sheet and an auditor's report thereon for distribution to shareholders before the annual meeting. This requirement was removed in an 1862 Act, but reinstated in a 1900 Act. In 1929 a requirement to produce a profit and loss account was introduced.

9   In 1900 the New York Stock Exchange required companies applying for listing to prepare financial statements showing the results of their operations as well as details about their financial position. In 1926 the exchange further required that all listed companies provide their shareholders with an annual financial report in advance of the companies' annual general meetings. The report did not have to be audited.

10   Five of the identified principles subsequently formed the basis of Chapter 1 of *Accounting Research Bulletin No. 43*, as issued by the Committee on Accounting Procedure.

DEVELOPMENT OF DISCLOSURE REGULATIONS

In the United States it was not until 1934 that specific disclosures of financial information were required by organisations seeking to trade their securities. The *Securities Exchange Act* of 1934, as administered by the Securities Exchange Commission (SEC), stipulated the disclosure of specific financial information. The SEC was given authority to stipulate accounting principles and reporting practices. However, it allowed the accounting profession to take charge of this activity as long as it could clearly indicate that it would perform such duties diligently. In an effort to convince the SEC that it could identify acceptable accounting practices, the American Institute of Accountants (one of the predecessors of the AICPA) released, in 1938, a study by Sanders, Hatfield and Moore entitled *A Statement of Accounting Principles*.

In 1938 the SEC stated (within Accounting Series Release No. 4) that it would accept only those financial statements that had been prepared in accordance with the generally accepted accounting principles of the accounting profession, thereby giving a great deal of power to the profession. In part, ASR No. 4 stated:

> In cases where financial statements filed with the Commission ... are prepared in accordance with accounting principles for which there is no substantial authoritative support, such financial statements will be presumed to be misleading or inaccurate despite disclosures contained in the certificate of the accountant or in footnotes to the statements provided the matters are material. In cases where there is a difference of opinion between the Commission and the registrant as to proper principles of accounting to be followed, disclosure will be accepted in lieu of correction of the financial statements themselves, only if the points involved are such that there is substantial authoritative support for the practices followed by the registrant and the position of the Commission has not previously been expressed in rules, regulations, or other releases of the Commission, including the published opinion of its chief accountant.

While the above statement does indicate that the SEC was to allow the accounting profession to determine acceptable practice, many considered that the SEC was also warning the accounting profession that it must take an authoritative lead in developing accounting standards, otherwise the SEC would take over the role (Zeff, 1972). From 1939 the Committee on Accounting Procedure, a committee of the accounting profession, began issuing statements on accounting principles, and between 1938 and 1939 it released twelve *Accounting Research Bulletins* (Zeff, 1972).

Development by the accounting profession of mandatory accounting standards is a relatively recent phenomenon. In the United Kingdom it was not until 1970, when the Accounting Standards Steering Committee was established (later to become the Accounting Standards Committee and then the Accounting Standards Board), that UK accountants had to conform with professionally developed mandatory accounting standards. Prior to this time the ICAEW had released a series of 'recommendations' to members. In the United States, although there had been *Accounting Research Bulletins* (released by the Committee on Accounting Procedure, formed in 1938) and Opinions (released by the Accounting Principles Board (APB), formed in 1959), these Bulletins and Opinions were not mandatory. Rather they indicated perceived best practice. There tended to be many corporate departures from these Bulletins and Opinions and, as a result, in 1965 a rule (Rule 203 of the AICPA) was introduced that required departures from principles published in APB Opinions to be disclosed in footnotes to financial statements.

From 1 July 1973 the APB was replaced by the Financial Accounting Standards Board (FASB), which has subsequently released many accounting standards that are mandatory.

As might be expected given overseas experience, the history of accounting regulation within Australia is quite recent. In 1946 the Institute of Chartered Accountants in Australia (ICAA) released five *Recommendations on Accounting Principles*, which were largely based on documents released by the Institute of Chartered Accountants in England and Wales (ICAEW). In 1956 a number of recommendations were released by the Australian Society of Accountants (now known as CPA Australia). In later years the two bodies agreed to issue statements and recommendations jointly through the Australian Accounting Research Foundation (AARF), a body jointly funded by the ICAA and CPA Australia. In 2005 the AARF was disbanded. Its elimination placed the development of accounting standards in the hands of the government (through the Australian Accounting Standards Board), rather than in the hands of the accounting profession, thereby effectively reducing the ability of the accounting profession to 'self-regulate'. Further, with the adoption of International Financial Reporting Standards (IFRSs) within Australia from 2005, a great deal of the work involved in developing accounting standards has been centralised with the International Accounting Standards Board (located in London), such that the scope for the AASB to develop accounting standards independently within Australia has been greatly reduced.

The development of accounting regulation in Europe is also worthy of consideration. As will be explored in greater depth in Chapter 4, financial accounting practices (and therefore the regulation of financial accounts) in many European countries were not primarily focused on the provision of information to aid investment decisions by external shareholders in capital markets. The regulation of accounting through professionally developed standards is therefore an even more recent phenomenon in large parts of continental Europe than it is, for example, in the United Kingdom. However, regulation through accounting standards of the consolidated financial statements of all companies whose shares are traded on any stock exchange in the European Union (EU) became compulsory from 1 January 2005.

A further significant change in the accounting regulatory frameworks of many countries occurred following several high-profile accounting and audit failures in the United States in 2001 and 2002 (such as Enron and WorldCom). Although, as Unerman and O'Dwyer (2004) point out, these were not the first large-scale accounting failures to occur since the inception of regulation through professional accounting standards, they were much larger than previous failures and occurred at a time of sharply falling stock markets. Private investors who were already losing confidence in stock markets due to their financial losses on falling share prices now perceived accounting failures as contributing to even larger losses. In this climate, politicians came under pressure to make accounting regulation more rigorous, and they passed legislation (such as the US *Sarbanes–Oxley Act* of 2002) to give greater legal force to many existing and new regulations.

THE RATIONALE FOR REGULATING FINANCIAL ACCOUNTING PRACTICE

As indicated above, even though financial reports have been in existence for hundreds of years, the regulation of accounting in economies dominated by capital markets (with large numbers of external investors) is a fairly recent phenomenon. Early moves for regulation of accounting were introduced in the United States around the 1930s and followed events such as the Wall Street stock-market crash of 1929. Rightly or wrongly, it was argued that problems inherent to accounting led to many poor and uninformed investment decisions (Boer, 1994; Ray, 1960), and this fuelled the public desire for information generated by companies to be subject to greater regulation.

In most countries with developed capital markets and large numbers of external investors, there is a multitude of accounting regulations covering a broad cross-section of issues. But do we need all this regulation? As the next chapter discusses, there are two broad schools of thought on this issue. There are parties who argue that regulation is necessary, and their reasons include the following:

- Markets for information are not efficient and without regulation a sub-optimal amount of information will be produced.
- While proponents of the 'free-market' (or 'anti-regulation') approach may argue that the capital market *on average* is efficient, such 'on average' arguments ignore the rights of individual investors, some of whom can lose their savings as a result of relying on unregulated disclosures.
- Some parties who demand information about an organisation can obtain their desired information due to the power they possess as a result of their control over scarce resources required by the organisation. Conversely, parties with limited power (limited resources) will generally be unable to secure information about an organisation, even though that organisation may impact on their existence.
- Investors need protection from fraudulent organisations that may produce misleading information, which, due to information asymmetries, cannot be known to be fraudulent when used.
- Regulation leads to uniform methods being adopted by different entities, thus enhancing comparability.

favour regulation

Other parties argue that regulation is not necessary, particularly to the extent that it currently exists. Some of the reasons cited against accounting regulation include the following:

- Accounting information is like any other good, and people (financial statement users) will be prepared to pay for it to the extent that it has use. This will lead to an optimal supply of information by entities.[11,12]
- Capital markets require information, and any organisation that fails to provide information will be punished by the market; an absence of information will be deemed to imply bad news.[13]

---

11 Advocates of a regulated approach would argue, however, that accounting information is a public good and, as a result, many individuals will obtain the information for free (this is often referred to as the 'free-rider' problem). Once this occurs, reliance on market-mechanism arguments tends to be flawed and the usual pricing mechanisms of a market cannot be expected to operate (Cooper & Keim, 1983).

12 This 'free-market' perspective is adopted by researchers who work within the agency theory paradigm. This paradigm is discussed in Chapter 7.

13 Accepting this perspective, and consistent with Akerlof (1970), companies that fail to produce the necessary information, particularly if the information is being produced by other entities, will be viewed as 'lemons' (a 'lemon' is something of inferior quality), and these 'lemons' will find it more costly to attract funds than other ('non-lemon') entities.

- Because users of financial information typically do not bear its cost of production, regulation will lead to an over-supply of information (at a cost to the producing firms) as users will tend to overstate the need for the information.
- Regulation typically restricts the accounting methods that may be used. This means that some organisations will be prohibited from using accounting methods that they believe most efficiently reflect their particular performance and position. This is considered to impact on the efficiency with which the firm can inform the markets about its operations.[14]

regulation protects public from inefficient markets

When regulation is introduced, there are various theories available to describe who benefits from such regulation. There is the *public interest theory* of regulation, which proposes that regulation be introduced to protect the public. This protection may be required as a result of inefficient markets. Public interest theory assumes that the regulatory body (usually government) is a neutral arbiter of the 'public interest' and does not let its own self-interest impact on its rule-making processes. According to Scott (2003, p. 448), following public interest theory, the regulator 'does its best to regulate so as to maximise social welfare. Consequently, regulation is thought of as a trade-off between the costs of regulation and its social benefits in the form of improved operation of markets'.

regulation controlled to protect self-interested groups

A contrary perspective of regulation is provided by *capture theory*, which argues that, although regulation is often introduced to protect the public, the regulatory mechanisms are often subsequently controlled (captured) so as to protect the interests of particular self-interested groups within society, typically those whose activities are most affected by the regulation. That is, the 'regulated' tend to capture the 'regulator'. Posner (1974, p. 342) argues that 'the original purposes of the regulatory program are later thwarted through the efforts of the interest group'. Empirical evidence of a regulator making individual decisions that favour the groups that it regulates is not sufficient to demonstrate regulatory capture (as each of these decisions might be regarded as the most appropriate in the circumstances). Rather, most of the regulator's whole program of regulation needs to work in the interests of the regulated, and usually against the interests of those who the regulator is intended to protect. This implies that accounting regulations can have a different impact on different people or groups, and there is evidence (discussed in the next chapter) showing that specific accounting regulations do have social and/or economic consequences that vary between different groups.

As an example of capture theory, Walker (1987) argues that in less than two years following the establishment of the Accounting Standards Review Board in Australia (subsequently replaced by the Australian Accounting Standards Board) the Australian accounting profession (the 'industry' subject to the regulation) was able to control, or capture, the ASRB's regulatory process. Walker provides evidence to support this claim, including the subsequent merger of the Australian Accounting Research Foundation (the professionally funded body) with the AASB

---

14   For example, pursuant to AASB 138 'Intangibles' (which is equivalent to IAS 38 'Intangibles'), all expenditure on research has to be expensed as incurred. This means that all companies have to adopt the same 'one size fits all' approach, even though some entities may have undertaken very valuable research that will lead to significant future economic benefits. On the basis of efficiency this regulation is deemed to be inappropriate, as it does not allow annual report readers to differentiate between companies with or without valuable research.

(the government body), and that the great majority of issues to be addressed in accounting standards were raised by the accounting profession itself.[15]

Both public interest theories and capture theories of regulation assert that initially regulation is put in place to protect the public (capture theory simply asserts that the regulated will then subsequently attempt to control the regulatory process). Another view, which is often referred to as *private interest theory* (or *economic interest group theory*), is proposed by researchers such as Stigler (1971) and Peltzman (1976). This theory relaxes the assumption that regulations are initially put in place to protect the public interest, as well as the assumption that government regulators are neutral arbiters not driven by self-interest. Stigler (1971) proposes that governments are made up of individuals who are self-interested and will introduce regulations more likely to lead to their re-election. In deciding on a particular regulation they will consider the impacts on key voters, as well as on election campaign finances. Individuals with an interest in particular legislation are deemed more likely to get their preferred legislation if they can form themselves into large organised groups with strong cohesive voting power. These theories of regulation (public interest theory, capture theory and private interest theory), as well as others, are further considered in Chapter 3.

If we are to accept the need for accounting regulation, a further issue to consider is who should be responsible for the regulation: should it be in the hands of the private sector (such as the accounting profession), or in the hands of the public (government) sector?[16] Can private sector regulators be expected to put in place regulations that are always in the public interest, or will they seek to put in place rules that favour their own constituency? Obviously, the answer to such a question will be dependent on our particular view of the world (and our own view of the world will in turn influence which particular theory of regulation we are more likely to embrace). Advocates of private sector accounting standard-setting would argue that the accounting profession is best able to develop accounting standards because of its superior knowledge of accounting, and because of the greater likelihood that its rules and regulations would be accepted by the business community. Proponents of public sector accounting standard-setting argue that government has greater enforcement powers, hence the rules of government are more likely to be followed. It might also be less responsive to pressures exerted by business, and more likely to consider the overall public interest.

What is demonstrated in subsequent chapters is that the regulation of accounting (or indeed an absence of regulation) can have many economic and social consequences. As such, the accounting standard-setting process is typically considered to be a very political process, with various interested parties lobbying the standard-setters.

---

15 The establishment of the ASRB in the first place, however, can be explained by a public interest theory perspective. Prior to the establishment of the ASRB, accounting standards in Australia were released by a private sector body, the Australian Accounting Research Foundation (AARF). The AARF, which was not a government body, had limited ability to impose sanctions against entities that did not follow the AARF standards. This was believed to be a major cause of the numerous corporate non-compliances, and the associated social and economic costs that such non-compliances might cause. The ASRB, a government body, was established to give legal backing to accounting standards through the operation of the Corporations Law. With renewed confidence in the information being produced, there was also a view that the capital markets would function more efficiently—which would be considered to be in the public interest.

16 In some countries, accounting regulation is in the hands of both private sector and public sector entities. As an example, within the European Union, accounting regulations are developed by the International Accounting Standards Board (private sector) but have to be endorsed by the Accounting Regulatory Committee (public sector) before they are enforced for EU companies. In the United States, both the Financial Accounting Standards Board (private sector) and the SEC (public sector) have released accounting standards. In Australia, and following the restructuring that has occurred in recent years, accounting standard-setting is now in the hands of the AASB, a government body.

THE ROLE OF PROFESSIONAL JUDGEMENT IN FINANCIAL ACCOUNTING

As we know from studying accounting, the process involved in generating accounts depends on many professional judgements. While the accounting treatment of many transactions and events is regulated, a great deal of accounting treatment pertaining to other transactions and events is unregulated. Even when particular regulations are in place, for example that buildings must be depreciated, there is still scope to select the useful life of the building and the residual value. Many such judgements must be made. Should an item be capitalised or expensed? This in turn will depend on crucial assessments as to whether the expenditure is likely to generate future economic benefits.

At the core of the accounting process is an expectation that accountants should be objective and free from bias when performing their duties. The information being generated should *represent faithfully* the underlying transactions and events and it should be neutral and complete (Paragraphs 33, 36 and 38 of the *Framework for the Preparation and Presentation of Financial Statements* issued by the Australian Accounting Standards Board in July 2004).[17,18] However, can we really accept that accounting can be 'neutral' or objective? Throughout the world, several national accounting standard-setters have explicitly considered the economic and social implications of possible accounting standards prior to their introduction. (The consideration of economic and social consequences prior to the release of an accounting standard is specifically referred to in the *Framework for the Preparation and Presentation of Financial Statements*.) In these countries, if the economic or social implications of a particular accounting standard have been deemed to be significantly negative, then it is likely that the introduction of the standard would have been abandoned, even though the particular standard may have been deemed to reflect more accurately particular transactions or events. While it is difficult to criticise a process that considers potential impacts on others, it is nevertheless difficult to accept that accounting standards are neutral or unbiased. In a sense the acceptance of the need to consider economic and social consequences as part of the standard-setting process has created a dilemma for standard-setters. According to Zeff (1978, p. 62):

> The board (FASB) is thus faced with a dilemma which requires a delicate balancing of accounting and non-accounting variables. Although its decisions should rest—and be seen to rest—chiefly on accounting considerations, it must also study—and be seen to study—the possible adverse economic and social consequences of its proposed

---

17 The AASB Framework is based on the Conceptual Framework developed by the International Accounting Standards Committee (IASC) in 1989. It is also referred to as the *Framework for the Preparation and Presentation of Financial Statements*. The IASC was subsequently replaced by the International Accounting Standards Board (IASB) and in 2001 the Framework was formally adopted by the IASB. Parts of the pre-existing Australian Conceptual Framework (specifically, SAC 3 and SAC 4) were replaced by the *Framework for the Preparation and Presentation of Financial Statements*. As already indicated, a revised conceptual framework is currently being jointly developed by the IASB and the FASB.

18 According to Hines (1991, p. 330), it is in the accounting profession's interest to promote publicly, perhaps through conceptual frameworks, a perspective of objectivity. As she states, 'the very talk, predicated on an assumption of an objective world to which accountants have privileged access via their "measurement expertise", serves to construct a perceived legitimacy for the profession's power and autonomy'.

actions ... What is abundantly clear is that we have entered an era in which economic and social consequences may no longer be ignored as a substantive issue in the setting of accounting standards. The profession must respond to the changing tenor of the times while continuing to perform its essential role in the areas in which it possesses undoubted expertise.

However, this willingness to take into account the possible wider social and economic consequences in developing accounting standards has decreased in several countries in recent years. For example, in the United Kingdom in 2001 and 2002, many large companies blamed (possibly unfairly) the rules in a controversial new accounting standard on pension costs for their decisions to withdraw elements of their pension schemes from many employees. This can be considered to have been a significant negative social consequence from the new accounting standard for these employees, but the UK accounting regulator refused to change the accounting standard (despite considerable political pressure).

Chapters 7 and 8 consider various theoretical perspectives proposed as explanations for why particular accounting methods may be implemented by a reporting entity (remember, the accounting treatment of many transactions and events is not subject to accounting standards). Consistent with a perspective of objectivity is a view that organisations are best served by selecting accounting methods that best reflect their underlying performance. This is referred to as an 'efficiency perspective' (derived from Positive Accounting Theory, which is explained in Chapter 7). The efficiency perspective asserts that different organisational characteristics explain why different firms adopt different accounting methods (Jensen & Meckling, 1976). For example, firms that have different patterns of use in relation to a particular type of asset will be predicted to adopt different amortisation policies. Advocates of the efficiency perspective argue that firms should be allowed to choose those accounting methods that best reflect their performance, and that accounting regulations that restrict the set of available accounting techniques will be costly. For example, if a new accounting standard is released that bans a particular accounting method being used by a reporting entity, this will lead to inefficiencies as the resulting financial statements may no longer provide the best reflection of the performance of the organisation. It would be argued that management is best able to select which accounting methods are appropriate in given circumstances, and government or other bodies should not intervene in the standard-setting process. This perspective, however, does not consider that some financial statement preparers may be less than objective (that is, as with Enron or WorldCom, they may be *creative*) when preparing the financial reports. The efficiency perspective also dismisses the comparability benefits that may arise if standard-setters reduce the available set of accounting methods.

An alternative perspective to explain why particular accounting methods are selected (and which is also derived from Positive Accounting Theory) is the 'opportunistic perspective'. This perspective does not assume that those responsible for selecting accounting methods will be objective. Rather, it assumes that they will be driven by self-interest (Watts & Zimmerman, 1978). This perspective provides an explanation of the practice of creative accounting, which is defined as an approach to accounting wherein objectivity is not employed, but rather refers to a situation where those responsible for the preparation of accounts select accounting methods that provide the result desired by the preparers. As an example, an organisation might, like Enron, opportunistically elect to structure certain transactions in a manner designed to remove specific assets and related liabilities from its balance sheet (a technique known as *off balance sheet funding*). This is not because these assets and liabilities do not 'belong' to the organisation, but perhaps because this off balance sheet funding has the effect of reducing the reported debt to equity (capital gearing) ratio at a time when the organisation is close to breaching particular accounting-based agreements negotiated with external parties, such as loan agreements that have a stipulated minimum allowable debt to equity ratio, below which particular assets of the reporting entity may be seized.

Apart from the efficiency and opportunistic perspectives, there are a number of other theoretical perspectives proposed to explain why an entity may select particular accounting and disclosure policies (other perspectives include Legitimacy Theory, Political Economy Theory, Institutional Theory and Stakeholder Theory). Chapter 8 further explores some of the alternative theoretical perspectives. However, what is being emphasised at this point is that, although there is much accounting regulation in place (and there are various theories to explain the existence of regulation), there are also many accounting decisions that are unregulated (giving rise to various theories to explain the choice of particular accounting methods from the set of available alternatives).

HOW POWERFUL IS THE ACCOUNTANT?

The idea of accountants being very powerful individuals within society is probably not an idea that is shared by many people. Indeed, accountants might be unfairly seen as being rather boring, unimaginative and methodical individuals. Certainly this is the stereotype that is attributed to accountants.[19] According to Bougen (1994), such a view is, in large part, driven by the interdependency between accounting and bookkeeping. Reflecting on the work of Bougen, Dimnik and Felton (2006, p. 133) state:

> Although much accounting work requires judgment, imagination and creativity, bookkeeping is boring and routine. Bougen suggests that historically accountants may have been willing to accept a personally disparaging, often laughable image because it was in their professional interest to do so. Since bookkeeping is also identified with positive characteristics such as objectivity, accuracy and conservatism, the stereotype of the unimaginative, harmless, methodical number cruncher may have actually heightened the accountant's reputation for dependability, giving the profession more credibility with the public.

Following from this quote, it could be argued that accountants might actually have decided to embrace an unimaginative and harmless persona because of the financial benefits associated with being seen as 'dependable' and 'credible'. How clever! Nevertheless, accountants are frequently the subject of many a cruel joke. They are often portrayed as small, weak individuals with poor social skills. For example, consider the depictions of accountants in various movies and television programs. In the (in)famous Monty Python lion tamer sketch, in which John Cleese is cast as a

---

19 According to Dimnik and Felton (2006, p. 131), a stereotype may be defined as a collection of attributes believed to describe the members of a social group.

recruitment consultant who interviews Michael Palin (who plays Mr Anchovy, the accountant and aspiring lion tamer), Cleese describes the accountant as:

An extremely dull fellow, unimaginative, timid, lacking in initiative, spineless, easily dominated ... Whereas in most professions these would be considerable drawbacks, in accountancy they are a positive boon.[20]

Some of us might also remember such characters as Louis Tully, the 'nerd' accountant in *Ghostbusters* (1984), who invites business associates to a party rather than friends so as to make the party tax-deductible, and Leo Getz, the bumbling accountant who constantly annoys two police officers in *Lethal Weapon 2* (1989) and *Lethal Weapon 3* (1992). While accountants may be the subject of such (poorly informed and unpleasant) depictions and taunts, we can rest in the knowledge that we accountants are indeed very powerful individuals.[21] The assertion that accountants are *powerful* (which is obviously more flattering than being seen as dull and unimaginative) is based on a number of perspectives, as follows:

■ The output of the accounting process (for example, *profits* or *net asset backing per share*) impacts on many decisions, such as whether to invest in or lend funds to an entity, whether to lobby for increased wages based on profitability, whether to place an entity into technical default for failure to comply with previously agreed accounting-based restrictions, whether to lobby government for intervention because of excessive *profits*, and so on. That is, many transfers of funds (and therefore wealth) arise as a result of reports generated by accountants through the accounting process. Many extremely large companies throughout the world have had to cease operations because they have breached various borrowing agreements, ones that are directly tied to numbers generated by the accountant (for example, organisations might have entered an agreement that restricts the amount of debt they can borrow relative to their total assets). Because accounting is heavily reliant on professional judgement, the judgement of the accountant can directly impact on various parties' wealth.

■ There is also a perspective that accountants, in providing objective information to interested parties, can, in a sense, provide or transfer to them a source of 'power' to drive changes to corporations' behaviour. That is, accounting information informs people about certain aspects of an organisation's performance and this information—compiled by accountants—might motivate the people to take various actions that might be advantageous or disadvantageous to the organisation. Such actions might not be initiated in the absence of the accounting information. As Gray (1992, p. 404) states:

... power can be exercised in some degree by all ... external parties. For that power to be exercised there is a basic need for information (as an essential element of the participatory democratic process ...) and this information will be an extension of that currently available. That is, the widest possible range of participants must be emancipated and enabled through the manifestation of existing but unfulfilled rights to information.

---

20   Smith and Briggs (1999) provide a comprehensive overview of how accountants have been portrayed in movies and on television. Other research that looks at how accountants are depicted in movies includes Cory (1992), Beard (1994) and Holt (1994).

21   In further research, Dimnik and Felton (2006) undertook a review of 121 movies and, while many accountants are depicted as 'plodders' (having low-level jobs with little status) or 'dreamers' (deemed to be out of touch with reality), a number of movies actually portray the accountant as a hero.

Accountants generate information that is used to guide the actions of many people throughout society. Indeed, a deal of the 'language' used in business is directly tied to the work undertaken by the accountant.

■ By emphasising particular performance attributes (such as profits), accountants can give legitimacy to organisations that otherwise may not be deemed to be legitimate. The financial press often praises companies because of their reported profits. That is, profitability might tend to be a 'proxy' for legitimacy. However, profitability is also often used as a basis for criticising a company. For example, consumer groups or employee groups might use the reported profits of a company as a justification for demanding that the company reduce the costs of its goods or services, or pay higher salaries to its workforce. What is being emphasised here is that the output of the accounting system is used in many different ways throughout society, which is further evidence of the influence of accounting and therefore of accountants.

Further reflecting on the above points, consider the work of Hines (1988, 1991). Hines (1991, p. 313) stresses a perspective that 'financial accounting practices are implicated in the construction and reproduction of the social world'. What she is arguing is that by emphasising a measure such as profits (which ignores many negative social and environmental impacts) accounting can cause people to support organisations that may not otherwise be supported. By holding profitability out as some ideal in terms of performance, profitable companies are often considered to be good companies despite the fact that they might generate various negative social and environmental impacts.

Consider Accounting Headline 2.1. The newspaper report emphasises the record profits of the Commonwealth Bank. If profits increase from one period to the next (or if the profits are larger than those of other organisations in the industry), this is typically portrayed as a sign of sound management. The earning of profits tends to be seen as consistent with a notion of legitimacy—profits are reported and emphasised as some form of objective measure of performance. But as we know, and what the media typically neglects to note, the measure of profits really depends on the assumptions and judgements made by the particular team of accountants involved. As can be seen from Accounting Headline 2.1, no mention is made of the accounting methods employed by the bank. This is typical of media coverage given to corporate performance, with accounting results (such as profits) being apparently promoted as hard, objective calculations. Financial accounting can engender such views because it is promoted (through such media as conceptual frameworks) as being objective and reliable and having the capacity to reflect accurately underlying facts.[22] As Hines (1991, p. 315) states in relation to conceptual framework projects:

It appears that the ontological assumption underpinning the CF is that the relationship between financial accounting and economic reality is a unidirectional, reflecting or faithfully reproducing relationship: economic reality exists objectively, inter-subjectively, concretely and independently of financial accounting practices; financial accounting reflects, mirrors, represents or measures this pre-existent reality.

What also should be appreciated is that the measures of profit calculated for the Commonwealth Bank (and also other organisations) ignore many social and environmental externalities caused

---

22 Authors such as Molotch and Boden (1985) provide a view that a form of social power is attributed to those people and professions that are able to 'trade on the objectivity assumption' (p. 281).

Age, 10 August 2005

Commonwealth Bank nets $4bn profit

The Commonwealth Bank of Australia (CBA) has posted a record annual net profit of nearly $4 billion.

In his last results announcement as chief executive, David Murray has delivered a better-than-expected 55 per cent rise in net profit to $3.99 billion for the bank.

In cash terms, profit was up 31 per cent to $3.54 billion.

Mr Murray has also reaffirmed that CBA's three-year restructuring program called 'Which new Bank' is on track to deliver its anticipated cost savings and earnings growth by the time it wraps up in June next year.

The program has involved the refurbishment of 253 branches so far, as well as the overhaul of CBA's IT system.

'Our strong result reflects the underlying momentum created by Which new Bank's progress, which has significantly enhanced the bank's already strong competitive position,' Mr Murray said.

'I am confident that the momentum which now exists throughout the business will be maintained and will continue to deliver substantial future benefits as the post–Which new Bank strategy is developed and implemented.'

The new strategy will be developed by incoming CEO Ralph Norris, who starts on September 23.

Looking ahead, CBA expects to continue to match or beat its peers in terms of its earnings per share (EPS) growth.

'As a consequence, the bank expects dividend per share to further increase in the 2006 fiscal year, subject to the factors considered in its dividend policy,' the bank said.

The bank declared a second half dividend of $1.12 compared to $1.04 for the previous corresponding period, taking total dividends for the year to $1.97 from $1.83 previously.

The bank said its profit for 2004/05 was helped by a strong performance of its core banking operations, despite the intensifying competition.

Its funds management and insurance businesses also grew profits, as well as receiving a $778 million uplift in appraisal valuation which helped boost the bank's bottom line.

Revenue was up 17.5 per cent to $26.08 billion for the year to June 30, 2005.

However the Finance Sector Union (FSU) said the big profit masked a sorry legacy for Mr Murray, who they say presided over 20,000 job losses during his 13 years as chief executive.

The union also said the bank had 'an unsustainable addiction to short term profit'.

'Mr Murray's departure provides an opportunity for a new direction where workers are treated with dignity and their choices are respected—particularly when it comes to bargaining collectively,' FSU national assistant secretary Sharron Caddie said.

---

by the reporting entity. For example, the bank continued to retrench workers and, while this might have positive impacts on reported profit, such retrenchments cause various social costs for the unemployed (and they also cause costs for governments—and hence taxpayers—in terms of unemployment benefits). Accounting, however, ignores these externalities.

A counterview to the perspective provided in conceptual frameworks of accounting (that accounting is *objective* and provides an accurate reflection of a pre-existent reality) is the view adopted by Hines that accountants can, in a sense, create different realities, depending on the particular judgements taken, the accounting standards available, and so on. That is, accounting does not objectively reflect a particular reality—it creates it. This view is also supported by Handel (1982, p. 36), who states:

> Things may exist independently of our accounts, but they have no human existence until they become accountable. Things may not exist, but they may take on human significance

by becoming accountable ... Accounts define reality and at the same time they are that reality ... The processes by which accounts are offered and accepted are the fundamental social process ... Accounts do not more or less accurately describe things. Instead they establish what is accountable in the setting in which they occur. Whether they are accurate or inaccurate by some other standards, accounts define reality for a situation in the sense that people act on the basis of what is accountable in the situation of their action. The account provides a basis for action, a definition of what is real, and it is acted on so long as it remains accountable.

While one team of accountants may make various accounting assumptions and judgements that lead to a profit being reported, it is possible that another team of accountants will make different assumptions and judgements that lead to the same organisation (with the same transactions and events) reporting a loss. Recording a loss may generate many negative reactions from various stakeholder groups (shareholders, media and analysts) and may cause real, negative cash-flow consequences for the reporting entity. Hines (1991, p. 20) further reflects on the power of the accounting profession:

If, say, auditors qualify their report with respect to the going-concern assumption, and/ or insist that a corporation's financial statements be prepared on the basis of liquidation values, this in itself may precipitate the failure of a company which may otherwise have traded out of its difficulties.

Another point to be made (which is related to the above point), and one that is discussed further in Chapter 3, is that few, if any, accounting standards are introduced without some form of economic and social impact (which as we know from previous discussion in this chapter is considered by many accounting standard-setters). As an example, consider the various arguments that were raised over the implementation of International Accounting Standard IAS 39 Financial Instruments: Recognition and Measurement by several EU countries, and its equivalent standard, AASB 139, within Australia. Many Australian and European banks argued that implementation of AASB 139/ IAS 39 would require them to value certain financial assets and liabilities in a manner that would not reflect the underlying economic reality of many financial transactions, and this would result in unrepresentative and highly volatile profit or loss figures and substantially weakened statements of financial position (or as they have traditionally been known, balance sheets). It was further argued that these weakened balance sheets and highly volatile reported profits would impact on market perceptions of banks' creditworthiness, thus increasing their cost of capital. A number of Australian organisations lobbied the AASB and the IASB to change the requirements of IAS 39; however, such lobbying was not successful. As will be seen in Chapter 4, as part of its regulatory process the European Union established the Accounting Regulatory Committee (ARC) whose task is to scrutinise all international accounting standards and recommend whether they should be enforced in the European Union. Successful lobbying by banks in Italy, Spain, Belgium and France led to these countries' members of the ARC voting against EU adoption of IAS 39 in July 2004, apparently because of its potential negative economic impact.

Because of the wider social and economic impacts that are potentially created by new accounting standards, perspectives of accounting as being neutral in its effects are now widely dismissed (Zeff, 1978). Many national standard-setting bodies throughout the world explicitly state in their various documents (which often form part of their respective conceptual frameworks) that economic and social implications of particular pronouncements must be considered prior to the introduction of new accounting rules. As Zeff (1978, p. 60) states:

> The issue of economic consequences has, therefore, changed from one having only procedural implications for the standard-setting process to one which is now firmly a part of the standard-setters' substantive policy framework.

The IASB, which has now effectively taken over the accounting standard-setting process of many countries (including all members of the European Union, and also many of the standard-setting functions previously carried out by the AASB in Australia), does not have a formal requirement to consider the broader social and economic implications of its accounting rules. However, members of both the IASB and its supervisory body (the International Accounting Standards Committee Foundation) must be aware that, in practice, if they develop too many accounting standards that have widespread negative social and/or economic impacts, governments are likely to reduce or withdraw their support for the continued use of International Financial Reporting Standards in their nations.

Hence, while the notion of objectivity and neutrality is promoted within various conceptual frameworks (perhaps, as Hines suggests, as a means of constructing a perceived legitimacy for the accounting profession), factors such as the possible economic and social implications and the potential influences of management self-interest (culminating in some form of *creative accounting*) can lead us to question such claims of objectivity. Also, despite the various stereotypes of accountants, accountants are actually a very powerful group of individuals. Many decisions with real economic and social implications are made on the basis of accounting information. Whether the supply of accounting information should be left to market forces, or whether accounting should be subject to regulation, is an issue that is investigated further in the next chapter.

CHAPTER SUMMARY

This chapter explored how the output of the financial accounting process is used in many different decisions by parties both within and outside an organisation. Because the financial accounting process provides information to parties external to the organisation who otherwise would not have the information, and because this information is used as the basis for many decisions, it is generally accepted that it is necessary to regulate the practice of financial accounting.

Financial accounting practices are heavily regulated. However, in countries dominated by strong capital markets (with large numbers of external investors), the history of financial accounting regulation is relatively recent and there was a general absence of such regulation prior to the twentieth century. In the early parts of the twentieth century, accounting research often involved documenting commonly used accounting practices. This research led to the development and acceptance of broad principles of accounting that all accountants were expected to follow. Over time, broad principles gave way to the development of specific accounting standards. Accounting standards began to be released by various accounting professional bodies throughout the world around the 1970s and standard-setting activity has tended to increase since then. Financial accounting practices throughout the world today are generally regulated by a large number of accounting standards.

The act of regulating accounting practices through the continual release of new and revised accounting standards has led to various arguments for and against regulation. The arguments range from the belief that there is no need to regulate accounting practices (the 'free-market' approach) to a view that regulation is necessary to protect the interests of those parties with a stake in a reporting entity. Those who argue against regulation often rely on the view that the output of the financial accounting system should be treated like any other good, and if the market is left to operate freely, optimal amounts of accounting information will be produced. They say that introducing regulation leads to an oversupply of accounting information and can cause organisations to use accounting methods that do not efficiently reflect their actual operations, financial position and financial performance. As will be seen in subsequent chapters, such 'free-market' arguments are challenged by many people.

This chapter has also briefly considered various theories about who is likely to benefit from regulation once it is introduced (Chapter 3 extends much of this discussion). Public interest theory proposes that regulation is introduced to protect the public and, when putting regulation in place, regulators seek to maximise the overall welfare of the community (which obviously requires trade-offs of particular costs and benefits). Capture theory proposes that, while regulation might initially be introduced for the public's benefit, ultimately the group that is regulated will gain control of the regulation process. That is, the group will eventually 'capture' the regulatory process. Private interest theories of regulation propose that the regulators introduce regulation that best serves the regulators' own private interest. That is, regulators are motivated not by the public interest but by their own self-interest. For example, politicians will introduce regulation likely to generate enough support to ensure their re-election.

The chapter also considered issues associated with the 'power' of accountants. Arguments were advanced to support a view that accountants hold a very powerful position in society (which is in contrast to how they are often portrayed in the media). Accountants provide information that is used in many decisions and they are able to highlight or downplay particular facets of an organisation's performance.

QUESTIONS

2.1 What expectations do accounting standard-setters have about the accounting knowledge of financial statement readers?

2.2 Do you think that users of financial reports should have a sound working knowledge of the various accounting standards in use? Explain your answer.

2.3 Do you believe that the media portray accounting numbers, such as profits, as some sort of 'hard' and objective performance indicator? Why do you think they might do this, and, if they do, what are some of the implications that might arise as a result of this approach?

2.4 Briefly outline some arguments in favour of regulating the practice of financial accounting.

2.5 Briefly outline some arguments in favour of eliminating the regulation pertaining to financial accounting.

2.6 Do you think that a general increase in the extent of separation between the ownership and management of organisations leads to a greater or a lesser amount of accounting regulation? Why?

2.7 Pursuant to capture theory, *how*, *by whom* and *why* would a regulator be captured?

2.8 Stigler (1971) proposes a theory (private interest theory) in which it is proposed that regulatory bodies (including accounting standard-setters) are made up of individuals who are self-interested, and these individuals will introduce regulation that best serves their own self-interest. Under this perspective, the view that regulators act in the public interest is rejected. From your experience, do you think this is an acceptable assumption? Would rejecting this central assumption have implications for whether you would be prepared to accept any predictions generated by the theory?

2.9 If regulators acted in accordance with predictions provided by the *private interest theory* of regulation, which assumes that all individuals (including politicians and regulators) are motivated by their own economic self-interest, what is the likelihood of the introduction of regulations aimed at reducing the problems associated with climate change—particularly if business corporations opposed such regulations?

2.10 If you believed that regulators acted in accordance with either capture theory or the private interest theory of regulation, would you believe that accounting standard-setters will develop accounting standards that most fairly present information about the financial position or performance of a reporting entity?

2.11 Because accounting standard-setters throughout the world typically consider the potential economic and social consequences of the accounting standards they develop, it has been argued that reports developed in accordance with the accounting standards cannot be considered neutral or unbiased. Do you agree with this perspective? Is this perspective consistent with the qualitative attributes typically promoted in accounting conceptual framework projects?

2.12 Why would 'free-market' advocates argue that the regulation of financial reporting leads to an oversupply of accounting rules and standards?

2.13 What is the basis of an argument that states that accounting regulation can act to undermine the efficiency with which the reporting entities present information about their financial performance and position?

2.14 According to Hines (1991), it is in the interest of the accounting profession to promote publicly a view that the information it generates is 'objective'. Why do you think this is the case?

2.15 Solomons (1978, p. 69) quotes the American Accounting Association:

> Every policy choice represents a trade-off among differing individual preferences, and possibly among alternative consequences, regardless of whether the policy-makers see it that way or not. In this sense, accounting policy choices can never be neutral. There is someone who is granted his preference, and someone who is not.

Evaluate this statement.

2.16 'While it is difficult to criticise a process that considers potential impacts on others, at the same time it is difficult to accept that accounting standards are neutral or unbiased.' Evaluate this statement.

2.17 Hines (1991, p. 313) stresses a view that 'financial accounting practices are implicated in the construction and reproduction of the social world'. What does Hines mean by this statement? Do you agree or disagree with her, and why?

2.18 Why might accountants be construed as being powerful individuals?

2.19 Explain what the following statement by Handel (1982, p. 36) means and provide an argument to either support or oppose the contention.

> Things may exist independently of our accounts, but they have no human existence until they become accountable. Things may not exist, but they may take on human significance by becoming accountable ... Accounts define reality and at the same time they are that reality ... The processes by which accounts are offered and accepted are the fundamental social process.

REFERENCES

Akerlof, G. A. (1970), 'The market for "lemons": quality uncertainty and the market mechanism', *Quarterly Journal of Economics,* 84, pp. 488–500.

Beard, V. (1994), 'Popular culture and professional identity: accountants in the movies', *Accounting, Organizations and Society,* 19(3), pp. 308–18.

Boer, G. (1994), 'Five modern management accounting myths', *Management Accounting* (January), pp. 22–27.

Bougen, P. D. (1994), 'Joking apart: the serious side to the accountant stereotype', *Accounting, Organizations and Society,* 19(3), pp. 319–35.

Cooper, K. & G. Keim (1983), 'The economic rationale for the nature and extent of corporate financial disclosure regulation: a critical assessment', *Journal of Accounting and Public Policy,* 2.

Cory, S. N. (1992), 'Quality and quantity of accounting students and the stereotypical accountant: is there a relationship?', *Journal of Accounting Education,* 10, pp. 1–24.

Dimnik, T. & S. Felton (2006), 'Accountant stereotypes in movies distributed in North America in the twentieth century', *Accounting, Organizations and Society,* 31(2), pp. 129–55.

Gilman, S. (1939), *Accounting Concepts of Profits,* New York: Ronald Press.

Goldberg, L. (1949), 'The development of accounting', in C. T. Gibson, C. G. Meredith & R. Peterson (eds), *Accounting Concepts Readings,* Melbourne: Cassell.

Gray, R. (1992), 'Accounting and environmentalism: an exploration of the challenge of gently accounting for accountability, transparency and sustainability', *Accounting, Organizations and Society,* 17(5), pp. 399–426.

Handel, W. (1982), *Ethnomethodology: How People Make Sense,* Hemel Hempstead: Prentice Hall.

Hatfield, H. R. (1924), 'An historical defense of bookkeeping', *Journal of Accountancy,* 37(4), pp. 241–53.

Hendriksen, E. S. & M. F. Van Breda (1992), *Accounting Theory,* 5th edn, Homewood: Irwin.

Hines, R. (1988), 'Financial accounting: in communicating reality, we construct reality', *Accounting, Organizations and Society,* 13(3), pp. 251–62.

Hines, R., (1991), 'The FASB's conceptual framework, financial accounting and the maintenance of the social world',

Accounting, Organizations and Society, 16(4), pp. 313–51.

Holt, P. E. (1994), 'Stereotypes of the accounting professional as reflected in popular movies, accounting students and society', *New Accountant,* April, pp. 24–25.

International Accounting Standards Board (2002), *Preface to International Financial Reporting Standards,* London: International Accounting Standards Board.

International Accounting Standards Board (2008), *Exposure Draft of an Improved Conceptual Framework for Financial Reporting,* London: International Accounting Standards Board.

International Accounting Standards Committee (1989), *Framework for the Preparation and Presentation of Financial Statements,* London: International Accounting Standards Committee.

Jensen, M. C. & W. H. Meckling (1976), 'Theory of the firm: managerial behavior, agency costs and ownership structure', *Journal of Financial Economics,* 3 (October), pp. 305–60.

Mathews, M. R. & M. H. B. Perera (1996), *Accounting Theory and Development,* 3rd edn, Melbourne: Thomas Nelson.

Molotch, H. L. & D. Boden (1985), 'Talking social structure: discourse, domination and the Watergate hearings', *American Sociological Review,* pp. 477–86.

Paton, W. A. (1922), *Accounting Theory,* Kansas: Scholars Book Co., reprinted 1973.

Paton, W. A. & A. C. Littleton (1940), *An Introduction to Corporate Accounting Standards,* USA: American Accounting Association.

Peltzman, S. (1976), 'Towards a more general theory of regulation', *Journal of Law and Economics* (August), pp. 211–40.

Posner, R. A. (1974), 'Theories of economic regulation', *Bell Journal of Economics and Management Science,* 5 (Autumn), pp. 335–58.

Ray, D. D. (1960), *Accounting and Business Fluctuations,* USA: University of Florida Press.

Sanders, T. H., H. R. Hatfield & U. Moore (1938), *A Statement of Accounting Principles,* reprinted AAA 1959 edn, USA: American Institute of Accountants.

Scott, W. R. (2003), *Financial Accounting Theory,* 3rd edn, Toronto: Pearson Education.

Smith, M. & S. Briggs (1999), 'From beancounter to action hero', *Charter,* 70(1), pp. 36–39.

Solomons, D. (1978), 'The politicisation of accounting', *Journal of Accountancy,* 146(5), pp. 65–72.

Stigler, G. J. (1971), 'The theory of economic regulation', *Bell Journal of Economics and Management Science* (Spring), pp. 2–21.

Unerman, J. & B. O'Dwyer (2004), 'Enron, WorldCom, Andersen et al: a challenge to modernity', *Critical Perspectives on Accounting,* 15(6–7), pp. 971–93.

Walker, R. G. (1987), 'Australia's ASRB: a case study of political activity and regulatory capture', *Accounting and Business Research,* 17(67), pp. 269–86.

Watts, R. & J. Zimmerman (1978), 'Towards a positive theory of the determination of accounting standards', *The Accounting Review,* 53(1), pp. 112–34.

Zeff, S. A. (1972), *Forging Accounting Principles in Five Countries,* Champaign: Stipes Publishing Co.

Zeff, S. A. (1978), 'The rise of economic consequences', *Journal of Accountancy,* 146(6), pp. 56–63.

THE REGULATION OF FINANCIAL ACCOUNTING

LEARNING OBJECTIVES

On completing this chapter readers should:

- understand some of the various theoretical arguments that have been proposed in favour of reducing the extent of regulation of financial accounting;
- understand some of the various theoretical arguments for regulating the practice of financial accounting;
- understand various theoretical perspectives that describe who are likely to gain the greatest advantage from the implementation of accounting regulation;
- understand that accounting standard-setting is a very political process which seeks the views of a broad cross-section of financial statement users;
- understand the relevance to the accounting standard-setting process of potential economic and social impacts arising from accounting regulations.

OPENING ISSUES

1. Prior to the widely publicised accounting 'scandals' at Enron and other large companies there were numerous calls for a reduction in accounting regulations (these calls used such terminology as 'accounting standard overload'). But if financial accounting had been deregulated, what could some of the implications have been?

2. If financial accounting were to be deregulated, what incentives or mechanisms might operate to cause an organisation to produce publicly available financial statements? Would these mechanisms operate to ensure that an optimal amount of reliable information was produced? What is the 'optimal' amount of information?

INTRODUCTION

Chapter 2 briefly considered a number of theories to explain the existence of accounting regulation. This chapter extends that discussion. While financial accounting is quite heavily regulated in many countries, with the level of regulation generally increasing in the aftermath of the high-profile accounting failures at Enron, Worldcom, HIH Insurance, Parmalat and other companies, it is nevertheless interesting to consider arguments for and against the continued existence of, and general growth in, regulation. It is also useful to look at various theories that explain what drives the imposition of regulation. By considering such theories we will be better placed to understand why some of the accounting prescriptions become formal regulations while others do not. Perhaps some proposed accounting regulations did not have the support of parties that have influence (or power) over the regulatory process. At issue here is whether issues of 'power' could or should be allowed to impact on the implementation of regulations, including accounting regulations. Is it realistic to expect that the interests of various affected parties will not impact on the final regulations? We will see that the accounting standard-setting process is a very political process. While some proposed requirements might appear technically sound and logical, we will see that this is not sufficient for them to be mandated. What often seems to be important is whether various parts of the constituency, who might be affected either socially or economically by the regulations, are in favour of them.

In considering accounting regulations, the chapter examines arguments for reducing or eliminating regulation, many of which propose that accounting information should be treated like any other good and that forces of *demand* and *supply* should be allowed to determine the optimal amount of information to be produced. Proponents of this 'free-market' approach (that is, proponents of the view that the provision of accounting information should be based on the laws of supply and demand rather than on regulation) have at times relied on the work of the eighteenth-century economist Adam Smith, and his much cited notion of the 'invisible hand'. However, Smith actually proposed the need for some regulation to support the interests of those individuals who would otherwise be disadvantaged by the functioning of unregulated market systems.

The chapter also considers a number of perspectives that explain why regulation might be necessary. The *public interest theory of regulation* is reviewed. Public interest theory provides an explanation of why regulation is necessary to protect the rights of the public, whereas there are other theories (for example, *capture theory* and *economic interest theory of regulation*) that provide explanations of why regulations might be put in place that actually serve the interests of some groups at the expense of others (rather than serving the 'public interest'). The chapter looks at how perceptions about the economic and social consequences of potential accounting requirements affect the decisions of standard-setters. It also discusses whether, in the light of regulators considering economic and social consequences, financial accounting should ever be expected to have qualitative characteristics such as *neutrality* and *representational faithfulness* (as proposed in conceptual frameworks of accounting, such as the *IASB Framework for the Preparation and Presentation of Financial Statements*).

WHAT IS REGULATION?

As this chapter considers various theories of regulation, and various arguments for and against regulation, it is useful to first define what we actually mean by 'regulation'. The *Oxford Dictionary* defines regulation in terms of a 'prescribed rule' or 'authoritative direction'. This is similar to the definition provided by the *Macquarie Dictionary*, which defines regulation as 'a rule of order, as for conduct, prescribed by authority; a governing direction or law'. Therefore, on the basis of these definitions we can say that regulation is designed to control or govern conduct. Hence, in discussing regulations relating to financial accounting we are discussing rules that have been developed by an independent authoritative body that has been given the power to govern how financial statements are to be prepared, and the actions of the authoritative body will have the effect of restricting the accounting options that would otherwise be available to an organisation.[1] The regulation would also be expected to incorporate a basis for monitoring and enforcing compliance with the specific regulatory requirements.

THE 'FREE-MARKET' PERSPECTIVE

As indicated in Chapter 2, a fundamental assumption underlying a 'free-market' perspective on accounting regulation is that accounting information should be treated like other goods, and demand and supply forces should be allowed to freely operate so as to generate an optimal supply of information about an entity. A number of arguments have been used in support of this perspective. One such argument, based on the work of authors such as Jensen and Meckling (1976), Watts and Zimmerman (1978), Smith and Warner (1979) and Smith and Watts (1982), is that, even in the absence of regulation, there are private economics-based incentives for the organisation to provide credible information about its operations and performance to certain parties outside the organisation, otherwise the costs of the organisation's operations would rise. The basis of this view is that, in the absence of information about the organisation's operations, other parties, including the owners of the firm (shareholders) who are not involved in the management of the organisation, will assume that the managers might be operating the business for their own benefit.[2] That is, rather than operating with the aim of maximising the value of the organisation, the managers will be assumed to be operating for their own personal gain (there

---

1   While our definition of reporting refers to an independent authoritative body, capture theory (to be discussed shortly) would question whether, in the longer run, regulators will be able to maintain their independence from those individuals or groups that are subject to the regulations.

2   The costs that arise from the perspective of the owner when the owner (or principal) appoints a manager (the agent) include those associated with the agent shirking (being idle) or consuming excessive perquisites (using the organisation's funds for the manager's private purposes). These are called agency costs. Agency costs can be defined as costs that arise as a result of the delegation of decision making from one party, for example the owner, to another party, for example the manager (representing an agency relationship). Agency costs are more fully considered in Chapter 7, which discusses agency theory. Another agency cost that might arise when decision making is delegated to the agent is the cost associated with the manager using information that is not available to the owners for the manager's personal gain. Smith and Watts (1982) provide an overview of the various conflicts of interest that arise between managers and owners.

is assumed to be a lack of alignment of goals between the external owners and the managers).[3] It is further assumed that potential 'external' shareholders will expect the managers to be opportunistic, and in the absence of safeguards will reduce the amount they will pay for the shares. Likewise, under this economics-based perspective of 'rationality' (self-interest), potential lenders (such as banks and bondholders) are assumed to expect managers—like everybody else—to undertake opportunistic actions with the funds the lenders might advance, and therefore in the absence of safeguards the lenders will charge the organisation a higher price for their funds.[4] That is, the lenders will 'price-protect', such that the higher the perceived risk, the higher the demanded return.

The expectations noted above (which are based on the rather pessimistic assumption that *all* parties will assume that others will work in their own self-interest unless constrained to do otherwise) will have the effect of increasing the operating costs of the organisation—the cost of attracting capital will increase and this will have negative implications for the value of the organisation.[5] In situations where managers have large investments in their organisation's shares (that is, where they are a type of 'internal' shareholder), it will be in the interests of the managers to maximise the value of the firm, as they will often gain more economically from an increase in the value of their investment than they would gain in direct 'spoils' from opportunistic behaviour. To achieve this maximisation of share value, managers will voluntarily enter into contracts with shareholders and lenders which make a clear commitment that certain management strategies, such as those that might be against the interests of the shareholders and lenders, will not be undertaken. For example, management might make an agreement with debtholders that they will keep future debt levels below a certain percentage of total assets (the view being that, all things being equal, the lower the ratio of debt to assets, the lower the risk that the organisation will default on paying the debtholders). To safeguard the debtholders' assets further, the organisation might agree to ensure that profits will cover interest expense by a specified number of times (referred to as an 'interest coverage clause'). In relation to concerns that the manager might 'shirk' (which might be of particular concern to shareholders, given that shareholders will share in any profits generated by the actions of the managers), the organisation might require managers to be rewarded on the basis of a bonus tied to profits, so the higher the profit (which is in the interests of shareholders and lenders), the higher the rewards that will be paid to managers. Most private corporations give their managers (particularly the more senior managers) some form of profit share (Deegan, 1997) as well as being involved in negotiated agreements with lenders (such as debt to asset constraints and interest coverage requirements).

3   What should be appreciated at this point is that these arguments are based on a central assumption that individuals will act in their own self-interest, which, in itself, is a cornerstone of many economic theories. If an individual acts with the intention of maximising personal wealth, this is typically referred to as being 'economically rational'. 'Economic rationality' is a theoretical assumption and, as might be expected, it is challenged by advocates of alternative views about what drives or motivates human behaviour.

4   In considering the relationship between managers and lenders, actions that would be detrimental to the interests of lenders include managers paying excessive dividends; taking on additional and possibly excessive levels of debt; and using the advanced funds for risky ventures, thereby reducing the probability of repayment. Smith and Warner (1979) provide an overview of some of the conflicts of interest that arise between managers and lenders.

5   This is based on the assumption that the value of an organisation is the present value of its expected future net cash flows. A higher cost of capital will result in a decreased net present value of future cash flows.

What should be obvious from this brief discussion is that such contractual arrangements are tied to accounting numbers (for example, paying the manager a bonus based on a percentage of *profits*). Hence the argument by some advocates of the 'free-market' perspective is that in the absence of regulation there will be private incentives to produce accounting information. That is, proponents of this view (based on agency theory, which is more fully discussed in Chapter 7) assert that there will (naturally) be conflicts between external owners and internal managers, and the costs of these potential conflicts will be mitigated through the process of private contracting and associated financial reporting.[6] Organisations that do not produce information will be penalised by higher costs associated with attracting capital, and this will damage the financial interests of those managers who own shares in their organisation. Further, depending on the parties involved and the types of assets in place, the organisation will be best placed to determine what information should be produced to increase the confidence of external stakeholders (thereby decreasing the organisation's cost of attracting capital). Imposing regulation that restricts the available set of accounting methods (for example, banning a particular method of depreciation or amortisation which has previously been used by some organisations) will decrease the efficiency with which negotiated contracts will reduce agency costs.[7] Given the theoretical economics-based assumption that managers will act in their own self-interest, there will also be a contractual demand to have the accounting reports audited by an external party. Such an activity will increase the perceived reliability of the data, and this in turn is expected to reduce the perceived risk of the external stakeholders, thus further decreasing the organisation's cost of capital (Francis & Wilson, 1988; Watts, 1977; Watts & Zimmerman, 1983). That is, financial statement audits can also be expected to be undertaken, even in the absence of regulation, and evidence indicates that many organisations did have their financial statements audited prior to any legislative requirement to do so (Morris, 1984).[8]

Hence, if we accept these arguments, we can propose that, in the presence of a limited number of contracting parties, reducing regulation might seem reasonable given the view that various items of financial information (as negotiated between the various parties) will be provided. Further, such information will be expected to be subject, where deemed necessary by the contracting parties, to an audit by an independent third party. However, in the presence of a multitude of different parties this argument that private incentives will lead to optimal amounts of accounting information (and a reduced need for regulation) seems to break down. As Scott (2003, p. 416) states:

> Unfortunately, while direct contracting for information production may be fine in principle, it will not always work in practice ... In many cases there are simply too many parties

---

6   This is consistent with the usual notion of 'stewardship' wherein management is expected to provide an account of how it has used the funds that have been provided.

7   It has also been argued that certain mandated disclosures will be costly to the organisation if they enable competitors to take advantage of certain proprietary information. Hakansson (1977) used this argument to explain costs that would be imposed as a result of mandating segmental disclosures.

8   As Cooper and Keim (1983, p. 199) indicate, to be an effective strategy 'the auditor must be perceived to be truly independent and the accounting methods employed and the statements' prescribed content must be sufficiently well-defined'. Public perceptions of auditor independence have been damaged as a result of revelations such as those in 2002 relating to the large auditing firm Arthur Andersen and its role in both designing and auditing complex accounting transactions at Enron (Unerman & O'Dwyer, 2004), and this could have implications for the benefits a firm derives from having its financial statements audited.

for contracts to be feasible. If the firm manager were to attempt to negotiate a contract for information production with every potential investor, the negotiation costs alone would be prohibitive. In addition, to the extent that different investors want different information, the firm's cost of information production would also be prohibitive. If, as an alternative, the manager attempted to negotiate a single contract with all investors, these investors would have to agree on what information they wanted. Again, given the disparate information needs of different investors, this process would be extremely time-consuming and costly, if indeed, it was possible at all. Hence, the contracting approach only seems feasible when there are few parties involved.

MARKET-RELATED INCENTIVES

While the 'free-market' (or anti-regulation) arguments are based on a private contracting perspective, there are further arguments for reducing or eliminating accounting regulation which are based on various market-related incentives, principally tied to the 'market for managers' and the 'market for corporate takeovers'. The 'market for managers' argument (see Fama, 1980) relies on an assumption of an efficient market for managers and that managers' previous performance will impact on how much remuneration (payment for services) they command in future periods, either from their current employer or elsewhere. Adopting this perspective, it is assumed that, even in the absence of regulations controlling management behaviour and in the absence of other contractual requirements, managers will be encouraged to adopt strategies to maximise the value of their organisation (which provides a favourable view of their own performance) and these strategies would include providing an optimal amount of financial accounting information. However, arguments such as this are based on assumptions that the managerial labour market operates efficiently, and that information about past managerial performance will not only be known by other prospective employers but will also be fully impounded in future salaries. It also assumes that the capital market is efficient when determining the value of the organisation and that effective managerial strategies will be reflected in positive share price movements. In reality, these assumptions will clearly not always be met. Markets will not always be efficient. The arguments can also break down if the managers involved are approaching retirement, in which case future market prices for their services in the 'market for managers' may be irrelevant.

The 'market for corporate takeovers' argument works on the assumption that an under-performing organisation will be taken over by another entity that will subsequently replace the existing management team. With such a perceived threat, managers would be motivated to maximise firm value to minimise the likelihood that outsiders could seize control of the organisation at low cost. The 'market for corporate takeovers' and the 'market for managers' arguments assume that information will be produced to minimise the organisation's cost of capital and thereby increase the value of the organisation. Therefore, the arguments assume that management will know the *marginal costs* and *marginal benefits* involved in providing information, and, in accordance with economic theories about the production of other goods, management will provide information to the point where the marginal cost equals the marginal benefit. While the disclosure of accounting Information will be in the interests of shareholders, it will also be in the interests of managers—there will be an alignment of interests. However, working out the marginal costs and marginal benefits of information production will be difficult, and to assume that the majority of corporate managers have the expertise to determine such costs and benefits is, again, somewhat unrealistic.

There is also a perspective that, even in the absence of regulation, organisations would still be motivated to disclose both good and bad news about their financial position and performance. Such a perspective is often referred to as the 'market for lemons' perspective (Akerlof, 1970), the view being that in the absence of disclosure the capital market will assume that the organisation is a 'lemon'.[9] That is, the failure to provide information is viewed in the same light as providing bad information. Hence, even though the firm may be worried about disclosing bad news, the market may make an assessment that silence implies that the organisation has very bad news to disclose (otherwise they would disclose it). This 'market for lemons' perspective provides an incentive for managers to release information in the absence of regulation, as failure to do so will have implications for the manager's wealth (perhaps in the form of current lower remuneration and a decreased value in the market for managers). That is, 'non-lemon owners or managers have an incentive to communicate' (Spence, 1974, p. 93).

Drawing on arguments such as those adopted in the 'lemons' argument and applying them to preliminary profit announcements, Skinner (1994, p. 39) states:

> Managers may incur reputational costs if they fail to disclose bad news in a timely manner. Money managers, stockholders, security analysts, and other investors dislike adverse earnings surprises, and may impose costs on firms whose managers are less than candid about potential earnings problems. For example, money managers may choose not to hold the stocks of firms whose managers have a reputation for withholding bad news and analysts may choose not to follow these firms' stocks ... Articles in the financial press suggest that professional money managers, security analysts, and other investors impose costs on firms when their managers appear to delay bad news disclosures. These articles claim that firms whose managers acquire a reputation for failing to disclose bad news are less likely to be followed by analysts and money managers, thus reducing the price and/or liquidity of their firms' stocks.

Reviewing previous studies, Skinner (p. 44) notes that there is evidence that managers disclose both good and bad news forecasts voluntarily. These findings are supported by his own empirical research which shows that when firms are performing well managers make 'good news disclosures' to distinguish their firms from those doing less well, and when firms are not doing so well managers make pre-emptive bad news disclosures consistent with 'reputational-effects' arguments (p. 58).

Evidence provided by Barton and Waymire (2004) showed that shareholders of US firms that made higher quality disclosures preceding the stock-market crash of 1929 experienced significantly smaller losses during the crash. Prior to the crash there was a general absence of

---

9   Something is a 'lemon' if it initially appears or is assumed (due to insufficient information) to be of a quality comparable to other products but later turns out to be inferior. Acquiring the 'lemon' will be the result of information asymmetry in favour of the seller.

disclosure regulation. In an argument that supports a 'free-market' (anti-regulation) approach to accounting regulation, Barton and Waymire state (p. 69):

> Viewed collectively, our evidence suggests that managers respond to investor demand for information and that managers' voluntary financial reporting choices can promote investor protection. That is, economic forces in advanced markets provide managers with incentives for beneficial financial reporting even in the absence of regulatory mandate.

These authors argue that economic forces operate to motivate managers to provide information to investors even in the absence of regulation.

Arguments that the market will penalise organisations for failure to disclose information (which may or may not be bad) of course assumes that the market knows that the manager has particular information to disclose. As has been seen with the many apparently unforeseen accounting failures in recent years (such as Enron, WorldCom and Parmalat), this expectation might not always be realistic, as the market will not always know that there is information available to disclose. That is, in the presence of information asymmetry (unequal distribution of information) the manager might know of some bad news but the market might not expect any information disclosures at that time. However, if it does subsequently come to light that news had been available that was not disclosed, we could perhaps expect the market to react (and in the presence of regulation, we could expect regulators to react, as failure to disclose information in a timely manner may be in contravention of particular laws in that jurisdiction). Also, at certain times, withholding information (particularly of a proprietary nature) could be in the interests of the organisation. For example, the organisation may not want to disclose information about certain market opportunities for fear of competitors using such information.

So, in summary to this point, there are various arguments or mechanisms in favour of reducing accounting regulation (including private contracting, markets for managers, markets for corporate takeovers and the 'market for lemons'), as even in the absence of regulation firms will have incentives to make disclosures. We now consider some arguments in favour of regulating financial accounting practice.

THE 'PRO-REGULATION' PERSPECTIVE

We have considered a number of reasons in favour of reducing or eliminating regulation. One of the simplest arguments is that if somebody really desired information about an organisation they would be prepared to pay for it (perhaps in the form of reducing their required rate of return), and the forces of supply and demand should operate to ensure an optimal amount of information is produced. Another perspective was that if information is not produced there will be greater uncertainty about the performance of the entity and this will translate into increased costs for the organisation. (For example, in the absence of sufficient information about an organisation, such an organisation will be considered to be of higher risk, and riskier organisations find it relatively more expensive to attract capital.) With this in mind, organisations would, it is argued, elect to produce information to reduce costs. However, arguments in favour of a 'free market' rely on users paying for the goods or services that are being produced and consumed. Such arguments break down when we consider the consumption of 'free' or 'public' goods.

Accounting information is a public good—once available, people can use it without paying and can pass it on to others. Parties that use goods or services without incurring some of the associated production costs are referred to as 'free riders'. In the presence of free riders, true demand is understated, because people know they can obtain the goods or services without paying for them. Few people will then have an incentive to pay for the goods or services, as they know that they themselves might be able to act as free riders. This dilemma in turn is argued to provide a lack of incentive for producers of the particular good or service, which in turn leads to an underproduction of information. As Cooper and Keim (1983, p. 190) state:

> Market failure occurs in the case of a public good because, since other individuals (without paying) can receive the good, the price system cannot function. Public goods lack the exclusion attribute, i.e., the price system cannot function properly if it is not possible to exclude nonpurchasers (those who will not pay the asked price) from consuming the good in question.

To alleviate this underproduction, regulation is argued to be necessary to reduce the impacts of market failure.[10] In specific relation to the production of information, Demski and Feltham (1976, p. 209) state:

> Unlike pretzels and automobiles, [information] is not necessarily destroyed or even altered through private consumption by one individual ... This characteristic may induce market failure. In particular, if those who do not pay for information cannot be excluded from using it and if the information is valuable to these 'free riders', then information is a public good. That is, under these circumstances, production of information by any single individual or firm will costlessly make that information available to all ... Hence, a more collective approach to production may be desirable.

However, as we often come to expect, there are counter-arguments to the perspective that the supply of 'free goods' should be regulated. Some economists argue that free goods are often overproduced as a result of regulation. The argument is that segments of the public (the users of the good or service), knowing that they do not have to pay for the free good, will overstate their need for the good or service. This argument could perhaps be applied to investment analysts. Investment analysts will typically be a main user of accounting information. If they lobby for additional regulation which requires further disclosure, they will tend to receive a disproportionate amount of the benefits relative to the costs of producing this further information. When considering the consumption of free goods it is argued by some that non-users effectively subsidise the consumers of the public good as, like other parties, the non-users pay towards the production of the good without benefiting from its consumption. The result of concerted lobbying by particular parties, such as analysts, could in turn lead to the existence of what has been termed an *accounting standards overload* which creates a cost for companies in terms of compliance. However, if we do not regulate, then in the presence of the 'free riders' we could arguably have an underproduction of accounting information. Clearly, this is not an easy thing to balance and we can start to understand the difficult position in which regulators find

---

10 In relation to the supply of information, Scott (1997, p. 329) defines market failure as 'an inability of market forces to produce a socially "right" amount of information, that is, to produce information to the point where its marginal cost to society equals its marginal benefit'.

themselves. Accounting Headline 3.1 refers to 'regulation overload' as it potentially relates to the insurance industry. The argument is that in response to major corporate collapses of insurance companies—such as HIH Insurance within Australia—the government reacted (or perhaps over-reacted) by introducing additional regulations. As we can imagine, it would be a difficult task to determine the 'right amount' of regulation to put in place.

Regulators often use the 'level playing field' argument to justify putting regulations in place. From a financial accounting perspective, this means that everybody should (on the basis of fairness) have access to the same information. This is the basis of laws that prohibit insider trading, which rely on an acceptance of the view that there will not be, or perhaps should not be, transfers of wealth between parties simply because one party has access to information that others do not.[11] Putting in place greater disclosure regulations will increase the confidence of external stakeholders that they are playing on a 'level playing field'. If this helps build or sustain confidence in the capital markets, then it is often deemed to be in 'the public interest'. However,

Accounting Headline 3.1 An example of perceived 'regulation overload'

Sydney Morning Herald, 18 June 2005

Insurers suffering 'regulation overload'

LISA MURRAY

More than four years after HIH collapsed in a $5.3 billion heap, insurance companies are still fighting with the regulator about new rules aimed at strengthening the industry to ensure it doesn't happen again.

Leading insurance executives including Insurance Australia Group CEO Michael Hawker, QBE chief financial officer Neil Drabsch and Promina CFO Harold Bentley told a conference on Friday that some of the proposed rules were too prescriptive and costly.

The Australian Prudential Regulation Authority first issued a discussion paper on the new rules in 2003, addressing recommendations that came out of the HIH Royal Commission. Since then a number of draft papers have been released following discussions with the industry. The regulator hopes to finalise and issue its new prudential standards by January.

Under the new regime, insurers will have to beef up their corporate governance and provide APRA with a number of documents outlining their risk management and reinsurance strategies. Actuaries will also have to sign a financial condition report.

'We are all bearing the costs of increased supervision,' Mr Drabsch said on Friday. 'We don't like it, our shareholders don't like it, but we have to do it.'

He warned that some small companies would not be able to cope with the extra compliance costs.

Mr Hawker said the industry had to be careful of 'regulation overload'.

Mr Bentley said that he was most concerned about the level of detail required in the risk management strategy report and questioned whether it was worth the effort.

APRA was also drilled at the conference over the increased disclosure required on reinsurance contracts. Financial reinsurance has been a hot issue in the industry following the AIG scandal in the US, and local investigations into Zurich and General Re Australia.

Financial reinsurance is not illegal but if it is not accounted for correctly, it can be used to falsely boost profits. APRA has proposed that any new financial reinsurance contracts be approved by the regulator and that more detailed information be required on existing contracts.

APRA chairman John Laker said the regulator needed 'to get the right balance between effective prudential supervision and excessive regulation'.

---

11 There is also the view (Ronen, 1977) that extensive insider trading will erode investor confidence such that market efficiency will be impaired.

we will always be left with the issue as to what is the socially 'right' level of information. Arguably, such a question cannot be answered with any level of certainty.

Many theories that argue in favour of free-market approaches to accounting regulation rely on the work of the eighteenth-century economist Adam Smith (originally published in 1776 but republished in 1937). Adam Smith has become famous for his notion of the 'invisible hand'. The 'invisible hand', which was mentioned only once in his five-book treatise, *The Wealth of Nations*, appears in Book Four, referring to the distribution of capital in society: 'the annual revenue ... is always equal to the whole product of its industry ... as every individual attempts to employ his [her] capital ... every individual necessarily endeavors the capital as great as he can ... he intends only his own industry ... his own gain ... led by an invisible hand by it'.[12]

Subsequent free-market exponents have drawn on the notion of the 'invisible hand' to promote a belief in 'market omnipotence', arguing against state involvement because it 'disturbs the spontaneous order and the spontaneous society' (Lehman, 1991, p. xi). That is, without regulatory involvement, productive resources will, as a result of individuals pursuing their own self-interest, somehow, as if by an 'invisible hand', find their way to their most productive uses. Some writers actually went to the next step by arguing that leaving activities to be controlled by market mechanisms will actually protect market participants. For example, Milton Friedman (1962, p. 82) states:

> The central feature of the market organisation of economic activity is that it prevents one person from interfering with another in respect of most of its activities. The consumer is protected from coercion by the seller because of the presence of other sellers with whom he can deal. The seller is protected from coercion by the consumer because of other consumers to whom he can sell.

These views ignore market failures (such as unequal access to information) and uneven distributions of power. Adam Smith was concerned with particular problems that occur in monopolistic situations where prices for needed goods might be driven up by suppliers. According to Collison (2003, p. 864):

> Smith ... was against legislation that protected the strong and the privileged either by conferring monopoly powers over consumers, or by worsening the already weak position of employees. He did not counsel against steps taken to protect the weak and was not against regulation per se.

Smith did not advocate that there should be no regulatory intervention. He was aware of the problems that might arise in an unregulated free market, and, although it is rarely mentioned by the advocates of the 'free market', he actually wrote of the need for the government to be involved in the 'public interest' to protect the more vulnerable. As Lehman (1991, p. x) states:

> Among the passages revealing Smith's concern for harmful unintended consequences [of the free-market approach] are those appearing in Book V, Chapter 1, where Smith writes that in the progress of the division of labour, the progress of the great body of people will be the man [or woman] who spends much time doing a few simple operations, with no invention, with no tender sentiment, incapable of judging, incapable of defending the

---

12 This quote is reproduced from Lehman (1991).

country in war. In every society, the great body of people will fall this way, 'unless the government takes some pains to prevent it'.

This view is also supported by Collison (2003, p. 863), who states:

Adam Smith himself was well aware that conditions in the world he inhabited did not conform to the competitive ideal: he was not opposed to government action in pursuit of general welfare; indeed he favoured it, and was acutely conscious of the danger of undue power in the hands of the capitalist class.

So if we accept that Smith's work has been misrepresented as a treatise in favour of the 'free market' (as a number of authors suggest), why has it been misrepresented? Collison (2003) argues that it is in the interests of many businesses that regulatory interference (such as the introduction of minimum wage controls, or disclosure requirements) be reduced. As such, he provides a view that many businesses used the work of acclaimed economists (such as Adam Smith and Milton Friedman) as a form of 'propaganda' to support their arguments for reduced regulation.[13,14]

According to Collison, arguments such as those presented by famous economists such as Smith or Friedman, and 'the corporate propaganda which is used to sell it to the public', were anticipated by Adam Smith, who warned of the negative impacts that could be caused by economically powerful interests, particularly when they are unrestrained due to an absence of adequate regulation or competition. According to Smith (as quoted in Collison, 2003):

The clamour and sophistry of merchants and manufacturers easily persuade ... that the private interest of a part, and of a subordinate part of the society is the general interest of the whole (Smith, 1776/1880, Bk I, Ch. X, Pt II, p. 101).

In other words, as far back as 1776 Adam Smith wrote that it is predictable that business managers will argue that what is in the interests of the business organisations will actually be in the interests of the society as a whole—an argument that is still heard today, more than 230 years later. That is, it is in the interests of managers to argue that if business prospers then society will also prosper. This perspective is consistent with the economic interest theory of regulation, which is discussed later in the chapter.

In relation to how business will oppose the need for regulation on the basis of the argument that 'what benefits business will also benefit society', we can consider a recent Australian government inquiry into corporate social responsibility and associated reporting. In 2005 the federal government established through its Parliamentary Joint Committee on Corporations and Financial Services (PJCCFS) (under the auspices of the *Australian Securities and Investments Commission Act 2001*) an *Inquiry into Corporate Responsibility*. Public submissions were invited,

---

13   Other authors (such as Carey, 1997) have argued that many larger businesses were able to influence academics (through the provision of funding) to support particular views. The results of the academic research studies, which often supported the views held by the groups that provided the research funding, were then provided to government to substantiate or support particular positions.

14   Collison also argues that the works of other well-respected economists have been misrepresented by vested interests. For example, the works of Berle and Means (1937) have 'become identified with conflicts of interest between owners and controllers of wealth when they explicitly argued that both should be subservient to wider interests ... They commended public policy rather than self interest as the proper mechanism for allocating corporate income streams. As with Adam Smith, their names have arguably become misleadingly linked with a particular agenda'.

with submissions being received up to early 2006. The purpose of the inquiry was to consider the merit of introducing greater regulatory requirements in relation to corporate social responsibility and associated reporting (an issue that is investigated in Chapter 9). Deegan and Shelly (2007) undertook an analysis of the submissions that were made to the inquiry. In summary, the analysis indicated that business corporations and related associations overwhelmingly favoured an anti-regulation ('free market') approach whereby corporations would be left to voluntarily determine their social responsibilities and the associated accountabilities, the view being that markets will ultimately penalise organisations with poor social and environmental records. (That is, the business organisations argued that if people in the marketplace expect a corporation to perform soundly in relation to its social and environmental activities and the organisation subsequently does not perform in accordance with these expectations then market participants will penalise the organisation.) For example, Deegan and Shelly quoted from the submission made to the inquiry by QBE Insurance, one of Australia's largest insurance companies. QBE Insurance stated: 'The market is the natural mechanism under which the issue of corporate social responsibility will continue to thrive.'

Seeing the market as 'a natural mechanism' is an interesting perspective. In stark contrast, social and environmental groups, consumer associations, employee groups and individuals who made submissions to the inquiry tended to adopt a pro-regulation view; they believed that regulation needs to be put in place to protect the interests of various stakeholders and that, when left to the 'invisible hand' of the market, corporations do not operate in the 'public interest' (other than perhaps when they are persuaded through 'enlightened self-interest').

Deegan and Shelly made specific reference to statements in various organisations' submissions to the inquiry. Of particular interest was a submission made by the Chamber of Commerce and Industry of Western Australia. The Chamber of Commerce was particularly critical of calls for the introduction of legislation in relation to corporate social responsibilities and associated reporting, stating:

> Above all, it (calls for regulation to require corporations to undertake certain social activities and to provide information about their social and environmental performance) is indicative of a lack of faith in the capacity of the 'invisible hand' of the free market to deliver a better economic, environmental and social outcome than the good intentions of business leaders, suitably stiffened by laws, incentives and stakeholder responsibilities ... But those who doubt the efficacy of markets have never yet been able to point to an economy or society where a 'visible hand' has done better, whether that hand is guided by the state, a plurality of stakeholders, or well-intentioned business leaders.
>
> ... The advocates of mandated corporate social responsibility and stakeholder entitlements would impede the business sector's capacity to make this valuable contribution to the economy and society.

It is interesting that a number of submissions to the inquiry made specific reference to the works of Adam Smith (and the 'invisible hand') to justify their particular anti-regulation viewpoint. Deegan and Shelly also found that many of the submissions made by business organisations suggested that the introduction of legislation was against the interests of Australia, as it would 'stifle' any form of innovation in social and environmental reporting. For example, the Australian Institute of Company Directors' submission stated:

> The AICD believes that reporting on corporate social responsibility in Australia is at a very early stage and mandating any particular approach is likely to stifle innovation and

experimentation by companies and to lead to a mentality where directors and management focus on compliance only.

Deegan and Shelly challenged the view that introducing mandatory reporting requirements would stifle innovation. Rather, they believed that regulation would simply establish a minimum level of disclosure which organisations could elect to exceed.

Evidence provided by Deegan and Shelly indicates that it is common for business organisations to oppose the introduction of various forms of legislation, and it is also common for business leaders to argue that if society expects corporations to undertake particular actions then corporations will undertake these actions because failure to do so will impose costs on the organisation. For example, if society expects a company to adopt high standards of environmental performance, and the company is then shown to be damaging the environment, consumers will elect not to buy the company's products, banks will not lend funds to the organisation, people will not want to work for the company, and so forth. The argument is that regulation is not needed and will actually impede the 'natural functioning' of the market. The market is seen as the best mechanism to discipline poorly performing managers.

With these arguments in mind, companies driven by 'enlightened self-interest' will be expected to respond to community concerns.[15] Interestingly, at the completion of the inquiry into corporate social responsibility, the government decided against introducing any regulation to specifically identify corporate social responsibilities. In justifying the conclusion that there was no need to introduce additional legislation, the final report of the inquiry made specific reference to the benefits of allowing 'enlightened self-interest' to dictate behaviour (PJCCFS, 2006, p. xiv):

> This 'enlightened self-interest' interpretation is favoured by the committee. Evidence received suggests that those companies already undertaking responsible corporate behaviour are being driven by factors that are clearly in the interests of the company … Maintaining and improving company reputation was cited as an important factor by companies, many of whom recognise that when corporate reputation suffers there can be significant business costs. Evidence also strongly suggested that an 'enlightened self-interest approach' assists companies in their efforts to recruit and retain high quality staff, particularly in the current tight labour market.

Hence, in relation to corporate social responsibilities, the government clearly favoured an anti-regulation approach, driven perhaps by the 'free market' arguments discussed in this chapter. Not surprisingly, there were many individuals and groups that criticised the decision made by the government and that favoured the introduction of regulation, perhaps driven by the 'pro-regulation' perspectives discussed in this chapter.[16] Again, as emphasised throughout

15 As an example of the 'enlightened self interest', Deegan and Shelly (2007) note that Origin Energy made the following submission to the inquiry: 'Successful companies can obtain competitive advantage by being considerate of wider 'duties' that may not be the subject of specific legislation. Companies that ignore these wider duties may suffer disadvantage in their product or investment markets and may suffer loss of value through damage to their reputation.'

16 As an example of the 'pro-regulation' perspective, Deegan and Shelly (2007) note that Amnesty International made the following submission to the inquiry: 'There are numerous cases of Australian companies that have acted with gross disregard of the environment and the communities in which they operate. It is also apparent that none of the supposed controls on corporate malfeasance—enlightened self interest, enlightened shareholder value, corporate reputation, voluntary commitments, personal ethics—were sufficient to prevent these events.'

this book, there will be different views about different issues, in this case about the advantages or disadvantages of regulation. Whether we personally favour one approach or the other will be based on our own values and about whether we are prepared to accept the arguments (and theories) proposed by 'free market' proponents or those proposed by 'pro-regulation' proponents.

Accounting Headline 3.2 reproduces a newspaper article which referred to Adam Smith's work. The article considers regulation of the superannuation industry and discusses some arguments for and against the regulation of that industry.

Only a brief overview has been provided here of the free-market versus the pro-regulation argument. This is an argument that is ongoing in respect of many activities and industries, with various vested interests putting forward many different and often conflicting arguments

---

Accounting Headline 3.2 Some arguments for and against industry regulation

Courier-Mail 8 August 2005

Effective regulation a challenge

TIM HUGHES

EACH person pursuing their own self-interest acts in the interests of the whole.

That is the basic premise behind the success of capitalist economies. It was laid down by the founder of modern economics, Adam Smith, in his seminal tome *An Inquiry into the Nature and Causes of the Wealth of Nations* in 1776.

The idea behind it is that each person working as hard as they can to their own advantage creates the energy, efficiency and competition required to drive the whole economy forward in the best possible way.

Of course, humans being what we are, many also seek to add unfair advantage to their circumstances through all sorts of misleading, deceptive or downright illegal behaviour or through the misuse of market power.

This is why corporate laws and regulations are absolutely vital to the efficient workings of the economy and to the maximisation of national wealth, provided of course that they work to enhance, rather than limit, those essential competitive forces between economic entities that Smith wrote about.

However, corporate law is clearly a huge challenge for all involved. One major Australian company recently told me that it had more than 2000 pieces of legislation and regulation that it had to comply with. Not an easy job.

On the other hand we now have a fierce war brewing between the various parties involved in the superannuation industry. It is a battleground ripe for all sorts of efficiency-destroying behaviour and it is coming thick and fast.

First we have the high-fee, profit-driven super providers trying to use the regulator to stop the current TV campaign of the not-for-profit industry super funds.

Given that the investment divisions of the commercial funds manage some of the monies of the industry funds and are paid many millions of dollars a year in fees to do so, this has led to some fairly ugly scenes as some of the industry funds have expressed their displeasure in no uncertain way, with some implicit threats to change managers.

More recently, ASIC has made the quite amazing discovery

that financial planners are not necessarily providing their clients with independent advice when it comes to super.

Then there are all of the less obvious deceptions.

It is abundantly clear that our regulators have an absolutely huge challenge on their hands if they are going to make choice-of-fund work. With virtually every working Australian involved and with total super monies in Australia heading towards $1000 billion, this is not a minor matter.

No one can argue against having a choice of super fund. However, with super now by far the largest pool of savings in our economy, it is vital to our economic future that it be invested as efficiently as possible and that means the law has to be up to the job.

As with some other recent examples, our corporate and super regulators appear to be well behind the game.

Tim Hughes is a director of Value Capital Management.

for or against regulation. It is an argument that is often the subject of heated debate within university economics and accounting departments throughout the world. What do you think? Should financial accounting be regulated, and, if so, how much regulation should be put in place?

As an example of another, post-Enron, perspective on the 'regulate or not to regulate' debate, consider Accounting Headline 3.3, which argues that regulation can introduce inefficiencies into the market. It questions whether the increasing amount of accounting regulation has been effective in protecting investors.

Having discussed the arguments for and against regulation, we will now consider a number of theories that describe why regulation is put in place, and discuss which stakeholders are expected to benefit from regulation. The following theories might assist our understanding of why, in particular situations, decisions were made for legislative reform. For example, according to Barton and Waymire (2004, p. 67):

> The October 1929 market crash is seen as among the most significant financial crises in US history (Galbraith, 1972) and was followed within five years by the most extensive changes in financial reporting requirements in US history.

Accounting Headline 3.3 Perspectives about the regulation of accounting

Future Enrons will result from over regulation of accountancy says IEA study

Institute of Economic Affairs, press release, London, 25 June 2004. This article is available free from www.iea.org.uk

Referring to the recent Enron and WorldCom scandals, David Myddelton, Professor of Finance and Accounting at Cranfield Business School, says that such events are more likely, not less likely, to occur in the future as a result of increased regulation of accounting. The UK and EU are increasingly following the failed approach of the US in prescribing in detail how companies produce accounts.

'In nine years the volume of accounting regulation has increased by 150%, from an already high level, at a huge cost to companies, without any corresponding benefit', says Myddelton in [his book] *Unshackling Accountants*. Sometimes regulators impose standards that are wrong and even dangerous.

Myddelton is highly critical of new regulations, such as the International Standards, being imposed by professional bodies, by international organisations and by government regulators. He suggests that radical new approaches to accounting are not generally accepted by the profession and are likely to lead to greater risk of financial and accounting scandals.

At the very least, increasingly prescriptive approaches to accounting lull users into a false sense of security and prevent auditors and accountants from using their judgement to ensure that accounts provide a reasonable picture of a company's financial situation. Users of accounts should understand that they come with 'health warnings' attached and interpret accounts with caution. Increasing the regulation of accounting shifts responsibility away from users and gives them a false sense of security. It also prevents the evolution of new and better accounting practices to deal with a changing world.

Why would there be such reform? Barton and Waymire further state (2004, p. 69):

Regulators often cite investor protection as a basis for more stringent financial reporting requirements enacted after financial crises. The investor protection justification has a long history dating back at least to British legislation passed in the wake of corporate bankruptcies in the 19th century (Littleton, 1933, pp. 272–87). Investor protection arguments surfaced in the US after the 1929 stock market crash as justification for the financial reporting requirements embodied in the *Securities Act* of 1933 and the *Securities Exchange Act* of 1934 (Pecora, 1939; Parrish, 1970). The intent of the *Securities Acts* was to protect investors from exploitation by informed traders in the large-scale securities markets that developed to support financing of enterprises with diffuse ownership structures (Berle & Means, 1932). More recently, the US Congress and Securities and Exchange Commission (SEC) have cited investor protection as the basis for recent reporting rules following the market decline of the past few years (US House, 2002). Implicit in the investor protection justification for financial reporting regulation is that higher quality reporting would have lessened investor losses during the recent crisis and that managers lacked incentives to supply higher quality financial information voluntarily.[17,18]

However, legislators might have justified the introduction of new legislation in terms of protecting investors, but does this mean that investor protection was their real motivation? Or did they have other *private* incentives? The following theories provide different perspectives on why the 'extensive changes' were made. For example, *public interest theory of regulation* would propose that such regulatory changes were brought about in the interest of the public—which would be consistent with an 'investor protection' style of argument. By contrast, *economic interest theories of regulation* would suggest that the regulations might have been put in place so that regulators themselves, who would have been under pressure due to the large losses that had been suffered, look like they are doing something and this might help them retain their positions as regulators (and therefore help them retain their related income stream). In such an explanation the introduction of the legislation is not so much about the *public interest* as about the *private interests* of those in charge of introducing the legislation. Again, as emphasised throughout this book, there are different ways of looking at the same phenomenon: some researchers may view the introduction of legislation as being in the public interest (a view embodied within public interest theory), whereas other researchers may consider that the same action was taken because it best served the private interests of those in control of introducing the legislation (economic interest group theory of regulation).

---

17 Consistent with a free-market approach to accounting information, Barton and Waymire (2004, p. 70) note: 'of course, mandatory disclosure requirements need not be the sole source of investor protection—self-interested managers supply information voluntarily to reduce agency costs (Jensen & Meckling, 1976; Watts & Zimmerman, 1986) and information costs in securities markets (Dye, 2001; Verecchia, 2001)'.

18 Interestingly, the US Securities and Exchange Commission website (as accessed January 2009) states: 'The mission of the U.S. Securities and Exchange Commission is to protect investors, maintain fair, orderly, and efficient markets, and facilitate capital formation'. It is interesting that the mission of the SEC does not embrace a responsibility to stakeholders other than investors—such as local communities, employees, and so forth. Perhaps there is a view that if 'investors' are protected the rest of society will benefit. This issue will be explored more fully in Chapter 9.

PUBLIC INTEREST THEORY

According to Posner (1974, p. 335), public interest theory 'holds that regulation is supplied in response to the demand of the public for the correction of inefficient or inequitable market practices'. That is, regulation is initially put in place to benefit society as a whole, rather than particular vested interests, and the regulatory body is considered to be a neutral arbiter that represents the interests of the society in which it operates, rather that the private interests of the regulators.[19] The enactment of legislation is considered a balancing act between the social benefits and the social costs of the regulation. Applying this argument to financial accounting, and accepting the existence of a capitalist economy, society needs confidence that capital markets efficiently direct (or allocate) resources to productive assets. Regulation is deemed to be an instrument to create such confidence.

Many people are critical of this fairly simplistic perspective of why regulation is introduced (for example, Peltzman, 1976; Posner, 1974; Stigler, 1971). Posner (1974) questions the 'assumptions that economic markets are extremely fragile and apt to operate very inefficiently (or inequitably) if left alone; the other that government regulation is virtually costless' (p. 336). Posner also criticises arguments that legislation is typically initially put in place for 'the public good' but only fails to achieve its aims due to government ineptitude, mismanagement or a lack of funds. As he states (p. 337):

> [There is] a good deal of evidence that the socially undesirable results of regulation are frequently desired by groups influential in the enactment of the legislation setting up the regulatory scheme ... Sometimes the regulatory statute itself reveals an unmistakable purpose of altering the operation of markets in directions inexplicable on public interest grounds ... The evidence that has been offered to show mismanagement by the regulatory body is surprisingly weak. Much of it is consistent with the rival theory that the typical regulatory agency operates with reasonable efficiency to attain deliberately inefficient or inequitable goals set by the legislature that created it.

Proponents of the economics-based assumption of 'self-interest' would argue against accepting that any legislation was put in place by particular parties because they genuinely believed that it was in the public interest. Rather, they consider that legislators will put in place legislation only because it might increase their own wealth (perhaps through increasing their likelihood of being re-elected), and people will lobby for particular legislation only if it is in their own self-interest. Obviously, as with most theoretical assumptions, this self-interest assumption is one that (hopefully!) does not always hold. The private interest group theory of regulation is considered later in the chapter. In the following section the regulatory capture theory of regulation is discussed. Unlike the private interest group theory of regulation, capture theory admits the possibility that regulation might initially be put in place for the public interest. However, it argues that the regulation will ultimately become controlled by those parties who it was supposed to control.

---

19 This perspective would not be accepted by advocates of the 'rational economic person' assumption, as they would argue that all activities, including the activities of regulators and politicians, are primarily motivated by a desire to maximise personal wealth rather than any notion of acting in the public interest.

CAPTURE THEORY

Researchers who embrace capture theory (capture theorists) would typically argue that, although regulation might be introduced with the aim of protecting the 'public interest' (as argued in public interest theory briefly described above), this laudable aim will not ultimately be achieved because, in the process of introducing regulation, the organisations that are subject to the regulation will ultimately come to control the regulator. The regulated industries will seek to gain control of the regulatory body because they know that the decisions made by the regulator will potentially have a significant impact on their industry. The regulated parties or industries will seek to take charge of (capture) the regulator with the intention of ensuring that the regulations subsequently released by the regulator (post-capture) will be advantageous to their industry. As an example of possible regulatory capture, consider a recent newspaper article entitled 'Aviation industry "captured" safety body' (*Canberra Times*, 4 July 2008), in which it was stated:

> A former senior legal counsel to the Civil Aviation Safety Authority for more than a decade has accused the regulator of failing as a safety watchdog because it is too close to the industry. Peter Ilyk, who left the authority in 2006, told a Senate inquiry into CASA's administration and governance the authority had been 'captured' by the industry, making it reluctant to deal decisively with air operators who fell short of safety regulations ... Another former staff member, Joseph Tully, who was policy manager general aviation before he left last year, agreed CASA was too close to the industry. 'You have got to keep a professional distance when you're a regulator ... we have become more of a partner than a regulator in the last few years,' Mr Tully said.

Another example of a possible case of regulatory capture can be seen in a newspaper article entitled 'More alcohol, more often is hardly the solution to a growing problem', which appeared in the *Sydney Morning Herald* (20 April 2007). The article stated:

> Research recently released by the NSW Bureau of Crime Statistics shows that the only criminal offence that became more common in the state in the past two years was malicious damage to property. Other research by the bureau has found that a substantial proportion of these offences were committed by intoxicated males late at night on weekends in the vicinity of licensed premises ... NSW—along with other state governments—has liberalised liquor licensing laws because the Competition Commission has decreed they are 'anti-competitive', that is, they do not allow licensed sellers of alcohol to compete through longer trading hours, and because restrictions on the number of new licences act as barriers to market entrants. The result of treating alcohol like any other commodity has been more licensed premises in our cities, and more pubs and clubs trading for up to 24 hours ... State and federal governments have developed 'partnerships' with the alcohol industry to change drinking culture and reduce alcohol-related problems, resulting in 'regulatory capture' with governments increasingly accepting the industry's diagnosis, and preferred remedies, for the problem ... Instead of acting on recommendations supported by independent research, state governments have adopted the paradoxical idea promoted by the industry that allowing drinking for

up to 24 hours a day, seven days a week, will reduce binge drinking and public disorder ... The State Government should heed the lessons of the alcohol summit and avoid worsening these problems, by tightening rather than liberalising liquor regulations. If it chooses instead to reward the liquor lobby for its generous support in the recent election campaign, one hopes the Bureau of Crime Statistics has the funding necessary to evaluate the effects of more liberal alcohol policies on future rates of malicious damage and assault.

Obviously there are economic benefits to an industry (such as the aviation industry or the alcohol industry) if it is able to 'capture' the body that regulates it. According to Mitnick (1980), there are at least five ways in which a regulated entity or industry will be able to capture a regulatory body (Mitnick, 1980, p. 95, as reproduced in Walker, 1987, p. 281):

1. Capture is said to occur if the regulated interest controls the regulation and the regulated agency;
2. or if the regulated parties succeed in coordinating the regulatory body's activities with their activities so that their private interest is satisfied;
3. or if the regulated party somehow manages to neutralise or ensure non-performance (or mediocre performance) by the regulating body;
4. or if in a subtle process of interaction with the regulators the regulated party succeeds (perhaps not even deliberately) in co-opting the regulators into seeing things from their own perspective and thus giving them the regulation they want;
5. or if, quite independently of the formal or conscious desires of either the regulators or the regulated parties, the basic structure of the reward system leads neither venal nor incompetent regulators inevitably to a community of interests with the regulated party.

Thus, while the introduction of regulation can in many cases be explained in terms of protecting the 'public interest', it is argued that inevitably it will be difficult for a regulator to remain independent of those parties or industries being regulated, as the survival of the regulatory body over a period of time often depends on satisfying the expectations of those parties or groups being regulated. Further, the greater the industry's total resources relative to those of the regulator, the greater will be the chance that the regulator will ultimately be unable to remain independent.

Accounting Headline 3.4 provides commentary on how it appears that one industry—involved in the production of asbestos—was able to continue operating when evidence suggested that it was in the public interest for regulation to be introduced that curtailed the use of asbestos. The evidence suggests that the industry was able to 'capture' the regulatory process and thereby allow asbestos use to continue—to the advantage of the industry, but to the detriment of society.

As with various industries, at various times and in various jurisdictions, it has been argued that large accounting firms have captured the accounting standard-setting process. This was of such concern in the United States that in 1977 the United States Congress investigated whether the (then) Big Eight accounting firms had 'captured' the standard-setting process (Metcalf Inquiry). In the Australian context, Walker (1987) argued that the Australian Accounting Standards Review Board (ASRB) (which was subsequently replaced by the Australian Accounting Standards Board)

Asbestos: key question hasn't been answered

ALAN MITCHELL

Australian Financial Review, 9 August 2004

The dangers of asbestos emerged in the 1920s. Why did successive governments fail to protect us, asks economics editor Alan Mitchell.

There's one question that the inquiry into James Hardie will not answer. Why did successive federal and state governments sit back and allow thousands of Australians to be poisoned by exposure to asbestos?

We must answer that question if we are to have any hope of avoiding similar disasters in the future.

On the face of it, the history of asbestos in Australia, the US and Europe looks like a monumental example of 'regulatory capture'. Regulatory capture is a common phenomenon in which regulators, governments, regulatory authorities and professional bodies come to identify more with the interests of the people they are supposed to be regulating than with the interests of the people they are supposed to protect.

On the question of asbestos, Australian governments appear to have taken their lead from the US and Europe. The failure of US federal and state governments to protect their citizens against asbestos is outlined by Michelle White, professor of economics at the University of California at San Diego, in the spring edition of the *Journal of Economic Perspectives*.

According to White, physicians recognised that exposure to asbestos caused disease, and asbestosis was named and described in British medical journals, in the 1920s. About the same time insurance companies in the US and Canada stopped selling life insurance to asbestos workers.

Safer substitutes for many uses were known as early as the 1930s, yet US consumption of asbestos did not peak until 1974.

Workers' compensation became available in the US from the 1930s, but asbestos producers successfully lobbied state governments for low levels of compensation and restrictive eligibility rules. In the 1970s, the newly established US Occupational Health and Safety Administration (OSHA) began regulating the exposure of workers to asbestos. But when studies showed that the new regulation was too lax, the OSHA was slow to respond, allegedly because of industry concerns.

In the late 1970s the Consumer Product Safety Commission pressured manufacturers to remove asbestos voluntarily from products such as hairdryers, but these efforts were halted under the Reagan administration. In the late 1980s the Environmental Protection Agency proposed a ban on asbestos use, but the ban was overturned by the federal court on technical grounds in 1991 and the agency never appealed.

White concludes that US governments were slow to limit asbestos exposure because the large asbestos producers were able to capture the regulators.

And yet, despite this failure, the US appears to have done considerably better than Europe. Levels of asbestos exposure were higher in Europe and consumption of asbestos products declined more slowly.

European death rates from mesothelioma are almost twice those in the US, and while the US rate appears to have peaked, death rates in the major European countries are expected to double over the next 20 years.

As in the US, the problem appears to have been regulatory capture. But in the US court-awarded damages appear to have curbed the use of asbestos.

What about Australia? Until 1966, Australia was a major producer of crocidolite, the type of asbestos fibre most strongly associated with mesothelioma. During the 1960s, Australia was one of the highest consumers of chrysotile asbestos per head of population.

The Productivity Commission notes in its 2004 report on workers' compensation that 'asbestos exemplifies the delayed response of government authorities to the incidence of disease'.

'Although there was reasonable scientific knowledge about the risks of exposing workers to asbestos by the 1950s, it was not until much later that governments in Australia introduced legislation to control the use of asbestos.'

Participants in the commission's inquiry complained that governments were still slow to implement controls of chemical hazards in the workplace.

What are the lessons from the asbestos saga?

The most important lesson is that we should never completely trust governments and their regulatory authorities. We should think carefully when we clip the wings of the courts and opportunistic lawyers. For years they appear to have been more effective than politicians at curbing the use of asbestos in the US.

Perhaps we also should be wary of the repeated attempts by our politicians to concentrate the ownership of Australia's media in the hands of a few friendly industrialists.

was apparently 'captured' by the accounting profession.[20] He cites a variety of evidence in support of this argument, concluding that within two years of its formation:

> the profession had managed to influence the procedures, the priorities and the output of the Board. It was controlling both the regulations and the regulatory agency; it had managed to achieve coordination of [its] activities; and it appears to have influenced new appointments so that virtually all members of the Board might reasonably be expected to have some community of interests with the professional associations. (Walker, 1987, p. 282)

As we know, proponents of capture theory typically argue that regulation is usually introduced, or regulatory bodies are established, to protect the public interest. For example, from an accounting perspective new regulatory systems and regimes are often established in response to high-profile accounting failures, where members of the public are perceived to have suffered a financial loss and where it is argued that new regulations will help prevent a repeat of the accounting failures. This happened with the establishment of the Securities and Exchange Commission in the United States in the early 1930s, which was formed in response to the Wall Street Crash of 1929, with the establishment of the UK Accounting Standards Steering Committee in the early 1970s following negative publicity over accounting failures at some large UK companies in the late 1960s, with the establishment of the Accounting Standards Board in the United Kingdom in 1990 following further large-scale accounting failures in the late 1980s, and with many tighter accounting and corporate governance regulations being imposed in many countries following the accounting failures at Enron, WorldCom, Parmalat and other companies in the early 2000s. While the resultant regulatory bodies are often portrayed as 'objective' and 'independent', in the past their members have predominantly been professional accountants and finance directors (the preparers of accounts who these regulatory bodies are meant to be regulating!), which Walker (1987) argues is an important component of regulatory capture. However, in recent years there has been a movement towards ensuring greater independence of accounting regulators. For example, the fourteen members of the International Accounting Standards Board (IASB) all have to work full time and exclusively for the board, and are required to sever their ties with previous employers. They are also appointed by a board of trustees, who represent a broad cross-section of interests and who have all agreed that they will act in the public (not their own private) interest. While this may help in giving an image of detached and impartial objectivity to the IASB standard-setting process (which is discussed in the next chapter), it should be remembered that the members of the IASB are still mostly professionally qualified accountants whose views are bound to be conditioned to a certain extent by their previous experiences and training. In these circumstances, it is reasonable to question how independent and impartial the accounting standard-setting process can be.

Returning to Walker's analysis of the 'capture' of accounting standard-setting within Australia, Walker argues that prior to the establishment of the ASRB, accounting standards were issued by

---

20   Walker was a member of the ASRB from 1984 to 1985. In commenting on his motivation for documenting the case study of the ASRB, Walker states (p. 285) that: 'The main concern was to highlight the way that a set of standard setting arrangements designed to permit widespread consultation and participation were subverted by some likeable, well-meaning individuals who were trying to promote the interests of their fellow accountants'.

the accounting profession and sanctions for non-compliance (which were very rarely imposed) could only be made against members of the profession. Walker (p. 270) notes that throughout the 1970s (which was prior to the establishment of the ASRB in 1984) monitoring activities by government agencies revealed a high incidence of non-compliance with profession-sponsored accounting rules.[21] This non-compliance was argued to reduce the confidence of the public in the capital market, which was not in itself deemed to be in the public interest. Government-sponsored standards, with associated legal sanctions, should, it was thought, increase the level of compliance and hence the confidence of the public in company reporting practices. Interestingly, in the 1970s the profession acknowledged the high level of non-compliance, but argued that the best alternative was to give automatic statutory backing to professionally developed standards (thereby increasing the 'force' of the standards, but leaving the standard-setting process in the hands of the profession).

While discussions proceeded relating to the establishment of the ASRB (a government body), suggestions were received by government from various sources that the possibility of statutory accounting standards being developed other than by the accounting profession should be considered. It was also suggested that the ASRB be given the power to determine the priorities of various standard-setting issues, as well as to appoint a 'research director'. The accounting profession was quite vocal in its opposition to such moves, as it was against the idea of government itself (through the ASRB) being involved in the actual development of accounting standards. The accounting profession wanted to retain control over the standard-setting rather than having the power transferred to government. According to Walker (1987, p. 271):

> The accounting profession strongly opposed the 'costly and possibly bureaucratic step' of involving government in the preparation of accounting rules. It publicised counter-proposals that existing rules contained in Schedule 7 of the Companies Act and Codes should be scrapped and that legislative backing be extended to the profession's own standards. The files of the Commonwealth Attorney-General's Department relating to the establishment of the ASRB (copies of which were obtained in terms of Commonwealth Freedom of Information legislation) record that National Companies and Securities Commission Chairman Leigh Masel referred to a 'concerted lobby by the accounting profession' on these matters.

According to Walker, Masel telexed members of the Commonwealth government's Ministerial Council advising that the NCSC had received submissions opposing the profession's proposals. Part of the message stated:

> A particular concern expressed in discussions with some respondents was that, if the accounting profession's proposals are accepted, the status and income on the profession would, effectively, be accorded statutory protection without any corresponding requirement for public reporting and accountability by that profession. For reasons readily apparent, there are many in the profession who would welcome the safe harbour which legislative recognition would provide.

---

21 According to Walker, the New South Wales Corporate Affairs Commission reviewed the financial statements of 8699 companies during the period 1978–82, and found that 3528 (41%) had failed to comply with one or more professionally sanctioned accounting standards.

After reviewing the available evidence, Walker argues that 'the ASRB's early history can be considered a case study in regulatory capture'. He provides the following evidence (p. 282):

1. Before the board was established the accountancy bodies lobbied to ensure that the government body (the ASRB) would not have an independent research capability, would not have an academic as chairperson, and would be provided with an administrative officer rather than a research director (all of which would undermine its capabilities); all of these objectives were achieved.

2. In 1984 the board established its priorities on the basis of public submissions; by November 1985 its agenda represented the standards that the Australian Accounting Research Foundation intimated it was prepared to submit (the AARF was a professionally sponsored body funded by the accounting profession—that is, it was under the direct control of the accounting profession); in December 1985 new ASRB procedures ensured that 'priorities would only be set after consultation with the Australian Accounting Research Foundation' (the profession's own research body).

3. In 1984 the board published a set of procedures (Release 200) which placed the AARF and other interests groups on a similar footing. Accordingly, the board refused to place a standard submitted earlier by the Australian Shareholders' Association on its agenda, on the ground that the association had not provided all the supporting documentation and an assignment of copyright as required by Release 200. Yet in November 1985 an ASRB advertisement announced that the board would be reviewing a series of standards yet to be submitted by the AARF; the board, while abandoning the requirement of Release 200 for the AARF, continued to impose it on the Australian Shareholders' Association. In December 1985 the ASRB reported that it had adopted 'fast-track' procedures for handling standards, but after six months had applied these only to submissions from the AARF, while it imposed more stringent requirements on submissions from other sources.

4. Prior to its establishment, it was suggested that the ASRB would be independent of the accounting profession and representative of a wide range of community interests. In 1984 the board membership included nominees of the Australian Council of Trade Unions, the Australian Shareholders' Association and (it is understood) the Australian Merchant Bankers Association. The 1986 membership consisted of two former national presidents of the Australian Society of Accountants[22] (including one who was a current member of AARF's Accounting Standards Board), a former national president of the Institute of Chartered Accountants in Australia, a former state president of the Australian Society of Accountants, a state councillor of the Australian Society of Accountants (and former chairperson of the AARF), an academic active in committee work for the Australian Society of Accountants, and only one other (the executive director of the Australian Associated Stock Exchanges).

In providing a concluding comment on the ASRB's 'capture', Walker (p. 282) states:

During 1984–5 the profession had ensured the non-performance of the ASRB and by the beginning of 1986 the profession had managed to influence the procedures, the priorities and the output of the Board. It was controlling both the regulations and the regulatory agency; it had managed to achieve co-ordination of the ASRB's activities;

---

22 The Australian Society of Accountants later became CPA Australia.

and it appears to have influenced new appointments so that virtually all members of the Board might reasonably be expected to have some community of interests with the professional associations. The ASRB had been 'captured' by the profession within only 24 months.

Chand and White (2007) also consider the issue of regulatory capture. In doing so they explain government involvement in the accounting standard-setting process, and explain why in the Australian context the Financial Reporting Council was established to oversee the activities of the Australian Accounting Standards Board. Chand and White (p. 612) state:

> Some jurisdictions, notably the US and Australia, have taken the regulatory process under the wing of a government agency, to efface or avoid its being captured by the profession. For example, the US has taken steps through the Sarbanes–Oxley legislation to strengthen the regulator's independence (Herz, 2002; Schipper, 2003). Similarly, in Australia the new standard setting arrangements were introduced in 1997, including the Financial Reporting Council to oversee the Australian Accounting Standards Board (Haswell and McKinnon, 2003, p. 10). Such remedial measures were seen as necessary in these countries, demonstrating that the regulatory process may have been captured.

Accounting Headline 3.5 provides information about another possible example of regulatory capture. It refers to the alleged capture of the regulation relating to the alcohol industry in the United Kingdom (as was argued to be the case in Australia, as demonstrated earlier). Consistent with regulatory capture, the methods proposed by the alcohol industry to address problems associated with the excess consumption of alcohol were embraced by government, with the government not supporting policies that appear to be more likely to be effective in reducing 'problem drinking'.

While a particular theory, such as capture theory, may be embraced by some researchers, there will be others who oppose such theories. Posner (1974), an advocate of the economic (private interest) theory of regulation (which is looked at next), argues against a regular sequence wherein the original purposes of a regulatory program are subsequently thwarted through the efforts of the regulated group. He states (p. 340):

> No reason is suggested as to why the regulated industry should be the only interest group to influence an agency. Customers of the regulated firm have an obvious interest in the outcome of the regulatory process—why may they not be able to 'capture' the agency as effectively as the regulated firms, or more so? No reason is suggested as to why industries are able to capture only existing agencies—never to procure the creation of an agency that will promote their interests—or why an industry strong enough to capture an agency set up to tame it could not prevent the creation of the agency in the first place.

A key component underlying all the perspectives on regulatory capture is that different groups will have different interests and that accounting regulations will have an impact on these social and/or economic interests. If particular groups did not perceive a potential threat (or opportunity) from a regulator to their specific social or economic interests, why would they devote resources to attempting to capture the regulator? The remainder of this chapter discusses perspectives on the impact of these private interests on the regulatory process.

Government 'too close to alcohol industry': medical journal attacks plans for 24-hour pub licensing

SARAH BOSELEY HEALTH EDITOR

The government is too close to the drinks industry to deal with growing alcohol-related problems, an article in the *British Medical Journal* says.

Wayne Hall, a professor in Queensland University's office of public policy and ethics, offers a savage critique of policies for dealing with excessive drinking that leads to violence and deaths. He says Australia has brought alcohol consumption down over the past two decades, while it has soared in the UK.

'The UK government's new alcohol policy, which includes "partnership" with the alcohol industry, shows all the hallmarks of regulatory capture in that it embraces the industry's diagnosis and preferred remedies for the alcohol problem,' he writes.

'The problem, in the industry's view, is a "minority" of drinkers who engage in antisocial behaviour and put their health at risk; the preferred remedies are public education about safe drinking, improved policing, better treatment for alcohol problems and self regulation by the alcohol industry— the policies which evidence suggests are the least likely to reduce problem drinking.'

The government, he says, has failed to introduce the most effective measure—imposing higher taxes on higher strength alcoholic drinks.

'It justifies this decision by saying that increased price has not been shown definitely to reduce harm due to alcohol, an assertion at odds with the views of the world's leading researchers on alcohol.'

Instead of reducing access to alcohol, the government 'embraces the paradoxical idea that allowing drinking for up to 24 hours a day will reduce binge drinking and public disorder,' he writes.

He points to the different approach taken in Australia. Although the Australian government also adopted liberalisation policies, it imposed lower taxes on low-alcohol beer, those with less than 3.8%. It also set a tougher drink-driving level of 0.05% alcohol in the blood instead of 0.08% as in the UK, and introduced random breath tests.

The rise of alcohol sales in Britain is probably the result of lowering the cost while increasing its availability, coupled to heavy promotion by the industry, he says.

Alcohol abuse is thought to cost the economy £30bn a year and alcohol dependency rates in the UK are among the highest in Europe, at 7.5% of men and 2.1% of women.

'If the UK government remains deaf to the arguments of its critics, it should honour its promise to evaluate the effects of its policies,' he writes.

'Then it would have the necessary evidence to drop policies that have failed and replace them with policies that have a chance of reducing (rather than merely preventing further rises in) alcohol-related harm.' He believes the UK should also invest in treatment for those with problems.

The *BMJ* also features papers by researchers who claim two psychosocial interventions would save society five times as much as they cost.

The two interventions—social behaviour and network therapy and motivational enhancement therapy—both give counselling and social support to heavy drinkers without them having to 'dry out' in a residential clinic.

Alcohol Concern called on the government to spend money to save money. 'We welcome the publication of such comprehensive research backing up what we have known for years: treatment works,' said Geethika Jayatilaka, its director of policy and public affairs.

'Every year thousands of people access help and support from specialist alcohol services and are able to turn their lives around. But without adequate funding agencies are struggling to survive and there are still too many people who cannot access the treatment.'

Almost three times more people die from alcohol than from drugs, she said, and yet alcohol services receive only a fifth of the funding.

ECONOMIC AND SOCIAL IMPACTS OF ACCOUNTING REGULATION

Before examining various theories that address the influence of private interests on the accounting regulatory process, it is necessary to establish whether accounting regulations can and do have a social and/or economic impact on the interests of preparers or users of accounts. Although many people might argue that accounting regulations only affect how underlying economic transactions and events are reflected in the financial reports, without any impact on the nature or shape of this underlying economic reality, there is a considerable body of evidence that accounting regulations have real social and economic consequences for many organisations and people.

For example, one of the first new accounting standards issued by the IASB as an International Financial Reporting Standard (IFRS) dealt with the accounting treatment of share options (IFRS 2, which subsequently became AASB 2 'Share-based Payment' within Australia). Although many companies use large numbers of share options as part of their management remuneration and incentive plans, prior to the release of IFRS 2 in 2005 most companies simply ignored the costs associated with issuing share options to employees when calculating their annual profit or loss. The justification for this practice was that when executives exercised the share options, and the company issued new shares to these executives at below market value, this did not apparently cost the company itself anything—despite it diluting the value of existing shareholders' investments. However, the IASB view was that, by granting valuable share options to employees, companies were able to pay these employees a lower amount of money than if they had not been granted the share options. As the company receives valuable services from employees in exchange for these options, which would have been recorded as an expense if they had been paid for in cash, under IFRS 2 and AASB 2 the fair value of share options now has to be recognised as an expense in the statement of comprehensive income. Although implementation of IFRS 2 should have had no direct impact on underlying cash flows, during the development of IFRS 2 it was extensively argued that it would have many indirect negative economic and social consequences for a multitude of people. As some companies would be required to recognise a potentially large share option expense each year, some people maintained that these companies would be less likely to use share options as part of their pay and rewards packages. If valuable share options are an effective way to motivate managers and help align their self-interests with those of shareholders, a reduction in use of this form of incentive could lead to less-motivated executives (or a less-motivated workforce overall if share options were granted to many employees). This could lead to a reduction in underlying company performance, simply because IFRS 2 changed the manner in which a specific item was reflected in the financial statements. Therefore, while it was argued that IFRS 2 (in common with most, if not all, other accounting standards) should not lead to any direct changes in underlying business performance or cash flows, its indirect economic consequences could be potentially large and negative.

As another example, with the adoption of International Financial Reporting Standards (IFRSs) in many countries, companies were required to follow IAS 38 'Intangibles' (which in Australia is known as AASB 138 'Intangibles'). This standard is particularly harsh on assets such as internally developed brand names, mastheads and research expenditure. Effectively, it requires expenditure on such assets to be written off as an expense when incurred. Previously, within many countries—such as Australia—there was no accounting standard preventing such expenditure from being recognised as an asset. As a result of the introduction of this accounting standard, many accounting commentators argued that expenditure on such items would be expected to reduce given the adverse impact that such expenditure would have on reported profits. It can be imagined how a reduction in expenditure on research could cause social and economic impacts that would flow throughout the society. Accounting Headline 3.6 briefly describes some concerns

Accounting Headline 3.6 A consideration of the economic consequences of an accounting standard

Firms to fight writedown rules—new standards could wipe $50 billion from balance sheets

MICHAEL WEST

Australian, 16 February 2004

AUSTRALIA'S biggest companies are fighting a rearguard action to win an exemption from new international accounting rules that will carve up to $50 billion off the value of corporate balance sheets next year.

The Group of 100, an industry body linked to the Business Council of Australia that represents the nation's finance executives, has written to the Australian Accounting Standards Board seeking an exemption from the new rules that from January 1, 2005, will force writedowns on intangible assets such as brand names, licence agreements and management rights.

G100 chairman John Stanhope, who is Telstra's chief financial officer, said the group had been lobbying Canberra to quarantine existing balance sheet intangibles, with a final decision on the new standards in the hands of Treasurer Peter Costello and his parliamentary secretary, Ross Cameron.

'It will have a big impact on some of Australia's major companies and therefore we should reflect on the national interests when making this decision,' he said.

Coca-Cola Amatil, Foster's Lion Nathan, The News Corporation Ltd, Publishing & Broadcasting and Seven Network are among the most obvious candidates for large writedowns as Australia moves to adopt the International Accounting Standards Board (IASB) standards on the valuation of intangible assets on January 1 next year.

The changes will affect all companies that have revalued any intangible assets for which there is not an active and liquid market. This includes their brand names, licence agreements, newspaper mastheads and management rights at property trusts.

Wayne Longeran, managing director of consulting firm Lonergan Edwards & Associates, said most large corporates would comfortably absorb the writedowns as they did not represent a cash loss.

But the reforms would reverberate all the way down the corporate food chain to smaller companies, whose return on equity, return on assets, debt gearing levels and banking covenants could be affected. A reduction in retained profits caused by the removal of intangible assets could also affect a company's ability to pay dividends, which could hit its share price.

'Try explaining to your bank manager that that $100 million asset is now worth zero,' Mr Longeran said. He estimates collective writedowns for Australian companies of between $40 billion and $50 billion.

Although most finance executives agree with the idea that Australia must step into line with global accounting practice, many corporates have baulked at complying with the new International Accounting Standard Board rules on assets.

The G100 wants intangible assets already on company balance sheets to be 'grandfathered' from the new rules.

Mr Stanhope has written to AASB chairman David Boymal seeking an exemption from the standard. Mr Boymal responded that the AASB was obliged to act on directives from the Financial Reporting Council—the international regulator that monitors accounting standards—and has passed the letter on to the FRC. The FRC has sympathy with the plight of the corporates; however, the march towards international compliance is likely to override the demand for exemption.

in relation to the introduction of the accounting standard on intangible assets within Australia. Before the release of the standard, it was argued that its introduction would 'reverberate' throughout society and would impact on the ability of companies to pay dividends and also affect corporate relationships with banks.

There are many other examples of accounting standards that have potential indirect economic and social impacts. Indeed, some people might argue that all accounting regulations will have an impact on managerial decisions (as managers will seek to manage their business so as to optimise their reported accounting numbers), and the resulting changes in managerial decisions will have a social and/or economic impact on those affected by the decisions. Several academic studies, which are discussed in the next section, have illustrated how the consideration of the potential economic consequences of proposed accounting standards motivated particular organisations to lobby regulators either in opposition to particular accounting standards or in support. This lobbying attempts to shape the regulations in a manner that will maximise the expected positive, or minimise the expected negative, economic consequences from the new accounting regulations for the lobbying organisations.

LOBBYING AND THE ECONOMIC INTEREST GROUP THEORY OF REGULATION

The economic interest group theory of regulation (or, as it is sometimes called, the private interest theory of regulation) assumes that groups will form to protect particular economic interests. Different groups, with incompatible or mutually exclusive interests and objectives, are viewed as often being in conflict with each other and they will lobby government or other regulators to put in place legislation that economically benefits them (at the expense of the others). As an example, consumers might lobby government for price protection, or producers might lobby government for tariff protection. This theoretical perspective adopts no notion of *public interest*—rather, private interests are considered to dominate the legislative process.[23]

In relation to financial accounting, particular industry groups may lobby the regulator (the accounting standard-setter) to accept or reject a particular accounting standard. For example, Hope and Gray (1982) show how a small number of aerospace companies were successful, during a consultation process, in changing the detailed requirements of a UK accounting standard on research and development in favour of their (private) interests. This was despite the overwhelming majority of participants in the consultation process not sharing the objections that had been made to the original proposals by the aerospace companies. These original proposals required all research and development expenditure to be charged as an expense in the year in which it had been incurred. The aerospace companies successfully argued that in certain circumstances they should be allowed to treat development expenditure as a form of capital expenditure, and charge it as an expense in future years by matching it against the income that it eventually generated. Although the impact on reported profits over the life of a project would be nil (the accounting treatment simply allowed a deferral of the expenditure between years), this accounting treatment

---

23   As Posner (1974) states, 'the economic theory of regulation is committed to the strong assumptions of economic theory generally, notably that people seek to advance their self-interest and do so rationally'.

resulted in higher net assets being reported in the balance sheet (statement of financial position) each year during a project than would have been the case if the development expenditure had been charged against profits in the year it was incurred. At the time, the prices that these aerospace companies could charge the UK government for large defence contracts was based on a percentage return on net assets. Clearly, the higher the reported net assets in any particular year, the more a company could charge the government for a contract, so it was clearly in the private interests of the aerospace companies that the accounting standard permitted deferral of development expenditure.

A more recent example of successful lobbying of an accounting regulator by an industry group, apparently seeking outcomes that were in the industry's own interests, has been the lobbying by some European banks against the revised provisions of International Accounting Standard (IAS) 39. Banks in several European countries, as in Australia, argued that some of the provisions of IAS 39 (AASB 139 within Australia) would result in their accounts showing significant volatility that did not reflect the underlying economic reality, and this could be damaging to a bank's perceived financial stability. The IASB made some limited changes in response to the banks' concerns, but refused to change IAS 39 substantially. As will be seen in the next chapter, from 1 January 2005 accounting standards issued by the IASB became the accounting regulations that must be followed by Australian companies as well as all companies that have their shares traded on any stock exchange in the European Union (EU). However, as part of the EU accounting regulatory process, for any accounting regulation to be mandated for use by EU companies it has first to be endorsed by the European Commission. The endorsement of each IAS/IFRS follows advice from the Accounting Regulatory Committee (ARC), which has one member from each of the twenty-five EU member states. At a meeting of the ARC in July 2004, four member states voted against full EU endorsement of IAS 39 and a further six states abstained, principally objecting to the elements of IAS 39 that banks in their countries had lobbied against. The fifteen states that voted in favour of full endorsement were insufficient to form the two-thirds majority of the ARC required for approval by the European Union of an IAS.[24] By comparison, while Australian banks lobbied against AASB 139 within Australia, the full requirements of IAS 39 were incorporated within AASB 139. Hence, unlike their European counterparts, Australian banks were unable to coerce the local regulator into amending the requirements of IAS 39.

In an early study on lobbying of accounting regulators, Watts and Zimmerman (1978) reviewed the lobbying behaviour of US corporations in relation to a proposal for the introduction of general price level accounting—a method of accounting that, in periods of inflation, would lead to a reduction in reported profits. They demonstrated that large politically sensitive firms favoured the proposed method of accounting, which led to reduced profits. This was counter to normal expectations that companies generally would prefer to show higher rather than lower earnings. It was explained on the (self-interest) basis that it was the larger firms which could be subject to negative public sentiment (and pressures for regulation of their prices) if their profits were seen to be abnormally high, and they might therefore be seen more favourably if they reported lower profits. Hence, by reporting lower

---

24 In recent years, environmental groups have also lobbied government to introduce a requirement for companies to report various items of social and environmental information. Such submissions could perhaps prove a problem for advocates of the view that lobbying behaviour will be dictated by private concerns about wealth maximisation (the rational economic person assumption). Perhaps (and we are clutching at straws here!) to maintain support for their 'self-interest' view of the world, proponents of the economic interest theory of regulation might argue that the submissions are made by officers of the environmental lobby group in an endeavour to increase their probability of reappointment.

profits there was less likely to be negative wealth implications for the organisations (perhaps in the forms of government intervention, consumer boycotts or claims for higher wages).

Accounting firms also make submissions as part of the accounting standard-setting process. If the economic interest group theory of regulation were to be embraced, we would argue that these submissions can be explained as efforts to protect the interests of professional accountants. Perhaps auditors favour rules that reduce the risk involved in an audit, as more standardisation and less judgement reduces the risk of an audit and therefore the potential for costly lawsuits. Evidence in Deegan, Morris and Stokes (1990) also supports the view that audit firms are relatively more likely to lobby in favour of particular accounting methods if those methods are already in use by a number of their clients. Analysts also frequently lobby regulators for increased disclosure, perhaps because they can use the information in their job but pay only a very small amount for it (other non-users will effectively subsidise the costs of the information—part of the free-rider issue discussed earlier in the chapter).

Under the economic interest group theory of regulation, the regulator itself is an interest group—one that is motivated to embrace strategies to ensure re-election, or to ensure the maintenance of its position of power or privilege within the community. For example, Broadbent and Laughlin (2002) argue that in the UK lobbying surrounding the development of accounting regulations applicable to governmental accounting for projects involving private sector provision of public services (known as Private Finance Initiative projects, or public private partnerships), various regulatory bodies adopted positions that could be interpreted as seeking to defend or enhance their standing with the groups who appoint them and give them legitimacy. It should be remembered that regulatory bodies can be very powerful.

The regulatory body, typically government controlled or influenced, has a resource (potential regulation) that can increase or decrease the wealth of various sectors of the constituency. As Stigler (1971, p. 3) states:

> The state—the machinery and power of the state—is a potential resource or threat to every industry in society ... Regulation may be actively sought by an industry, or it may be thrust upon it ... as a rule, regulation is acquired by the industry and is designed and operated primarily for its benefit ... We propose the general hypothesis: every industry or occupation that has enough political power to utilise the state will seek to control entry.

Under this 'economic interest' perspective of regulation, rather than regulation initially being put in place for the *public interest* (as is initially assumed within capture theory and also in public interest theory), it is proposed that regulation is put in place to serve the *private interests* of particular parties, including politicians who seek re-election. According to Posner (1974, p. 343), economic interest theories of regulation insist that economic regulation serves the private interests of politically effective groups. Further, Stigler (1971, p. 12) states:

> The industry which seeks regulation must be prepared to pay with the two things a party needs: votes and resources. The resources may be provided by campaign contributions, contributed services (the businessman heads a fund-raising committee), and more indirect methods such as the employment of party workers. The votes in support of the measure are rallied, and the votes in opposition are dispersed, by expensive programs to educate (or uneducate) members of the industry and other concerned industries ... The smallest industries are therefore effectively precluded from the political process unless they have

some special advantage such as geographical concentration in a sparsely settled political subdivision.[25]

Under the economic interest theory of regulation, the regulation itself is considered to be a commodity subject to the economic principles of supply and demand. According to Posner (1974, p. 344):

> Since the coercive power of government can be used to give valuable benefits to particular individuals or groups, economic regulation—the expression of that power in the economic sphere—can be viewed as a product whose allocation is governed by laws of supply and demand ... There are a fair number of case studies—of trucking, airlines, railroads, and many other industries—that support the view that economic regulation is better explained as a product supplied to interest groups than as an expression of the social interest in efficiency or justice.

Posner's position is consistent with that adopted by Peltzman (1976), who states (p. 212):

> The essential commodity being transacted in the political market is a transfer of wealth, with constituents on the demand side and their political representatives on the supply side. Viewed in this way, the market here, as elsewhere, will distribute more of the good to those whose effective demand is the highest ... I begin with the assumption that what is basically at stake in the regulatory process is a transfer of wealth.

The idea being promoted by the advocates of economic interest group theories of regulation is that if a particular group (perhaps a minority) does not have sufficient power (which might be reflected by the numbers of controlled votes, or by the potential funds available to support an election campaign) then that group will not be able to effectively lobby for regulation that might protect its various interests. This view is compatible with some of the arguments used by a number of critical theorists (discussed in Chapter 12), who often contend that the legislation supporting our social system (including Corporations Law and accounting standards) acts to protect and maintain the position of those with power (capital) and suppresses the ability of others (those without financial wealth) to exert a great deal of influence within society. Consistent with this view, advocates of the economic interest group theory of regulation would also argue that regulators will use their power to regulate to transfer wealth from those people with low levels of political power (who have a limited ability to influence the appointment of the regulator) to those parties with greater levels of political power. Reflective of this possibility, in a review of the United States *Securities Acts* of 1933 and 1934, Merino and Neimark (1982, p. 49) conclude that 'The security acts were designed to maintain the ideological, social and economic status quo while restoring confidence in the existing system and its institutions'. They further state (p. 51) that the establishment of the *Securities Acts* 'may have further contributed to the virtual absence of any serious attempts to ensure corporate accountability by broadening the set of transactions for which corporations are to be held accountable'.

The works of some critical theorists are discussed in greater depth in Chapter 12.

---

25 As an example, Stigler (1971, p. 8) refers to the railroad industry. 'The railroad industry took early cognizance of this emerging competitor, and one of the methods by which trucking was combated was state regulation. By the early 1930s all states regulated the dimensions and weights of trucks.'

ACCOUNTING REGULATION AS AN OUTPUT OF A POLITICAL PROCESS

If we accept that accounting standard-setting is a political process, then the view that financial accounting should be *objective*, *neutral* and *apolitical* (as espoused internationally within various conceptual framework projects such as the IASB's Framework for the Preparation and Presentation of Financial Statements) is something that can be easily challenged. As seen in the previous section, because financial accounting affects the distribution of wealth within society it consequently will be political.[26]

Standard-setting bodies typically encourage various affected parties to make submissions on draft versions of proposed accounting standards. This is deemed to be part of the normal 'due process'.[27] If the views of various parts of the constituency are not considered, the implication might be that the very existence of the regulatory body could be challenged. As Gerboth (1973, p. 497) states:

> When a decision making process depends for its success on the public confidence, the critical issues are not technical; they are political ... In the face of conflict between competing interests, rationality as well as prudence lies not in seeking final answers, but rather in compromise—essentially a political process.

In the earlier example of objections made by banks in some EU countries to certain detailed provisions of IAS 39, the failure of the IASB to compromise or concede to the wishes of these banks, and the willingness of certain EU governments to fight the banks' case, led to a confrontation between two regulators—the EU and the IASB. At the time, this confrontation was seen as potentially highly damaging to both regulators. If the EU endorsed a revised EU regulation on accounting for financial instruments that had important (although possibly only small) differences from IAS 39, then rules underlying the accounts of EU companies would be different from the rules underlying the accounts of non-EU companies, and this would frustrate the objectives of international accounting standardisation (which is discussed in the next chapter). A common accounting regulation required both sides to compromise.

An obstacle to reaching compromise between two powerful (and sometimes apparently intransigent) international regulatory bodies is that, as discussed earlier in the chapter, accounting standards (and therefore financial accounting reports themselves) are the result of various social and economic considerations.[28] Hence, they are very much tied to the values, norms and expectations of the society in which the standards are developed. Therefore, it is

---

26   For example, whether dividends are paid to shareholders will be dependent on whether there are reported profits. Further, whether a company incurs the costs associated with defaulting on an accounting-based debt agreement (such as a debt to asset constraint, or an interest coverage requirement) may be dependent on the accounting methods it is permitted to apply.

27   Due process can be defined as a process wherein the regulator involves those parties likely to be affected by the proposed regulation in the discussions leading to the regulation; it provides an opportunity to 'be heard'.

28   The perspective adopted by the economic interest group theory of regulation will not be pursued at this point. If we had persisted with this perspective, we would argue that the standard-setters would support those submissions which best served the standard-setters' self-interest.

questionable whether financial accounting can ever claim to be *neutral* or *objective* (Hines, 1988, 1991). While it is frequently argued within conceptual frameworks that proposed disclosures should be useful for decision making, this in itself is not enough. The proposed requirements must be acceptable to various parts of the constituency, and the benefits to be derived from the proposals must, it is argued, exceed the costs that might arise. Obviously, determining these costs and benefits is very problematic and this is an area where academic advice and academic research are often used. According to Beaver (1973, p. 56), 'without a knowledge of consequences ... it is inconceivable that a policy-making body ... will be able to select optimal accounting standards'.

May and Sundem (1976, p. 750) take the argument further, stating, 'If the social welfare impact of accounting policy decisions were ignored, the basis for the existence of a regulatory body would disappear'.

As noted above, while accounting standard-setters need in principle to consider the potential costs and benefits of particular accounting requirements before they are put in place, this is not a straightforward exercise. As the IASB stated in an exposure draft released in 2008 (released as part of a joint process between the IASB and the US Financial Accounting Standards Board to develop a new conceptual framework of financial reporting):

> The boards (IASB and FASB) observed that the major problem for standard-setters in conducting rigorous cost–benefit analyses in financial reporting is the inability to quantify the benefits of a particular reporting requirement, or even to identify all of them. However, obtaining complete, objective quantitative information about the initial and ongoing costs of a requirement, or the failure to impose that requirement, would also be extremely difficult. Regardless of the difficulty, standard-setters should endeavour to take into account both the benefits and the costs of proposed financial reporting requirements (p. 61).

Any consideration of possible economic consequences (the costs and the benefits) necessarily involves a trade-off between the various consequences. For example, if neutrality/representational faithfulness is sacrificed to reduce potential negative impacts on some parties (for example, preparers who might have otherwise been required to disclose proprietary information, or to amend their accounting policies with the implication that they will default on existing debt contracts), this may have negative consequences for users seeking to make decisions on the basis of information provided.

While it is accepted that accounting standards are developed having regard to social and economic consequences, it is also a requirement in many jurisdictions—including Australia— that corporate financial statements be 'true and fair'. Australian research indicates (Deegan, Kent & Lin, 1994) that auditors generally consider that compliance with accounting standards is necessary and often sufficient for them to decide that the auditee's financial statements are true and fair. But can we really say they are *true* when the standards are determined depending on various economic and social consequences? Perhaps it is easier to say they are *fair* in the sense that they are drawn up in accordance with the rules incorporated in accounting standards. 'Truth' itself is obviously a difficult concept to define and this might explain why in some jurisdictions it was decided that 'true and fair' was achieved if financial reports simply complied with relevant accounting regulations and generally accepted accounting practice.

As another issue to consider, would it be reasonable to assume that users of financial reports generally know that accounting reports are the outcome of various political pressures, or would they expect that the reports are objective and accurate reflections of an organisation's performance and financial position? There could in fact be an accounting report *expectations gap* in this regard, although there is limited evidence of this.[29] According to Solomons (1978, p. 71), 'It is perfectly proper for measurements to be selected with particular political ends if it is made clear to users of the measurement what is being done.' However, is it realistic or practical to assume that users of financial statements would be able or prepared to accept that financial accounting necessarily needs to accommodate political considerations? Further, could or would users rely on financial statements if they had such knowledge? Would there be a reduction of confidence in capital markets?

The argument that economic consequences need to be taken into account before new rules are introduced (or existing rules are changed) also assumes that in the first instance (before any amendments are to be made) there was some sort of equity that did not need addressing or rebalancing. As Collett (1995, p. 27) states:

> The claim that all affected parties such as the preparers of reports are entitled to have their interest taken into account in deciding on a standard, and not only dependent users, assumes that the position immediately prior to implementing the standard was equitable. If, however, users were being misled prior to the standard—for example, because certain liabilities were being kept off the balance sheet—then the argument that the interests of preparers of reports were being neglected in the standard-setting process would lose its force.

This was the case at Enron, where substantial liabilities were 'hidden' from users of the financial accounts through complex financial arrangements which resulted in these liabilities 'being kept off the balance sheet'. As Unerman and O'Dwyer (2004) explain, the false image portrayed by Enron's financial statements led many people, including Enron's employees, to lose money which they would probably not have invested if they had been aware of the true extent of Enron's liabilities. The senior executives ultimately responsible for preparing Enron's financial statements appear to have provided misleading information, which resulted in the economic resources of external parties being allocated in a highly inefficient manner—but a manner that might have been perceived at the time by Enron's senior executives as being in their own personal interests. Perhaps, the absence of adequate regulation had very real and significant economic consequences in this case, which potentially demonstrates that regulation might be needed in some instances to protect the interests of less powerful stakeholders.

As a further related issue for readers to ponder, is it appropriate for regulators to consider the views of financial statement preparers when developing accounting standards, given that accounting standards are put in place to limit what preparers are allowed to do, that is, to regulate their behaviour in the public interest? As we can see, regulating accounting practice requires many difficult assessments.

---

29 Liggio (1974) and Deegan and Rankin (1999) provide definitions of the expectations gap. An expectations gap is considered to exist when there is a difference between the expectations users have with regard to particular attributes of information and the expectations preparers believe users have in regard to that information.

CHAPTER SUMMARY

▪▬

This chapter considered various arguments that either supported or opposed the regulation of financial accounting. Advocates of the 'free-market' (anti-regulation) approach argue that there are private economic incentives for organisations to produce accounting information voluntarily, and imposing accounting regulation leads to costly inefficiencies. To support their argument for a reduction in financial accounting regulation, the 'free-market' advocates rely on such mechanisms as private contracting (to reduce agency costs), the market for managers and the market for corporate takeovers.

By contrast, advocates of the 'pro-regulation' perspective argue that accounting information should not be treated like other goods. As it is a 'public good', it is unrealistic to rely on the forces of supply and demand. Because users of financial information can obtain the information at zero cost (they can be 'free riders'), producers will tend to produce a lower amount of information than might be socially optimal (which in itself is obviously difficult to determine). Further, there is a view that the stakeholders of an organisation have a right to various information about an entity, and regulation is typically needed to ensure that this obligation is adhered to by all reporting entities. Regulation itself is often introduced on the basis that it is in the 'public interest' to do so, the view being that regulators balance the costs of the regulation against the economic and social benefits that the legislation will bring. Clearly, assessments of costs and benefits are difficult to undertake and will almost always be subject to critical comment.

There are alternative views as to why regulation is introduced in the first place. There is one perspective (referred to above) that legislation is put in place for the *public interest* by regulators who are working for the interests of the constituency (public interest theory). Public interest theory does not assume that individuals are primarily driven by their own *self-interest*. (Hence public interest theory makes assumptions that are not in accordance with economic theories that have as their core assumption that all individuals are driven by self-interest, with this self-interest being tied to efforts to maximise personal wealth.) However, an assumption of self-interest is made by other researchers who argue in favour of an economic interest theory of regulation. They argue that *all* action by *all* individuals can be traced back to self-interest in which *all people* will be seeking to increase their own economic wealth.[30] Under this perspective, regulators will be seeking votes and election funding/support, and through embracing self-interest will tend to provide the legislation to groups who can pay for it in terms of either providing votes or providing funds to support the regulators' re-election.

Capture theory provides another perspective on the development of regulation. It argues that, while regulation might initially be put in place for well-intentioned reasons (for example, in the 'public interest'), the regulated party will, over time, tend to gain control of (or capture) the regulator so that the regulation will ultimately favour those parties that the regulation was initially intended to control.

---

30 There are, of course, many researchers who oppose this (rather cynical) view of human behaviour. Authors such as Gray, Owens and Adams (1996) refer to this perspective as being 'morally bankrupt' and providing very little hope for efforts to address pressing global problems such as ongoing global environmental deterioration. Some of these alternative perspectives are discussed in Chapters 8 and 9.

This chapter has also considered how perceptions about potential economic and social consequences impact on the development of accounting standards. In the light of this, the chapter has questioned whether financial accounting reports can really be considered as neutral, objective and representationally faithful—as the IASB/AASB *Framework for the Preparation and Presentation of Financial Statements* would suggest.

QUESTIONS

3.1 What is regulation?

3.2 As this chapter indicates, some people argue that the extent of regulation relating to financial accounting is excessive and should be reduced.
(a) What arguments do these people use to support this view?
(b) How would you rate the arguments in terms of their logic?

3.3 What is the basis of the 'market for lemons' argument?

3.4 Given the process involved in developing accounting standards, do you believe that accounting standards can be considered to be 'neutral' (that is, not serving the interests of some constituents over others)?

3.5 The website of the FASB (as at the end of 2008) states:

> The FASB is committed to following an open, orderly process for standard setting that precludes placing any particular interest above the interests of the many who rely on financial information. The Board believes that this broad public interest is best served by developing neutral standards that result in accounting for similar transactions and circumstances in a like manner and different transactions and circumstances should be accounted for in a different manner.

Do you agree with this statement? That is, do you believe that the FASB will not favour any particular interests or that accounting standards are ultimately 'neutral'? Clearly identify the theoretical basis that you have applied in arriving at your answer.

3.6 What is meant by saying that financial accounting information is a 'public good'?

3.7 Is regulation more likely to be required in respect of public goods than other goods? Why?

3.8 Why would an 'accounting standards overload' occur?

3.9 Can regulatory intervention be explained on fairness or equity grounds? If so, what is the basis of this argument?

3.10 It is argued by some researchers that even in the absence of information organisations have an incentive to provide credible information about their operations and performance to certain parties outside the organisation, otherwise the costs of the organisations' operations would rise. What is the basis of this belief?

3.11 Would you expect independent financial statement audits to exist for listed companies even in the absence of regulation requiring them to be undertaken? Why?

3.12 Some companies argue that introducing mandatory reporting requirements will tend to stifle innovation in relation to the reporting. Do you believe that the introduction of mandatory reporting requirements in relation to a particular area of reporting (for example, social and environmental reporting) will act to stifle innovation in reporting? Explain your view.

3.13 Read and evaluate the following paragraph extracted from Cooper and Keim (1983, p. 202):

> It should also be noted that the nature and degree of the effect of disclosure requirements (and other aspects of security regulation) on public confidence in the financial markets is unknown. Investors who have never read a prospectus or even thumbed through a 10-K report may have a great deal more confidence in the capital markets because the SEC and its regulations are an integral aspect of the financial system. The salutary effect of such enhancement of the perceived integrity and credibility of the investment process is to reduce the cost of capital for all firms, and the magnitude of this effect may be quite significant.

3.14 Private contractual incentives will assist in ensuring that, even in the absence of regulation, organisations will provide such information as is demanded by its respective stakeholders. Evaluate this argument.

3.15 Why would the managerial labour market motivate the manager to provide information voluntarily to outside parties?

3.16 What is the 'market for corporate takeovers' and how would its existence encourage organisations to make accounting disclosures even in the absence of regulation?

3.17 Market failure has been defined as the inability of market forces to produce a socially 'right' amount of information, that is, to produce information to the point where its marginal cost to society equals its marginal benefit. While in theory this calculation may be possible, in reality there are problems with applying such a definition of market failure. What are some of the problems?

3.18 A newspaper article entitled 'Hannes "knew of TNT valuation"' (*Australian*, 18 June 1999, p. 24) reported a case involving a person who was before the courts on a charge of insider trading. In part, the article stated:

> Macquarie Bank executive director Simon Hannes learnt of the value the bank had placed on TNT shares three months before the transport giant was subject to a takeover bid by Dutch company KPN, a jury heard yesterday
>
> The Crown has alleged that Mr Hannes, using the alias Mark Booth, used that confidential information to make a $2 million profit trading in TNT options at the time of the October 1996 takeover offer. Macquarie was advising TNT on the bid and the Downing Centre District Court jury has previously heard Mr Hannes claimed to have had only a general knowledge of a possible transaction involving TNT. Mr Hannes, 39, has pleaded not guilty to one charge of insider trading and two of structuring bank withdrawals to avoid reporting requirements.

(a) Which of the theoretical perspectives of regulation reviewed in this chapter might best explain the existence of laws that prohibit insider trading?

(b) How would advocates of a 'free-market' approach justify the removal of legislation pertaining to insider trading?

3.19 What assumptions are made about the motivations of the regulators in:

    (a) the public interest theory of regulation?

    (b) the capture theory of regulation?

    (c) the economic interest theory of regulation?

3.20 Is it realistic to assume, in accordance with 'public interest theory', that regulators will not be driven by their own self-interest when designing regulations?

3.21 Is it in the public interest for regulators to be driven by their own self-interest?

3.22 Identify and evaluate the key negative economic and social consequences that might potentially arise following the introduction of an accounting standard with which you are familiar.

3.23 Under the economic interest theory of regulation, what factors will determine whether a particular interest group is able to secure legislation that directly favours that group above all others?

3.24 What do we mean when we say that financial accounting standards are the outcome of a political process? Why is the process 'political'?

3.25 Is the fact that accounting standard-setters consider the economic and social consequences of accounting standards consistent with a view that accounting statements, if compiled in accordance with accounting standards and other generally accepted accounting principles, will be neutral and objective?

3.26 If an accounting standard-setter deems that a particular accounting standard is likely to adversely affect some preparers of financial statements, what do you think it should do? Justify your view.

3.27 Read Accounting Headline 3.7 overleaf, and explain the Senate committee's concerns from a capture theory perspective.

3.28 Assume that a government regulator makes a decision that all companies with a head office in Australia must separately disclose, within their annual financial report, the amount of expense incurred in relation to the training of employees. The companies must also spend at least 5 per cent of their reported profits on training employees. You are required to:

    (a) explain the decision made by the regulator in terms of *public interest theory*

    (b) explain the decision made by the regulator in terms of the *economic interest group theory of regulation.*

3.29 Accounting Headline 3.8 discusses how European banks were able to lobby the European Union (EU) so as to be regulated by a 'watered-down' version of the accounting standard IAS 39. Explain whether the decision of the EU to embrace a 'watered-down' version of the standard is consistent with a 'public interest theory of regulation perspective', or whether it can be explained by an alternative theoretical perspective (which you should attempt to identify).

3.30 Read Accounting Headline 3.9 and, using a particular theory of regulation (choose the most appropriate one), explain what factors might be motivating the then president Jacques Chirac to lobby against the accounting standards in question.

Age, 6 August 2004

Chief scientist's dual roles damaging to office, committee finds

ORIETTA GUERRERA

The position of the Federal Government's chief scientist should be full-time, a Senate committee has recommended after it found there was a conflict between Robin Batterham's duties in the role and his role as chief technologist for mining giant Rio Tinto.

The committee, which has been investigating the potential for a conflict between Dr Batterham's two part-time positions, said the public's faith in the office had been eroded because of his dual roles.

However, it concluded there was no evidence that Dr Batterham 'had behaved inappropriately or improperly'.

The committee initiated the inquiry after the Government did not allow Dr Batterham to appear before a Senate Estimates Committee to answer conflict of interest allegations.

Greens leader Bob Brown has raised concerns about Dr Batterham's advice on the largely untested process of burying greenhouse gas emissions, which is favoured by the coal mining industry. Yesterday Senator Brown called for Dr Batterham's resignation—which the report did not recommend.

The majority report, supported by Labor, the Democrats and Greens, made four recommendations, including that the position be made full-time and that it be subject to the same accountability measures as other senior public servant offices.

The committee said that 'potential and apparent conflicts of interests' which arose from Dr Batterham's dual roles were as damaging to the Office of Chief Scientist as 'any real conflict of interest'. However, in a dissenting report, Government senators rejected that there was a conflict.

3.31 Read Accounting Headline 3.10, and then answer these questions:

What theory of regulation seems to explain the actions of Sir David Tweedie?

What theories of regulation would appear to explain the lobbying efforts of the European banks?

What theories of regulation would appear to explain the lobbying efforts of the European insurance companies?

Do Ruth Picker's actions appear to be consistent with a view that she has been 'captured' by business organisations? Explain your answer.

3.32 One of the most pressing problems confronting the world is global warming. To effectively address this issue, governments across the world will be required to introduce regulations to mitigate the impacts of business activities on the environment. This regulation would necessarily require corporations to make significant changes to how they operate and this will undoubtedly have negative implications for the profitability of many organisations. (However, in the long-run no organisations will exist and there will be no profits if action is not taken.) You are required to describe whether the various theories discussed in this chapter provide hope, or otherwise, that regulations will be introduced that will ultimately benefit future generations but that will require corporations to change how they do business.

Accounting Headline 3.8 An example of corporate lobbying on an accounting standard

IAS 39 dawns for local firms

MARK FENTON-JONES

The European Union's decision to accept a modified version of the contentious international accounting standard on valuing financial instruments is unlikely to be adopted here as companies are warned to step up their pace of preparation for the introduction of global standards in January.

Last Friday, after a year-long impasse, EU member states adopted the International Financial Reporting Standards (IFRS) with a watered-down version of IAS 39.

This particular standard deals with accounting for financial instruments such as derivatives, guarantees and loans. The modified version excludes provisions relating to hedge accounting and the fair-value option for financial assets and liabilities.

The modified rule will become part of the new IFRS that will come into force for about 7000 EU stockmarket-listed companies on January 1, 2005.

Those outstanding issues dealing with the option to fair-value all financial assets and liabilities, and to hedge accounting, are still the subject of further discussions between the International Accounting Standards Board, the European Central Bank, prudential supervisors and the banking industry.

EU officials, who argue that the changes leave about 95 per cent of IAS 39 intact, expect the problems with the carved-out provisions to be resolved over the next year.

On its website, the EU says that 'It is therefore the objective to arrive as soon as possible and if at all possible no later than around the end of 2005 at a situation whereby an amended IAS 39 can be adopted in full by the commission'.

Countries wanting to apply the hedge accounting provisions as set out in IAS 39 by the IASB, the London-based accounting rule-maker that developed IFRS, can still do so.

Warren McGregor, the Australian member of the IASB board, expects that European banks listed in the US will apply the full IAS 39.

'The carve-out will be used by a small number of banks in Europe,' said Mr McGregor, who also expects Australian banks to comply fully with IAS 39.

Australian standard setters have already stated that companies here will have to comply with the March 2004 version of IAS 39 from January 1, 2005 and catch up later with any further amendments.

New Zealand has not yet issued its final version of IAS 39, which will be compulsory only from 2007.

Allen Blewitt, the London-based chief executive of the Association of Chartered Certified Accountants, said the debate around IAS 39 had opened up the scope for lobbying by interest groups and for political interference in the standard-setting process.

Opposition to IAS 39 in its original form was driven mostly by the French banks, which were concerned that valuing derivatives at market prices rather than at cost as required by the rule could cause harmful volatility in their accounts.

The European Commission, the EU's executive arm and initiator of financial regulation, hopes to adopt the diluted form of IAS 39 by the end of November, after its translation into all 20 official EU languages.

'There should be no effect on Australian and New Zealand companies. Australia and New Zealand will hopefully progress with full IFRS and not be tempted down the road of tinkering with the standards in the way the EU now proposes,' Mr Blewitt said.

A PricewaterhouseCoopers' survey of 39 companies, the majority listed, also revealed that, while 90 per cent understood the importance of IFRS implementation, 85 per cent said they were not confident they had the skills and resources to complete the changes in time.

The study also showed that 75 per cent of companies surveyed felt they had significant work ahead of them to correctly identify missing information that would be needed to complete their first 2005 IFRS report.

Robert Baker, PwC's project office leader on IFRS, said the results were a warning bell for companies to step up the pace of preparation for IFRS.

3.33 Let us assume that the government has become concerned that existing disclosure regulation tends to fixate on the financial performance of organisations but fails to address other aspects of corporate performance, including a failure to provide information about corporate social and environmental impacts as well as about various initiatives and investments an organisation has undertaken to improve its social and environmental performance. As such, the government has decided to

EU defers accounting standards

ANTONIA SENIOR

Australian, 4 February 2004

THE EU Commission caved in to lobbying from bankers and the French Government yesterday when it pledged to postpone new derivative accounting standards drafted following the Enron affair.

Frits Bolkestein, the EU commissioner responsible for leading the drive towards pan-European financial services, said he would shelve plans to impose the two new accounting standards next year if the warring parties could not reach an agreement by next month.

The disputed measures, drawn up by the International Accounting Standards Board, would have forced firms to account for derivative losses or gains on their books.

Most companies account for financial instruments such as derivatives by quoting how much it cost to acquire them. This technique means derivatives often do not appear on company accounts.

Banks and insurers are lobbying against the standards amid fears the new rules would create massive holes in their balance sheets.

Mr Bolkestein said he would establish a committee of 'industry specialists' this month to examine the disputed standards: 'We will see what we can settle before the mid-March deadline and we will park what now cannot be settled and get a high-level committee to look at it and come up with solutions.'

If Mr Bolkestein acts on his threat to put the outstanding standards on hold, EU companies would have to implement the bulk of the new accounting standards but continue to account for their financial instruments the same way they do now.

Mr Bolkestein's comments follow intense lobbying against the new rules, which has gained the public support of the French Government. President Jacques Chirac wrote to the European Commission last year, saying that the new standards 'would have harmful consequences on financial stability'.

But proponents of the accounting standards say they are essential to understanding companies' true financial health. They say that the new rules would have made it impossible for Enron, the US energy company, to shift its underperforming assets into private partnerships, known as special purpose vehicles. The firm collapsed after the sudden disclosure of huge debts that had not been revealed in its accounts.

The IASB made concessions on the standards at the end of last year but critics said the revisions did not go far enough. The IASB is wedded to the concept of 'fair value' which involves putting a market value on all assets held by a company. Observers fear that the two sides may be too entrenched to reach a compromise over the accounting principles at stake.

The IASB is concerned that any moves to water down the rules would stop European accounts becoming compatible with American standards, the long-term goal of the project.

All European companies must use new international accounting standards to report their figures from 2005. But the IASB will not publish the final details on the two disputed standards until mid-March. The EU, which has adopted the bulk of the IASB's proposals, must endorse any version of the rules on derivatives before they become compulsory.

An IASB spokesman said: 'The board is in continuing discussions with many interested parties and our expectation is to conclude the deliberations by the end of March.'

---

introduce legislation that will require business corporations to provide information about the social and environmental impacts of their operations, as well as the social and environmental initiatives undertaken by the corporations. You are required to do the following:

(a) Explain from a public interest theory perspective the rationale for the government introducing the legislation and how the government will ultimately assess whether any proposed legislation should actually be introduced.

(b) Predict from a capture theory perspective the types of constituents that will benefit in the long run from any social and environmental disclosure legislation.

Tweedie The Unrelenting

BY BRUCE ANDREWS

Business Review Weekly, 28 August 2003

Global standards will be released early next year come what may, says IASB chairman Sir David Tweedie.

European and Australian companies are wary of adopting some of the new international accounting standards, fearing the effects they will have on balance sheets and profit-and-loss statements. However, the chairman of the International Accounting Standards Board (IASB), Sir David Tweedie, is determined to have all the new standards released by the first quarter of next year.

He is meeting resistance. The zeal for reform that followed the collapse of companies such as Enron, WorldCom, HIH and One. Tel has slowed in Australia. After compromising with European banks on the standard for financial instruments, Tweedie's fight to have the rest of the standards adopted without further changes is now against European insurance companies. Tweedie has been in Australia to iron out any misunderstandings in government and business about the standards.

The conflict between Tweedie and the big European corporations has created uncertainty about the content of the final standards, making it difficult for accountants to advise their clients. A financial-services partner at PricewaterhouseCoopers, Ian Hammond, says the uncertainty is causing some Australian companies to procrastinate over preparing for the new standards.

A survey of the finance managers of 150 Australian companies, recently published by the recruitment firm Robert Half Management Resources, found that 33% have not started preparing for the adoption of the new standards and 13% do not even have plans to prepare. The Financial Reporting Council committed Australia to adopt the new standards on January 1, 2005, but many companies will have to use them from July 1, 2004, when recording their financial data for comparisons.

Tweedie has already backed down in one fight with big business. In June, European banks—grouped together under the banner of the European Banking Federation—successfully lobbied the IASB to amend the new accounting standard for financial instruments to allow all banks to continue the practice of macro-hedging. They can continue to hedge against risk across their entire portfolio of loans. The standard had called for the banks to hedge against risk for each individual loan or face putting their hedges on to their profit-and-loss statements, resulting in greater volatility in reported profits. The IASB will release a draft of the amended standard for public comment later this year. The standard is due to be released in March 2004.

Tweedie says he has not caved in to the European banks, even though the standard for financial instruments will now be incompatible with the United States standard. The amended international standard will allow banks to macro-hedge their risks; the US financial accounting standard (FAS) 133 does not. Tweedie says the international standard for financial instruments is a half-way house and as soon as it is introduced, he will be working with the US accounting standards-setters to write its replacement. 'That will take five years.'

Insurers, encouraged by seeing the banks winning concessions, called for talks of their own. In late July, a group of chief executives from European insurance companies called for a meeting with the IASB to change the standard on financial instruments that the banks had fought over. The insurers are also concerned that the standard will add volatility to their reported profits, because it calls for them to measure investment assets by market value and record the gains and losses from these assets on profit-and-loss statements.

Tweedie insists he will not back down to pressure from big business unless he is proved wrong. He says some European companies, unhappy about having to adopt the new standards for financial instruments, are waging a personal campaign against him. 'They have been telling politicians that I don't listen, that I don't understand industry. I understand industry too well.'

Tweedie is also battling the Australian Accounting Standards Board (AASB). Its acting chairperson, Ruth Picker, wants to negotiate with the IASB for an easier transition to the new rules on valuing internally generated intangibles. Australian business supports the board's efforts. John Stanhope, president of the Group of 100, which represents the chief financial officers of 93 of Australia's largest companies and government-owned entities, says the group wrote to Tweedie this year to express its members' concerns about the effect the IASB's decision on intangibles will have on Australian business.

Tweedie says Australia's standard on valuing intangibles is 'deplorable'. 'You are the only ones who account for intangibles this way.'

When the new accounting standards are introduced in 2005, Australian companies will have to write off the value of the intangi-

(continued)

bles on their balance sheets that were generated internally or were revalued after being acquired, because they do not follow the IASB's rules for valuing intangibles. In 1999, Ernst & Young calculated that Australian companies had about $40 billion of intangibles (such as mastheads, licences, trademarks and intellectual property) on their books.

Picker says Tweedie's criticism is unfair. She says: 'For almost every single standard we are giving up in Australia and taking the international one, we are giving up a superior standard and taking on a worse one. The only exceptions are the standards for intangibles and financial instruments. And that is because we don't have a standard for financial instruments.'

Picker says the AASB is being compelled to negotiate with Tweedie and the IASB over the transition to the intangibles standard by founding legislation that says it must act in the best interests of the Australian economy. It does not regard wiping up to $40 billion from Australian balance sheets as in the economy's best interests.

'It will affect companies' abilities to pay dividends ... it might affect share prices, it will affect loan covenants, and it will affect interest deductions,' Picker says.

Hammond doubts that the AASB can win this battle. 'We are telling our clients, "Don't assume that the negotiations will get anywhere and keep planning for the introduction of what the standard says now".' The IASB has listened to Australia's protests about the standard for intangibles and has given the AASB an opportunity to write a new one. Picker says this project is not due for completion until after 2005. 'We won't get to start on it until probably this time next year. We are going to go right back to basics and start with a clean sheet of paper.'

Picker says she is negotiating with the IASB to change the new accounting standards to allow companies to adopt some of them in stages before they are required to, making the transition smoother. She says Australia's *Acts Interpretation Act* prohibits regulations (such as accounting standards) from referring to other

regulations that do not exist at the time they are implemented.

The first international accounting standard, IFRS One, refers to subsequent standards. Tweedie sympathises with Picker's complaints but refuses to relent. 'I have been approached about this [issue of early adoption of the standards] from boards in Europe and elsewhere ... But I've decided that we have to go with the "Big Bang" approach for everyone when adopting the rules.'

Picker and Stanhope say that Australian companies still support adopting the new standards because of the long-term benefits they will bring. Overseas investors will be more inclined to invest their capital in Australia when they can easily compare the financial reports of Australian and overseas companies. However, Picker says that the European banks' success in lobbying against the standard on financial instruments might encourage Australian companies to join in the lobbying of Tweedie and the IASB for more changes to the international standards.

(c) Predict from an economic interest group theory perspective of regulation whether any potential legislation to be introduced will lead to an increase in the accountability of corporations in relation to their social and environmental performance despite any implications that this increased corporate accountability might have for the financial success of large but heavily polluting organisations.

REFERENCES

Akerlof, G. A. (1970), 'The market for "lemons": quality uncertainty and the market mechanism', *Quarterly Journal of Economics*, 84, pp. 488–500.

Barton, J. & G. Waymire (2004), 'Investor protection under unregulated financial reporting', *Journal of Accounting and Economics*, 38, pp. 65–116.

Beaver, W. H. (1973), 'What should be the FASB's objectives?', *Journal of Accountancy*, 136, pp. 49–56.

Berle, A. A. & G. C. Means (1937), *The Modern Corporation and Private Property*, New York, NY: Macmillan.

Broadbent, J. & R. Laughlin (2002), 'Accounting choices: technical and political trade-offs and the UK's private finance initiative', *Accounting, Auditing & Accountability* Journal, 15(5), pp. 622–54.

Carey, A. (1997), *Taking the Risk out of Democracy: Corporate Propaganda Versus Freedom and Liberty*, USA: University of Illinois Press.

Chand, P. & M. White (2007), 'A critique of the influence of globalization and convergence of accounting standards in Fiji', *Critical Perspectives on Accounting*, 18, pp. 605–22.

Collett, P. (1995), 'Standard setting and economic consequences: an ethical issue', *ABACUS*, 31(1), pp. 18–30.

Collison, D. J. (2003), 'Corporate propaganda: its implications for accounting and accountability', *Accounting, Auditing & Accountability Journal*, 16(5), pp. 853–86.

Cooper, K. & G. Keim (1983), 'The economic rationale for the nature and extent of corporate financial disclosure regulation: a critical assessment', *Journal of Accounting and Public Policy*, 2.

Deegan, C. (1997), 'The design of efficient management remuneration contracts: a consideration of specific human capital investments', *Accounting and Finance*, 37(1), pp. 1–40.

Deegan, C., P. Kent & C. Lin (1994), 'The true and fair view: a study of Australian auditors' application of the concept', *Australian Accounting Review*, Issue 7, 4(1), pp. 2–12.

Deegan, C., R. Morris & D. Stokes (1990), 'Audit firm lobbying on proposed accounting disclosure requirements', *Australian Journal of Management*, 15(2), pp. 261–80.

Deegan, C. & M. Rankin (1999), 'The environmental reporting expectations gap: Australian evidence', *British Accounting Review*, 31(3).

Deegan, C. & M. Shelly (2007), 'Corporate social responsibilities: alternative perspectives about the need to legislate', European Accounting Association Annual Conference, Lisbon, Portugal.

Demski, J. & G. Feltham (1976), *Cost Determination: A Conceptual Approach*, USA: The Iowa State University Press.

Fama, E. (1980), 'Agency problems and the theory of the firm', *Journal of Political Economy*, 88, pp. 288–307.

Francis, J. R. & E. R. Wilson (1988), 'Auditor changes: a joint test of theories relating to agency costs and auditor differentiation', *The Accounting Review*, 63(4), pp. 663–82.

Friedman, M. (1962), *Capitalism and Freedom*, Chicago: University of Chicago Press.

Gerboth, D. L. (1973), 'Research, intuition, and politics in accounting inquiry', *The Accounting Review* (July).

Gray, R.,D. Owen & C. Adams (1996), *Accounting and Accountability: Changes and Challenges in Corporate Social and Environmental Reporting*, London: Prentice Hall.

Hakansson, N. H. (1977), 'Interim disclosure and public forecasts: an economic analysis and framework for choice', *The Accounting Review* (April), pp. 396–416.

Hines, R. (1988), 'Financial accounting: in communicating reality, we construct reality', *Accounting, Organizations and Society*, 13(3), pp. 251–62.

Hines, R. (1991), 'The FASB's conceptual framework, financial accounting and the maintenance of the social world', *Accounting, Organizations and Society*, 16(4), pp. 313–51.

Hope, T. & R. Gray (1982), 'Power and policy making: the development of an R & D standard', *Journal of Business Finance and Accounting*, 9(4), pp. 531–58.

International Accounting Standards Board (2008), *Exposure Draft of an Improved Conceptual Framework for Financial Reporting*, London: IASB.

Jensen, M. C. & W. H. Meckling (1976), 'Theory of the firm: managerial behavior, agency costs and ownership structure', *Journal of Financial Economics*, 3 (October), pp. 305–60.

Lehman, C. (1991), 'Editorial: The invisible Adam Smith', *Advances in Public Interest Accounting*, 4, pp. ix–xiv.

Liggio, C. D. (1974), 'The expectations gap: the accountants' Waterloo', *Journal of Contemporary Business*, 3(3), pp. 27–44.

May, R. G. & G. L. Sundem (1976), 'Research for accounting policy: an overview', *The Accounting Review*, 51(4), pp. 747–63.

Merino, B. & M. Neimark (1982), 'Disclosure regulation and public policy: a socio-historical appraisal', *Journal of Accounting and Public Policy*, 1, pp. 33–57.

Mitnick, B. M. (1980), *The Political Economy of Regulation*, USA: Columbia University Press.

Morris, R. (1984), 'Corporate disclosure in a substantially unregulated environment', *ABACUS* (June), pp. 52–86.

Parliamentary Joint Committee on Corporations and Financial Services (PJCCFS) (2006), *Corporate Responsibility: Managing Risk and Creating Value*, Commonwealth of Australia, Canberra, June.

Peltzman, S. (1976), 'Towards a more general theory of regulation', *Journal of Law and Economics* (August), pp. 211–40.

Posner, R. A. (1974), 'Theories of economic regulation', *Bell Journal of Economics and Management Science*, 5 (Autumn), pp. 335–58.

Ronen, J. (1977), 'The effect of insider trading rules on information generation and disclosure by corporations', *The Accounting Review*, 52, pp. 438–49.

Scott, W. R. (1997), *Financial Accounting Theory*, New Jersey: Prentice Hall.

Scott, W. R. (2003), *Financial Accounting Theory*, 3rd edn, Toronto: Pearson Education Canada Inc.

Skinner, D. J. (1994), 'Why firms voluntarily disclose bad news', *Journal of Accounting Research*, 32(1), pp. 38–60.

Smith, A. (1937), *The Wealth of Nations*, originally published in 1776 edn, New York: Modern Library.

Smith, C. W. & J. B. Warner (1979), 'On financial contracting: an analysis of bond covenants', *Journal of Financial Economics* (June), pp. 117–61.

Smith, C. W. & R. Watts (1982), 'Incentive and tax effects of executive compensation plans', *Australian Journal of Management* (December), pp. 139–57.

Solomons, D. (1978), 'The politicisation of accounting', *Journal of Accountancy*, 146(5), pp. 65–72.

Spence, A. (1974), *Market Signalling: Information Transfer in Hiring and Related Screening Processes*, USA: Harvard University Press.

Stigler, G. J. (1971), 'The theory of economic regulation', *Bell Journal of Economics and Management Science* (Spring), pp. 2–21.

Unerman, J. & B. O'Dwyer (2004), 'Enron, WorldCom, Andersen et al: a challenge to modernity', *Critical Perspectives on Accounting*, 15(6–7), pp. 971–93.

Walker, R. G. (1987), 'Australia's ASRB: a case study of political activity and regulatory capture', *Accounting and Business Research*, 17 (67), pp. 269–86.

Watts, R. L. (1977), 'Corporate financial statements: a product of the market and political processes', *Australian Journal of Management* (April), pp. 53–75.

Watts, R. & J. Zimmerman (1978), 'Towards a positive theory of the determination of accounting standards', *The Accounting Review*, 53(1), pp. 112–34.

Watts, R.L. & J. L. Zimmerman (1983), 'Agency problems: auditing and the theory of the firm: some evidence', *Journal of Law and Economics*, 26 (October), pp. 613–34.

CHAPTER 4

INTERNATIONAL ACCOUNTING

LEARNING OBJECTIVES

On completing this chapter readers should:

- understand the background to recent actions by the International Accounting Standards Board and other standard-setting bodies to implement the adoption of a uniform set of accounting standards for worldwide use (this set of accounting standards being known as International Financial Reporting Standards or, in abbreviated form, IFRS);

- understand some of the perceived advantages and disadvantages for countries that adopt IFRS;

- appreciate that prior to many countries adopting IFRS there were a number of important differences between the accounting policies and practices adopted within various countries; such differences are decreasing as countries elect to adopt accounting standards released by the International Accounting Standards Board;

- understand various theoretical explanations about why countries might adopt particular accounting practices in preference to others, and be able to evaluate whether, in light of the various theories, it is appropriate to have one globally standardised set of accounting standards;

- be able to explain what is meant by the terms 'harmonisation' and 'standardisation' of accounting;

- be able to identify and explain some of the perceived benefits of, and obstacles to, harmonising or standardising accounting practices on an international scale;

- understand the key factors that are leading to greater international harmonisation of accounting.

OPENING ISSUES

Since the start of 2005, accounting standards issued by the International Accounting Standards Board (IASB) have become the accounting standards that are to be followed within Australia and a number of other countries (including member states of the European Union). Do you believe that diftferent countries should adopt the same accounting standards—that is, that a 'one size fits all' approach to financial accounting is appropriate despite differences in cultures, legal systems and financial systems? What are some of the advantages and disadvantages that arise as a result of a country adopting the accounting standards issued by the IASB?

The previous chapters looked at how regulation can shape the practice of financial reporting. We saw that various factors can influence the actions of regulators (for example, the regulators' perceptions about what is in the 'public interest' or about what the economic implications of a newly proposed accounting standard might be), and that various theoretical perspectives can be applied when making a judgement about the factors that will be likely to impact on a regulator's ultimate decision to support or oppose particular financial accounting requirements. We saw how differences in, or changes to, accounting regulations can result in different accounting 'numbers' being reported for a given underlying transaction or event, and how these differences in reported accounting results can lead to both positive and negative social and economic consequences. Clearly, therefore, any differences in accounting regulations between different countries are likely to result in the accounting outcomes reported from a specific set of transactions and/or events varying from country to country.

This chapter discusses theoretical explanations as to why, in the absence of efforts to globally harmonise or standardise accounting practices, accounting regulations and practices could be expected to vary between different countries. It explains why there was a large degree of variation in accounting practices internationally prior to recent decisions by many countries to adopt the accounting standards issued by the International Accounting Standards Board (IASB). In light of previous research that indicates that people in different countries or from different cultures will have different information demands and expectations, the chapter explores the logic of recent global efforts to establish one set of accounting standards for worldwide use. It addresses the question of whether it makes sense that organisations in diverse countries all adopt the same accounting standards in an apparent acceptance of a 'one size fits all' approach to financial reporting.

The chapter provides a discussion of recent initiatives undertaken, principally driven by the IASB, to establish a uniform set of accounting standards for global use. More than 100 countries have adopted the accounting standards issued by the IASB, even though these standards often represented a significant change to the accounting standards that had been developed domestically within the respective countries. A significant exception to this general trend has been the United States, which has decided against adopting the accounting standards released by the IASB. To date, the United States continues to use its own domestic standards, those issued by the Financial Accounting Standards Board (FASB), although in 2008 the US Securities and Exchange Commission (SEC) did pass a ruling allowing foreign listed entities that are also listed on the US stock exchange to lodge their reports in accordance with International Financial Reporting Standards (IFRS) without the necessity to provide a reconciliation to US generally accepted accounting procedures. The FASB and the IASB have entered into an arrangement whereby they are trying to eliminate major differences between their respective standards (converge their standards) and once this is achieved then the SEC has indicated a possibility that domestic companies will thereafter be required to also follow IFRS, as is the case in most other countries. However, the timing of any move by the United States to adopt IFRS is far from certain.

The chapter begins with a brief discussion of the international differences that existed between various countries' accounting practices prior to the countries' recent adoption of IFRS.

EVIDENCE OF INTERNATIONAL DIFFERENCES IN ACCOUNTING PRIOR TO RECENT STANDARDISATION INITIATIVES

In recent years many countries (including Australia and countries in the European Union) have elected to adopt the accounting standards issued by the IASB, with such implementation typically being effective from 2005. However, to understand how different nations' accounting rules had led to vastly different accounting results prior to the recent standardisation efforts (and hence to put into context some of the arguments for standardisation), it is useful to consider some actual examples of how a particular company's results varied dramatically depending on which nation's accounting standards were being used to account for its various transactions.

In research undertaken prior to the recent widespread adoption of IFRS, Nobes and Parker (2004, p. 4) compared the results of a small number of European-based multinationals which reported their results in accordance with both their home nation's accounting rules and US accounting rules. Their comparative analysis shows, for example, that the underlying economic transactions and events of the Anglo-Swedish drug company AstraZeneca in the year 2000 produced a profit of £9521 million when reported in conformity with UK accounting rules but a profit of £29 707 million when reported pursuant to US accounting rules — a difference of 212 per cent in reported profits from an identical set of underlying transactions and events! Extending this analysis to a more recent period, the 2003 annual report of AstraZeneca shows that a profit of $3036 million derived from applying UK accounting rules became a profit of $2268 million when calculated in accordance with US accounting rules—this time a difference of 25 per cent. In its balance sheet (or, as it is also known, its statement of financial position), AstraZeneca's shareholders' equity at 31 December 2003 was $13 178 million when reported in accordance with UK accounting rules, but this became $33 654 million when determined in accordance with US accounting rules, a difference of 155 per cent. Although percentage differences of this size might be unusual, an examination of the financial reports of almost any company that reported its results in accordance with more than one nation's set of accounting regulations will have shown differences between the profits reported under each set of regulations and between the financial position reported under each set of regulations. In this regard, consider the following statement from an article in the *Australian Financial Review* (25 November 1998):

> From time to time, the fundamental differences in accounting and reporting standards among the various countries of the western world hit the headlines. This was never more dramatically demonstrated than when Daimler-Benz achieved a listing on the New York Stock Exchange (the first German company to do so) in October 1993.
>
> When the group accounts were converted from German accounting rules to US GAAP (generally accepted accounting practice), a DM168 million profit for the first half year became a staggering DM949 million loss.
>
> More recently, German conglomerate Hoechst, which had adopted international accounting standards (IAS) in 1994, also listed in New York. In the process of reconciling its accounts with US GAAP an IAS profit of DM1.7 billion became a loss of DM57 million.

News learns wealthy lesson: don't move to US

FINOLA BURKE

US accounting principles have turned The News Corporation Ltd's $1.92 billion net profit in fiscal 2000 into a $329 million loss, according to documents filed with the US Securities and Exchange Commission.

While the US loss does not change the profit reported by News at the end of last financial year, it does demonstrate how different News's accounts would look if it moved its headquarters to the US.

The net difference before minority interests to the way in which News reported its income last year was a $2.4 billion loss.

Under US Generally Accepted Accounting Principles (US GAAP), companies are not allowed to capitalise start-ups, book abnormal losses or gains, or revalue mastheads or television licences. Depreciation is also treated differently.

US GAAP would have had News making a loss rather than its near $2 billion profit and shaved its operating income back to $1.5 billion from the reported $2.74 billion the company made under Australian accounting rules.

Australian, 15 November 2000, p. 32

Accounting Headline 4.1 also illustrates how a large accounting profit according to Australian accounting standards became a significant loss for the Australian company News Corporation Ltd when US accounting standards were applied.

A further dramatic example of the existence of differences between the accounting rules of different countries is provided by the US corporation Enron. As Unerman and O'Dwyer (2004) explain, in the aftermath of the collapse of Enron many accounting regulators, practitioners and politicians in European countries claimed that the accounting practices that enabled Enron to 'hide' vast liabilities by keeping them off their US balance sheet would not have been effective in Europe. In the United Kingdom this explanation highlighted the differences between the UK approach and the US approach to accounting regulation. It was argued that under UK accounting regulations these liabilities would not have been treated as off balance sheet, thus potentially producing significant differences between Enron's balance sheet under UK and US accounting practices.

We can now consider whether the fact that different countries' accounting rules can generate significantly different profits or losses is a justification for the decision by many countries to adopt accounting standards issued by the IASB. Obviously, if various countries adopted the same accounting rules the differences between the results that would be reported in different countries would disappear. What do you think? Is removing international differences in accounting results sufficient justification for standardising international accounting? Certainly, this justification has been used by the IASB and regulators within the European Union and in other countries (such as Australia) to justify the use of IFRS.

The following section looks at some of the factors that have been used to justify efforts to standardise accounting internationally. However, it should be appreciated that there are many accounting researchers who argue that there are very good reasons for accounting rules to be different in different countries (underlying national differences in culture, legal systems, finance systems and so forth). The theoretical reasons given to explain why international differences are expected to exist, and perhaps *should* still exist, can in turn be used as possible arguments against the international standardisation of accounting—something that nevertheless has been actively pursued by the IASB. Towards the end of the chapter the various theoretical arguments that have been proposed in opposition to standardising international accounting are considered.

DOES IT REALLY MATTER IF DIFFERENT COUNTRIES USE DIFFERENT ACCOUNTING METHODS?

Before considering some of the perceived advantages associated with having a standardised system of accounting it is useful to first clarify some important terminology. Nobes and Parker (2004, p. 77) distinguish between 'harmonisation' and 'standardisation' of accounting. They define 'harmonisation' as 'a process of increasing the compatibility of accounting practices by setting bounds to their degree of variation'.

'Standardisation' of accounting is explained as a term that 'appears to imply the imposition of a more rigid and narrow set of rules [than harmonisation]' (p. 77). Therefore, harmonisation seems to allow more flexibility than standardisation, but, as Nobes and Parker (2004) point out, the two terms have been used almost synonymously in international accounting. Nevertheless, what appears to be happening through the efforts of the IASB is a process of standardisation.

Nobes and Parker (2004) explain that the reasons for the recent efforts to increase international *standardisation* of financial accounting are similar to the reasons previously used to justify standardising financial accounting within an individual country. If investors are increasingly investing in companies from diverse countries, and these investors use financial statements as an important source of information on which to base their investment decisions, there is a view held by many people (but not all people) that standardisation is important to enable them to understand the financial statements, and to have a reasonable basis for comparing the financial accounting numbers of companies from different countries. Just as is the case domestically (see the arguments in Chapters 2 and 3), the *understandability* and *interpretation* of financial accounting information should be more effective if all accounts are compiled using the same set of underlying assumptions and accounting rules. If an international investor has to understand numerous different sets of accounting assumptions, rules and regulations, the task of making efficient and effective international investment decisions becomes considerably more complicated.

Further, if the long-term finance needs of a multinational company are too great for the providers of finance in a single country, the country may need to raise finance by listing its securities on the stock exchanges of more than one country. For reasons of domestic investor protection, the stock exchange regulators in a particular country might be reluctant to permit a company's shares to be traded on its exchange if that company does not produce financial reports that are readily comparable with the financial reports of all other companies whose shares are traded on that exchange—that is, reports that have been prepared using comparable assumptions (or rules). Also, where a company has to produce financial accounting reports in accordance with the accounting rules of each of the stock exchanges where its shares are traded, its accounting procedures would be considerably simplified if there was a single set of internationally recognised accounting rules that were acceptable to all the stock exchanges where its shares are traded. It makes sense to use a single set of international accounting rules and regulations for all companies listed on any stock exchange.

A further reason for the international standardisation of accounting provided by Nobes and Parker (2004) is that it will facilitate greater flexibility and efficiency in the use of experienced staff by multinational firms of accountants and auditors. Without standardisation, the different accounting regulations in different countries act as a barrier to the transfer of staff between countries. However, whether such a factor provides real benefits to parties other than accounting firms and multinational companies is not clear.

Reflective of the perceived advantages of international standardisation, the Australian government was concerned for a number of years about the differences between Australian accounting standards and their international counterparts. In response to this concern, from 1995 Australia was involved in a process that would harmonise (but not initially 'standardise') Australian accounting standards with accounting standards being released by the International Accounting Standards Committee (the forerunner to the IASB). The 'harmonisation process' required Australian accounting standards to be as compatible as possible with International Accounting Standards (IAS), but still allowed some divergence where the Australian treatment was considered to be more appropriate than the international counterpart. A document released in 1997 as part of the Australian government's Corporate Law Economic Reform Program (entitled *Accounting Standards: Building International Opportunities for Australian Business*) discussed the rationale for the harmonisation efforts. It stated (p. 15):

> There is no benefit in Australia having unique domestic accounting standards which, because of their unfamiliarity, would not be understood by the rest of the world. Even if those standards were considered to represent best practice, Australia would not necessarily be able to attract capital because foreign corporations and investors would not be able to make sensible assessments, especially on a comparative basis, of the value of the Australian enterprises.[1] The need for common accounting language to facilitate investor evaluation of domestic and foreign corporations and to avoid potentially costly accounting conventions by foreign listed companies are powerful arguments against the retention of purely domestic financial reporting regimes.

This view was also consistent with the view provided in Policy Statement 6: International Harmonisation Policy (issued in April 1996 by the Australian Accounting Standards Board), which emphasised the need for international comparability of financial statements. As Policy Statement 6 noted in paragraph 1.2:

> The globalisation of capital markets has resulted in an increased demand for high quality, internationally comparable financial information. The Boards believe that they should facilitate the provision of this information by pursuing a policy of international harmonisation of Australian accounting standards. In this context the international harmonisation of Australian accounting standards refers to a process which leads to those

---

1   The view that harmonisation might lead to Australia abandoning particular standards that might represent 'best practice' is very interesting. It implies that harmonisation might lead to systems of accounting that are less than ideal. Also, moving away from 'best practice' obviously has implications for qualitative characteristics such as representational faithfulness and neutrality.

standards being made compatible, in all significant respects, with the standards of other national and international standard-setters.

Ball (2006, p. 11) identifies a number of other advantages that are often advanced to support the case for the global standardisation of financial reporting. First, the adoption of IFRS might be done on the premise that the decision will lead to more accurate, comprehensive and timely financial statement information, relative to the information that would have been generated from the national accounting standards they replaced. To the extent that the resulting financial information would not be available from other sources, this should lead to more-informed valuations in the equity markets, and hence lower the risks faced by investors. Another perceived benefit of adopting IFRS relates to the increased financial information that would be available to small and large investors alike. Small investors might be less likely than larger investment professionals to be able to access or anticipate particular financial statement information from other sources. Improving financial reporting quality will allow smaller investors to compete more fully with professional (larger) investors, and hence will reduce the risk that smaller investors are trading with better-informed professional investors (such a risk is known as 'adverse selection').[2]

While there are many perceived advantages as well as those given above that could be listed in relation to standardising international accounting, it is obviously very difficult to quantify such benefits or advantages. For example, Australia has now adopted IFRS because of the perceptions that various economic benefits would follow, but there is no real evidence that the country is any better off economically than it would have been had the use of domestically developed accounting standards been maintained. As Ball (2006, p. 9) states, 'There is very little empirical research or theory that actually provides evidence of the advantages or disadvantages of uniform accounting rules nationally, or internationally.'

Hence, it is not at all clear from an empirical perspective whether the decision made by the Financial Reporting Council (FRC) back in 2002 (that Australia would adopt IFRS in 2005) was the 'right' one. Also, it is a matter of conjecture whether the benefits of adopting IFRS are shared by a majority of corporations within a country or whether the benefits are confined to large multinational corporations. If it is only the larger organisations that benefit, then perhaps we may need to question the equity associated with a process that requires all companies within a country to switch from domestic standards to IFRS. In this regard, Chand and White (2007) question the relevance of IFRS to a small, less-developed country such as Fiji, which has a relatively small capital market. They ask (p. 607):

Why would a developing country such as Fiji that does not have a well-established capital market adopt the IFRSs? Questions concerning the effects of harmonized accounting standards on domestic users and local communities have largely been left unanswered.

Having identified some of the perceived advantages relating to standardisation (some perceived disadvantages will be discussed later in the chapter), it is useful now to consider the main organisation involved in standardising accounting on an international basis—the IASB.

---

2   'Adverse selection' is an economics term that represents a situation in a market where buyers cannot accurately gauge the quality of the product they are buying, but where sellers have knowledge about the quality of the product they are selling.

A BRIEF OVERVIEW OF THE IASB AND ITS GLOBALISATION ACTIVITIES

The following pages describe recent initiatives that have been implemented to standardise financial accounting on a global basis. A brief description and history of the IASB—the organisation at the centre of the global standardisation of accounting—is provided, along with a brief description of the standardisation efforts in the European Union and Australia.

In describing the history of the IASB, we perhaps need to go back over fifty years and make reference to a former president of the Institute of Chartered Accountants of England and Wales (ICAEW), Henry Benson. Benson was elected president of the ICAEW in 1966. He was the grandson of one of the four brothers who, in 1854, founded the accounting firm Coopers (which through various mergers and so forth has become part of PricewaterhouseCoopers). Veron (2007, p. 10) outlines Benson's influence on international accounting:

> When elected (in 1966), Benson gave a short address to the Institute's Council, in which he mentioned invitations he had received to visit his counterparts at the Canadian Institute of Chartered Accountants and the American Institute of Certified Public Accountants. He then added: 'I have had the feeling for a long time that our relations with those Institutes were very friendly but somewhat remote and, with the Council's approval, I shall see whether I can perhaps get them on to a more intimate basis'.
>
> These characteristically understated words marked the beginning of international accounting standard-setting. Benson recalls the moment in his autobiography, published in 1989 under the title *Accounting for Life*:
>
> > My private but unstated ambition at that stage was to make it, as I think it turned to be, a turning point in the history of the accountancy profession. The United Kingdom, America and Canada were the three most important countries at that time in the world of accountancy, but there was very little dialogue between them. No attempt had been made to make them closer together to advance the interests of the profession as a whole or to get a common approach to accountancy and audit problems. The Canadian institute was closer to the American institute than we were because of their geographical position but each of the three pursued its own policies without reference or collaboration with the other two. I hoped to change this.
>
> Following Benson's visits, the three bodies jointly established an Accountants' International Study Group in February 1967, which soon published papers on accounting topics and gradually developed its own doctrinal framework. This then formed the basis for the creation in 1973 of the International Accounting Standards Committee (IASC) by an extended array of accounting bodies from Australia, France, Germany, Japan, Mexico and the Netherlands, in addition to Canada, the United Kingdom (plus Ireland associated with it), and the United States. The IASC's stated aim was to issue international standards of reference which would guide the convergence of national standards over time. Benson was duly elected the IASC's first chairman, and opened its offices in London.

When the IASC was established in 1973 it had the stated objectives of:

formulating and publishing in the public interest accounting standards to be observed in the presentation of financial statements and promoting their worldwide acceptance and observance; and working generally for the improvement and harmonisation of regulations, accounting standards and procedures relating to the presentation of financial statements (IASC, 1998, p. 6).

Veron (2007) provides a description of the work performed by the IASC in the years following its formation in 1973 (p. 11):

In the ensuing years, the IASC prepared and published a growing number of documents constituting an increasingly comprehensive body of rules, eventually completed in 1998 as a set of 39 so-called 'core' International Accounting Standards (IAS). Simultaneously, its governance evolved constantly to accommodate a growing and increasingly diverse stakeholder base. Belgium, India, Israel, New Zealand, Pakistan and Zimbabwe joined as associate members as early as 1974, and many other countries later followed suit. In 1981, the IASC's Consultative Group was formed with representatives of the World Bank, United Nations, OECD, and various market participants. This group was joined in 1987 by the International Organisation of Securities Commissions (IOSCO, which brings together the SEC and its national counterparts around the world), and in 1990 by the European Commission and FASB, the US standard-setting body, as these two organisations joined IASC meetings as observers. In 2000, IOSCO recommended the use of IAS for cross-border offerings or listings. By the same time, a number of developing countries had taken the habit of using them as the reference for drafting their own national standards. Some, like Lebanon and Zimbabwe, had even made their use a requirement for banks or publicly listed companies. Several developed countries, such as Belgium, France, Italy and Germany, had also adopted laws allowing large listed companies to publish consolidated accounts using IAS or standards very similar to them, without having to 'reconcile' them with national standards. Following the Asian crisis of the late 1990s, international accounting standards were also endorsed by the G7 Group of industrialised countries and by the Financial Stability Forum, a group of financial regulators hosted by the Bank for International Settlements in Basel.

In the late 1990s there were significant changes made to how the IASC conducted its operations. The IASC Foundation was created and this body, through a group of trustees, was established to supervise the operations of the newly created International Accounting Standards Board which began operations in 2001.[3] The trustees of the IASC Foundation are responsible for the IASB's governance and oversight, including funding. However, the trustees are not to be involved in any technical matters relating to the standards. The responsibility for technical matters associated with accounting standards rests solely with the IASB.

The trustees of the IASC Foundation also appoint the members of the IASB, the International Financial Reporting Interpretations Committee (IFRIC) (which was established at the same time

---

3   The IASC Foundation has twenty-two trustees, of which six are appointed from North America, six from Europe, six from the Asia/Oceania region, and four from any area, subject to establishing overall geographical balance.

as the IASB) and the Standards Advisory Council. Briefly, and according to the IASB's website, the IFRIC is the interpretative body of the IASC Foundation and its mandate is to review on a timely basis widespread accounting issues that have arisen within the context of current International Financial Reporting Standards (IFRS). The work of the IFRIC is aimed at reaching consensus on the appropriate accounting treatment for particular transactions and events (IFRIC interpretations) and providing authoritative guidance on those issues. The IFRIC comprises fourteen members who are drawn from a variety of countries and professional backgrounds. IFRIC interpretations are subject to IASB approval and have the same authority as a standard issued by the IASB. IFRIC interpretations may be released when reporting entities appear to be applying a particular reporting requirement in a variety of ways.

According to the IASB's website, the Standards Advisory Council (SAC) is a forum for the International Accounting Standards Board (IASB) to consult a wide range of representatives from user groups, preparers, financial analysts, academics, auditors, regulators and professional accounting bodies that are affected by and interested in the IASB's work. The SAC meets three times a year to advise the IASB on a range of issues, including the IASB's agenda and work program. It should be noted that in 2008 the IASC released a document entitled 'Review of the Constitution: Public Accountability and the Composition of the IASB—Proposals for Change', which, as part of a regular five-year review, proposed a number of changes to how the IASB will be organised and governed in the future. Regular changes to the functioning of the IASB can be expected in the future.

The IASB has fourteen members, twelve of whom are full time and two of whom are part time. According to the IASC Foundation constitution, IASB members must:

> comprise a group of people representing, within that group, the best available combination of technical skills and background experience of relevant international business and market conditions in order to contribute to the development of high quality, global accounting standards.

To approve a standard, a two-thirds majority of the fourteen members of the IASB needs to be in favour of the relevant requirements. It should be noted, however, that the IASB does not have the power to enforce the use of the standards in particular jurisdictions. As will be seen later in the chapter, the IASB's inability to enforce accounting standards has meant that there is a potential that different countries will enforce the requirements of various IFRS in a less than uniform manner.

The IASB's approach to accounting regulation essentially followed the Anglo-American model (which is explained later in the chapter), but initially many of the International Accounting Standards (IAS) it published permitted a wide range of accounting options. As such, they were not particularly effective at *standardising* accounting practices internationally, as different companies (or countries) could use substantially different accounting policies while still being able to state that they complied with the single set of IAS regulations. Therefore, compliance with IASs did not ensure or enhance the *comparability* or *understandability* of financial accounts—a key purpose of accounting regulation—and was not accepted by stock exchanges as a basis for the preparation of financial reports to support a listing on their exchange.[4]

In the late 1980s the International Organization of Securities Commissions (IOSCO), a body representing government securities regulators worldwide, recognised that to encourage a

---

4   The IASB's *Framework for the Preparation and Presentation of Financial Statements* identifies comparability and understandability as two primary qualitative characteristics of financial information (the other two being relevance and reliability).

greater number of multinational companies to raise funds from stock exchanges in more than one country it would be useful to have a single set of rigorous international accounting standards, compliance with which would be acceptable to any stock exchange regulated by an IOSCO member. This would reduce the costs for companies that were currently producing a different set of financial accounting results for each of the countries in which their shares were listed. However, to be acceptable for this purpose, the IAS would have to be much more effective at standardising accounting practice, and would therefore need to permit a much narrower set of accounting practices or options.

Accordingly, the IASC (which subsequently became the IASB) embarked on a *comparability and improvements project* to reduce the range of permitted options in IAS and thereby make them acceptable to IOSCO (Purvis, Gernon & Diamond, 1991). This project culminated in the publication of a revised core set of IAS by 1999, which was then accepted by IOSCO members—with the important exception of the US Securities and Exchange Commission. After this endorsement by IOSCO, any company that drew up its accounts in accordance with the revised IAS could use this single set of IAS-based accounts to support its listing on any stock exchange regulated by an IOSCO member anywhere in the world—again, with the exception of the United States.

After completion of the core of the comparability and improvements project, the IASC was replaced in 2001 by the IASB, which adopted all existing IAS and from 2001 has published new regulations in the form of International Financial Reporting Standards (IFRS).[5] The IASB has a structure that is considerably more independent and rigorous than the former IASC (although there are still some concerns about the independence of the IASB, as discussed later in the chapter).

Despite the reforms to the IASB, IFRSs/IASs have still not been accepted by the US Securities and Exchange Commission as an adequate basis for the preparation by US companies of financial statements to support a listing on a US stock exchange.[6] However, the IASB and the US standard-setter (the Financial Accounting Standards Board) have been working to reduce the differences between the international standards and US accounting standards, in what is referred to as its 'convergence project' (Nobes & Parker, 2004). We will return to a discussion of the project shortly.

A very significant participant in the process of standardising accounting practices internationally was the European Union (EU).[7] A key reason for the EU becoming involved in accounting regulation at the EU level (rather than leaving this to individual member states) is that a founding principle of the EU is freedom of movement within the EU of people, goods and capital. As discussed earlier, differing accounting principles in different countries have acted

---

5   When the IASC issued accounting standards they were referred to as International Accounting Standards (IASs). When the IASB now issues accounting standards they are referred to as International Financial Reporting Standards (IFRSs). Many of the IASC standards are still in existence, although a lot have been modified or updated by the IASB. These modified standards are still referred to as IASs and retain the same title and number, rather than becoming an IFRS, such that at the international level there are many IASs as well as numerous newly released IFRSs. A list of the currently applicable accounting standards can be found on the IASB's website, www.iasb.org.

6   As noted elsewhere in the chapter, foreign listed companies are allowed to lodge their financial statements within the United States in accordance with IFRS. This concession, however, is not extended to US companies.

7   The European Union was formerly known as the European Community (and prior to that it was known as the Common Market). It is an intergovernmental organisation of twenty-seven Western European nations created by the Maastricht Treaty of December 1993 with its own institutional structures and decision–making framework. It comprises Austria, Belgium, Bulgaria, Cyprus, the Czech Republic, Estonia, Great Britain, Denmark, Finland, France, Germany, Greece, Hungary, Ireland, Italy, Latvia, Lithuania, Luxembourg, Malta, the Netherlands, Poland, Portugal, Romania, Spain, Slovakia, Slovenia and Sweden.

European Commission press release, Reference: IP/02/827, Date: 7 June 2002

Agreement on International Accounting Standards will help investors and boost business in EU

The European Commission has welcomed the Council's adoption, in a single reading, of the Regulation requiring listed companies, including banks and insurance companies, to prepare their consolidated accounts in accordance with International Accounting Standards (IAS) from 2005 onwards (see IP/01/200 and MEMO/01/40). The Regulation will help eliminate barriers to cross-border trading in securities by ensuring that company accounts throughout the EU are more reliable and transparent and that they can be more easily compared. This will in turn increase market efficiency and reduce the cost of raising capital for companies, ultimately improving competitiveness and helping boost growth. The IAS Regulation was proposed by the Commission in February 2001. It is a key measure in the Financial Services Action Plan, on which significant progress has been made in the last few weeks (see IP/02/796). Unlike Directives, EU Regulations have the force of law without requiring transposition into national legislation. Member States have the option of extending the requirements of this Regulation to unlisted companies and to the production of individual accounts. Although the Commission put

forward the IAS proposal long before the Enron affair, this is one of a series of measures which will help to protect the EU from such problems. Others include the Commission's recent Recommendation on Auditor Independence (see IP/02/723) and its proposal to amend the Accounting Directives (see IP/02/799).

Internal Market Commissioner Frits Bolkestein said: 'I am delighted that the IAS Regulation has been adopted in a single reading and am grateful for the positive attitude of both the Parliament and the Council. I believe IAS are the best standards that exist. Applying them throughout the EU will put an end to the current Tower of Babel in financial reporting. It will help protect us against malpractice. It will mean investors and other stakeholders will be able to compare like with like. It will help European firms to compete on equal terms when raising capital on world markets. What is more, during my recent visit to the US, I saw hopeful signs that the US will now work with us towards full convergence of our accounting standards.'

To ensure appropriate political oversight, the Regulation establishes a new EU mechanism to assess IAS adopted by the

International Accounting Standards Board (IASB), the international accounting standard-setting organisation based in London, to give them legal endorsement for use within the EU. The Accounting Regulatory Committee chaired by the Commission and composed of representatives of the Member States, will decide whether to endorse IAS on the basis of Commission proposals.

In its task, the Commission will be helped by EFRAG, the European Financial Reporting Advisory Group; a group composed of accounting experts from the private sector in several Member States.

EFRAG provides technical expertise concerning the use of IAS within the European legal environment and participates actively in the international accounting standard setting process. The Commission invites all parties interested in financial reporting to contribute actively to the work of EFRAG. The Commission recently proposed amendments to the Accounting Directives which would complement the IAS Regulation by allowing Member States which do not apply IAS to all companies to move towards similar, high quality financial reporting (see IP/02/799).

as an impediment to investors seeking to understand and compare the financial statements of companies in different countries, and thereby acted as an impediment to them freely investing their capital in companies from different EU member states (an inhibition to the free movement of capital). The approach towards harmonisation of accounting in the EU has historically differed from the IASC/IASB approach. This should be of little surprise, given that most countries in the EU, by definition, follow a continental European system of accounting (to be discussed shortly) rather than the Anglo-American model of the IASC/IASB, so the EU approach to accounting harmonisation has historically been through legislation. This legislation has primarily been in the form of EU directives on company law, which have to be agreed on by the EU and then implemented in the domestic legislation of each EU member state. This is a very lengthy process, and during the 1990s the EU recognised that it was far too inflexible to respond to the requirements of a dynamic business environment where financial accounting practices need to adapt quickly to rapidly changing business practices—especially for companies that rely on 'outsider' forms of finance, as an increasing number of the largest companies in many continental European nations do. ('Outsider forms of finance' refers to finance received from parties, such as shareholders, that do not get involved in the management of the organisation.)

Following proposals made in 2000, the EU agreed in 2002 that from 1 January 2005 all companies whose shares were traded on any stock exchange in the EU would have to compile their consolidated accounts in accordance with IASs/IFRSs.[8] This was seen as ensuring that accounting rules were flexible enough to suit the needs of a dynamic business environment and that the financial accounts of EU-listed companies maintained international credibility. Further details regarding the EU adoption of IASs/IFRSs are shown in Accounting Headline 4.2, which is a press release issued by the European Commission when this route for accounting regulation was formally adopted in 2002.

Accounting Headline 4.2 demonstrates that the views being embraced in favour of the adoption of IAS/IFRS are based on beliefs about the information people need in making various decisions (which can be tied back to decision usefulness theories—some of which are considered in Chapters 5 and 6), beliefs about how individuals and capital markets react to accounting information (which can be tied back to behavioural and capital markets research—the topics of Chapters 10 and 11), and a view that the adoption of IAS/IFRS is in the public interest, rather than being driven by the private interests of particular constituents (public interest theories and private interest theories are discussed in Chapter 3). There also appears to be a view that new accounting methods will be embraced in a similar manner across different countries (which perhaps differs from some of the assertions in this chapter—for example, that religion, culture or taxation systems influence the usefulness of various alternative accounting approaches).

Despite the European Commission's enthusiasm for the adoption of IAS/IFRS, there were concerns that, for both legal and political reasons, the EU could not be seen to endorse in advance regulations that could be developed at any time in the future by an international body not under control of the EU (Nobes & Parker, 2004). That is, the EU was unwilling to give a blanket approval covering all future IFRSs (that would apply to many EU companies) without considering the details of those IFRSs. Therefore, as can be seen in Accounting Headline 4.2, the EU established a mechanism whereby each IAS/IFRS would have to be endorsed separately by the EU before becoming mandatory for listed companies in the EU. This endorsement process involves an eleven-member committee entitled the European Financial Reporting Advisory Group (EFRAG), whose members are drawn from the preparers and users of financial statements, and who comment on each IAS/IFRS to a new EU Accounting Regulatory Committee (ARC).[9] The ARC has a member from each EU state, and the members vote on whether to recommend approval of the IAS/IFRS to the EU Commission, a two-thirds majority of the twenty-seven members being required to recommend approval. This mechanism was used in 2004 to block recommendation of full EU endorsement of IAS 39 (on financial instruments) by governments

8   For a small number of companies, the deadline was 2007 instead of 2005.

9   For details of EFRAG and the ARC, see the following websites respectively: www.efrag.org and http://ec.europa.eu/internal_market/accounting/committees_en.htm.

who argued that aspects of IAS 39 were unrealistic and would have potentially significant negative economic consequences on banks in their nations. It is interesting to speculate whether this action by the EU to modify an accounting standard issued by the IASB (and thereby move away from full standardisation) will undermine the efforts being undertaken by the IASB to encourage other countries, most notably the United States, to adopt IFRS. The benefits of international standardisation are potentially reduced when some countries—such as the member countries of the EU—decide to make alterations to the standards issued by the IASB.

The efforts undertaken within Australia to harmonise or standardise Australian accounting practice with international practice are now considered. As indicated earlier, from the mid-1990s Australia adopted a policy of harmonisation. This process led to revised Australian accounting standards which, although not the same, were very comparable with those issued by the IASC. Once these revisions were almost complete and many revised accounting standards had been issued, a decision was made in 2002 by the Financial Reporting Council (FRC) that Australia would 'adopt' accounting standards being issued by the IASB and no divergence was to be acceptable (that is, there was a shift from harmonisation to standardisation).[10] This led to yet another set of accounting standards being released, for application in 2005. This was a very frustrating time for Australian accountants. Just as they were getting used to a new set of accounting standards that had been released to harmonise Australian accounting standards with IASs, the revised (harmonised) standards were dumped in favour of a standardisation process that involved the adoption of IASs. The *Bulletin* released by the FRC outlining its direction on the *adoption* of international accounting standards is reproduced in Accounting Headline 4.3. As can be seen, there is much similarity between the arguments in favour of standardisation provided in Accounting Headline 4.3 and the supporting arguments expressed in Accounting Headline 4.2. However, as has already been mentioned, there have been no known attempts to quantify the costs and benefits of these standardising activities.

THE UNITED STATES' ROLE IN THE INTERNATIONAL STANDARDISATION OF FINANCIAL ACCOUNTING

The major event that triggered the adoption of IFRS by more than 100 countries was the decision taken by the European Union to adopt IFRS as the accounting standards to be used for preparing the consolidated financial statements of publicly listed companies from 2005.[11] In Australia, the Financial Reporting Council (FRC) followed the lead of the European Union and in 2002 decided that Australia would adopt IFRS from 2005. Prior to the adoption of IFRS, these countries used accounting standards that were typically developed on a domestic basis.

---

10 The FRC has an oversight function in regards to the Australian Accounting Standards Board (and the Australian Auditing Standards Board) and appoints members of the AASB (other than the chairperson). There are nineteen members on the FRC inclusive of the chairperson. See www.frc.gov.au for more details about the FRC.

11 The proposal to adopt IFRS was confirmed in a regulation of the European Parliament and European Council released on 19 July 2002. IFRS and IFRIC interpretations, once adopted by the IASB, need to be specifically acknowledged (and translated into various languages) by the European Commission to become part of EU law. National standards are still commonly used in European countries for individual (non-consolidated) financial statements.

Adoption of International Accounting Standards by 2005

The Chairman of the Financial Reporting Council (FRC), Mr Jeffrey Lucy, AM, today announced that the FRC has formalised its support for the adoption by Australia of international accounting standards by 1 January 2005.

Subject to the Government's support at the appropriate time for any necessary amendments of the *Corporations Act*, this will mean that, from 1 January 2005, the accounting standards applicable to reporting entities under the Act will be the standards issued by the International Accounting Standards Board (IASB). After that date, audit reports will refer to companies' compliance with IASB standards.

The FRC considered the issue at its meeting on 28 June and formally endorsed the 2005 objective, in line with statements made recently by the Parliamentary Secretary to the Treasurer, Senator the Hon. Ian Campbell. Mr Lucy paid tribute to the Government's strong leadership over the last five years in pressing for the international convergence of accounting standards. This objective is reflected in the Government's 1997 Corporate Law Economic Reform Program initiative (CLERP 1) and amendments made in 1999 to the *Australian Securities and Investments Commission Act 2001*.

The FRC fully supports the Government's view that a single set of high-quality accounting standards which are accepted in major international capital markets will greatly facilitate cross-border comparisons by investors, reduce the cost of capital, and assist Australian companies wishing to raise capital or list overseas.

Mr Lucy said he understood that the 1 January 2005 timing is somewhat later than the Government would have liked. However, it is determined by the decision of the European Union to require EU listed companies to prepare their consolidated accounts in accordance with IASB standards from that date, in support of the EU single market objective. Australia certainly cannot afford to lag [behind] Europe in this regard, Mr Lucy said. He also expressed his support for efforts to encourage the United States to further converge its standards with IASB standards with a view to eventual adoption.

Mr Lucy was pleased to note that the Chairman of the IASB, Sir David Tweedie, had issued a statement in London welcoming the FRC's decision. Sir David said that the FRC's announcement demonstrates growing support for the development and implementation of a single set of high-quality global accounting standards by 2005.

'This vote of confidence is a reflection of the leadership role that Australia continues to play in standard-setting, and will increase momentum for convergence towards high-quality international standards. The input and active participation of interested parties in Australia and the Australian Accounting Standards Board (AASB), under the leadership of Keith Alfredson, are and will remain a vital element in ensuring the IASB's success. It is through national standard-setters, such as the AASB, and the members of our various committees that we are able jointly to develop high-quality solutions to accounting issues, leverage resources to research topics not yet on the international agenda so as to expedite conclusions, reach interested parties throughout the world and better understand differences in operating environments, thus fulfilling our role as a global standard-setter.'

The full statement is available on the IASB's website www.iasb.org.uk.

While there will be a need for business and the accounting profession to adapt to significant changes in some standards, and to some complex new standards, the AASB has been harmonising its standards with those of the IASB for some years, resulting in substantial synergies between the two.

Nevertheless, Mr Lucy urged the accounting bodies to prepare for the changeover through their programs of professional development and their influence on accounting education. He also urged the business community to participate fully in commenting on exposure drafts of IASB standards issued in Australia in the period ahead.

Mr Lucy noted that implementation issues would also need to be considered by the FRC (to the extent they did not involve the content of particular standards) and the AASB between now and 2005. These could relate, for example, to the timing of introduction of particular IASB standards in Australia before 1 January 2005 (which would be AASB standards until that date), as well as to issues of interpretation.

The FRC and AASB will be doing everything they can to keep constituents informed about these issues and to communicate an overall strategy for adoption, Mr Lucy said.

Mr Lucy also confirmed that Australia would be making a substantial financial contribution, through the FRC, to the International Accounting Standards Committee (IASC) Foundation in 2002–03. This

(continued)

contribution will be sourced from funds available to the FRC for the standard-setting process contributed by the Commonwealth, State and Territory governments, the three accounting bodies, the Australian Stock Exchange, and from the Financial Industry Development Account (as announced by Senator Campbell on 12 June).

Among the FRC's functions are to further the development of a single set of accounting standards for world-wide use and to promote the adoption of international best practice accounting standards in Australia if doing so would be in the best interests of both the private and public sectors in the Australian economy.

The IASB, which is based in London, is committed to developing, in the public interest, a single set of high-quality, global accounting standards that require transparent and comparable information in financial statements. In pursuit of this objective, the IASB cooperates with national standard-setters, including the AASB, to achieve convergence in accounting standards around the world.

The AASB has been harmonising its standards with IASB standards for a number of years and is now working in close partnership with the IASB as a liaison standard-setter, aligning its work program with that of the IASB and standing ready to allocate resources to lead or support projects on the IASB agenda. Recently, the AASB issued to its Australian constituents invitations to comment on a number of exposure drafts of IASB standards.

Australians are actively involved in the work of the IASB. Mr Ken Spencer is a member of the oversight body for the IASB, the IASC Foundation Trustees (and Chairman of the Foundation's Nominating Committee). Mr Warren McGregor is a member of the IASB, also designated the Liaison Member for Australia and New Zealand. Mr Kevin Stevenson, a former director of the Australian Accounting Research Foundation, is the IASB's Director of Technical Activities. Australians are also on the IASB's Standards Advisory Council (Mr Peter Day and Mr Ian Mackintosh) and its Interpretations Committee (Mr Wayne Lonergan).

One notable exception to the global adoption of IFRS is the United States. But before considering the US position on global standardisation, it is useful to briefly consider the two main bodies responsible for accounting regulation within the United States, the Securities and Exchange Commission and the Financial Accounting Standards Board. In relation to their history, following the US stock-market crash of 1929 the newly established US securities legislation of 1933 and 1934 led to the creation of the Securities and Exchange Commission (SEC). The SEC was given the authority to develop accounting regulation, but it decided to rely on the expertise of the US accounting profession to develop accounting standards. Over the following decades the US accounting profession developed various documents that became known as 'generally accepted accounting principles' (GAAP). In 1973 the SEC entrusted the task of developing accounting standards to the newly formed Financial Accounting Standards Board (FASB).[12] The FASB is a private-sector body that was established to act in the 'public interest'. While the FASB was established as an independent body, the SEC has the power to override the accounting standards issued by the FASB should it see fit to do so.[13]

In the United States, reliance is still placed on accounting standards issued by the FASB, rather than on the standards issued by the IASB. That is, unlike many other countries, the United States has not yet adopted IFRS. Given that the United States represents the world's major capital market, its non-involvement represents a significant limitation in the global acceptance

---

12 Prior to this time, the Accounting Principles Board (a committee of the American Institute of Certified Practicing Accountants) was responsible for developing US GAAP.

13 See the following websites for further information about the SEC and FASB respectively: www.sec.gov and www.fasb.org.

of IFRS. The United States was very strong in its resolve not to adopt IFRS, believing that its 'rules-based' standards were superior to the more 'principles-based' standards of the IASB.[14] However, this resolve appeared to diminish around 2001–2002 with the various 'accounting scandals' involving organisations such as Enron.[15] As Veron (2007, p. 23) states:

> The context was profoundly modified by the Enron bankruptcy in December 2001 and other accounting scandals that erupted in 2002, following the bursting of the late-1990s stock market bubble. Before this wave of controversy, specific US GAAP standards had been occasionally criticised but overall it was widely considered, in the US and elsewhere, that US GAAP as a whole were the best available set of accounting standards ... But Enron's collapse shattered the perception of high quality. It exposed the shortcomings of some detailed US GAAP rules, most notably those on consolidation which gave Enron enough leeway to hide its now famous 'special-purpose entities' (with their funny names such as Chewco, Raptor, Jedi, or Big Doe) off its balance sheet, packing them with real debts backed by flimsy assets ... In February 2002, a Senate Committee investigating the Enron debacle heard the testimony of IASB Chairman David Tweedie who explicitly criticised the rules-based approach which is prevalent in US GAAP, contrasting it with the more principles-based stance adopted by the IASB. Shortly thereafter, the *Sarbanes–Oxley Act* specifically mandated the SEC to study how a more principles-based system (such as IFRS) could be introduced in the United States.

With the perceived limitations of some US accounting requirements in mind, the FASB and the IASB entered a joint agreement in 2002 to converge and improve the standards of both the IASB and the FASB. The ultimate consequence of the Convergence Project would be that the United States adopted IFRS. As Veron (2007, p. 24) states:

> Since the early 2000s the FASB has been working with the IASB to narrow the differences between US GAAP and IFRS—a process they call 'convergence', but which in fact is very different from the unilateral convergence of, say, Australian or South Korean accounting standards towards IFRS. The premise, enshrined in the so-called Norwalk Agreement of September 2002[16] and renewed by a FASB–IASB Memorandum of Understanding in February 2006, is that both the FASB and the IASB would need to move some way

---

14   In basic terms, rules-based accounting standards tend to be relatively lengthy and provide explicit guidelines on how to account for specific attributes of different transactions and events. By contrast, principles-based accounting standards tend to be less detailed and more concise. Rather than providing detailed rules for particular transactions and events, in principles-based standards reference is made to general principles that should be followed. These principles might be incorporated within a conceptual framework of accounting. Principles-based accounting standards require the exercise of greater levels of professional judgement relative to rules-based accounting standards. As an example of the difference, a rules-based accounting standard might say that a particular type of intangible asset should be amortised over twenty years, whereas a principles-based standard might require that the intangible assets be amortised to the extent that the economic value of the asset has declined since the beginning of the accounting period. Accounting standards released by the FASB are generally considered to be more rules-based that accounting standards issued by the IASB (which are considered to be principles-based).

15   Enron was an energy company based in Texas. Prior to its bankruptcy in late 2001, it employed approximately 22 000 people and was one of the world's leading electricity, natural gas, pulp and paper, and communications companies, with reported revenues of $111 billion in 2000. At the end of 2001, it became apparent that the company's financial position was generated through extensive accounting fraud. Enron represented one of the biggest and most complex bankruptcy cases in US history.

16   It was signed in FASB's home city of Norwalk, Connecticut, hence becoming known as the Norwalk Agreement.

towards each other. In this process, on some issues FASB adopts standards identical or near identical to existing IFRS (e.g. for stock option expensing); on other issues the IASB adopts standards identical or near identical to existing US GAAP rules, as with the IFRS 8 standard on 'operating segments'; and on yet other issues the two bodies jointly develop entirely new projects.

Although there appears to be a long-term aim that ultimately there will be one set of standards used internationally, including within the United States, the timing of when (and some people still question 'if') the United States will adopt IFRS is far from certain. Obviously, for the IASB to achieve its aim of developing 'a single set of high-quality, understandable and international financial reporting standards (IFRSs) for general purpose financial statements' (as stated on the IASB website), it will need to encourage the United States to adopt its standards. However, at this point the US adoption of IFRS for use by US companies appears to be a number of years away. The adoption of IFRS will be contingent ultimately on whether the SEC and the FASB are satisfied with the results generated by the IASB/FASB Convergence Project. Nevertheless, from late 2007 the SEC adopted rules that permit foreign private issuers (but not US domestic companies) to lodge, with the SEC, their financial statements prepared in accordance with IFRS without the need to provide a reconciliation to generally accepted accounting principles (GAAP) as used in the United States. That is, foreign companies that are listed across a number of stock exchanges internationally, including within the United States, can now lodge their reports in the United States even though the reports have *not* been prepared in accordance with US accounting standards and do not provide a reconciliation to US GAAP. The ruling of the SEC requires that foreign private issuers that take advantage of this option must state explicitly and unreservedly in the notes to their financial statements that such financial statements are in compliance with IFRS as issued by the IASB (without modifications) and they must also provide an unqualified auditor's report that explicitly provides an opinion that the financial statements have been compiled in accordance with IFRS as issued by the IASB. In explaining the basis for its decision to provide this concession to foreign companies, the SEC stated (2007, p. 16):

> As discussed in the Proposing Release, continued progress towards convergence between U.S. GAAP and IFRS as issued by the IASB is another consideration in our acceptance of IFRS financial statements without a U.S. GAAP reconciliation. We believe that investors can understand and work with both IFRS and U.S. GAAP and that these two systems can co-exist in the U.S. public capital markets in the manner described in this rule making, even though convergence between IFRS and U.S. GAAP is not complete and there are differences between reported results under IFRS and U.S. GAAP.

Hence, effectively there are two types of financial statements being lodged within the United States (as is the case in many other countries). Foreign companies can lodge their reports within the United States in accordance with IFRS, whereas domestic US companies must lodge their reports in accordance with US GAAP. It is interesting that the SEC states that these two systems can co-exist. If different systems can co-exist, does that question the need for all countries to adopt IFRS? What do you, the reader, think? Does the US position of supporting dual reporting systems undermine the view of the FRC in Australia, which argued back in 2002 that if Australia retained its own accounting standards (which were fundamentally similar to IFRS) it would be damaging to Australian capital markets?

The following two press releases provide additional information about the decision taken in 2002 for the IASB and FASB to work towards converging their respective accounting standards, and the decision taken in late 2007 by the SEC to remove the requirement for foreign companies to provide a reconciliation to US GAAP.

As noted above, there is resistance in the United States in relation to the adoption of IFRS by US-based organisations. Although there is a view that IFRS will eventually be adopted, the adoption may be some years away. This is best summed up by a submission made by the US Financial Accounting Foundation (FAF)[17] in 2007 to the SEC in response to a concept release issued by the SEC which called for opinions about the United States ultimately adopting IFRS:

> The Concept Release asks, 'could comentators foresee a scenario under which it would be appropriate for the Securities and Exchange Commission to call for all remaining U.S.

JOINT NEWS RELEASE FROM THE FASB AND IASB

29 October 2002

FASB and IASB agree to work together toward convergence of global accounting standards.

LONDON, United Kingdom—The Financial Accounting Standards Board (FASB) and International Accounting Standards Board (IASB) have issued a *memorandum of understanding* marking a significant step toward formalizing their commitment to the convergence of U.S. and international accounting standards. The FASB and IASB presented the agreement to the chairs of leading national standard setters at a two-day meeting being held in London. The agreement between the FASB and IASB represents their latest commitment, following their September joint meeting, to adopt compatible, high-quality solutions to existing and future accounting issues.

The agreement follows the decisions recently reached by both Boards to add a joint short-term convergence project to their active agendas. The joint short-term convergence project will require both Boards to use their best efforts to propose changes to U.S. and international accounting standards that reflect common solutions to certain specifically identified differences. Working within each Board's due process procedures, the FASB and IASB expect to issue an Exposure Draft to address some, and perhaps all, of those identified differences by the latter part of 2003. The elimination of those differences, together with the commitment by both Boards to eliminate or reduce remaining differences through continued progress on joint projects and coordination of future work programs, will improve comparability of financial statements across national jurisdictions.

Robert H. Herz, Chairman of the FASB, commented, 'The FASB is committed to working toward the goal of producing high-quality reporting standards worldwide to support healthy global capital markets. By working with the IASB on the short-term convergence project—as well as on longer-term issues—the chances of success are greatly improved. Our agreement provides a clear path forward for working together to achieve our common goal.'

Hailing the agreement, Sir David Tweedie, Chairman of the IASB, remarked, 'This underscores another significant step in our partnership with national standard setters to reach a truly global set of accounting standards. While we recognize that there are many challenges ahead, I am extremely confident now that we can eliminate major differences between national and international standards, and by drawing on the best of U.S. GAAP, IFRSs and other national standards, the world's capital markets will have a set of global accounting standards that investors can trust.'

---

17 The Financial Accounting Foundation was established in 1972 and is the independent, private-sector organisation with responsibility for the oversight, administration and finances of the FASB. It also selects the members of the FASB.

IASB PRESS RELEASE

15 November 2007

The IASB welcomes SEC vote to remove reconciliation requirement.

The International Accounting Standards Board (IASB) welcomed the decision taken today by the US Securities and Exchange Commission (SEC) to remove the requirement for non-US companies reporting under International Financial Reporting Standards (IFRSs) as issued by the IASB to reconcile their financial statements to US generally accepted accounting principles (GAAP).

The development of a single, high-quality language for financial reporting that is accepted throughout the world's capital markets has been the primary goal of the IASB since its inception in 2001 and today's decision is an important step towards achieving that objective.

The adoption of IFRSs by the European Union with effect from 2005, and similar decisions by Australia, Hong Kong and South Africa, led the way in a process that has resulted in over 100 countries now requiring or permitting the use of IFRSs. The SEC's decision follows those announced by other leading countries in 2007 to establish time lines for the acceptance of IFRSs in their domestic markets or accelerate convergence of national standards with IFRSs. Among those are Canada, India and Korea, all of which will adopt IFRSs by 2011. In Brazil listed companies will have to comply with IFRSs from 2010, and convergence between Japanese GAAP and IFRSs is expected by 2011. At the beginning of this year China introduced a completely new set of accounting standards that are intended to produce the same results as IFRSs.

Commenting on the SEC's decision Sir David Tweedie, Chairman of the IASB, said:

We are delighted that the US Securities and Exchange Commission has decided to allow non-US issuers to file under IFRSs without the need for reconciliation to US GAAP. The IASB remains strongly committed to its joint work with the US Financial Accounting Standards Board set out in the Memorandum of Understanding in February 2006 in order to achieve our goal of providing the world's integrating capital markets with a common language for financial reporting.

[non governmental] issuers to move their financial reporting to IFRS?'. We believe the answer to that question is 'yes'. In our view, now is the time to develop a plan for moving all U.S. public companies to an improved version of IFRS. We are not recommending immediate adoption of existing IFRS because various elements of the U.S. financial reporting system need to change before moving to IFRS, and those changes will take several years to complete. In addition, further improvements to IFRS are needed before U.S. public companies transition to IFRS (FAF, 2007, p. 5).

Hence, while the FAF considers that the ultimate adoption of IFRS within the United States is a sound idea, the adoption should not in its opinion happen for a number of years, to give enough time for IFRS to be further improved and for the US reporting systems to be properly prepared for the transition. The FAF made the following suggestion (2007, p. 7):

We propose transitioning from U.S. GAAP to IFRS via a two-pronged 'improve-and-adopt' process.

• The first part of the process involves working with the IASB to improve areas where neither U.S. GAAP nor IFRS is considered to be of sufficiently high quality. The 2006 Memorandum of Understanding identifies a number of those areas (e.g. leases, financial statement presentation, revenue recognition), but other areas such as completing key aspects of the conceptual framework also should be considered. The blueprint would establish a timetable for producing a new common high-quality standard in each of the improvement areas.

- The second part of the process involves the FASB adopting applicable IFRS in all other areas that are not the subject of the improvements program. This will move U.S. public companies to most of the IASB's standards in an orderly fashion while allowing the IASB and FASB to focus their resources on providing significant improvements in financial reporting.

We support the improve-and-adopt approach for several reasons.

- Both existing U.S. GAAP and IFRS require improvement in several major areas. A cooperative effort between the IASB and the FASB to develop improved standards in those areas will benefit financial statement users both here and abroad.
- This approach results in the adoption of IFRS standards over several years, which avoids or minimizes the capacity constraints that might develop in an abrupt mandated switch to IFRS.
- This approach allows other infrastructure elements to improve and converge while IFRS are improved or adopted.
- The improve-and-adopt approach avoids the added cost and complexity to U.S. capital market participants of dealing with two accounting systems.

Hence, if the SEC takes note of the concerns of the FAF, a deal of work will need to be undertaken to improve the IFRS before the United States will be prepared to adopt them. It is interesting that many other countries (including Australia) were prepared to adopt the IFRS before many of the current 'improvement projects' were completed.

The FAF also raised concerns about the perceived independence of the IASB, and it wanted certain changes to be made to the governance policies of the IASB before the United States would be willing to adopt IFRS (which emanate from the IASB). Of particular concern was the uncertain nature of the funding being received by the IASB and the fact that a great deal of the funding comes from the Big 4 accounting firms who each donate $1 million to the IASB—organisations that are directly affected by the operations of the IASB. The FAF (2007, p. 8) called for mechanisms to be established 'to provide the IASB with sufficient and stable funding and staffing levels, thereby ensuring its sustainability as an independent setter of high-quality accounting standards'. The FAF further stated (2007, p. 8) that it did not 'support moving U.S. public companies to IFRS until mechanisms to adequately fund the IASB's activities over the long term are developed'.

The FAF was also concerned that in many jurisdictions amendments are being made to IFRS at a local level before the standards are used in that particular country. This has the obvious implications of undermining the consistency of accounting being undertaken across countries that otherwise state they have adopted IFRS. As the FAF (2007, p. 3) states:

Agreements are needed to eliminate the separate review and endorsement processes that various jurisdictions apply to each IFRS after it is issued by the IASB. These after-the-fact jurisdictional processes are inconsistent with the objective of a single set of high-quality international accounting standards, as evidenced by the local variants of IFRS that have developed in some jurisdictions.

In 2008 the IASC Foundation proposed a number of changes to the IASB's organisational and governance practices.[18] Whether such changes will be sufficient to satisfy the concerns of various stakeholders such as the FAF will become clearer in future years.

DOES THE INTERNATIONAL STANDARDISATION OF ACCOUNTING STANDARDS NECESSARILY LEAD TO THE INTERNATIONAL STANDARDISATION OF ACCOUNTING PRACTICE?

The standardisation of accounting standards by a multitude of different countries, with different enforcement mechanisms, different forms of capital markets, different cultures and so forth, might be considered to lead to the standardisation of accounting practice. Certainly this seems to be a central assumption of the IASB. But is this a realistic belief? Will international standardisation of accounting standards lead to international standardisation of accounting practice? The discussion that follows will show that there are a number of reasons why the standardisation of accounting standards will not necessarily lead to standardisation in practice. Hence, consistent with Nobes (2006), the study of international differences in accounting (and the reasons and motivations for them) will remain an important area of research despite the ongoing standardisation efforts of the IASB.[19] It will be seen that there are various reasons why international differences will survive beyond the introduction of IFRS.

DIFFERENCES IN TAXATION SYSTEMS
Nobes (2006, p. 235) uses a comparison of differences in taxation systems between Germany and the United Kingdom to identify why financial accounting practices in the two countries might be systematically different despite both countries adopting IFRS. As he states:

> In Germany, companies are required to continue to prepare unconsolidated financial statements under the conventional rules of the *Handelsgesetzbuch* (HGB) for calculations of taxable income and distributable income. This is irrespective of any use of IFRS for consolidated or unconsolidated statements (Haller and Eierle, 2004). In some areas, the tax-driven accounting choices of the unconsolidated statements might flow through to consolidated IFRS statements. For example, asset impairments are tax deductible in Germany (but not in the UK), so there is a bias in favour of them. They might survive into IFRS consolidations in Germany, given the room for judgment in IFRS impairment procedures.

---

18 As indicated previously, in July 2008 the IASC Foundation released a report entitled 'Review of the Constitution: Public Accountability and the Composition of the IASB—Proposals for Change'. Public comments were to be received by 20 September 2008, with changes to be implemented in 2009.

19 As Nobes (2006) noted, there has historically been a number of accounting researchers who specialised in studying the reasons and rationale for differences in the accounting methods or practices adopted in different countries. Many such researchers considered that their area of specialisation might become defunct as a result of the global adoption of IFRS. However, as this section demonstrates, despite the widespread adoption of IFRS there will continue to be many differences in the accounting methods adopted across different countries, and hence many areas to consider for research into international accounting differences.

In the UK, IFRS is allowed for individual company financial statements and therefore as a starting point for calculations of taxable income. The tax authorities generally expect the statements of a parent and other UK group members to use the same accounting policies as group statements. To take an example, the recognition and measurement of intangible assets has tax implications. Consequently, given that IFRS requires considerable judgment in this area, individual companies using IFRS will have an incentive to make interpretations of IAS 38 (Intangible Assets) in order to minimise capitalisation and therefore tax, and then these will flow through to consolidated financial statements.

DIFFERENCES IN ECONOMIC AND POLITICAL INFLUENCES ON FINANCIAL REPORTING

There is also an expectation that differences in the economic and political forces operating within a country will have implications for various decisions and judgements made throughout the accounting process. As Ball (2006, p. 15) states:

> The fundamental reason for being sceptical about uniformity of implementation in practice is that the incentives of preparers (managers) and enforcers (auditors, courts, regulators, boards, block shareholders, politicians, analysts, rating agencies, the press) remain primarily local. All accounting accruals (versus simply counting cash) involve judgments about future cash flows. Consequently, there is much leeway in implementing accounting rules. Powerful local economic and political forces therefore determine how managers, auditors, courts, regulators and other parties influence the implementation of rules. These forces have exerted a substantial influence on financial reporting practice historically, and are unlikely to suddenly cease doing so, IFRS or no IFRS. Achieving uniformity in accounting standards seems easy in comparison with achieving uniformity in actual reporting behaviour. The latter would require radical change in the underlying economic and political forces that determine actual behaviour.

MODIFICATIONS MADE TO IFRS AT A NATIONAL LEVEL

As indicated earlier, an issue that is of concern to the Financial Accounting Foundation in the United States is that the IASB has no ability to enforce the application of its accounting standards in countries that have made the decision to adopt IFRS. The effect of this is that regulatory bodies in particular countries may make a decision to modify a particular IFRS before it is released. This was the case in the European Union in relation to its acceptance of IFRS 39. If modifications to IFRS are made at a national level, the result will be international inconsistencies in accounting practice. As Ball (2006, p. 16) states:

> The most visible effect of local political and economic factors on IFRS lies at the level of the national standard adoption decision. This already has occurred to a minor degree, in the EU 'carve out' from IAS 39 in the application of fair value accounting to interest rate hedges. The European version of IAS 39 emerged in response to considerable political pressure from the government of France, which responded to pressure from domestic banks concerned about balance sheet volatility. Episodes like this are bound to occur in the future, whenever reports prepared under IFRS produce outcomes that adversely affect local interests.

In relation to local modifications to IFRS, Veron (2007) also makes the following comment (p. 41):

> If implementation is guided by nationally determined recommendations, then they may gradually diverge from one country to another ... The main promise of IFRS, of making the accounts of companies comparable for investors to make the right choices across countries and sectors, would be in jeopardy. The SEC's Chairman recently insisted that 'We have got to be able to demonstrate that IFRS is indeed a single set of international accounting standards, and not a multiplicity of standards going by the same name'.

DIFFERENCES IN IMPLEMENTATION, MONITORING AND ENFORCEMENT

The argument here is that unless there is consistency in the implementation of accounting standards and subsequent enforcement mechanisms then we cannot expect accounting practices to be uniform despite the actions of the IASB. That is, inconsistencies internationally in how the adoption of accounting standards is implemented, monitored and enforced will lead to inconsistencies in how the standards are applied, which in turn will diminish the international comparability of financial reports. In relation to the implementation of accounting standards, different countries will have varying levels of expertise in applying IFRS. Using China as an example, Veron (2007, p. 20) states:

> In China as in other developing economies, any reference to financial statements prepared 'in accordance with IFRS' needs to be taken with a pinch of salt. The most daunting challenge there is not the standards' adoption, but their proper enforcement in a context of massive underdevelopment of the accounting profession, both quantitatively and qualitatively: China has no more than 70,000 practising accountants (many of them poorly trained), while the size of its economy would probably require between 300,000 and one million.

As Nobes (2006, p. 242) explains when considering differences between accounting practice in Germany and the United Kingdom:

> Enforcement (including monitoring) of compliance with IFRS remains a national matter within the EU. It has been suggested (La Porta et al., 1997) that enforcement of accounting rules is stronger in the UK than in Germany. Hope (2003) constructed an index of compliance and registered Germany substantially lower than the UK. Furthermore, a great deal of evidence has been amassed that compliance by German groups with international standards was lax despite an audited statement of compliance by directors (e.g. Street and Bryant, 2000; Street and Gray, 2001). By contrast, compliance with standards in the UK since the creation of the Financial Reporting Review Panel (FRRP) in 1990 is generally regarded as having been high (Brown and Tarea, 2005).

Questioning the logic behind any belief that the efforts of the IASB will realistically lead to international consistencies in accounting practice, Ball (2006, p. 16) states:

> Does anyone seriously believe that implementation will be of an equal standard in all the nearly 100 countries that have announced adoption of IFRS in one way or another? The

list of adopters ranges from countries with developed accounting and auditing professions and developed capital markets (such as Australia) to countries without a similarly developed institutional background (such as Armenia, Costa Rica, Ecuador, Egypt, Kenya, Kuwait, Nepal, Tobago and Ukraine). Even within the EU, will implementation of IFRS be at an equal standard in all countries? The list includes Austria, Belgium, Cyprus, Czech Republic, Denmark, Germany, Estonia, Greece, Spain, France, Ireland, Italy, Latvia, Lithuania, Luxembourg, Hungary, Malta, Netherlands, Poland, Portugal, Slovenia, Slovakia, Finland, Sweden and the UK. It is well known that uniform EU economic rules in general are not implemented evenly, with some countries being notorious standouts. What makes financial reporting rules different?

Accounting accruals generally require at least some element of subjective judgment and hence can be influenced by the incentives of managers and auditors. Consider the case of IAS 36 and IAS 38 which require periodic review of long-term tangible and intangible assets for possible impairment to fair value. Do we seriously believe that managers and auditors will comb through firms' asset portfolios to discover economically impaired assets with the same degree of diligence and ruthlessness in all the countries that adopt IFRS? Will auditors, regulators, courts, boards, analysts, rating agencies, the press and other monitors of corporate financial reporting provide the same degree of oversight in all IFRS-adopting countries? In the event of a severe economic downturn creating widespread economic impairment of companies' assets, will the political and regulatory sectors of all countries be equally likely to turn a blind eye?

Will they be equally sympathetic to companies failing to record economic impairment on their accounting balance sheets, in order to avoid loan default or bankruptcy (as did Japanese banks for an extended period)? Will local political and economic factors cease to exert the influence *on actual financial reporting practice* that they have in the past? Or will convergence among nations in adopted accounting standards lead to an offsetting divergence in the extent to which they are implemented?

Ball (2006) also discusses how the recent general trend inherent within IFRS of adopting asset measurement bases tied to 'fair value' will in itself create inconsistencies, because in many countries there is an absence of markets for many types of assets, including financial assets. In countries with 'thinly trading markets', relatively more estimation of 'fair values' will be required. Ball (p. 17) states:

> To make matters worse, the countries in which there will be greater room to exercise judgment under fair value accounting, due to lower-liquidity markets and poorer information about asset impairment, are precisely the countries with weaker local enforcement institutions (audit profession, legal protection, regulation, and so on). Judgment is a generic property of accounting standard implementation, but worldwide reliance on judgment has been widely expanded under IFRS by the drift to fair value accounting and by the adoption of fair value standards in countries with illiquid markets.

The ultimate implication of the potential variation in accounting practice (for the reasons discussed in this section) is that investors might be misled into believing that IFRS adoption has created a consistency in international accounting practices. That is, the adoption of IFRS might (incorrectly) be construed as a signal that a country has improved its quality of reporting. In a sense, the adoption of IFRS brings a level of legitimacy to a country's financial reporting despite any limitations in the level of enforcement of the standards. Ball (pp. 22–23) states:

> Substantial international differences in financial reporting quality are inevitable, and my major concerns are that investors will be misled into believing that there is more uniformity in practice than actually is the case and that, even to sophisticated investors, international differences in reporting quality now will be hidden under the rug of seemingly uniform standards ... But the problem with IFRS adoption, as a signal to investors about the financial reporting quality of a preparer, is that it is almost costless for *all* countries to signal that they are of high quality: i.e., to adopt the highest available accounting standards on paper. Worse. IFRS adoption most likely costs less to the lower-quality countries, for two reasons. First, the lower-quality regimes will incur fewer economic and political costs of actually enforcing the adopted standards. It is the higher quality reporting regimes that are more likely to incur the cost of actually enforcing IFRS. Because they have the institutions (such as a higher-quality audit profession, more effective courts system, better shareholder litigation rules) that are more likely to require enforcement of whatever standards are adopted. Second, by wholesale adoption of IFRS, the lower-quality regimes can avoid the costs of running their own standard-setting body, which likely are proportionally higher than in larger economies.

Ball discusses the 'free rider' problem associated with IFRS.[20] If a 'symbol of legitimacy'—such as IFRS—can be acquired at low cost, some countries with low accounting proficiency will make the choice to adopt IFRS because of the reputational benefits such a choice may generate. However, such a choice will have costly implications for countries with higher levels of accounting proficiency and who put in place appropriate implementation, monitoring and enforcement mechanisms. As Ball (p. 23) states:

> A classic 'free rider' problem emerges: it is essentially costless for low-quality countries to use the IFRS 'brand name,' so they all do. If IFRS adoption is a free good, what companies or countries will not take it? When it is costless to say otherwise, who is going to say: 'We will not adopt high standards'?

As a potential solution to the problem, Ball (p. 24) makes the following proposal:

> The only way to make the IFRS signal informative about quality is for the worldwide financial reporting system to incorporate a cost of signalling that the lower-quality agents are not prepared to pay. This would necessitate an effective worldwide enforcement mechanism under which countries that adopt but do not effectively implement IFRS are either penalised or prohibited from using the IFRS brand name. In the absence of an effective worldwide enforcement mechanism it is essentially costless for low-quality countries to use the IFRS brand name, and local political and economic factors inevitably will exert substantial influence on local financial reporting practice, IFRS adoption notwithstanding. If allowing all countries to use the IFRS label discards the information in accounting standards about reporting quality differences, then the

---

20 As explained in Chapter 3, a free-rider can be defined as a party that takes advantage of particular goods or services without incurring some of the associated production or establishment costs.

available quality signal could become the quality of the enforcement of standards, not standards per se.

Accounting Headline 4.4 provides an example of a European company that appeared to depart from an IASB standard, and the article emphasises the inability of the IASB to force compliance with its standards. The article also makes reference to inconsistencies in how IFRSs are applied internationally.

Given the material in this section, the belief that the global adoption of IFRS will lead to consistency in international accounting practices could be questioned. There will continue to be international differences in accounting practice and such differences will continue to provide an interesting area of research for accounting academics. However, at a more fundamental level, is it really a good idea to have global consistency in accounting practice anyway? That is, is the central

---

Accounting Headline 4.4 A European company departs from an IASB standard

New York Times, 7 March 2008, p. C1

Loophole lets bank rewrite the calendar

FLOYD NORRIS

It is not often that a major international bank admits it is violating well-established accounting rules, but that is what Société Générale has done in accounting for the fraud that caused the bank to lose 6.4 billion euros—now worth about $9.7 billion—in January.

In its financial statements for 2007, the French bank takes the loss in that year, offsetting it against 1.5 billion euros in profit that it says was earned by a trader, Jérôme Kerviel, who concealed from management the fact he was making huge bets in financial futures markets.

In moving the loss from 2008—when it actually occurred—to 2007, Société Générale has created a furor in accounting circles and raised questions about whether international accounting standards can be consistently applied in the many countries around the world that are converting to the standards.

While the London-based International Accounting Standards Board writes the rules, there is no international organization with the power to enforce them and assure that companies are in compliance.

In its annual report released this week, Société Générale invoked what is known as the 'true and fair' provision of international accounting standards, which provides that 'in the extremely rare circumstances in which management concludes that compliance' with the rules 'would be so misleading that it would conflict with the objective of financial statements', a company can depart from the rules.

In the past, that provision has been rarely used in Europe, and a similar provision in the United States is almost never invoked. One European auditor said he had never seen the exemption used in four decades, and another said the only use he could recall dealt with an extremely complicated pension arrangement that had not been contemplated when the rules were written.

Some of the people who wrote the rule took exception to its use by Société Générale.

'It is inappropriate,' said Anthony T. Cope, a retired member of both the I.A.S.B. and its American counterpart, the Financial Accounting Standards Board. 'They are manipulating earnings.'

John Smith, a member of the I.A.S.B., said: 'There is nothing true about reporting a loss in 2007 when it clearly occurred in 2008. This raises a question as to just how creative they are in interpreting accounting rules in other areas.' He said the board should consider repealing the 'true and fair' exemption 'if it can be interpreted in the way they have interpreted it'.

Société Générale said that its two audit firms, Ernst & Young and Deloitte & Touche, approved of the accounting, as did French regulators. Calls to the international headquarters of both firms were not returned, and Société Générale said no financial executives were available to be interviewed.

In the United States, the Securities and Exchange Commission has the final say on

(continued)

whether companies are following the nation's accounting rules. But there is no similar body for the international rules, although there are consultative groups organized by a group of European regulators and by the International Organization of Securities Commissions. It seems likely that both groups will discuss the Société Générale case, but they will not be able to act unless French regulators change their minds.

'Investors should be troubled by this in an I.A.S.B. world,' said Jack Ciesielski, the editor of *The Analyst's Accounting Observer*, an American publication. 'While it makes sense to have a "fair and true override" to allow for the fact that broad principles might not always make for the best reporting, you need to have good judgment exercised to make it fair for investors. SocGen and its auditors look like they were trying more to appease the class of investors or regulators who want to believe it's all over when they say it's over, whether it is or not.'

Not only had the losses not occurred at the end of 2007, they would never have occurred had the activities of Mr Kerviel been discovered then. According to a report by a special committee of Société Générale's board, Mr Kerviel had earned profits through the end of 2007, and entered 2008 with few if any outstanding positions.

But early in January he bet heavily that both the DAX index of German stocks and the Dow Jones Euro Stoxx index would go up. Instead they fell sharply. After the bank learned of the positions in mid-January, it sold them quickly on the days when the stock market was hitting its lowest levels so far this year.

In its annual report, Société Générale says that applying two accounting rules—IAS 10, 'Events After the Balance Sheet Date', and IAS 39, 'Financial Instruments: Recognition and Measurement'— would have been inconsistent with a fair presentation of its results. But it does not go into detail as to why it believes that to be the case.

One rule mentioned, IAS 39, has been highly controversial in France because banks feel it unreasonably restricts their accounting. The European Commission adopted a 'carve out' that allows European companies to ignore part of the rule, and Société Générale uses that carve out. The commission ordered the accounting standards board to meet with banks to find a rule they could accept, but numerous meetings over the past several years have not produced an agreement.

Investors who read the 2007 annual report can learn the impact of the decision to invoke the 'true and fair' exemption, but cannot determine how the bank's profits would have been affected if it had applied the full IAS 39.

It appears that by pushing the entire affair into 2007, Société Générale hoped both to put the incident behind it and to perhaps de-emphasize how much was lost in 2008. The net loss of 4.9 billion euros it has emphasized was computed by offsetting the 2007 profit against the 2008 loss.

It may have accomplished those objectives, at the cost of igniting a debate over how well international accounting standards can be policed in a world with no international regulatory body.

quest of the IASB that there be global standardisation of accounting standards logically flawed? Is it appropriate to have a global 'one size fits all' approach to financial reporting when there are international differences in the nature of capital, labour and product markets; differences in monitoring and enforcement mechanisms; differences in economic and political influence; and differences in cultures? The next section explores various reasons why, in the absence of globalisation efforts such as those being undertaken by the IASB, we would expect to find international differences in accounting practices.

EXPLANATIONS OF DIFFERENCES IN ACCOUNTING

Will financial accounting standards developed in London by the IASB necessarily meet the information needs of financial report users in all countries? Does it make sense that a given suite of accounting standards will be equally applicable for a service company operating in South

America as it would for a mining company operating in Australia or a manufacturing company in China? What do you, the reader, think? In this regard, Chand and White (2007, p. 606) make the following comment:

> Once the IFRSs are adopted by a particular country, both the multinational and domestic enterprises may be required to follow the standards. A suite of standards developed with the needs of international users of financial reports in mind, specifically those seeking international comparability, will not necessarily meet the needs of users in a particular jurisdiction. The IASB cannot take cognisance of the individual national, cultural and political factors of all its member nations while preparing IFRSs. Transporting IASB standards to developing countries—which have their own disparate group of external information users that operate within internationally diverse cultural, social, and political environments—should not be expected to have optimum results (Hopwood, 2000; Ngangan et al., 2005). Therefore, of critical importance is the fundamental question, who gains the most from harmonization/convergence?

Chand and White's point is interesting. Given that more than 100 countries have now adopted IFRS, is there any clear evidence that all of the countries have benefited from the adoption, or that the benefits are spread across different types or sizes of organisations within particular countries? Authors such as Perera (1989) have argued that accounting practices within particular countries have traditionally evolved to suit the circumstances of a particular society at a particular time. While there was a large variation in accounting systems used in different countries prior to 2005 (when many, but not all, countries adopted IFRS), it has been commonly accepted that there were two main models of financial accounting that had evolved within economically developed countries: the Anglo-American model and the continental European model (Mueller, 1967; Nobes, 1984).[21] The Anglo-American model is characterised by a system of accounting that is strongly influenced by professional accounting bodies rather than government; it emphasises the importance of capital markets (the entities within the countries that use this model of accounting are typically very reliant on public sources of equity and debt finance), and relies on terms such as 'true and fair' or 'presents fairly', which in turn are based on considerations of economic substance over and above legal form (legal form being bound by legislation).

The continental European model of accounting, on the other hand, typically is characterised by a relatively small input from the accounting profession, little reliance on qualitative requirements such as true and fair, and stronger reliance on government. The accounting methods tend to be heavily associated with the tax rules in place, and the information tends to be of a nature that protects the interest of creditors rather than investors per se. (The entities within countries that use the continental European model have historically tended to obtain most of their long-term funds from family sources, governments or lenders, often banks.)

Over time, numerous reasons have been given for the differences in the accounting methods of different countries. Mueller (1968) suggests that such differences might have been caused

---

21 For example, France, Italy, Spain and Germany are often presented as examples of the continental European group, while countries such as the United States, the United Kingdom, Ireland, the Netherlands, Canada, Australia and New Zealand are often presented as examples of the Anglo-American group.

by differences in the underlying laws of the country, the political systems in place (for example, a capitalistic/free-market system versus a centralised/communistic system), or their level of development from an economic perspective. As Mueller (p. 95) explains:

> In society, accounting performs a service function. This function is put in jeopardy unless accounting remains, above all, practically useful. Thus, it must respond to the ever-changing needs of society and must reflect the social, political, legal and economic conditions within which it operates. Its meaningfulness depends on its ability to mirror these conditions.

Other factors such as tax systems, level of education and level of economic development have also been suggested as explanations for historical differences in accounting practices (Doupnik & Salter, 1995). At present there is no single clear theory that explains why, in the absence of efforts to standardise accounting, we would expect to find international differences in accounting practices. Many different causes have been suggested. Nobes (1998) reviewed the literature and confirmed that numerous reasons have been proposed to explain the differences:

1. Nature of business ownership and financing system
2. Colonial inheritance
3. Invasions
4. Taxation
5. Inflation
6. Level of education
7. Age and size of accountancy profession
8. Stage of economic development
9. Legal systems
10. Culture
11. History
12. Geography
13. Language
14. Influence of theory
15. Political systems, social climate
16. Religion

According to Nobes, many of the factors are interrelated. A number are deemed to be 'institutional' and a number relate to the broader notion of culture. The next sections look more closely at some of the factors. Again, it is emphasised that many differences in accounting practices have been eliminated due to many countries adopting IFRS. After reading the material, readers might question whether it was appropriate for such a diverse group of countries to adopt one set of accounting standards.

CULTURE

Culture is a broad concept that would be expected to impact on legal systems, tax systems, the way businesses are formed and financed, and so on. For many years culture has been used in the psychology, anthropology and sociology literatures as the basis for explaining differences in social systems (Hofstede, 1980). In recent decades it has also been used to try to explain international differences in accounting systems. An early paper that considered the impact of culture on accounting was one by Violet (1983), who argued that accounting is a 'socio-technical activity' that involves interaction between both human and non-human resources. Because the two interact, Violet claims that accounting cannot be considered culture-free. Relating accounting to culture, Violet (p. 8) claims:

> Accounting is a social institution established by most cultures to report and explain certain social phenomena occurring in economic transactions. As a social institution, accounting has integrated certain cultural customs and elements within the constraints of cultural postulates. Accounting cannot be isolated and analyzed as an independent component of a culture. It is, like mankind and other social institutions, a product of culture and contributes to the evolution of the culture which employs it. Since accounting is culturally determined, other cultural customs, beliefs, and institutions influence it.

Takatera and Yamamoto (1987) have defined culture as 'an expression of norms, values and customs which reflect typical behavioural characteristics'. Hofstede (1980, p. 25) has defined culture as 'the collective programming of the mind which distinguishes the members of one human group from another'. It describes a system of societal or collectively held values (Gray, 1988, p. 4) rather than values held at an individual level. 'Values' are deemed to determine behaviour. Gray (p. 4) explains that the term 'culture' is typically reserved for societies as a whole, or nations, whereas 'subculture' is used for the level of an organisation, profession (such as the accounting profession) or family. It is expected that different subcultures within a particular society will share common characteristics. In the discussion that follows the work of Professor Sid Gray is explored in some depth. This work is generally acknowledged as constituting some of the most rigorous research into accounting's relationship to, and to some extent dependence on, national culture.

Gray (p. 5) argues that 'a methodological framework incorporating culture may be used to explain and predict international differences in accounting systems and patterns of accounting development internationally'. Any consideration of culture necessarily requires difficult choices as to the aspects of culture that are important to the issue under consideration, and, in turn, how one goes about measuring the relevant cultural attributes. As Perera (1989, p. 43) states, 'the study of culture is characterized by a unique problem arising from the inexhaustible nature of its components'.[22] Gray used the work of Hofstede (1980, 1983). Gray (1988, p. 5) explains:

> Hofstede's (1980, 1983) research was aimed at detecting the structural elements of culture and particularly those which most strongly affect known behaviour in work situations in organizations and institutions. In what is probably one of the most extensive cross-cultural studies ever conducted, psychologists collected data about 'values' from the employees of a multinational corporation located in more than fifty

---

22 Perera (1989, p. 43) further states that 'it is essential, therefore, that in analyzing the impact of culture upon the behaviour of the members of any particular subculture, a researcher must select the cultural components or dimensions most pertinent to the particular facet of cultural behaviour being studied'. This is clearly not a straightforward task.

countries. Subsequent statistical analysis and reasoning revealed four underlying societal value dimensions along which countries could be positioned. These dimensions, with substantial support from prior work in the field, were labeled Individualism, Power Distance, Uncertainty Avoidance, and Masculinity. Such dimensions were perceived to represent a common structure in cultural systems. It was also shown how countries could be grouped into culture areas, on the basis of their scores on the four dimensions.[23]

Gray argues that the value systems of accountants will be derived from and related to societal values (which are reflected by Hofstede's cultural dimensions of Individualism, Power Distance, Uncertainty Avoidance and Masculinity).[24] These social values that are also held by accountants (which Gray terms the 'accounting subculture') will in turn, it is believed, impact on the development of the respective accounting systems at the national level. Therefore, at this point we can perhaps start to question whether accounting systems can be developed in a 'one size fits all' perspective—an approach that the International Accounting Standards Board (IASB) has adopted. However, while it is argued that there should be some association between various value systems and accounting systems, many events would typically have occurred over time that confound this possible relationship. For example, in relation to developing countries, Baydoun and Willett (1995, p. 72) state:

> It is quite possible that had accounting systems evolved independently in developing countries they would have a rather different form from any we now witness in present day Europe. However, most accounting systems used in developing countries have been directly imported from the West through a variety of channels: by colonialism in the past; and through Western multinational companies, the influence of local professional associations (usually founded originally by Western counterpart organizations) and aid and loan agencies from the industrialised countries.

Returning to the work of Hofstede, the four societal value dimensions identified by Hofstede can be summarised as follows (quoted from Hofstede, 1984):

■ Individualism versus collectivism

> Individualism stands for a preference for a loosely knit social framework in society wherein individuals are supposed to take care of themselves and their immediate families only. Its opposite, Collectivism, stands for a preference for a tightly knit social framework in which individuals can expect their relatives, clan, or other in-group to look after them in exchange for unquestioning loyalty (it will be clear that the word 'collectivism' is not used here to describe any particular social system). The fundamental issue addressed by this dimension is the degree of interdependence a society maintains among individuals. It relates to people's self concept: 'I' or 'we'.

---

23 Hofstede's work is based on international surveys conducted within IBM. The attitude surveys were conducted between 1967 and 1973 and resulted in 117 000 responses from 88 000 employees in sixty-six countries (Baskerville, 2003). Hofstede was the senior researcher in charge of the survey.

24 Hofstede's theory, while being applied to accounting issues, is from the cross-cultural psychology literature and was of itself not directly concerned with accounting.

With regard to the cultural dimension of individualism versus collectivism, it is interesting to note that a great deal of economic theory is based on the notion of self-interest and the rational economic person (one who undertakes action to maximise personal wealth at the expense of others). This is very much based in the individualism dimension. In a culture that exhibited collectivism, it is expected that members of the society would look after each other and issues of loyalty would exist.[25]

■ Large versus small power distance

Power Distance is the extent to which the members of a society accept that power in institutions and organisations is distributed unequally. This affects the behaviour of the less powerful as well as of the more powerful members of society. People in Large Power Distance societies accept a hierarchical order in which everybody has a place, which needs no further justification. People in Small Power Distance societies strive for power equalisation and demand justification for power inequities. The fundamental issue addressed by this dimension is how a society handles inequalities among people when they occur. This has obvious consequences for the way people build their institutions and organisations.

■ Strong versus weak uncertainty avoidance

Uncertainty Avoidance is the degree to which the members of a society feel uncomfortable with uncertainty and ambiguity. This feeling leads them to beliefs promising certainty and to sustaining institutions protecting conformity. Strong Uncertainly Avoidance societies maintain rigid codes of belief and behaviour and are intolerant towards deviant persons and ideas. Weak Uncertainty Avoidance societies maintain a more relaxed atmosphere in which practice counts more than principles and deviance is more easily tolerated. The fundamental issue addressed by this dimension is how a society reacts to the fact that time only runs one way and that the future is unknown: whether it tries to control the future or to let it happen. Like Power Distance, Uncertainty Avoidance has consequences for the way people build their institutions and organisations.

■ Masculinity versus femininity

Masculinity stands for a preference in society for achievement, heroism, assertiveness, and material success. Its opposite, Femininity, stands for a preference for relationships, modesty, caring for the weak, and the quality of life. The fundamental issue addressed by this dimension is the way in which a society allocates social (as opposed to biological) roles to the sexes.

---

25 Positive Accounting Theory, a theory developed by Watts and Zimmerman (and which is discussed in depth in Chapter 7), attempts to explain and predict managers' selection of accounting methods. In developing their theory, Watts and Zimmerman assume that individuals will always act in their own self-interest. Such an assumption would be invalid in a community that embraces a collectivist perspective. In a similar vein, Hamid, Craig and Clarke (1993) suggest that finance theories developed in Western cultures will not apply in Islamic cultures. According to these authors, the Islamic principles do not allow the payment of interest. They argue (p. 146) therefore that 'much of Western finance theory, in particular the capital asset pricing model, which draws upon interest-dependent explanations of risk, cannot be part of the (Islamic) accounting and finance package'.

Again, when countries are given scores on the four value dimensions, a number of countries can be clustered together, reflecting that they have similar cultural values.[26,27] Having considered Hofstede's value dimensions, the next step for Gray was to relate them to the values that he perceived to be in place within the accounting subculture. Gray developed four accounting values that were deemed to relate to the accounting subculture, with the intention that the accounting values would then be directly linked to Hofstede's four societal values (discussed above). Gray's four accounting values were defined as follows (1988, p. 8):

■ Professionalism versus statutory control

A preference for the existence of individual professional judgement and the maintenance of professional self-regulation, as opposed to compliance with prescriptive legal requirements and statutory control.

■ Uniformity versus flexibility

A preference for the enforcement of uniform accounting practices between companies and the consistent use of such practices over time, as opposed to flexibility in accordance with the perceived circumstances of individual companies.

■ Conservatism versus optimism

A preference for a cautious approach to measurement so as to cope with the uncertainty of future events, as opposed to a more optimistic, laissez-faire, risk-taking approach.

■ Secrecy versus transparency

A preference for confidentiality and the restriction of disclosure of information about the business only to those who are closely involved with its management and financing, as opposed to a more transparent, open and publicly accountable approach.

Gray (1988) then developed a number of hypotheses relating Hofstede's four societal cultural dimensions to each one of his four accounting values.[28] His first hypothesis was:

Hypothesis 1: The higher a country ranks in terms of *Individualism* and the lower it ranks in terms of *Uncertainty Avoidance* and *Power Distance*, then the more likely it is to rank highly in terms of *Professionalism*.

The basis for the first hypothesis was that a preference for applying judgement (for example, determining whether something is true and fair) rather than strict rules is more likely where

---

26 For example, of the many groups, one group with similar scores on each of the four societal values comprises Australia, Canada, Ireland, New Zealand, the United Kingdom and the United States. Another group is Denmark, Finland, the Netherlands, Norway and Sweden, while another group comprises Indonesia, Pakistan, Taiwan and Thailand. The view is that people within these various groupings of countries share a similar culture and therefore share similar norms and value systems.

27 A number of authors have been critical of Hofstede's work. One particular criticism is that Hofstede equated nations with cultures (that is, each nation was deemed to be one culture), when in fact numerous cultures can exist within a particular country (Baskerville, 2003).

28 Although Gray (1988) developed four hypotheses, he did not test them empirically. To test them, as others have subsequently done, one must determine whether an accounting system scores high or low in a particular country on the four dimensions developed by Gray.

people tend to be individualistic, where people are relatively more comfortable with people using their own judgement, rather than conforming to rigid codes of rules, and where different people are allowed to make judgements rather than relying on strict rules 'from above' (lower power distance).

Gray's second hypothesis was:

Hypothesis 2: The higher a country ranks in terms of *Uncertainty Avoidance* and *Power Distance* and the lower it ranks in terms of *Individualism*, then the more likely it is to rank highly in terms of *Uniformity*.

The basis for the second hypothesis is that communities that prefer to avoid uncertainty prefer more rigid codes of behaviour and greater conformity. A desire for uniformity is also deemed to be consistent with a preference for *Collectivism* (as opposed to *Individualism*) and an acceptance of a relatively more *Power Distance* society in which laws are more likely to be accepted.

Gray's third hypothesis was:

Hypothesis 3: The higher a country ranks in terms of *Uncertainty Avoidance* and the lower it ranks in terms of *Individualism* and *Masculinity*, then the more likely it is to rank highly in terms of *Conservatism*.

As noted previously, Conservatism implies that accountants favour notions such as prudence (which traditionally means that profits and assets are calculated in a conservative manner with a tendency towards understatement rather than overstatement). The basis for the third hypothesis is that communities that have strong Uncertainty Avoidance characteristics tend to prefer a more cautious approach to cope with existing uncertainties. On the other hand, Conservatism is expected to be associated with communities that care less about individual achievement. Communities that tend to demonstrate masculine tendencies emphasise achievement—hence the expectation that lower levels of Masculinity will lead to higher preferences for conservative accounting principles. A more highly masculine community would be deemed to prefer to use methods of accounting that lead to higher levels of performance being reported.

Gray's fourth hypothesis was:

Hypothesis 4: The higher a country ranks in terms of *Uncertainty Avoidance* and *Power Distance* and the lower it ranks in terms of *Individualism* and *Masculinity*, then the more likely it is to rank highly in terms of *Secrecy*.

The basis for the fourth hypothesis is that communities that have a higher preference for Uncertainty Avoidance prefer not to disclose too much information because this could lead to conflict, competition and security problems. Also, communities that accept higher Power Distance would accept restricted information, as this acts to preserve power inequalities. Also, a community that prefers a collective approach, as opposed to an individualistic approach, would prefer to keep information disclosures to a minimum to protect those close to the firm and to reflect limited concern for those external to the organisation. A more Masculine community would be expected to provide more information about its financial position and performance to enable comparisons of the level of performance of different entities. (Masculine communities would be deemed to be more concerned with issues such as ranking the performance of one entity against another.) However, as a caveat to the general position that more Masculine communities disclose more accounting information, Gray (1988, p. 11) argues that 'a significant but less important link with Masculinity also seems likely to the extent that more caring societies, where more emphasis is given to the quality of life, people and the environment, will tend to be more open, especially as regards socially related information'.[29] Table 4.1 summarises the hypothesised relationships between Gray's accounting values and Hofstede's cultural values.

Table 4.1 Summary of the hypothesised relationships between Gray's accounting values and Hofstede's cultural values

Cultural values (from Hofstede)	Accounting values (from Gray)			
	Professionalism	Uniformity	Conservatism	Secrecy
Power Distance	–	+	?	+
Uncertainty Avoidance	–	+	+	+
Individualism	+	–	–	–
Masculinity	?	?	–	–

Note: '+' indicates a positive relationship; '–' indicates a negative relationship; and '?' indicates that the direction of the relationship is unclear.

Gray (1988) further hypothesised that relationships can be established between accounting values and the authority and enforcement of accounting systems (the extent to which they are determined and enforced by statutory control or professional means), and the measurement and disclosure characteristics of the accounting systems. According to Gray (p. 12):

> Accounting value systems most relevant to the professional or statutory authority for accounting systems and their enforcement would seem to be the professionalism and uniformity dimensions, in that they are concerned with regulation and the extent of enforcement and conformity ... Accounting values most relevant to the measurement practices used and the extent of information disclosed are self-evidently the conservatism and the secrecy dimensions.

Gray's linkage between societal values, accounting values and accounting practice are summarised in Figure 4.1.

Perera (1989, p. 47) provides additional discussion in respect of the relationships summarised in Figure 4.1. He states:

> The higher the degree of professionalism the greater the degree of professional self-regulation and the lower the need for government intervention. The degree of uniformity preferred in an accounting sub-culture would have an effect on the manner in which the accounting system is applied. The higher the degree of uniformity the lower the

---

29 Socially related information would relate to such issues as health and safety, employee education and training, charitable donations, support of community projects and environmental performance. A more Feminine (less Masculine) society would tend to consider these issues more important. Hence, while Femininity might be associated with less financial disclosure, it is assumed to be associated with greater social disclosure.

FIGURE 4.1 Gray's hypothesised relationships between society values, accounting values and accounting practice

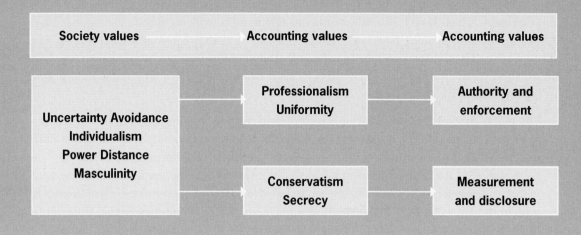

Society values	Accounting values	Accounting values
Uncertainty Avoidance Individualism Power Distance Masculinity	Professionalism Uniformity	Authority and enforcement
	Conservatism Secrecy	Measurement and disclosure

Source: H. H. E. Fechner & A. Kilgore (1994), 'The influence of cultural factors on accounting practice', *International Journal of Accounting*, 29, p. 269.

extent of professional judgment and the stronger the force applying accounting rules and procedures. The amount of conservatism preferred in an accounting sub-culture would influence the measurement practices used. The higher the degree of conservatism the stronger the ties with traditional measurement practices. The degree of secrecy preferred in an accounting sub-culture would influence the extent of the information disclosed in accounting reports. The higher the degree of secrecy, the lower the extent of disclosure.

One objective of Gray's research was to explain how differences between countries in respect of their culture may either impede any moves towards international harmonisation of accounting standards or bring into question efforts to generate some form of harmonisation or standardisation. While some of the above material might appear a little confusing (perhaps not), it does represent quite an intellectual body of research, which is attempting to relate a fairly difficult to measure construct, culture, to differences in values of the accounting subculture, and ultimately to differences in the systems of accounting employed. While we might not be able to remember all the hypothesised relationships described, what is important is that we appreciate how researchers have attempted to link cultural measures to accounting practice.

A number of other authors have also used Hofstede's cultural dimensions.[30] Zarzeski (1996) provides evidence that supports a view that entities located in countries classified as relatively

30 Baydoun and Willett (1995, p. 72) identify a number of problems in testing the Hofstede–Gray theory. They emphasise that many accounting systems are imported from other countries with possibly different cultures. As they state: 'Due to the interference in what would otherwise have been the natural evolution of financial information requirements there are no uncontaminated examples of modern accounting practices in developing countries. Consequently great care has to be taken in using data from developing countries to draw inferences about relevance on the basis of the Hofstede–Gray framework.'

more Individualistic and Masculine and relatively less in terms of Uncertainty Avoidance provide greater levels of disclosure. Zarzeski also considered issues associated with international profile and found that those entities with a relatively higher international profile tend to be less secretive than other entities. Further, entities from continental European countries, such as France and Germany, which have historically tended to rely more heavily on debt financing than, say, Anglo-American companies, have lower levels of disclosure than Anglo-American companies. In relation to the issue of secrecy, Zarzeski shows that local enterprises are more likely to disclose information commensurate with the secrecy of their culture than are international enterprises. In explaining this, she states (p. 20):

> The global market is just a different 'culture' than the one the firm faces at home. When a firm does business in the global market, it is operating in a different 'culture' and therefore may need to have different 'practices'. Higher levels of financial disclosures may be necessary for international survival because disclosure of quality operations should result in lower resource costs. When enterprises from more secretive countries perceive economic gain from increasing their financial disclosures, cultural borrowing may occur. The culture being borrowed will be a 'global market culture,' rather than a specific country culture.

Perera (1989) considered both Hofstede's cultural dimensions and Gray's accounting subcultural value dimensions and uses them to explain historical differences in the accounting practices adopted in continental European countries and Anglo-American countries. According to Perera (p. 51), many countries in continental Europe are characterised by relatively high levels of uncertainty avoidance, where rules or 'social codes' tend to shape behaviour, while the opposite applies in Anglo-American countries:

> The presence of these rules satisfied people's emotional needs for order and predictability in society, and people feel uncomfortable in situations where there are no rules. Therefore, in general, one can expect more formalization and institutionalization of procedures in strong uncertainty avoidance societies than in weak uncertainty avoidance countries.
>
> There is a preference for the existence of individual professional judgement, the maintenance of professional self-regulation, and flexibility in accordance with the perceived circumstances of individual companies in the accounting sub-culture of Anglo-American countries, whereas there is a preference for compliance with prescriptive legal requirements and statutory control, the maintenance of uniform accounting practices between companies, and the consistent application of such practices over time in the accounting sub-cultures of Continental Europe. Also, there is more support in the latter group for a prudent and cautious approach to income measurement to cope with the uncertainty of future events and the confidentiality of the information by restricting disclosures to only those involved with the management and financing of the organization.
>
> These characteristics, in turn, tend to influence the degree of disclosure expected in the respective accounting systems or practices. For example, in France and West Germany, where the level of professionalism is relatively low and the preference for conservatism and secrecy is relatively high, the combined effect on the degree of disclosure will be negative. On the other hand, the collectivist or anti-individualist values of the society require business enterprises to be accountable to society by way of providing information.

Therefore, it becomes necessary for the Government to intervene and prescribe certain disclosure requirements, including those in regard to social accounting. Furthermore, this situation is not likely to be rejected by the accounting profession, because here is a preference for compliance with prescriptive legal regulation and statutory control in the accounting sub-culture. By comparison, in the United States and U.K., although the relatively high level of professionalism and low level of preference for conservatism and secrecy tend to have a positive combined effect on the degree of disclosure in accounting practices, the individualistic values of the society are more concerned with the provision of information to shareholders or investors than those issues involving accountability to society at large.

Baydoun and Willett (1995) used the Hofstede–Gray theory to investigate the use of the French United Accounting System (which was ranked lowly in terms of Professionalism and highly in terms of Uniformity as well as being considered quite conservative) in Lebanon. According to Baydoun and Willett, following World War I the Allied Supreme Council granted France a mandatory authority over Lebanon. Lebanon was a French colony until 1943 and French troops remained there until 1946. Strong trading relations between France and Lebanon continued to exist and in 1983 the French government sponsored the transfer of the French Uniform Accounting System (UAS) to Lebanon. What was of interest was whether the French system was actually suited to the Lebanese cultural environment. Baydoun and Willett provided evidence to suggest that Lebanon and France ranked in a relatively similar manner in terms of Power Distance and Individualism. However, Lebanon was considered to rank lower in terms of Uncertainty Avoidance and higher in terms of Masculinity. On this basis (refer back to Table 4.1), Baydoun and Willett (p. 81) conclude that 'it would appear that Lebanon's requirements are for less Uniformity, Conservatism and Secrecy in financial reporting practices'.[31] They further state (p. 87):

Assuming that cultural relevance is or should be a factor in determining the form of financial statements, we would expect Lebanese financial statements to be less uniform across time and between entities, to contain more market value information and provide more items of disaggregated information. Normal publication dates should be relatively flexible and there should be less call for conservative valuation rules such as lower of cost and market. It would appear that these and other similar prescriptions cannot be tested directly at present. Since 1983 all Lebanese firms have been required to follow UAS and this system has not yet been modified to accommodate any cultural differences between France and Lebanon ... However, our analysis suggests that modifications along the lines described above either will or should take place in Lebanese accounting in the future.

Chand and White (2007) explored various cultural attributes within Fijian society to determine whether the recent adoption of IFRS within the Fijian context made sense. Their view was that

---

31 In undertaking their work, Baydoun and Willett were, in a number of respects, critical of Gray's work. For example, they state (p. 82) that 'all of Gray's accounting values are defined in terms of preferences for particular courses of action, rather than in terms of apparent attributes of financial statements, such as the qualitative characteristics described in the FASB's conceptual framework project'. Also they state that Gray's theory does not clearly indicate what forms of financial statements might be preferred.

rules-based standards would be more appropriate than the principles-based standards that have been developed by the IASB. As they state (p. 616):

Fiji is a society that is dominated by two ethnic groups—indigenous Fijians and Indo-Fijians. Both groups exhibit cultural characteristics of uncertainly avoidance and a preference for a society that adheres to rules as opposed to one that expects the individual to act appropriately by personal initiative and professional judgment (see Chand, 2005). Fijian society is also characterized by the presence of a strong power distance between leaders in all capacities and their constituents. A number of entities have been established in Fiji with a stated remit to foster the indigenous population's participation in the economy. Educated and articulate principals who have the temerity to question financial reports are typically reminded that Fijian society does not tolerate such challenges. The adoption of IFRSs leads to principles-based financial reports that require the exercise of professional judgment and introduces ambiguity in the reporting process, thus clouding rather than enhancing accountability (Davie, 1999, 2000). Managers of such entities drawn from the Fijian elite caste, as many are, who are beyond the challenge by non-elites, may 'request' the accountant to exercise judgment in such a way that the entity reports a stronger financial position than economic reality. Cultural values would require a Fijian accountant to accede to the 'request'. Rule-based standards would protect the accountant from such 'requests'. In Fiji, rule-based standards may reduce the potential relevance of financial reports, but should improve their transparency and the confidence that principals will place in them.

RELIGION

A great deal of the culture-based research, particularly that based on the work of Hofstede and Gray, tends to lead to countries being grouped together in terms of both community and accounting subculture; this is perceived as providing insights into the appropriateness of the harmonisation/standardisation process and, particularly, in identifying limits therein. That is, a feature of the work of Gray is that it relies on indigenous characteristics which are confined within the boundaries of the countries under review. In subsequent work, Hamid, Craig and Clarke (1993) considered the influence of one cultural input or factor, *religion*, on accounting practices. As they indicate, religion transcends national boundaries. They looked at how Islamic cultures, which exist in numerous countries, had typically failed to embrace 'Western' accounting practices and they reflected on how issues of religion had previously occupied minimal space in the accounting literature. They state (p. 134):

The existing literature dealing with the interaction of business activity and Islam needs extending to capture the particular effects which compliance with Islamic beliefs have on the structure of business and finance within an Islamic framework. In particular, the incompatibility of many Western accounting practices with Islamic principles requires explanation. For jurisprudential Islamic law influences the conduct of businesses in a manner not accommodated automatically by Anglo-American accounting practice. And many Western accounting practices draw upon assumptions which conflict with the tenets of Islam … There seems to be little understanding that, unlike the Western tradition, fundamental business ethics flow automatically from the practices of the religion, rather than from the codes (mainly of etiquette) devised and imposed upon members by professional associations.

Hamid, Craig and Clarke point out that the Islamic tradition does have notions of stewardship—but to God rather than to suppliers of equity or debt capital. That is, Muslims believe that they hold assets not for themselves but in trust for God. There are also other fundamental differences—for example, Islam precludes debt financing and prohibits the payment of interest, and this prohibition has significant implications for processes aimed at the international harmonisation of accounting standards, particularly:

> ... in-so-far as harmonisation is perceived necessary to entail implementation of many standard Western accounting procedures in which interest calculations are integral. Many past and present Western standards entail discounting procedures involving a time value of money concept, which is not admitted by Islam (p. 144).[32]

Hence, Hamid, Craig and Clarke appear to provide a logical argument that religion can have a major impact on the accounting system chosen. Religion can potentially affect how people do business and how they make decisions. As will be seen in Chapter 6, the conceptual framework projects developed in countries such as the United States, Australia, Canada, the United Kingdom and New Zealand (which, interestingly, have all been grouped together by Hofstede), and by the IASB's predecessor (the International Accounting Standards Committee, or IASC), are based on the underlying objective that financial report users require financial information as the basis for making rational economic decisions (and what is 'rational' may be culturally dependent). Such rational economic decisions also take into account the time value of money, which necessarily requires considerations of appropriate interest or discount rates. In some societies, such as Islamic states, this may not be a relevant objective. Further, any claims that particular frameworks of accounting are superior to others should only be made after considering the environments in which the frameworks are to be used.

Having examined several theories that seek to explain international accounting differences in terms of broad cultural (including religious) influences, we now move on to explore five of the more concrete institutional factors which some theorists believe influence the shape of accounting practices in any nation at any point in time. As you will appreciate when reading the following sections, these institutional factors are interrelated and they can be linked to the broader cultural influences just examined. A useful exercise to help develop your understanding of both the cultural factors and the institutional factors is for you to attempt, while reading the following sections, to associate (in a broad way) the institutional factors with cultural influences.

LEGAL SYSTEMS

The legal systems operating in different countries can be divided into two broad categories: common law and Roman law systems. In common law systems, there have historically been relatively few prescriptive statutory laws. Instead, the body of law has been developed by judges applying both the limited amount of statutory law and the outcomes of previous judicial decisions to the facts of a specific case. Each judgement then becomes a legal precedent for future cases. Common law originated in England and spread to its former colonies (such as the United States, Canada, Australia and New Zealand). Conversely, in Roman law systems,

---

32 For example, notions of discounting are found in 'Western' accounting standards dealing with employee benefits, lease capitalisation, impairment of assets, and general insurers.

parliamentary (statutory) law tends to be very detailed and covers most aspects of daily life. The implications of this for accounting is that in common law countries we would expect to find relatively few detailed accounting laws guiding accounting practices, and therefore historically the development of accounting practices would have been left much more to the professional judgement of accountants (and auditors). With Roman law systems, by contrast, we would expect to find a body of codified accounting laws prescribing in detail how each type of transaction or event should be treated in the accounts. In this type of system there was therefore much less need or scope for the use of professional judgement in preparing accounts or developing accounting practices.

As Nobes and Parker (2004) explain, the common law system was developed in England after the Norman Conquest of 1066, whereas the Roman law system was developed in continental European countries and spread to the former colonies of Belgium, France, Germany, Italy, Portugal and Spain. Countries where the development of legal systems and practices were heavily influenced by England tend to have common law systems. Conversely, most continental European countries, along with countries whose legal systems were developed under the influence of these countries, tend to have Roman law systems. Such countries include most members of the European Union (other than England, Wales and Ireland) and many countries in other parts of the world that were former colonies of continental European nations.[33]

Therefore, in the European Union we would expect England, Wales, Ireland and (partially) Scotland historically to have had relatively few codified accounting laws, with the development of accounting practices being left to the professional judgement of accountants. In the remainder of the European Union we would expect accounting practice to have historically been developed through detailed codified accounting laws (or legally recognised regulations) with relatively little input from professional accountants. The adoption of IFRSs—which are often considered to be principles based—would have represented a significant change in practice for countries with Roman law systems relative to countries with common law systems.

BUSINESS OWNERSHIP AND FINANCING SYSTEM

A second key institutional factor which researchers have demonstrated has historically had an impact on the shape of a nation's accounting practices is the business ownership and financing system. Similarly to legal systems, this factor can be broadly divided into two distinct types—'outsider' systems and 'insider' systems.

In 'outsider' systems, external shareholders (that is, those who are not involved in the management of the company) are a significant source of finance for much business activity. As these external shareholders will not be involved in the detailed management of the company, and will therefore not have access to the company's detailed management accounting information, they will need to be provided with separate financial accounting information to help them make their investment decisions. They may invest in the shares of a number of companies, and they need a basis on which to evaluate the performance of any company—for example, by comparing it to the performance of other companies. To help ensure an effective and

---

33 Nobes and Parker (2004) point out that a very small number of countries (such as Scotland, South Africa and Israel) have developed legal systems that incorporate aspects of both common law and Roman law.

efficient allocation of finance to different companies in this type of outsider-financed system, it is important for external investors (and potential investors) to be provided with financial accounting information that reflects the underlying economic performance of a business in a fair, balanced and unbiased manner. Thus, given the significance of outsider finance, financial accounting will have historically developed with a primary aim of providing this fair, balanced and unbiased information to external shareholders—a process that requires rather extensive use of professional judgement (Nobes, 1998), for example to handle regular developments or innovations in business practices that cannot easily be foreseen when writing accounting codes or legislation.

Conversely, in 'insider' systems of finance, provision of finance by external shareholders is much less significant. Instead, there has been a dominance of family-owned businesses, and/or the dominant providers of long-term finance have historically been either banks or governments (Zysman, 1983). With family-owned businesses, the owners will tend to have access to the detailed internal management accounting information of the business, so there is no obvious need for financial statements to provide information to aid investment decision making by shareholders. In some countries (such as Germany) where banks have historically been the dominant source of long-term finance for large companies (rather than external shareholders), banks and companies have tended to develop long-term supportive relationships. These involve banks having a representative on the supervisory board of companies to whom they are major lenders, and these representatives are provided with the detailed management accounting information available to all members of the supervisory board. In the case of family-owned businesses, given that the predominant providers of finance are effectively 'insiders' to the business and have access to detailed management information, there will have been little pressure for financial accounting to have developed to provide information to aid external investment decisions (Nobes, 1998).[34] Nobes and Parker (2004) explain that, in systems where governments provide a significant amount of long-term business finance, government representatives will often become directors of the state-funded companies, and will thus have access to the inside management information. Thus, a characteristic shared by all countries in which insider systems of finance predominate is that the primary role of accounting has historically not been to provide fair, balanced and unbiased information to help outside investors make efficient and effective investment decisions. Financial accounting in these countries has developed to fulfill a different role than in outsider-financed countries. One such role, which is explored in the next section, is the provision of information to calculate taxation liabilities.

Countries that have historically been dominated by insider systems of finance have tended also to be countries with Roman law systems, while outsider-financed countries usually have common law systems (La Porta et al., 1997). Thus, most continental European countries (a notable exception being the Netherlands, which has a Roman law system but a large amount of outsider finance) have historically relied on insider forms of finance, with the result that financial accounting in these nations did not develop to serve the needs of investment decisions in capital markets. Conversely, the United Kingdom and Ireland (and the United States, Australia and New Zealand among other non-European states) have relied to a much greater extent on outsider forms of finance, with a

---

34 As such, the entities would not be considered to be reporting entities. The topic of 'reporting entities' is addressed in Chapter 6. Reporting entities produce general purpose financial statements for parties with a stake in the organisation and that are unable to command information to satisfy their specific information needs.

primary role of accounting historically being to service the information needs of capital markets with fair, balanced and unbiased information.[35]

As an example of empirical research linking financing systems with differences in accounting practices, Pratt and Behr (1987) compared the standard-setting processes adopted in the United States and Switzerland. Differences in the standards and processes adopted were explained by differences in 'size, complexity, and diversity of capital transactions, the wide distribution of ownership, and the opportunistic nature of the capital market participants'.

Chand and White (2007) consider the ownership and financing systems that are common in Fiji and argue that the recent adoption of IFRS in Fiji has created a level of inefficiency not previously experienced. That is, they argue that there is an inappropriate match between IFRS and the financing systems inherent in Fiji. As they state (p. 615):

> The financial institutions and in particular the commercial banks dominate Fiji's capital markets. It is on these institutions that almost all of Fiji's domestically controlled business enterprises rely for financing. Two commercial banks control 75% of the banking market and exercise duopoly powers (Ministry of Finance, 1999). Many business enterprises therefore need to provide financial reports to their banks, the banks being their prime financiers. Banks in Fiji, as in other jurisdictions, are concerned with assessing the financial stability and security that can be offered by prospective borrowers and compliance with loan covenant agreements by established clients. They typically require their borrowers to adopt a conservative approach to asset valuation and gearing measures, inter alia, as a bonding exercise (Watts, 2003). Banks seek reports from their clients that conform to a particular framework and a set of rules that the banks themselves impose. The banks operating in a non-competitive environment are able to require clients to reconstruct their financial reports on terms determined by the banks in order both to secure and retain financing. The banks acquire the accounting information the way they need it, without having to lobby the regulator to set reporting standards that address those needs. Kanaenabogi (2003) provides evidence that bank's in Fiji typically take a conservative view of asset valuations offered as security in assessing loan applications. Banks use asset valuations, which are determined by applying conservative assumptions, taking these as proxies for orderly liquidation values, where formal independent valuations have not been secured.
>
> Accounting values determined by applying Fiji's current reporting regulations and IFRS are not accepted in assessing entities' capacities to repay loans. Therefore, Kanaenabogi argues that complying with two sets of audited financial statements imposes an unnecessary financial burden on business enterprises. Consequently, the more conservative financial reporting models applied by France, Germany and Japan (Briston, 1978; Radebaugh and Gray, 2002) may be more appropriate for Fiji's domestic economy than the IASB model.

Before leaving the discussion of the impact of different financing systems on the shape of accounting practices, we should emphasise that, with the increasing scale of globalised businesses, multinational corporations based in any country are increasingly relying on financing from more

---

35 As will be seen in the final chapter of this book, many critical accounting theorists strongly disagree that accounting information is fair, balanced or unbiased.

than one nation. The funding needs of many companies in countries that have traditionally relied on insider forms of finance have grown beyond the funding capacity of the insider sources of finance, and several companies are now increasingly also relying on outsider finance—from shareholders in both their home country and other nations. Thus, the information requirements associated with outsider-financed systems are now becoming applicable to many large companies in continental European countries (Nobes & Parker, 2004).

TAXATION SYSTEMS

In countries with predominantly outsider systems of finance, financial accounting practices historically developed to provide a fair, balanced and unbiased representation of the underlying economic performance of a business to help improve the effectiveness of investment allocation decisions by external shareholders. Such a system requires that accounting reflects some sort of economic reality; for example, a business selects a depreciation method that most closely reflects the manner in which it uses its fixed assets.

Conversely, in countries with largely insider systems of finance this pressure for financial reports to have developed to reflect fairly some form of underlying economic reality is not present. Rather, financial reports have developed for different purposes, and one important purpose is the calculation of tax (Nobes & Parker, 2004). In most continental European countries that have traditionally relied heavily on insider forms of finance, for a company to claim an allowance for tax this allowance must be included in its financial reports. For example, if a company wishes to reduce its tax liability by taking advantage of the maximum permitted taxable depreciation allowances, it has to include the tax depreciation allowances in its financial reports. The tax depreciation allowances will be determined by taxation law, and will not necessarily bear any relationship to the amount of the fixed assets that have actually been used in any particular year. The financial accounting results will therefore be expected to be substantially affected and determined by the provisions of taxation law in many continental European countries that have historically relied on insider systems of finance.

In outsider-financed countries, the tax accounts have historically been separate from the financial accounts. Thus, if a company wished to claim the maximum tax depreciation allowances permitted by taxation law in these countries, this would not affect the calculation of its reported profits in its financial statements. These financial statements can therefore include a fair depreciation charge reflecting the utilisation of assets without affecting the company's ability to claim the maximum tax depreciation allowances in its tax accounts, and the provisions of taxation law have not therefore exerted much influence on the financial statements.

Given that there has tended to be a high correlation between insider-financed systems and Roman law countries (La Porta et al., 1997), the detailed provisions of taxation law have effectively become a large part of the detailed accounting regulations in many continental European countries that have codified Roman law systems (with the notable exception of the Netherlands). Again, the adoption of IFRS in such countries represented a significant change to their traditional accounting practices.

STRENGTH OF THE ACCOUNTING PROFESSION

The strength of the accounting profession in any country has historically been determined by, and helped to reinforce, the influence on financial accounting systems of the institutional factors discussed above (Nobes & Parker, 2004). In a common law country, which has a predominantly outsider system of long-term finance and where tax law has had little influence on financial accounting, there will have been relatively few statutory laws determining the contents of financial statements. The primary purpose of these financial statements will have been to provide a fair, balanced and unbiased representation of the underlying economic performance of the business, and this will have required the exercise of professional judgement to cope with each different situation. Thus, in these countries there will have historically been a demand for a large number of accountants who are able to apply professional judgement to determine the most suitable way of reflecting unique sets of transactions and events in financial accounting reports of companies. This need for accountants who are able to, and have scope to, exercise professional judgement has led to the development of large and strong accounting professions in countries such as the United Kingdom, Ireland, the United States, Canada, Australia and New Zealand. As seen in Chapter 2, strong accounting professions have been effective in lobbying governments to ensure that accounting regulatory systems give scope for the exercise of professional judgement, thus possibly reinforcing the strength and influence of the accounting profession.

Conversely, in Roman law countries that have largely insider systems of finance and where compliance with the details of tax laws exerts a substantial influence on the shape of financial accounts, there will have been little need or scope for the use of professional judgement when drawing up financial accounting statements. There has therefore been much less impetus for the development of accounting professions compared to outsider-financed common law systems. The accounting professions in many continental European countries have historically been smaller and weaker (in terms of influence) than their counterparts in the United Kingdom, Ireland, Australia or the United States. Nobes and Parker (2004) argue that these weaker accounting professions have had an impact in reinforcing accounting practices that require little exercise of professional judgement, because the effective implementation of flexible accounting practices requires a reasonably large accounting profession that is comfortable with (and has sufficient experience of) applying professional judgements to complex accounting issues.

ACCIDENTS OF HISTORY

As indicated at the beginning of this section, accounting systems tend to be regarded as following either an Anglo-American model or a continental European model. The cultural and institutional differences discussed so far in this chapter support this view, with countries following the Anglo-American model tending to have common law systems, outsider financing, little influence of taxation law on financial accounting and a strong accounting profession accustomed to exercising a considerable amount of professional judgement—with the opposite applying in countries following the continental European model. If we accept that these influences are significant in shaping a nation's accounting practices, we should expect accounting practices in countries with Anglo-American systems to have historically been broadly similar. However, this is not consistent with the evidence presented in the first section of this chapter, when, for example, we saw that both the reported profits and the net assets of the multinational pharmaceutical company AstraZeneca were significantly different when calculated in accordance with UK accounting rules than when calculated in accordance with US rules. If the cultural and institutional influences examined so far in this chapter, and that are broadly similar in the United Kingdom and the United States, are significant in shaping accounting practices, there must be an important additional influencing factor which varies between the United Kingdom and the United States.

Nobes and Parker (2004) point to the importance of the additional factor of 'accidents of history', whose influence will be restricted to the accounting systems of the individual countries affected by the accidents. For example, following the Wall Street crash of 1929, the United States established securities exchange legislation aimed at investor protection, while there was no such development at the time in the United Kingdom. This legislation included certain accounting requirements, which have been delegated to private sector accounting standard-setting bodies and which have produced a detailed set of US accounting rules (as we would expect to see in a Roman law country). In contrast, following a series of high-profile accounting failures in the United Kingdom in the late 1980s, the United Kingdom established a more principles-based system of accounting regulation. As Unerman and O'Dwyer (2004) highlight, in the aftermath of accounting failures at Enron in 2001, it was claimed by many in the United Kingdom that the different regulatory systems would have prevented Enron using the creative accounting techniques in the United Kingdom that it followed in the United States. Going back to the case of AstraZeneca, studying the reconciliation provided in the financial reports between the results calculated using UK accounting rules and those calculated using US accounting rules, it is apparent that a substantial difference between the two sets of accounting regulations (in the case of this company) arises from differences between the US and the UK accounting treatment of mergers and acquisitions (including the calculation of goodwill). Different pressures in the United Kingdom (possibly including different lobbying efforts by interested parties in each country) resulted in UK and US accounting rules for mergers and acquisitions being somewhat different, although these differences are likely to reduce substantially in the future given the ongoing convergence efforts of the IASB and the FASB.

Summarising this chapter so far, a number of reasons have been advanced to explain the accounting systems in place in different countries, including culture, religion (which is a subset of culture) and institutional factors (which we could also imagine would be influenced by culture). The discussion has by no means been exhaustive in identifying the many factors proposed to explain why historically there were international differences in accounting systems; nevertheless, the referenced research indicates that one general approach to accounting, such as that used in the United Kingdom, Ireland, the Netherlands, the United States, Australia, New Zealand or Canada, may suit one particular environment but not others. Therefore, it is probably somewhat naive to claim that there is one 'best' system of accounting. With this in mind, we can reflect on the claim by a former chairperson of the US Financial Accounting Standards Board, Dennis Beresford, that the US accounting and reporting system was regarded by many as 'the most comprehensive and sophisticated system in the world' (as quoted in Wyatt and Yospe, 1993). Perhaps in some countries (perhaps the majority) the US system would be considered to be sophisticated, but in others it might be considered to be quite irrelevant on cultural, religious or institutional grounds.

Despite various factors that provide a logical rationale for international differences in accounting practices, there have been extensive efforts over several decades to reduce the differences between accounting systems in different countries. A great deal of this effort culminated in many diverse countries adopting IFRS. The material in this chapter will have given the reader a good understanding of why accounting systems in different countries were dissimilar prior to efforts to standardise financial accounting. The reader might also have formed an opinion about whether the global standardisation of accounting is appropriate. What do you, the reader, think? Is it appropriate for diverse countries with different cultural attributes, different financing sytems, different religions, different taxation systems, different histories and so forth to all adopt the same accounting standards? The next section provides some concluding comments on the obstacles to ongoing standardisation of accounting.

CONCLUDING COMMENTS ABOUT OBSTACLES TO THE ONGOING STANDARDISATION OF FINANCIAL ACCOUNTING

As discussed, one key obstacle to the establishment and maintenance of the international standardisation of accounting is the international cultural and institutional differences that caused financial accounting to vary in the first place. As argued earlier, if these causal factors continue to vary between countries, it is difficult to see how a single set of accounting rules— such as those published by the IASB—will be appropriate or suitable for all countries. That is, as accounting traditionally varied between different countries for reasons that could be theoretically explained (such as cultural, religious or institutional reasons), a key impediment to the continued standardisation of accounting is the fact that these good reasons for accounting differences arguably continue to exist. While many countries have either adopted IFRSs or plan to adopt them in the near term, there is nothing that strictly stops them from abandoning IFRSs should it become apparent that they are not very relevant to their countries' financial accounting information needs. Of course it would be costly and difficult for a country to abandon IFRSs, but it is possible.

As an example of the obstacle to maintaining standardisation efforts, Perera (1989, p. 52) considers the success of transferring accounting skills from Anglo-American countries to developing countries. He notes: 'The skill[s] so transferred from Anglo-American countries may not work because they are culturally irrelevant or dysfunctional in the receiving countries' context.'

Perera also argues that international accounting standards themselves are strongly influenced by Anglo-American accounting models and, as such, they tend to reflect the circumstances and patterns of thinking in a particular group of countries. He argues that these standards are likely to encounter problems of relevance in countries with different environments from those found in Anglo-American countries. Thus, for example, if the majority of German companies continue to rely on 'insider' forms of finance, and Germany continues to use a Roman law system, its previously used codified accounting regulations would probably be more appropriate for most German companies than the imposition of a form of the Anglo-American accounting system.[36] Nobes and Parker (2004) suggest that in such circumstances it might be more appropriate to have a dual system, where all companies in each country are required to prepare financial reports in accordance with their historically developed domestic system, and companies that raise funds internationally can prepare an additional set of financial reports (probably only

36 In a similar way, the imposition of a detailed codified accounting system would not be appropriate for Australia, the United Kingdom, the United States or New Zealand, for example, where the 'outsider' system of finance requires financial accounts to provide fair and balanced information reflecting some form of underlying economic reality.

the consolidated or group accounts) in accordance with Anglo-American-style international accounting rules.[37]

A further obstacle to harmonisation, identified by Nobes and Parker (2004), is the lack in some countries of a developed accounting profession. Thus, in countries where strong accounting professions have not developed there are likely to be initial problems implementing international accounting regulations based on the Anglo-American professional judgement model (such as IFRS). Furthermore, some countries might have nationalistic difficulties in being seen to implement a system of international accounting standards that are regarded as being closely aligned to the Anglo-American systems.

A final potential and significant obstacle to the ongoing standardisation of accounting is that, as seen in Chapters 2 and 3, accounting regulations can and do have economic consequences (Nobes & Parker, 2004). Across time, governments of individual countries may regret giving the control of a process—accounting standard-setting—that has real economic consequences to an international body (the IASB) over which they have little influence. (Indeed, this was a concern in Australia, where the AASB's role in developing accounting standards has effectively been transferred to the IASB—although the AASB provides input to the standards being developed by the IASB.) It was seen in Chapter 3 how this can impact on the process of international standardisation, in the recent difficulties experienced with the refusal of some EU countries to endorse fully the provisions of the revised IAS 39, partly because of the potential negative economic impact that these provisions might have on banks in their countries.

CHAPTER SUMMARY

This chapter identified and considered historical differences in international accounting practices and looked at numerous reasons (generated from different theoretical perspectives) that have been advanced to explain why such differences arose (including differences in culture, religions as a subset of culture, legal systems, financing systems, taxation systems, the strength of the accounting profession and accidents of history). Much of the research into comparative international accounting questions whether it is appropriate to have one system of accounting that is adopted uniformly throughout the world (a long-term objective of the IASB).

While many researchers question the relevance of 'Western-style' accounting standards for all countries, efforts by a number of international organisations are nevertheless continuing to encourage quite culturally disparate countries to adopt IASs/IFRSs. This implies that the members of some international organisations are either unaware of the literature or, alternatively, choose to reject it as irrelevant. As efforts by a number of countries, for example Australia and some members of the European Union, continue in relation to the domestic implementation of international standards, it is to be expected that this debate will continue.

---

37 In this regard, although companies in member states of the European Union are required to follow accounting standards released by the IASB for the purposes of their consolidated financial reports, the requirement is restricted to companies listed on a stock exchange.

QUESTIONS

4.1 In the context of financial accounting, what is harmonisation and/or standardisation?

4.2 Global standardisation of accounting requires the United States to adopt IFRS. Do you think it is likely that the United States will embrace IFRS in the near term, and what do you think are some of the factors that might discourage the country from adopting IFRS?

4.3 Identify some factors that might be expected to explain why different countries use different systems of accounting.

4.4 Does the adoption of IFRS by different countries necessarily mean that the accounting procedures and practices they adopt will be consistent and comparable internationally?

4.5 After considering the Hofstede–Gray model, briefly explain the hypothesised link between society values, accounting values and accounting practice.

4.6 Any effort towards standardising accounting practices on an international basis implies a belief that a 'one size fits all' approach is appropriate. Is this naive?

4.7 While it is often argued that within particular countries there should be some association between various value systems and accounting systems, it is also argued (for example, by Baydoun and Willett, 1995) that over time many events would typically have occurred that confound this expected relationship. What type of events might confound the expected relationship?

4.8 Baydoun and Willett (1995, p. 72) identify a number of problems in testing the Hofstede–Gray theory. They emphasise that many accounting systems are imported from other countries with possibly different cultures. As they state: 'Due to the interference in what would otherwise have been the natural evolution of financial information requirements, there are no uncontaminated examples of modern accounting practices in developing countries. Consequently great care has to be taken in using data from developing countries to draw inferences about relevance on the basis of the Hofstede–Gray framework.' Explain Baydoun and Willett's point of view. Do you believe that they are correct?

4.9 As noted in this chapter, Hamid, Craig and Clarke (1993) provide an argument that religion can have a major impact on the accounting system chosen by a particular country and that before 'Western' methods of accounting are exported to particular countries it must be determined whether particular religious beliefs will make the 'Western' accounting policies irrelevant. Explain their argument.

4.10 Nobes (1998) suggests that for countries that have organisations that rely relatively heavily on equity markets, as opposed to other sources of finance, there will be a greater propensity for such organisations to make public disclosures of information. Evaluate this argument.

4.11 In the early 1990s, the US Financial Accounting Standards Board's chairperson Dennis Beresford claimed that the US accounting and reporting system was regarded by many as 'the most comprehensive and sophisticated system in the world'. Evaluate this statement. How do you think its validity might have changed in the aftermath of accounting failures at Enron, WorldCom and Andersen in 2001–02? Do you think that the US system would be regarded as sophisticated in all cultural contexts?

4.12 Do you think it is realistic to expect that there will eventually be an internationally uniform set of accounting standards? What factors would work for or against achieving and maintaining this aim?

4.13 Prior to recent international actions to adopt IFRS, would you expect that large international companies domiciled in a particular country would have adopted different accounting policies from companies that operated only within the confines of that country? Explain your answer.

4.14 Evaluate how reasonable it is to assume that the inflow of foreign investment into Australia would have been restricted if Australia, through the decision of the Financial Reporting Council, had not made the decision to adopt IFRS from 2005.

4.15 Explain barriers to ongoing standardisation of financial accounting across all EU member states. Given these barriers, do you think that the European Union has been naive in embracing the standardisation process for all member states?

4.16 What are some perceived benefits that flow from the decision that a country will adopt IFRS?

4.17 On the basis of recent actions to standardise accounting across countries, does it appear that organisations such as the AASB and the IASB are ignoring academic research that signals why we would expect to find international differences in financial accounting practices?

4.18 It is often argued that the accounting standards of the FASB are rule-based, whereas the accounting standards issued by the IASB are principles-based. Rules-based standards by their nature can be quite complex, particularly if they seek to cover as many situations as possible. Do you think it would be easier to circumvent the requirements of rules-based or principles-based accounting standards?

4.19 Is it appropriate for accounting standard-setting bodies to consider culture and religion when devising accounting regulations, particularly given that the output of financial reporting is expected to be objective and unbiased? Explain your view.

4.20 What are some possible reasons for historical differences in accounting rules operating within Australia, the United States and the United Kingdom?

4.21 Does the standardisation of accounting standards on a global basis necessarily equate with a standardisation in accounting practice?

4.22 The website of the FASB (www.fasb.org) has a section entitled 'Facts about FASB', in which there is information about how accounting standards are developed (as accessed in early 2009). In part, it states:

> Each FASB Statement or Interpretation is issued in draft form (Exposure Draft) for public comment. When the Board has reached conclusions on the issues, it directs the staff to prepare a proposed Exposure Draft for consideration by the Board. After further discussion and revisions, Board members vote by written ballot to issue the Exposure Draft. A majority vote of the Board is required to approve a document for issuance as an Exposure Draft. Alternative views, if any, are explained in the document and posted on the FASB website.
>
> The Exposure Draft sets forth the proposed standards of financial accounting and reporting, the proposed effective date and method of transition, background information, and an explanation of the basis for the Board's conclusions.

At the end of the exposure period, which is determined at the discretion of the Board but should never be less than 30 days, all comment letters and position papers are analyzed by the staff. This is a search for new information and persuasive arguments regarding the issues; it is not intended to be simply a 'nose count' of how many support or oppose a given point of view. In addition to studying this analysis, Board members review the comment letters to help them in reaching conclusions.

Further Deliberation of the Board

After the comments have been analyzed and studied, the Board redeliberates the issues. As in earlier stages of the process, all Board meetings are open to public observation. The Board considers comments received on the Exposure Draft and often incorporates suggested changes in the final document. If substantial modifications appear to be necessary, the Board may decide to issue a revised Exposure Draft for additional public comment. When the Board is satisfied that all reasonable alternatives have been considered adequately, the staff is directed to prepare a draft of a final document for consideration by the Board. A vote is taken on the final document, again by written ballot. A simple majority of four votes is required for adoption of a pronouncement.

Statements of Financial Accounting Standards

The final product of most technical projects is a Statement of Financial Accounting Standards. Like the Exposure Draft, the Statement sets forth the actual standards, the effective date and method of transition, background information, a brief summary of research done on the project, and the basis for the Board's conclusions, including the reasons for rejecting significant alternative solutions. It also identifies members of the Board voting for and against its issuance and includes reasons for any dissents.

Given the process involved in developing accounting standards—which involves asking constituents to make submissions on exposure drafts—do you think that accounting standards developed within the United States would be the same as accounting standards developed in another country? Provide an explanation for your answer

4.23 The IASC (1998, p. 50) stated that 'many developing and newly industrialised countries are using International Accounting Standards as their national requirements, or as the basis for their national requirements. These countries have a growing need for relevant and reliable financial information to meet the requirements both of domestic users and of international providers of the capital that they need'. Do you think that IASs/IFRSs will provide 'relevant and reliable information' that meets the needs of all financial statement users in all countries?

4.24 In considering the relevance of IFRS to developing countries, Chand and White (2007, p. 606) state:

While the forces of globalisation and convergence are moving accounting practices towards a unified, or at least harmonised regulatory framework for financial reporting, this is unlikely to best serve the diverse interests of the disparate user groups of financial reports.

Explain the reasons behind Chand and White's claim.

4.25 Ball (2006, p. 17) makes the following comment:

In sum, even a cursory review of the political and economic diversity among IFRS-adopting nations, and of their past and present financial reporting practices, makes the notion that uniform standards alone will produce uniform financial reporting seem naive.

Explain the basis of Ball's comments.

4.26 Irvine (2008, p. 127) makes the following comment:

Global accounting technologies, including IFRS, provide developing nations with legitimacy. Similarly, emerging economies, if they wish to gain credence in global capital markets, need to adopt western accounting technologies.

Explain the basis of Irvine's comments.

4.27 The website of the FASB (as at early 2009) states:

The Board's work on both concepts and standards is based on research aimed at gaining new insights and ideas. Research is conducted by the FASB staff and others, including foreign national and international accounting standard-setting bodies. The Board's activities are open to public participation and observation under the 'due process' mandated by formal Rules of Procedure. The FASB actively solicits the views of its various constituencies on accounting issues.

The FASB says that it considers the views of its constituents. Do you think that the financial information demands or expectations of 'constituents' in the United States would be different from the financial information demands or expectations of people in other countries? Why?

4.28 The website of the FASB (as at early 2009) states that FASB intends:

To promulgate standards only when the expected benefits exceed the perceived costs. While reliable, quantitative cost–benefit calculations are seldom possible, the Board strives to determine that a proposed standard will meet a significant need and that the costs it imposes, compared with possible alternatives, are justified in relation to the overall benefits.

Do you think that cost–benefit considerations will be different in different countries? If so, how would cost–benefit considerations be determined by a global accounting standard-setter such as the IASB?

4.29 Ball (2006, p. 17) states:

Under its constitution, the IASB is a standard setter and does not have an enforcement mechanism for its standards: it can cajole countries and companies to adopt IFRS in name, but it cannot require their enforcement in practice. It cannot penalise individual companies or countries that adopt its standards, but in which financial reporting practice is of low quality because managers, auditors and local regulators fail to fully implement the standards. Nor has it shown any interest in disallowing or even dissuading low-quality companies or countries from using its 'brand name'. Individual countries remain primarily regulators of their own financial markets. EU member countries included. That exposes IFRS to the risk of adoption in name only.

Evaluate Ball's comments and provide an argument as to whether you agree or disagree with his view.

4.30 Ball (2006, p. 22) provides the following statement:

> In the presence of local political and economic factors that exert substantial influence on local financial reporting practice, and in the absence of an effective worldwide enforcement mechanism, the very meaning of IFRS adoption and the implications of adoption are far from clear. In the enthusiasm of the current moment, the IFRS 'brand name' currently is riding high, and IFRS adoption is being perceived as a signal of quality. I am not sure how long that perception will last.

Provide an argument as to whether you are inclined to agree or disagree with Ball's scepticism about the future 'value' associated with embracing IFRS.

4.31 The European Commission made the following statement in a press release issued in 2002:

> European Commission has welcomed the Council's adoption, in a single reading, of the Regulation requiring listed companies, including banks and insurance companies, to prepare their consolidated accounts in accordance with International Accounting Standards (IAS) from 2005 onwards (see IP/01/200 and MEMO/01/40). The Regulation will help eliminate barriers to cross-border trading in securities by ensuring that company accounts throughout the EU are more reliable and transparent and that they can be more easily compared. This will in turn increase market efficiency and reduce the cost of raising capital for companies, ultimately improving competitiveness and helping boost growth.

You are required to evaluate the above statement. In particular you should consider whether the adoption of IFRS in different countries, with different overview and enforcement mechanisms, necessarily leads to the generation of financial information that is more 'reliable' and 'comparable'.

REFERENCES

Ball, R. (2006), 'International financial reporting standards (IFRS): pros and cons for investors', *Accounting and Business Research*, International Accounting Policy Forum, pp. 5–27.

Baskerville, R. (2003), 'Hofstede never studied culture', *Accounting, Organizations and Society*, 28, pp. 1–14.

Baydoun, N. & R. Willett (1995), 'Cultural relevance of Western accounting systems to developing countries', *ABACUS*, 31(1), pp. 67–92.

Chand, P. & M. White (2007), 'A critique of the influence of globalization and convergence of accounting standards in Fiji', *Critical Perspectives on Accounting*, 18, pp. 605–22.

Doupnik, T. S. & S. B. Salter (1995), 'External environment, culture, and accounting practice: a preliminary test of a general model of international accounting development', *International Journal of Accounting*, 30(3), pp. 189–207.

European Commission (1992), *Towards Sustainability: A Community Programme of Policy and Action in Relation to the Environment and Sustainable Development*, Brussels: European Commission.

Fechner, H. H. E. & A. Kilgore (1994), 'The influence of cultural factors on accounting practice', *International Journal of Accounting*, 29, pp. 265–77.

Financial Accounting Foundation, (2007), 'FASB/FAF response to SEC releases—November 2007', Norwalk, CT: FAF.

Gray, S. J. (1988), 'Towards a theory of cultural influence on the development of accounting systems internationally', *ABACUS*, 24(1), pp. 1–15.

Hamid, S., R. Craig & F. Clarke (1993), 'Religion: a confounding cultural element in the international harmonization of accounting?', *ABACUS*, 29(2), pp. 131–48.

Hofstede, G. (1980), *Culture's Consequences: International Differences in Work-Related Values*, Beverly Hills, CA: Sage Publications.

Hofstede, G. (1983), 'Dimensions of national cultures in fifty countries and three regions', in J. B. Derogowski, S. Dziuraweic & R. Annis (eds), *Expiscations in Cross-Cultural Psychology*, Lisse, the Netherlands: Swets & Zeitlinger.

Hofstede, G. (1984), 'Cultural dimensions in management and planning', *Asia Pacific Journal of Management*, 1(2), pp. 81–98.

IASC (2008) 'Review of the Constitution: Public Accountability and the Composition of the IASB—Proposal for Change', London: International Accounting Standards Committee.

IASC (1998), 'Shaping IASC for the Future', London: International Accounting Standards Committee.

Irvine, H., (2008), 'The global institutionalization of financial reporting: The case of the United Arab Emirates', *Accounting Forum*, 32, pp. 125–42.

La Porta, R., F. Lopez-de-Silanes, A. Shleifer & R. W. Vishny (1997), 'Legal determinants of external finance', *Journal of Finance*, 52(3), pp. 1131–50.

Mueller, G. G. (1967), *International Accounting*, New York: Macmillan.

Mueller, G. G. (1968), 'Accounting principles generally accepted in the United States versus those generally accepted elsewhere', *International Journal of Accounting Education and Research*, 3(2), pp. 91–103.

Nobes, C. (1984), *International Classification of Financial Reporting*, London: Croom Helm.

Nobes, C. (1998), 'Towards a general model of the reasons for international differences in financial reporting', *ABACUS*, 34(2), pp. 162–187.

Nobes, C. (2006), 'The survival of international differences under IFRS: towards a research agenda', *Accounting and Business Research*, 36(3), pp. 233–45.

Nobes, C. & R. Parker (2004), *Comparative International Accounting*, Harlow: Pearson Education Limited.

Perera, H. (1989), 'Towards a framework to analyze the impact of culture on accounting', *International Journal of Accounting*, 24(1), pp. 42–56.

Pratt, J. & G. Behr (1987), 'Environmental factors, transaction costs, and external reporting: A cross national comparison', *International Journal of Accounting Education and Research* (Spring), pp. 1–24.

Purvis, S. E. C., H. Gernon & M. A. Diamond (1991), 'The IASC and its comparability project', *Accounting Horizons*, 5(2), pp. 25–44.

Securities and Exchange Commission (2007), 'Acceptance from Foreign Private Issuers of Financial Statements Prepared in Accordance with International Financial Reporting Standards without Reconciliation to U.S. GAAP', RIN 3235-AJ90, Washington: SEC.

Takatera, S. & M. Yamamoto (1987), 'The cultural significance of accounting in Japan', Seminar on Accounting and Culture, European Institute for Advanced Studies in Management: Brussels.

Unerman, J. & B. O'Dwyer (2004), 'Basking in Enron's reflexive goriness: mixed messages from the UK profession's reaction', paper presented at Asia Pacific Interdisciplinary Research on Accounting Conference, Singapore.

Veron, N., (2007), *The Global Accounting Experiment*, Brussels, Belgium: Bruegel Publishers.

Violet, W. J. (1983), 'The development of international accounting standards: an anthropological perspective', *International Journal of Accounting Education and Research*, 18(2), pp. 1–12.

Wyatt, A. R. & J. F. Yospe (1993), 'Wake-up call to American business; International Accounting Standards are on the way', *Journal of Accountancy*, July, pp. 80–85.

Zarzeski, M. T. (1996), 'Spontaneous harmonization effects of culture and market forces on accounting disclosure practices', *Accounting Horizons*, 10(1), pp. 18–37.

Zysman, J. (1983), *Government, Markets and Growth: Financial Systems and the Politics of Change*, USA: Cornell University Press.

CHAPTER 5

NORMATIVE THEORIES OF ACCOUNTING—THE CASE OF ACCOUNTING FOR CHANGING PRICES

LEARNING OBJECTIVES

On completing this chapter readers should:

- be aware of some particular limitations of historical cost accounting in terms of its ability to cope with various issues associated with changing prices;
- be aware of a number of alternative methods of accounting that have been developed to address problems associated with changing prices;
- be able to identify some of the strengths and weaknesses of the various alternative accounting methods;
- understand that the calculation of income under a particular method of accounting will depend on the perspective of capital maintenance that has been adopted.

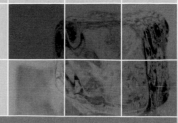

OPENING ISSUES

Various asset valuation approaches are often adopted in the financial statements of large corporations. Non-current assets acquired (or perhaps revalued) in different years will simply be added together to give a total dollar value, even though the various costs or valuations might provide little reflection of the current values of the respective assets. For example, pursuant to IAS 16/AASB 116 'Property, Plant and Equipment' it is permissible for some classes of property, plant and equipment to be measured at cost, less a provision for depreciation, whereas another class of property, plant and equipment is allowed to be measured at fair value.[1] The different measurements are then simply added together to give a total value of property, plant and equipment—with the total representing neither cost nor fair value.

Issues to consider:

- What are some of the criticisms that can be made in relation to the practice of accounting wherein assets that have been acquired or valued in different years are added together, without adjustment, when the purchasing power of the dollar in those years was conceivably quite different?
- What are some of the alternative methods of accounting (alternatives to historical cost accounting) that have been advanced to cope with the issue of changing prices, and what acceptance have these alternatives received from the accounting profession?
- What are the strengths and weaknesses of the alternatives to historical cost?

---

1   Throughout this chapter, where reference is made to an accounting standard, reference will be made to both the International Accounting Standard and its Australian equivalent. For example, in relation to property, plant and equipment the international standard is IAS 16 and the Australian equivalent is AASB 116. The relevant standard would therefore be referenced as IAS 16/ AASB 116.

Chapter 3 considered various theoretical explanations for why regulation might be put in place. Perspectives derived from *public interest theory, capture theory* and the *economic interest theory of regulation* did not attempt to explain what form of regulation was most optimal or efficient. Rather, by adopting certain theoretical assumptions about individual behaviour and motivations, the theories attempted to explain which parties were most likely to try to affect the regulatory process, and perhaps succeed in doing so.

This chapter considers a number of *normative* theories of accounting. Based on particular judgements about the types of information people *need* (which could be different from what they *want*), the various normative theories provide prescriptions about how the process of financial accounting *should* be undertaken.[2]

Across time, numerous normative theories of accounting have been developed by a number of well-respected academics. However, these theories have typically failed to be embraced by the accounting profession or to be mandated within financial accounting regulations. Relying in part on material introduced in Chapter 3, this chapter considers why some proposed methods of accounting are ultimately accepted by the profession and/or accounting standard-setters, while many are dismissed or rejected. It questions whether the rejection is related to the *merit* of the arguments (or lack thereof), or due to the *political nature* of the standard-setting process wherein various vested interests and economic implications are considered. The chapter specifically considers various prescriptive theories of accounting (normative theories) that were advanced by various people on the basis that historical cost accounting had too many shortcomings, particularly in times of rising prices. Some of these shortcomings were summarised by the International Accounting Standards Committee (which was subsequently replaced by the International Accounting Standards Board) in IAS 29 (paragraph 2):

> In a hyperinflationary economy, reporting of operating results and financial position in the local currency without restatement is not useful. Money loses purchasing power at such a rate that comparison of amounts from transactions and other events that have occurred at different times, even within the same accounting period, is misleading.

---

2   Positive theories, by contrast, attempt to explain and predict accounting practice without seeking to prescribe particular actions. Positive accounting theories are the subject of analysis in Chapters 7 and 8.

LIMITATIONS OF HISTORICAL COST ACCOUNTING IN TIMES OF RISING PRICES

Over time, criticisms of historical cost accounting have been raised by a number of notable scholars, particularly in relation to its inability to provide useful information in times of rising prices.[3] For example, criticisms were raised by Sweeney, MacNeal, Canning and Paton in the 1920s and 1930s. From the 1950s the level of criticism increased, with notable academics (such as Chambers, Sterling, Edwards and Bell) prescribing different models of accounting that they considered provided more useful information than was available under conventional historical cost accounting. Such work continued through to the early 1980s but declined thereafter as levels of inflation throughout the world began to drop. Nevertheless, the debate continues.[4]

Historical cost accounting assumes that money holds a constant purchasing power. As Elliot (1986, p. 33) states:

> An implicit and troublesome assumption in the historical cost model is that the monetary unit is fixed and constant over time. However, there are three components of the modern economy that make this assumption less valid than it was at the time the model was developed.[5]
>
> One component is specific price-level changes, occasioned by such things as technological advances and shifts in consumer preferences; the second component is general price-level changes (inflation); and the third component is the fluctuation in exchange rates for currencies. Thus, the book value of a company, as reported in its financial statements, only coincidentally reflects the current value of assets.

Again it is emphasised that under our current accounting standards many assets can or must be measured at historical cost. (For example, inventory must be measured at cost—or net realisable value if it is lower—and property, plant and equipment can be valued at cost where an entity has adopted the 'cost model' for a class of property, plant and equipment pursuant to IAS 16/AASB 116.) While there was much criticism of historical cost accounting during the high-inflation periods of the 1970s and 1980s, there were also many people who supported historical cost accounting. The method of accounting predominantly used today is still based on historical cost accounting, although the conceptual frameworks discussed in the next chapter, and some recent accounting standards, have introduced elements of current value—or fair

---

3   Across time, these criticisms appear to have been accepted by accounting regulators—at least on a piecemeal basis. In recent years various accounting standards have been released that require the application of fair values when measuring assets. For example, financial instruments (pursuant to IAS 39/AASB 139), property, plant and equipment (where the fair value model has been adopted pursuant to IAS 16/AASB 116—this accounting standard gives financial statement preparers a choice between the cost model and the fair value model in the measurement of property, plant and equipment), some intangible assets (where there is an 'active market' pursuant to IAS 38/AASB 138), investment properties (pursuant to IAS 14/AASB 114) and biological assets (pursuant to IAS 41/AASB 141) are required to be valued at fair value as opposed to historical cost.

4   For example, there is a great deal of debate about whether inventory measurement rules (which require inventory to be measured at the lower of cost and net realisable value pursuant to IAS 2/AASB 102) provide relevant information in situations where the market (fair) value of the inventory greatly exceeds its cost.

5   As indicated in Chapter 2, the historical cost method of accounting was documented as early as 1494 by the Franciscan monk Pacioli in his famous work *Summa de Arithmetica, Geometrica, Proportioni et Proportionalita*.

value—measurements. Hence, the accounting profession and reporting entities have tended to maintain at least partial support for the historical cost approach.[6] The very fact that historical cost accounting has continued to be applied by business entities has been used by a number of academics to support its continued use (which in a sense is a form of accounting-Darwinism perspective—the view that those things that are most efficient and effective will survive over time). For example, Mautz (1973) states:

> Accounting is what it is today not so much because of the desire of accountants as because of the influence of businessmen. If those who make management and investment decisions had not found financial reports based on historical cost useful over the years, changes in accounting would long since have been made.[7,8]

It has been argued (for example, Chambers, 1966) that historical cost accounting information suffers from problems of irrelevance in times of rising prices. That is, it is questioned whether it is useful to be informed that something cost a particular amount many years ago when its current value (as perhaps reflected by its replacement cost, or current market value) might be considerably different. It has also been argued that there is a real problem of additivity. At issue is whether it is logical to add together assets acquired in different periods when those assets were acquired with dollars of different purchasing power.[9]

In a number of countries, organisations are permitted to revalue their non-current assets. What often happens, however, is that different assets are revalued in different periods (with the local currency—for example dollars or euros—having different purchasing power in each period), yet the revalued assets might all be added together, along with assets that have continued to be valued at cost, for the purposes of balance sheet (also known as the statement of financial position) disclosure.[10]

---

6   IAS 16/AASB 116 provides reporting entities with an option to adopt either the 'cost model' (measuring property, plant and equipment at historical cost) or the 'fair value model' for measuring classes of property, plant and equipment. The 'fair value model' requires the revaluation of the assets to their fair value (which in itself means that a modified version of historical cost accounting can be used), which is one way to take account of changing values. Basing revised depreciation on the revalued amounts is one limited way of accounting for the effects of changing prices.

7   However, because something continues to be used does not mean that there is nothing else that might not be better. This is a common error made by proponents of decision usefulness studies. Such studies attempt to provide either support for, or rejection of, something on the basis that particular respondents or users indicated that it would, or would not, be useful for their particular purposes. Often there are things that might be more 'useful'—but they are unknown by the respondents. As Gray, Owen and Adams (1996, p. 75) state: 'Decision usefulness purports to describe the central characteristics of accounting in general and financial statements in particular. To describe accounting as useful for decisions is no more illuminating than describing a screwdriver as being useful for digging a hole—it is better than nothing (and therefore "useful") but hardly what one might ideally like for such a task.'

8   Reflective of the lack of agreement in the area, Elliot (1986) adopts a contrary view. Still relying on metaphors associated with evolution, Elliot (p. 35) states: 'There is growing evidence in the market place ... that historical cost-basis information is of ever declining usefulness to the modern business world. The issue for the financial accounting profession is to move the accounting model toward greater relevance or face the fate of the dinosaur and the messenger pigeon.'

9   Again, under existing accounting standards, assets such as property, plant and equipment can be measured at fair value or at cost. IAS 16/AASB 116 gives reporting entities the choice between applying the fair value model or the cost model to the different classes of property, plant and equipment. Hence, we are currently left with a situation where, even within a category of assets (for example, property, plant and equipment), some assets might be measured at cost while others might be measured at fair value.

10 In relation to property, plant and equipment, IAS 16/AASB 116 requires that where revaluations to fair value are undertaken, the revaluations must be made with sufficient regularity to ensure that the carrying amount of each asset in the class does not differ materially from its fair value at the reporting date. Nevertheless, there will still be instances where some assets have not been revalued for three to five years but they will still be aggregated with assets that have been recently revalued.

There is also an argument that methods of accounting that do not take account of changing prices, such as historical cost accounting, can tend to overstate profits in times of rising prices, and that distribution to shareholders of historical cost profits can actually lead to an erosion of operating capacity. For example, assume that a company commenced operations at the beginning of the year 2010 with $100 000 in inventory comprising 20 000 units at $5.00 each. If at the end of the year all the inventory had been sold, there were assets (cash) of $120 000 and throughout the year there had been no contributions from owners, no borrowings and no distributions to owners, then profit under an historical cost system would be $20 000. If the entire profit of $20 000 was distributed to owners in the form of dividends, the financial capital would be the same as it was at the beginning of the year. Financial capital would remain intact.[11]

However, if prices had increased throughout the period, the actual operating capacity of the entity may not have remained intact. Let us assume that the company wishes to acquire another 20 000 units of inventory after it has paid $20 000 in dividends, but finds that the financial year-end replacement cost has increased to $5.40 per unit. The company will be able to acquire only 18 518 units with the $100 000 it still has available. By distributing its total historical cost profit of $20 000, with no adjustments being made for rising prices, the company's ability to acquire goods and services has fallen from one period to the next. Some advocates of alternative approaches to accounting would prescribe that the profit of the period is more accurately recorded as $120 000 less 20 000 units at $5.40 per unit, which equals $12 000. That is, if $12 000 is distributed to owners in dividends, the company can still buy the same amount of inventory (20 000 units) as it had at the beginning of the period—its purchasing power remains intact.[12] Despite the problems associated with measuring inventory at historical cost, organisations are still required to measure their inventory at cost (or net realisable value if it is lower than cost) pursuant to IAS 2/AASB 102.

In relation to the treatment of changing prices, we can usefully, and briefly, consider IAS 41 'Agriculture' (or AASB 141 within Australia). IAS 41 provides the measurement rules for biological assets (for example, for grapevines or cattle). The accounting standard requires that changes in the fair value of biological assets from period to period be treated as part of the period's profit or loss. In the development of the accounting standard there were arguments by some researchers (Roberts, Staunton & Hagan, 1995) that the increases in fair value associated with changing prices should be differentiated from changes in fair value that are due to physical changes (for example, changes in the size or number of the biological assets). The argument was that only the physical changes should be treated as part of profit or loss. Although IAS 41 treats the total change in fair value as part of income, it is interesting to note that IAS 41 'encourages' disclosures that differentiate between changes in the fair values of the biological assets that are based upon price changes and those based on physical changes. As paragraph 51 of IAS 41 states:

> The fair value less estimated point-of-sale costs of a biological asset can change due to both physical changes and price changes in the market. Separate disclosure of physical

---

11 While it might be considered that measuring inventory at fair value would provide relevant information, IAS 2/AASB 102 'Inventories' prohibits the revaluation of stock. Specifically, IAS 2/AASB 102 requires inventory to be measured at the lower of cost and net realisable value.

12 In some countries, such as the United States, a cost-flow assumption based on the last-in-first-out (LIFO) method can be adopted (this cost-flow assumption is not allowed under IAS 2/AASB 102). The effect of employing LIFO is that cost of goods sold will be determined on the basis of the latest cost, which in times of rising prices will be higher, thereby leading to a reduction in reported profits. This does provide some level of protection (although certainly not complete) against the possibility of eroding the real operating capacity of the organisation.

and price changes is useful in appraising current period performance and future prospects, particularly when there is a production cycle of more than one year. In such cases, an entity is encouraged to disclose, by group or otherwise, the amount of the change in fair value less estimated point-of-sales costs included in profit or loss due to physical changes and due to price changes. This information is generally less useful when the production cycle is less than one year (for example, when raising chickens or growing cereal crops).

In relation to the above disclosure guidance, it is interesting to consider why the regulators considered that financial statement users would benefit from separate disclosure of price changes and physical changes in relation to agricultural assets when similar suggestions are not provided within other accounting standards relating to other categories of assets. This is somewhat inconsistent.

Returning to the use of historical cost in general, it has also been argued that historical cost accounting distorts the current year's operating results by including in the current year's income holding gains that actually accrued in previous periods.[13] For example, some assets may have been acquired at a very low cost in a previous period (and perhaps in anticipation of future price increases pertaining to the assets), yet under historical cost accounting the gains attributable to such actions will only be recognised in the subsequent periods when the assets are ultimately sold. As an illustration, let us assume that a reporting entity acquired some land in 2002 for $1 000 000. Its fair value increased to $1 300 000 in 2006 and then $1 700 000 in 2009. A decision is made to sell the land in 2010 for its new fair value of $1 900 000. If the land had been measured at cost, the entire profit of $900 000 would be shown in the 2010 financial year even though the increase in fair value accrued throughout the previous eight years. Arguably, placing all the gain in the last year's profits distorts the results of that financial period as well as the results of preceding periods. Another potential problem of historical cost accounting is that it can lead to a distortion of 'return-on-asset' measures. For example, consider an organisation that acquired some machinery for $1 million and returned a profit of $100 000. Such an organisation would have a return on asset of 10 per cent. If another organisation later acquired the same type of asset at $2 million (due to rising prices) and generated a profit of $150 000, then on the basis of return on assets the second organisation would appear less efficient, pursuant to historical cost accounting.

There is a generally accepted view that dividends should be paid only from profits (and this is enshrined within the corporations laws of many countries). However, one central issue relates to how we measure profits. There are various definitions of profits. One famous definition, provided by Hicks (1946), is that profits (or 'income', as he referred to it) is the maximum amount that can be consumed during a period while still expecting to be as well off at the end of the period as at the beginning of the period. Any consideration of 'well-offness' relies on a notion of capital maintenance—but which one? Different notions will provide different perspectives of profit.

There are a number of perspectives of capital maintenance. One version of capital maintenance is based on maintaining financial capital intact, and this is the position taken in historical cost accounting. Under historical cost accounting, dividends should normally be paid only to the extent that the payment will not erode financial capital, as illustrated in the previous example where

---

13 Holding gains are those that arise while an asset is in the possession of the reporting entity.

$20 000 is distributed to owners in the form of dividends and no adjustment is made to take account of changes in prices and the related impact on the purchasing power of the entity.

Another perspective of capital maintenance is one that aims at maintaining purchasing power intact.[14] Under this perspective, historical cost accounts are adjusted for changes in the purchasing power of the dollar (typically by use of the price index), which, in times of rising prices, will lead to a reduction in income relative to the income calculated under historical cost accounting. As an example, under general price level adjustment accounting (which is considered more fully later in the chapter) the historical cost of an item is adjusted by multiplying it by the chosen price index at the end of the current period, divided by the price index at the time the asset was acquired. For example, if some land, which was sold for $1 200 000, was initially acquired for $1 000 000 when the price index was 100, and the price index at the end of the current period is 118 (reflecting an increase in prices of 18 per cent), the adjusted cost would be $1 180 000. The adjusted profit would be $20 000 (compared with an historical cost profit of $200 000).[15] What should be realised is that under this approach to accounting where adjustments are made by way of a general price index, the value of $1 180 000 will not necessarily (except due to chance) reflect the current market value of the land. Various assets will be adjusted using the same general price index.

Use of actual current values (as opposed to adjustments to historical cost using price indices) is made under another approach to accounting which seeks to provide a measure of profits which, if distributed, maintains physical operating capital intact. This approach to accounting (which could be referred to as current cost accounting) relies on the use of current values, which could be based on present values, entry prices (for example, replacement costs) or exit prices.

Reflective of the attention that the impact of inflation was having on financial statements, Accounting Headline 5.1 is an article that appeared in the *Australian* in April 1975 (a period of high inflation and a time when debate in this area of accounting was widespread).

In the discussion that follows, a number of different approaches to undertaking financial accounting in times of rising prices are considered. This discussion is by no means exhaustive but does give an insight into some of the models that have been prescribed by various parties.[16]

---

14 Gray, Owen and Adams (1996, p. 74) also provide yet another concept of capital maintenance—one that includes environmental capital. They state, 'it is quite a simple matter to demonstrate that company "income" contains a significant element of capital distribution—in this case "environmental capital". An essential tenet of accounting is that income must allow for the maintenance of capital. Current organisational behaviour clearly does not maintain environmental capital and so overstates earnings. If diminution of environmental capital is factored into the income figure it seems likely that no company in the western world has actually made any kind of a profit for many years.' This issue is considered further in Chapter 9.

15 Hence, if $20 000 is distributed as dividends, the entity would still be in a position to acquire the same land that it had at the beginning of the period (assuming that actual prices increased by the same amount as the particular price index used).

16 For example, we will not be considering one approach to determining income based on present values, which did not have wide support but would be consistent with Hicks' income definition (and which might be considered as a true income approach). A present value approach would determine the discounted present value of the firm's assets and liabilities and use this as the basis for the financial statements. Under such an approach the calculated value of assets will depend on various expectations, such as expectations about the cash flows the asset would return through its use in production (its value in use) or its current market value (value in exchange). Such an approach relies on many assumptions and judgements, including the determination of the appropriate discount rate. Under a present value approach to accounting, profit would be determined as the amount that could be withdrawn yet maintain the present value of the net assets intact from one period to the next.

Australian, 11 April 1975, p. 12

Call for inflated books

BRIAN MAHONEY

With their capitalist ship slowly sinking from the weight of inflation, company directors and accountants are at last doing something about the problem.

They are not exactly finding a way to overcome it, but they have decided on a way of recording the effects of inflation in company accounts.

Members of the Institute of Chartered Accountants in Australia at the annual Victorian congress last weekend and a panel of directors at the Institute of Directors in Australia in Sydney on Wednesday called for the introduction of some form of accounting for inflation.

At present there is a preliminary exposure draft of one such form of accounting—Changes in the Purchasing Power of Money—distributed by the Institute of Chartered Accountants and the Australian Society of Accountants.

Under CPP, figures are adjusted by an index to a constant purchasing power.

Another such draft of another form of inflation accounting—Replacement Cost—is expected within a few months and hopefully some decision will be made after that as to what form of accounting will be encouraged.

RC accounting aims at showing the replacement value of non-monetary assets expected to be replaced, with consequential adjustments to profits.

As the ICAA pointed out at its Victorian meeting, a company reporting a steady profit in times of 20 per cent inflation would show adjusted earnings actually 20 per cent lower under the new schemes.

The present historical cost accounting, where companies compared different value dollars without converting them by any 'inflation exchange rate', has led some companies effectively to pay dividends out of capital.

Over 200 directors at the institute's seminar at the Wentworth Hotel, Sydney, were told until companies start to show the real effect of inflation on their earnings they could not hope to see any government moves similar to that of Finland where an index of inflation is declared each quarter.

Mr R. N. H. Denton, an accountant with Irish, Young and Outhwaite, told them: 'I prophesise that more and more companies will be seeking capital issues merely to maintain their level of operations.

'This is in a capital market where confidence has been severely shaken and which is in doubt as to whether industry can now earn an adequate return to service capital in real terms.

'To add to the problem, no recognition is given to our taxation policy to the effect that inflation exerts. The rate of 45 per cent, after a hopelessly inadequate reduction of 2.5 per cent, is really significantly higher on real earnings,' he said.

CURRENT PURCHASING POWER ACCOUNTING

Current purchasing power accounting (or, as it is also called, general purchasing power accounting, general price level accounting, or constant dollar accounting) can be traced to the early works of such authors as Sweeny (1964, but originally published in 1936) and has since been favoured by a number of other researchers. Current purchasing power accounting (CPPA) has also, at various times, been supported by professional accounting bodies throughout the world (but more in the form of supplementary disclosures to accompany financial statements prepared under historical cost accounting principles). CPPA was developed on the basis of a view that, in times of rising prices, if an entity were to distribute unadjusted profits based on historical costs the result could be a reduction in the real value of an entity—that is, in real terms the entity could risk distributing part of its capital.

In considering the development of accounting for changing prices, the majority of research initially related to restating historical costs to account for changing prices by using historical cost accounts as the basis, but restating the accounts by use of particular price indices. This is the approach considered in this section of the chapter. The literature then tended to move towards current cost accounting (which is considered later in the chapter), which changed the basis of measurement to current values as opposed to restated historical values. Consistent with this trend, the accounting profession initially tended to favour price-level-adjusted accounts (using indices), but then tended to switch to current cost accounting, which required the entity to find the current values of the individual assets held by the reporting entity.[17,18]

CPPA, with its reliance on the use of indices, is generally accepted as being easier and less costly to apply than methods that rely on current valuations of particular assets.[19] It was initially considered by some people that it would be too costly and perhaps unnecessary to attempt to find current values for all the individual assets. Rather than considering the price changes of specific goods and services, it was suggested on practical grounds that price indices be used.

CALCULATING INDICES

When applying general price level accounting, a price index must be applied. A price index is a weighted average of the current prices of goods and services relative to a weighted average of prices in a prior period, often referred to as a 'base period'. Price indices may be broad or narrow—they may relate to changes in prices of particular assets within a particular industry (a specific price index), or they might be based on a broad cross-section of goods and services that are consumed (a general price index, such as the Consumer Price Index (CPI) in Australia).

But which price indices should be used? Should we use changes in a general price index (for example, as reflected in Australia by the CPI) or should we use an index that is more closely tied to the acquisition of production-related resources? There is no clear answer. From the shareholders' perspective the CPI may more accurately reflect their buying pattern—but prices will not change by the same amount for shareholders in different locations. Further, not everybody will have the same consumption patterns as is assumed when constructing a particular index. The choice of an index can be very subjective. Where CPPA has been recommended by particular professional bodies, CPI-type indices have been suggested.

Because CPPA relies on the use of price indices, it is useful to consider how such indices are constructed. To explain one common way that indices may be constructed we can consider the following example which is consistent with how the Australian CPI is determined. Let us assume

---

17 Current values could be based on entry or exit prices. As we will see, there is much debate as to which 'current' value is most appropriate.

18 The professional support for the use of replacement costs appeared to heighten around the time of the 1976 release of ASR 190 within the United States.

19 However, many questions can be raised with regard to what the restated value actually represents after being multiplied by an index such as the general rate of inflation. This confusion is reflected in studies that question the relevance of information restated for changes in purchasing power.

that there are three types of commodities (A, B and C) that are consumed in the following base year quantities and at the following prices:

Year	Commodity A		Commodity B		Commodity C	
	Price ($)	Quantity	Price ($)	Quantity	Price ($)	Quantity
Base year (2010)	10.00	100	15.00	200	20.00	250
2011	12.00		15.50		21.20	

From the above data we can see that prices have increased. The price index in the base year is frequently given a value of 100 and it is also frequently assumed that consumption quantities thereafter remain the same, such that the price index at the end of year 2011 would be calculated as:

$$100 \times \frac{(12.00 \times 100) + (15.50 \times 200) + (21.20 \times 250)}{(10.00 \times 100) + (15.00 \times 200) + (20.00 \times 250)}$$

$$= 106.67100$$

From the above calculations we can see that the prices within this particular 'bundle' of goods have been calculated as rising on average by 6.67 per cent from the year 2010 to the year 2011. The reciprocal of the price index represents the change in general purchasing power across the period. For example, if the index increased from 100 to 106.67, as in the above example, the purchasing power of the dollar would be 93.75 per cent (100/106.67) of what it was previously. That is, the purchasing power of the dollar has decreased.

PERFORMING CURRENT PURCHASING POWER ADJUSTMENTS

When applying CPPA, all adjustments are done at the end of the period, with the adjustments being applied to accounts prepared under the historical cost convention. When considering changes in the value of assets as a result of changes in the purchasing power of money (due to inflation) it is necessary to consider monetary assets and non-monetary assets separately. Monetary assets are those assets that remain fixed in terms of their monetary value, for example cash and claims to a specified amount of cash (such as trade debtors and investments that are redeemable for a set amount of cash). These assets will not change their monetary value as a result of inflation. For example, if we are holding $10 in cash and there is rapid inflation, we will still be holding $10 in cash, but the asset's purchasing power will have decreased over time.

Non-monetary assets can be defined as those assets whose monetary equivalents will change over time as a result of inflation, and would include such things as plant and equipment and inventory. For example, inventory may cost $100 at the beginning of the year, but the same inventory could cost, say, $110 at the end of the year due to inflation. Relative to monetary assets, the purchasing power of non-monetary assets is assumed to remain constant even in the presence of inflation.

Most liabilities are fixed in monetary terms (there is an obligation to pay a pre-specified amount of cash at a particular time in the future independent of the change in the purchasing power of the particular currency) and hence liabilities would typically be considered as monetary items (monetary liabilities). Non-monetary liabilities, on the other hand, although less common, would include obligations to transfer goods and services in the future, items that could change in terms of their monetary equivalents.

Net monetary assets would be defined as monetary assets less monetary liabilities. In times of inflation, holders of monetary assets will lose in real terms as a result of holding the monetary assets, as the assets will have less purchasing power at the end of the period relative to what they had at the beginning of the period (and the greater the level of general price increases, the greater the losses). Conversely, holders of monetary liabilities will gain, given that the amount they have to repay at the end of the period will be worth less (in terms of purchasing power) than it was at the beginning of the period.

Let us consider an example to demonstrate how gains and losses might be calculated on monetary items (and under CPPA, gains and losses will relate to net monetary assets rather than net non-monetary assets). Let us assume that an organisation holds the following assets and liabilities at the beginning of the financial year:

	$
Current Assets	
Cash	6 000
Inventory	9 000
	15 000
Non-current Assets	
Land	10 000
Total Assets	25 000
Liabilities	
Bank loan	5 000
Owners' Equity	20 000

Let us also assume that the general level of prices has increased 5 per cent since the beginning of the year and let us make a further simplifying assumption (which will be relaxed later) that the company did not trade during the year and that the same assets and liabilities were in place at the end of the year as at the beginning. Assuming that general prices, perhaps as reflected by changes in the CPI, have increased by 5 per cent, the CPI-adjusted values would be:

	Unadjusted $	Price adjustment factor $	Adjusted $
Current Assets			
Cash	6 000		6 000
Inventory	9 000	0.05	9 450
	15 000		15 450
Non-current Assets			
Land	10 000	0.05	10 500
Total Assets	25 000		25 950
Liabilities			
Bank loan	5 000		5 000
Owners' Equity	20 000		20 950

Again, monetary items are not adjusted by the change in the particular price index because they will retain the same monetary value regardless of inflation. Under CPPA there is an assumption that the organisation has not gained or lost in terms of the purchasing power attributed to the non-monetary assets, but, rather, it will gain or lose in terms of purchasing power changes attributable to its holdings of the net monetary assets. In the above example, to be as 'well off' at the end of the period the entity would need $21 000 in net assets (which equals $20 000 × 1.05) to have the same purchasing power as it had one year earlier (given the general increase in prices of 5 per cent). In terms of end-of-year dollars, in the above illustration the entity is $50 worse off in adjusted terms (it has net assets with an adjusted value of $20 950, which does not have the same purchasing power as $20 000 did at the beginning of the period). As indicated above, this $50 loss relates to the holdings of net monetary assets and not to the holding of non-monetary assets, and is calculated as the balance of cash, less the balance of the bank loan, multiplied by the general price level increase. That is, ($6000 − $5000) × 0.05. If the monetary liabilities had exceeded the monetary assets throughout the period, a purchasing power gain would have been recorded. If the amount of monetary assets held was the same as the amount of monetary liabilities held, no gain or losses would result.

Again, it is stressed that under CPPA no change in the purchasing power of the entity is assumed to arise as a result of holding non-monetary assets. Under general price level accounting, non-monetary assets are restated to current purchasing power and no gain or loss is recognised. Purchasing power losses arise only as a result of holding net monetary assets. As noted at paragraph 7 of Provisional Statement of Standard Accounting Practice 7 (PSSAP 7), issued in the United Kingdom in 1974:

> Holders of non-monetary assets are assumed neither to gain nor to lose purchasing power by reason only of inflation as changes in the prices of these assets will tend to compensate for any changes in the purchasing power of the pound.

An important issue to consider is how the purchasing power gains and losses should be treated for income purposes. Should they be treated as part of the period's profit or loss, or should they be transferred directly to a reserve? Generally, where this method of accounting has been recommended it has been advised that the gain or loss should be included in income. Such recommendations are found in the US *Accounting Research Bulletin* No. 6 (issued in 1961), in the Accounting Principles Board (APB) Statement No. 3 (issued in 1969 by the American Institute of Certified Public Accountants (AICPA)), in the Financial Accounting Standards Board's (FASB) exposure draft entitled 'Financial Reporting in Units of General Purchasing Power', and within Provisional Statement of Accounting Practice No. 7 issued by the Accounting Standards Steering Committee (UK) in 1974.

As a further example of calculating gains or losses in purchasing power pertaining to monetary items, let us assume four quarters with the following CPI index figures:

At the beginning of the year	120
At the end of the first quarter	125
At the end of the second quarter	130
At the end of the third quarter	132
At the end of the fourth quarter	135

Let us also assume the following movements in net monetary assets (total monetary assets less total monetary liabilities):

Opening net monetary assets		$100 000
Inflows:		
First quarter net inflow	20 000	
Second quarter net inflow	24 000	
Total inflows		**44 000**
Outflows:		
Third quarter net outflow	(17 000)	
Fourth quarter net outflow	(13 000)	
Total outflows		(30 000)
Closing net monetary assets		**$114 000**

In terms of year-end purchasing power dollars, the purchasing power gain or loss can be calculated as:

	Unadjusted dollars		Price index		Adjusted dollars
Opening net monetary assets	$100 000	×	135/120	=	$112 500
Inflows:					
First quarter net inflow	$20 000	×	135/125	=	$21 600
Second quarter net inflow	$24 000	×	135/130	=	$24 923
Outflows:					
Third quarter net outflow	$(17 000)	×	135/132	=	$(17 386)
Fourth quarter net outflow	$(13 000)	×	135/135	=	$(13 000)
Net monetary assets adjusted for changes in purchasing power					$128 637

What the above calculation reflects is that, to have the same purchasing power as when the particular transactions took place, in terms of end-of-period dollars, $128 637 in net monetary assets would need to be on hand at year end.[20] The actual balance on hand, however, is $114 000. Hence, there is a purchasing power loss of $14 637 which under CPPA would be treated as an expense and included within the profit or loss of the period.

Let us now consider a more realistic example of CPPA adjustments. The financial statements will be restated to reflect purchasing power as at the end of the current financial year. Let us assume that the entity commenced operation on 1 January 2010 and the unadjusted balance sheet (statement of financial position) is as follows:

CPP Limited Statement of Financial Position as at 1 January 2010

Current Assets

Cash	10 000	
Inventory	25 000	35 000

(continued)

20 For example, we can consider the initial net monetary asset balance of $100 000 at the beginning of the period. For illustration, assume that this was represented by cash of $100 000. Given the inflation which has caused general prices to rise from a base of 120 to 135, to have the same general purchasing power at the end of the period an amount of cash equal to $112 500 would need to be on hand. The difference between the required amount of $112 500 and the actual balance of $100 000 is treated as a purchasing power loss relating to holding the cash. Conversely, if the net monetary balance had been ($100 000), meaning that monetary liabilities exceeded monetary assets, we would have gained, as the purchasing power of what we must pay has decreased over time.

Non-current Assets		
Plant and equipment	90 000	
Land	75 000	165 000
Total Assets		200 000
Current Liabilities		
Bank overdraft	10 000	
Non-current Liabilities		
Bank loan	10 000	
Total Liabilities		20 000
Net Assets		180 000
Represented by:		
Shareholders' Funds		
Paid-up capital		180 000

As a result of its operations for the year, CPP Limited had the historical cost income statement and statement of financial position at year end as shown below:

CPP Limited Income Statement for year ended 31 December 2010		
Sales revenue		200 000
Less:		
Cost of goods sold		
Opening inventory	25 000	
Purchases	110 000	
	135 000	
Closing inventory	35 000	100 000
Gross profit		100 000
Other expenses		
Administrative expenses	9 000	
Interest expense	1 000	
Depreciation	9 000	19 000
Operating profit before tax		81 000
Tax		26 000

(continued)

CPP Limited Income Statement for year ended 31 December 2010 (continued)

Operating profit after tax		55 000
Opening retained earnings		0
Dividends proposed		15 000
Closing retained earnings		40 000

CPP Limited Statement of Financial Position as at 31 December 2010

Current Assets		
Cash	100 000	
Trade debtors	20 000	
Inventory	35 000	155 000
Non-current Assets		
Plant and equipment	90 000	
Accumulated depreciation	(9 000)	
Land	75 000	156 000
Total Assets		311 000
Current Liabilities		
Bank overdraft	10 000	
Trade creditors	30 000	
Tax payable	26 000	
Provision for dividends	15 000	81 000
Non-current Liabilities		
Bank loan	10 000	10 000
Total Liabilities		91 000
Net Assets		220 000
Represented by:		
Shareholders' Funds		
Paid-up capital		180 000
Retained earnings		40 000
		220 000

As already stated, under CPPA gains or losses occur only as a result of holding net monetary assets. To determine the gain or loss, we must consider the movements in the net monetary assets. For example, if the organisation sold inventory during the year, this will ultimately impact on cash. However, over time, the cash will be worth less in terms of its ability to acquire goods and services, hence there will be a purchasing power loss on the cash that was received during the year. Conversely, expenses will decrease cash during the year. In times of rising prices, more cash would be required to pay for the expense, hence in a sense we gain in relation to those expenses that were incurred earlier in the year (the logic being that if the expenses were incurred later in the year, more cash would have been required).

We must identify changes in net monetary assets from the beginning of the period until the end of the period.

Movement in net monetary assets from 1 January 2010 to 31 December 2010		
	1 January 2010	31 December 2010
Monetary assets		
Cash	10 000	100 000
Trade debtors	–	20 000
	10 000	120 000
Less:		
Monetary liabilities		
Bank overdraft	10 000	10 000
Trade creditors		30 000
Tax payable		26 000
Provision for dividends		15 000
Bank loan	10 000	10 000
	20 000	91 000
Net monetary assets	(10 000)	29 000

To determine any adjustments in CPP Limited, we must identify the reasons for the change in net monetary assets.

Reconciliation of opening and closing net monetary assets	
Opening net monetary assets	(10 000)
Sales	200 000
Purchase of goods	(110 000)
Payment of interest	(1 000)

(continued)

Reconciliation of opening and closing net monetary assets *(continued)*	
Payment of administrative expenses	(9 000)
Tax expense	(26 000)
Dividends	(15 000)
Closing net monetary assets	29 000

What we need to determine is whether, had all the transactions taken place at year end, the company would have had to transfer the same amount, measured in monetary terms, as it actually did. Any payments to outside parties throughout the period would have required a greater payment at the end of the period if the same items were to be transferred. Any receipts during the year will, however, be worth less in purchasing power.

To adjust for changes in purchasing power we need to have details about how prices have changed during the period, and we also need to know when the actual changes took place. We make the following assumptions:

- The interest expense and administrative expenses were incurred uniformly throughout the year.
- The tax liability did not arise until year end.
- The dividends were declared at the end of the year.
- The inventory on hand at year end was acquired in the last quarter of the year.
- Purchases of inventory occurred uniformly throughout the year.
- Sales occurred uniformly throughout the year.

We also assume that the price level index at the beginning of the year was 130. Subsequent indices were as follows:

31 December 2010	140
Average for the year	135
Average for first quarter	132
Average for second quarter	135
Average for third quarter	137
Average for fourth quarter	139

Rather than using price indices as at the particular dates of transactions (which would generally not be available) it is common to use averages for a particular period.

	Unadjusted	Index	Adjusted
Opening net monetary assets	(10 000)	140/130	(10 769)
Sales	200 000	140/135	207 407
Purchase of goods	(110 000)	140/135	(114 074)
Payment of interest	(1 000)	140/135	(1 037)

(continued)

Payment of administrative expenses	(9 000)	140/135	(9 333)
Tax expense	(26 000)	140/140	(26 000)
Dividends	(15 000)	140/140	(15 000)
Closing net monetary assets	29 000		31 194

The difference between $29 000 and the amount of $31 194 represents a loss of $2194. It is considered to be a loss, because to have the same purchasing power at year end as when the entity held the particular net monetary assets, the entity would need the adjusted amount of $31 194, rather than the actual amount of $29 000. This loss of $2194 will appear as a 'loss on purchasing power' in the price-level-adjusted income statement (see below).

Price-level-adjusted Income Statement for year ended 31 December 2010			
Sales revenue	200 000	140/135	207 407
Less **Cost of goods sold**			
Opening inventory	25 000	140/130	26 923
Purchases	110 000	140/135	114 074
	135 000		140 997
Closing inventory	35 000	140/139	35 252
	100 000		105 745
Gross profit	100 000		101 662
Other expenses			
Administrative expenses	9 000	140/135	9 333
Interest expense	1 000	140/135	1 037
Depreciation	9 000	140/130	9 692
	19 000		20 062
Profit before tax	81 000		81 600
Tax	26 000	140/140	26 000
Profit after tax	55 000		55 600
Loss on purchasing power			2 194
			53 406
Opening retained earnings	0		0
Dividends proposed	15 000	140/140	15 000
Closing retained earnings	40 000		38 406

Price-level-adjusted Statement of Financial Position as at 31 December 2010

Current Assets

Cash	100 000		100 000
Trade debtors	20 000		20 000
Inventory	35 000	140/139	35 252
Total Current Assets	155 000		155 252
Non-current Assets			
Plant and equipment	90 000	140/130	96 923
Accumulated depreciation	(9 000)	140/130	(9 692)
Land	75 000	140/130	80 769
Total Non-current Assets	156 000		168 000
Total Assets	311 000		323 252
Current Liabilities			
Bank overdraft	10 000		10 000
Trade creditors	30 000		30 000
Tax payable	26 000		26 000
Provision for dividends	15 000		15 000
Non-current Liabilities			
Bank loan	10 000		10 000
Total Liabilities	91 000		91 000
Net Assets	220 000		232 252
Represented by:			
Shareholders' Funds			
Paid-up capital	180 000	140/130	193 846
Retained earnings	40 000		38 406
	220 000		232 252

From the above statement of financial position (balance sheet) we can again emphasise that the non-monetary items are translated into dollars of year-end purchasing power, whereas the monetary items are already stated in current purchasing power dollars, and hence no changes are made to the reported balances of monetary assets.

One main strength of CPPA is its ease of application. The method relies on data that would already be available under historical cost accounting and does not require the reporting entity to incur the cost or effort involved in collecting data about the current values of the various non-monetary assets. CPI data would also be readily available. However, and as indicated previously, movements in the prices of goods and services included in a general price index might not be reflective of price movements involved in the goods and services involved in different industries. That is, different industries may be affected differently by inflation.

Another possible limitation is that the information generated under CPPA might actually be confusing to users. They might consider that the adjusted amounts reflect the specific value of specific assets (and this is a criticism that can also be made of historical cost information). However, as the same index is used for all assets this will rarely be the case. Another potential limitation considered at the end of the chapter is that various studies (which have looked at such things as movements in share prices around the time of disclosure of CPPA information) have failed to find much support for the view that the data generated under CPPA are relevant for decision making (the information when released caused little if any share price reaction).

Following the initial acceptance of CPPA in some countries in the 1970s, there was a move towards methods of accounting that used actual current values rather than revised values being based on the application of indices. Support for CPPA declined. Such approaches are now considered.

CURRENT COST ACCOUNTING

Current cost accounting (CCA) is one of the alternatives to historical cost accounting that has tended to gain the most acceptance. Notable advocates of the approach have included Paton (1922) and Edwards and Bell (1961). Such authors decided to reject historical cost accounting and CPPA in favour of a method that considered actual valuations. As we will see, unlike historical cost accounting, CCA differentiates between profits from trading and those gains that result from holding an asset.

Holding gains can be considered as realised or unrealised. If a financial capital maintenance perspective is adopted with respect to the recognition of income, then holding gains or losses can be treated as income. Alternatively, they can be treated as capital adjustments if a physical capital maintenance approach is adopted.[21] Some versions of CCA, such as that proposed by Edwards and Bell, adopt a physical capital maintenance approach to income recognition. In this approach, which determines valuations on the basis of replacement costs,[22] operating income represents realised revenues, less the replacement cost of the assets in question. It is considered that this generates a measure of income which represents the maximum amount that can be distributed, while maintaining operating capacity intact. For example, assume that an entity acquired 150 items of inventory at a cost of $10.00 each and sold 100 of the items for $15 each when the replacement cost to the entity was $12 each. Assume also that the replacement cost of the 50 remaining items of inventory at year end was $14. Under the Edwards and Bell approach the operating profit that would be available for dividends would be $300, which is

---

21 In some countries non-current assets can be revalued upward by way of an increase in the asset account and an increase in a reserve, such as a revaluation surplus account. This increment is typically not treated as income and therefore the treatment is consistent with a physical capital maintenance approach to income recognition (this approach is embodied within IAS 16/AASB 116 as it relates to property, plant and equipment, and within IAS 38/AASB138 as it relates to intangible assets).

22 We will also see later in this chapter that there are alternative approaches to current cost accounting that rely on exit (sales) prices.

$100 \times (\$15 - \$12)$. There would be a realised holding gain on the goods that were sold, which would amount to $100 \times (\$12 - \$10)$, or \$200, and there would be an unrealised holding gain in relation to closing inventory of $50 \times (\$14 - \$10)$, or \$200. Neither the realised nor the unrealised holding gain would be considered to be available for dividend distribution.[23]

In undertaking CCA, adjustments are usually made at year end using the historical cost accounts as the basis of adjustments. If the Edwards and Bell approach to profit calculation is adopted, operating profit is derived after ensuring that the operating capacity of the organisation is maintained intact. Edwards and Bell believe that operating profit is best calculated by using replacement costs.[24,25] As noted above, in calculating operating profit, gains that accrue from holding an asset (holding gains) are excluded and are not made available for dividends—although they are included when calculating what is referred to as business profit. For example, if an entity acquired goods for \$20 and sold them for \$30, business profit would be \$10, meaning that \$10 could be distributed and still leave financial capital intact (this would be the approach taken in historical cost accounting). But if at the time the goods were sold their replacement cost to the entity was \$23, then \$3 would be considered a holding gain, and to maintain physical operating capacity only \$7 could be distributed—current cost operating profit would be \$7. No adjustment is made to sales revenue. This \$7 distribution can be compared with what could be distributed under historical cost accounting. Because historical costs accounting adopts a financial capital maintenance approach, \$10 could be distributed in dividends, thereby maintaining financial capital (but nevertheless causing an erosion in the operating ability of the organisation).

In relation to non-current assets, for the purposes of determining current cost operating profit, depreciation is based on the replacement cost of the asset. For example, if an item of machinery was acquired in 2009 for \$100 000 and had a projected life of 10 years and no salvage value, then, assuming the straight-line method of depreciation is used, its depreciation expense under historical cost accounting would be \$10 000 per year. If at the end of 2010 its replacement cost had increased to \$120 000, then under current cost accounting a further \$2000 would be deducted to determine current cost operating profit. However, this \$2000 would be treated as a realised cost saving (because historical cost profits would have been lower if the entity had not already acquired the asset) and would be recognised in business profit (it would be added back below operating profit) and the other \$18 000 would be treated as an unrealised cost saving and would also be included in business profit. As with CPPA, no restatement of monetary assets is required as they are already recorded in current dollars and hence in terms of end-of-period purchasing power dollars.

As an example of one version of CCA (consistent with the Edwards and Bell proposals) let us consider the following example. CCA Limited's statement of financial position (balance sheet) at the commencement of the year is provided below. This is assumed to be the first year of CCA Limited's operations.

---

23 Comparing this approach to income calculations under historical cost accounting, we see that, if we add CCA operating profit of \$300 and the realised holding gain of \$200, this will give the same total as we would have calculated for income under historical cost accounting.

24 In a sense, the Edwards and Bell approach represents a 'true income' approach to profit calculation. They believe that profit can only be correctly measured (that is, 'be true') after considering the various asset replacement costs.

25 Those who favour a method of income calculation that requires a maintenance of financial capital (advocates of historical cost accounting) treat holding gains as income, while those who favour a maintenance of physical capital approach to income determination (such as Edwards and Bell) tend to exclude holding gains from income. A physical capital perspective was adopted by most countries in their professional releases pertaining to CCA.

CCA Limited Statement of Financial Position as at 1 January 2010

Current Assets

Cash	10 000	
Inventory	25 000	35 000
Non-current Assets		
Plant and equipment	90 000	
Land	75 000	165 000
Total Assets		200 000
Current Liabilities		
Bank overdraft	10 000	
Non-current Liabilities		
Bank loan	10 000	
Total Liabilities		20 000
Net Assets		180 000
Represented by:		
Shareholders' Funds		
Paid-up capital		180 000

The unadjusted income statement and statement of financial position for CCA Limited after one year's operations are provided below.

CCA Limited Income Statement for year ended 31 December 2010

Sales revenue		200 000
Less:		
Cost of goods sold		
Opening inventory	25 000	
Purchases	110 000	
	135 000	
Closing inventory	35 000	100 000
Gross profit		100 000

(continued)

CCA Limited Income Statement for year ended 31 December 2010 *(continued)*

Other expenses

Administrative expenses	9 000	
Interest expense	1 000	
Depreciation	9 000	19 000
Operating profit before tax		81 000
Tax		26 000
Operating profit after tax		55 000
Opening retained earnings		0
Dividends proposed		15 000
Closing retained earnings		40 000

CCA Limited Statement of Financial Position as at 31 December 2010

Current Assets

Cash	100 000	
Trade debtors	20 000	
Inventory	35 000	155 000
Non-current Assets		
Plant and equipment	90 000	
Accumulated depreciation	(9 000)	
Land	75 000	156 000
Total Assets		311 000
Current Liabilities		
Bank overdraft	10 000	
Trade creditors	30 000	
Tax payable	26 000	
Provision for dividends	15 000	81 000
Non-current Liabilities		
Bank loan	10 000	10 000
Total Liabilities		91 000
Net Assets		220 000
Represented by:		

(continued)

Shareholders' Funds		
Paid-up capital		180 000
Retained earnings		40 000
		220 000

We will assume that the inventory on hand at year end comprised 3500 units that cost $10 per unit. The replacement cost at year end was $11.00 per unit. We will also assume that the replacement cost of the units actually sold during the year was $105 000 (as opposed to the historical cost of $100 000) and that the year-end replacement cost of the plant and equipment increased to $115 000. The plant and equipment has an expected life of 10 years with no residual value. The replacement cost of the land is believed to be $75,000 at year end.

CCA Limited Income Statement for year ended 31 December 2010

Adjusted by application of current cost accounting

Sales revenue		200 000
Less:		
Cost of goods sold		105 000
		95 000
Other expenses		
Administrative expenses	9 000	
Interest expense	1 000	
Tax	26 000	
Depreciation (115 000 × 1/10)	11 500	47 500
Current cost operating profit		47 500
Realised savings		
Savings related to inventory actually sold		5 000
Savings related to depreciation actually		
incurred [(115 000 – 90 000) × 1/10]		2 500
Historical cost profit		55 000
Unrealised savings		
Gains on holding inventory—yet to be realised		3 500
Gains on holding plant and machinery—not yet realised through the process of depreciation [(115 000 – 90 000) × 9/10)]		22 500

(continued)

CCA Limited Income Statement for year ended 31 December 2010 *(continued)*

Business profit		81 000
Opening retained earnings		0
Dividends proposed		15 000
Closing retained earnings		66 000

CCA Limited Statement of Financial Position as at 31 December 2010

Adjusted by application of current cost accounting

Current Assets		
Cash	100 000	
Trade debtors	20 000	
Inventory (3500 × $11.00)	38 500	158 500
Non-current Assets		
Plant and equipment	115 000	
Accumulated depreciation	(11 500)	
Land	75 000	178 500
Total Assets		337 000
Current Liabilities		
Bank overdraft	10 000	
Trade creditors	30 000	
Tax payable	26 000	
Provision for dividends	15 000	81 000
Non-current Liabilities		
Bank loan	10 000	10 000
Total liabilities		91 000
Net Assets		246 000
Represented by:		
Shareholders' Funds		
Paid-up capital		180 000
Retained earnings		66 000
		246 000

Consistent with the CCA model prescribed by Edwards and Bell, all non-monetary assets have to be adjusted to their respective replacement costs. Unlike historical cost accounting, there is no need for inventory cost flow assumptions (such as last-in-first-out, first-in-first-out, weighted average). Business profit shows how the entity has gained in financial terms from the increase in cost of its resources—something typically ignored by historical cost accounting. In the above illustration, and consistent with a number of versions of CCA, no adjustments have been made for changes in the purchasing power of net monetary assets (in contrast to CPPA).[26]

The current cost operating profit before holding gains and losses, and the realised holding gains, are both tied to the notion of realisation, and hence the sum of the two equates to historical cost profit.

Differentiating operating profit from holding gains and losses (both realised and unrealised) has been claimed to enhance the usefulness of the information being provided. Holding gains are deemed to be different from trading income as they are due to market-wide movements, most of which are beyond the control of management. Edwards and Bell (1961, p. 73) state:

> These two kinds of gains are often the result of quite different decisions. The business firm usually has considerable freedom in deciding what quantities of assets to hold over time at any or all stages of the production process and what quantity of assets to commit to the production process itself ... The difference between the forces motivating the business firm to make profit by one means rather than by another and the difference between the events on which the two methods of making profit depend require that the two kinds of gain be separated if the two types of decisions involved are to be meaningfully evaluated.

As with CPPA, the CCA model described above has been identified as having a number of strengths and weaknesses. Some of the criticisms relate to its reliance on replacement values. The CCA model just described uses replacement values, but what is the rationale for replacement cost? Perhaps it is a reflection of the 'real' value of the particular asset. If people in the market are prepared to pay the replacement cost, and if we assume economic rationality, then the amount paid must be a reflection of the returns it is expected to generate. However, it might not be worth that amount (the replacement cost) to all firms—some firms might not elect to replace a given asset if they have an option. Further, past costs are sunk costs and if the entity were required to acquire new plant it might find it more efficient and less costly to acquire different types of assets. If it did buy it, this might reflect that it is actually worth much more. Further, replacement cost does not reflect what it would be worth if the firm decided to sell it.

As indicated previously, it has been argued that separating holding gains and losses from other results provides a better insight into management performance, as such gains and losses are due to impacts generated outside the organisation; however, this can be criticised on the basis that acquiring assets in advance of price movements might also be part of efficient operations.

---

26 Some variants of CCA do include some purchasing power changes as part of the profit calculations. For example, if an entity issued $1 million of debt when the market required a rate of return of 6 per cent, but that required rate subsequently rises to 8 per cent, the unrealised savings would include the difference between what the entity received for the debt and what it would receive at the new rate. This unrealised saving would benefit the organisation throughout the loan as a result of the lower interest charges.

Another potential limitation of CCA is that it is often difficult to determine replacement costs. The approach also suffers from the criticism that allocating replacement cost via depreciation is still arbitrary, just as it is with historical cost accounting.

An advantage of CCA is better comparability of various entities' performance, as one entity's profits are not higher simply because it bought assets years earlier and therefore would have generated lower depreciation under historical cost accounting.

Chambers, an advocate of CCA based on exit values, was particularly critical of the Edwards and Bell model of accounting. He states (1995, p. 82) 'In the context of judgement of the past and decision making for the future, the products of current value accounting of the Edwards and Bell variety are irrelevant and misleading'.

The next section looks at the alternative accounting model prescribed by Chambers and a number of others—a model that relies on the use of exit values.

EXIT PRICE ACCOUNTING: THE CASE OF CHAMBERS' CONTINUOUSLY CONTEMPORARY ACCOUNTING

Exit price accounting has been proposed by researchers such as MacNeal, Sterling and Chambers. It is a form of current cost accounting that is based on valuing assets at their net selling prices (exit prices) at the reporting date and on the basis of orderly sales. Chambers coined the term 'current cash equivalent' to refer to the cash that an entity would expect to receive through the orderly sale of an asset, and he had the view that information about current cash equivalents was fundamental to effective decision making. He labelled his method of accounting Continuously Contemporary Accounting, or CoCoA.

Although Chambers generated some much-cited research throughout the 1950s (such as Chambers, 1955) a great deal of his work culminated in 1966 in the publication of *Accounting, Evaluation and Economic Behavior*. This document stressed that the key information for economic decision making relates to capacity to adapt—a function of current cash equivalents. The balance sheet (statement of financial position) is considered to be the prime financial statement and should show the net selling prices of the entity's assets. Profit would directly relate to changes in adaptive capital, with adaptive capital reflected by the total exit values of the entity's assets.

As indicated previously, how one calculates income is based, in part, on how one defines wealth. According to Sterling, an advocate of exit price accounting (1970b, p. 189):

The present [selling] price is the proper and correct valuation coefficient for the measurement of wealth at a point in time and income is the difference between dated wealths so calculated.

Consistent with the views of Sterling, Chambers (1966, p. 91) states:

At any present time, all past prices are simply a matter of history. Only present prices have any bearing on the choice of an action. The price of a good ten years ago has no more relation to this question than the hypothetical price 20 years hence. As individual prices may change even over an interval when the purchasing power of money does not, and as the general purchasing power of money may change even though some individual prices do not, no useful inference may be drawn from past prices which has a necessary bearing on present capacity to operate in a market. Every measurement of a financial property for the purpose of choosing a course of action—to buy, to hold, to sell—is a measurement at a point in time, in the circumstances of the time, and in the units of currency at that time, even if the measurement process itself takes some time.

Excluding all past prices, there are two prices which could be used to measure the monetary equivalent of any non-monetary good in possession: the buying price and the selling price. But the buying price, or replace price, does not indicate capacity, on the basis of present holdings, to go into a market with cash for the purpose of adapting oneself to contemporary conditions, whereas the selling price does. We propose, therefore, that the single financial property which is uniformly relevant at a point of time for all possible future actions in markets is the market selling price or realizable price of any goods held. Realizable price may be described as current cash equivalent. What men wish to know, for the purpose of adaptation, is the numerosity of the money tokens which could be substituted for particular objects and for collections of objects if money is required beyond the amount which one already holds.[27]

We can see that Chambers has made a judgement about what people need in terms of information. Like authors such as Edwards and Bell, and unlike some of the earlier work which documented existing accounting practices to identify particular principles and postulates (descriptive research),[28] Chambers set out to develop what he considered was a superior model of accounting—a model that represented quite a dramatic change from existing practice. We call this 'prescriptive' or 'normative' research. The research typically highlighted the limitations of historical cost accounting and then proposed an alternative on the basis that it would enable better decision making. Chambers adopts a decision usefulness approach and within this approach he adopts a decision-models perspective.[29]

Chambers' approach is focused on new opportunities; the ability or capacity of the entity to adapt to changing circumstances and the most important item of information to evaluate future decisions is, according to Chambers, current cash equivalents. Chambers makes an assumption about the objective of accounting—to guide future actions. Capacity to adapt is the key and the capacity to adapt to changing circumstances is dependent on the current cash equivalents of the

27 As quoted in Riahi-Belkaoui (2004, pp. 496–97).

28 As a specific example of the inductive (descriptive) approach to theory development, consider the work of Grady (1965). This research was commissioned by the American Institute of Certified Public Accountants and documented the generally accepted conventions of accounting at the time.

29 As indicated in Chapter 1, decision usefulness research can be considered to have two branches, these being the decision-makers emphasis and the decision-models emphasis. The decision-makers emphasis relies on undertaking research that seeks to ask decision makers what information they want. Proponents of the decision-models emphasis, on the other hand, develop models based on the researchers' perceptions about what is necessary for efficient decision making. Information prescriptions follow (for example, that information should be provided about the market value of the reporting entity's assets). This branch of research typically assumes that different classes of stakeholders have identical information needs. Unlike the decision-makers emphasis, the decision-models emphasis does not ask the decision makers what information they want, but, instead, it concentrates on what types of information are considered by the researcher to be useful for decision making.

assets on hand. The higher the current market value of the entity's assets, the greater the ability of the organisation to adapt to changing circumstances.

As stated previously, in Chambers' model profit is directly tied to the increase (or decrease) in the current net selling prices of the entity's assets. No distinction is drawn between realised and unrealised gains. Unlike some other models of accounting, all gains are treated as part of profit. Profit is that amount that can be distributed while maintaining the entity's adaptive ability (adaptive capital). CoCoA abandons notions of realisation in terms of recognising revenue, and hence revenue recognition points change relative to historical cost accounting. Rather than relying on sales, revenues are recognised at such points as production or purchase.

Unlike the Edwards and Bell approach to CCA, within CoCoA there is an adjustment to take account of changes in general purchasing power, which is referred to as a 'capital maintenance adjustment'. The capital maintenance adjustment also forms part of the period's income, with a corresponding credit to a capital maintenance reserve (which forms part of owners' equity). In determining the capital maintenance adjustment, the opening residual equity of the entity (that is, the net assets) is multiplied by the proportionate change in the general price index from the beginning of the period to the end of the financial period. As an example, if opening residual equity (or owners' equity) was $5 000 000 and the price index increased from 140 to 148, then the capital maintenance adjustment (in the case of increasing prices, an expense) would be calculated as $5 000 000 × 8/140 = $285 714. According to Chambers (1995, p. 86):

> Deduction of that amount, a capital maintenance or inflation adjustment, from the nominal difference between opening and closing capitals, would give the net increment in purchasing power, the real income, of a period. The inflation adjustment would automatically cover gains and losses in purchasing power from net holdings of money and money's worth. Net real income would then be the algebraic sum of (a) net realised revenues based on consummated transactions, or net cash flows, (b) the aggregate of price variation adjustments, the unrealised changes in value of assets on hand at balance date, and (c) the inflation adjustment. The amount of the inflation adjustment would be added proportionately to the opening balances of contributed capital and undivided surplus, giving closing amounts in units of up to date purchasing power.

Some of the above points are summarised in Accounting Headline 5.2, which is an article that appeared in the *Australian Financial Review* (10 May 1973). It reported some of Chambers' concerns with regards to historical cost accounting.

As a simple illustration of CoCoA, consider the following information. Assume that Cocoa Limited had the following statements of financial position as at 30 June 2010, one compiled using historical cost accounting and the other using CoCoA.

We assume that in the financial year ending on 30 June 2011, all the opening inventory was sold for $16 000 and the same quantity of inventory was reacquired at a cost of $11 000 (and which had a retail price of $18 000). There were salaries of $2000 and historical cost depreciation was based on 5 per cent of book value of plant and equipment. Prices rose generally throughout the period by 10 per cent and the net market value of the plant and equipment was assessed as $29 000.

Where company reports fail— Prof Chambers

Australian Financial Review, 10 May 1973, p. 30

Financial reports of companies generally failed to give a fair idea of their financial positions and profits, Professor R. J. Chambers, professor of accounting at the University of Sydney, said last night.

He called for amplification of the law on company reporting to ensure that balance sheets recognise changes in the prices of specific assets and profit and loss accounts reflect changes in the general purchasing power of money.

The accounting rules used were so different in effect that comparisons between companies were often quite misleading.

These rules had been debated for years among accountants but never yet had accountants settled on rules which gave consistent and up-to-date information year by year.

Addressing the university's Pacioli Society, Professor Chambers outlined specific amendments to the Companies Acts which are contained in his new book, 'Securities and Obscurities'.

Professor Chambers' amendment to the laws governing balance sheet reporting was that no balance sheet should be deemed to give a true and fair view of the state of affairs of a company unless the amounts shown for the several assets were the best possible approximations of the net selling prices in the ordinary course of business.

Debts receivable should be the best possible approximations to the amounts expected at the date of the balance sheet to be receivable or recoverable.

On the profit and loss account, Professor Chambers urged that it be deemed to give a true and fair view only if the profit or loss was calculated so as to include changes during the year in the net selling prices of assets and the effects during the year of changes in the purchasing power of the unit of account as specified in the Schedule of the Act.

Professor Chambers said thousands of shareholders had lost millions of dollars on security investments made on the basis of out-of-date information or on fictions which were reported as facts.

Cocoa Limited Historical Cost Statement of Financial Position as at 30 June 2010

Assets	
Cash	6 000
Inventory	10 000
Plant and equipment	24 000
Total Assets	40 000
Liabilities	
Bank loan	10 000
Net Assets	30 000
Represented by:	
Shareholders' Funds	
Paid-up capital	10 000
Retained earnings	20 000
	30 000

Cocoa Limited CoCoA Statement of Financial Position as at 30 June 2010

Assets	
Cash	6 000
Inventory	16 000
Plant and equipment	28 000
Total Assets	50 000
Liabilities	
Bank loan	10 000
Net Assets	40 000
Represented by:	
Shareholders' Funds	
Paid-up capital	10 000
Retained earnings	22 000
Capital maintenance reserve	8 000
	40 000

The income determined for the year ended 30 June 2011 under historical cost accounting and CoCoA can be calculated as follows:

Cocoa Limited Historical Cost Profit and Loss Statement for year ended 30 June 2011	
Sales	16 000
Cost of goods sold	(10 000)
Gross margin	6 000
Salaries expense	(2 000)
Depreciation	(1 200)
Net profit	2 800
Opening retained earnings	20 000
Closing retained earnings	22 800

Cocoa Limited CoCoA Profit and Loss Statement for year ended 30 June 2011	
Sale price of inventory	18 000
Cost of inventory	11 000
Trading income	7 000
Salaries expense	(2 000)
Increase in exit value of plant	1 000
Capital maintenance	
Adjustment (40 000 × 0.10)	(4 000)
Net profit	2 000
Opening retained earnings	22 000
Closing retained earnings	24 000

Cocoa Limited Historical Cost Statement of Financial Position as at 30 June 2011	
Assets	
Cash	9 000
Inventory	11 000
Plant and equipment (net)	22 800
Total Assets	42 800
Liabilities	
Bank loan	10 000
Net Assets	32 800
Represented by:	
Shareholders' Funds	
Paid-up capital	10 000
Retained earnings	22 800
	32 800

Cocoa Limited CoCoA Statement of Financial Position as at 30 June 2011	
Assets	
Cash	9 000
Inventory	18 000
Plant and equipment	29 000
Total Assets	56 000
Liabilities	
Bank loan	10 000
Net Assets	46 000
Represented by:	
Shareholders' Funds	
Paid-up capital	10 000
Retained earnings	24 000
Capital maintenance reserve	12 000
	46 000

What must be remembered is that, under CoCoA, when the inventory recorded above is sold for $18 000, no profit or loss will be recognised. Such gain was recognised when the inventory was purchased, with the gain being the difference between the expected retail price (net of related expenses) and the cost to Cocoa Limited. Hence, it is again emphasised, CoCoA involves a fundamental shift in revenue recognition principles compared with historical cost accounting.

As with other methods of accounting, a number of strengths and weaknesses have been associated with CoCoA. Considering the strengths, advocates of CoCoA have argued that by using one method of valuation for all assets (exit value) the resulting numbers can logically be added together (this is often referred to as 'additivity').[30] When CoCoA is adopted, there is also no need for arbitrary cost allocations for depreciation as depreciation will be based on movements in exit price.

Considering possible limitations, CoCoA has never gained widespread acceptance, despite being supported by a small number of widely respected academics (there was more support for replacement costs). Also, if CoCoA was implemented it would involve a fundamental and major shift in financial accounting (for example, including major shifts in revenue recognition points and major adjustments to asset valuations) and this in itself could lead to many unacceptable social and economic consequences.

The relevance of exit prices has also been questioned, particularly if we do not expect to sell assets (just as the relevance of replacement costs was questioned if we do not expect to replace the asset). Further, under CoCoA, assets of a specialised nature (such as a blast furnace) are considered to have no value because they cannot be separately disposed of. This is an assertion that is often challenged because it ignores the 'value in use' of an asset.[31] Further, is it appropriate to value all assets on the basis of their exit values if the entity is considered to be a going concern? Determination of exit values can also be expected to introduce a degree of subjectivity into the financial statements (relative to historical cost), particularly if the assets are unique.

CoCoA also requires assets to be valued separately with regard to their current cash equivalents, rather than as a bundle of assets. Hence, CoCoA would not recognise goodwill as an asset because it cannot be sold separately. Evidence shows that the value of assets sold together can be very different from the total amount that would be received if they were sold individually (Larson & Schattke, 1966).

Just as Chambers was critical of the Edwards and Bell model, Edwards and Bell were also critical of Chambers' approach. For example, Edwards (1975, p. 238) states:

> I am not convinced of the merit of adopting, as a normal basis for asset valuation in the going concern, exit prices in buyer markets. These are unusual values suitable for unusual situations. I would not object in principle to keeping track of such exit prices at all times and, as Solomons (1966) has suggested, substituting them for entry values when they are

---

30   This can be contrasted with the current situation where it is common to find that various classes of assets are valued using a different approach (for example, for inventory—lower of cost and net realisable value; for marketable securities—at fair value; for buildings—at cost or fair value; for debtors—at face value, less a provision for doubtful debts), yet they are simply added together to give a total asset amount.

31   In considering 'value in use', logically, if an asset's 'value in use' exceeds its market value, it will be retained, otherwise it will be sold. 'Value in use' is defined in IAS 36/AASB 136 as the present value of the future cash flows expected to be derived from an asset. Hence, the point might be that there has actually been a choice not to sell the assets that the entity has on hand (Solomons, 1966). Further, specialised assets might be of particular value to one entity but not to any others.

the lesser of the two and the firm has taken a definite decision not to replace the asset, or even the function it performs.

THE DEMAND FOR PRICE-ADJUSTED ACCOUNTING INFORMATION

One research method often used to assess the usefulness of particular disclosures is to look for a stock-market reaction (share price reaction) around the time of the release of the information, the rationale being that if share prices react to the disclosures then such disclosures must have information content. That is, the information impacts on the decisions made by individuals participating in the capital market. A number of studies have looked at the stock-market reaction to current cost and CPPA information. Results are inconclusive, with studies such as Ro (1980, 1981), Beaver, Christie and Griffin (1980), Gheyara and Boatsman (1980), Beaver and Landsman (1987), Murdoch (1986), Schaefer (1984), Dyckman (1969), Morris (1975) and Peterson (1975) finding limited evidence of any price changes around the time of disclosure of current cost information. (However, Lobo and Song (1989) and Bublitz, Freka and McKeown (1985) provide limited evidence that there is information content in current cost disclosures.)

While the majority of share price studies show little or no reaction to price-adjusted accounting information, it is possible that the failure to find a significant share price reaction might have been due to limitations in the research methods used. For example, there could have been other information released around the time of the release of the CCA/CPPA information. However, with the weight of research that indicates little or no reaction by the share market, it would be reasonable to believe that the market does not value such information when disclosed within the annual report. Of course there are a number of issues in why the capital market might not react to such information. Perhaps individuals or organisations are able to obtain this information from sources other than corporate annual reports, and hence, as the market is already aware of the information, no reaction would be expected when the annual reports are released.

Apart from analysing share price reactions, another way to investigate the apparent usefulness of particular information is to undertake surveys. Surveys of managers (for example, Ferguson and Wines, 1986) have indicated limited corporate support for CCA, with managers citing such issues as the expense, the limited benefits from disclosure, and the lack of agreement as to the appropriate approach to explain the limited support for CCA.

In the United States, and in relation to the relevance of FASB Statement No. 33 (which required a mixture of CCA and CPPA information), Elliot (1986, p. 33) states:

> FASB Statement No. 33 requires the disclosure of value information on one or two bases, either price level adjusted or current cost. Surveys taken since this rule became effective suggest that users do not find the information helpful, don't use it, and they say it doesn't tell them anything they didn't already know. Preparers of the information complain that it is a nuisance to assemble.

Given the above results, it could be said that, in general, there is limited evidence to support the view that the methods used to account for changing prices have been deemed to be successful in providing information of relevance to financial statement users. This is an interesting outcome, particularly given that many organisations over time have elected to provide CCA/CPPA information in their annual reports even when there was no requirement to do so, and also given that many organisations have actively lobbied for or against the particular methods of accounting. Adopting the method for disclosure purposes, or lobbying for it, implies that corporate management, at least, considered that the information was relevant and likely to impact on behaviour—a view at odds with some of the surveys and share price studies reported earlier.

In relation to research that has attempted to analyse the motivations underlying the corporate adoption of alternative accounting methods, an influential paper was one prepared by Watts and Zimmerman (1978). That paper is generally considered to be one of the most important papers in the development of Positive Accounting Theory (which is discussed in Chapter 7). The authors investigated the lobbying positions taken by corporate managers with respect to the FASB's 1974 discussion memorandum on general price level accounting (current purchasing power accounting). As this chapter has discussed, if general price level accounting were introduced, reported profits in times of rising prices would be reduced relative to profits reported under historical cost conventions. The reduction in profits would be due to such effects as higher depreciation and purchasing power losses due to holding net monetary assets.

Watts and Zimmerman proposed that the political process was a major factor in explaining which corporate managers were more likely to favour or oppose the introduction of general price level accounting. The political process itself is seen as a competition for wealth transfers. For example, some groups may lobby government to transfer wealth away from particular companies or industries (for example, through increased taxes, decreased tariff support, decreased subsidies, increases in award wages, more stringent licensing arrangements) and towards other organisations or groups otherwise considered to be poorly treated. Apart from government, groups such as consumer groups (perhaps through product boycotts), employee groups (through wage demands or strikes) and community interest groups (through impeding operations or lobbying government) can act to transfer wealth away from organisations through political processes.

The perspective of Watts and Zimmerman was that entities deemed to be politically visible are more likely to favour methods of accounting that allow them to reduce their reported profits. High profitability itself was considered to be one attribute that could lead to the unwanted (and perhaps costly) attention and scrutiny of particular corporations.

The corporate lobbying positions in the submissions made to the FASB are explained by Watts and Zimmerman on the basis of self-interest considerations (rather than any consideration of such issues as the 'public interest').[32] The study suggests that large firms (and large firms are considered to be more politically sensitive) favour general price level accounting because it enables them to report lower profits.[33,34]

---

32 As discussed in Chapter 7, and as already mentioned in earlier chapters, one of the central assumptions of Positive Accounting Theory is that all individual action is motivated by self-interest considerations, with that interest being directly tied to the goal of maximising an individual's own wealth.

33 Ball and Foster (1982), however, indicate that size can be a proxy for many things other than political sensitivity (such as industry membership).

34 Within the Watts and Zimmerman study many of the respondents were members of the oil industry and such industry members were also inclined to favour the introduction of general price level accounting. Consistent with the political cost hypothesis, 1974 (the time of the submissions) was a time of intense scrutiny of oil companies.

Other research has also shown that companies might support CCA for the political benefits it provides. In times of rising prices, the adoption of CCA (as with general price level accounting) can lead to reduced profits. In a New Zealand study, Wong (1988) investigated the accounting practices of New Zealand companies between 1977 and 1981 and found that corporations that adopted CCA had higher effective tax rates and larger market concentration ratios than entities that did not adopt CCA, both variables being suggestive of political visibility. In a UK study, Sutton (1988) found that politically sensitive companies were more likely to lobby in favour of CCA. Sutton investigated lobbying submissions made in the United Kingdom in relation to an exposure draft of a proposed accounting standard that recommended the disclosure of CCA information. Applying a Positive Accounting Theory perspective, he found support for a view that organisations that considered they would benefit from the requirement tended to lobby in support of it. Those expected to benefit were:

- capital-intensive firms, because it was expected that the adoption of CCA would lead to decreased profits (due to higher depreciation) and this would be particularly beneficial if the method was accepted for the purposes of taxation; and
- politically sensitive firms, as it would allow them to show reduced profits.

Examining possible perceived political 'benefits' of inflation-adjusted accounting information from a different perspective, Broadbent and Laughlin (2005) draw on debates in the United Kingdom in the 1970s to argue that the then British government considered CPPA as likely to produce undesirable economic impacts compared with CCA. The main issue was that the government believed CPPA accounts could foster divestment at a time when the UK economy needed investment. In support of their argument, Broadbent and Laughlin (2005) quote Bryer and Brignall (1985, p. 32) who state that in launching a governmental committee of inquiry to examine inflation accounting a government minister had commented that:

> inflation accounting ... involved issues much broader than pure accounting matters. The committee would 'take into account a broad range of issues including the implications for investment and efficiency; allocation of resources through the capital market; the need to restrain inflation in the UK'.[35]

PROFESSIONAL SUPPORT FOR VARIOUS APPROACHES TO ACCOUNTING FOR CHANGING PRICES

Over time, varying levels of support have been given to different approaches to accounting in times of rising prices. CPPA was generally favoured by accounting standard-setters from the 1960s to the mid-1970s, with a number of countries, including the United States, the United Kingdom, Canada, Australia, New Zealand, Ireland, Argentina, Chile and Mexico, issuing documents that supported the approach. For example, in the United States the American Institute of Certified

---

35 This quotation indicates the existence of broader perceived economic impacts of accounting regulation, as discussed in Chapter 3.

Public Accountants (AICPA) supported general price level restatement in Accounting Research Study No. 6 released in 1961. The Accounting Principles Board also supported the practice in Statement No. 3. Early in its existence, the FASB also issued an exposure draft supporting the use of general purchasing power—'Financial Reporting in Units of General Purchasing Power'—which required CPPA to be disclosed as supplementary information.

From about 1975, preference tended to shift to CCA. In 1976 the SEC released ASR 190 which required certain large organisations to provide supplementary information about 'the estimated current replacement cost of inventories and productive capacity at the end of the fiscal year for which a balance sheet is required and the approximate amount of cost of sales and depreciation based on replacement cost for the two most recent full fiscal years'. In Australia, a Statement of Accounting Practice (SAP 1) entitled 'Current Cost Accounting' was issued in 1983. Although not mandatory, SAP 1 recommended that reporting entities provide supplementary CCA information. In the United Kingdom, support for CCA was demonstrated by the Sandilands Committee (a government committee) in 1975. In 1980 the Accounting Standards Committee (UK) issued SSAP 16 which required supplementary disclosure of current cost data (SSAP 16 was withdrawn in 1985).

In the late 1970s and early 1980s many accounting standard-setters issued recommendations that favoured disclosure based on a mixture of CPPA and CCA. Such 'mixed' reporting recommendations were released in the United States, the United Kingdom, Canada, Australia, New Zealand, Ireland, West Germany and Mexico. For example, in 1979 the FASB released SFAS 33, which required a mixture of information, including:

- purchasing power gains and losses on net monetary assets;
- income determined on a current cost basis; and
- current costs of year-end inventory and property plant and equipment.

Around the mid-1980s, generally a time of falling inflation, accounting professions worldwide tended to move away from issues associated with accounting in times of changing prices. For example, in 1984 a member of the Accounting Standards Review Board (subsequently to become the Australian Accounting Standards Board), Mr Ron Cotton, was reported (*Australian Financial Review*, 19 January 1984) as saying that 'there are far more important things for the board to look at when current cost accounting does not have the support of the public or the government'. Mr Cotton also said he would be 'surprised and disappointed' if the board put current cost accounting high on the list of priorities when it met for the first time next in January 1984.

It is an interesting exercise to consider why particular methods of accounting did not gain and maintain professional support. Perhaps it was because (as indicated in Broadbent and Laughlin, 2005) the profession, like a number of researchers, questioned the relevance of the information, particularly in times of lower inflation. If they did question the relevance of the information to various parties (such as the capital market), it would be difficult for them to support regulation from a 'public interest' perspective, given the costs that would be involved in implementing a new system of accounting.[36]

---

36 Broadbent and Laughlin (2005) argue that the conception of 'public interest' will vary from person to person (or interest group to interest group) and will also change over time.

Even in the absence of concerns about the relevance of the information, standard-setters might have been concerned that a drastic change in our accounting conventions could cause widespread disruption and confusion in the capital markets and therefore might not be in the public interest. Although there have been numerous accounting controversies and disputes (for example, how to account for goodwill or research and development, or how to account for investments in associates), such controversies typically impact on only a small subset of accounts. Adopting a new model of accounting would have much more widespread effects, which again might not have been in the public interest.

It has also been speculated that the adoption of a new method of accounting could have consequences for the amount of taxation that the government ultimately collects from businesses. As Zeff and Dharan (1996, p. 632) state:

> Some governments fear that an accounting regimen of generally lower reported profits under current cost accounting (with physical capital maintenance) would lead to intensified pressure for a concomitant reform of corporate income tax law.

Throughout the 1970s and 1980s, many organisations opposed the introduction of alternative methods of accounting (alternative to historical cost). Corporate opposition to various alternative methods of accounting could also be explained by the notion of self-interest as embraced within the economic interest theory of regulation. Under historical cost accounting, management has a mechanism available to manage its reported profitability. Holding gains might not be recognised for income purposes until such time as the assets are sold. For example, an organisation might have acquired shares in another organisation some years earlier. In periods in which reported profits are expected to be lower than management wants, management could elect to sell some of the shares to offset other losses. If alternative methods of accounting were introduced, this ability to manipulate reported results could be lost.[37] Hence such corporations might have lobbied government, the basis of the submissions being rooted in self-interest. Because there are typically corporate or business representatives on most standard-setting bodies, there is also the possibility that corporations/ business interests were able to capture the standard-setting process (Walker, 1987).

As already seen in this chapter, there is some evidence that accounting information adjusted to take account of changing prices might not be relevant to the decision-making processes of those parties involved in the capital market (as reflected by various share price studies) and hence the alternative models of accounting might not be favoured by analysts. (Accepting the private economic interest theory of regulation, analysts might have little to gain personally if the alternative methods of accounting were introduced.)

Of course we will never know for sure why particular parties did not favour particular accounting models, but what we can see is that alternative explanations can be provided from public interest theory, capture theory or the economic interest theory of regulation—theories that were discussed at greater length in earlier chapters.

Throughout the CCA/CPPA debates a number of key academics continued to promote their favoured methods of accounting (and some continued to do so throughout the 1990s), even going as far as to release their own exposure drafts (see Accounting Headline 5.3). One can speculate about what drove them—was it the public interest or was it self-interest? What do you think?

---

37 In recent years the discretion of management in relation to the measurement of equity investments has been reduced. IAS 39/AASB 139 stipulates a general requirement that such investments shall be measured at fair value.

Australian, 3 November 1975, p. 5

Chambers drafts a final method

Professor R. J. Chambers of the University of Sydney has dropped a bombshell on the accounting profession by issuing his own 'exposure draft' on accounting for inflation.

Professor Chambers' pet method —dubbed Continuously Contemporary Accounting (CoCoA)—rivals the two exposure drafts already issued by the Institute of Chartered Accountants and the Australian Society of Accountants.

These cover current purchasing power (CPP) and current value accounting (CVA). The drafts are open for comment and suggestions from the profession until December 31.

Professor Chambers' stand is certain to fragment even further the profession's very lively debate on the most acceptable method. Up until now CVA has been acknowledged to have a slight lead over CPP.

He includes an evaluation of the three methods in his exposure draft. Answering a series of rhetorical questions, his own method comes out clearly on top.

He also says CPP and CVA lead to odd consequences in accounts because they are only partial treatments of changes in prices and price levels.

'The prices of the particular assets of a firm cannot be expected to move at the same rate (or even in the same direction) as a general price index.

CoCoA realises this fact, which is ignored by CPP—and also takes into account the fall in purchasing power of actual net assets which is ignored by CVA', he says.

The debate is far from settled as to which method of accounting is most appropriate in accounting for changing prices. While debate in this area has generally abated since the mid-1980s, it is very possible that, if levels of inflation return to their previously high levels, such debates will again be ignited. Various authors have developed accounting models that differ in many respects. Some of these differences are due to fundamental differences of opinion about the role of accounting and the sort of information necessary for effective decision making. Because information generated by systems of accounting based on the historical cost convention is used in many decisions, major change in accounting conventions would conceivably have widespread social and economic impacts. This in itself will restrict any major modifications/changes to our (somewhat outdated) accounting system. This perspective was reflected in the 1960s, and arguably the perspective is just as relevant now.

As an example of how the profession has typically been reluctant to implement major reforms, consider activities undertaken in 1961 and 1962, when the Accounting Research Division of the American Institute of Certified Public Accountants (AICPA) commissioned studies by Moonitz (1961) and by Sprouse and Moonitz (1962). In these documents the authors proposed that accounting measurement systems be changed from historical cost to a system based on current values. However, prior to the release of the Sprouse and Moonitz study the Accounting Principles Board of the AICPA stated in relation to the Moonitz and the Sprouse and Moonitz studies that 'while these studies are a valuable contribution to accounting principles, they are too radically different from generally accepted principles for acceptance at this time' (Statement by the Accounting Principles Board, AICPA, April 1962).

While this chapter has emphasised various issues and debates associated with how best to measure the financial performance of an entity in times when prices are changing, it must be remembered that financial performance is only one facet of the total performance of an entity.

As seen in Chapter 9, there is much debate about how to measure and report information on the social and environmental performance of reporting entities, and as with the debate considered in this chapter, that debate is far from settled. The practice of accounting generates a multitude of interesting debates.

CHAPTER SUMMARY

This chapter has explored different models of accounting that have been developed to provide financial information in periods of rising prices. These models have been developed because of the perceived limitations of historical cost accounting, particularly in times of rising prices. Critics of historical cost accounting suggest that, because historical cost adopts a capital maintenance perspective which is tied to maintaining financial capital intact, it tends to overstate profits in periods of rising prices. Historical cost accounting adopts an assumption that the purchasing power of currency remains constant over time. Debate about the best model of accounting to use in periods of rising prices was vigorous in the 1960s through to the mid-1980s. During this time, inflation levels tended to be relatively high. Since then, inflation levels internationally have tended to be low and the debate about which model to adopt to adjust for rising prices has waned. Nevertheless, there has been a general movement by regulators such as the International Accounting Standards Board (IASB) and the Australian Accounting Standards Board (AASB) towards the use of fair values in various accounting standards—although the adoption of fair value tends to be on a piecemeal basis as particular accounting standards are developed. With this said, however, there are still various assets that are measured on the basis of historical costs.[38]

A number of alternative models have been suggested. For example, current purchasing power accounting (CPPA) was one of the earlier models to be developed. CPPA was supported by a number of professional accounting bodies during the 1960s and 1970s, although support then shifted to current cost accounting. CPPA uses numbers generated by the historical cost accounting as the basis of the financial statements, and at the end of each period CPPA applies a price index, typically a general price index, to adjust the historical cost numbers. For balance sheet (statement of financial position) purposes, adjustments are made to non-monetary assets. Monetary items are not adjusted by the price index. However, although monetary items are not adjusted for disclosure purposes, holding monetary items will lead to gains or losses in purchasing power that are recognised in the period's profit or loss. No gains or losses are recorded in relation to holding non-monetary items. One of the advantages of using CPPA is that it is easy to apply. It simply uses the historical cost accounting numbers that are already available and applies a price index to these numbers. A disadvantage is that the adjusted prices may provide a poor reflection of the actual value of the items in question.

Another model of accounting is current cost accounting (CCA). It uses actual valuations of assets, typically based on replacement costs, and operating income is calculated after consideration of the replacement costs of the assets used in the production and sale cycle. Non-monetary assets are adjusted to take account of changes in replacement costs, and depreciation

---

38 For example, inventory and property, plant and equipment where the entity has elected to adopt the 'cost model'.

expenses are also adjusted on the basis of changes in replacement costs. While not in use today, CCA attracted support from professional accounting bodies in the early 1980s. Opponents of CCA argued that replacement costs have little relevance if an entity is not considering replacing an asset, and, further, that replacement costs might not accurately reflect the current market values of the assets in question.

The final model of accounting considered was Continuously Contemporary Accounting (CoCoA). One key objective of CoCoA was to provide information about an entity's capacity to adapt to changing circumstances, with profit being directly related to changes in adaptive capacity. Profit is calculated as the amount that can be distributed while maintaining the adaptive capital intact. CoCoA does not differentiate between realised and unrealised gains. In support of CoCoA, it requires only one type of valuation for all assets (based on exit prices). There is no need for arbitrary cost allocations, such as for depreciation. Criticisms of CoCoA include the relevance of values based on exit (selling) prices if there is no intention of selling an item. Also, many people have challenged the perspective that if an asset cannot be sold separately it has no value (for example goodwill). It has also been argued that valuing items on the basis of sales prices can introduce an unacceptable degree of subjectivity into accounting, particularly if the items in question are quite specialised and rarely traded.

QUESTIONS

5.1 What assumptions, if any, does historical cost accounting make about the purchasing power of the currency?

5.2 List some of the criticisms that can be made of historical cost accounting when it is applied in times of rising prices.

5.3 Why do you think that corporate management might prefer to be allowed to use historical costs rather than being required to value assets on the basis of current values?

5.4 As shown in this chapter, Mautz (1973) made the following statement:
> Accounting is what it is today not so much because of the desire of accountants as because of the influence of businessmen. If those who make management and investment decisions had not found financial reports based on historical cost useful over the years, changes in accounting would long since have been made.

Evaluate the statement.

5.5 What is the 'additivity' problem that Chambers refers to?

5.6 Explain the difference between income derived from the viewpoint of maintaining financial capital (as in historical cost accounting) and income derived from a system of ensuring that physical capital remains intact.

5.7 In current purchasing power accounting:
(a) Why is it necessary to consider monetary assets separately from non-monetary assets?
(b) Why will holding monetary assets lead to a purchasing power loss, but holding non-monetary assets not lead to a purchasing power loss?

5.8 What is the basis of Chambers' argument against valuing assets on the basis of replacement costs?

5.9 If Continuously Contemporary Accounting is adopted and an organisation is involved with selling goods, when would the profit from the sale of goods be recognised? How does this compare with historical cost accounting?

5.10 What are holding gains, and how are holding gains treated if current cost accounting is applied? Do we need to differentiate between realised and unrealised holding gains?

5.11 Should 'profits' that result from holding gains be allowed to be distributed to shareholders? Explain your view.

5.12 What are some of the major strengths and weaknesses of historical cost accounting?

5.13 What are some of the major strengths and weaknesses of current purchasing power accounting?

5.14 What are some of the major strengths and weaknesses of current cost accounting (applying replacement costs)?

5.15 What are some of the major strengths and weaknesses of Continuously Contemporary Accounting?

5.16 Evaluate the statement of Chambers (1995, p. 82) that 'in the context of judgement of the past and decision making for the future, the products of Current Value Accounting of the Edwards and Bell variety are irrelevant and misleading. No budget can properly proceed except from an up-to-date statement of the amount of money's worth available to enter the budget period'.

5.17 Evaluate the statement of Edwards (1975, p. 238) that 'I am not convinced of the merit of adopting, as a normal basis for asset valuation in the going concern, exit prices in buyer markets. These are unusual values suitable for unusual situations. I would not object in principle to keeping track of such exit prices at all times and, as Solomons (1966) has suggested, substituting them for entry values when they are the lesser of the two and the firm has taken a definite decision not to replace the asset or even the function it performs'.

5.18 Despite the efforts of authors such as Chambers, Edwards and Bell, and Sterling, historical cost accounting has maintained its position of dominance in how we do financial accounting. Why do you think that historical cost accounting has remained the principal method of accounting?

5.19 As indicated in this chapter, various studies have provided support for a view that CCA/CPPA is of little relevance to users of financial statements. Nevertheless, numerous organisations lobbied in support of the methods, as well as voluntarily providing such information in their annual reports. Why do you think this is so?

5.20 The IASB *Framework for the Preparation and Presentation of Financial Statements* does not prescribe a specific approach to measurement. However, in recent years accounting standards have been released which have shown a movement away from historical costs and a movement towards the use of fair values. Why do you think this is occurring? Further, why do you think that conceptual frameworks have not been amended to suggest an alternative to historical costs—such as the use of fair values?

5.21 According to Watts and Zimmerman (1978), what factors appeared to motivate corporate management to lobby in support of general price level accounting (current purchase power accounting)?

REFERENCES

Ball, R. & G. Foster (1982), 'Corporate financial reporting: a methodological review of empirical research', *Studies on Current Research Methodologies in Accounting: A Critical Evaluation,* supplement to *Journal of Accounting Research,* 20(Supplement), pp. 161–234.

Beaver, W., A. Christie & P. Griffin (1980), 'The information content of SEC ASR 190', *Journal of Accounting and Economics,* 2.

Beaver, W. & W. Landsman, (1987), 'The Incremental Information Content of FAS 33 Disclosures', Research Report, Stamford: FASB.

Broadbent, J. & R. Laughlin (2005), 'Government concerns and tensions in accounting standard setting: the case of accounting for the private finance initiative in the UK', *Accounting and Business Research,* 21(1), pp. 75–97.

Bryer, R. & S. Brignall, (1985), 'The GAAP in inflation accounting debate', *Accountancy,* pp. 32–33.

Bublitz, B., T. Freka & J. McKeown (1985), 'Market association tests and FASB statement 33 disclosures: a re-examination', *Journal of Accounting Research* (Supplement), pp. 1–23.

Canning, J. B. (1929), *The Economics of Accountancy: A Critical Analysis of Accounting Theory,* New York: Ronald Press.

Chambers, R. J. (1955), 'Blueprint for a theory of accounting', *Accounting Research* (January), pp. 17–55.

Chambers, R. J. (1966), *Accounting, Evaluation and Economic Behavior,* Englewood Cliffs, NJ: Prentice Hall.

Chambers, R. J. (1995), 'An introduction to price variation and inflation accounting research', in S. Jones, C. Romana & J. Ratnatunga (eds), *Accounting Theory: A Contemporary Review,* Sydney: Harcourt Brace.

Dyckman, T. R. (1969), *Studies in Accounting Research No. 1: Investment Analysis and General Price Level Adjustments,* USA: American Accounting Association.

Edwards, E. (1975), 'The state of current value accounting', *The Accounting Review,* 50(2), pp. 235–45.

Edwards, E. O. & P. W. Bell (1961), *The Theory and Measurement of Business Income,* Berkeley: University of California Press.

Elliot, R. K. (1986), 'Dinosaurs, passenger pigeons, and financial accountants', *World,* pp. 32–35, as reproduced in S. A. Zeff & B. G. Dharan (1996), *Readings and Notes on Financial Accounting,* 5th edn, New York: McGraw-Hill.

Ferguson, C. & G. Wines (1986), 'Incidence of the use of current cost accounting in published annual financial statements', *Accounting Forum* (March).

Gheyara, K. & J. Boatsman (1980), 'Market reaction to the 1976 replacement cost disclosures', *Journal of Accounting and Economics,* 2(2), pp. 107–25.

Grady, P. (1965), *An Inventory of Generally Accepted Accounting Principles for Business Enterprises, Accounting Research Study No. 7,* New York: AICPA.

Gray, R., D. Owen & C. Adams (1996), *Accounting and Accountability: Changes and Challenges in Corporate Social and Environmental Reporting,* London: Prentice Hall.

Hicks, J. R. (1946), *Value and Capital,* Oxford: Oxford University Press.

Larson, K. & R. Schattke (1966), 'Current cash equivalent, additivity and financial action', *The Accounting Review,* 41(4), pp. 634–41.

Lobo, G. & I. Song (1989), 'The incremental information in SFAS 33 income disclosures over historical cost income and its cash and accrual components', *The Accounting Review,* 64(2), pp. 329–43.

MacNeal, K. (1970), *Truth in Accounting,* originally published in 1939 edn, Kansas: Scholars Book Company.

Mautz, R. K. (1973), 'A few words for historical cost', *Financial Executive* (January), pp. 23–27 and 93–98.

Moonitz, M. (1961), *The Basic Postulates of Accounting, Accounting Research Study No. 1,* New York: AICPA.

Morris, R. C. (1975), 'Evidence of the impact of inflation on share prices', *Accounting and Business Research* (Spring), pp. 87–95.

Murdoch, B. (1986), 'The information content of FAS 33 returns on equity', *The Accounting Review,* 61(2), pp. 273–87.

Paton, W. A. (1922), *Accounting Theory,* Kansas: Scholars Book Co, reprinted 1973.

Peterson, R. J. (1975), 'A portfolio analysis of general price-level restatement', *The Accounting Review,* 50(3), pp. 525–32.

Riahi-Belkaoui, A. (2004), *Accounting Theory,* 5th edn, London: Thomson Learning.

Ro, B. T. (1980), 'The adjustment of security returns to the disclosure of replacement cost accounting information', *Journal of Accounting and Economics,* 2(2), pp. 159–89.

Ro, B. T. (1981), 'The disclosure of replacement cost accounting data and its effect on transaction volumes', *The Accounting Review,* 56(1), pp. 70–84.

Roberts, D. L., J. J. Staunton & L. L. Hagan (1995), *Accounting for Self-Generating and Regenerating Assets, Discussion Paper No. 23,* Melbourne: Australian Accounting Research Foundation.

Schaefer, T. (1984), 'The information content of current cost income relative to dividends and historical cost income', *Journal of Accounting Research,* 22(2), pp. 647–56.

Solomons, D. (1966), 'An overview of exit price accounting', *ABACUS* (December).

Sprouse, R. & M. Moonitz (1962), *A Tentative Set of Broad Accounting Principles for Business Enterprises, Accounting Research Study No. 3,* New York: American Institute of Certified Public Accountants.

Sterling, R. R. (1970a), 'On theory construction and verification', *The Accounting Review,* 45(4), pp. 444–57.

Sterling, R. R. (1970b), *Theory of the Measurement of Enterprise Income,* USA: University of Kansas Press.

Sutton, T. G. (1988), 'The proposed introduction of current cost accounting in the UK: determinants of corporate preference', *Journal of Accounting and Economics,* 10(2), pp. 127–49.

Sweeney, H. W. (1964), *Stabilised Accounting,* originally published in 1936, Holt Rinehart & Winston.

Walker, R. G. (1987), 'Australia's ASRB: a case study of political activity and regulatory capture', *Accounting and Business Research,* 17(67), pp. 269–86.

Watts, R. & J. Zimmerman (1978), 'Towards a positive theory of the determination of accounting standards', *The Accounting Review,* 53(1), pp. 112–34.

Wong, J. (1988), 'Economic incentives for the voluntary disclosure of current cost financial statements', *Journal of Accounting and Economics,* 10(2), pp. 151–67.

Zeff, S. A. & B. G. Dharan (1996), *Readings and Notes on Financial Accounting,* 5th edn, New York: McGraw-Hill.

CHAPTER 6

NORMATIVE THEORIES OF ACCOUNTING—THE CASE OF CONCEPTUAL FRAMEWORK PROJECTS

LEARNING OBJECTIVES

On completing this chapter readers should:

- understand the role that conceptual frameworks can play in the practice of financial reporting;
- be aware of the history of the development of the various existing conceptual framework projects;
- be able to identify, explain and critically evaluate the various building blocks that have been developed within various conceptual framework projects;
- be able to identify some of the perceived advantages and disadvantages that arise from the establishment and development of conceptual frameworks;
- be aware of some recent initiatives being jointly undertaken by the International Accounting Standards Board and the Financial Accounting Standards Board to develop an improved conceptual framework of financial reporting;
- be able to identify some factors, including political factors, that might help or hinder the development of conceptual framework projects;
- be able to explain which groups within society are likely to benefit from the establishment and development of conceptual framework projects.

OPENING ISSUES

For many years the practice of financial accounting lacked a generally accepted theory that clearly enunciated the objectives of financial reporting, outlined the required qualitative characteristics of financial information, or provided clear guidance as to when and how to recognise and measure the various elements of financial accounting. In the absence of an accepted theory, accounting standards tended to be developed in a rather *ad hoc* manner, with inconsistencies between the various standards. For example, some accounting standards relating to different classes of assets used different recognition and measurement criteria. It has been argued that the development of a conceptual framework would lead to improved financial reporting, and this improved reporting would provide benefits to financial statement readers as it would enable them to make more informed resource allocation decisions. Do you agree with this argument, and what is the basis of your view?

INTRODUCTION

Chapter 5 considered a number of normative theories developed by some notable accounting academics to address various accounting issues associated with how financial accounting should be undertaken in the presence of changing prices (typically increasing prices associated with inflation). These theories included current purchasing power accounting, current cost accounting and Continuously Contemporary Accounting (or exit price accounting). As revealed in Chapter 5, the normative theories, which represented quite significant departures from existing accounting practice, failed to be embraced by professional accounting bodies and regulators throughout the world, and with the decline in levels of inflation within most countries the debate about the relative benefits of alternative approaches of accounting for changing prices has subsided. However, in recent times there has nevertheless been an increasing propensity for accounting standard-setters to adopt fair value as the basis for measuring many assets, and to thereby move away from the use of historical cost. The adoption of fair value will take into account many of the effects of changing prices.

While the various normative theories discussed in Chapter 5, and which were advanced to deal with changing prices, did not ultimately gain the support of accounting professions, professional accounting bodies in countries such as the United States, the United Kingdom, Canada, Australia and New Zealand, as well as the International Accounting Standards Committee (which subsequently became the International Accounting Standards Board), have developed conceptual frameworks for accounting, which in themselves can be considered to constitute *normative theories of accounting*. This chapter considers what is meant by the term 'conceptual framework' and why particular professional bodies thought there was a need to develop them. There are numerous perceived advantages and disadvantages associated with conceptual frameworks, and the chapter looks at certain arguments that suggest that conceptual frameworks play a part in *legitimising* the existence of the accounting profession. Within Australia, the conceptual framework released by the International Accounting Standards Board, which is known as the *IASB Framework for the Preparation and Presentation of Financial Statements* (or simply the IASB Framework), is used*. Therefore, a deal of the discussion in the chapter refers to the guidance provided in the IASB Framework. However, as the chapter explains, there is currently a joint initiative being undertaken by the IASB and the US Financial Accounting Standards Board (FASB) to develop a revised conceptual framework. This work is being undertaken in a number of stages and the expectation is that the framework will not be completed for a number of years. Some recent publications that have already emanated from the joint efforts of the IASB and the FASB are referred to at various points in the chapter, as such publications provide an indication of what prescriptions might be embodied within a future conceptual framework.

WHAT IS A CONCEPTUAL FRAMEWORK OF ACCOUNTING?

There is no definitive view of what constitutes a 'conceptual framework'. The Financial Accounting Standards Board (FASB) in the United States, which developed one of the first conceptual frameworks in accounting, defined its conceptual framework as 'a coherent system of interrelated objectives and fundamentals that is expected to lead to consistent standards' (Statement of Financial Accounting Concepts No. 1: *Objectives of Financial Reporting by Business Enterprises*, 1978).

Chapter 1 provided a definition of 'theory' (from the *Oxford English Dictionary*) as 'A scheme or system of ideas or statements held as an explanation or account of a group of facts or phenomena'. This definition was similar to that provided by the accounting researcher Hendriksen (1970, p. 1). He defined a theory as 'a coherent set of hypothetical, conceptual and pragmatic principles forming the general framework of reference for a field of inquiry'. Looking at these definitions of 'theory' and looking at the FASB's definition of its conceptual framework, it is reasonable to argue that the conceptual framework attempts to provide a theory of accounting, and one that appears quite structured. Because conceptual frameworks provide a great deal of prescription (that is, they prescribe certain actions, such as when to recognise an asset for financial statement purposes) they are considered to have normative characteristics. According to the FASB, the conceptual framework 'prescribes the nature, function and limits of financial accounting and reporting' (as stated in Statement of Financial Accounting Concepts No. 1: *Objectives of Financial Reporting by Business Enterprises*, 1978). As we know from earlier chapters, a theory that 'prescribes' practice is considered to be a normative theory.

In recent years, the US Financial Accounting Standards Board (FASB) and the International Accounting Standards Board (IASB) have been undertaking an initiative to develop, on a joint basis, an improved conceptual framework for financial reporting. In July 2006 the FASB and the IASB jointly published a discussion paper, *Preliminary Views on an Improved Conceptual Framework for Financial Reporting: The Objective of Financial Reporting and Qualitative Characteristics of Decision-useful Financial Reporting Information*. That paper was the first in a series of publications developed by the two boards as part of the project to develop a common conceptual framework for financial reporting. The boards received nearly 200 responses to the discussion paper and after considering the various comments they released an exposure draft in May 2008. The document was entitled *Exposure Draft of an Improved Conceptual Framework for Financial Reporting* and this phase of the project specifically addressed the objective of financial reporting and the qualitative characteristics and constraints of decision-useful financial reporting information. According to the exposure draft, the conceptual framework is:

> a coherent system of concepts that flow from an objective. The objective of financial reporting is the foundation of the framework. The other concepts provide guidance on identifying the boundaries of financial reporting; selecting the transactions, other events and circumstances to be represented; how they should be recognised and measured (or disclosed); and how they should be summarised and communicated in financial reports.

As this definition indicates, the objective of financial reporting is the fundamental building block for the conceptual framework being developed by the IASB and the FASB. Hence, if particular individuals or parties disagreed with the objective identified by the IASB and the FASB, they would most likely disagree with the various prescriptions provided within the revised conceptual framework.[1]

The view taken by people involved in developing conceptual frameworks tends to be that if the practice of financial reporting is to be developed logically and consistently (which might be important for creating public confidence in the practice of financial accounting) there first needs to be some consensus on important issues such as what is actually meant by *financial reporting* and what its scope should be, what organisational characteristics or attributes indicate that an entity should produce general purpose financial statements, what the objective of financial reporting is, what *qualitative characteristics* financial information should possess, what the elements of financial reporting are, what measurement rules should be employed in relation to the various elements of accounting, and so forth. It has been proposed that unless there is some agreement on fundamental issues, such as those mentioned, accounting standards will be developed in a rather *ad hoc* or piecemeal manner, with limited consistency between the various accounting standards developed over time.

It is perhaps somewhat illogical to consider how to account for a particular item of expenditure if there has not been agreement in the first place on what the *objective* of financial accounting actually is, or indeed on issues such as what an *asset* is or what a *liability* is. Nevertheless, for many years accounting standards were developed in many countries in the absence of conceptual frameworks. For example, the United Kingdom's Accounting Standards Board initiated a conceptual framework development project in 1991. Within Australia the first Statement of Accounting Concept (SAC 1: Definition of the Reporting Entity) was released in 1990. The Australian conceptual framework—until 2005—was comprised of four Statements of Accounting Concepts (SACs). However, recommendations related to the practice of accounting first started being released in both countries in the 1940s, followed some years later by accounting standards. By the time the United Kingdom's conceptual framework (entitled *The Statement of Principles*) was issued in 1999, there were already many accounting standards in place. A similar situation existed within Australia, with many accounting standards already being in place prior to the release of SAC 1 in 1990. In the absence of a conceptual framework, and reflective of the lack of agreement in many key areas of financial reporting, there was a degree of inconsistency between the various accounting standards that were being released in the United Kingdom and in Australia. This absence of a conceptual framework led to a great deal of criticism. As Horngren (1981, p. 94) states:

> All regulatory bodies have been flayed because they have used piecemeal approaches, solving one accounting issue at a time. Observers have alleged that not enough tidy rationality has been used in the process of accounting policymaking. Again and again, critics have cited a need for a conceptual framework.

In developing a conceptual framework for accounting, there are a number of 'building blocks' that must be developed. The framework must be developed in a particular order, with some

---

1   The objective of financial reporting as provided in the draft conceptual framework document released by the IASB and FASB in 2008 is stated as follows: 'The objective of general purpose financial reporting is to provide financial information about the reporting entity that is useful to present and potential equity investors, lenders and other creditors in making decisions in their capacity as capital providers. Information that is decision-useful to capital providers may also be useful to other users of financial reporting who are not capital providers.'

issues necessarily requiring agreement before work can move on to subsequent 'building blocks'. Figure 6.1 provides an overview of the framework developed in the late 1980s by the International Accounting Standards Committee (IASC), and which was later adopted by the IASC's successor— the International Accounting Standards Board (IASB). While initially referred to as the IASC Framework, it is now referred to as the *IASB Framework for the Preparation and Presentation of Financial Statements* (or simply the IASB Framework). This is the framework that Australia and other countries that have adopted International Financial Reporting Standards (IFRSs) are to use until such time as the new conceptual framework being developed by the IASB and the FASB is released. In Australia the IASB Framework is referred to as the AASB Framework.

At this point it should be noted that within Australia the Australian Accounting Standards Board (AASB) had been responsible for the development of a conceptual framework of accounting, with the framework seeking to define the nature, subject, purpose and broad content of general purpose financial reporting. As a result of the 2002 decision by the Australian Financial

Figure 6.1 Components of a conceptual framework (based on the IASC/IASB Framework)

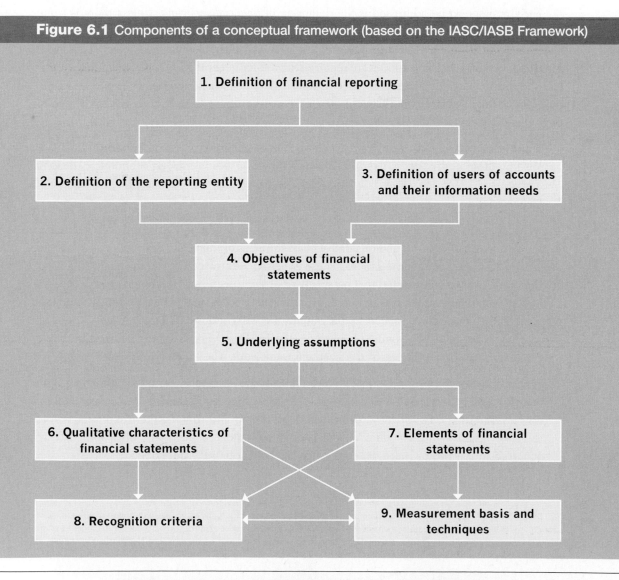

Reporting Council (FRC) that Australia would adopt accounting standards issued by the IASB by 2005, there was a related requirement that Australia also adopt the conceptual framework that had been developed by the IASB (or, more precisely, by its predecessor, the IASC). In some respects this represented somewhat of a backward step, as it is generally considered that the Australian conceptual framework was more robust than the IASB Framework. However, as IFRSs have been developed in accordance with the IASB Framework, and as Australia adopted IFRSs, then Australia also had to adopt the IASB Framework. This is also the case in a number of other countries that have adopted IFRSs. As already noted, and as discussed later in the chapter, in 2005 the IASB and FASB commenced joint efforts to develop a revised conceptual framework. The timing of the completion of the revised conceptual framework is uncertain.

The IASC/IASB view of a conceptual framework is also broadly consistent with the definitions in the conceptual frameworks developed by some individual countries, although the relative emphasis given to the different components tends to vary slightly from one framework to another.

The first issue to be addressed is the definition of *financial reporting*. Unless there is some agreement on this it would be difficult to construct a framework for financial reporting. Having determined what financial reporting means, attention is then turned to the subject of financial reporting, specifically which entities are required to produce general purpose financial statements[2] and the likely characteristics of the users of these statements. Attention is then turned to the objective of financial reporting. The objective of general purpose financial reporting provided in the IASB Framework is deemed to be:

> to provide information about the financial position, performance and changes in financial position of an entity that is useful to a wide range of users in making economic decisions (paragraph 12 of the IASB *Framework for the Preparation and Presentation of Financial Statements*).

If it is accepted that this is the objective of financial reporting, the next step is to determine the basic underlying assumptions and qualitative characteristics of financial information necessary to allow users to make economic decisions. These issues are addressed later in the chapter.

Over time, it is to be expected that perspectives of the role of financial reporting will change. Consistent with this view, there is an expectation by many people, including accounting standard-setters, that the development of conceptual frameworks will continue. They will evolve over time. This view is consistent with comments made by the IASB and FASB in relation to work being undertaken in developing the revised conceptual framework. They state (IASB 2008a, p. 9):

> To provide the best foundation for developing principle-based common standards, the boards have undertaken a joint project to develop a common and improved conceptual framework. The goals for the project include updating and refining the existing concepts to reflect changes in markets, business practices and the economic environment that occurred in the two or more decades since the concepts were developed.

---

2   Conceptual frameworks of accounting relate to general purpose financial reporting (which meets the needs of a multitude of user groups, many of which have information needs in common) as opposed to special purpose financial reports (special purpose financial reports are specifically designed to meet the information needs of a specific user or group). We consider definitions of general purpose financial reporting in more depth later in this chapter.

In the discussion that follows, the history of the development of conceptual frameworks in different countries is considered. It will be seen that conceptual frameworks are largely prescriptive, or normative in approach, for example indicating how the elements of accounting (the elements being assets, liabilities, income, expenses and equity) are defined and when they should be recognised. However, in certain cases, because of apparent coercion by powerful interest groups, parts of some conceptual frameworks became descriptive of current practice, with limited implications for changing existing accounting practices.

A BRIEF OVERVIEW OF THE HISTORY OF THE DEVELOPMENT OF CONCEPTUAL FRAMEWORKS

A number of countries, such as the United States, the United Kingdom, Ireland, Canada, Australia and New Zealand, have undertaken various activities directed to the development of a conceptual framework. The IASC also undertook work to develop a conceptual framework. There are many similarities in (and some differences between) the various conceptual frameworks developed in the different jurisdictions.[3] It is arguable whether any standard-setter anywhere in the world has developed what could be construed as a complete conceptual framework.

One country particularly active in developing frameworks in relation to financial reporting was the United States. Initially, some of the work involved developing *prescriptive theories* of how accounting *should* be undertaken, while other research related to the development of *descriptive theories* of how accounting was generally performed. For example, in 1961 and 1962 the Accounting Research Division of the American Institute of Certified Public Accountants (AICPA) commissioned studies by Moonitz (1961) and Sprouse and Moonitz (1962). These theorists prescribed that accounting practice should move towards a system based on current values rather than historical cost. This work was considered 'too radically different from generally accepted principles' (AICPA, 1973) and was abandoned by the profession. The AICPA then commissioned Grady to develop a theory of accounting. Grady's theory (1965) was basically descriptive of existing practice (it was based on inductive reasoning—as described in Chapter 1 of this book), thereby being quite uncontroversial. His work led to the release of Accounting Principles Board (APB) Statement No. 4, *Basic Concepts and Accounting Principles Underlying the Financial Statements of Business Enterprises*, in 1970. As it was not controversial and simply

---

3 This raises issues associated with the possible duplication of effort and whether it might have been more cost efficient for the various countries to pool their resources and develop one unified conceptual framework. However, as Kenneth Most states in Staunton (1984, p. 87) when comparing the Australian and US conceptual frameworks, 'a conceptual framework differs from a straight-jacket; one size does not fit all. The kind of doctrinaire thinkers who have dominated the standard-setting process in this country (United States) are not subject to the same economic, sociological, and professional influences that would affect Australians faced with a similar task'. Consistent with this view, Chapter 4 considered how issues such as culture are used to explain differences between the rules released by standard-setters in different countries. However, with the increasing use of IFRSs internationally, and the related adoption of the IASB Framework, it appears that global uniformity (and therefore a 'one size fits all' approach), is deemed by accounting regulators to be more important than the cultural differences that might influence the information requirements of particular nations or cultures. It would also appear that, given the joint work being undertaken by the IASB and the FASB, in future years we will see the introduction of a single conceptual framework for use internationally—again ignoring the view that different countries have different information demands and expectations.

reflected generally accepted accounting principles of the time, APB Statement No. 4 had a high probability of being acceptable to the AICPA's constituency (Miller & Reading, 1986).

THE TRUEBLOOD REPORT

Although APB Statement No. 4 did not cause great controversy, the accounting profession was under some criticism for the apparent lack of any real theoretical framework.[4] The generally accepted accounting principles of the time allowed for much diversity in accounting treatments and this was seen by many to be a problem. There was an absence of agreement on key issues about the role and objectives of financial reporting, appropriate definition, recognition and measurement rules for the elements of accounting, and so on. Responding to the criticism, the AICPA formed the Trueblood Committee (named after the committee chairperson, Robert Trueblood) in 1971. The committee produced *The Trueblood Report* (released in 1973 by the AICPA), which listed twelve objectives of accounting and seven qualitative characteristics that financial information should possess (relevance and materiality, form and substance, reliability, freedom from bias, comparability, consistency, understandability).

Objective 1 of the report was that financial statements are to provide information useful for making economic decisions. That is, there was a focus on the information needs of financial statement users. This objective, which was carried forward to subsequent documents, indicated that decision usefulness (as opposed to concepts such as stewardship) was a primary objective of financial statements.[5,6] This can be contrasted with previous perspectives of the role of accounting. For example, Accounting Terminology Bulletin No.1 issued in 1953 by the AICPA made no reference to the information needs of users. It stated:

> Accounting is the art of recording, classifying and summarizing in a significant manner and in terms of money, transactions and events which are in part at least of a financial character, and interpreting the results thereof.

Objective 2 provided by the Trueblood Committee stated that financial statements are primarily to serve those users who have limited authority, ability or resources to obtain information and who rely on financial statements as the principal source of information about an organisation's activities. This objective, which was also carried forward in subsequent work, was interesting in that it tended to be a departure from much research that was being carried out at the time. A great deal of research being undertaken in the late 1960s and thereafter had embraced the *Efficient Markets Hypothesis* (discussed more fully in Chapter 10) that markets react quickly to impound the information content of publicly available information, whenever that information first becomes publicly available. Researchers working with the Efficient Markets Hypothesis considered that, as long as the information was publicly available to somebody, and

---

4   In relation to APB Statement No. 4, Peasnell (1982, p. 245) notes that 'at best it was a defensive, descriptive document'.

5   This focus on decision users' needs was also embraced in an earlier document, *A Statement of Basic Accounting Theory*, issued by the American Accounting Association in 1966. It was also embraced in APB Statement No. 4 released in 1970.

6   'Decision usefulness' and 'stewardship' are two terms that are often used in relation to the role of financial information. The 'decision usefulness' criterion is considered to be satisfied if particular information is useful (decision-useful) for making particular decisions, such as decisions about the allocation of scarce resources. From an accounting perspective, 'stewardship' refers to the process wherein a manager demonstrates how he or she has used the resources that have been entrusted to them. Traditionally, this was seen as one of the key roles of historical cost accounting.

given an assumption of market efficiency, the information would quickly be dispersed among all interested users. The Trueblood Committee and subsequent committees responsible for the development of conceptual frameworks in the United States and elsewhere did not appear to embrace this view of market efficiency.

The Trueblood Committee acknowledged that a variety of different valuation methods were used for different classes of assets and liabilities. This had been an issue that had concerned a number of researchers, such as Raymond Chambers (as indicated in Chapter 5). However, the Trueblood Committee considered that different valuation rules were relevant for different classes of assets, thereby ignoring the 'additivity problem' raised by individuals such as Chambers. As will be seen shortly, prescribing a particular valuation or measurement approach is an activity that those responsible for developing conceptual frameworks have been reluctant to undertake.

THE FASB CONCEPTUAL FRAMEWORK PROJECT

In 1974 the Accounting Principles Board within the United States was replaced by the Financial Accounting Standards Board (FASB). The FASB embarked on its conceptual framework project early in its existence and the first release, Statement of Financial Accounting Concepts (SFAC) No. 1: *Objectives of Financial Reporting by Business Enterprises*, occurred in 1978. This was followed by the release of six more SFACs, with the latest one, SFAC No. 7: *Using Cash Flow Information and Present Values in Accounting Measurement*, being issued in 2000. The initial SFACs were quite normative (that is, they attempted to prescribe how accounting should be undertaken). However, when SFAC No. 5: *Recognition and Measurement in Financial Statements of Business Enterprises* was released in 1984 the FASB appeared to opt for an approach largely descriptive of current practice. Rather than prescribe a particular valuation approach, the FASB described some of the various valuation approaches commonly used or suggested: historical cost, current cost (replacement cost), current market value (exit value), net realisable value (amount gained from sale, less costs associated with the sale) and the present (discounted) value of future cash flows. The failure to take the lead and actually prescribe a particular valuation approach was referred to as a 'cop-out' by Solomons (1986). This view was also embraced by a number of others. For example, Nussbaumer (1992, p. 238) states:

> ... the issuance of SFAC 5 (December 1984) marked the greatest disappointment of the FASB's project for the conceptual framework. It did nothing more than describe present practice; it was not prescriptive at all. The recognition and measurement issues, which the FASB promised to deal with in SFAC 5, were not settled, and the measurement issue was sidestepped ... If the FASB cannot reach an agreement when there are only seven members, it is unlikely that the profession as a whole will come to agreement on these issues either. The FASB should provide leadership to the profession on these issues and not compromise them for the sake of expediency.

In a similar vein, Miller (1990) argued that the FASB conceptual framework in accounting initially provided much needed reform to accounting. For example, SFAC No. 1 explicitly put financial report users' needs at the forefront of consideration. However, when SFAC No. 5 was released, 'momentum was lost when FASB did not have sufficient political will to face down the counter-reformation and endorse expanded use of current values in the recognition and measurement phase of the project' (Miller, 1990, p. 32). Interestingly, since SFAC 5 was released there has been very limited activity in the FASB conceptual framework project. SFAC 6 was released in 1985, but this was primarily a replacement of an early statement (SFAC 3). Only one further SFAC (SFAC 7) was released (in 2000). It would appear that measurement issues represented a real stumbling block for the project. Had the FASB supported one valuation method over and above others, this would have been a dramatic departure from current accounting practice and may not have been palatable to its constituents.[7] Although this is conjecture, perhaps the FASB went as far as it could politically. This issue is considered in more depth later in the chapter.

THE (UK) CORPORATE REPORT

The degree of progression of other conceptual framework projects has also been slow. In the United Kingdom, an early move towards developing guidance in relation to the objectives and the identification of the users of financial statements, as well as the methods to be used in financial reporting, was provided by *The Corporate Report*, a discussion paper released in 1975 by the Accounting Standards Steering Committee of the Institute of Chartered Accountants in England and Wales. *The Corporate Report* was particularly concerned with addressing the rights of the community in terms of access to financial information about the entities operating in the community. The view taken was that if the community gives an organisation permission to operate, then that organisation has an accountability to the community and this accountability includes an obligation to provide information about its financial performance. This perspective of financial statement users was broader than that adopted in frameworks being developed in other countries and involved groups that did not have a direct financial interest in the organisation but were nevertheless affected by its ongoing operations.

The Corporate Report was also part of a UK Government Green Paper on Law Reform. The report ultimately did not become enshrined in law and its contents were generally not accepted by the accounting profession. In 1991 the UK Accounting Standards Board embarked on a project to develop a conceptual framework, largely consistent with the main principles underlying the FASB and IASC frameworks, and thereby abandoned the broader notions of *users' rights* raised in *The Corporate Report*.

DEVELOPMENT OF CONCEPTUAL FRAMEWORKS
IN AUSTRALIA AND ELSEWHERE

Other countries such as Australia, Canada and New Zealand have devoted resources to the development of a conceptual framework. In Australia, work on the conceptual framework started in the 1980s, with the first of four Statements of Accounting Concept being issued in 1990. The Australian conceptual framework had a number of similarities to the FASB project and, as with the FASB, prescribing a particular measurement principle was a major stumbling block.[8] In Canada,

---

7   Current accounting practice requires that different measurement approaches be used for different classes of assets. For example, the lower of cost and net realisable value is used for inventory, whereas marketable securities are to be valued at fair value. If a conceptual framework was released that required one basis of asset measurement for all assets, this would have significant implications for the revision of various accounting standards.

8   As indicated earlier, since 2005 Australia has embraced the IASB conceptual framework. This move was based on the view that as Australia elected to adopt IASs/IFRSs from 2005—many of which represented significant changes from Australia accounting standards—it also had to embrace the IASB Framework, given that IASs, and more recently IFRSs, are based, at least in part, on the contents of the IASB Framework. As with the loss of control in developing accounting standards, in adopting IFRSs Australia has also lost control in the development of a conceptual framework. When finally completed, Australia will embrace the new conceptual framework developed by the IASB and the FASB, a framework that Australia has had relatively little input in developing.

initial efforts were incorporated in a document entitled *Corporate Reporting: Its Future Evolution*, which was released in 1980. This report was written by Edward Stamp and became known as *The Stamp Report*. The report appeared to rely heavily on *The Corporate Report* (which was unsurprising, as Stamp was one of its authors), and like *The Corporate Report* was not embraced by the accounting profession. Subsequently, further work was undertaken towards developing a conceptual framework with a number of similarities to the FASB project. In 1990 the Accounting Research and Standards Board in New Zealand also commenced work related to a conceptual framework, which has many similarities to other frameworks developed in other countries. At the international level, the IASC published a conceptual framework in 1989, entitled *Framework for the Preparation and Presentation of Financial Statements*, which is also similar in many respects to the conceptual frameworks developed in Australia, Canada and New Zealand. Given the new centrality of International Accounting Standards/International Financial Reporting Standards in European and global financial reporting (particularly since January 2005), some argue that the IASB needs a more up-to-date conceptual framework to guide its accounting standard-setting process, which the IASB has responded to by jointly undertaking the initiative with the FASB to develop a new conceptual framework.

What this information demonstrates is that a number of countries have devoted resources to the development of a conceptual framework. What also is apparent is that those responsible for the frameworks have either been reluctant to promote significant changes from accounting practice (which obviously limits their ability to generate significant changes in financial reporting) or, where frameworks have suggested significant changes, such changes have not been embraced by the accounting professions and many of their constituents. The reasons for this are provided in the discussion that follows.

CURRENT EFFORTS OF THE IASB AND THE FASB

From 2005 the IASB and the FASB have been jointly working towards the development of a revised conceptual framework that will be used by both parties. The need for this revised framework has arisen because of the 'convergence project', in which the IASB and the FASB are working together to converge their two sets of accounting standards. The ultimate aim is that the accounting standards of both the IASB and the FASB will be of such a comparable nature that the United States will ultimately adopt IFRSs and there will be one set of accounting standards (IFRS) that are used globally. As indicated in Chapter 4, unlike many other countries, at this time the United States has not adopted IFRSs and has retained the use of its own domestically developed accounting standards.

Prior to convergence many differences existed between the respective standards released by the IASB and the FASB. There were also many differences between the conceptual frameworks developed by the respective boards. Given that efforts are under way to converge accounting standards being released by the IASB with those being released by the FASB, there is a need for one uniform conceptual framework. In explaining the need for a revised conceptual framework, the FASB and IASB (2005, p. 2) state:

> The Boards will encounter difficulties converging their standards if they base their decisions on different frameworks ... The FASB's current Concepts Statements and the IASB's Framework, developed mainly during the 1970s and 1980s, articulate concepts that go a long way toward being an adequate foundation for principles-based standards ... Although

the current concepts have been helpful, the IASB and FASB will not be able to realise fully their goal of issuing a common set of principles-based standards if those standards are based on the current FASB Concepts Statements and IASB Framework. That is because those documents are in need of refinement, updating, completion, and convergence. There is no real need to change many aspects of the existing frameworks, other than to converge different ways of expressing what are in essence the same concepts. Therefore, the project will not seek to comprehensively reconsider all aspects of the existing Concepts Statements and the Framework. Instead, it will focus on areas that need refinement, updating, or completing, particularly on the conceptual issues that are more likely to yield standard-setting benefits soon.

In regards to the amount of time it will take to develop the converged conceptual framework, the FASB and IASB (2005, p. 16) state:

This joint project is a major undertaking for both Boards and will take several years. In the intervening period, the Boards will look to their existing frameworks for guidance in setting standards.

Work on the conceptual framework is being undertaken in eight phases, as listed below. At the beginning of 2009, phases A, B, C and D were active:

Phase	Topic
A	Objectives and qualitative characteristics.
B	Definitions of elements, recognition and derecognition
C	Measurement
D	Reporting entity concept
E	Boundaries of financial reporting, and presentation and disclosure
F	Purpose and status of the framework
G	Application of the framework to not-for-profit entities
H	Remaining issues, if any

Details of the progress on the revised conceptual framework can be found on the IASB's website (www.iasb.org) by following the links to the conceptual framework project.

BUILDING BLOCKS OF A CONCEPTUAL FRAMEWORK

This section looks at some of the guidance that has already been produced in existing conceptual framework projects. Topics discussed include the definition of a reporting entity, the perceived users of financial statements, the objectives of general purpose financial reporting, the qualitative characteristics that general purpose financial statements should possess, the elements of financial statements, and possible approaches to recognition and measurement of the elements of financial statements. The focus is primarily on the IASB Framework that is currently in place, as this is the framework that is guiding accounting practice in those countries, such as Australia, that made the decision to adopt IFRS. Where appropriate, reference is also made to current work being undertaken in the joint IASB/FASB conceptual framework project, given that this work provides an indication of possible future guidance.

DEFINITION OF THE REPORTING ENTITY

One key issue in any discussion about financial reporting is what characteristics of an entity provide an indication of an apparent need for it to produce general purpose financial statements. The term *general purpose financial statements* refers to financial statements that comply with accounting standards and other generally accepted accounting principles and are released by *reporting entities* to satisfy the information demands of a varied cross-section of users. These financial statements can be contrasted with special purpose financial statements, which are provided to meet the information demands of a particular user or group of users. As stated earlier, the guidance that is considered in this chapter relates to general purpose financial statements.

Some researchers, such as Walker (2003), have been critical of the practicality of conceptual frameworks directed at general purpose financial statements, as a single set (or framework) of accounting concepts is unlikely to be able to address the diversity of information needs from a heterogeneous range of different stakeholders.

Clearly, not all entities should be expected to produce general purpose financial statements. For example, there would be limited benefits in requiring an owner/manager of a small corner shop to prepare general purpose financial statements (that comply with the numerous accounting standards). There would be few external users with a significant stake or interest in the organisation. Limited guidance is provided by some conceptual frameworks regarding the types of entities to whose financial statements the conceptual framework is relevant. For example, paragraph 8 of the IASC *Framework for the Preparation and Presentation of Financial Statements*—and remember that this framework has now been adopted as the IASB Framework (as well as the AASB Framework)—states that:

> The Framework applies to the financial statements of all commercial, industrial and business reporting entities, whether in the public or private sectors. A reporting entity is an entity for which there are users who rely on the financial statements as their major source of financial information about the entity.

Consistent with the discussion above, general purpose financial statements are considered in the IASB Framework (paragraph 6) to be statements that 'are directed towards the common information needs of a wide range of users'.

The conceptual framework developed within Australia provided more detail about the reporting entity concept relative to the IASB Framework. The Australian framework also provided more detail about the objectives of general purpose financial reporting. Hence, when the IASB Framework was adopted in Australia in 2005, it was also decided that Australia would retain the use of two of the four SACs that had been developed as part of the Australian Conceptual Framework Project. That is, in 2005 the Australian Conceptual Framework became a mixture of the IASB Framework and two of the Australian SACs. Specifically, Australia retained the use of SAC 1 'Definition of the Reporting Entity' and SAC 2 'Objective of General-Purpose Financial Reporting'. The IASB Framework replaced the other two SACs, these being SAC 3 'Qualitative Characteristics of Financial Reporting' and SAC 4 'Definition and Recognition of the Elements of Financial Statements'.

In the work being undertaken by the IASB and the FASB, it is expected that Australia's SAC 1 will be used, at least in part, to develop further the reporting entity concept in the joint IASB and FASB conceptual framework. Specifically, FASB and IASB (2005, p.13) state:

> The Australian accounting standards boards did issue in 1990 a concepts statement, *Definition of the Reporting Entity*, that defined an economic entity as a group of entities under common control, with users who depend on general purpose financial reports to make resource allocations decisions regarding the collective operation of the group and examined the implications of that concept. The boards may find that Concepts Statement useful in developing a complete, converged concept of reporting entity.

In May 2008 the IASB released a document entitled *Preliminary Views—Conceptual Framework for Financial Reporting: The Reporting Entity* as part of the work being undertaken by the IASB and the FASB. In providing background to the report, IASB state (2008b, p. 1):

> The boards' existing conceptual frameworks do not include a reporting entity concept. The IASB's *Framework for the Preparation and Presentation of Financial Statements* defines the reporting entity in one sentence with no further explanation. The FASB's *Statements of Financial Accounting Concepts* do not contain a definition of a reporting entity or discussion of how to identify one. As a result, neither framework specifically addresses the reporting entity concept. The objective of this phase (Phase D) of the project is to develop a reporting entity concept for inclusion in the boards' common conceptual framework.

For further clarification of what constitutes a reporting entity, SAC 1 states that general purpose financial statements should be prepared by all reporting entities. General purpose financial statements are considered to be statements that comply with conceptual framework pronouncements and accounting standards. Paragraph 6 of SAC 1 further defines general purpose financial statements as financial statements 'intended to meet the information needs common to users who are unable to command the preparation of reports tailored so as to satisfy, specifically, all of their information needs'.

Further, paragraph 8 of SAC 1 states that general purpose financial statements should be prepared when there are users 'whose information needs have common elements, and those users cannot command the preparation of information to satisfy their individual information needs'.

If an entity is not deemed to be a reporting entity (that is, there is a general absence of users dependent on general purpose financial statements), it will not be required to produce general purpose financial statements—that is, it will not necessarily be required to comply with accounting standards.

Hence, whether an entity is classified as a reporting entity is determined by the information needs of the users and relies on professional judgement. When information relevant to decision making is not otherwise accessible to users who are judged to be dependent on general purpose financial statements to make and evaluate resource-allocation decisions, the entity is deemed to be a reporting entity. Where dependence is not readily apparent, SAC 1 suggests factors that may indicate a reporting entity (and hence a need to produce general purpose financial statements). These factors include:

- the separation of management from those with an economic interest in the entity (paragraph 20)—as the spread of ownership increases and/or the separation of management and ownership increases, the greater the likelihood becomes that an entity will be considered to be a reporting entity;

- the economic or political importance/influence of the entity to/on other parties (paragraph 21)—as the entity's dominance in the market increases and/or its potential influence over the welfare of external parties increases, the greater the likelihood is that an entity will be considered to be a reporting entity;
- the financial characteristics of the entity (paragraph 22)—as the amount of sales, value of assets, extent of indebtedness, number of customers and number of employees increases, the greater the likelihood is that an entity will be considered to be a reporting entity.

Clearly, the approach adopted within Australia towards defining a reporting entity is highly subjective and could lead to conflicting opinions about whether an entity is a reporting entity or not. Interestingly, Australian law developed more objective criteria for determining when a company is required to provide financial statements that comply with accounting standards, and these criteria, which are written within the *Corporations Act*, are related to measures such as gross revenue, dollar value of assets and number of employees.

USERS OF FINANCIAL REPORTS

If conceptual frameworks are designed to meet the 'information needs of a wide range of users', to be effective it is necessary for the frameworks to identify the potential users and their main information needs. The definition of users provided at paragraph 9 of the IASB Framework encompasses investors, employees, lenders, suppliers, customers, government and their agencies, and the public, and is thereby broader than that used by the FASB in the United States. In the FASB's SFAC 1, the main focus of financial reports is present and potential investors and other users (with either a direct financial interest or somehow related to those with a financial interest, for example stockbrokers, analysts, lawyers or regulatory bodies). Within SFAC 1 there appears to be limited consideration of the public being a legitimate user of financial reports. However, in the IASB Framework, even though a range of users (along with the nature of their likely information needs) is identified, it is proposed that accounting information designed to meet the information needs of investors will usually also meet the needs of the other user groups identified. This claim is justified on the basis that 'investors are providers of risk capital to the entity' (paragraph 10), but the framework does not explain why information designed to be useful to the providers of risk capital is also likely to be useful to the other types of stakeholders in most circumstances.

In Australia, SAC 2 'Objective of General-Purpose Financial Reporting' identifies three primary user groups of general purpose financial statements: resource providers, recipients of goods and services, and parties performing a review or oversight function. Resource providers are defined as including employees, lenders, creditors, suppliers, investors and contributors, while the recipients of goods and services are deemed to include customers and beneficiaries. Parties performing a review or oversight function include parliaments, governments, regulatory agencies, analysts, labour unions, employer groups, media and special interest groups.

Hence, the definition of users provided by SAC 2 is quite broad, and through reference to such parties as 'special interest groups' could be construed as embracing the 'public'. While perhaps not as broad as the definition provided by *The Corporate Report* (UK), which considered 'rights' to information that is not necessarily linked to resource allocation decisions, the definition of users provided in the Australian document is broader than that provided by the FASB and the IASB. In SFAC 1 the main focus of financial reports is present and potential investors and other users (with either a direct financial interest or somehow related to those with a financial interest, for example stockbrokers, analysts, lawyers or regulatory bodies). Within SFAC 1 there appears to be limited consideration of the public in terms of the public being considered as a legitimate user of financial reports.

The issue as to which groups should be considered to be legitimate users of financial information about an organisation is an argument that has attracted a great deal of debate. There are many, such as the authors of *The Corporate Report*, who hold that all groups affected by an organisation's operations have *rights* to information about the reporting entity, including financial information, regardless of whether they are contemplating resource allocation decisions.

Indeed, many would question whether the need for information to enable 'resource allocation decisions' is the only or dominant issue to consider in determining whether an organisation has a public obligation to provide information about its financial performance.[9] Organisations, particularly large corporations, have many social and environmental impacts on society, and these impacts are not restricted to those people who are investors or who are considering investing in the organisation. In large part, the extent of an organisation's impact, and its ability to minimise harmful impacts, will be tied to the financial resources under its control. As such, a reasonable argument can be made that various groups within society have a legitimate interest in information about an organisation's financial position and performance and to restrict the definition of users to investors does seem too simplistic. The 2008 exposure draft released by the IASB as part of the conceptual framework project states (IASB 2008a, p. 16):

> The primary user group includes both present and potential equity investors, lenders and other creditors, regardless of how they obtained, or will obtain, their interests. In the framework, the terms *capital providers* and *claimants* are used interchangeably to refer to the primary user group.
>
> Managers and the governing board of an entity (herein collectively referred to as management) are also interested in financial information about the entity. However, management's primary relationship with the entity is not that of a capital provider. Management is responsible for preparing financial reports; management is not their intended recipient. Other users who have specialised needs, such as suppliers, customers and employees (when not acting as capital providers), as well as governments and their agencies and members of the public, may also find useful the information that meets the needs of capital providers; however, financial reporting is not primarily directed to these other groups because capital providers have more direct and immediate needs.

As we can see from this quote, the current work of the IASB and FASB appears to maintain a restricted view of the users of general purpose financial statements and tends to disregard information rights or needs of users who do not have a direct financial interest in the organisation.

In regards to the issue of the level of expertise expected of financial report readers, it has generally been accepted that readers are expected to have some proficiency in financial accounting. As a result, accounting standards are developed on this basis. The FASB conceptual framework refers to the 'informed reader'. In the IASB Framework, paragraph 25 explains that 'users are assumed to have a reasonable knowledge of business and economic activities and

9   This issue is discussed further in Chapter 9.

accounting and a willingness to study the information with reasonable diligence'. Consistent with this, in the recent conceptual framework project, the IASB (2008a, p. 40) states:

> Users of financial reports are assumed to have a reasonable knowledge of business and economic activities and to be able to read a financial report. In making decisions, users also should review and analyse the information with reasonable diligence.

In considering the required qualitative characteristics that financial information should possess (for example, relevance, understandability), some assumptions about the ability of report users are required. It would appear that those responsible for developing conceptual frameworks have accepted that individuals without any expertise in accounting are not the intended audience of reporting entities' financial statements (even though such people may have a considerable amount of their own wealth invested). Having established the audience for general purpose financial statements, we now consider the objectives of such statements aimed at these users.

OBJECTIVES OF GENERAL PURPOSE FINANCIAL REPORTING

Over time, a number of objectives have been attributed to information provided within financial statements.[10] A traditionally cited objective was to enable outsiders to assess the *stewardship* of management—that is, whether the resources entrusted to management have been used for their intended or appropriate purposes. It is generally accepted that historical cost accounting enables management to report effectively on the stewardship of the resources provided to the reporting entity.

Another objective of financial reporting, and one that has become a commonly accepted goal of financial reporting, is to assist in report users' economic decision making. That is, in recent times less emphasis has been placed on the stewardship function of financial reports. For example, the FASB notes in SFAC 1 that a major objective of financial reporting is that it:

> ... should provide information that is useful to present and potential investors and creditors and other users in making rational investment, credit and similar decisions.

This objective refers to 'rational' decisions. It is commonly accepted in the economics and accounting literature that a 'rational decision' is one that maximises expected utility, with this utility typically considered to be related to the maximisation of wealth. The FASB framework emphasises the information needs of those who have a financial stake in the reporting entity. For example, the above objective refers to the needs of present and potential investors and creditors. It also refers to the needs of 'others', but the 'others' are also explained in terms of having financial interests in the reporting entity.

This focus on the information needs of financial report users has also been embraced in other conceptual frameworks. For example, in the IASB Framework the objective of financial reporting is 'to provide information about the financial position, performance, and changes in financial position of an enterprise that is useful to a wide range of users in making economic decisions' (paragraph 12).[11] This is consistent with SAC 2 as released within Australia, which

---

10 In a FASB discussion memorandum released in 1974, the FASB defines an objective as 'something toward which effort is directed, an aim, or end of action, a goal'. It is perhaps questionable whether information itself can have objectives. Certainly, users of information can have objectives that can be achieved (or not) as a result of using information. Nevertheless, it is common for accounting standard-setters to talk about the objectives of financial information and, as such, we maintain this convention.

states that the objective of general purpose financial reporting is 'to provide information to users that is useful for making and evaluating decisions about the allocation of scarce resources'.

The IASB Framework explains that economic decisions should be based on an assessment of an enterprise's future cash flows, indicating that the main objective of general purpose financial statements is to assist stakeholders in judging likely future cash flows. Moving towards a system of reporting a range of cash-flow forecasts would clearly be a significant change to existing accounting practices, which focus on reporting (some of) the effects of past transactions and events. However, the IASB Framework (paragraph 15) then explains that:

> Users are better able to evaluate this ability to generate cash and cash equivalents if they are provided with information that focuses on the financial position, performance and changes in financial position of an entity.

Therefore, while the objective of financial statements is to aid economic decisions that will be based on an evaluation of future cash flows, the IASB Framework argues that this objective of enabling stakeholders to evaluate cash flows will be effectively addressed through the information contained in balance sheets (or as they are also known, statements of financial position), income statements (or as they are becoming known, statements of comprehensive income) and cash flow/ funds flow statements. Thus, there is no need for a radical change in the types of main financial statements that are needed if the objective of the financial statements as a whole (that is, the annual report and accounts) is to provide information that is useful for making economic decisions.

Once we move towards this notion of *decision usefulness*, an objective embraced within all conceptual framework projects, we might question whether historical cost information (which arguably is useful for assessing stewardship) is useful for financial report users' decisions, such as whether to invest in, or lend funds to, an organisation. Arguably, such decisions could be more effectively made if information on current market values was made available. Within Chambers' model of accounting, Continuously Contemporary Accounting, which is covered in Chapter 5, one objective of financial accounting is to provide information about the *adaptive capacity* of an entity. Historical cost information does not help meet this objective. It is interesting to note that, although the IASB Framework does not really address measurement issues, many recently released accounting standards require assets to be valued on the basis of 'fair values', and also various liabilities to be valued on the basis of present values. In effect, accounting regulators appear to be sidestepping the use of the conceptual framework as the foundation of developing the measurement principles of general purpose financial reporting and instead are using the ongoing release of new accounting standards as the means of bringing major change to accounting measurement principles. Such an approach seems to be inconsistent with the reasons for conceptual frameworks being established.

Apart from *stewardship* and *decision usefulness*, another commonly cited objective of financial reporting is to enable reporting entities to demonstrate *accountability* between the entity and those parties to which the entity is deemed to be accountable. Gray, Owen and Adams (1996, p. 38) provide a definition of accountability, this being: 'the duty to provide an account or reckoning of those actions for which one is held responsible'. Issues that arise here are *to whom* is a reporting entity accountable and *for what*? There are a multitude of opinions on this. Within

---

11 The more traditional stewardship role of financial statements is explicitly recognised as an additional objective in the IASB Framework, where paragraph 14 states that 'Financial statements also show the results of the stewardship of management, or the accountability of management for the resources entrusted to it'.

the FASB project it would appear that those responsible for developing a framework considered that there is a duty to provide an account of the entity's financial performance to those parties who have a direct financial stake in the reporting entity. Emphasis seems to be placed on economic efficiencies. This can be contrasted with the guidance provided by *The Corporate Report* (UK), which argues that society effectively allows organisations to exist as long as they accept certain responsibilities, one being that they are accountable for their actions to society generally, rather than solely to those who have a financial stake in the entity. *The Corporate Report* makes the following statement at paragraph 25:

> The public's right to information arises not from a direct financial or human relationship with the reporting entity but from the general role played in our society by economic entities. Such organisations, which exist with the general consent of the community, are afforded special legal and operational privileges; they compete for resources of manpower, materials and energy and they make use of community owned assets such as roads and harbours.

Although *The Corporate Report* emphasised an accountability perspective of financial reporting, it was generally not accepted, and the UK position (through the ASB's subsequent conceptual framework project) was basically one of acceptance of the decision-makers emphasis, with prime consideration being given to the needs of those with a financial interest or stake in the organisation.

To understand the 'current thinking' of the IASB and the FASB in relation to the objective of financial reporting, it is useful to consider the exposure draft released by the IASB as part of the ongoing efforts to develop a revised conceptual framework. In relation to the objective of financial reporting, it states (IASB, 2008a, p. 14):

> The objective of general purpose financial reporting is to provide financial information about the reporting entity that is useful to present and potential equity investors, lenders and other creditors in making decisions in their capacity as capital providers. Information that is decision-useful to capital providers may also be useful to other users of financial reporting who are not capital providers.

As a normative theory of accounting, whether we are likely to accept the prescriptions provided by the new conceptual framework will be dependent on whether we agree with the underlying key assumptions and objectives adopted as the basis of developing the theory. Hence, if we disagree with the objective of financial reporting as noted above, we would probably be inclined to dismiss much of the contents of the revised conceptual framework.

Before moving on to consider some of the suggested *qualitative characteristics* of financial information, for the sake of completeness mention should be made of the underlying assumptions set out as a separate section in the IASB's framework but not given such prominence in most other conceptual framework projects. These underlying assumptions are simply that for financial statements to meet the objectives of providing information for economic decision making they should be prepared on the accrual and 'going concern' basis. Specifically, paragraphs 22 and 23 of the IASB Framework currently state:

> 22. In order to meet their objectives, financial reports are prepared on the accrual basis of accounting. Under this basis, the effects of transactions and other events are

recognised when they occur (and not as cash or its equivalent is received or paid) and they are recorded in the accounting records and reported in the financial reports of the periods to which they relate. Financial reports prepared on the accrual basis inform users not only of past transactions involving the payment and receipt of cash but also of obligations to pay cash in the future and of resources that represent cash to be received in the future. Hence, they provide the type of information about past transactions and other events that is most useful to users in making economic decisions.

23. Financial reports are normally prepared on the assumption that an entity is a going concern and will continue in operation for the forseeable future. Hence, it is assumed that the entity has neither the intention nor the need to liquidate or curtail materially the scale of its operations; if such an intention or need exists, the financial report may have to be prepared on a different basis and, if so, the basis used is disclosed.

QUALITATIVE CHARACTERISTICS OF FINANCIAL REPORTS

If it is accepted that financial information should be useful for economic decision making, as conceptual frameworks indicate, then a subsequent issue to consider (or in terms of the terminology used earlier, a subsequent 'building block' to consider) is the qualitative characteristics (attributes or qualities) that financial information should have if it is to be useful for such decisions (implying that an absence of such qualities would mean that the central objectives of general purpose financial statements would not be met).

Conceptual frameworks have dedicated a great deal of their material to discussing qualitative characteristics of financial information. The four primary qualitative characteristics that have been identified in the IASB Framework are *understandability*, *relevance*, *reliability* and *comparability*.

Understandability

In the IASB Framework, information is considered to be *understandable* if it is likely to be understood by users with some business and accounting knowledge (as discussed earlier in the chapter). However, this does not mean that complex information that is relevant to economic decision making should be omitted from the financial statements just because it might not be understood by some users. Given that conceptual frameworks have been developed primarily to guide accounting standard-setters in the setting of accounting rules (rather than as a set of rules to which entities must refer when compiling their financial statements), this qualitative characteristic of *understandability* is perhaps best seen as a requirement (or challenge) for standard-setters to ensure that the accounting standards they develop for dealing with complex areas produce accounting disclosures that are understandable (irrespective of the complexity of the underlying transactions or events). Based on your knowledge of accounting practice, how successful do you think accounting standard-setters have been in this task?

Relevance

Under the IASB Framework, information is regarded as relevant if it:

... influences the economic decisions of users by helping them evaluate past, present or future events or confirming, or correcting, their past evaluations (paragraph 26).

There are two main aspects to relevance—for information to be relevant it should have both *predictive value* and *feedback* (or *confirmatory*) *value*, the latter referring to the information's utility in confirming or correcting earlier expectations.

Materiality

Closely tied to the notion of *relevance* is the notion of *materiality*. This is embodied in various conceptual framework projects. For example, paragraph 30 of the IASB Framework states that an item is material if:

> ... its omission or misstatement could influence the economic decisions of users taken on the basis of the financial statements ... Materiality provides a cut-off point rather than being a primary qualitative characteristic which information must have if it is to be useful.

Considerations of materiality provide the basis for restricting the amount of information provided to levels that are comprehensible to financial statement users. It would arguably be poor practice to provide hundreds of pages of potentially relevant and reliable information to report readers—this would only result in an overload of information. Nevertheless, materiality is a heavily judgemental issue and at times we could expect that it might actually be used as a justification for failing to disclose some information that might be deemed to be potentially harmful to the reporting entity.

Reliability

Turning to another primary qualitative characteristic, something is deemed to be reliable if it 'is free from material bias and error and can be depended upon by users to represent faithfully' the underlying items it claims to represent (IASB Framework, paragraph 31). Within the United States, SFAC 2 defines reliability as 'the quality of information that assures that information is reasonably free from error and bias and faithfully represents what it purports to represent'. SFAC 2 notes that reliability is a function of *representational faithfulness*, *verifiability* and *neutrality*. According to SFAC 2, *representational faithfulness* refers to the 'correspondence or agreement between a measure or description and the phenomenon that it purports to represent'. *Verifiability* is defined in SFAC 2 as 'the ability through consensus among measurers to ensure that information represents what it purports to represent, or that the chosen method of measurement has been used without error or bias'. *Neutrality* implies that the information was not constructed or compiled to generate a predetermined result.

In addition to freedom from bias and material error, the IASB Framework assesses reliability in terms of *faithful representation*, *substance over form*, *neutrality*, *prudence* and *completeness*. Where the economic substance of a transaction is inconsistent with its legal form, *substance over form* requires that the accounting represents the economic substance (or impact) of the transaction. *Prudence* in paragraph 37 of the IASB Framework requires 'a degree of caution in the exercise of judgement needed in making the estimates required under conditions of uncertainty', but this does not extend to 'excessive provisions, the deliberate understatement of assets or income, or the deliberate overstatement of liabilities or expenses', as this would conflict with the requirement of neutrality.

Introducing notions of *prudence* with the associated notions of *neutrality* and *representational faithfulness* has implications for how financial accounting has traditionally been practised. Traditionally, accountants adopted the doctrine of conservatism or prudence. In practice, this meant that asset values should never have been shown at amounts in excess of their realisable values (but they could be understated), and liabilities should never have been understated (although it was generally acceptable for liabilities to be overstated). That is, there was traditionally a bias towards undervaluing the net assets of an entity. It would appear that such a doctrine is not consistent with the qualitative characteristic of 'freedom from bias', as financial statements should, arguably, not be biased in one direction or another. In more recent conceptual framework projects (such as the UK ASB's *Statement of Principles* and the Australian conceptual framework project) and recently developed accounting standards in many jurisdictions, the requirement of prudence was 'softened' in favour of a greater focus on neutrality and representational faithfulness.

Comparability

The final primary qualitative characteristic in the IASB Framework is *comparability*. To facilitate the comparison of the financial statements of different entities (and for a single entity over a period of time), methods of measurement and disclosure must be consistent—but should be changed if no longer relevant to an entity's circumstances. Drawing on studies by Loftus (2003) and Booth (2003), Wells (2003) argues that a key role of a conceptual framework should be to produce consistent accounting standards which lead to comparable accounting information between different entities, as without such comparability it is difficult for users to evaluate accounting information.

Desirable characteristics such as consistency thus imply that there are advantages in restricting the number of accounting methods that can be used by reporting entities. However, other academics have argued that any actions which result in a reduction in the accounting methods that can be used by reporting entities lead potentially to reductions in the efficiency with which organisations operate (Watts & Zimmerman, 1986). For example, management might elect to use a particular accounting method because it believes that for the particular and perhaps unique circumstances the specific method of accounting best reflects the underlying performance. Restricting the use of the specific method can result in a reduction in how efficiently external parties can monitor the performance of the entity, and this in itself has been assumed to lead to increased costs for the reporting entity. (The 'efficiency perspective', which has been applied in Positive Accounting Theory, is explored in Chapter 7.)

If it is assumed, consistent with the *efficiency perspective*, that firms adopt particular accounting methods because the methods best reflect the underlying economic performance of the entity, then it is argued by some theorists that the regulation of financial accounting imposes unwarranted costs on reporting entities. For example, if a new accounting standard is released that bans an accounting method being used by a particular organisation, this will lead to inefficiencies, as the resulting financial statements will no longer provide the best reflection of the performance of the organisation. Many theorists would argue that management is best able to select the appropriate accounting methods in given circumstances, and government and/or others should not intervene.

BALANCING RELEVANCE AND RELIABILITY

Returning to the specific requirements of the IASB Framework, it is considered important for information to possess each of the four primary qualitative characteristics if it is to be useful in aiding economic decision making. However, it appears that the IASB Framework gives greater prominence to *reliability* and *relevance* than to *understandability* or *comparability*. In balancing relevance and reliability, paragraph 32 notes that 'Information might be relevant but so unreliable in nature or representation that its recognition may be potentially misleading'.

Another consideration that needs to be addressed when deciding whether to disclose particular information is thus the potential constraints on producing relevant and reliable information. The IASB Framework discusses two such constraints: *timeliness* and *balancing costs and benefits*. In relation to the former, paragraph 43 recognises that for much accounting information there will be a trade-off between being able to produce information quickly (and thereby enhancing the relevance of the information) and measuring this information accurately (and therefore *reliably*), as the production of accurate information often requires corroboration that occurs sometime later. In these circumstances, it is a matter of judgement as to how to balance *relevance* and *reliability* (that is, how long to wait against the extent of reliability required).

That is, the longer we take to ensure information is reliable (perhaps through various forms of auditing) the less relevant the information becomes.

The other major constraint, consideration of costs and benefits of disclosure, is a highly subjective activity and requires decisions about many issues. Paragraph 44 of the IASB Framework requires that 'the benefits derived from information should exceed the cost of providing it'. But from whose perspective are we to consider costs and benefits? Are costs and benefits attributable to some user groups more or less important than others, and so on? Any analysis of costs and benefits is highly judgemental and open to critical comment.

It is interesting to consider the 'latest thinking' of the IASB and FASB in relation to the desired qualitative characteristics of financial reporting. In the exposure draft released in 2008 as part of the joint initiative of the IASB and FASB (IASB, 2008a) it is stated:

> For financial information to be useful, it must possess two fundamental qualitative characteristics—*relevance* and *faithful representation*.

Therefore, although the existing *IASB Framework for the Preparation and Presentation of Financial Statements* has four primary qualitative characteristics of financial reporting (relevance, reliability, understandability and comparability), the draft conceptual framework being developed by the IASB and FASB has reduced the four 'primary qualitative characteristics' to two 'fundamental qualitative characteristics': *relevance* and *faithful representation*.

Within the 2008 exposure draft the qualitative characteristic of reliability had been replaced by 'faithful representation'; in previous documents 'faithful representation' had been seen as a component of reliability. In relation to faithful representation, the exposure draft states (IASB 2008a, p. 36):

> Faithful representation is attained when the depiction of an economic phenomenon is complete, neutral, and free from material error. Financial information that faithfully represents an economic phenomenon depicts the economic substance of the underlying transaction, event or circumstances, which is not always the same as its legal form.

In explaining why it has been proposed that 'relevance' be replaced as a primary qualitative characteristic of financial reporting, the exposure draft states (IASB 2008a, p. 47):

> Given the nature and extent of the longstanding problems with the qualitative characteristic of *reliability*, as well as previous efforts to address them, the boards concluded that the term itself needed reconsideration. Because further efforts to explain what *reliability*

means were not likely to be productive, the boards sought a term that would more clearly convey the intended meaning.

Faithful representation—the faithful depiction in financial reports of economic phenomena—is essential if information is to be decision-useful. To represent economic phenomena faithfully, accounting representations must be complete, neutral and free from material error. Accordingly, the boards proposed that 'faithful representation' encompasses all the key qualities that the previous frameworks included as aspects of reliability.

The other two primary qualitative characteristics identified in the IASB Framework, *understandability* and *comparability*, have been renamed as 'enhancing qualitative characteristics' in the draft document released by the IASB. Two additional 'enhancing qualitative characteristics' have also been included (thereby giving a total of four 'enhancing qualitative characteristics), these being *verifiability* and *timeliness*. IASB (2008a, p. 38) explains:

> Enhancing qualitative characteristics are complementary to the fundamental qualitative characteristics. Enhancing qualitative characteristics distinguish more useful information from less useful information. The enhancing qualitative characteristics are *comparability*, *verifiability*, *timeliness* and *understandability*. These characteristics enhance the decision-usefulness of financial reporting information that is relevant and faithfully represented.

CAN FINANCIAL STATEMENTS PROVIDE NEUTRAL AND UNBIASED ACCOUNTS OF AN ENTITY'S PERFORMANCE AND POSITION?

A review of existing conceptual frameworks such as the IASB Framework or the framework proposed in joint work currently being undertaken by the IASB and the FASB, as reflected by some of the material discussed above, indicates that conceptual frameworks support a perspective that accounting can, if performed properly, provide an *objective* (*neutral* and *representationally faithful*) view of the performance and position of a reporting entity. Reflecting on this apparent perspective, Hines (1991, p. 314) states:

> ... it appears that the ontological assumption underpinning the Conceptual Framework is that the relationship between financial accounting and economic reality is a unidirectional, reflecting or faithfully reproducing relationship: economic reality exists objectively, intersubjectively, concretely and independently of financial accounting practices; financial accounting reflects, mirrors, represents or measures the pre-existent reality.

In fact, the role of a well-functioning system of accounting has been compared with that of cartography (map-making). That is, just as an area can be objectively 'mapped', some have argued that so can the financial position and performance of an organisation (Solomons, 1978). But, as can be appreciated, the practice of accounting is heavily based on professional judgement. As will be seen in the subsection dealing with recognition, the elements of financial accounting are, in some jurisdictions and in the IASB Framework, explicitly tied to assessments of probabilities. Clearly, there is a degree of subjectivity associated with such assessments. Cartography is not based on subjective assessments of probabilities.[12]

---

12 If it was, we could imagine the carnage that might occur if a map of the ocean simply told a ship's captain that it was probable that a reef was safe for crossing.

Although conceptual frameworks argue for attributes such as neutrality and representational faithfulness, is it valid or realistic to believe that financial accounting provides an objective perspective of an entity's performance? Chapter 3 looked at research that investigated the economic consequences of accounting regulations. It was explained that before an accounting standard-setting body releases new or amended reporting requirements it attempts to consider the economic consequences that would follow from the decision to release an accounting standard. Even if a proposed accounting rule was considered the best way to account (however this is determined—which of course would be an issue provoking much debate), if this proposed accounting rule would lead to significant costs being imposed on particular parties (for example, preparers) then plans to require the approach could be abandoned by the standard-setters. Once a profession starts considering the economic consequences of particular accounting standards it is difficult to perceive that the accounting standards, and therefore accounting, can really be considered objective or neutral.

Tied to issues associated with economic implications, there is a body of literature (Positive Accounting Theory, which has already been briefly discussed and which is considered in Chapter 7) that suggests that those responsible for preparing financial statements will be driven by self-interest to select accounting methods that lead to outcomes that provide favourable outcomes for their own personal wealth. That is, this literature predicts that managers and others involved in the accounting function will always put their *self-interest* ahead of that of others.[13] If we accept this body of literature, we would perhaps dismiss notions of objectivity or neutrality as being unrealistic. Self-interest perspectives are often used to explain the phenomenon of 'creative accounting'—a situation where those responsible for the preparation of financial statements select accounting methods that provide the most desired outcomes from their own perspective (such as apparently occurred at Enron).

Accounting standards and conceptual frameworks form the foundation of general purpose financial reporting. As noted in earlier chapters, accounting standards and conceptual frameworks are developed through public consultation, which involves the release of exposure drafts and, subsequently, a review of the written submissions made by various interested parties, including both the preparers and the users of the financial information. Consequently, the process leading to finalised accounting standards and conceptual frameworks can be considered to be political. The political solutions and compromises impact on the financial information being presented and that information is, therefore, an outcome of a political process—a process where parties with particular attributes (power) may be able to have a relatively greater impact on final reporting requirements than other parties. This can be considered to have implications for the objectivity or neutrality of the financial information being disclosed. Hines (1989, p. 80) argues that many individuals not involved in the standard-setting process would be very surprised to find out just how political the development of accounting standards actually is. She states: 'an accounting outsider might find it remarkable that accounting knowledge should be articulated not only by professional accountants, but also by accounting information users—much like doctors and patients collaborating on the development of medical knowledge'.

---

13 One example that is often provided by proponents of Positive Accounting Theory is managers being provided with a bonus tied to the output of the accounting system, for example, to profits. It would be argued in such a case that managers will have incentives to increase reported profits, rather than be objective.

Hines is one author who has written quite a deal of material on what she sees as the apparent 'myth' of accounting neutrality. Hines (1988) argues that parties involved in the practice and regulation of accounting impose their own judgements about what attributes of an entity's performance should be emphasised (for example, *profits* or *return on assets*), and, also, what attributes of an entity's operations (for example, expenditure on employee health and safety initiatives) are not important enough to emphasise or highlight separately. The accountant can determine, under the 'guise' of objectivity, which attributes of an entity's operations are important and which can be used as a means of comparing the performance of different organisations. For example, we are informed in the United States' SFAC No. 1 that reported earnings measures an *enterprise's performance* during a period (paragraph 45)—but clearly there are other perspectives of organisational performance (clearly some that would take a more social, as opposed to financial, form).[14] Hines (1991, p. 322) emphasises that in *communicating reality* accountants simultaneously *construct reality*.

> If people take a definition or description of reality, for example, an organisational chart, or a budget, or a set of financial statements, to be reality, then they will act on the basis of it, and thereby perpetuate, and in so doing validate, that account of reality. Having acted on the basis of that definition of reality, and having thereby caused consequences to flow from that conception of reality, those same consequences will appear to social actors, in retrospect, to be proof that the definition of reality on which they based their actions was real ... Decisions and actions based on that account predicate consequences, which, in retrospect, generally confirm the validity of the subsequent account. For example, say an investigator, or a newspaper report, suggested that a 'healthy' set of financial statements is not faithfully representational, and that a firm 'really' is in trouble. If this new definition of reality is accepted by, say, creditors, they may panic and precipitate the failure of the firm, or, through the court, they may petition for a liquidation. A new definition of reality, if accepted, will be 'real in its consequences', because people will act on the basis of it.

Until accountants determine that something is worthy of being the subject of the accounting system, the issue or item, in a sense, does not exist. There is no transparency, and as such there is no perceived accountability in relation to the item. This perspective is adopted by Handel (1982, p. 36), who states:

> Things may exist independently of our accounts, but they have no human existence until they become accountable. Things may not exist, but they may take on human significance by becoming accountable ... Accounts define reality and at the same time they are that reality ... The processes by which accounts are offered and accepted are the fundamental social process ... Accounts do not more or less accurately describe things. Instead they establish what is accountable in the setting in which they occur. Whether they are accurate or inaccurate by some other standards, accounts define reality for a situation in the sense that people act on the basis of what is accountable in the situation of their action. The account provides a basis for action, a definition of what is real, and it is acted on so long as it remains accountable.[15]

14   And of course financial 'performance' is very much tied to the judgements about which particular accounting methods should be employed, over how many years an asset should be amortised, and so forth. Further, because accounting rules can change over time, this in itself can lead to a change in reported profits and hence a change in apparent 'performance'.

15   As quoted in Hines (1991).

Hence, we can see that there are a number of arguments that suggest that characteristics such as neutrality, while playing a part in the development of conceptual frameworks, do not, and perhaps may never be expected to, reflect the underlying characteristics of financial statements. As with much of the material presented in this book, whether we accept these arguments is a matter of personal opinion. As a concluding comment to challenge the belief in the objectivity or neutrality of accounting practice, reflect on the following statement of Baker and Bettner (1997, p. 293):

> Accounting's capacity to create and control social reality translates into empowerment for those who use it. Such power resides in organizations and institutions, where it is used to instill values, sustain legitimizing myths, mask conflict and promote self-perpetuating social orders. Throughout society, the influence of accounting permeates fundamental issues concerning wealth distribution, social justice, political ideology and environmental degradation. Contrary to public opinion, accounting is not a static reflection of economic reality, but rather is a highly partisan activity.[16]

DEFINITION OF THE ELEMENTS OF FINANCIAL REPORTING

Having considered perspectives on the required qualitative characteristics of financial information, the next building block to consider is how the elements of financial reporting are defined. The definitions provided within conceptual frameworks indicate the characteristics or attributes that are required before an item can be considered as belonging to a particular class of element (for example, before it can be considered to be an asset). Recognition criteria (considered in the next subsection of this chapter), on the other hand, are employed to determine whether the item can actually be included within the financial statements (that is, whether a particular transaction or event should be recognised as affecting the accounts).

Alternative approaches have been adopted in defining the elements of financial reporting. In the United States, ten elements of financial reporting are identified in SFAC 3, and subsequently in SFAC 6.[17] These elements are assets, liabilities, equity, investments, distributions, comprehensive income, revenues, expenses, gains and losses. The IASC's 1989 Framework (which subsequently became the IASB Framework) identifies five elements, split into two broad groups. The first group comprises elements relating to *financial position*, the elements of *assets*, *liabilities* and *equity*. The second group includes elements relating to *performance* and comprises *income* and *expenses*. In the United Kingdom, the elements defined in the ASB's 1999 framework were somewhere between the US framework and the IASB Framework, being *assets*, *liabilities*, *ownership interest*, *gains*, *losses*, *contributions from owners* and *distributions to owners*. The Australian conceptual framework, through SAC 4 (which has now been replaced by the IASB Framework), identified five elements: assets, liabilities, equity, revenue and expenses.

In the FASB conceptual framework, rather than simply having a single element entitled *income* (or *gains* as in the ASB's framework), two elements are provided, *revenues* and *gains*, where revenues relate to the 'ongoing major or central operations' of the entity, while gains relate to 'peripheral

---

16 The view that the practice of accounting provides the means of maintaining existing positions of power and wealth by a favoured 'elite' is further investigated in Chapter 12, which considers the works of a body of theorists who are labelled 'critical theorists'.

17 SFAC 3 was superseded by SFAC 6. SFAC 3 related to business enterprises. SFAC 6 includes non-business entities.

or incidental transactions'. Clearly, the FASB classification system requires a judgement to be made about whether an item does or does not relate to the central operations of the entity. Such differentiation admits the possibility that managers might opportunistically manipulate whether items are treated as part of the ongoing operations of the entity or are treated as peripheral or incidental.

There are different approaches that can be applied to determining profits (revenues less expenses). Two such approaches are commonly referred to as the *asset/liability approach* and the *revenue/expense approach*. The asset/liability approach links profit to changes that have occurred in the assets and liabilities of the reporting entity, whereas the revenue/expense approach tends to rely on concepts such as the matching principle, which is very much focused on actual transactions and gives limited consideration to changes in the values of assets and liabilities. Most conceptual framework projects, including the IASB Framework and the FASB framework, adopt the asset/liability approach. Within these frameworks the definitions of elements of financial statements must thus start with definitions of assets and liabilities, as the definitions of all other elements flow from these definitions. This should become apparent as each of the elements of accounting is considered—as is now about to be done. In relation to the 'asset and liability view' of profit determination, the FASB and IASB (2005, pp. 7 and 8) state:

> In both [FASB and IASB] frameworks, the definitions of the elements are consistent with an 'asset and liability view,' in which income is a measure of the increase in the net resources of the enterprise during a period, defined primarily in terms of increases in assets and decreases in liabilities. That definition of income is grounded in a theory prevalent in economics: that an entity's income can be objectively determined from the change in its wealth plus what is consumed during a period (Hicks, pp. 178–179, 1946). That view is carried out in definitions of liabilities, equity, and income that are based on the definition of assets, that is, that give 'conceptual primacy' to assets. That view is contrasted with a 'revenue and expense view,' in which income is the difference between outputs from and inputs to the enterprise's earning activities during a period, defined primarily in terms of revenues (appropriately recognized) and expenses (either appropriately matched to them or systematically and rationally allocated to reporting periods in a way that avoids distortion of income) ... Some recent critics advocate a shift back to the revenue and expense view. However, in a recent study about principle-based standards, mandated by the 2002 Sarbanes–Oxley legislation, the U.S. Securities and Exchange Commission said the following:
>
> > ... the revenue/expense view is inappropriate for use in standard-setting—particularly in an objectives-oriented regime ... Historical experience suggests that the asset/liability approach most appropriately anchors the standard setting process by providing the strongest conceptual mapping to the underlying economic reality (page 30).
> >
> > ... the FASB should maintain the asset/liability view in continuing its move to an objectives-oriented standard setting regime (page 42).

DEFINITION OF ASSETS

In the IASB Framework, paragraph 49(a) defines an asset as:

> ... a resource controlled by the entity as a result of past events and from which future economic benefits are expected to flow to the entity.

This definition, which is similar to that adopted by the FASB, identifies three key characteristics:

1. There must be an expected future economic benefit.
2. The reporting entity must *control* the resource giving rise to these future economic benefits.
3. The transaction or other event giving rise to the reporting entity's control over the future economic benefits must have occurred.

The IASB Framework makes clear that the future economic benefits can be distinguished from the source of the benefit—a particular object or right. The definition refers to the benefit and not the source. Thus, whether an object or right is disclosed as an asset will be dependent on the likely economic benefits flowing from it. In the absence of the benefits, the object should not be disclosed as an asset. As paragraph 59 of the IASB Framework states:

> There is a close association between incurring expenditure and generating assets but the two do not necessarily coincide. Hence, when an entity incurs expenditure, this may provide evidence that future economic benefits were sought but is not conclusive proof that an item satisfying the definition of an asset has been obtained.

Conceptual frameworks do not require that an item must have a value in exchange before it can be recognised as an *asset*. The economic benefits may result from its ongoing use (often referred to as *value in use*) within the organisation. This approach can be contrasted with the model of accounting proposed by Raymond Chambers: *Continuously Contemporary Accounting* (considered in Chapter 5). Under Chambers' approach to accounting, if an asset does not have a current market value (value in exchange) it is to be excluded from the financial statements regardless of its value-in-use.

The characteristic of *control* relates to the capacity of a reporting entity to benefit from the asset and to deny or regulate the access of others to the benefit. The capacity to control would normally stem from legal rights. However, legal enforceability is not a prerequisite for establishing the existence of control. Hence, it is important to realise that control, and not legal ownership, is required before an asset can be shown within the body of an entity's statement of financial position (balance sheet). Frequently, controlled assets are owned but this is not always the case. As paragraph 57 of the IASB Framework states:

> In determining the existence of an asset, the right of ownership is not essential; thus, for example, property held on a lease is an asset if the entity controls the benefits which are expected to flow from the property. Although the capacity of an entity to control benefits is usually the result of legal rights, an item may nonetheless satisfy the definition of an asset even where there is no legal control.

While the above definition of an asset is the definition that currently must be used within countries that have adopted IFRSs (such as Australia), it should be noted that the definition might change in future years. Given the central importance of the asset definition to financial reporting, any change will conceivably have broad implications for financial reporting. In relation to joint work being undertaken by the FASB and the IASB, the FASB and IASB released a 'Project Update: Conceptual Framework—Phase B: Elements and Recognition', which noted that the existing definition of assets, which relies on the terms 'control', 'expected' and 'flow' of benefits, has a number of shortcomings. The boards noted the following (FASB, 2008):

> The Boards agreed that the current frameworks' existing asset definitions have the following shortcomings:
>
> Some users misinterpret the terms 'expected' (IASB definition) and 'probable' (FASB definition) to mean that there must be a high likelihood of future economic benefits for the definition to be met; this excludes asset items with a low likelihood of future economic benefits.
>
> The definitions place too much emphasis on identifying the future flow of economic benefits, instead of focusing on the item that presently exists, an economic resource.
>
> Some users misinterpret the term 'control' and use it in the same sense as that used for purposes of consolidation accounting. The term should focus on whether the entity has some rights or privileged access to the economic resource.
>
> The definitions place undue emphasis on identifying the past transactions or events that gave rise to the asset, instead of focusing on whether the entity had access to the economic resource at the balance sheet date.
>
> After consulting technical experts, the Boards decided to consider the following working definition of an asset:
>
> An *asset* of an entity is a present economic resource to which, through an enforceable right or other means, the entity has access or can limit the access of others.

Whether this definition replaces the existing definition is something that future years will reveal. Certainly the definition does seem to have some limitations of its own.

DEFINITION OF LIABILITIES

Paragraph 49(b) of the IASB Framework defines a liability as:

> ... a present obligation of the entity arising from past events, the settlement of which is expected to result in an outflow from the entity of resources embodying economic benefits.

This definition is also very similar to the definition provided in other conceptual frameworks and, as with the definition of assets, there are three key characteristics:

1. There must be an expected future disposition or transfer of economic benefits to other entities.
2. It must be a present obligation.
3. A past transaction or other event must have created the obligation.

As indicated, the definition of a liability does not restrict 'liabilities' to situations where there is a legal obligation. Liabilities should also be recognised in certain situations where equity or usual business practice dictates that obligations to external parties currently exist. As paragraph 60 of the *Framework for the Preparation and Presentation of Financial Statements* (the IASB Framework) states:

> An essential characteristic of a liability is that the entity has a present obligation. An obligation is a duty or responsibility to act or perform in a certain way. Obligations may be legally enforceable as a consequence of a binding contract or statutory requirement.

This is normally the case, for example, with amounts payable for goods and services received. Obligations also arise, however, from normal business practice, custom and a desire to maintain good business relations or act in an equitable manner. If, for example, an entity decides as a matter of policy to rectify faults in its products even when these become apparent after the warranty period has expired, the amounts that are expected to be expended in respect of goods already sold are liabilities.

Hence, the liabilities that appear within an entity's balance sheet (or, as it is also called, the statement of financial position) might include obligations that are legally enforceable as well obligations that are deemed to be equitable or constructive. When determining whether a liability exists, the intentions or actions of management need to be taken into account. That is, the actions or representations of the entity's management or governing body, or changes in the economic environment, directly influence the reasonable expectations or actions of those people outside the entity and, although they have no legal entitlement, they might have other sanctions that leave the entity with no realistic alternative but to make certain future sacrifices of economic benefits. Such present obligations are sometimes called 'equitable obligations' or 'constructive obligations'. An equitable obligation is governed by social or moral sanctions or custom rather than legal sanctions. A constructive obligation is created, inferred or construed from the facts in a particular situation rather than contracted by agreement with another entity or imposed by government.

Determining whether an equitable or a constructive obligation exists is often more difficult than identifying a legal obligation, and in most situations judgement is required to determine if an equitable or a constructive obligation exists. One consideration is that the entity has no realistic alternative to making the future sacrifice of economic benefits and this implies that there is no discretion. In cases where the entity retains discretion to avoid making any future sacrifice of economic benefits, a liability does not exist and is not recognised. It follows that a decision of the entity's management or governing body, of itself, is not sufficient for the recognition of a liability. Such a decision does not mark the inception of a present obligation since, in the absence of something more, the entity retains the ability to reverse the decision and thereby avoid the future sacrifice of economic benefits. For example, an entity's management or governing body may resolve that the entity will offer to repair a defect it has recently discovered in one of its products, even though the nature of the defect is such that the purchasers of the product would not expect the entity to do so. Until the entity makes public that offer, or commits itself in some other way to making the repairs, there is no present obligation, constructive or otherwise, beyond that of satisfying the existing statutory and contractual rights of customers.

Requiring liability recognition to be dependent upon there being a present obligation to other entities has implications for the disclosure of various provision accounts, such as a provision for maintenance. Generally accepted accounting practice in some countries has required such amounts to be disclosed as a liability, even though it does not involve an obligation to an external party. This issue is partially addressed in paragraph 64 of the IASB Framework, which states:

> ... when a provision involves a present obligation and satisfies the rest of the definition, it is a liability even if the amount has to be estimated. Examples include provisions for payments to be made under existing warranties and provisions to cover pension obligations.

Thus, the IASB Framework requires estimated (and therefore uncertain) present obligations, which have resulted from past events and are likely to result in an outflow of economic resources, to be treated as liabilities. In more recent conceptual frameworks (such as the ASB's UK and Irish framework and the Australian Accounting Standards Board's framework—both of which have now effectively been superseded by the older IASB Framework given the adoption of IASs/IFRSs in both the European Union and Australia from 2005) there tends to be an explicit requirement that uncommitted provisions not be classified as liabilities. For example, paragraph 60 of the Australian SAC No 4 stated:

> Some entities that carry out overhauls, repairs and renewals relating to major items of property, plant and equipment regularly 'provide' in their financial reports for such work to be undertaken in the future, with concomitant recognition of an expense. These provisions do not satisfy the definition of liabilities, because the entity does not have a present obligation to an external party... Also, some entities create 'provisions' for uninsured future losses (sometimes known as 'self-insurance provisions') for the purpose of retaining funds in the entity to meet losses which may arise in the future. In these situations, the entity does not have an obligation to an external party.[18]

As with the asset definition, the IASB and FASB have recently suggested a revised definition of a liability. As IASB (2008b) states:

> The Boards agreed that the current frameworks' existing liability definitions have the following shortcomings:
>
> Some users misinterpret the terms 'expected' (IASB definition) and 'probable' (FASB definition) to mean that there must be a high likelihood of future outflow of economic benefits for the definition to be met; this excludes liability items with a low likelihood of a future outflow of economic benefits.
>
> The definitions place too much emphasis on identifying the future outflow of economic benefits, instead of focusing on the item that presently exists, an economic obligation.
>
> The definitions place undue emphasis on identifying the past transactions or events that gave rise to the liability, instead of focusing on whether the entity has an economic obligation at the balance sheet date. The Boards considered the following working definition of a liability:
>
> "A *liability* of an entity is a present economic obligation that is enforceable against the entity."

Again, as with the proposed definition of assets, the suggested change in the liability definition could potentially have significant implications for financial reporting. For example, the definition could act to exclude constructive or equitable obligations that are not enforceable against the entity. This would be a major departure from existing practice. Again, whether the proposed definition ultimately becomes part of the revised conceptual framework is a matter of debate.

DEFINITION OF EQUITY

Paragraph 49(c) of the IASB Framework defines equity as 'the residual interest in the assets of the entity after deducting all its liabilities'. That is, equity equals assets minus liabilities (and in a company equity would be represented by 'shareholders' funds'). This definition is essentially the

---

18 As previously indicated, within Australia SAC 4 was replaced in 2005 by the IASB Framework.

same as that provided by the FASB and the ASB (and within the former conceptual framework in Australia). The residual interest is a claim or right to the net assets of the reporting entity. As a residual interest, it ranks after liabilities in terms of a claim against the assets of a reporting entity. Consistent with the *asset/liability approach* to determining profits (discussed earlier), the definition of equity is directly a function of the definitions of assets and liabilities. Profit or loss, income and expenses are then calculated in terms of changes in equity (that is, changes in net assets).

DEFINITION OF INCOME

Consistent with the *asset/liability approach*, the definition of income (and expenses) provided in the IASB Framework is dependent upon the definitions given to assets and liabilities. Paragraph 70(a) defines income as:

> ... increases in economic benefits during the accounting period in the form of inflows or enhancements of assets or decreases of liabilities that result in increases in equity, other than those relating to contributions from equity participants.

This definition is broadly consistent with that provided by the FASB, except that the FASB definition in SFAC 3 and SFAC 6 restricts revenues to the transaction or events that relate to the 'ongoing major or central operations' of the entity.

Income can therefore be considered as relating to transactions or events that cause an increase in the net assets of the reporting entity, other than owner contributions. Strictly speaking, applying the definition of income, increases in the market values of all assets could be treated as income. However, this is not always the case.

Within the IASB Framework, income can be recognised from normal trading relations, as well as from non-reciprocal transfers such as grants, donations, bequests or where liabilities are forgiven.

The IASB Framework further subdivides income into *revenues* and *gains*. Pursuant to the IASB Framework, 'revenue' arises in the course of the ordinary activities of an entity and is referred to by a variety of different names, including sales, fees, interest, dividends, royalties and rent. 'Gains' represent other items that meet the definition of income and may, or may not, arise in the course of the ordinary activities of an enterprise. Gains include, for example, those arising on the disposal of non-current assets. There will be a degree of professional judgement involved in determining whether a component of income should be classified as revenue or as a gain. Conceptually, it is not clear why the IASB Framework subdivides income into revenues and gains and there is minimal justification provided for this subdivision within the framework.

DEFINITION OF EXPENSES

As with income, the definition of expenses is dependent upon the definitions of assets and liabilities. Paragraph 70(b) of the IASB Framework defines expenses as:

> ... decreases in economic benefits during the accounting period in the form of outflows or depletions of assets or incurrences of liabilities that result in decreases in equity, other than those relating to distributions to equity participants.

There is no reference within the IASB Framework to traditional notions of 'matching' expenses with related revenues. The definition provided by the FASB in SFAC 3 and SFAC 6 is also similar, but restricts expenses to transactions or events relating to 'ongoing major or central operations'.[19]

Expenses may therefore be considered as transactions or events that cause reductions in the net assets or equity of the reporting entity, other than those caused by distributions to the owners. They include losses (reductions in net assets) caused by events that are not under the control of an entity—such as the uninsured element of losses caused by fires or floods, or losses caused by unhedged changes in foreign exchange rates.

Reviewing the above definition of expenses (which we know is a direct function of the definitions given to assets and liabilities), we can see that if a resource is used up or damaged by an entity, but that entity does not control the resource—that is, it is not an asset of the entity—then to the extent that no liabilities or fines are imposed, no expenses will be recorded by the entity. For example, if an entity pollutes the environment but incurs no related fines, no expense will be acknowledged and reported profits will not be affected, no matter how much pollution was emitted or how much damage was done to resources that are shared with others (and hence not controlled by the reporting entity). This has been seen as a limitation of financial accounting and a number of experimental approaches have been adopted by a number of entities to recognise the externalities their operations can generate but which would normally be ignored by traditional systems of accounting, including those proposed by the various conceptual framework projects. (Approaches used to incorporate externalities into financial accounting, often referred to as *full-cost accounting*, are explored in Chapter 9.)

The IASB Framework does not have a separate definition of profits, but, rather, only defines income and expenses as elements of performance. Profit is a presentational issue and is represented as the difference between the two elements, income and expenses.

RECOGNITION OF THE ELEMENTS OF FINANCIAL REPORTING

Having considered definitions of the elements of financial reporting (assets, liabilities, equity, income and expenses), the next building block to consider is the recognition criteria for these elements. Recognition criteria are employed to determine whether an item can actually be included within any of the elements of the financial statements. For example, should an item of expenditure be recognised as an asset? Issues of recognition are tied to issues of measurement, which are considered in the next subsection of this chapter. Under conceptual frameworks such as the IASB Framework, an item cannot be recognised if it cannot be reliably measured.

Paragraph 83 of the IASB Framework specifies in relation to all elements of accounting that:

An item that meets the definition of an element should be recognised if:

(a) it is probable that any future economic benefit associated with the item will flow to or from the entity; and

(b) the item has a cost or value that can be measured with reliability.

Thus, recognition is dependent upon the degree of probability that a future flow of economic benefits will arise that can be reliably measured. Obviously, considerations of *probability* can be very subjective, such that different people in different organisations might make different

---

19 The definition of expenses provided in SFAC 3 and 6 is 'outflows or other using up of the assets of the entity or incurrences of liabilities of an entity (or a combination of both) during a period that result from delivering or producing goods, rendering services, or carrying out other activities that constitute the entity's ongoing major or central operations'.

probability assessments for similar items. This will have implications for issues such as comparability—a qualitative characteristic of financial reporting. The IASB Framework provides relatively little guidance in judging probability, other than stating (in paragraph 85) that:

> Assessments of the degree of uncertainty attaching to the flow of future economic benefits are made on the basis of the evidence available when the financial statements are prepared.

Even though the determination of 'probable' is central to the recognition criteria applied to the elements of financial statements—as indicated above—the IASB Framework unfortunately does not define 'probable' (perhaps they think it is obvious). For guidance we can refer to the superseded Australian document, SAC 4. Paragraph 40 of SAC 4 defined 'probable' as 'more likely rather than less likely'.

Other paragraphs in the IASB Framework also mention that recognition depends on materiality, and that given the interconnectedness of the definitions of the various elements, recognition of a transaction or event in respect of one element requires recognition in all elements related to that transaction or event. For example, if an event occurs which leads to the recognition that the value of a fixed asset has decreased (for example, depreciation), the impact of this event on both assets and expenses must be recognised.

As noted above, issues of recognition are often regarded as standing side-by-side with issues of measurements. For example, Sterling (1985) argues that it is illogical to discuss how or when to recognise an element of accounting if we are not sure what measurement characteristics are to be recognised in relation to assets. What do you think of Sterling's argument that considering recognition issues in advance of measurement issues is akin to 'putting the cart before the horse'?

MEASUREMENT PRINCIPLES

While the recognition of the elements of financial reporting requires that the elements must be measurable with reasonable accuracy, conceptual frameworks have tended to provide very limited prescription in relation to measurement issues. Assets and liabilities are often (and certainly in practice under IASs/IFRSs) measured in a variety of ways depending on the particular class of assets or liabilities being considered, and given the way assets and liabilities are defined this has direct implications for reported profits. For example, liabilities are frequently recorded at present value, face value or on some other basis. In relation to assets, there are various ways these are measured; for example, inventory is to be measured at the lower of cost and net realisable value, some non-current assets such as property, plant and equipment can be measured at historical cost less a provision for depreciation, while other assets such as financial assets are to be measured at fair value.

Issues associated with measurement appeared to represent a stumbling block in the development of the FASB conceptual framework. While the FASB framework was initially promoted as being prescriptive, when SFAC 5 was issued in 1984 the FASB appeared to sidestep the difficult measurement issues; instead, the statement provided a description of various approaches to measuring the elements of accounting. SFAC 5 simply notes that there are generally accepted to be five alternative measurement bases applied in practice: historical cost, current replacement cost, current market value, net realisable value and present value. As noted previously, such a descriptive approach was generally considered to represent a 'cop-out' on behalf of the FASB (Solomons, 1986). The IASB Framework explicitly recognises the same variety of acceptable measurement bases as the FASB framework, with the exception of current market value (which could be regarded as comprising elements of current replacement cost and net realisable (sale) value).

As previously indicated, the IASB and the FASB are currently involved in joint efforts to develop a new refined conceptual framework. In relation to measurement, FASB and IASB (2005, p. 12) state:

> Measurement is one of the most underdeveloped areas of the two frameworks ... Both frameworks (the IASB and FASB Frameworks) contain lists of measurement attributes used in practice. The lists are broadly consistent, comprising historical cost, current cost, gross or net realizable (settlement) value, current market value, and present value of expected future cash flows. Both frameworks indicate that use of different measurement attributes is expected to continue. However, neither provides guidance on how to choose between the listed measurement attributes or consider other theoretical possibilities. In other words, the frameworks lack fully developed measurement concepts ... The long-standing unresolved controversy about which measurement attribute to adopt— particularly between historical-price and current-price measures—and the unresolved puzzle of unit of account are likely to make measurement one of the most challenging parts of this project.

Phase C of the joint IASB and FASB conceptual framework project is to address measurement issues. In this work the IASB and FASB have identified nine potential measurement bases: *past entry price, past exit price, modified past amount, current entry price, current exit price, current equilibrium price, value in use, future entry price* and *future exit price*. However, it is expected that it will be a number of years before any conclusion is reached about the most appropriate measurement basis for assets and liabilities.

Having considered the definition, recognition and measurement of the elements of financial statements, we will now consider some potential benefits that arise as a result of the development of conceptual frameworks.

BENEFITS ASSOCIATED WITH HAVING A CONCEPTUAL FRAMEWORK

Conceptual frameworks are costly to develop and open to many forms of political interference. In some respects their degree of progress, while initially promising, was for many years rather slow and disappointing. It will be interesting to see how successful the joint initiative of the IASB and the FASB is relative to previous initiatives. Is it worth continuing with these frameworks? This section considers some perceived advantages that have been advanced by standard-setting bodies as being likely to follow from the development of a conceptual framework (some criticisms will also be discussed). The perceived advantages include:

1. Accounting standards should be more consistent and logical because they are developed from an orderly set of concepts. That is, the accounting standards will be developed on the basis

of agreed principles. The view is that in the absence of a coherent theory the development of accounting standards could be somewhat *ad hoc*. As the FASB and IASB (2005, p. 1) state:

> To be principles-based, standards cannot be a collection of conventions but rather must be rooted in fundamental concepts. For standards on various issues to result in coherent financial accounting and reporting, the fundamental concepts need to constitute a framework that is sound, compehensive, and internally consistent.

2. The standard-setters should be more accountable for their decisions because the thinking behind specific requirements should be more explicit, as should any departures from the concepts that may be included in particular accounting standards.

3. The process of communication between the standard-setters and their constituents should be enhanced because the conceptual underpinnings of proposed accounting standards will be more apparent when the standard-setters seek public comment on them. Preparers and auditors will have a better understanding of why they are reporting/auditing. There is also a perspective that having a conceptual framework should alleviate some of the political pressure that might otherwise be exerted when accounting standards are developed—the conceptual framework could, in a sense, provide a defence against political attack.

4. The development of accounting standards should be more economical because the concepts developed will guide the standard-setters in their decision making.

5. Where accounting concepts cover a particular issue, there might be a reduced need for developing additional accounting standards.

6. Conceptual frameworks have had the effect of emphasising the 'decision usefulness' role of financial reports, rather than just restricting concern to issues associated with stewardship.

In terms of some possible disadvantages of conceptual frameworks, as with all activities based, at least in part, on lobbying processes and political actions, there will always be some parties potentially disadvantaged relative to others.

Perhaps some smaller organisations feel that they are overburdened by reporting requirements because analysts have been able to convince regulators that particular information was necessary for an efficiently functioning economy.

Another criticism raised regarding the conceptual framework projects relates to their focus. Being principally economic in focus, general purpose financial statements typically ignore transactions or events that have not involved market transactions or an exchange of property rights. That is, transactions or events that cannot be linked to a 'market price' are not recognised. For example, a great deal of recent literature has been critical of traditional financial accounting for its failure to recognise the environmental externalities caused by business entities (see Deegan & Rankin, 1997; Gray & Bebbington, 2001; Gray et al., 1996; Rubenstein, 1992).

Following on from this point, it has been argued that, by focusing on economic performance, this in itself further reinforces the importance of economic performance relative to various levels of social or environmental performance—and this is becoming more of a problem as it becomes increasingly apparent that organisations should be embracing the concept of sustainable development. Several writers, such as Hines (1988) and Gray and Bebbington (2001), have argued that the accounting profession can play a large part in influencing the forms of social conduct acceptable to the broader community. As has been indicated previously, accounting can both reflect and construct social expectations. For example, if profits and associated financial data are promoted as the best measure of organisational success, it could be argued that dominant consideration—by both the organisation and the community—will be given to activities that impact on this measure. If accountants were encouraged to embrace other types of performance indicators, including those that relate to environmental and other social performance, this may conceivably filter through to broadening people's expectations about organisational performance. Nevertheless, at the present time, profitability, as indicated by the output of the accounting system, is typically used as a guide to the success of an organisation.

Another criticism of conceptual frameworks is that they simply represent a codification of existing practice (Dean & Clarke, 2003; Hines, 1989), putting in place a series of documents that describe existing practice, rather than prescribing an 'ideal' or logically derived approach to accounting. Hines (1989) also argues that accounting regulations, as generated by the accounting regulators, are no more than the residual of a political process and as such do not represent any form of ideal model.

It has also been argued that conceptual frameworks have a more important objective from the perspective of the accounting standard-setters and one that does not provide benefits to financial statement users. Hines (1989) provides evidence that conceptual framework projects were actually initiated at times when professions were under threat—that they are 'a strategic manoeuvre for providing legitimacy to standard-setting boards during periods of competition or threatened government intervention' (1989, p. 89).

In supporting her case, Hines referred to the work undertaken in Canada. The Canadian Institute of Chartered Accountants (CICA) had done very little throughout the 1980s in relation to its conceptual framework project. It had begun the development of a framework in about 1980, a period Hines claimed was 'a time of pressures for reform and criticisms of accounting standard-setting in Canada' (1989, p. 88). However, interest 'waned' until another Canadian professional accounting body, the Certified General Accountants Association, through its Accounting Standards Authority of Canada, began developing a conceptual framework in 1986. This was deemed to represent a threat to CICA, 'who were motivated into action'. Solomons (1983) also provides an argument that conceptual frameworks are a defence against political interference by other interest groups.

CONCEPTUAL FRAMEWORKS AS A MEANS OF LEGITIMISING STANDARD-SETTING BODIES

While accounting standard-setters have promoted the benefits of conceptual frameworks, some of which have been discussed above, a number of writers (including Hines and Solomons, as identified above) have suggested that conceptual frameworks are created primarily to provide benefits to the parties that actually develop or commission the frameworks. It has been argued that conceptual frameworks have been used as devices to help ensure the ongoing existence of the accounting profession by 'boosting' their public standing (Dopuch & Sunder, 1980, p. 17). As Hines (1989, p. 74) suggests:

One of the main obstacles against which accountants have continually had to struggle in the professionalism quest has been the threat of an apparent absence of a formal body of accounting knowledge, and that creating the perception of possessing such knowledge has been an important part of creating and reproducing their social identity as a profession … Viewing these attempts (at establishing conceptual frameworks) as claims to accounting knowledge, which are used as a political resource in reducing the threat of government intervention and competing with other groups, in order to maintain and increase professionalism and social mobility seems to explain these projects better than viewing them from a technical/functional perspective.

It is argued that conceptual frameworks provide a means of increasing the ability of a profession to self-regulate, thereby counteracting the possibility that government intervention will occur. Hines (1991, p. 328) states:

> Conceptual Frameworks presume, legitimise and reproduce the assumption of an objective world and as such they play a part in constituting the social world ... Conceptual Frameworks provide social legitimacy to the accounting profession.
>
> Since the objectivity assumption is the central premise of our society ... a fundamental form of social power accrues to those who are able to trade on the objectivity assumption. Legitimacy is achieved by tapping into this central proposition because accounts generated around this proposition are perceived as 'normal'. It is perhaps not surprising or anomalous then that Conceptual Framework projects continue to be undertaken which rely on information qualities such as 'representational faithfulness', 'neutrality', 'reliability', etc., which presume a concrete, objective world, even though past Conceptual Frameworks have not succeeded in generating Accounting Standards which achieve these qualities. The very talk, predicated on the assumption of an objective world to which accountants have privileged access via their 'measurement expertise', serves to construct a perceived legitimacy for the profession's power and autonomy.

If we accept Hines' argument, we would perhaps reject the notion that the accounting profession was attempting to uncover any *truths* or *ideals*, and, rather, we would consider that the development of conceptual frameworks was a political action to ensure the survival of the profession. Reflecting on the role of conceptual frameworks in assisting a professional accounting body to survive, Horngren (1981, p. 87) notes:

> The useful life of the FASB is not going to rest on issues of technical competence. The pivotal issue will be the ability of the board to resolve conflicts among the various constituencies in a manner perceived to be acceptable to the ultimate constituent, the 800-pound gorilla in the form of the federal government, particularly the SEC (of course, the federal gorilla is also subject to pressure from its constituents). The ability will be manifested in the FASB's decisions, appointments and conceptual framework. So the conceptual framework is desirable if the survival of the FASB is considered to be desirable. That is, the framework is likely to help provide power to the board. After all, the board has no coercive power. Instead, the board must really rely on power by persuasion.

CHAPTER SUMMARY

This chapter has considered the development of conceptual frameworks. Conceptual frameworks are made up of a number of building blocks that cover issues of central importance to the financial reporting process. From a technical or functional perspective it has been argued by accounting standard-setters that the development of a conceptual framework will lead to improvements in financial reporting practices, which will in turn lead to financial statements that are deemed more useful for the economic decisions made by the financial statements users. With a well-formulated conceptual framework there is an expectation that information will be generated that is of more relevance to financial statements users, as well as being more reliable. The use of a logically derived conceptual framework will also lead to the development of accounting standards that are consistent with each other. Further, there is a view that conceptual frameworks will allow constituents to understand more fully how and why particular accounting standards require specific approaches to be adopted, and will provide preparers with guidance when no specific accounting standards exist.

In considering the success of conceptual frameworks, there are numerous authors who suggest that the frameworks have been a failure and have questioned whether such work should continue (Dopuch & Sunder, 1980). Issues such as those relating to measurement have been very real stumbling blocks for the ongoing development of conceptual frameworks. The progress, or in some cases the lack of it, emphasises the political nature of the accounting standard-setting process and shows that where constituents do not support particular approaches the standard-setters will quite often abandon particular endeavours.

While we can question the technical accomplishments of conceptual frameworks, some authors have suggested that technical advances were not the goal of the standard-setters. Rather, they have suggested that conceptual frameworks are actually established to bolster the ongoing existence and position of accountants in society. As Hines (1989, p. 79) states:

> Since professional powers, professional prestige and financial rewards are legitimised in society by being assumed to be founded on a formal body of knowledge unique to the profession, the possibility of the loss of this mystique poses a threat to the successful advancement or social reproduction of the profession. The phenomenon of the proliferation of conceptual framework projects in the UK, USA, Canada and Australia is better understood as a response to such a threat than in the functional/technical terms in which the Conceptual Frameworks have been articulated and discussed.

Whether we accept that conceptual frameworks are developed to improve the practice of accounting, or that such frameworks are primarily created to assist those within the accounting profession, is obviously a matter of personal opinion. Having read this chapter you should be better informed to make a judgement.

QUESTIONS

6.1 What is a conceptual framework of accounting?

6.2 Do you think we need conceptual frameworks? Explain your answer.

6.3 Why did Australia adopt the IASB Framework effective from 2005?

6.4 What advantages or benefits have been advanced by standard-setters to support the development of conceptual framework projects? Do you agree that in practice such benefits will be achieved?

6.5 Conceptual framework projects identify a number of qualitative criteria that financial information should possess if it is to be useful for economic decision making. Two such attributes are *neutrality* and *representational faithfulness*. Do you believe that financial information can, in reality, be neutral and representationally faithful? Explain your answer.

6.6   Is the notion of 'prudence' as described in the IASB Framework consistent with the notion of 'neutrality' as also described within the IASB Framework?

6.7   The two main qualitative characteristics that financial information should possess have been identified as *relevance* and *reliability*. Is one more important than the other, or are they equally important?

6.8   What are some possible objectives of general purpose financial reporting? Which objective appears to have been embraced within existing conceptual framework projects?

6.9   Which groups within society are likely to benefit from the development of a conceptual framework of accounting?

6.10 Would you consider that conceptual frameworks have been successful in achieving their stated objectives? Why, or why not?

6.11 Conceptual frameworks have yet to provide prescription in relation to measurement issues. Why do you think this is the case?

6.12 Hines (1989, p. 89) argues that conceptual frameworks are 'a strategic manoeuvre for providing legitimacy to standard-setting boards during periods of competition or threatened government intervention'. Explain the basis of her argument and consider whether the history of the development of conceptual frameworks supports her position.

6.13 *The Corporate Report* (UK) referred to the 'public's right to information'. How does this differ from the perspectives adopted in other conceptual framework projects?

6.14 According to the IASB Framework, what level of proficiency in accounting are financial statement readers expected to possess? Do you agree with this position?

6.15 Hines (1991) states that 'in communicating reality, accountants simultaneously create reality'. What does she mean?

6.16 This chapter discussed how accounting standard-setters typically find it difficult to get support for newly developed requirements if those requirements represent major changes to existing practice. Why do you think this is the case and do you think the potential lack of support would influence the strategies adopted by accounting standard-setters?

6.17 Do you think that the newly proposed definitions of assets and liabilities, as proposed in the joint work being undertaken by the IASB and FASB (and reproduced in this chapter), will have major implications for general purpose financial reporting if ultimately adopted? Why?

6.18 The definition of financial statement users provided at paragraph 9 of the IASB Framework encompasses investors, employees, lenders, suppliers, customers, government and their agencies, and the public. How much consideration, in your opinion, is given within the IASB Framework to the information needs and expectations of 'the public'? Does the conceptual framework really prescribe the disclosure of information that members of the community would find useful in assessing the contribution that a corporation makes to the community?

6.19 Within the joint conceptual framework project being undertaken by the IASB and FASB, the following objective of general purpose financial reporting has been proposed (IASB, 2008a, p. 14):

> The objective of general purpose financial reporting is to provide financial information about the reporting entity that is useful to present and potential equity investors, lenders and other creditors in making decisions in their capacity as capital providers. Information that is decision-useful to capital providers may also be useful to other users of financial reporting who are not capital providers.

Given the above definition, would general purpose financial reports be of relevance to people who are trying to assess the social and environmental performance of an organisation?

6.20 Do you agree with a 'one size fits all' approach to international financial accounting—that is, that all countries should adopt the same accounting standards and conceptual framework? Explain your answer.

6.21 Read the following quote from the FASB and IASB (2005, p. 5) and evaluate the view that 'reliability should be the dominant characteristic of financial statement measures'.

> Some FASB and IASB constituents have questioned some of the trade-offs between relevance and reliability that the Boards have made in setting particular accounting standards. For example, those constituents have questioned the appropriateness of trade-offs made in requiring financial statement measures that reflect fair values rather than historical costs. Their underlying presumption seems to be that historical costs, although arguably not as relevant as fair values, are more reliable. In those instances, those constituents assert that the trade-off between relevance and reliability should favour historical costs rather than fair values or, more generally, that reliability should be the dominant characteristic of financial statement measures.

6.22 The FASB and IASB (2005, p. 12) state:

> The long-standing unresolved controversy about which measurement attribute to adopt—particularly between historical-price and current-price measures—and the unresolved puzzle of unit of account are likely to make measurement one of the most challenging parts of this project.

Provide an explanation of why measurement will be one of the most 'challenging' components of the conceptual framework being jointly developed by the FASB and the IASB.

6.23 Hines (1991, p. 328) made the following statement:

> Conceptual Frameworks presume, legitimise and reproduce the assumptions of an objective world and as such they play a part in constituting the social world ... Conceptual Frameworks provide social legitimacy to the accounting profession. Since the objectivity assumption is the central premise of our society ... a fundamental form of social power accrues to those who are able to trade on the objectivity assumption. Legitimacy is achieved by tapping into this central proposition because accounts generated around this proposition are perceived as 'normal'. It is perhaps not surprising or anomalous then that Conceptual

Framework projects continue to be undertaken which rely on information qualities such as 'representational faithfulness', 'neutrality', 'reliability', etc., which presume a concrete, objective world, even though past Conceptual Frameworks have not succeeded in generating Accounting Standards which achieve these qualities. The very talk, predicated on the assumption of an objective world to which accountants have privileged access via their 'measurement expertise', serves to construct a perceived legitimacy for the profession's power and autonomy.

You are to explain and evaluate Hines' statement.

REFERENCES

Accounting Standards Steering Committee (1975), *The Corporate Report*, London: Institute of Chartered Accountants in England and Wales.

AICPA (1973), *Report of Study Group on Objectives of Financial Statements*, The Trueblood Report, New York: American Institute of Certified Public Accountants.

Baker, C. & M. Bettner (1997), 'Interpretive and critical research in accounting: a commentary on its absence from mainstream accounting research', *Critical Perspectives on Accounting*, 8(1), pp. 293–310.

Booth, B. (2003), 'The conceptual framework as a coherent system for the development of accounting standards', *ABACUS*, 39(3), pp. 310–24.

Chambers, R. J. (1966), *Accounting, Evaluation and Economic Behavior*, Englewood Cliffs, NJ: Prentice Hall.

Dean, G. W. & F. L. Clarke (2003), 'An evolving conceptual framework?', *ABACUS*, 39(3), pp. 279–97.

Deegan, C. (2007), *Australian Financial Accounting*, 5th edn, Sydney: McGraw-Hill.

Deegan, C. M. & M. Rankin (1997), 'The materiality of environmental information to users of accounting reports', *Accounting, Auditing and Accountability Journal*, 10(4), pp. 562–83.

Dopuch, N. & S. Sunder (1980), 'FASB's statements on objectives and elements of financial accounting: a review', *The Accounting Review*, 55(1), pp. 1–21.

Financial Accounting Standards Board and International Accounting Standards Board (2005) *Revisiting the Concepts: A New Conceptual Framework Project*, Norwalk, USA: FASB.

Financial Accounting Standards Board (2006), *Preliminary Views—Conceptual Framework for Financial Reporting: Objective of Financial Reporting and Qualitative Characteristics of Decision-Useful Financial Reporting Information*, FASB, Norwalk, CT.

Financial Accounting Standards Board (2008), *Project Update: Conceptual Framework—Phase B: Elements and Recognition*, FASB, Norwalk, CT.

Grady, P. (1965), *An Inventory of Generally Accepted Accounting Principles for Business Enterprises, Accounting Research Study No. 7*, New York: AICPA.

Gray, R. & J. Bebbington (2001), *Accounting for the Environment*, London: Sage Publications Ltd.

Gray, R., D. Owen & C. Adams (1996), *Accounting and Accountability: Changes and Challenges in Corporate Social and Environmental Reporting*, London: Prentice Hall.

Handel, W. (1982), *Ethnomethodology: How People Make Sense*, Hemel Hempstead: Prentice Hall.

Hendriksen, E. (1970), *Accounting Theory,* Illinois: Richard D. Irwin.

Hines, R. (1988), 'Financial accounting: in communicating reality, we construct reality', *Accounting, Organizations and Society,* 13(3), pp. 251–62.

Hines, R. (1989), 'Financial accounting knowledge, conceptual framework projects and the social construction of the accounting profession', *Accounting, Auditing and Accountability Journal,* 2(2), pp. 72–92.

Hines, R. (1991), 'The FASB's conceptual framework, financial accounting and the maintenance of the social world', *Accounting, Organizations and Society,* 16(4), pp. 313–51.

Horngren, C. T. (1981), 'Uses and limitations of a conceptual framework', *Journal of Accountancy,* 151(4), pp. 86–95.

International Accounting Standards Board (2008a), *Exposure Draft of an Improved Conceptual Framework for Financial Reporting,* IASB, London.

International Accounting Standards Board (2008b), *Discussion Paper—Preliminary Views on an Improved Conceptual Framework for Financial Reporting: The Reporting Entity,* London: IASB.

Loftus, J. A. (2003), 'The CF and accounting standards: the persistence of discrepancies', *ABACUS,* 39(3), pp. 298–309.

Miller, P. B. W. (1990), 'The conceptual framework as reformation and counterreformation', *Accounting Horizons* (June), pp. 23–32.

Miller, P. B. W. & R. Reading (1986), *The FASB: The People, the Process, and the Politics,* Illinois: Irwin.

Moonitz, M. (1961), *The Basic Postulates of Accounting, Accounting Research Study No. 1,* New York: AICPA.

Nussbaumer, N. (1992), 'Does the FASB's conceptual framework help solve real accounting issues?', *Journal of Accounting Education,* 10(1), pp. 235–42.

Peasnell, K. V. (1982), 'The function of a conceptual framework for corporate financial reporting', *Accounting and Business Research,* 12(4), pp. 243–56.

Rubenstein, D. B. (1992), 'Bridging the gap between green accounting and black ink', *Accounting, Organizations and Society,* 17(5), pp. 501–8.

Solomons, D. (1978), 'The politicization of accounting', *Journal of Accountancy,* 146(5), pp. 65–72.

Solomons, D. (1983), 'The political implications of accounting and accounting standard setting', *Accounting and Business Research,* 13(56), pp. 107–18.

Solomons, D. (1986), 'The FASB's conceptual framework: an evaluation', *Journal of Accountancy,* 161(6), pp. 114–24.

Sprouse, R. & M. Moonitz (1962), *A Tentative Set of Broad Accounting Principles for Business Enterprises, Accounting Research Study No. 3,* New York: American Institute of Certified Public Accountants.

Stamp, E. (1980), *Corporate Reporting: Its Future Evolution,* Toronto: Canadian Institute of Chartered Accountants.

Staunton, J. (1984), 'Why a conceptual framework of accounting?', *Accounting Forum,* 7(2), pp. 85–90.

Sterling, R. R. (1985), 'An essay on recognition', University of Sydney Accounting Research Centre.

Walker, R. G. (2003), 'Objectives of financial reporting', *ABACUS,* 39(3), pp. 340–55.

Watts, R. L. & J. L. Zimmerman (1986), *Positive Accounting Theory,* Englewood Cliffs, NJ: Prentice Hall.

Wells, M. (2003), 'Forum: the accounting conceptual framework', *ABACUS,* 39(3), pp. 273–78.

CHAPTER 7

POSITIVE ACCOUNTING THEORY

LEARNING OBJECTIVES

On completing this chapter readers should understand:

- how a positive theory differs from a normative theory;
- the origins of Positive Accounting Theory (PAT);
- the perceived role of accounting in minimising the transaction costs of an organisation;
- how accounting can be used to reduce the costs associated with various political processes;
- how particular accounting-based agreements with parties such as debtholders and managers can provide incentives for managers to manipulate accounting numbers;
- some of the criticisms of PAT.

OPENING ISSUES

Corporate management often expends considerable time and effort making submissions to accounting regulators on proposed introductions of, or amendments to, mandated accounting requirements (for example, accounting standards). For instance, in 2005 Australia adopted a new accounting standard pertaining to intangible assets, AASB 138. AASB 138 'Intangible Assets', which is based on the International Accounting Standard IAS 38, required that many intangible assets—such as internally generated brand names, trademarks and research expenditure—be removed from the statement of financial position (or, as it is also known, the balance sheet). Australian companies had previously been allowed to include such assets on the statement of financial position. This new requirement had a significant impact on the statement of financial position, with many assets having to be removed. Before the new accounting standard became effective, an article in the *Australian* on 19 June 2004 (entitled '$40 billion in write-offs expected') predicted that 'about $40 billion will be wiped from the value of Australia's top 180 companies'. Before the implementation of the new standard, numerous corporate submissions were made to the Australian Accounting Standards Board and the International Accounting Standards Board arguing that elements of AASB 138/IAS 38 failed to take account of the underlying economic realities of the assets in question, and would result in financial statements that did not reflect the underlying economic reality. Executives of many organisations lobbied against the introduction of AASB 138 in Australia. What would have motivated such opposition?

INTRODUCTION

Previous chapters of this book have considered numerous issues as they relate to financial accounting, including theories to explain the needs and demand for financial accounting regulations as well as explanations for international differences in financial accounting. Normative theories of accounting have also been considered—specifically theories that prescribe how to undertake financial accounting in times of changing prices, and conceptual framework projects that provide prescription about how elements of accounting should be defined and measured, and when they should be recognised.

This chapter changes focus and considers a theory that seeks to explain *why* managers within organisations elect to adopt particular accounting methods in preference to others. That is, it does not consider theories (normative theories) that tell us how financial accounting *should* be undertaken.

Quite often in financial accounting we will have a choice between alternative accounting methods to account for a particular transaction or event—that is, even with the many accounting standards there is still a degree of flexibility in how to account for specific items or events. The theory discussed in this chapter—Positive Accounting Theory—provides a particular perspective about why managers, when confronted with a choice between competing accounting methods, would elect to adopt or support particular accounting methods in preference to others. Positive Accounting Theory relies in large part on assumptions from the economics literature. For example, the theory assumes that 'markets' are efficient and that all individual action is driven by self-interest. As with most theories of accounting, there will be supporters of the theory and there will also be opponents. The chapter concludes with a review of some criticisms of Positive Accounting Theory.

POSITIVE ACCOUNTING THEORY DEFINED

As indicated in Chapter 1, a *positive theory* is a theory that seeks to explain and predict particular phenomena. According to Watts (1995, p. 334), the use of the term *positive research* was popularised in economics by Friedman (1953) and was used to distinguish research that sought to *explain* and *predict* (which is positive research) from research that aimed to provide *prescription* (as explained in previous chapters, prescriptive research is often labelled *normative* research). Positive Accounting Theory, the topic discussed in this chapter and the theory popularised by Watts and Zimmerman, is one of several positive theories of accounting.[1] As indicated in Chapter 1, this text uses lower-case when referring to the general class of theories that attempt to explain and predict accounting practice (that is, 'positive theories of accounting'), and uses

---

1   Legitimacy Theory, Institutional Theory and Stakeholder Theory, all covered in Chapter 8, are other examples of positive theories. For example, Legitimacy Theory predicts that in certain circumstances organisations will use positive or favourable disclosures in an effort to gain, maintain or restore the legitimacy of an organisation. These other positive theories are not grounded in classical economic theory, whereas Positive Accounting Theory is.

upper-case when referring to Watts and Zimmerman's particular theory of accounting, Positive Accounting Theory. Hence, while it might be confusing, we must remember that Watts and Zimmerman's Positive Accounting Theory is an example of one particular positive theory of accounting. This confusion might not have arisen had Watts and Zimmerman elected to adopt an alternative name (or 'trademark') for their particular theory. According to Watts and Zimmerman (1990, p. 148):

> We adopted the label 'positive' from economics where it was used to distinguish research aimed at explanation and prediction from research whose objective was prescription. Given the connotation already attached to the term in economics we thought it would be useful in distinguishing accounting research aimed at understanding accounting from research directed at generating prescriptions ... The phrase 'positive' created a trademark and like all trademarks it conveys information. 'Coke', 'Kodak', 'Levi's' convey information.

As Watts and Zimmerman (1986, p. 7) state, Positive Accounting Theory (hereafter referred to as PAT):

> ... is concerned with explaining accounting practice. It is designed to explain and predict which firms will and which firms will not use a particular method ... but it says nothing as to which method a firm should use.[2]

Positive theories can be contrasted with normative theories. Chapters 5 and 6 considered different normative theories of accounting. Normative theories prescribe how a particular practice *should* be undertaken and this prescription might be a significant departure from existing practice. A normative theory is generated as a result of the particular theorist applying some norm, standard or objective against which actual practice should strive to achieve. For example, under Chambers' theory of accounting, which he labelled Continuously Contemporary Accounting, *all* assets *should* be measured at net market value; according to Chambers, such information is more useful for informed decision making than information based on historical costs, which may actually be misleading. Chambers made a judgement about the role of accounting (to provide information about an entity's *capacity to adapt* to changing circumstances) and as a result of this judgement he prescribed a particular accounting practice.

Returning to PAT, this chapter reveals that PAT focuses on the relationships between the various individuals involved in providing resources to an organisation and how accounting is used to assist in the functioning of these relationships. Examples are the relationships between the owners (as suppliers of equity capital) and the managers (as suppliers of managerial labour), or between the managers and the firm's debt providers (that is, the creditors). Many relationships involve the delegation of decision making from one party (the principal) to another party (the agent)—this is referred to as an agency relationship.

When decision-making authority is delegated, this can lead to some loss of efficiency and consequent costs. For example, if the owner (principal) delegates decision-making authority to a manager (agent) it is possible that the manager may not work as hard as would the owner, given

---

2   Similarly, in Chapter 8 we see that three other positive theories, Stakeholder Theory (the managerial version), Institutional Theory and Legitimacy Theory, provide alternative explanations (alternative to PAT) about what drives an organisation to make particular disclosures. These theoretical perspectives also do not prescribe particular actions or methods of disclosure.

that the manager might not share directly in the results of the organisation. Any potential loss of profits brought about by the manager under-performing is considered to be a cost that results from the decision-making delegation within this agency relationship—an agency cost. The agency costs that arise as a result of delegating decision-making authority from the owner to the manager are referred to in PAT as *agency costs of equity*.

PAT, as developed by Watts and Zimmerman and others, is based on the central economics-based assumption that all individuals' actions are driven by *self-interest* and that individuals will always act in an opportunistic manner to the extent that the actions will increase their wealth. Notions of loyalty, morality and the like are not incorporated in the theory (as they typically are not incorporated in other accounting or economic theories). Given an assumption that self-interest drives *all* individual actions (which in many people's mind is an overly simplistic assumption), PAT predicts that organisations will seek to put in place mechanisms that align the interests of the managers of the firm (the agents) with the interests of the owners of the firm (the principals). As discussed later in the chapter, some of these methods of aligning interests will be based on the output of the accounting system (such as providing the manager with a share of the organisation's *profits*). Where such accounting-based 'alignment mechanisms' are in place, there will be a need for financial statements to be produced. Managers are predicted to 'bond' themselves to prepare these financial statements.[3] This is costly in itself, and in PAT would be referred to as a 'bonding cost'. If we assume that managers (agents) will be responsible for preparing the financial statements, then PAT also would predict that there would be a demand for those statements to be audited or monitored, otherwise agents would, assuming self-interest (a maintained assumption of PAT), try to overstate profits, thereby increasing their absolute share of profits. In PAT, the cost of undertaking an audit is referred to as a 'monitoring cost'.

To address the agency problems that arise within an organisation, there may be various bonding and monitoring costs incurred. If it was assumed, contrary to the assumptions of PAT, that individuals *always* worked for the benefit of their employers, there would not be a demand for such activities—other than perhaps to review the efficiency with which the manager was operating the business. As PAT assumes that not all opportunistic actions of agents can be controlled by contractual arrangements or otherwise, there will always be some residual costs associated with appointing an agent.

Having provided this introductory overview of PAT, we now turn to the origins and development of PAT. The issue of how accounting can be used to reduce conflicts within the firm is returned to later in the chapter. The following discussion shows that PAT developed out of the economics literature and was heavily reliant on assumptions about the efficiency of markets (from the Efficient Markets Hypothesis), on research that considered the reactions of capital markets to accounting information (which was developed from models such as the Capital Assets Pricing Model), and on the role of contractual arrangements in minimising conflicts within an organisation (from agency theory).

---

3   From the PAT perspective, bonding occurs when the agent gives a guarantee to undertake, or not to undertake, certain activities.

THE ORIGINS AND DEVELOPMENT OF POSITIVE ACCOUNTING THEORY

Positive research in accounting started coming to prominence around the mid-1960s and appeared to become the dominant research paradigm within financial accounting in the 1970s and 1980s. Prior to this time the dominant type of accounting research was normative accounting research—research that sought to provide prescription based on the theorists' perspective of the underlying objective of accounting. High-profile normative researchers of this time included Sterling, Edwards, Bell and Chambers and the focus of much of the research was how to undertake accounting in times of rising prices.[4] Such normative research did not rely on examining existing practice—that is, it did not tend to be empirical.

Watts (1995, p. 299) provides an insight into the trends in accounting research that occurred from the 1950s to the 1970s. As evidence of the trends, and relying on the works of Dyckman and Zeff (1984), he documents the number of publications accepted by two dominant academic accounting journals—*The Accounting Review* and the *Journal of Accounting Research*.[5] He states:

> The introduction of positive research into accounting in the mid-1960s represented a paradigm shift. Prior to that time, the most common type of paper published in the leading English language academic journal of the time (*The Accounting Review*) was normative (like the works of Edwards and Bell, Chambers and Sterling). In the period 1956–1963, 365 of *Accounting Review* articles were of this type. These papers use assumptions about phenomena and objectives to deduce their prescriptions. They do not use systematic evidence and/or advance hypotheses for formal testing. Only 3% of the articles published in *Accounting Review* in 1956–1963 were empirical and most were not designed to test hypotheses. Virtually none of the papers in this time period were attempts to explain current accounting using mathematical modelling or less formal techniques. Today, almost all papers in *Accounting Review* are in the positive tradition and the same is true of most other leading academic journals (all of which started in 1963 or later).[6]

---

4   The work of these theorists was considered in Chapter 5. As indicated in Chapter 5 as well as in Chapter 1, researchers such as Sterling, Chambers and many others were particularly critical of positive research, and particularly of Positive Accounting Theory. Among their many criticisms was the criticism that PAT, while attempting to explain and predict accountants' behaviour, provided no prescription about what methods accountants should adopt to provide useful information to the readers of accounting reports.

5   By relying on only two journals it could easily be argued, given that there are many other accounting journals, that the data may not be representative of all accounting research being undertaken. Further, evidence would indicate that the editors of these journals developed an extremely favourable disposition towards positive research, a disposition not necessarily shared by editors of other journals. Nevertheless, there was certainly a significant movement towards positive research in the 1960s and 1970s.

6   As we might imagine, there are many researchers who do not favour the positive research paradigm, and hence would challenge Watts' view that journals that publish positive research are 'leading' academic journals.

In reflecting on what caused the shift in paradigm from normative to positive research, Watts (1995, p. 299) argues that:

> The paradigm shift is associated with changes in US business schools in the late 1950s and early 1960s. Reports on business education commissioned by the Ford Foundation and the Carnegie Corporation of New York were catalysts for those changes ... Hypothesis forming and testing were viewed as essential for good research.[7]

The quote refers to the 'essential' nature of 'hypothesis forming and testing'. This in itself represents a biased view about what constitutes 'good research'. A hypothesis would be formed to test a prediction, for example that under specific conditions accountants would select a particular method of accounting—this type of issue is something that fascinates researchers working within a PAT framework. The reason that normative researchers, on the other hand, would not form and test hypotheses is that such researchers would not be as concerned with *what is* (which could be tested empirically); rather, they would be concerned with *what should be*. Hence, normative researchers do not necessarily develop any predictive hypotheses, but this in itself should not be used to dismiss their work as not being 'good research'.

Nevertheless, there was a view from opponents of normative research that, in failing to provide 'falsifiable' predictions (or hypotheses), normative researchers failed to meet the requirements necessary to advance knowledge. As indicated in Chapter 1, there is a subset of the research community known as the falsificationists (the leader of which was considered to be Karl Popper). They consider that knowledge develops through trial and error and that 'sound research' should generate propositions or hypotheses that are of a form that allows them to be rejected if evidence supporting the propositions or hypotheses is not available (that is, the hypothesis should be falsifiable). If falsifiable hypotheses are not generated from the theory, then falsificationists would believe that the theory is deficient.

It was also argued that around the mid-1960s and throughout the 1970s computing facilities improved markedly, such that it became increasingly practical to undertake large-scale statistical analysis—an approach used within the positive research paradigm. As Watts and Zimmerman (1986, p. 339) state:

> Computers and large machine-readable data bases (CRSP and Compustat) became available in the 1960s. And, partially in response to the lowered cost of empirical work, finance and economic positive theories became available for accounting researchers' use. This led to the development of positive accounting research and to researchers trained in the methodology of positive theory.[8]

---

7   As indicated in Chapter 1, a paradigm can be described as an approach to knowledge advancement that adopts particular theoretical assumptions, research goals and research methods (Kuhn, 1962).

8   Chapter 12 (which considers the views of the critical theorists) provides alternative views about why positive accounting flourished in the 1970s and 1980s. These theorists (for example, Mouck, 1992; Tinker et al., 1991) believe that many accounting researchers provide research results and perspectives that aim to legitimise and maintain particular political ideologies. As an example, in the late 1970s and in the 1980s, there were moves by particular governments around the world towards deregulation. This was particularly the case in the United States and the United Kingdom. Around this time researchers working within the Positive Accounting Theory framework, and researchers who embraced the Efficient Markets Hypothesis, came to prominence. The researchers typically took an anti-regulation stance, a stance that matched the views of the government of the time. Coincidentally, perhaps, the critical theorists show that such research, which supported calls for deregulation, tended to attract considerable government-sourced research funding, thereby providing further resources for the theory's development.

Watts considers that a paper that was crucial to the acceptance of the positive research paradigm was one by Ball and Brown (1968). According to Watts (1995, p. 303), the publication of this paper in the *Journal of Accounting Research* caused widespread interest in accounting-related capital markets research (research that seeks to explain and predict share price reaction to the public release of accounting information), and led to ever-increasing numbers of papers being published in the area (this paper will be considered shortly). Reflecting on the subsequent shift in publications towards positive research, Watts (1995, p. 303) states:

> Empirical papers as a proportion of papers published in *Journal of Accounting Research* rose from 13 per cent in 1967 to 31 per cent in 1968 and to 60 per cent by 1972. Normative papers in *Journal of Accounting Research* fell from 24 per cent in 1967 to seven per cent in 1968 and by 1972 to zero. *The Accounting Review* (which is another leading journal) followed suit and stopped publishing normative papers. The empirical papers in the capital markets area were in the positivist tradition. The normativists challenged the evidence and its interpretation, but did not supply their own counter-evidence. They did not have the training nor likely the desire to compete in this dimension.

ROLE OF THE EFFICIENT MARKETS HYPOTHESIS

One development from the 1960s that was crucial to the development of PAT was the work of theorists such as Fama, particularly work that related to the development of the Efficient Markets Hypothesis (EMH). The EMH is based on the assumption that capital markets react in an efficient and unbiased manner to publicly available information.[9] The perspective taken is that security prices reflect the information content of publicly available information and this information is not restricted to accounting disclosures. The capital market is considered to be highly competitive, and as a result newly released public information is expected to be quickly impounded into share prices. As Watts and Zimmerman (1986, p. 6) state:

> Underlying the EMH is competition for information. Competition drives investors and financial analysts to obtain information on the firm from many sources outside the firm's accounting reports and even outside the firm itself. For example, analysts obtain weekly production data on automobile firms and interview management. Analysts also interview competitors about a corporation's sales and creditors about the corporation's credit standing.

If accounting results are released by an organisation, and these results were already anticipated by the market (perhaps as a result of interim announcements), the expectation is that the price of the security will not react to the release of the accounting results. Consistent with traditional finance theory, the price of a security is determined on the basis of beliefs about the present value of future cash flows pertaining to that security and when these beliefs change

---

9   Research that subsequently tested the EMH predominantly adopted the assumption of semi-strong form market efficiency. Under the assumption of semi-strong form efficiency, the market price of a firm's securities reflects all publicly available information. According to Watts and Zimmerman (1986, p. 19), the available evidence is generally consistent with the semi-strong form of EMH. Two other forms of market efficiency (with less empirical support) have also been advanced. A weak form of market efficiency assumes that existing security prices simply reflect information about past prices and trading volumes. The strong form of market efficiency assumes that security prices reflect all information known to anyone at that point in time (including information that is not publicly available). Capital markets research (and the EMH) is considered more fully in Chapter 9.

(as a result of particular 'new' information becoming available) the expectation is that the security's price will also change.[10]

Because share prices are expected to reflect information from various sources (as the information relates to predicting future cash flows), there was a view that management cannot manipulate share prices by changing accounting methods in an opportunistic manner. If the change in accounting method does not signal a change in cash flows, then early proponents of the EMH would argue that the capital market will not react. Further, because there are many sources of data used by the capital market, if managers make less than truthful disclosures, which are not corroborated or contradict other available information, then, assuming that the market is efficient, the market will question the integrity of the managers. Consequently, the market will tend to pay less attention to subsequent accounting disclosures made by such managers. Watts and Zimmerman (1986) rely on this perspective to argue against the need for extensive accounting regulation. Because accounting information is only one source of information, because markets are assumed to be efficient in evaluating information, and because of the existence of other potentially non-corroboratory evidence, there is believed to be limited benefit in imposing accounting regulation.[11]

SHARE PRICE REACTIONS TO UNEXPECTED EARNINGS ANNOUNCEMENTS

Researchers such as Ball and Brown (1968) and Beaver (1968) sought to investigate empirically stock-market reactions to accounting earnings announcements. Using monthly information about earnings announcements in the *Wall Street Journal* and information about share returns, Ball and Brown investigated whether unexpected changes in accounting earnings lead to abnormal returns on an organisation's securities. Relying on the EMH, Ball and Brown proposed that, if the earnings announcements were useful to the capital market (there was new or unexpected information in the announcement), share prices would adjust to reflect the new information. As they stated (1968, p. 159):

> If security prices do in fact adjust rapidly to new information as it becomes available, then changes in security prices will reflect the flow of information to the market. An observed revision of stock prices associated with the release of the income report would thus provide evidence that the information reflected in income numbers is useful.

Hence Ball and Brown needed to determine whether the earnings announcement contained any information that was unexpected and therefore potentially 'useful'. Using statistical modelling, they calculated an estimate of what the *expected earnings* of the entity were in the absence of the earnings announcement. They also needed a model to estimate what the market return from holding the entity's securities would have been in the absence of the information. That is, they needed to be able to determine what *normal* returns would have been on the securities so

---

10   In studies that investigate the reaction of the capital market to earnings announcements, it is generally assumed that accounting earnings are highly correlated with cash flows, hence new information about accounting earnings is deemed to indicate new information about cash flows.

11   As indicated in Chapter 3, advocates of a 'free-market' approach to regulation (that is, people who adopt an anti-regulation stance) typically use arguments that various markets (such as capital markets and managerial labour markets) are efficient and will penalise managers who fail to provide information that efficiently reflects the performance of their organisation. Hence, markets will 'encourage' full disclosure and there is therefore perceived to be no need for regulatory requirements or intervention.

that they could then determine whether any *abnormal* returns arose (which would have been assumed to relate to the information disclosure).

In determining what normal returns would have been had there been no unexpected information in the earnings announcement, reliance is placed on the market model which is derived from the Capital Asset Pricing Model (CAPM).[12] These models are more fully discussed in Chapter 10. Briefly, on the basis of past information, the CAPM provides an indication of the expected rate of return on securities by applying a linear model.[13] The expected return on a particular stock is calculated by considering the risk-free rate of return (for example, the return from holding government bonds), plus a risk/return component that is based on how the returns on the particular security have fluctuated historically relative to the movements in the overall (diversified) stock market. The difference between the expected return and the actual return constitutes the abnormal return. The results of the Ball and Brown study were generally supportive of the view that, if earnings (or profit) announcements provided unexpected information, the capital market reacted to the information, the reaction taking the form of abnormal returns on the entity's securities.

By indicating that earnings (or profit) announcements (mainly based on historical cost accounting) were impacting on share prices, Ball and Brown provided evidence that they considered was consistent with a view that historical cost information was useful to the market.[14] This was in direct conflict with various normative theorists (such as Chambers) who had argued that historical cost information is rather useless and misleading.[15] The capital market apparently thought otherwise (if we accept that the change in share price reflected the usefulness of the accounting information).[16] In this respect, Watts and Zimmerman (1986, p. 161) state:

> Some critics charge that, because earnings are calculated using several different methods of valuation (e.g. historical cost, current cost, and market value), the earnings numbers are meaningless and stock prices based on those numbers do not discriminate between efficient and less efficient firms. Given the EMH, evidence is inconsistent with this criticism. Positive stock price changes are associated with positive unexpected

---

12 Share returns would generally be calculated by taking into account the change in price of the security during the period, as well as any dividends received during the period.

13 The development of the CAPM is generally credited to the works of Sharpe (1964) and Lintner (1965).

14 Much research has followed Ball and Brown (1968). For example, subsequent research has shown that the relationship between the information content in earnings announcements and changes in share prices tends to be more significant for small firms. That is, in general, larger firms' earnings announcements have relatively less information content (for example). This is consistent with the EMH and is explained by the fact that larger firms tend to have more information being circulated about them, as well as attracting more attention from such parties as security analysts. Hence, on average, earnings announcements for larger firms tend to be more anticipated, and hence already impounded in the share price prior to the earnings announcement.

15 Ball and Brown's results were also considered to be important because they emphasise that accounting numbers were not the sole (or predominant) source of information about an organisation. This was in contrast to the views held by many normative theorists who considered that accounting data were the sole, or at least the most important, source of information about an organisation, hence their concerns about getting the accounting numbers 'right'.

16 What should also be appreciated is that research such as that undertaken by Ball and Brown and subsequent researchers actually represents a joint test of the EMH as well as the procedures used to estimate expected returns and normal returns. That is, failure to generate significant results (or indeed, success in generating significant results) may be due to misspecification problems in the calculation of expected earnings and normal returns, rather than problems with the hypothesis itself.

earnings and negative stock prices with negative unexpected earnings. Therefore, since the stock price is an unbiased estimate of value, earnings changes are measures of value changes.

Throughout the 1970s and subsequent years, many other studies were published that documented the relationship between accounting earnings and security returns (and a number of these are considered in Chapter 10). However, while supportive of the EMH, the literature was unable to explain *why* particular accounting methods might have been selected in the first place. That is, the research provided no hypotheses to *predict* and *explain* accounting choices—rather the existing research simply considered the market's reaction to the ultimate disclosures.

USE OF AGENCY THEORY TO HELP EXPLAIN AND PREDICT MANAGERIAL CHOICE OF ACCOUNTING POLICIES

Much of the research based on the EMH assumed that there were zero contracting and information costs, as well as assuming that the capital market could efficiently 'undo' the implications of management selecting different accounting methods.[17] For example, if an entity elected to switch its inventory cost-flow assumptions and this led to an increase in reported income, the market was assumed to be able to 'see through' this change, and, to the extent that there were no apparent cash-flow implications (for example, through changing taxes), there would be no share price reaction. Hence, if the particular accounting method had no direct taxation implications, and assuming that markets were efficient and able to understand the effects of using alternative accounting methods, there was an inability to explain why one method of accounting was selected by management in preference to another. As Watts and Zimmerman (1990, p. 132) state:

> An important reason that the information perspective (e.g. Ball and Brown, 1968) failed to generate hypotheses explaining and predicting accounting choice is that in the finance theory underlying the empirical studies, accounting choice per se could not affect firm value. Information is costless and there are no transaction costs in the CAPM frameworks. Hence if accounting methods do not affect taxes they do not affect firm value. In that situation there is no basis for predicting and explaining accounting choice. Accounting is irrelevant.

Yet, evidence indicated that corporate managers expended considerable resources lobbying regulators in regard to particular accounting methods that could potentially be included in accounting standards. To such individuals, the choice of accounting method *did* matter. Further, there was evidence (for example, Kaplan & Roll, 1972) that firms within an entire industry often elected to switch accounting methods at a particular time.

---

17 As shown later in the chapter, however, subsequent arguments were developed to support a contrary view that a change in accounting method may have cash-flow consequences (and therefore, consequences for share prices). For example, the new accounting method may be considered to provide information more efficiently about the performance of the firm, and hence may enable the firm to attract more funds at lower cost (perhaps because investors consider the available information to be more reliable). Further, and as shown shortly, many contractual arrangements with associated cash flows (for example, there might be an agreement that the manager gets paid a percentage of profits) are tied to accounting numbers and hence changing those numbers can ultimately change cash flows (and hence, firm value if we believe that the value of a firm's securities represent expectations about the net present value of the future expected cash flows of the firm).

A key to explaining managers' choice of particular accounting methods came from agency theory. Agency theory provided a necessary explanation of why the selection of particular accounting methods might matter, and hence was an important facet in the development of PAT. Agency theory focused on the relationships between principals and agents (for example, the relationship between shareholders and corporate managers), a relationship which, due to various information asymmetries, created much uncertainty. Agency theory accepted that transaction costs and information costs exist.

Jensen and Meckling (1976) was a key paper in the development of agency theory and was a paper that Watts and Zimmerman greatly relied on when developing PAT. Jensen and Meckling defined the agency relationship (1976, p. 308) as:

> A contract under which one or more (principals) engage another person (the agent) to perform some service on their behalf which involves delegating some decision making authority to the agent.[18]

Relying on traditional economics literature (including accepting assumptions such as that all individuals are driven by a desire to maximise their own wealth), Jensen and Meckling considered the relationships and conflicts between agents and principals and how efficient markets and various contractual mechanisms can assist in minimising the cost to the firm of these potential conflicts.

Within agency theory, a well-functioning firm was considered to be one that minimises its agency costs (those costs inherent in the principal–agent relationship). As indicated earlier, if there is no mechanism to make an agent pay for actions that are undertaken and which adversely impact on the owners (principals), that agent (or manager) will, it is assumed, have an incentive to consume many perquisites, as well as to use confidential information for personal gain at the expense of the principals (the owners). It is the incentive problems that are at the heart of agency theory. As Lambert (2001) states:

> Agency theory models are constructed based on the philosophy that it is important to examine incentive problems and their 'resolution' in an economic setting in which the potential incentive problem actually exists. Typical reasons for conflicts of interest include (i) effort aversion by the agent, (ii) the agent can divert resources for his private consumption or use, (iii) differential time horizons, e.g., the agent is less concerned about the future period effects of his current period actions because he does not expect to be with the firm or the agent is concerned about how his actions will affect others' assessments of his skill, which will affect compensation in the future, or (iv) differential risk aversion on the part of the agent.

It is assumed within agency theory that principals will assume that the agent (like the principal, and, indeed, all individuals) will be driven by self-interest, and therefore the principals will anticipate that the manager, unless restricted from doing otherwise, will undertake self-serving activities that could be detrimental to the economic welfare of the principals. In the absence of any contractual mechanisms to restrict the agents' potentially opportunistic behaviour, the principal will pay the

---

18 This contract does not have to be a written contract. That is, it may simply constitute implicit terms about how the principal expects the manager to behave.

agent a lower salary in anticipation of the opportunistic actions.[19] This lower salary will compensate the owners for the adverse actions that the managers are considered likely to undertake (this is referred to as *price protection*). Hence, the perspective is that it is the agents who, on average, pay for the principals' expectations of their opportunistic behaviour. The agents are therefore assumed to have an incentive to enter into contractual arrangements that appear to be able to reduce their ability to undertake actions detrimental to the interests of the principals. Consistent with this, Watts and Zimmerman (1986, p. 184) state:

> This (perspective) provides the prime insight in the Jensen and Meckling analysis: the agent, not the principal, has the incentive to contract for monitoring. The outside shareholders do not care if monitoring (often involving accounting and auditing) is conducted. Competition in the capital markets leads to price protection and ensures that outside investors earn a normal return. Owner-managers (the agents) have the incentive to offer guarantees to limit their consumption of perks, for owner-managers receive all the gains ... With competition and rational expectations, owner-managers who have incentives to take value reducing actions (opportunistic actions) such as over-consuming perks, shirking, or stealing when they sell outside shares, bear the costs of those dysfunctional actions. Hence they have incentives to contract to limit those actions and to have their actions monitored. The incentive is reduced (but not eliminated) by price protection in managerial labour markets.[20]

That is, if it is assumed that managers would prefer higher salaries, there will be an incentive for them to agree to enter into contractual arrangements that minimise their ability to undertake activities that might be detrimental to the interests of the owners (many of these contractual arrangements will be tied to accounting numbers). The managers (agents) will have incentives to provide information to demonstrate that they are not acting in a manner detrimental to the owners (principals).[21]

In reflecting on why many accounting researchers embraced agency theory as part of their research, Lambert (2001, p. 4) states:

> The primary feature of agency theory that has made it attractive to accounting researchers is that it allows us to explicitly incorporate conflicts of interest, incentive problems, and mechanisms for controlling incentive problems into our models. This is important because much of the motivation for accounting and auditing has to do with the control of incentive problems. For example, the reason we insist on having an 'independent' auditor is that

---

19 Or if shares are being sold in a company, the shareholders will, in the absence of contractual constraints on the manager, pay a lower price for shares in the organisation.

20 In this context, reference is made to the owner–manager to imply that the manager might have some ownership in the organisation but does not own the entire organisation. This quote also reflects the beliefs that Positive Accounting theorists have about the efficiency of markets—such as capital markets or labour markets. It is assumed that such markets can efficiently adjust required rates of return to anticipated levels of risk—such as the risks associated with managers being opportunistic.

21 These arguments about managers' opportunistic behaviour are 'on average' arguments. Principals would not know with certainty whether specific agents will adopt particular opportunistic strategies that are detrimental to the principals' economic welfare. Rather, the principals who believe that everybody is motivated by their own self-interest will assume, on average, that the agent will adopt such strategies, and the principal will price protect accordingly. Hence, agents who do not commit to restrict the available set of actions will be penalised (in the form of lower salary) even though they individually may not ultimately elect to undertake actions detrimental to the principal.

we do not believe we can trust managers to issue truthful reports on their own. Similarly, much of the motivation for focusing on objective and verifiable information and for conservatism in financial reporting lies with incentive problems. At the most fundamental level, agency theory is used in accounting research to address two questions: (i) how do features of information, accounting, and compensation systems affect (reduce or make worse) incentive problems and (ii) how does the existence of incentive problems affect the design and structure of information, accounting, and compensation systems?

THE PERSPECTIVE OF THE FIRM AS A 'NEXUS OF CONTRACTS'

In the agency theory literature, the firm itself is considered to be a nexus of contracts and these contracts are put in place with the intention of ensuring that all parties, acting in their own self-interest, are at the same time motivated towards maximising the value of the organisation. The view of the firm as a nexus of contracts is consistent with Smith and Watts' (1983, p. 3) definition of a corporation. They define the corporation as:

> ... a set of contracts among various parties who have a claim to a common output. These parties include stockholders, bondholders, managers, employees, suppliers and customers. The bounds of the corporation are defined by the set of rights under the contracts. The corporation has an indefinite life and the set of contracts which comprise the corporation evolves over time.

Agency theory does not assume that individuals will ever act other than in self-interest, and the key to a well-functioning organisation is to put in place mechanisms (contracts) that ensure that actions that benefit the individual also benefit the organisation.[22] The firm will have many contracts negotiated with various individuals and parties and these contracts will aim to reduce the many conflicts of interests and related uncertainties that might otherwise arise (that is, the firm will be a nexus of contracts). Apart from internal mechanisms (for example, compensation contracts with managers that pay managers a bonus tied to accounting profits), there will be other market-wide mechanisms that are also assumed to constrain the opportunistic actions of the managers. That is, apart from the effects of various contractual arrangements within 'the firm', the literature of the 1970s also proposed that various markets, such as the *market for corporate control* and the *market for managers*, provided incentives for managers to work in the interests of the owners (Fama, 1980).[23] As Bushman and Smith (2001, p. 238) state:

> Corporate control mechanisms are the means by which managers are disciplined to act in the investors' interest. Control mechanisms include both internal mechanisms, such as managerial incentive plans, director monitoring, and the internal labor market, and external mechanisms, such as outside shareholder or debtholder monitoring, the market for corporate control, competition in the product market, the external managerial

---

22 As shown later in this chapter, one way to align the interests of the manager with those of the owners of the firm might be for the manager to be given a share of profits in the organisation. Hence, the manager would be motivated to increase profits (to increase his or her own wealth) and such self-interested activity will also provide benefits to the owners, who, all things being equal, will benefit from higher accounting earnings.

23 See Chapter 3 for an overview of the implications for managers that flow from an efficiently functioning 'market for managers' and 'market for corporate takeovers'. Chapter 3 shows that an assumption about efficiency in these markets provides a justification for some people to argue against regulating accounting disclosures.

labor market, and securities laws that protect outside investors against expropriation by corporate insiders.

As indicated above, agency theory provides an explanation for the existence of the firm. The establishment of the firm is seen as an alternative and efficient way to produce or supply goods and services relative to individuals dealing with 'the market' by way of a series of separate transactions.[24] As Emanuel, Wong and Wong (2003, p. 151) state:

> The firm is an alternative to the market when the costs of using the market become excessive. When a firm replaces the market, authority substitutes for the price mechanism in determining how decisions are made ... Accounting, together with employment contracts, compensation arrangements, debt contracts and the board of directors including its audit and compensation committees comprise a package of structures that have evolved to govern the firm. These institutional devices become the firm's efficient contracting technology. As accounting is part of that contracting technology, the accounting controls and systems and board structures that evolve and get implemented are efficient and the accounting methods that are used in calculating the numbers in the contractual arrangements are, likewise, efficient.

In explaining the existence of firms from an agency theory perspective, reliance is often placed on the early work of Ronald Coase. As Emanuel, Wong and Wong (2003, p. 152) state:

> Coase (1937) suggests that the firm is an alternative form of organisation for managing the very same transactions [that otherwise could be made with market participants]. For example, a firm could make its raw materials as opposed to acquiring them through the market. Coase indicates that firms exist because there are costs of using the pricing mechanism. Examples of these costs are the costs of discovering what the relevant prices are, the costs of determining quality, and the costs of negotiating and concluding a separate contract for each exchange transaction. Further, there are costs associated with drawing up a long-term contract because, due to uncertainty (i.e., where knowledge of future possible states of the world and all involved relationships are incomplete) and bounded rationality (i.e., the limitations of humans to make economic decisions because of their limited ability to receive, store, retrieve, and process information), complete contracting is not feasible (Williamson, 1975, 1985, 1988, 1996). Coase suggests that economies of scale in long-term contracting are what cause activity to be organised in firms ... The Coasian and Williamson analysis suggests that firms exist because they are contracting-cost-efficient. Economic Darwinism ensures that competition will weed out inefficient structures and ill-designed organisations. Over the long-term, the institutional structure that survives is the firm's efficient contracting technology. As accounting is part of that contracting technology, the accounting controls and systems that the firm uses and the accounting methods that are used to reduce conflicts of interests between parties

---

24 For example, if we wanted a new car we can either buy it from a firm that specialises in making cars (and which has developed efficient contracting mechanisms between the various providers of the factors of production) or we can individually negotiate via 'the market' with suppliers of tyres, seats, engines, windscreens, radios, frames, mechanics, and so forth. It is accepted that it is more efficient, because of contracting efficiencies inherent within a firm, to acquire the car from a firm specialising in car production rather than to coordinate the production of the car ourselves.

to the firm and that align with the firm's value-increasing activities are, likewise, efficient. In respect of the accounting methods, Watts and Zimmerman (1990, p. 134) describe these procedures as efficient accounting choices because they 'are the result of a similar economic equilibrium'.

Firms therefore exist because they are an efficient way to coordinate the activities of various agents. As explained, each of the agents employed within a firm is assumed to act in his or her own 'self-interest'. Principals will be aware of this self-interest. Unless agents can show that they are working in the interests of the principals, the principals will pay the agents lower rewards for their work in anticipation of the agent taking actions that are costly to the principal. Knowing this, agents are predicted to have an incentive to provide information to show they are working for the benefit of the owners (principals) so as to receive higher payments. This prediction (from agency theory), combined with the view that markets were efficient, was traditionally used by researchers as a basis for arguments against the regulation of accounting. Managers (agents) are deemed, even in the absence of regulation, to have incentives to provide information that best reflects the underlying performance of the entity. Failure to do so will have negative implications for their reputation and hence will negatively impact on the total amount of income they can receive from within the organisation, or elsewhere. Referring to the work of Fama, Watts and Zimmerman (1986, p. 192) argue:

> Fama (1980) suggests that information on managers' opportunistic value-reducing behavior eventually becomes known and affects their reputation. As a consequence, if managers consume a large quantity of perks (e.g., shirks), it eventually becomes known and they acquire a reputation. Such managers are expected to over-consume perks in the future, and their future compensation is reduced. Hence, even if managers' compensation is not adjusted in the period in which they over-consume, they still bear a cost for that over-consumption—the present value of the reductions in their future compensation. This effect is mitigated if the manager is close to retirement and does not have any deferred compensation (i.e., compensation paid after retirement).

THE EMERGENCE OF POSITIVE ACCOUNTING THEORY

By the mid to late 1970s, the theory had therefore been developed that proposed that markets were efficient and that contractual arrangements were used as a basis for controlling the efforts of self-interested agents. The existence of firms was also explained on the basis of the firms' efficiency in terms of reducing total transaction costs. This research provided the necessary basis for the development of PAT. PAT emphasised the role of accounting in reducing the agency costs of an organisation (including the conflicts that exist between owners and managers). It also emphasised that efficiently written contracts, with many being tied to the output of the accounting system, were a crucial component of an efficient corporate governance structure.

One of the first papers to document how considerations of contracting costs,[25] as well as considerations of the political process, impacted on the choice of accounting methods was

---

25 Contracting costs are costs that arise as a result of 'contracting' or formulating an agreement with another party (for example, a manager) wherein one party provides a particular service for a particular payment. The contracting costs include: the costs of finding the other party to the contract; negotiating the agreement; costs associated with monitoring that the agreement has been carried out in the manner expected; possible renegotiation costs; and so on.

Watts (1977), which did not attract much attention. However, in the subsequent year, Watts and Zimmerman (1978a) published a paper that has become accepted as the key paper in the development and acceptance of PAT. It attempted to explain the lobbying positions taken by US corporate managers in relation to the FASB's 1974 discussion memorandum on general price level adjustments (GPLAs). According to Watts and Zimmerman (1978a, p. 113):

> In this paper, we assume that individuals act to maximise their own utility. In doing so they are resourceful and innovative. The obvious implication of this assumption is that management lobbies on accounting standards based on its own self-interest.[26]

As indicated in Chapter 5, general price level accounting, through the use of a general price index, makes adjustments to historical cost profits to take into account the effects of changing prices. In times of inflation this typically has the effect of decreasing income as well as increasing assets.

Watts and Zimmerman considered how particular organisational attributes might affect whether the managers of an organisation supported, or opposed, a particular accounting requirement. Among the factors considered, one was the possibility that managers were paid bonuses tied to reported profits (which they referred to as the management compensation hypothesis), and another was the possibility that the organisation was subject to high levels of political scrutiny (which they referred to as the political cost hypothesis). In relation to the issue of political scrutiny and the associated costs, Watts and Zimmerman (1978a, p. 115) state:

> To counter potential government intrusions, corporations employ a number of devices, such as social responsibility campaigns in the media, government lobbying and selection of accounting procedures to minimise reported earnings. By avoiding the attention that 'high' profits draw because of the public's association of high reported profits and monopoly rents, management can reduce the likelihood of adverse political actions and, thereby, reduce its expected costs (including the legal costs the firm would incur opposing the political actions). Included in political costs are the costs labour unions impose through increased demands generated by large reported profits. The magnitude of the political costs is highly dependent on firm size.

Watts and Zimmerman's (1978a) results did not provide support for the management compensation hypothesis.[27] This was probably due to the fact that the discussion memorandum required GPLA disclosures to be provided as a supplement to the financial statements and did not require the financial statements themselves to be altered (and the bonus plans were expected to be tied to the numbers presented in the financial statements). However, significant findings

---

26 Watts and Zimmerman, like many other economists, ignored non-financial aspects of an individual's utility function and simply assumed that an individual's utility, or well-being, is maximised when their wealth is maximised. Perhaps non-financial aspects of an individual's utility function were ignored because such aspects were considered too difficult to model.

27 Specifically, the prediction provided within Watts and Zimmerman (1978a, p. 116) in relation to management compensation plans was that 'a change in accounting standards which increase the firm's reported earnings would, *ceteris paribus*, lead to greater incentive income. But this would reduce the firm's cashflows and share prices would fall. As long as per manager present value of the after tax incentive income is greater than the decline in each manager's share portfolio, we expect management to favour such an accounting change'.

were presented in relation to the political cost hypothesis.[28] More specifically, larger firms (who were deemed to be subject to higher political scrutiny) tended to support the discussion memorandum—an approach which would indicate (in times of rising prices) that the profits of the firm, adjusted for the effects of inflation, were lower than were otherwise reported.[29] The view of Watts and Zimmerman was that, by presenting lower adjusted profits, these firms would attract less political attention and hence there would be less likelihood that parties would attempt to transfer wealth away from the firm (perhaps in the form of calls for increased taxes, for less tariff protection, for higher wages and so on). In concluding their paper, Watts and Zimmerman (p. 131) state:

> The single most important factor explaining managerial voting behavior on General Price Level Accounting is firm size (after controlling for the direction of change in earnings). The larger firms, *ceteris paribus*, are more likely to favour GPLA if earnings decline. This finding is consistent with our government intervention argument since the larger firms are more likely to be subjected to government interference and, hence, have more to lose than smaller organisations.

Following the work of Watts and Zimmerman (1978a), research in the area of PAT flourished. Much of this research sought to address some of the limitations inherent in Watts and Zimmerman's work. For example, subsequent research acknowledged that reported profits are affected by many different accounting choices (rather than just the one choice, such as the choice to use GPLA), some of which may be income increasing, while others are income decreasing (thereby potentially offsetting each other). Zmijewski and Hagerman (1981) undertook research in an endeavour to predict managements' choice in relation to four accounting methods choices, those relating to how to account for depreciation, stock (or inventory), investment tax credits and past pension costs.

In 1990 Watts and Zimmerman published an article in *The Accounting Review* that considered ten years of development of Positive Accounting Theory ('Positive Accounting Theory: a ten year perspective'). They identified three key hypotheses that had become frequently used in the PAT literature to explain and predict whether an organisation would support or oppose a particular accounting method. These hypotheses can be called the 'management compensation hypothesis' (or 'bonus plan hypothesis'), the 'debt hypothesis' (or 'debt/equity hypothesis') and the 'political cost hypothesis'. Watts and Zimmerman (1990, p. 138) explain these hypotheses as follows:

> The bonus plan hypothesis is that managers of firms with bonus plans [tied to reported income] are more likely to use accounting methods that increase current period reported income. Such selection will presumably increase the present value of bonuses

---

28 Political costs are costs that particular groups external to the organisation may be able to impose on the organisation as a result of particular political actions. The costs could include increased taxes, increased wage claims or product boycotts.

29 The prediction provided by Watts and Zimmerman (1978a, p. 118) in relation to political costs was 'that managers have greater incentives to choose accounting standards which report lower earnings (thereby increasing cash flows, firm value and their welfare) due to tax, political, and regulatory considerations than to choose accounting standards which report higher earnings and, thereby, increase their incentive compensation. However, this prediction is conditional upon the firm being regulated or subject to political pressure. In small (i.e., lower political costs) unregulated firms, we would expect that managers do have incentives to select accounting standards which report higher earnings, if the expected gain in incentive compensation is greater than the forgone expected tax consequences. Finally, we expect managers to also consider the accounting standard's impact on the firm's bookkeeping costs (and hence their own welfare)'.

if the compensation committee of the board of directors does not adjust for the method chosen. The choice studies to date find results generally consistent with the bonus plan hypothesis.

Hence, all things being equal, this hypothesis predicts that, if a manager is rewarded in terms of a measure of performance such as accounting profits, that manager will prefer accounting methods that have a greater impact on increasing profits to the extent that this leads to an increase in his or her bonus. In relation to the 'debt hypothesis', they state (p. 139):

> The debt/equity hypothesis predicts [that] the higher the firm's debt/equity ratio, the more likely managers use accounting methods that increase income. The higher the debt/equity ratio, the closer (i.e. tighter) the firm is to the constraints in the debt covenants.[30] The tighter the covenant constraint, the greater [is] the probability of a covenant violation and of incurring costs from technical default. Managers exercising discretion by choosing income increasing accounting methods relax debt constraints and reduce the costs of technical default.[31]

Hence, all things being equal, if a firm has entered into agreements with lenders, and these agreements involve accounting-based debt covenants (such as stipulating a maximum allowable debt/equity or debt/asset constraint), managers have an incentive to adopt accounting methods that relax the potential impacts of the constraints (such as adopting accounting methods that increase reported income and assets). In relation to the third hypothesis of their study—the 'political costs hypothesis'—Watts and Zimmerman state (1990, p.139):

> The political cost hypothesis predicts [that] large firms rather than small firms are more likely to use accounting choices that reduce reported profits. Size is a proxy variable for political attention. Underlying this hypothesis is the assumption that it is costly for individuals to become informed about whether accounting profits really represent monopoly profits and to 'contract' with others in the political process to enact laws and regulations that enhance their welfare. Thus rational individuals are less than fully informed. The political process is no different from the market process in that respect. Given the cost of information and monitoring, managers have incentive to exercise discretion over accounting profits and the parties in the political process settle for a rational amount of ex post opportunism.

Hence, all things being equal, if managers consider that they are under a deal of political scrutiny, this could motivate them to adopt accounting methods that reduce reported income.

---

30 In this chapter there are a number of instances when reference is made to debt covenants. Covenants can be considered as undertakings provided by a borrower as part of a contract associated with a loan, and these undertakings (covenants) either specifically restrict the borrower from taking particular actions or specifically require the borrower to take particular actions.

31 As indicated here, Watts and Zimmerman made the assumption that 'the higher the debt/equity ratio, the closer (i.e. tighter) the firm is to the constraints in the debt covenants'. This assumes that all organisations have entered into debt agreements that have covenants restricting the amount of total debt relative to the amount of total assets or total equity. While this assumption might have been reasonable back in the 1970s/1980s when most large companies had entered into such arrangements, Mather and Peirson (2006) provide evidence that, while the majority of large companies do still agree to debt covenants, less than half of the recently negotiated covenants restrict total liabilities to a proportion of either total assets or equity. Hence the predictive power of the hypotheses may not be as great as it once was. Nevertheless, it provides a useful prediction for companies known to have leverage constraints.

Daily Telegraph, 2 February 2008

$35bn Shell says thank you

Australian families have helped drive petrol giant Shell into the record books with a staggering $35.5 billion global annual profit.

The NRMA said yesterday the company owed a thank you to Australian motorists, after it turned a profit of almost $4 million every hour last year.

Shell's full-year net profit is an all-time record for a European company.

'Shell is a very rich company today and when they're allowed to charge Australian motorists whatever they want for petrol, it's not hard to see why,' NRMA president Alan Evans said.

'When we consider that motorists in Sydney are paying as much as $1.47 a litre for petrol ... a note from Shell Australia to all motorists, thanking them for contributing to their astronomical profits, would not go astray.'

Mr Evans said the soon-to-be-appointed petrol commissioner, announced by the Federal Government, must be given the power to penalise oil companies for overcharging for petrol.

'Oil companies will continue to make obscene profits until something is done about the way petrol is priced in Australia,' he said.

Reducing reported profits could decrease the possibility that people will argue that the organisation is exploiting other parties by applying business practices that generate excessive profits for the benefit of owners while at the same time providing limited returns to other parties involved in the transactions, such as employees. As an indication of how reported profits can be used as a means to criticise companies for charging consumers too much for their products, and how the profits can also be used to justify a call for government action against a company, consider Accounting Headline 7.1, which is critical of Shell and its 'obscene profits'. Read the article and then decide whether the position taken by Mr Evans would have been as strong if Shell had not recorded such high profits.

Researchers using the three hypotheses (the management bonus hypothesis, the debt/equity hypothesis and the political cost hypothesis), and there have been many such researchers, often adopted the perspective that managers (or agents) will act opportunistically when selecting particular accounting methods (for example, managers will select particular accounting methods because the choice will lead to an increase in profit and therefore to an increase in their bonus). Watts and Zimmerman's study (1978a) was mainly grounded in the opportunistic perspective. However, a deal of the subsequent PAT research also adopted an efficiency perspective. This perspective proposes that managers will elect to use a particular accounting method because the method most efficiently provides a record of how the organisation performed. For example, the manager might have selected a particular depreciation method not because it would have led to an increase in his or her bonus (the opportunistic perspective) but because the method most correctly reflected the use of the underlying asset. The following discussion considers the opportunistic and efficiency perspectives of PAT. In practice it is often difficult to determine whether opportunistic or efficiency considerations drove the managers' choice of a particular method—and this has been one limitation of much of this research.

OPPORTUNISTIC AND EFFICIENCY PERSPECTIVES

■ ■

As noted above, research that applies PAT typically adopts either an *efficiency perspective* or an *opportunistic perspective*. Within the efficiency perspective, researchers explain how various contracting mechanisms can be put in place to minimise the agency costs of the firm, that is, the costs associated with assigning decision-making authority from the principal (for example, the owner) to the agent (for example, the manager). The efficiency perspective is often referred to as an *ex ante* perspective—*ex ante* meaning 'before the fact'—as it considers what mechanisms are put in place *up front*, with the objective of minimising future agency and contracting costs. For example, many organisations throughout the world voluntarily prepared publicly available financial statements before there was any regulatory requirement to do so. These financial statements were also frequently subjected to an audit, even when there also was no regulatory requirement to do so (Morris, 1984).[32] Researchers such as Jensen and Meckling (1976) argue that the practice of providing audited financial statements leads to real cost savings as it enables organisations to attract funds at a lower cost. As a result of the audit, external parties have more reliable information about the resources and obligations of the organisation, which therefore enables the organisation to attract funds at a lower cost than would otherwise be possible, thereby increasing the value of the organisation.

Within this efficiency (*ex ante*) perspective of PAT it is also argued that the accounting practices adopted by firms are often explained on the basis that such methods best reflect the underlying financial performance of the entity. Different organisational characteristics are used to explain why different firms adopt different accounting methods. For example, the selection of a particular asset depreciation rule from among alternative approaches is explained on the basis that it best reflects the underlying use of the asset. Firms that have different patterns of use in relation to an asset will be predicted to adopt different depreciation or amortisation policies. That is, organisations will differ in the nature of their business, and these differences will in turn lead to differences in the accounting methods (as well as other policies) being adopted. By providing measures of performance that best reflect the underlying performance of the firm, it is argued that investors and other parties will not need to gather as much additional information from other sources. This will consequently lead to cost savings.

As an illustration of research that adopts an efficiency perspective, Whittred (1987) sought to explain why firms voluntarily prepared publicly available consolidated financial statements in a period when there was no regulation that required them to do so. He found that when companies borrowed funds, security for debt often took the form of guarantees provided by other entities within the group of organisations. Consolidated financial statements were described as being a more efficient means of presenting information about the group's ability

---

32 Benston (1969) provides evidence that all the firms listed on the New York Stock Exchange in 1926 published balance sheets when there was no direct requirement to do so. Further, 82 per cent were audited by a CPA when there was also no direct statutory requirement to do so.

to borrow and repay debts than providing lenders with separate financial statements for each entity in the group.[33]

If it is assumed, consistent with the efficiency perspective, that firms adopt particular accounting methods because the methods best reflect the underlying economic performance of the entity (thereby reducing the risks of investors and therefore decreasing the firm's cost of capital), it is argued by PAT theorists that the regulation of financial accounting imposes unwarranted costs on reporting entities. For example, if a new accounting standard is released that bans an accounting method being used by particular organisations, this will lead to inefficiencies, as the resulting financial statements will no longer provide the best reflection of the performance of the organisation. Many PAT theorists would argue that management is best able to select the appropriate accounting methods in given circumstances, and government should not intervene in the process.[34]

The opportunistic perspective of PAT, on the other hand, takes as given the negotiated contractual arrangements of the firm (some of which are discussed later in the chapter) and seeks to explain and predict certain opportunistic behaviours that will subsequently occur. Initially, the particular contractual arrangements might have been negotiated because they were considered to be most efficient in aligning the interests of the various individuals within the firm, thereby providing cost savings for the firm. However, it is not possible or efficient to write complete contracts that provide guidance on all accounting methods to be used in all circumstances— hence there will always be some scope for managers to be opportunistic.

The opportunistic perspective is often referred to as an *ex post* perspective—*ex post* meaning after the fact—because it considers opportunistic actions that could be undertaken once various contractual arrangements have been put in place. For example, in an endeavour to minimise agency costs (an efficiency perspective), a contractual arrangement might be negotiated that provides the managers with a bonus based on the profits generated by the entity. Once it is in place, the manager could elect to adopt particular accounting methods that increase accounting profits and therefore the size of the bonus (an opportunistic perspective). Managers might elect to adopt a particular asset depreciation method that increases income (for example, electing to depreciate an asset over a longer useful life), even though it might not reflect the actual use of the asset. It is assumed within PAT that managers will opportunistically select particular accounting methods whenever they believe that this will lead to an increase in their personal wealth. PAT also assumes that principals would predict a manager to be opportunistic. With this in mind,

---

33 These results were also supported by Mian and Smith (1990). Using US data they found that the inclusion of financial subsidiaries in consolidated financial statements prior to Financial Accounting Standard 94 (which required the subsidiaries to be included within consolidated statements) was directly related to whether guarantees of debt were in existence between members of the group of companies. As Watts (1995, p. 332) indicates, the fact that two independent studies (Mian and Smith, 1990; Whittred, 1987) in different time periods and in different countries found the same results provides a stronger case that the efficiency perspective appears to explain this type of accounting choice.

34 In this regard we can consider AASB 138 'Intangibles' (which is based on IAS 38 'Intangibles'). This accounting standard requires all research expenditure to be expensed as incurred regardless of whether the expenditure is considered likely to lead to future economic benefits (AASB 138 does, however, allow development expenditure to be carried forward subject to certain stringent requirements). The requirement that all research be expensed as incurred is highly conservative and does not allow financial report readers to differentiate between entities that have undertaken valuable research (in terms of generating future economic benefits) and those entities that have pursued failed research projects. For financial accounting purposes all research (good and bad) is to be treated the same. Arguably, this does not enhance the 'efficiency' of general purpose financial reports in terms of enabling an assessment of the past and future economic performance of respective reporting entities.

principals often stipulate the accounting methods to be used for particular purposes. For example, a bonus-plan agreement may stipulate that a particular depreciation or amortisation method such as straight-line amortisation be adopted to calculate income for the determination of the bonus. However, as noted previously, it is assumed to be too costly to stipulate in advance all accounting rules to be used in all circumstances. Hence PAT proposes that there will always be scope for agents opportunistically to select particular accounting methods in preference to others. There have been many reported cases of organisations that have been found to have overstated their reported earnings and assets. For example, consider Accounting Headline 7.2, which relates to a high-profile case of 'creative accounting' involving the organisation Harris Scarfe. In this situation the accountant was 'ordered to take part in creative accounting by his boss'. The results of the

Accounting Headline 7.2 An instance of creative accounting

Harris accountant jailed for $36m fraud

MARK STEENE

Courier-Mail, 27 June 2002

AN accountant who fiddled the books of a retail store chain to the tune of $36 million was yesterday jailed for a minimum of three years.

But Alan Hodgson, 57, who was Harris Scarfe's chief financial officer and secretary, claimed yesterday he had been ordered to take part in the creative accounting by his boss.

His counsel told the South Australian District Court that company executive chairman Adam Trescowthick pressured him into doctoring the books. He said Mr Trescowthick 'became insistent the balance sheet meet his expectations'.

Harris Scarfe collapsed in April last year with debts of $160 million, a figure that eventually blew out to $275 million before a management buy-out saved the company in November.

Hodgson, who earned more than $250,000 a year at Harris Scarfe, arrived at court for sentencing yesterday morning hand-in-hand with his wife Helen and carrying a small overnight bag.

Hodgson pleaded guilty to 24 counts of making false entries and eight counts of disseminating false information to the Australian Stock Exchange between September 1996 and February last year.

Although he did not personally benefit from the fraud, in which he wrote down company losses and wrote up company profits, Hodgson's activities had wide reaching ramifications, the court heard.

Judge David Bright said Hodgson falsely painted a picture the company was in good financial health, allowing it to raise $35 million through a new share issue and obtain $67 million in loans.

But he accepted Hodgson had not acted alone, stating: 'it seemed to jump off the pages' that others were involved.

Judge Bright said Hodgson's activities kept the company in business and that the resulting losses to people who invested in it must have amounted to tens of millions of dollars.

'I accept that you, like a gambler, continued to hope the company would trade its way out of difficulty,' he said. 'You say you were pressured. He was a forceful person. You succumbed.

'The image of integrity you once projected is now lost.'

Michael Boylan, for Hodgson, said his client loved working at Harris Scarfe and was immensely proud of its achievements. Mr Boylan said his client knew he had wrongly succumbed to the pressure from his boss.

'That pressure was regular,' he said.

'That is not put as an excuse.'

'He had a responsibility, even if it meant losing his job.'

'That's what should have happened.'

'I emphasise that what he did, he did for no personal gain.'

'He lost his job, his reputation and his family home.'

Prosecutor Thomas Muir said the court should send a warning to people like Hodgson. 'People in these positions can't follow these orders,' he said.

'They have ramifications everywhere. A message must be sent in that regard.'

Judge Bright sentenced Hodgson to a maximum of six years behind bars.

creative accounting were that profits and assets were significantly overstated. The opportunistic perspective provided by PAT provides some possible reasons for the overstatement of reported assets and profits. Perhaps the entity inflated its profits and assets in an attempt to circumvent restrictions that had been put in place by lenders—for example, lenders might have stipulated debt-to-asset constraints or minimum earnings requirements (perhaps in the form of negotiated interest-coverage clauses in a debt agreement). As the level of debt increases, the tendency towards opportunistic overstatement of assets and income would be expected to increase (if we accept the arguments provided by PAT). The extent of the opportunistic accounting activities often only becomes evident following corporate failure (as was the case with Harris Scarfe), at which time the extent of the asset overstatement will be highlighted.

The following discussion addresses the various contractual arrangements that may exist between owners and managers, and between debtholders and managers, particularly those contractual arrangements based on the output of the accounting system. Again, these contractual arrangements are initially assumed to be put in place to reduce the agency costs of the firm (the efficiency perspective). However, it is assumed by Positive Accounting theorists that once the arrangements are in place, parties will, if they can, adopt manipulative strategies to generate the greatest economic benefits to themselves (the opportunistic perspective). The following material also considers the political process and how firms might use accounting to minimise the costs of potential political scrutiny.

While some researchers tend to use either the efficiency perspective or the opportunistic perspective of PAT to explain particular accounting choices, it should be noted that in reality it is often difficult to conclude firmly that an accounting choice was driven solely by an efficiency or an opportunistic motivation. As Fields, Lys and Vincent (2001) state:

> Unconstrained accounting choice is likely to impose costs on financial statement users because preparers are likely to have incentives to convey self-serving information. For example, managers may choose accounting methods in self-interested attempts to increase the stock [share] price prior to the expiration of stock options they hold. On the other hand, the same accounting choices may be motivated by managers' objective assessment that the current stock price is undervalued (relative to their private information). In practice, it is difficult to distinguish between the two situations, but it is the presence of such mixed motives that makes the study of accounting choice interesting.

OWNER–MANAGER CONTRACTING

If the manager owned the firm, then that manager would bear the costs associated with his or her own perquisite consumption. Perquisite consumption could include consumption of the firm's resources for private purposes (for example, the manager may acquire an overly expensive company car, acquire overly luxurious offices, stay in overly expensive hotel accommodation) or the excessive generation and use of idle time. As the percentage ownership held by the manager decreases, that manager begins to bear less of the cost of his or her own perquisite consumption. The costs begin to be absorbed by the owners of the firm.

As noted previously, PAT adopts as a central assumption that all action by individuals is driven by self-interest, and that the major interest of individuals is to maximise their own wealth.

Such an assumption is often referred to as the 'rational economic person' assumption. If all individuals are assumed to act in their own self-interest, then owners would expect the managers (their agents) to undertake activities that may not always be in the interest of the owners (the principals). Further, because of their position within the firm, the managers will have access to information not available to the principals (this problem is frequently referred to as 'information asymmetry') and this may further increase managers' ability to undertake actions beneficial to themselves at the expense of the owners. The costs of the divergent behaviour that arises as a result of the agency relationship (that is, the relationship between the principal and the agent appointed to perform duties on behalf of the principal) are, as indicated previously, referred to as agency costs (Jensen and Meckling, 1976).

It is assumed in PAT that the principals hold expectations that their agents will undertake activities that may be disadvantageous to the value of the firm, and the principals will price this into the amounts they are prepared to pay the manager. That is, in the absence of controls to reduce the ability of the manager to act opportunistically, the principals expect such actions and, as a result, will pay the manager a lower salary. That is, the principals will price protect. This lower salary compensates the principals for the expected opportunistic behaviour of the agents. The manager will therefore bear some of the costs of the potential opportunistic behaviours (the agency costs) that they may, or may not, undertake. If it is expected that managers would derive greater satisfaction from additional salary than from the perquisites that they will be predicted to consume, then managers may be better off if they are able to commit themselves contractually not to consume perquisites. That is, they commit or bond themselves contractually to reducing their set of available actions (some of which would not be beneficial to owners). Of course, the owners of the firm would need to ensure that any contractual commitments can be monitored for compliance before agreeing to increase the amounts paid to the managers. In a market where individuals are perfectly informed, it could be assumed that managers would ultimately bear the costs associated with the bonding and monitoring mechanisms (Jensen & Meckling, 1976). However, markets are typically not perfectly informed.

Managers may be rewarded on a fixed basis (that is, a set salary independent of performance), on the basis of the results achieved, or on a combination of the two. If the manager was rewarded purely on a fixed basis, then, assuming self-interest, that manager would not want to take great risks as he or she would not share in any potential gains. There would also be limited incentives for the manager to adopt strategies that increase the value of the firm (unlike equity owners whose share of the firm may increase in value). Like debtholders, managers with a fixed claim would want to protect their fixed income stream. Apart from rejecting risky projects, which may be beneficial to those with equity in the firm, the manager with a fixed income stream may also be reluctant to take on optimal levels of debt, as the claims of the debtholders would compete with the manager's own fixed income claim.

Assuming that self-interest drives the actions of the managers, it may be necessary to put in place remuneration schemes that reward the managers in a way that is, at least in part, tied to the performance of the firm. This will be in the interest of the manager, as that manager will potentially receive greater rewards and will not have to bear the costs of the perceived opportunistic behaviours (which may not have been undertaken anyway). If the performance of the firm improves, the rewards paid to the manager correspondingly increase. Bonus schemes tied to the performance of the firm will be put in place to align the interests of the owners and the managers. If the firm performs well, both parties will benefit.

BONUS SCHEMES GENERALLY

It is common practice for managers to be rewarded in a way that is tied to the profits of the firm, the sales of the firm, or the return on assets, that is, for their remuneration to be based on the output of the accounting system. It is also common for managers to be rewarded in line with the market price of the firm's shares. This may be through holding an equity interest in the firm, or perhaps by receiving a cash bonus explicitly tied to movements in the market value of the firm's securities. Deegan (1997) lists some of the accounting performance measures used in Australia as a basis for rewarding managers:

- Percentage of after-tax profits of the last year
- Percentage of after-tax profits after adjustment for dividends paid
- Percentage of pre-tax profits of the last year
- Percentage of division's profit for the last year
- Percentage of division's sales for the last year
- Percentage of the last year's accounting rate of return on assets
- Percentage of previous year's division's sales, plus percentage of firm's after-tax profits
- Percentage of previous year's division's sales, plus percentage of division's pre-tax profits
- Percentage of previous two years' division's sales, plus percentage of last two years' division's pre-tax profit
- Percentage of previous year's firm's sales, plus a percentage of firm's after-tax profit
- Average of pre-tax profit for the last two years
- Average of pre-tax profit for the last three years
- Percentage of the last six months' profit after tax.

ACCOUNTING-BASED BONUS PLANS

As indicated above, the use of accounting-based bonus schemes is quite common. In considering their use in the United States, Bushman and Smith (2001, p. 250) state:

> The extensive and explicit use of accounting numbers in top executive compensation plans at publicly traded firms in the U.S. is well documented. Murphy (1999) reports data from a survey conducted by Towers Perrin in 1996–1997. The survey contains detailed information on the annual bonus plans for 177 publicly traded U.S. companies. Murphy reports that 161 of the 177 sample firms explicitly use at least one measure of accounting profits in their annual bonus plans. Of the 68 companies in the survey that use a single performance measure in their annual bonus plan, 65 use a measure of accounting profits. While the accounting measure used is often the dollar value of profits, Murphy also reports common use of profits on a per-share basis, as a margin, return, or expressed as a growth rate. Ittner, Larker and Rajan (1997), using proxy statements and proprietary survey data, collect detailed performance measure information for the annual bonus plans of 317 U.S. firms for the 1993–1994 time period. The firms are drawn from 48 different two-digit SIC codes. Ittner, Larker and Rajan document that 312 of the 317 firms report using at least one financial measure in their annual plans. Earnings per share, net income and operating income are the most common financial measure, each being used by more than a quarter of the sample.

Given that the amounts paid to the manager may be directly tied to accounting numbers (such as profits/sales/assets), any changes in the accounting methods being used by the organisation will affect the bonuses paid (unless the bonuses have been explicitly tied to the accounting numbers that would be derived from the use of the accounting methods in place when the bonus schemes were originally negotiated—this is sometimes referred to as using 'frozen GAAP').[35] Such a change may occur as a result of a new accounting standard being issued. For example, AASB 138 'Intangibles' (released in Australia in 2004 and effective from 2005) permits some development (but not research) expenditure to be capitalised as an intangible asset in certain circumstances. Consider the consequences if a new rule was issued that required all research and development expenditure to be written off. With such a change, profits for some firms that previously capitalised development expenditure could decline, and the bonuses paid to managers may also change. If it is accepted, consistent with classical finance theory, that the value of the firm is a function of the future cash flows of the firm, then the value of the organisation may change (perhaps because less expenditure will be incurred in relation to development). Hence, once we consider the contractual arrangements within a firm, Positive Accounting theorists would argue that we can start to appreciate that a change in accounting method can lead to a change in cash flows, and hence a change in the value of the organisation (because, as has already been emphasised, the value of an organisation is considered to relate directly to expectations about the present value of the organisation's future cash flows). This perspective is contrary to the views of early proponents of the EMH who argued that changes in accounting methods would not impact on share prices unless they had direct implications for expenses such as taxation.

As a recent case in point, we can speculate on how the adoption of IAS 38 'Intangibles' (or, within Australia, AASB 138) in some countries (among other things, this standard requires that all research expenditure must be expensed as incurred) will impact on the research and development activities of various organisations. For example, subject to certain requirements, Australian, New Zealand, French and Scandinavian listed companies could, prior to 2005, capitalise research expenditure. With the adoption of International Financial Reporting Standards (IFRSs) from 2005, this is no longer permitted and all research expenditure must be expensed as incurred (subject to certain requirements, development expenditure can be capitalised). As a result, there might be some expectation that the accounting standard will impact on the amount of research being conducted by some firms in those countries. With specific reference to the 'bonus hypothesis', there could be an expectation that if a manager is being paid a bonus tied to accounting profits, and given the 'harsh' treatment required in relation to research expenditure ('harsh' because it has to be written off as incurred), the existence of a management bonus may motivate managers to reduce the level of research expenditure, thereby increasing the size of their bonus. Such a strategy of reducing research expenditure might be even greater the closer the manager is to retirement—the reason for this being that the time lag between the research expenditure and the subsequent economic benefits might be longer than the period until the manager retires (we will return to this 'horizon problem' shortly). Through the related impacts on cash flows, such a change in research activity in turn can be expected to impact on the value of the reporting entities' equity (share price). This example demonstrates how a change in an accounting standard can have real implications for an organisation's share price.

---

35 Where an accounting-based contractual arrangement is to be calculated according to the accounting rules in place at reporting date (and these rules may change as new accounting standards are issued), then such agreements are considered to be relying on 'rolling GAAP' (also called 'floating GAAP').

Of course it is possible that the bonus may be based on the 'old' accounting rules in place at the time the remuneration contract was negotiated (perhaps through a clause in the management compensation contract) such that a change in generally accepted accounting principles will not impact on the bonus, but this will not always be the case. Contracts that rely on accounting numbers may rely on 'floating' generally accepted accounting principles. This would suggest that should an accounting rule change, and should it affect an item used within a contract negotiated by the firm, the value of the firm (through changes in related cash flows) might consequently change. PAT would suggest that if a change in accounting policy had no impact on the cash flows of the firm, then a firm would be indifferent to the change.

In explaining the use of accounting-based bonus schemes, Emanuel, Wong and Wong (2003, p. 155) state:

> Accounting earnings are often used to calculate the manager's payoff (Smith and Watts, 1982; Healy, 1985; Sloan, 1993) because it is a more efficient measure of the manager's performance than other measures such as stock prices and realised cash flows. There are two reasons for this. First, stock prices are influenced more by market factors that are outside the control of management and, hence, are less effective in isolating that part of performance that results from the manager's actions (Sloan, 1993). Secondly, realised cash flows do not take into account the manager's actions at the time those actions are put in place to increase the value of the firm. Hence, realised cash flows do not provide a timely measure of the effect of the manager's actions on firm performance, especially when performance is measured over short intervals (Dechow, 1994). Further, accounting earnings possess a variety of desirable characteristics that other performance measures do not have, including objectivity, reliability, verifiability and conservatism (Watts and Zimmerman, 1986, pp. 205–207). Since accounting earnings are efficient in measuring firm performance, they play an important role in determining the reward and punishment of performance. We observe the existence of earnings-based bonus plans that provide an efficient means of aligning the manager's and shareholders' interests so that the manager does not participate in activities that are opportunistic, because such actions detract from firm value maximisation. To the extent that earnings are a good measure of future cash flows and all things else are constant, higher earnings lead to higher firm value and more compensation to the manager. Besides compensation, accounting performance measures affect other rewards and punishments of the firm's employees, such as continued employment and promotion (Blackwell et al, 1994).

INCENTIVES TO MANIPULATE ACCOUNTING NUMBERS

In considering the costs of implementing incentive schemes based on accounting output, there is a possibility that rewarding managers on the basis of accounting profits may induce them to manipulate the related accounting numbers to improve their apparent performance and, importantly, their related rewards (the opportunistic perspective). That is, accounting profits may not always provide an unbiased measure of firm performance or value. Healy (1985) provides an illustration of when managers may choose to manipulate accounting numbers opportunistically due to the presence of accounting-based bonus schemes. He found that when schemes existed that rewarded managers after a pre-specified level of earnings had been reached, the managers would adopt accounting methods consistent with maximising that bonus. In situations where the profits were not expected to reach the minimum level required by the bonus plan, the managers appeared to adopt strategies that further reduced income in that period (frequently referred to as 'taking a bath') but would lead to higher income in subsequent periods—periods when the profits may be above the required threshold for the bonus to be paid. As an example, the manager may write off an asset in one period, when a bonus was not going to be earned anyway, such that there would be nothing further to depreciate in future periods when profit-related bonuses may be paid.[36]

Investment strategies that maximise the present value of the firm's resources will not necessarily produce uniform periodic cash flows or accounting profits. It is possible that some strategies may generate minimal accounting returns in early years, yet still represent the best alternatives available to the firm. Rewarding managers on the basis of accounting profits may discourage them from adopting such strategies. That is, it may encourage management to adopt a short-term, as opposed to a long-term, focus.

In Lewellen, Loderer and Martin (1987) it was shown that US managers approaching retirement were less likely to undertake research and development expenditure if their rewards were based on accounting-based performance measures such as profits. This was explained on the basis that all research and development had to be written off as incurred pursuant to US accounting standards, and hence undertaking research and development would lead directly to a reduction in profits. Although the research and development expenditure would be expected to lead to benefits in subsequent years, the retiring managers might not have been there to share in the gains. That is, the employment horizon of the manager is short relative to the 'horizon' relating to the continuation of the organisation (which might be assumed to be indefinite). This difference in 'horizons' is often referred to as an 'horizon problem'. Hence, the self-interested manager who was rewarded on the basis of accounting profits was predicted not to undertake research and development in the periods close to the point of retirement because the manager would not share in any associated gains. This may, of course, have been detrimental to the ongoing operations (and value) of the business. In such a case it would have been advisable from an efficiency perspective for an organisation that incurred research and development expenditure to take retiring managers off a profit-share bonus scheme, or alternatively to calculate 'profits' for the purpose of the plan after adjusting for research and development expenditures. Alternatively, managers approaching retirement could have been rewarded in terms of market-based schemes that are tied to the long-term performance of the organisation. For example, perhaps the manager of a company involved in research and development, and who is expected to retire in the near future, should be allocated options to buy shares in the company (share options) that cannot be exercised for, say, three or four years after he or she retires. In that way, the manager would be encouraged to put in place projects that would be successful after he or she leaves the organisation.

MARKET-BASED BONUS SCHEMES

Firms involved in mining, or high-technology research and development, may have accounting earnings that fluctuate greatly. Successful strategies may be put in place that will not provide

---

36 Holthausen, Larcker and Sloan (1995) used private data on firms' compensation plans also to investigate managers' behaviour in the presence of management compensation plans. Their results confirmed those of Healy (1985), except that they did not find any evidence to support the view that management will 'take a bath' when earnings are below the lower pre-set bound.

accounting earnings for a number of periods. In such industries, Positive Accounting theorists may argue that it is more appropriate to reward the manager in terms of the market value of the firm's securities, which are assumed to be influenced by expectations about the net present value of expected future cash flows. This may be done either by basing a cash bonus on any increases in share prices or by providing the manager with shares or options to shares in the firm. If the value of the firm's shares increases, both the manager and the owners will benefit (their interests will be aligned). Importantly, the manager will be given an incentive to increase the value of the firm. In a survey of Australian managers, Deegan (1997) provides evidence that 21 per cent of the managers surveyed held shares in their employer.

As already indicated, offering managers incentives that are tied to accounting profits might have the adverse effect of inducing them to undertake actions that are not in the interests of shareholders. This might particularly be the case in relation to expenditure on research and development. As already explained, within the United States all research and development is required to be expensed as incurred, and hence there is an immediate downward impact on profits when a firm undertakes research and development.[37] Apart from the initial impacts on profits, there is also evidence that capital markets frequently do not put a great amount of value on research and development expenditure because of the many uncertainties inherent in such expenditure (Kothari et al., 2002; Lev & Sougiannis, 1996)—that is, the market is considered to undervalue the benefits attributable to research and development. In relation to the personal motivations of chief executive officers (CEOs) in the United States, Cheng (2004, p. 307) states:

> CEOs consider the benefits and costs of R&D spending, and [consistent with the maintained assumption of self-interest] they invest in R&D only when the expected personal benefits dominate the personal costs. Their expected costs of R&D spending include the negative impact of R&D spending on short-term accounting and stock performance, since these measures affect CEO compensation and job security (Dechow and Skinner 2000; Murphy 1999). The negative impact of R&D spending on current accounting earnings is due to the fact that R&D spending is typically immediately expensed under US GAAP. Therefore, CEOs who want to boost current accounting earnings have incentives to reduce R&D spending (e.g., Baber et al., 1991; Dechow and Sloan 1991). In addition, CEOs may consider R&D investments as less desirable than other investments in terms of the impact of the investments on short-term stock prices [because of the tendency of capital markets to undervalue R&D expenditures]. Relative to other investments, R&D projects are associated with higher information asymmetry between managers and shareholders (e.g., Clinch, 1991) and greater uncertainty of the future benefits (e.g., Chan et al., 2001; Kothari et al., 2002). As a result, current stock prices likely do not fully reflect the future benefits of R&D spending (Lev and Sougiannis 1996). Therefore, CEOs concerned with short-term stock prices may reduce R&D spending to increase other investments with benefits more fully (or better) reflected in current stock prices.

---

37 By contrast, IAS 38 'Intangible Assets' (and, within Australia, AASB 138) requires expenditure on research to be expensed as incurred, but does allow development expenditure to be capitalised to the extent that future economic benefits are deemed 'probable' and the cost can be measured reliably.

These impacts are heightened as the manager approaches retirement. As Cheng (2004, p. 308) states:

> CEOs are concerned with short-term accounting and stock performance, and these concerns generate incentives for CEOs to reduce R&D spending. Such incentives become stronger when CEOs approach retirement or face earnings shortfalls (Baber et al. 1991; Dechow and Sloan 1991). As the CEO approaches retirement, it is less likely for the CEO to benefit from current R&D investments. Meanwhile, the CEOs career concern diminishes, and the CEO becomes more short-term oriented (Gibbons and Murphy 1992) due to weakened concern about the discipline from the managerial labor markets. Likewise, when facing deteriorating economic performance, the CEO is more concerned with the expected personal costs of R&D spending, since poor performance may trigger such results as job termination and corporate takeover, which may disentitle the CEO to the future of current R&D spending. Thus CEOs have incentives to reduce R&D spending in order to reverse a poor performance, especially if an expected shortfall is small and thus more easily reversed.

Given that there would conceivably be incentives for senior management to reduce spending on research and development (particularly if managers are offered bonuses tied to accounting profit), it is perhaps predictable that additional contractual agreements might be put in place to reduce this motivation to reduce research and development. One approach would be to have those people who are responsible for determining senior management salaries (often done by way of a compensation committee that is established within the organisation and on which non-managerial directors often serve) specifically adjust the salaries in such a way that the salary is directly tied to research and development activity. As Cheng (2004, p. 308) states:

> When CEO incentives to reduce R&D spending become stronger, compensation committees may adjust CEO compensation arrangements to mitigate such incentives. This adjustment should affect CEO's consideration of the expected personal benefits and expected personal costs of R&D spending in favour of R&D expenditures. One possible adjustment is to establish a greater positive association between changes in R&D spending and changes in CEO compensation. Such a greater association makes increasing R&D spending more beneficial to the CEO, and reducing R&D spending more costly to the CEO.

The results of Cheng (2004) indicate that compensation committees do often establish a link between changes in research and development spending and changes in CEOs' total compensation. Further, the compensation being offered to the retiring managers is often by way of the provision of share options. Granting share options increases the longer term focus of the managers, thereby further motivating them to embrace optimal levels of research and development activity.[38]

In considering the use of share options, and as with accounting-based bonus schemes, there are also problems associated with the manager being rewarded in ways that are influenced by

---

38 As a particular example of the use of share options, Cheng (2004, p. 321) refers to the options provided to the CEO of a large US corporation. According to Cheng, 'the CEO of the company was scheduled to retire on April 1, 2000 at age 64. The compensation committee approved to grant 1,500,000 stock options to the CEO in 1997 in order to provide a stock option-based incentive to continue his contributions to the improvement of the share price through and beyond retirement, and half the options would not become exercisable until the CEO became 66.'

share price movements. First, the share price will be affected not only by factors controlled by the manager but also by outside, market-wide factors. That is, share prices may provide a 'noisy' measure of management performance—'noisy' in the sense that they are affected not only by the actions of management but also largely by general market movements over which the manager has no control. Further, only the senior managers would be likely to have a significant effect on the cash flows of the firm and hence the value of the firm's securities. Therefore, market-related incentives may be appropriate only for senior management. Offering shares to lower-level management may be demotivational, as their own individual actions would have little likelihood (relative to senior management) of impacting on share prices and therefore their personal wealth. Consistent with this, it is more common for senior managers than other employees to hold shares in their employer. Within the Deegan (1997) sample, 35 per cent of the senior management, 16 per cent of the middle management and 6 per cent of the lower management held shares in their employer.

Reflecting the way executives often share in the performance of an organisation, Accounting Headline 7.3 shows how CSR Ltd rewards its CEO by way of short-term and long-term

Accounting Headline 7.3 An example of the use of short-term and long-term incentives

Australian, 16 June 2005

Life's sweet: $4m for CSR chief

TERESA OOI

CSR chief executive and managing director Alec Brennan has been rewarded for boosting earnings with a hefty 43 per cent pay rise this year to $4.1 million, up from $2.9 million in 2004.

Mr Brennan received $1.16 million in salary, $715.000 in short-term bonuses and $1.6 million in long-term incentives for the full year ending 31 March, compared with his total package of $2.9 million last year, which included $600,000 in short-term incentives and $393,018 in long-term bonuses.

Mr Brennan, who joined the sugar, building and construction materials company in 1969, has increased the company's net income by 79 per cent to $287 million.

The earnings lift came as sugar demand soared in Asia where a two-year drought in India and Thailand hit sugar crops and helped drive up raw sugar prices. Sugar earnings more than doubled to $89.8 million from $37.6 million a year ago.

Mr Brennan became managing director in 2003 after the company split with cement producer Rinker, leaving CSR with sugar, building materials and aluminium business.

At the time of the demerger CSR's market capitalisation was $1.5 billion. In two years it has grown to more than $2.2 billion.

Mark Ebbinghaus of UBS said CSR has performed strongly in a challenging market for the building materials company which also faced votalile sugar prices.

'Mr Brennan's performance has exceeded expectations. He is known for running the business very tightly and is respected as a long-sighted chief executive.'

The company explained that the majority of Mr Brennan's remuneration is 'dependent on increasing shareholder value'.

'Short-term incentive rewards performance in a given year—CSR's net profit before significant items was up 25.3 per cent to $201 million

(including significant items it was up 79 per cent to $287 million). Cash flow was also up 10.5 per cent to $321 million and dividend increased to 12c from 11c. Alec has chosen to acquire CSR shares with his total short-term incentive of $715,000 for the year.

'A long-term incentive of 750,000 shares ($1.6 million) was purchased during the year as CSR's total shareholder return (share price plus dividend) was in the top quartile of companies in the ASX 200 accumulation index.'

The company stressed that all shares purchased under the incentive scheme were bought on-market and 'therefore not dilutive to shareholders'.

Mr Brennan now has 3.1 million CSR shares.

CSR's shares rose 1c to close at $2.60 yesterday.

incentives. The short-term incentives relate to profit-sharing plans, whereas the longer term incentives relate to changes in share prices. It would be expected that rewarding the executives in the manner outlined should align the interests of the executives (agents) with those of the shareholders (principals)—a view consistent with agency theory and PAT. It would be expected that such schemes would be restricted to senior managers, as they have the greatest ability to affect share prices. However, there has been considerable criticism from shareholders in recent years of the size of executive share option schemes. From the perspective of PAT, this might indicate that shareholders believe that the size of some such schemes potentially dilutes the value of shareholders' existing shares (through the issue of new shares at a substantial discount to future market values) by so much that the agency benefits of the share options are outweighed by the cost to existing shareholders.

In general, it is argued that the likelihood of accounting-based or market-based performance measures or reward schemes being put in place will, in part, be driven by considerations of the relative 'noise' of market-based versus accounting-based performance measures. The relative reliance on accounting-based or market-based measures may potentially be determined on the basis of the relative sensitivity of either measure to general market (largely uncontrollable) factors. Sloan (1993) indicates that CEO salary and bonus compensation appears to be relatively more aligned with accounting earnings in those firms where:

- share returns are relatively more sensitive to general market movements (relatively noisy);
- accounting earnings have a high association with the firm-specific movement in the firm's share values;
- accounting earnings have a less positive (more negative) association with market-wide movements in equity values.

While the above arguments have discussed how or why managers might work in the interests of owners if they are offered rewards that are tied to the value of the shares of the organisation, there is also an argument that if managers are provided with an equity interest in the organisation this will have other positive impacts in terms of encouraging the managers to increase the level of disclosure. Without an equity interest in the organisation, managers might be motivated to withhold information from shareholders and other interested stakeholders. As Nagar, Nanda and Wysocki (2003, p. 284) state:

> Managers avoid disclosing private information because such disclosure reduces their private control benefits. For instance, a lack of information disclosure limits the ability of capital and labour markets to effectively monitor and discipline managers (Shleifer and Vishny, 1989). The disclosure agency problem can thus be regarded as a fundamental agency problem underlying other agency problems. Practitioners also echo the view that managers exhibit an inherent tendency to withhold information from investors, even in the 'high disclosure' environment of US capital markets. A panellist at the recent STERN Stewart Executive Roundtable states, 'all things equal, the managers of most companies would rather not disclose things if they don't have to. They don't want you to see exactly what they're doing; to see the little bets they are taking' (Stern Stewart, 2001, p. 37).

In relation to the concern that managers might be motivated to restrict disclosure, Nagar, Nanda and Wysocki (2003) suggest that providing managers with equity interests (for example, shares or share options) in the organisation will act to reduce the 'non-disclosure tendency'. Specifically, they state (p. 284):

Stock [share] price-based incentives elicit both good news and bad news disclosures from managers. Managers have incentives to release good news and bad news because it boosts stock price. On the other hand, the potential negative investor interpretation of silence (Verecchia, 1983; Milgrom, 1981), and litigation costs (which reduce the value of the managers' ownership interest) are incentives to release bad news. Therefore, we argue that managerial stock price-based incentives, both as periodic compensation and aggregate shareholdings, help align long-run managerial and investor disclosure preferences and mitigate disclosure agency problems ... Our basic premise is that stock price-based incentives are contractual mechanisms that align managerial disclosure preferences with those of shareholders.

The results of Nagar, Nanda and Wysocki's study are consistent with their expectations. Their results show that offering managers equity-based incentives increases the managers' propensity to disclose information. Specifically, they found that firm disclosures, measured by both the frequency of earnings forecasts and analysts' ratings of the firms' disclosures, increase as the proportion of CEO compensation tied to the share prices and the value of CEO shareholdings increase.

In considering the use of share-based versus accounting-based bonus schemes, accounting-based rewards have the advantage that the accounting results may be based on subunit or divisional performance, but one would need to ensure that individuals do not focus on their division at the expense of the organisation as a whole.

PAT assumes that if a manager is rewarded on the basis of accounting numbers (for example, on the basis of a share of profits) then the manager will have an incentive to manipulate the accounting numbers. Given such an assumption, the value of audited financial statements becomes apparent. Rewarding managers in terms of accounting numbers (a strategy aimed at aligning the interests of owners and managers) may not be appropriate if management was solely responsible for compiling those numbers. The auditor will act to arbitrate on the reasonableness of the accounting methods adopted. However, it must be remembered that there will always be scope for opportunism.

The above arguments concentrate on how management's rewards will be directly affected by the particular accounting methods chosen. Management might also be rewarded in other indirect ways as a result of electing to use particular accounting methods. For example, DeAngelo (1988) provided evidence that when individuals face a contest for their positions as managers of an organisation they will, prior to the contest, adopt accounting methods that lead to an increase in reported profits (and the increased reported earnings could not be associated with any apparent increase in cash flows), thereby bolstering their case for re-election. DeAngelo also showed that, where the existing managers were unsuccessful in retaining their positions within the organisation, the newly appointed managers were inclined to recognise many expenses as soon as they took office (that is, 'take a bath') in a bid to highlight the poor 'state of affairs' they had inherited. Such strategies would be consistent with the opportunistic perspective applied within PAT. The view that incoming CEOs may 'take a bath' was also confirmed by Wells (2002). Using Australian data Wells (p. 191) states:

There is support for the view that incoming CEOs take an 'earnings bath' in the year of the CEO change ... Tests of earnings management yield evidence of income decreasing earnings management in the year of the CEO change, with the strongest results for CEO changes categorised as 'non-routine'. In this setting, the incoming CEO is typically not associated with past decisions, implicit criticism of which may be embodied in downwards earnings management. Moreover, the outgoing CEO is unable to constrain such behaviour. This highlights an important corporate governance issue, namely the effect of the CEO succession process in constraining the opportunities for incoming management to undertake earnings management in the period subsequent to the CEO change.[39]

Apart from using particular incentive schemes to motivate employees to work in the interests of owners in the current period, particular remuneration plans can also be used to retain key employees. For example, offering managers share options that cannot be exercised for a number of years, and that would be forfeited on departure from the organisation, can not only act to motivate them to increase the organisation's value but can also act as an incentive for them to remain with the firm (Deegan, 1997). As Balsam and Miharjo (2007, p. 96) state:

> Equity compensation, or more precisely, forfeitable equity compensation, can reduce voluntary executive turnover by imposing a cost on the executive, which a prospective employer may not be willing to reimburse ... The vast majority of publicly traded corporations provide equity compensation, usually stock options, to their executives in an effort to retain them and motivate them to act in the shareholders' interests. Equity compensation provides a direct link between executive compensation and shareholder wealth and consequently aligns the interests of a firm's executives with those of its shareholders.

Balsam and Miharjo provide evidence that offering executives share options that cannot be exercised for a number of periods does have the effect of retaining strongly performing executives. By contrast, they provide little incentive for poorly performing managers to stay with a firm, as poor performance will translate to lower share prices and hence may make the options worthless—thereby eliminating any retention effects.

Having considered the contractual relationship between managers and principals, and how accounting can be used as a means of reducing the costs associated with potential conflict, we can now consider the relationship between debtholders and managers. It will be seen that accounting can be used to restrict the implications of this conflict and thereby enable an organisation to attract funds at a lower cost than might otherwise be possible.

DEBT CONTRACTING

When a party lends funds to another organisation, the recipient of the funds may undertake activities that reduce or even eliminate the probability that the funds will be repaid. These costs that relate to the divergent behaviour of the borrower are referred to in PAT as the *agency costs of debt* and, under PAT, lenders will anticipate divergent behaviour. For example, the recipient

---

39 Information reported on Crikey.com (entitled "ANZ boss joins the 'clear the decks' club", 26 October 2007) also provides evidence of how newly appointed chief executive officers of 13 large Australian listed companies—including ANZ Bank—made significant asset writedowns in the initial stages of their appointment.

of the funds may pay excessive dividends, leaving few assets in the organisation to service the debt. Alternatively, the organisation may take on additional and perhaps excessive levels of debt. The new debtholders would then compete with the original debtholder for repayment.

Further, the firm that has borrowed the funds may also invest in very high-risk projects. This strategy would also not be beneficial to the debtholders (who can also be referred to as 'creditors'). The debtholders have a fixed claim (that is, they are receiving a set rate of interest) and hence if the project generates high profits they will receive no greater return, unlike the owners, who will share in the increased value of the firm. If the project fails, which is more likely with a risky project, the debtholders may receive nothing. The debtholders therefore do not share in any 'upside' (the profits), but suffer the consequences of any significant losses (the 'downside').

In the absence of safeguards that protect the interests of debtholders, the holders of debt will assume that management will take actions—such as those described above—that might not always be in the debtholders' interest, and, as a result, it is assumed that they will require the firm to pay higher costs of interest to compensate the debtholders for the high-risk exposure (Smith & Warner, 1979).

If the firm agrees not to pay excessive dividends, not to take on high levels of debt and not to invest in projects of an excessively risky nature, it is assumed that this will reduce the risks of lenders and as a result the firm will be able to attract debt capital at a lower cost than would otherwise be possible. To the extent that the benefits of lower interest costs exceed the costs that may be associated with restricting how management can use the available funds, management will elect to sign agreements that restrict their subsequent actions. Again, signing such an agreement that includes restrictive debt covenants would be an efficient strategy from the firm's perspective as it will be likely to lead to a reduction in the firm's cost of attracting funds.

Apart from explicitly agreeing not to undertake certain actions (such as taking on excessive levels of debts or agreeing not to invest in particularly risky ventures), management might also agree to adopt particular accounting methods if such adoption leads to a reduction in the cost of attracting debt capital. For example, Zhang (2008) argues that managers might agree to adopt conservative accounting methods because they believe that this might reduce the perceived risks faced by the lender. Conservative accounting methods bias the organisation towards more readily recognising losses than gains, consistent with the traditional 'doctrine of conservatism'. Conservative accounting practices would also restrict the organisation from undertaking numerous (or perhaps, any) asset revaluations. The effect of conservative accounting methods is that both profits and net assets (and therefore equity) would tend to be understated (that is, they provide 'conservative measures' of financial position and financial performance) relative to organisations that do not adopt conservative accounting methods. It also means that debt covenants restricting the amount of debt relative to assets (or debt to equity), or the amount of times profits must cover interest (known as an 'interest coverage' clause), will tend to be more restrictive or binding for those organisations that adopt conservative accounting methods. As Zhang (2008) argues, the more binding covenants will provide an earlier warning of default risk, and will thereby reduce the risk exposure of the lending party (for example, a bank). The reason for this is that, because management will have less ability to circumvent restrictive covenants (for example, by undertaking asset revaluations), such covenants will create a technical default of a loan agreement earlier than if management has the scope to loosen the restrictions, perhaps through undertaking an asset revaluation. The earlier the lender can take action to safeguard its funds, the lower the risk of the lender.

Zhang (2008) reports that borrowers who adopt conservative accounting methods attract funds at lower rates of interest (a benefit to the borrower). This is consistent with Ahmed et al. (2002), who also found that adopting conservative accounting methods leads to a reduction in the cost of attracting capital. According to Zhang (2008), borrowers that adopt conservative accounting methods are also more likely to violate debt contracts and to violate them sooner (and the early default signal creates lower risk for lenders, which explains why they are prepared to lend the money at a lower cost).

Historical evidence on Australian public debt contracts is provided by Whittred and Zimmer (1986), who found that for public debt contracts written between 1962 and 1985:[40]

> ... with few exceptions, trust deeds for public debt place restrictions on the amount of both total and secured liabilities that may exist. The constraints were most commonly defined relative to total tangible assets; less often relative to shareholders' funds. The most frequently observed constraints were those limiting total and secured liabilities to some fraction of total tangible assets (p. 22).[41]

While Whittred and Zimmer provided information about public debt issues, Cotter (1998a) provided evidence of private debt contracts negotiated between Australian listed companies and banks between 1993 and 1995. Her findings reveal that (p. 187):

> Leverage covenants are frequently used in bank loan contracts, with leverage most frequently measured as the ratio of total liabilities to total tangible assets. In addition, prior charges covenants that restrict the amount of secured debt owed to other lenders are typically included in the term loan agreements of larger firms, and are defined as a percentage of total tangible assets.[42]

Hence, it is clear that for a number of years both private and public debt contracts within Australia have included restrictive covenants that are directly linked to accounting numbers. Where covenants restrict the total level of debt that may be issued—as was found by both Whittred and Zimmer (1986) and Cotter (1998a)—this is assumed to lead to a reduction in the risk to existing debtholders. It is further assumed to translate to lower interest rates being charged by the 'protected' debtholders. Where the covenants (or debt contract clauses) in a debt contract are breached, this is referred to as a 'technical default' of the borrowing agreement. Where such a breach occurs, and depending on the terms of the debt contract, the debtholder could have the right to demand immediate repayment or the right to seize particular assets over which it has security. Alternatively, the debtholder could agree to renegotiate the terms of the contract and

---

40 When we note that something is a 'public issue' it means that the particular security (such as a debenture, an unsecured note or a convertible note) was made available for the public to invest in (with the terms of the issue typically provided within a publicly available prospectus document). Investors in a public debt issue would have a trustee who is to act in the interests of all the public investors. By contrast, a private debt issue involves an agreement between a limited number of parties (perhaps just one party, such as a bank) to provide debt capital to an organisation.

41 It is common in debt contracts that the measure of assets to be used excludes intangible assets. In part, this is due to the concern that if an organisation becomes financially distressed then many of its intangible assets (such as brand names, patents and goodwill) may have little market value.

42 Cotter (1998a) notes that in the 1990s banks became the major source of corporate debt. This can be contrasted with the earlier period reviewed by Whittred and Zimmer (1986). In the early 1980s Australian corporations placed relatively greater reliance on raising debt through public funding, rather than privately dealing with institutions such as banks.

not enforce the conditions of the breach, but, as indicated below, renegotiation would typically be available only in the case of private debt agreements, given that the negotiation for privately raised debt would involve a limited number of parties.

In relation to debt restrictions incurred within debt contracts, Cotter (1998a) found that the definition of assets commonly used within debt agreements allowed for assets to be revalued. However, for the purposes of the debt restriction, some banks restricted the frequency of revaluations to once every two or three years, while others tended to exclude revaluations undertaken by directors of the firm. These restrictions lessened the ability of firms to loosen debt constraints by revaluing assets. Cotter (1998a) also found that apart from debt-to-assets constraints, interest coverage and current ratio clauses were frequently used in debt agreements. These clauses typically required that the ratio of net profit, with interest and tax added back, to interest expense be at least a minimum number of times. In the Cotter study, the number of times that interest had to be covered ranged from one and a half to four times. The current ratio clauses reviewed by Cotter required that current assets had to be between one and two times the size of current liabilities, depending on the size and industry of the borrowing firm.

In more recent research, Mather and Peirson (2006) undertook an analysis of Australian public and private debt issues made between 1991 and 2001. They reported that, relative to the earlier samples used by Whittred and Zimmer, public debt issues showed a 'significant reduction in the use of debt to asset constraints such as covenants restricting the total liabilities/total tangible assets, or total secured liabilities to total tangible assets, with only 28 per cent of the sample of recent contracts including these covenants' (p. 292). However, Mather and Peirson provide evidence that, while there is a reduction in the use of covenants that restrict the amount of total liabilities relative to assets, there appears to be a greater variety of covenants being used relative to earlier years. Among the other covenants they found in debt contracts were requirements stipulating required minimum interest coverage, minimum dividend coverage, minimum current ratio, and required minimum net worth. Again, if these minimum accounting-based requirements are not met, the borrower is considered to be in technical default of the debt agreement and the lenders may take action to retrieve their funds. As already discussed, the purpose of the various debt covenants is to provide lenders with regular and timely indicators of the possibility of a borrower defaulting on repayment of its debts. A violation of a debt covenant signals an increase in the likelihood of default. However, it needs to be appreciated that the covenant measures are simply indicators of the chances that an organisation will not repay borrowed funds, and an organisation being in technical default of a covenant is not a perfect indicator that it would not have repaid the borrowed funds.

When debt contracts are written, and where they use accounting numbers, the contract can rely on either the accounting rules in place when the contracts were signed (often called 'frozen GAAP') or the accounting rules in place at each year's reporting date (referred to as 'rolling GAAP' of 'floating GAAP'). Mather and Peirson found that, in all the public debt contracts other than one, rolling (or floating) GAAP was to be used to calculate the specific ratios used within the contracts. The use of rolling GAAP increases the risk to borrowers in the sense that, if a new accounting standard is released by the IASB (and thereafter by the AASB) that changes the treatment of particular assets, liabilities, expenses or income, this has the potential to cause an organisation to be in technical default of a loan agreement. For example, a new accounting standard might be released that requires a previously recognised asset to be fully expensed in the statement of comprehensive income, which could have obvious implications for debt to asset constraints or interest coverage requirements. This in itself could motivate an organisation to actively lobby accounting standard-setters against a particular draft accounting standard. As Mather and Peirson (p. 294) state:

> The use of rolling GAAP in Australia means that new (or revisions to) accounting standards might cause breaches of covenants not anticipated at the time of contract negotiation.

When comparing the use of covenants in public and private debt issues, Mather and Peirson (2006) found that the mean number of accounting-based covenants used in the sample of public debt contracts is smaller (mean of 1.5) than the mean number of covenants (mean of 3.5) found in the sample of private debt contracts. That is, there were more restrictions placed on privately negotiated debt agreements. Similarly, where debt covenants restricted total liabilities to total tangible assets, Mather and Peirson found that 'the limits imposed in public debt contracts (a mean total liabilities/total tangible assets of 82.2 per cent) appear to be less restrictive that those in private debt contracts (mean limit of 75.2 per cent)'. The fact that private debt contracts are more restrictive than public debt contracts can be explained from an efficiency perspective. Where a covenant is violated, an organisation is in technical default of the debt contract. If an organisation is in technical default, it often has the option to try to negotiate with the debtholders to come up with a compromise that does not involve immediate repayment of the debt. However, it is very difficult to come up with a negotiated outcome in a public debt issue as there are so many diverse parties involved, some of which might not even be able to be contacted, making it difficult or nearly impossible to have a successful renegotiation. Hence, we would expect to find less restrictive covenants in public debt contracts relative to private debt contracts.[43] As Mather and Peirson (p. 305) state:

> In comparison to our sample of recent public debt contracts, private debt contracts contain a greater number, variety and, collectively, more restrictive set of financial covenants. We also document differences in accounting rules associated with financial covenants used in these contracts. Tailoring of the definition of liabilities and earnings in private debt contracts make them more restrictive compared with the definitions in public debt contracts. Our findings support theory that suggests that covenant-restrictive and renegotiation-flexible contracts are more suited to borrowers contracting with financial intermediaries in private debt markets than in public debt markets that are characterized by diverse and numerous investors.

As with management compensation contracts, PAT assumes that the existence of debt contracts (which are initially put in place as a mechanism to reduce the agency costs of debt and can be explained from an efficiency perspective) provides management with a subsequent (*ex post*) incentive to manipulate accounting numbers, with the incentive to manipulate the numbers increasing as the accounting-based constraint approaches violation. As Watts (1995, p. 323) states:

> Early studies of debt contract-motivated choice test whether firms with higher leverage (gearing) are more likely to use earnings-increasing accounting methods to avoid default

---

43 As Mather and Peirson (2006) point out, a trustee would typically be appointed to look after the interests of individual investors in a public debt issue. However, individual investors would still be required to approve any course of action ensuing from a technical breach of a debt covenant.

(leverage hypothesis). The underlying assumptions are that the higher the firm's leverage the less [is the] slack in debt covenants and the more likely the firm is to have changed accounting methods to have avoided default. This change is usually interpreted as opportunistic since technical default generates wealth transfers to creditors but it could also be efficient to the extent that it avoids real default and the deadweight loss associated with bankruptcy.

For example, if the firm contractually agreed that the debt to total tangible assets ratio should be kept below a certain figure, then if that figure was likely to be exceeded (causing a technical default of the loan agreement), management may have an incentive either to inflate assets or deflate liabilities. This is consistent with the results reported in Christie (1990) and Watts and Zimmerman (1990). To the extent that such an action was not objective, management would obviously be acting opportunistically and not to the benefit of individuals holding debt claims against the firm. Debt agreements typically require financial statements to be audited.

Other research to consider how management might manipulate accounting numbers in the presence of debt agreements includes that undertaken by DeFond and Jiambalvo (1994) and Sweeney (1994). Both of these studies investigated the behaviour of managers of firms known to have defaulted on accounting-related debt covenants. DeFond and Jiambalvo (1994) provided evidence that the managers manipulated accounting accruals in the years before and the year after violation of the agreement. Similarly, Sweeney (1994) found that as a firm approaches violation of a debt agreement managers have a greater propensity to adopt income-increasing strategies relative to firms that are not approaching technical default of accounting-based debt covenants. The income-increasing accounting strategies included changing key assumptions when calculating pension liabilities and adopting last-in-first-out cost-flow assumptions for inventory.

Sweeney (1994) also showed that managers with an incentive to manipulate accounting earnings might also strategically determine when they will first adopt a new accounting requirement. When new accounting standards are issued, there is typically a transition period (which could be a number of years) in which organisations can voluntarily opt to implement a new accounting requirement. After the transitional period the use of the new requirement becomes mandatory. Sweeney showed that organisations that defaulted on their debt agreements tended to adopt income-increasing requirements early, and deferred the adoption of accounting methods that would lead to a reduction in reported earnings. Research by Dhaliwal (1982) and Holthausen (1990) has also shown that firms with high leverage ratios (debt to equity), and who are thereby assumed to be approaching the violation of debt agreements, tend to oppose the introduction of accounting methods that have the potential to introduce high variability in reported earnings. This is because the high variability might increase the possibility of defaulting on accounting-based debt agreements in particular years.

Debt contracts occasionally restrict the accounting techniques that may be used by the firm, hence requiring adjustments to published accounting numbers. For example, and as stated above, Cotter (1998a) showed that bank loan contracts sometimes did not allow the component related to asset revaluations to be included in the definition of 'assets' for the purpose of calculating ratios, such as 'debt to assets' restrictions. These revaluations were, however, permitted for external reporting purposes. Therefore, loan agreements sometimes require the revaluation component (or other accounting adjustments that are allowed by accounting standards) to be removed from the published accounting numbers prior to the calculation of any restrictive covenants included within the debt contract.

Within accounting, management usually has available a number of alternative ways to account for particular items. Hence, management has at its disposal numerous ways to minimise the effects of existing accounting-based restrictions. Therefore, it may appear optimal for debtholders to stipulate in advance all accounting methods that management must use. However, and as noted previously, it would be too costly, and for practical purposes impossible, to write 'complete' contracts up front. As a consequence, management will always have some discretionary ability, which may enable it to loosen the effects of debtholder-negotiated restrictions. The role of external auditors (if appointed) would be to arbitrate on the reasonableness of the accounting methods chosen.

Apart from debt covenants (such as debt-to-asset constraints or minimum interest coverage requirements), which may or may not be breached, another contractual mechanism is something known as 'performance pricing'. Referring to US data, Beatty and Weber (2003, p. 120) state:

> Performance pricing is a relatively new feature in bank debt contracts that explicitly makes the interest rate charged on a bank loan a function of the borrower's current creditworthiness. Asquith, Beatty and Webber (2002) document that performance-pricing features typically measure the borrower's creditworthiness using financial ratios such as debt to earnings before interest, taxes, depreciation and amortisation (EBITDA), leverage and interest coverage. That is, the interest rate charged in the contract does not remain fixed over the length of the loan, but varies inversely with changes in measures of financial performance. Compared to covenants under which accounting information affects loan rates only when the borrower violates a single threshold, performance pricing creates a more continuous and direct link between accounting information and interest rates. Thus, performance pricing likely gives managers additional incentives to make income-increasing accounting method changes.

Beatty and Weber (2003) explore whether the existence of accounting-based performance pricing increases borrowers' tendencies to adopt income-increasing accounting method changes.

Beatty and Weber also note that debt contracts often prohibit borrowers from using voluntary accounting method changes to affect contract calculations. Hence they expect that borrowers who change their accounting methods are more likely to make income-increasing changes if their debt contracts allow the changes to affect contract calculations.

It has previously been argued that borrowers would typically agree to various contractual restrictions (including restrictions on the accounting methods they are permitted to use) in an effort to reduce the interest costs and other borrowing costs that they are required to pay. However, Beatty and Weber (2003) also suggest that some borrowers might actually agree to pay higher costs of interest in return for being allowed greater flexibility in choosing accounting methods. That is, if we accept that restrictions placed on borrowers (which have the effect of reducing the ability of the borrower to transfer wealth away from the lenders and thereby potentially reduce the agency costs of debt) lead to a reduction in cost, then conversely we could speculate that in some circumstances some managers might be prepared to pay for increased flexibility—that is, there could be a value in having the ability to select alternative accounting measures.

Beattie and Weber found that 75 borrowers from their sample of 125 borrowing corporations had at least one contract that allowed voluntary accounting method changes to affect contract calculations. Predictably, they found that firms with contracts that allowed voluntary changes in the accounting methods used were more likely to adopt income-increasing accounting methods than firms that had debt contracts that did not allow debt covenants to be calculated using new accounting methods. Further, they found that the likelihood that such firms would adopt income-increasing methods increased as the cost of technical violation of debt contracts increased. In relation to the existence of accounting-based performance pricing, their results show that borrowers that change their accounting methods are more likely to make income-increasing accounting changes if their debt contracts include accounting-based performance pricing.

Having discussed how managers might have incentives to adopt income-increasing accounting methods, we can now briefly consider the role of independent auditors. In relation to auditors, and following discussion so far in this chapter, there would arguably be a particular demand for financial statement auditing (that is, monitoring by external parties) when:

■ management is rewarded on the basis of numbers generated by the accounting system (therefore giving managers an incentive to increase accounting numbers to increase personal financial rewards); and
■ the firm has borrowed funds, and accounting-based covenants are in place to protect the investments of the debtholders.

Consistent with this, it could also be argued that, as the managers' share of equity in the business decreases, and as the proportion of debt to total assets increases, there will be a corresponding increase in the demand for auditing. In this respect, Ettredge, Simon, Smith and Stone (1994) show that organisations that voluntarily elect to have interim financial statements audited tend to have greater leverage and lower management shareholding in the firm.

The next section considers how expectations about the political process can also impact on a manager's choice of accounting methods.

POLITICAL COSTS

As indicated previously, firms (particularly large ones) are sometimes under scrutiny by various groups, for example, by government, employee groups, consumer groups, environmental lobby groups and so on. The size of a firm is often used as an indication of market power and this in itself can attract the attention of regulatory bodies such as the Australian Competition and Consumer Commission, the Competition Commission in the United Kingdom or the Federal Trade Commission in the United States.

Government and interest groups may publicly promote the view that a particular organisation (typically large) is generating excessive profits and not paying its 'fair share' to other segments of the community (the wages it is paying are too low, its product prices are too high, its financial commitment to environmental and community initiatives is too low, its tax payments are too low, and so on). Watts and Zimmerman (1978b, 1986) highlight the highly publicised claims about US oil companies made by consumers, unions and government within the United States in the late 1970s. The claims were that oil companies were making excessive profits and were in effect exploiting the nation. Such claims may have led to the imposition of additional taxes in the form of 'excess profits' taxes.

Consistent with the early work of Watts and Zimmerman (1978b), it has been argued that to reduce the possibility of adverse political attention and the associated costs of this attention (the costs associated with increased taxes, increased wage claims or product boycotts), politically sensitive firms (typically large firms) will adopt accounting methods that lead to a reduction in reported profits.[44] However, the view that lower reported profits will lead to lower political scrutiny (and ultimately to lower wealth transfers away from the firm) assumes that parties involved in the political process are unable or not prepared to 'unravel' the implications of the managers' various accounting choices. That is, managers can somehow fool those involved in the political process by simply adopting one method of accounting (income decreasing) in preference to another. In this regard, Fields, Lys and Vincent (2001, p. 260) state:

> In order for earnings management to be successful the perceived frictions must exist and at least some users of accounting information must be unable or unwilling to unravel completely the effects of the earnings management ... Political cost-based motivations implicitly assume that users of accounting information (e.g, trade unions or government agencies) may be unable to undo completely the effects of earnings management.

But, why would it be the case that external parties can potentially be 'fooled' by management as a result of management's choices of alternative accounting methods when elsewhere it has been assumed (consistent with the EMH) that individuals within other markets, such as the capital market, can efficiently unravel management's choice of accounting methods?

In relation to political costs, and from an economic perspective, there is a view that in political markets there is limited expected 'pay-off' that can result from the actions of individuals (Downs, 1957). For example, if an individual seeks to know the real reasons why government elected to adopt a particular action from among many possible actions, the gathering of such information would be costly. Yet that individual's vote would have very little likelihood of affecting the existence of the government. Hence, individuals will elect to remain rationally uninformed. However, should particular interest groups form, then such information costs can be shared and the ability to investigate government actions can increase. A similar perspective is taken with groups other than government, for example representatives of labour unions, consumer bodies and so on. Officials of these bodies represent a diverse group of people, with the individual constituents again having limited incentive to be fully informed about the activities of the office-bearers.

Because PAT assumes that all actions by all individuals (including officials of interest groups, politicians and so on) are driven by self-interest, representatives of interest groups are predicted to adopt strategies that maximise their own welfare in the knowledge that their constituents will have limited motivation to be fully informed about their activities.

With the above arguments in mind, consider the actions of politicians. Because politicians know that highly profitable companies could be unpopular with a large number of their constituency, the politicians could 'win' votes by taking action against such companies. However, Watts and Zimmerman (1979) argue that politicians will claim that the actions they have taken

---

44 Difficulties with using firm size to proxy for political costs, including the likelihood that it can proxy for many other effects, such as industry membership, are discussed in Ball and Foster (1982).

were in the 'public interest', as obviously they need to disguise the fact that such actions best served the politicians' own interests. Watts and Zimmerman (p. 283) state:

> In recent years economists have questioned whether the public interest assumption is consistent with observed phenomena. They have proposed an alternative assumption— that individuals involved in the political process act in their own self-interest (the self-interest assumption). This assumption yields implications which are more consistent with observed phenomena than those based on the public interest assumption.[45]

To justify their actions, politicians may simply rely on the reported profits of companies to provide an excuse for their actions, knowing that individual constituents are unlikely to face the cost of investigating the politicians' motives, or the cost of investigating how the corporation's profits were determined (that is, whether the profit resulted because a particular accounting method was used in a less than objective manner). To reduce the excuses of politicians, potentially politically sensitive firms are predicted to anticipate politicians' actions and therefore managements of politically vulnerable firms have an incentive to reduce their reported profits. As Watts and Zimmerman (1979, p. 281) state:

> Government commissions often use the contents of financial statements in the regulatory process (rate setting, anti-trust, etc.). Further, Congress often bases legislative actions on these statements. This, in turn, provides management with incentives to select accounting procedures which either reduce the costs they bear or increase the benefits they receive as a result of the actions of government regulators and legislators.

Interestingly, when the media report a company's profitability they seldom give any attention to the accounting methods used to calculate the profit. In a sense, profit is held out as some form of objective measure of organisational performance (much like governments might rely on profits to support a particular action). Media reports of high corporate profitability can potentially trigger political costs for a firm. As discussed, representatives of interest groups might use profits as a justification for particular actions. In this respect, consider Accounting Headline 7.4. The article refers to the high profits of the Commonwealth Bank and questions how the bank could retrench so many employees when it makes such high profits. The high profits coupled with the loss of jobs for employees are seen as potentially 'double-daring' the government to introduce legislation to reduce the socially irresponsible behaviour of the banks. The union leader quoted in the article accuses the organisation of acting with 'incredible arrogance'. In a sense, the reported accounting profits could be used as an excuse to push for greater regulation of bank lending practices and to call for banks to pay higher wages and reduce the level of job redundancies. If reported profits were not so high, there might be less chance that demands for increased regulation or a reduction in job redundancies would be made. As Watts and Zimmerman (1978b, p. 115) state:

> By avoiding the attention that high profits draw because of monopoly rents, management can reduce the likelihood of adverse political actions and, thereby, reduce its expected

---

45   Chapter 3 of this book considered different theories of regulation. One theory, public interest theory, suggests that regulators are not driven by self-interest but, rather, elect to put in place regulations that are in the best interests of society. By contrast, economic interest group theories of regulation assume that everybody, including regulators, are motivated by their own self-interest and hence regulators put in place regulations that best serve themselves rather than society generally. This latter theory ties in best with the assumptions embodied within PAT.

Sydney Morning Herald, 22 August 2002

CBA cuts 1000 staff on record profit day

ANTHONY HUGHES

The main consumers' body accused the Commonwealth Bank of thumbing its nose at the Federal Government yesterday by revealing 1000 job cuts while reporting a record $2.6 billion annual profit.

The Australian Consumers' Association also expressed scepticism at the bank's promise to maintain its branch numbers at about 1000, accusing the bank of backtracking on such promises in the past and downgrading the level of services at many branches.

'They might keep a physical presence that's the same as now but the question is what level of services will be provided at these locations,' said the association's financial services policy officer, Catherine Wolthuizen.

'For the bank to make the joint announcement of the massive profit and the job cuts on the one day, it's almost double-daring the Government into whether it will regulate the industry.'

But the bank said the job cuts did not include staff who would be dealing directly with customers. The cuts, on top of 500 job losses announced recently, will include back office staff in branches and regional offices as well as staff involved in credit processes.

The CBA's managing director, David Murray, said the bank needed to improve its productivity to cope with an expected downturn in consumer lending and the possibility that a weakening US economy would stall a pick-up in business lending.

About 550 new jobs would be created in other areas, most likely in a division that serviced only 'premium' customers.

The bank's 11 per cent rise in net profit was driven by its banking arm and included a 6 per cent rise in commission and other fee income to $1.24 billion, thanks partly to a revamped fee structure on its main savings account.

The introduction of a flat $5 monthly fee earlier this year was touted by the bank as a more transparent structure for customers but independent analysts estimated it would add several hundred million dollars to the bank's annual revenue.

The Finance Sector Union's national secretary, Tony Beck, said his members' job security became more precarious as bank profits swelled.

'This is a corporation that purports to be a good corporate citizen, has a CEO that seeks to be a leader in the community and they behave with this incredible arrogance,' Mr Beck said.

The ANZ has already promised not to close any more rural branches, while Westpac has also put a 'moratorium' on closures.

'We knew that having completed all of the rationalisation of our branch system through two mergers (State Bank of Victoria and Colonial) ... that we have now a size of network that fits our customer requirements,' Mr Murray said.

Despite the job cuts, Mr Murray promised the bank would obtain better feedback from customers about service levels and address issues of queuing in branches.

The bank also used yesterday's profit announcement to call for higher corporate governance standards amid the global crisis of confidence in corporate accounting. The CBA yesterday became one of the few companies to abandon the issue of options to executives, with Mr Murray arguing they had led to negative 'behavioural consequences', particularly in the US.

But executives will still be rewarded with shares as incentives. Mr Murray also retains his 1.5 million options, which are estimated to be showing a profit of at least several million dollars assuming they meet share price performance hurdles.

costs (including the legal costs the firm would incur opposing the political actions). Included in political costs are the costs labour unions impose through increased demands generated by large reported profits.

As a further example of how reported profits can be used in a political debate, consider Accounting Headline 7.5. This article refers to a dispute between Qantas and both its engineers and the union representing the engineers. Note how the company's record profits are used to

Australian, 30 May 2008, p. 40

Deadlock in engineers' salary discussions

JOHN STAPLETON

The ACTU has called on Qantas to return to the negotiating table after it backed out of wage negotiations with its engineers. The company cancelled meetings over the wage claims scheduled for this week, prompting stopwork meetings in three states.

One hundred engineers held a four-hour stopwork meeting in Sydney yesterday morning, while another 100 stopped work from 6 pm to 10 pm last night. About 120 engineers are expected to stop work in Melbourne this morning. Management personnel and retirees were used to replace the engineers.

ACTU head Sharan Burrow said the airline engineers union, ALAEA, did not want to continue industrial action. 'We are asking Qantas to come to the bargaining table, they have refused,' she said. 'They cancelled the meeting. It is incredible. There can be no negotiation with a company that is showing no respect for workers by refusing to sit at the bargaining table.'

The engineers are calling for a 5 per cent wage increase, while the company is offering 3 per cent. Ms Burrow was cheered as she condemned the company's senior executives for their exploitation of the engineers' talent while granting themselves multi-million-dollar pay deals at a time of record profits. She said the company's profits had been increasing at twice the rate of wages.

Union officials said the company offer was below inflation, represented a pay cut and would reduce their living standards.

Ms Burrow said Qantas profits were expected to increase by 40 per cent this year to about $1.5 billion. Granting the engineers' claim would add an extra $2 million to the company's costs. 'It is shameful,' she said. 'The wages claim is as affordable as anything Qantas has ever done.'

Qantas chief executive Geoff Dixon had given himself a 22 per cent pay rise last year, bringing his salary to almost $7 million, she said. 'There is a simple principle at stake here: the engineers and other staff that are essential to keeping planes in the air and providing a high-quality service should not have to suffer a real wage cut while Qantas executives get big bonuses and the company heads for a record profit.

'Qantas management also need to be reminded that cuts to wages and costs would not attract more customers and could put at risk services and standards at the airline. Qantas engineers are highly skilled, highly professional people who deserve to be treated with dignity and respect.' ALAEA federal secretary Steve Purvinas distributed a flyer to the engineers saying Qantas managers were expecting them to sign off on a 3 per cent wages policy they did not apply to themselves.

'Due to taxing shift work, most Qantas engineers are the sole income providers to their families and work extensive overtime to pay their bills,' he said. 'Outdoor shift work through the night takes its toll. Most will have been divorced at least once and life expectancy is seven years less than the Australian average.'

On an average day, the engineers certified and were responsible for the safety of thousands of people. 'During their careers the average union engineer is required to pass more than 150 examinations, many of which required extensive study in the engineers' own time,' he said.

One engineer who spoke to the *Australian* said his base salary of $63,000 made bringing up his children and paying a mortgage in Sydney almost impossible. It was difficult for his wife to get a job because of the 'extreme' shift work he was asked to do. 'At any moment there are 5000 people cruising at high altitude and their lives depend on my work,' he said.

His job had once been considered a highly skilled occupation deserving of a healthy salary, but he was now paid little more than the average wage.

Shortly after speaking to the *Australian*, the engineer was phoned by management and warned off talking to the media, he said.

Qantas chief executive Geoff Dixon accused the union of being 'loose with the truth' and said he would not negotiate while strikes were ongoing.

'Their claim is out of order and we're not going to entertain it,' he said. 'We're prepared to wait this one out. We are not going to change our view on this. We've got the long-term future of the company in mind more than anything else and if it means that some of our passengers have some discomfort for a while, that will be the case. These people must know that whatever they do won't be enough for us to change our minds.'

Qantas has refused to reveal exactly how many flights were disrupted or cancelled yesterday as a result of the industrial action. Industry sources estimate about six flights were cancelled.

The airline said the vast majority of passengers were re-accommodated within 30 minutes of their original flight time.

justify the claim that Qantas is not paying enough in salaries. Again, consistent with the political cost hypothesis of PAT, it could be argued that had the company not reported such high profits such calls for increased salaries would not have been made.

Numerous studies have considered how particular accounting methods can be used in an endeavour to decrease political costs. As well as the work of Watts and Zimmerman, research has been undertaken by Jones (1991), who, in a US study, considered the behaviour of twenty-three domestic firms from five industries that were the subject of government import-related investigations over the period from 1980 to 1985. These investigations by the International Trade Commission sought to determine whether the domestic firms were under threat from foreign competition. Where such a threat is deemed to be unfair, the government can grant relief by devices such as tariff protection. In making its decision, the government relies on a number of factors, including economic measures such as profits and sales. The results of the study show that in the year of the investigations the sample companies selected accounting strategies that led to a decrease in reported profits. Such behaviour was not evidenced in the year before or the year after the government investigation (perhaps indicating that the politicians are fairly 'shortsighted' when undertaking investigations).

In a UK study, Sutton (1988) found that politically sensitive companies were more likely to lobby in favour of current cost accounting.[46] In a New Zealand study, Wong (1988) investigated the practice of New Zealand companies between 1977 and 1981 and found that those that adopted current cost accounting (which had the effect of reducing reported profits) had higher effective tax rates and larger market concentration ratios than other firms. Effective tax rates and market concentration rates were both used as a measure of political sensitivity.

Authors such as Ness and Mirza (1991) have argued that particular voluntary social disclosures in an organisation's annual report can be explained as an effort to reduce the political costs of the disclosing entities. Ness and Mirza studied the environmental disclosure practices of a number of UK companies. They considered that companies in the oil industry had developed particularly poor reputations for their environmental practices and that this reputation could be used by various interest groups to transfer wealth away from the firm (and presumably away from the managers). Such wealth transfers might be generated if certain groups lobbied government to impose particular taxes (perhaps related to their environmental performance), or if particular employee groups took action to insist that the companies put in place strategies to improve their environmental performance and reputation. Ness and Mirza argued that if firms voluntarily provide environmental disclosures (typically of a positive or self-laudatory nature) this may lead to a reduction in future wealth transfers away from the firm. They found, consistent with their expectations, that oil companies provided greater environmental disclosures within their annual reports than did companies operating in other industries. The authors believe that this was because oil companies had more potentially adverse wealth transfers at stake.

Before concluding the discussion on political costs it is useful to consider a headline that appeared in the *Age* newspaper on 4 February 2006 (p. 5): 'Shell cops heat as $31bn profit leaves

---

46 While a number of studies considered in this chapter investigate the choice between alternative accounting methods, it should be noted that in recent years there has been an increased focus on studying the manipulation of accounting accruals. Relative to investigating the selection of particular accounting methods (for example, the use of straight-line depreciation versus reducing-balance depreciation), the study of the accruals is more difficult and requires the use of modelling techniques to identify discretionary accruals (those controlled by management) and non-discretionary accruals (Jones, 1991). The use of accruals can also be explained from either an efficiency or an opportunistic perspective (Guay, Kothari & Watts, 1996).

many cold'. During 2005 and 2006 fuel prices had reached record levels worldwide. The high prices meant that many people had difficulty finding the money for such basic requirements as heating. Arguably, a time when high fuel costs were adversely affecting so many people was not the most politically favourable time for Shell to post record profits. The following is an extract from the article:

> Oil giant Shell has come under attack from consumers, trade unions and green groups after announcing on Thursday the biggest profit by a British company. Shell made £1.5 million ($A3.5 million) an hour on the back of soaring oil prices.
>
> 'It is high time the Government acted decisively and brought in a proper windfall tax,' said Tony Woodley, general secretary of the Transport and General Workers Union.
>
> 'At a stroke a windfall tax could strengthen the Financial Assistance Scheme and put some backbone into the Pension Protection Fund.'
>
> Meanwhile, poverty activists argued that Shell's profits came at the expense of one million more households falling into fuel poverty.
>
> The Road Haulage Association, representing British hauliers, also joined in the attack on Shell, urging the Government to 'take a little more' from the oil companies and use the cash to reduce fuel tax for road transport operators.

The *Age* article shows how accounting profits can be used to justify actions being taken against an organisation. If Shell's profits had not been so high, such calls for action might not have been made. This is consistent with Watts and Zimmerman's political cost hypothesis.

To this point, we have seen that PAT indicates that the selection of particular accounting methods may impact on the cash flows associated with debt contracts, the cash flows associated with management compensation plans, and the political costs of the firm, and these impacts can be used to explain why firms elect to use particular accounting methods in preference to others. PAT also indicates that the use of particular accounting methods may have opposing effects. For example, if a firm was to adopt a policy that increased income (for example, it may capitalise an item, rather than expensing it as incurred), this may reduce the probability of violating a debt constraint; however, it may increase the political visibility of the firm due to the higher profits. Managers are assumed to select the accounting methods that best balance the conflicting effects (and also that maximise their own wealth).

PAT became the dominant theory used by accounting researchers in the 1970s.[47] It represented a challenge to many normative theorists and conflicted with the views of many established researchers. Many individuals openly criticised PAT, and the concluding section of the chapter considers some of these criticisms.

SOME CRITICISMS OF POSITIVE ACCOUNTING THEORY

One widespread criticism of PAT is that it does not provide prescription and therefore does not provide a means of improving accounting practice. It is argued that simply explaining and

---

47 While its popularity is still high, many accounting schools are now actively promoting alternative theories.

predicting accounting practice—which is the aim of PAT—is not enough. Using a medical analogy, Sterling (1990, p. 130) states:

> PAT cannot rise above giving the same answers because it restricts itself to the descriptive questions. If it ever asked how to solve a problem or correct an error (both of which require going beyond a description to an evaluation of the situation), then it might go on to different questions and obtain different answers after the previous problem was solved. If we had restricted the medical question to the description of the smallpox virus, for example, precluding prescriptions to be vaccinated, we would need more and more descriptive studies as the virus population increased and mutations appeared. Luckily Edward Jenner was naughtily normative, which allowed him to discover how cowpox could be used as a vaccine so smallpox was eventually eliminated, which made room for different questions on the medical agenda.

Howieson (1996, p. 31) provides a view that, by failing to provide prescription, Positive Accounting theorists may alienate themselves from practising accountants. As he states:

> ... an unwillingness to tackle policy issues is arguably an abrogation of academics' duty to serve the community which supports them. Among other activities, practitioners are concerned on a day-to-day basis with the question of which accounting policies they should choose. Traditionally, academics have acted as commentators and reformers on such normative issues. By concentrating on positive questions, they risk neglecting one of their important roles in the community.

A second criticism of PAT is that it is not *value free*, as it asserts. A review of the various research that has adopted PAT will reveal a general absence of prescription (that is, there is no guidance as to what people *should* do—rather it explains or predicts what they *will* do). Positive Accounting theorists normally justify this by saying that they do not want to impose their views on others, but rather would prefer to objectively provide information about the expected implications of particular actions and let people decide for themselves what they should do. (For example, they may provide evidence to support a prediction that organisations close to breaching accounting-based debt covenants will adopt accounting methods that increase the firm's reported profits and assets.) However, as a number of accounting academics have pointed out, selecting a theory to adopt for research (such as PAT) is based on a value judgement; what to research is based on a value judgement; believing that all individual action is driven by self-interest is a value judgement; and so on.[48] Equally, whether one accepts that 'stealing by the owner-manager is analogous to the owner-manager's over-consumption of perks', as Watts and Zimmerman (1986, p. 185) note, is a matter of personal opinion. Also, Watts and Zimmerman appear to have taken a normative position when they identify the objective of accounting research. According to them, 'the objective of accounting theory is to explain and predict accounting practice' (1986, p. 2). Clearly, there are many other views about the role of accounting theory. Hence, no research, whether conducted under PAT or otherwise, is value free. While Watts and

---

48 In Chapter 12 it is noted that some researchers argue that Positive Accounting theorists adopt a conservative right-wing ideology in promoting the virtues of markets, the rights of shareholders (the capitalist class) and so on.

Zimmerman did continue to argue for a number of years that PAT was value free, they did eventually concede (1990, p. 146) that:

> Positive theories are value laden. Tinker et al. (1982, p. 167) argue that all research is value laden and not socially neutral. Specifically, 'Realism operating in the clothes of positive theory claims theoretical supremacy because it is born of fact, not values' (p. 172). We concede the importance of values in determining research: both the researcher's and user's preferences affect the process.

A third criticism of PAT relates to the fundamental assumption that all action is driven by a desire to maximise one's wealth. To many researchers such an assumption represents a far too negative and simplistic perspective of humankind. In this respect, Gray, Owen and Adams (1996, p. 75) state that PAT promotes 'a morally bankrupt view of the world'. Given that everybody is deemed to act in their own self-interest, the perspective of self-interest has also been applied to the research efforts of academics. For example, Watts and Zimmerman (1990, p. 146) argue that:

> Researchers choose the topics to investigate, the methods to use, and the assumptions to make. Researchers' preferences and expected payoffs (publications and citations) affect their choice of topic, methods, and assumptions.

Many academics would challenge this view and would argue that they undertake their research because of real personal interest in an issue. Another implication of the self-interest notion is that incorporation of the self-interest assumption into the teaching of undergraduate students (as has been done in many universities throughout the world) has the possible implication that students think that when they subsequently have to make decisions in the workplace it is both acceptable and predictable for them to place their own interests above those of others. It is questionable whether such a philosophy is in the interests of the broader community.[49] Nevertheless, while assuming that all action is driven by a desire to maximise one's own wealth is not an overly kind assumption about human nature, such an assumption has been the cornerstone of many past and existing theories used within the discipline of economics (and this is not a justification).

Another criticism of PAT is that since its general inception in the 1970s the issues being addressed have not shown great development. Since the early days of Watts and Zimmerman (1978b) there have been three key hypotheses: the debt hypothesis (which proposes that organisations close to breaching accounting-based debt covenants will select accounting methods that lead to an increase in profits and assets); the bonus hypothesis (which proposes that managers on accounting-based bonus schemes will select accounting methods that lead to an increase in profits); and the political cost hypothesis (which proposes that firms subject to political scrutiny will adopt accounting methods that reduce reported income). A review of the recent PAT literature indicates that these hypotheses continue to be tested in different

---

49 It certainly is not consistent with any quest towards ecologically and socially sustainable development—an issue addressed in Chapter 9. To embrace sustainable development—which is defined as development that meets the needs of the present world without compromising the ability of future generations to meet their own needs (World Commission on Environment and Development, 1987)—we need to consider the interests of future generations. If we accept and promote a view that self-interest drives all current actions—as PAT researchers and many other economics researchers do—such an assumption holds very little hope for any real quest towards sustainable development.

environments and in relation to different accounting policy issues—even after the passing of over thirty years since Watts and Zimmerman's paper (1978b). In this respect, Sterling (1990, p. 130) posed the following question:

> What are the potential accomplishments [of PAT]? I forecast more of the same: twenty years from now we will have been inundated with research reports that managers and others tend to manipulate accounting numerals when it is to their advantage to do so.

In commenting on the perceived lack of development of PAT, Fields, Lys and Vincent (2001, p. 301) state:

> Fundamentally, we believe it is necessary to step back from the current research agenda, and to develop the 'infrastructure' surrounding the field. In a sense, the accounting choice field has been a victim of its own perceived success, and has outrun the development of theories, statistical techniques and research design that are necessary to support it. We therefore are calling for a return to work in these basic areas, before the field is able to advance further.

Also, much of the research within PAT considers individual accounting choices (for example, whether an entity will revalue a particular class of non-current assets), when in practice the organisation will have a vast number of accounting choices, many of which might have opposing effects on financial performance and position. That is, while researchers might be studying whether an entity elects to adopt an accounting method that increases income, at the same time the entity might also be adopting another (unresearched) accounting method that reduces income. Considering one accounting method choice from the portfolio of all the accounting choices being made within the firm provides a very incomplete picture. In this regard Fields, Lys and Vincent (2001, p. 288) state:

> Most of the work [in PAT] examines the choice of a particular accounting method within the context of the goals driving the accounting choice, whereas managers may make multiple accounting method choices to accomplish a specific goal. As a result, examining only one choice at a time may obscure the overall effect obtained through a portfolio of choices.

Fields, Lys and Vincent (p. 290) further state:

> In addition to the problem of addressing multiple accounting choices, generally as reflected in accruals, there is also the issue of multiple, and potentially conflicting, motivations for the accounting choices. Most of the work discussed focuses on a single motive for accounting choice decisions. For example, the compensation literature focuses on the question of whether managers use accounting discretion to maximize their compensation. Implicitly, the results suggest that managers' actions come at the expense of shareholders. But if this is so, why do compensation contracts allow discretion? One plausible answer is that managers' actions are not only anticipated, but also desirable from shareholders' perspective. For example, the same accounting choices that maximize managers' compensation may also decrease bond covenant violations or increase asset valuations. However, such motives are typically not included in the analysis. By focusing on one goal at a time, much of the literature misses the more interesting question of the

interactions between and tradeoffs among goals. Moreover, it is not clear whether the conclusions are attributable to the specific motivation being analyzed; generally results consistent with one hypothesis are consistent with many. For example, what may appear to be an opportunistic choice of an earnings increasing accounting method choice (to benefit managers at the expense of other stakeholders in the firm), may be in fact a response to avoid a bond covenant violation (and thus benefits all other stakeholders at the expense of the creditors). Finally, with only few exceptions, research in the 1990s generally focuses on motives identified in the 1970s and 1980s. Typically the usual suspects are rounded up. However, we suspect that new insights may be gained by investigating additional motives. The problem of multiple conflicts can be viewed, in turn, as a special case of the familiar 'correlated omitted variable' problem in econometrics.

Another criticism is that the measurements or proxies being used within the literature are often far too simplistic. As Fields, Lys and Vincent (p. 272) state:

Most work investigating the debt hypothesis in the 1980s used crude proxies such as the leverage ratio for the proximity of the firm to violation of its debt covenants. However, Lys (1984) documents that because leverage is determined endogenously, it is a poor proxy for default risk, unless there is a control for the risk of the underlying assets. On the other hand, Duke and Hunt (1990) determine that the debt to equity ratio is a good proxy for the closeness to some covenant violations, including retained earnings, net tangible assets and working capital, but not for other covenants. In the 1990s researchers began studying firms that actually violated covenants in order to avoid the use of proxies.

A further criticism is that PAT is scientifically flawed. It has been argued that as the hypotheses generated pursuant to PAT (the debt hypothesis, the bonus hypothesis and the political cost hypothesis) are frequently not supported (they are falsified), then scientifically PAT should be rejected. Christenson (1983, p. 18) states:

We are told, for example, that 'we can only expect a positive theory to hold on average' [Watts and Zimmerman, 1978, p. 127, n. 37]. We are also advised 'to remember that as in all empirical theories we are concerned with general trends' [Watts and Zimmerman, 1978, pp. 288–9], where 'general' is used in the weak sense of 'true or applicable in most instances but not all' rather than in the strong sense of 'relating to, concerned with, or applicable to every member of a class' [*American Heritage Dictionary*, 1969, p. 548] ... A law that admits exceptions has no significance, and knowledge of it is not of the slightest use. By arguing that their theories admit exceptions, Watts and Zimmerman condemn them as insignificant and useless.

As a study of people, however (accounting is a process undertaken by people and the accounting process itself cannot exist in the absence of accountants), it is hard to consider that any model or theory could ever fully explain human action. In fact, ability to do so would constitute a dehumanising action. Are there any theories of human activity or choice processes that always hold? In defence of the fact that PAT predictions do not always hold, Watts and Zimmerman (1990, p. 148) state:

But accounting research using this methodology has produced useful predictions of how the world works. A methodology that yields useful results should not be abandoned purely because it may not predict all human behaviour. Do we discard something that works in some situations because it may not work in every circumstance?

Another criticism of PAT is that the positive researchers believe that they can generate laws and principles expected to operate in different situations, and that there is one underlying 'truth' that can be determined by an independent, impartial observer who is not influenced by individual perceptions, idiosyncrasies or biases (Tinker, Merino & Neimark, 1982, p. 167). That is, the apparent perspective is that reality exists objectively, and one observer's view of that reality will be the same as all other people's views. This is referred to as the 'realist philosophy'. A number of researchers have challenged this philosophy (for example, Hines, 1988). They have argued that, in undertaking large-scale empirical research, positive researchers ignore many organisation-specific relationships and the information collected is only the information that the researchers consider relevant. A different person would possibly consider that other information is more relevant. Many researchers critical of the 'realist perspective' argue that more insights might be gained by undertaking in-depth case studies. Positive researchers would provide a counter-argument, however, that case study research is very specific to a particular time and place and therefore cannot be generalised to a broader population. Such arguments about research methodology abound in the literature, with very little likelihood that researchers operating across different paradigms will ever agree on what constitutes valid research. As Watts and Zimmerman (1990, p. 149) concede when defending their research against numerous criticisms:

> To most researchers, debating methodology is a 'no win' situation because each side argues from a different paradigm with different rules and no common ground. Our reason for replying here is that some have mistaken our lack of response as tacit acceptance of the criticisms.

While the criticisms do, arguably, have some merit, PAT does continue to be used by many accounting researchers. Respected accounting research journals continue to publish PAT research (although the numbers appear to be declining). A number of the leading accounting research schools throughout the world continue to teach it. What must be remembered is that all theories of accounting will have limitations. They are, of necessity, abstractions of the 'real world'. Whether individually we prefer one theory of accounting in preference to another will be dependent upon our assumptions about many of the issues raised in this chapter.

CHAPTER SUMMARY

A positive theory seeks to explain and predict particular phenomena. This chapter considered Positive Accounting Theory (PAT), a theory that seeks to explain and predict managers' choices of accounting methods. PAT focuses on relationships between various individuals within and outside an organisation and explains how financial accounting can be used to minimise the costly implications associated with each contracting party operating in his or her own self-interest. The economic perspective that all individual behaviour is motivated by self-interest is central to PAT, and PAT predicts that contractual arrangements will be put in place to align the interests of the various self-interested parties. Many of these contractual arrangements will use the output of the accounting system.

PAT became a dominant research paradigm in the 1970s and 1980s and its development owed much to previous research work that had been undertaken, including work on the Efficient Markets Hypothesis (EMH) and agency theory. The EMH provided evidence that capital markets react to new information, but it provided little explanation for why managers might elect to use particular accounting methods in preference to others. PAT was developed to fill this void.

Applying agency theory, PAT focused on relationships between principals and agents. PAT proposed that agents have incentives to enter various contracts. Firms themselves were considered as a nexus of contracts between many self-interested individuals. The contractual arrangements are initially put in place for efficiency reasons, with well-developed contracts reducing the overall agency costs that could arise within the firm. Further, agents are predicted to adopt those accounting methods that most efficiently reflect their own performance. Regulation is considered to introduce unnecessary costs and inefficiencies into the contractual arrangements, particularly as it often acts to reduce the methods of accounting that would otherwise be adopted.

Early work within PAT relied on three central hypotheses: the bonus hypothesis, the debt hypothesis and the political cost hypothesis. The bonus hypothesis predicts that from an efficiency perspective many organisations will elect to provide their managers with bonuses tied to the performance of the firm, with these bonuses often being directly related to accounting numbers (for example, management might be rewarded with a share of profits). Offering performance-based rewards will motivate the self-interested manager to work also in the best interests of the owners. However, under the opportunistic perspective, PAT predicts that once bonus schemes are in place, managers will, to the extent that they can get away with it, manipulate performance indicators such as profits to generate higher individual rewards.

The debt hypothesis predicts that to reduce the cost of attracting debt capital firms will enter into contractual arrangements with lenders that reduce the likelihood that the managers can expropriate the wealth of the debtholders. Arranging such agreements prior to obtaining debt finance is deemed to be an efficient way to attract lower cost funds. However, once a debt contract is in place, the opportunistic perspective of PAT predicts that firms, particularly those close to breaching debt covenants, will adopt accounting methods that act to minimise or loosen the effects of the debt constraint.

The political cost hypothesis explores the relationships between a firm and various outside parties who, although perhaps not having any direct contractual relationships, can nevertheless impose various types of wealth transfers away from the firm. It is argued that high profits can attract adverse and costly attention to the firm, and hence managers of politically vulnerable firms look for ways to reduce the level of political scrutiny. One way is to adopt accounting methods that lead to a reduction in reported profits. Most tests of the political cost hypothesis use size of the firm as a proxy for the existence of political scrutiny.

The chapter also provided a number of criticisms of PAT. Included among the various criticisms was a challenge to the central PAT assumption that all individual action is driven by self-interest. Another major criticism was that PAT fails to provide prescriptions for practicing accountants in terms of how they should account for various transactions or events.

QUESTIONS

7.1 Early positive research investigated evidence of share price changes as a result of the disclosure of accounting information. However, such research did not explain why particular accounting methods were selected in the first place. How did Positive Accounting Theory fill this void?

7.2 Explain the *management bonus hypothesis* and the *debt hypothesis* of Positive Accounting Theory.

7.3 If a manager is paid a percentage of profits, does this generate a motive to manipulate profits? Would this be anticipated by principals and, if so, how would principals react to this expectation?

7.4 What is an *agency relationship* and what is an *agency cost*? How can agency costs be reduced?

7.5 Explain the *political cost hypothesis* of Positive Accounting Theory.

7.6 Explain the *efficiency perspective* and the *opportunistic perspective* of Positive Accounting Theory. Why is one considered to be *ex post* and the other *ex ante*?

7.7 Would managers who have negotiated debt contracts with accounting-based covenants based around 'rolling GAAP' be relatively more likely to lobby an accounting standard-setter about a proposed accounting standard than would a manager from a firm who has negotiated accounting-based debt covenants that use 'frozen GAAP'? Why?

7.8 Organisations typically have a number of contractual arrangements with debtholders, with many covenants written to incorporate accounting numbers.
   (a) Why would an organisation agree to enter into such agreements with debtholders?
   (b) On average, do debtholders gain from the existence of such agreements?

7.9 Positive Accounting theorists typically argue that managers can reduce political costs by simply adopting an accounting method that leads to a reduction in reported income. Does this imply anything about the perceived efficiency of those parties involved in the political process and, if so, what perception is held?

7.10 If a reporting entity has a choice of either *expensing* or *capitalising* an item of expenditure, and if the entity is subject to a high degree of political scrutiny, then what choice would be predicted by the *political cost hypothesis* of Positive Accounting Theory? Explain your answer.

7.11 Assume that Kahuna Company Ltd decides to undertake an upward revaluation of its non-current assets just prior to the end of the financial year, the effect being that the total assets of the company increases, as does the total shareholders' equity.
   (a) Explain the decision of management to undertake an asset revaluation in terms of the *debt hypothesis* of Positive Accounting Theory.
   (b) Explain the decision of management to undertake an asset revaluation in terms of the *management compensation hypothesis* of Positive Accounting Theory.

7.12 Mather and Peirson (2006) report that public debt contracts tend to have a lower average number of accounting-based debt covenants as well as less binding debt covenants. (For example, in relation to debt to assets constraints in both public and private debt agreements, the covenants in the public debt agreements were found to be 'looser', meaning that the ratio percentage is typically higher in the public debt contract.) Why would this be the case?

7.13 Positive Accounting Theory assumes that all individual action is driven by self-interest, with the self-interest being tied to wealth maximisation.

(a) Is this a useful and/or realistic assumption?

(b) Adopting this assumption, why would politicians introduce particular regulations?

(c) Why would researchers study particular issues?

7.14 What are some of the criticisms of PAT? Do you agree with them? Why or why not?

7.15 Zhang (2008) argues that if a borrower adopts conservative accounting methods this will reduce the risk exposure of the lender and will lead to a reduced interest cost for the borrower. What is the basis of this argument?

7.16 Read Accounting Headline 7.6. As you will see, Babcock and Brown had negotiated an agreement with lenders that its market capitalisation would not fall below an

---

Accounting Headline 7.6 An example of a debt covenant being breached

Australian, 16 June 2008, p. 29

Battered Babcock to meet bankers

RICHARD GLUYAS

Babcock & Brown investors face a nervous wait this week as a syndicate of 24 banks considers whether to call a formal review of a $2.8 billion lending facility.

Initial discussions between Babcock and its lenders are scheduled to take place today and tomorrow. A share-price rout late last week resulted in the stock falling through a minimum market capitalisation requirement of $2.5 billion or $7.50 a share.

Babcock shares sagged a further $1.65 on Friday to $5.25, wiping more than $450 million from the value of the stock, which only 12 months ago commanded a heady $34.63.

Trevor Loewensohn, head of capital markets for Babcock, said yesterday that the corporate-facility banks were notified last Thursday that the threshold had been reached.

'Reaching that threshold does not mean that the company has breached any debt covenant,' he said. 'We will soon meet with our banks to update them on the company's financial position.'

In the meantime, it was 'business as usual', Mr Loewensohn said, as the company proceeded with asset sales and other activities that were part of its normal business plan.

On the most optimistic scenario, the 25 banks will quickly decide that there has been no fundamental change in Babcock's cash flow, interest cover and the general operating position of its business since the facility was agreed to last April.

But there is a crisis of confidence surrounding Babcock, first triggered by a global aversion to leveraged stocks, and then fanned by concern about its business model and a debt crisis at one of its satellite funds, Babcock & Brown Power.

On Friday, Standard & Poor's downgraded Babcock & Brown International from BBB with negative implications to BB+, also on negative watch. S&P said the rating was supported by the fund's 'quality' assets, but that to stay at the new level, it would require certainty about the group's future business structure and funding arrangements, as well as the restoration of market confidence in Babcock.

If the banks call a review, a four-month period of consultation takes place. At the end of that period, if Babcock's market cap remains below $2.5 billion and there is no agreement with the lenders on a course of action, a minimum of two-thirds of the lenders have the right to serve notice on Babcock to repay the facility within 90 days.

Analysts have started to suggest that Babcock could be forced into a massive fire sale of global infrastructure assets to pare back $50 billion of debt in its group of 20 funds.

Among its assets are Eircom, Ireland's largest telco, a US gas pipeline, British ports, schools in NSW and power generators. UBS analyst Jonathan Mott said Babcock could sell off other parts of its wind development pipeline to generate extra revenue and repay debt.

Some observers have questioned why Babcock's senior executives have not backed their judgment by increasing their own holdings.

However, a spokesman said they were unable to trade during a blackout period that would remain in place until the release of Babcock's interim result in August.

agreed amount of $7.50 per share. However, the share price dipped below this agreed amount, meaning that the lenders could demand repayment of the funds if they choose to invoke their right to do so. From a PAT theory perspective, why would Babcock have agreed to this market capitalisation requirement rather than other types of covenants, such as a restriction on the organisation's total liabilities to total tangible assets? Further, why would the banks have negotiated to have this market capitalisation agreement included within the debt agreement?

7.17 Read Accounting Headline 7.7, and, adopting a Positive Accounting Theory perspective, consider the following issues:

(a) If a new accounting standard impacts on profits, should this impact on the value of the firm, and if so, why?

(b) Will the imposition of a particular accounting method have implications for the efficiency of the organisation?

Accounting Headline 7.7 Implications of the release of new accounting standards

Australian Financial Review, 30 July 2005

Foster's: less goodwill, higher earnings

ANTHONY HUGHES

The challenges facing investors seeking a true picture of a company's earnings during the impending profit reporting season were underlined again on Friday when Foster's flagged it would report a $1.2 billion reduction in net assets under new accounting standards.

The transition to international financial reporting standards (IFRS) means Foster's net assets will fall from $4.6 billion to $3.37 billion based on its last reported balance sheet, mainly as a result of the internally generated goodwill on brand names not being recognised.

The other major contributor to the reduction is the requirement to allow for deferred tax liabilities based on the difference between the carrying value of assets and their cost base.

Despite scepticism about the likely success of Foster's recent $3 billion acquisition of winemaker Southcorp and Foster's ability to extract sufficient merger synergies, the changes to the reported accounts do not relate to any issues with that acquisition. The brewing and winemaking group told analysts

the balance sheet adjustments wouldn't affect its cash flows or ability to pay dividends.

But reported profits will be higher than they otherwise would be because of the removal of goodwill amortisation charges.

Under the standards, goodwill is instead subject to an annual 'impairment test', with the elimination of amortisation expenses boosting reported profits. If the new standards were applied to Foster's half-year accounts to December 31, 2004, the company would have made a net profit of $783.2 million versus the $757 million reported.

The reduced asset base reported by companies such as Foster's will also mean they will report more favourable returns on these written-down asset values.

The transition to new standards has raised concerns that companies will announce potentially misleading profit numbers and will be reluctant to predict future profits because of the uncertainty around some aspects of the standards. There is also concern about how credit ratings

agencies will react to such wild swings in balance sheet values.

But the adoption of the standards will make it easier for investment analysts to compare companies to their global peers. In Foster's case, this means investment analysts will be able to better discern whether it is outperforming or underperforming global wine and brewing peers such as Diageo and Pernod Ricard.

ABN Amro Asset Management's Mark Nathan said: 'It differs by company and industry. There will be some concern over whether the new standards result in a less realistic portrayal of what's happening than the current Australian standards, but by and large it's an improvement.'

However, Goldman Sachs JBWere said in a note to clients that given the shortened period in which companies must now report their results, the new standards 'would only add to the data overload during the last two to three weeks of August'. Foster's closed 2¢ higher at $5.46.

7.18 Applying Positive Accounting Theory, and after reading Accounting Headline 7.8, which relates to an article published in the United Kingdom, answer the following questions:

(a) From an efficiency perspective, why could the introduction of new rules on share option accounting be costly for an organisation?

(b) Why could the introduction of the new rules on share option accounting be costly for a manager?

(c) What would motivate the regulators to develop the new rules?

7. 19 Read Accounting Headline 7.4 (earlier in the chapter) and explain why publicity such as this might be costly to an organisation. How would Positive Accounting theorists expect the banks to react to such publicity?

7.20 Read Accounting Headline 7.9, which discusses the accounting practices used at the Australian company Harris Scarfe. It has been shown that Harris Scarfe reported results that inappropriately overstated its assets and understated its liabilities. Discuss whether this is consistent with the opportunistic perspective provided by PAT and explain from a contracting perspective why an organisation might want to overstate its assets and understate its liabilities.

Accounting Headline 7.8 Introduction of accounting regulation for accounting for share options

Are you getting your fair shares?

JOANNA OSBORNE

SENIOR IFRS TECHNICAL PARTNER AT KPMG

Accountancy Age (UK), 8 March 2004

Last month, the IASB issued IFRS2 on share-based payment, which will affect UK-listed companies preparing their first group financial statements under IFRS and applies to share-based payments active at 1 January 2005.

In the UK, share-based payments are already required to be expensed under UITF17. But whereas this expense is the difference between the underlying share price at grant date and the employee contribution (intrinsic value), IFRS2 requires share-based payments to be expensed at fair value.

This, alongside other differences to current UK practice, will mean a significant increase in the frequency and amount of expenses recorded for share-based payments in company accounts from 2005.

IFRS2 seeks to measure the fair value of services received from employees by reference to the fair value of a share option, multiplied by the number of options that ultimately vest. This measure will mean a greater hit on the accounts, as the fair value of an option will be recorded as higher than the intrinsic value of the share.

To understand this, compare two different employee packages, one comprising cash plus an option to acquire a share at today's price in three years' time, and one comprising ownership of the share itself.

In the first package you can earn interest on the cash for three years, although you don't receive the generally small amount from dividends that you would in the second package. The major bonus of this package is the one-way nature of the share option.

In effect it is a free bet on whether the share price will be higher than today's price in three years' time. If you hold an actual share you suffer a loss if the price goes down. If you have an option, you don't have to exercise it and suffer that loss—you still have the cash and subsequent interest. If the share price rises you gain with either package.

It is, however, complicated to determine the fair value of a share option at grant date because it involves predicting, among other things, future share price movements. But there are well-established and accessible mathematical techniques, for example the Black–Scholes and the binomial models, that are used by option traders to predict the future movements in share price and therefore to derive the fair value of an option. ...

The long-awaited arrival of IFRS2 is going to make the means of payment of bonuses largely neutral in profit and loss account terms between cash and shares or share options. But a significant increase in the amount of expense recorded for share-based payments is inevitable.

The tremors left behind as a retail giant falls from grace

COLIN JAMES

Adelaide Advertiser, 14 April 2001

COLIN JAMES explains how the drama surrounding Harris Scarfe unfolded.

Harris Scarfe executive chairman Adam Trescowthick said he was stunned when senior managers approached him after the departure of the firm's most senior executive. They outlined allegations of irregularities in the company's financial accounts which had left its 35 stores across the country on the brink of collapse.

Mr Trescowthick, a 36-year-old businessman who inherited the Harris Scarfe chairmanship from his father, Sir Donald Trescowthick, immediately called in its external auditors, PricewaterhouseCoopers.

An investigation confirmed the worst: the company's assets had been overstated and its liabilities understated for up to six years, leaving it in the precarious position where it was unable to pay its debts.

Mr Trescowthick and his board of directors—former Independent Holdings managing director John Patten, former AFL chief executive Ross Oakley, former Young Rubicam and Mattingley chairman David Mattingley, Melbourne lawyer Roger Curtis and Sir Donald's youngest son, information technology consultant Mark—received the news on Friday, March 29.

Six days earlier, they had notified the Australian Stock Exchange of the resignation of Harris Scarfe chief operating officer Dan McLaughlin after 27 years with the company.

Then, on March 28, chief financial officer Alan Hodgson had informed them he was taking sick leave.

Later that day, Mr Trescowthick and the other directors resolved to call in accountants from international company KPMG, who told the board to take steps to ensure no further liabilities were incurred. They also advised Harris Scarfe not to pay any debts until the situation could be stabilised.

KPMG told Mr Trescowthick he had to immediately notify the company's biggest secured creditor, the ANZ Banking Group.

A meeting with the bank's Adelaide credit centre was scheduled for the following day, where Mr Trescowthick said that if urgent funds were not made available within 48 hours, Harris Scarfe would have to stop trading and appoint administrators.

A second meeting was held on Sunday, April 1, where KPMG representatives outlined the extent of the financial irregularities within Harris Scarfe.

The following day ANZ told the Harris Scarfe board it would not be providing any further funds. ANZ made it clear that if administrators were appointed, it would override the move by appointing a receiver to ensure its interests were protected.

Mr Trescowthick and his directors met the bank in a bid to avoid receivership, requesting more time to appoint administrators. The bank granted a temporary reprieve, enabling Harris Scarfe to appoint KPMG accountants Michael Dwyer and Lindsay Maxsted on Tuesday, April 3.

Three days later, the bank's patience expired. Exposed to potential losses of $67 million, ANZ appointed Adelaide insolvency specialist Bruce Carter as receiver, who, on Wednesday, announced Harris Scarfe would be sold to recover its debts.

The sale came as no surprise to Harris Scarfe's 1200 unsecured trade creditors, many of whom had been experiencing difficulties for several years with getting payments from Harris Scarfe.

Some had been forced to use debt collectors to ensure bills were paid. One credit company, Australian Business Research, had interviewed Mr Hodgson in January as part of a report which it completed for suppliers on March 23, the day Mr McLaughlin's resignation was announced to the ASX.

The ABR report, obtained by the *Advertiser*, said Mr Hodgson said Harris Scarfe was experiencing a difficult trading year because of the GST, interest rates, increasing petrol prices and the post-Olympic spending slump.

In its assessment of Harris Scarfe, ABR warned creditors to exercise caution when supplying stock to its stores in SA, New South Wales, Queensland, Victoria, Western Australia and Tasmania. According to figures provided by the company, ABR said its assets of $195,433,000 were 'predominantly funded through debts' of $118,576,000.

Observing this situation 'indicates a cause for concern'. ABR said the company was in 'a poor short position, meaning short-term debt is not covered by short-term asset position'.

This situation was confirmed on Tuesday when Mr Dwyer and Mr Maxsted presented their preliminary report to a creditors' meeting at Thebarton Theatre.

Mr Dwyer and Mr Maxsted said that after the ANZ and creditors had refused to supply further credit, a 'more thorough investigation' of Harris Scarfe's cash flow projections 'revealed that the liabilities of the company had been understated and the assets overstated'.

This 'systematic overstatement of profit has been funded by increased debt both to the (ANZ) bank and to creditors', they said.

Mr Dwyer and Mr Maxsted told creditors a 'more accurate financial position' could be reached by reducing assets by $17.2 million and increasing debts by $16.3 million.

Investigations were continuing into how these irregularities had occurred, they said.

Company records had been seized and copies sent to the Australian Securities and Investments Commission, which had been alerted by Mr Trescowthick following the appointment of Mr Dwyer and Mr Maxsted.

The two men are working closely with ASIC investigators in a bid to unravel what happened inside Harris Scarfe and how misleading financial accounts were allegedly maintained for up to six years.

Mr Trescowthick, who was on an internal audit committee with Mr Patten and Mr Hodgson charged with ensuring the accuracy of the company's financial records, has said senior management did not inform directors of the problems.

This situation will be closely examined as it is the legal responsibility of directors to ensure they fully inform themselves about the financial positions of companies they represent.

The ASIC also will investigate statements by the directors that they relied on the accuracy

of reports prepared by Harris Scarfe's auditors over the past seven years, Ernst and Young, and PricewaterhouseCoopers.

Both firms lodged formal declarations with the ASIC and ASX between 1996 and last year saying the accounts had been subjected to full audits 'conducted in accordance with Australian Auditing Standards'.

This included statements to the ASX which said 'our procedures included examination, on a test basis, of evidence supporting the amounts and other disclosures in the financial report, and the evaluation of accounting policies and significant accounting estimates'.

REFERENCES

Ahmed, A., B. Billings, R. Morton & M. Harris (2002), 'The role of accounting conservatism in mitigating bondholder–shareholder conflict over dividend policy and in reducing debt cost', *The Accounting Review*, 77, pp. 867–90.

Asquith, P, A. Beatty & J. Weber (2002), 'Performance pricing in private debt contracts', working paper, Massachusetts Institute of Technology, Cambridge, MA.

Ball, R. & P. Brown (1968), 'An empirical evaluation of accounting income numbers', *Journal of Accounting Research*, 6(2), pp. 159–78.

Ball, R. & G. Foster (1982), 'Corporate financial reporting: a methodological review of empirical research', *Studies on Current Research Methodologies in Accounting: A Critical Evaluation*, supplement to

Journal of Accounting Research, 20 (Supplement), pp. 161–234.

Balsam, S. & S. Miharjo (2007), 'The effect of equity compensation on voluntary executive turnover', *Journal of Accounting and Economics*, 43, pp. 95–119.

Beatty, A. & J. Weber (2003), 'The effects of debt contracting on Voluntary Accounting Method Changes', *The Accounting Review*, 78, pp. 119–42.

Beaver, W. (1968), 'The information content of annual earnings announcements', *Journal of Accounting Research*, 6 (Supplement), pp. 67–92.

Benston, G. J. (1969), 'The value of the SEC's accounting disclosure requirements', *The Accounting Review* (July), pp. 515–32.

Blackwell, D., J. Brickley & M. Weisbach (1994), 'Accounting information and internal performance evaluation: evidence from Texas banks', *Journal of Accounting and Economics*, 17, pp. 331–58.

Bushman, R. & A. Smith (2001), 'Financial accounting information and corporate governance', *Journal of Accounting and Economics*, 32, pp. 237–333.

Cheng, S. (2004), 'R&D expenditures and CEO compensation', *The Accounting Review*, 79, pp. 305–28.

Christenson, C. (1983), 'The methodology of positive accounting', *The Accounting Review*, 58 (January), pp. 1–22.

Christie, A. (1990), 'Aggregation of test statistics: an evaluation of the evidence on contracting and size hypotheses', *Journal of Accounting and Economics*, 12, pp. 15–36.

Clinch, G. (1991), 'Employee compensation and firms' research and development activity', *Journal of Accounting Research*, 29, pp. 59–78.

Coase, R. (1937), 'The nature of the firm', *Economica*, 4, pp. 386–406.

Cotter, J. (1998a), 'Asset revaluations and debt contracting', unpublished PhD thesis, University of Queensland, Australia.

Cotter, J. (1998b), 'Utilisation and restrictiveness of covenants in Australian private debt contracts', *Accounting and Finance*, 38(2), pp. 181–96.

DeAngelo, L. (1988), 'Managerial competition, information costs, and corporate governance: the use of accounting performance measures in proxy contests', *Journal of Accounting and Economics*, 10 (January), pp. 3–36.

Dechow, P. (1994), 'Accounting earnings and cash flows as a measure of firm performance: the role of accounting accruals', *Journal of Accounting and Economics*, 18, pp. 3–42.

Dechow, P. & D. Skinner (2000), 'Earnings management: reconciling the views of accounting academics, practitioners and regulators', *Accounting Horizons*, 14, pp. 235–50.

Dechow, P. & R. Sloan (1991), 'Executive incentives and horizon problems', *Journal of Accounting and Economics*, 14, pp. 51–89.

Deegan, C. (1997), 'The design of efficient management remuneration contracts: a consideration of specific human capital investments', *Accounting and Finance*, 37(1), pp. 1–40.

DeFond, M. & J. Jiambalvo (1994), 'Debt covenant violation and manipulation of accruals', *Journal of Accounting and Economics*, 17, pp. 145–76.

Dhaliwal, D., (1982), 'Some economic determinants of management lobbying for alternative methods of accounting: evidence from the accounting for interest case', *Journal of Business Finance and Accounting*, 9, pp. 255–65.

Downs, A. (1957), *An Economic Theory of Democracy*, New York: Harper & Row.

Duke, J. & H. Hunt (1990), 'An empirical examination of debt covenant restrictions and accounting-related debt proxies', *Journal of Accounting and Economics*, 12, pp. 45–64.

Dyckman, A. & S. Zeff (1984), 'Two decades of the *Journal of Accounting Research*', *Journal of Accounting Research*, 22, pp. 225–97.

Emanuel, D., J. Wong & N. Wong (2003), 'Efficient contracting and accounting', *Accounting and Finance*, 43, pp. 149–66.

Ettredge, M., D. Simon, D. Smith & M. Stone (1994), 'Why do companies purchase timely quarterly reviews?', *Journal of Accounting and Economics*, 18(2), pp. 131–56.

Fama, E. (1965), 'The behavior of stock market prices', *Journal of Business*, 38, pp. 34–105.

Fama, E. (1980), 'Agency problems and the theory of the firm', *Journal of Political Economy*, 88, pp. 288–307.

Fields, T., T. Lys & L. Vincent (2001), 'Empirical research on accounting choice', *Journal of Accounting and Economics*, 31, pp. 255–307.

Friedman, M. (1953), *The Methodology of Positive Economics, Essays in Positive Economics*, reprinted in 1966 by Phoenix Books edn, Chicago: University of Chicago Press.

Gibbons, R. & K. Murphy (1992), 'Optimal incentive contracts in the presence of career concerns: theory and evidence', *Journal of Political Economy*, 100, pp. 468–505.

Gray, R., D. Owen & C. Adams (1996), *Accounting and Accountability: Changes and Challenges in Corporate Social and Environmental Reporting*, London: Prentice Hall.

Guay, W. R., S. P. Kothari & R. L. Watts (1996), 'A market-based evaluation of discretionary accrual models', *Journal of Accounting Research*, 34 (Supplement), pp. 83–105.

Healy, P. M. (1985), 'The effect of bonus schemes on accounting decisions', *Journal of Accounting and Economics*, 7, pp. 85–107.

Hines, R. (1988), 'Financial accounting: in communicating reality, we construct reality', *Accounting, Organizations and Society*, 13(3), pp. 251–62.

Holthausen, R. W., (1990), 'Accounting method choice: opportunistic behaviour, efficient contracting and information perspectives', *Journal of Accounting and Economics*, 12, pp. 207–18.

Holthausen, R. W., D. F. Larcker & R. G. Sloan (1995), 'Annual bonus schemes and the manipulation of earnings', *Journal of Accounting and Economics*, 19.

Howieson, B. (1996), 'Whither financial accounting research: a modern-day Bo-peep?', *Australian Accounting Review*, 6(1), pp. 29–36.

Ittner, C., D. Larker & M. Rajan (1997), 'The choice of performance measures in annual bonus contracts', *The Accounting Review*, 72, pp. 231–55.

Jensen, M. C. & W. H. Meckling (1976), 'Theory of the firm: managerial behavior, agency costs and ownership structure', *Journal of Financial Economics*, 3 (October), pp. 305–60.

Jones, J. (1991), 'Earnings management during import relief investigations', *Journal of Accounting Research*, 29, pp. 193–228.

Kaplan, R. S. & R. Roll (1972), 'Investor evaluation of accounting information: some empirical evidence', *Journal of Business*, 45, pp. 225–57.

Kothari, S. P., T. Laguerre & A. Leone (2002), 'Capitalizing versus expensing: evidence on the uncertainty of future earnings from capital expenditure versus R&D outlay', *Review of Accounting Studies*, 7, pp. 355–82.

Kuhn, T. S. (1962), *The Structure of Scientific Revolutions*, Chicago: University of Chicago Press.

Lambert, R. (2001), 'Contracting theory and accounting', *Journal of Accounting and Economics*, 32, pp. 3–87.

Lev, B. & T. Sougiannis (1996), 'The capitalization, amortization, and value relevance of R&D', *Journal of Accounting and Economics*, 21, pp. 107–38.

Lewellen, R. A., C. Loderer & K. Martin (1987), 'Executive compensation and executive incentive problems', *Journal of Accounting and Economics*, 9, pp. 287–310.

Lintner, J. (1965), 'The valuation of risk assets and the selection of risky investments in stock portfolios and capital budgets', *Review of Economics and Statistics*, 47, pp. 13–37.

Lys, T. (1984), 'Mandated accounting changes and debt covenants: the case of oil and gas accounting', *Journal of Accounting and Economics*, 9, pp. 39–66.

Mather, P. & G. Peirson (2006), 'Financial covenants in the markets for public and private debt', *Accounting and Finance*, 46, pp. 285–307.

Mian, S. L. & C. W. Smith (1990), 'Incentives for consolidated financial reporting', *urnal of Accounting and Economics*, 12, pp. 141–71.

grom, P. (1981), 'Good news and bad news: representation theorems and applications', *Bell Journal of Economics*, 12, pp. 380–91.

Morris, R. (1984), 'Corporate disclosure in a substantially unregulated environment', *ABACUS* (June), pp. 52–86.

Mouck, T. (1992), 'The rhetoric of science and the rhetoric of revolt in the story of positive accounting theory', *Accounting, Auditing and Accountability Journal*, 5(4), pp. 35–56.

Murphy, K. (1999), 'Executive compensation', in *Handbook of Labor Economics*, 3B, North Holland, Amsterdam, The Netherlands.

Nagar, V., D. Nanda & P. Wysocki, (2003), 'Discretionary disclosure and stock-based incentives', *Journal of Accounting and Economics*, 34, pp. 283–309.

Ness, K. & A. Mirza (1991), 'Corporate social disclosure: a note on a test of agency theory', *British Accounting Review*, 23, pp. 211–17.

Sharpe, W. F. (1964), 'Capital asset prices: a review of market equilibrium under conditions of risk', *Journal of Finance*, 19, pp. 425–42.

Shleifer, A. & R. Vishny (1989), 'Management entrenchment: the case of manager-specific investments', *Journal of Accounting and Economics*, 25, pp. 8–41.

Sloan, R. G. (1993), 'Accounting earnings and top executive compensation', *Journal of Accounting and Economics*, 16, pp. 55–100.

Smith, C. W. & J. B. Warner (1979), 'On financial contracting: an analysis of bond covenants', *Journal of Financial Economics*, June, pp. 117–61.

Smith, C. W. & R. L. Watts (1982), 'Incentive and tax effects of executive compensation plans', *Australian Journal of Management*, 7, pp. 139–57.

Smith, C. W. & R. L. Watts (1983), 'The structure of executive contracts and the

control of management', unpublished manuscript, University of Rochester.

Sterling, R. R. (1990), 'Positive accounting: an assessment', *ABACUS*, 26(2), pp. 97–135.

Stern, S. (2001), 'Stern Stewart roundtable on capital structure and stock repurchase', *Journal of Applied Corporate Finance*, 14, pp. 8–41.

Sutton, T. G. (1988), 'The proposed introduction of current cost accounting in the UK', *Journal of Accounting and Economics*, 10, pp. 127–49.

Sweeney, A. P. (1994), 'Debt-covenant violations and managers accounting responses', *Journal of Accounting and Economics*, 17, pp. 281–308.

Tinker, A., C. Lehman & M. Neimark (1991), 'Corporate social reporting: falling down the hole in the middle of the road', *Accounting, Auditing and Accountability Journal*, 4(1), pp. 28–54.

Tinker, A. M., B. D. Merino & M. D. Neimark (1982), 'The normative origins of positive theories: ideology and accounting thought', *Accounting Organizations and Society*, 7(2), pp. 167–200.

Verecchia, R. (1983), 'Discretionary disclosure', *Journal of Accounting and Economics*, 5, pp. 179–94.

Watts, R. L. (1995), 'Nature and origins of positive research in accounting', in S. Jones, C. Romano & J. Ratnatunga (eds), *Accounting Theory: A Contemporary Review*, Sydney: Harcourt Brace, pp. 295–353.

Watts, R. L. (1977), 'Corporate financial statements: a product of the market and political processes', *Australian Journal of Management* (April), pp. 53–75.

Watts, R. & J. Zimmerman (1978a), 'Towards a positive theory of the determination of accounting standards', *The Accounting Review*, 53(1), pp. 112–34.

Watts, R. L. & J. L. Zimmerman (1978b), 'Towards a positive theory of the determinants of accounting standards', *The Accounting Review*, LIII(1), pp. 112–34.

Watts, R. L. & J. L. Zimmerman (1979), 'The demand for and supply of accounting theories: the market for excuses', *The Accounting Review*, LIV(2), pp. 273–305.

Watts, R. L. & J. L. Zimmerman (1986), *Positive Accounting Theory*, Englewood Cliffs, NJ: Prentice Hall.

Watts, R. L. & J. L. Zimmerman (1990), 'Positive Accounting Theory: a ten year perspective', *The Accounting Review*, 65(1), pp. 259–85.

Wells, P. (2002), 'Earnings management surrounding CEO changes', *Accounting and Finance*, 42(2), pp. 169–93.

Whittred, G. (1987), 'The derived demand for consolidated financial reporting', *Journal of Accounting and Economics*, 9 (December), pp. 259–85.

Whittred, G. & I. Zimmer (1986), 'Accounting information in the market for debt', *Accounting and Finance*, 28(1), pp. 1–12.

Williamson, O. E. (1975), *Markets and Hierarchies: Analysis and Antitrust Implications*, New York: The Free Press.

Williamson, O. E. (1985), *The Economic Institutions of Capitalism*, New York: The Free Press.

Williamson, O. E. (1988), 'Corporate finance and corporate governance', *Journal of Finance*, 43, pp. 567–91.

Williamson, O. E. (1996), *The Mechanisms of Governance*, New York: Oxford University Press.

Wong, J. (1988), 'Economic incentives for the voluntary disclosure of current cost financial statements', *Journal of Accounting and Economics*, 10(2), pp. 151–67.

World Commission on Environment and Development (1987), *Our Common Future* (The Brundtland Report), Oxford: Oxford University Press.

Zmijewski, M. & R. Hagerman (1981), 'An income strategy approach to the positive theory of accounting standard setting/choice', *Journal of Accounting and Economics*, 3, pp. 129–49.

Zhang, J., (2008), 'The contracting benefits of accounting conservatism to lenders and borrowers', *Journal of Accounting and Economics*, 45, pp. 27–54.

CHAPTER 8

UNREGULATED CORPORATE REPORTING DECISIONS: CONSIDERATIONS OF SYSTEMS-ORIENTED THEORIES

LEARNING OBJECTIVES

On completing this chapter readers should:

- understand how community or stakeholders' perceptions can influence the disclosure policies of an organisation;
- understand how Legitimacy Theory, Stakeholder Theory and Institutional Theory can be applied to help explain why an entity might elect to make particular voluntary disclosures;
- understand what we mean by organisational legitimacy and how corporate disclosures within such places as annual reports and corporate websites can be used as a strategy to maintain or restore the legitimacy of an organisation;
- understand how the respective power and information demands of particular stakeholder groups can influence corporate disclosure policies;
- understand the view that a successful organisation is one that is able to balance or manage the demands (sometimes conflicting), including information demands, of different stakeholder groups.

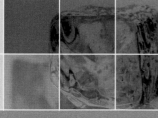

OPENING ISSUES

In the *Daily Telegraph* (Sydney) newspaper on 7 October 2008 a headline read: 'Banks Swipe Rates Cash—Homeowners robbed of $500,000 a day'. The article was particularly critical of the Australian banks for not passing on fully to customers the interest rate cut made by the Reserve Bank of Australia: 'Australia's major banks, which last financial year posted record profits of more than $10 billion, have refused to guarantee they will pass on the entire RBA cut ... Protecting the big banks' profits will cost hundreds of thousands of households dollars they can ill-afford in the lead-up to the bleakest Christmas in years.'

Would you expect the banks to react to such negative media publicity, and, if so, why? Further, would you expect the banks to make any disclosures within their annual reports or on their corporate websites in relation to the criticisms associated with the failure to pass on the full interest rate cut to their customers? What form would you expect these disclosures to take?

Chapter 7 considered a number of theoretical arguments as to why corporate management might elect voluntarily to provide particular information to parties outside the organisation. These arguments were grounded within Positive Accounting Theory. This chapter considers some alternative theoretical perspectives that address the issue, specifically Legitimacy Theory, Stakeholder Theory and Institutional Theory.

As has been stressed throughout this book, and particularly in Chapter 1, theories are abstractions of reality and hence particular theories cannot be expected to provide a full account or description of particular behaviour. Hence, it is sometimes useful to consider the perspectives provided by alternative theories. Different researchers might study the same phenomenon but elect to adopt alternative theoretical perspectives.[1] The choice of one theoretical perspective in preference to others will, at least in part, be due to particular value judgements of the authors involved. As O'Leary (1985, p. 88) states:

> Theorists' own values or ideological predispositions may be among the factors that determine which side of the argument they will adopt in respect of disputable connections of a theory with evidence.

Legitimacy Theory, Stakeholder Theory and Institutional Theory are three theoretical perspectives that have been adopted by a number of researchers in recent years. These theories are sometimes referred to as 'systems-oriented theories'. In accordance with Gray, Owen and Adams (1996, p. 45):

> ... a systems-oriented view of the organisation and society ... permits us to focus on the role of information and disclosure in the relationship(s) between organisations, the State, individuals and groups.

Systems-oriented theories have also been referred to as 'open-systems theories'. Commenting on the use of open-systems theorising, Suchman (1995, p. 571) states:

> Open-system theories have reconceptualised organisational boundaries as porous and problematic ... Many dynamics in the organisational environment stem not from technological or material imperatives, but rather, from cultural norms, symbols, beliefs and rituals. Corporate disclosure policies are considered to represent one important means by which management can influence external perceptions about their organisation.

Within a systems-based perspective, the entity is assumed to be influenced by, and in turn to have an influence on, the society in which it operates. This is simplistically represented in Figure 8.1.

Within Legitimacy Theory, Stakeholder Theory and Institutional Theory, accounting disclosure policies are considered to constitute a strategy to influence the organisation's

---

1   For example, some researchers operating within the Positive Accounting Theory paradigm (for example, Ness & Mirza, 1991) argue that the voluntary disclosure of social responsibility information can be explained as a strategy to reduce political costs. Social responsibility reporting has also been explained from a Legitimacy Theory perspective (for example, Deegan, Rankin & Tobin, 2002), and from a Stakeholder Theory perspective (for example, Swift, 2001).

Figure 8.1 The organisation viewed as part of a wider social system

relationships with the other parties with which it interacts. In recent times, Stakeholder Theory and Legitimacy Theory have frequently been applied to explain why organisations make certain social responsibility disclosures within their annual reports or within other corporate reports.[2] However, these theories could also be applied to explain why companies adopt particular financial accounting techniques. The two theories are the main focus of this chapter, but towards the end of the chapter some insights from the more recent application of Institutional Theory to the analysis of voluntary corporate reporting will also be explored. To the extent that these theories provide explanations for and predictions of particular managerial decisions, such as decisions to disclose information, they can also be considered to be positive theories (as opposed to normative theories, which are theories used to prescribe that certain activities should be undertaken).

POLITICAL ECONOMY THEORY

According to Gray, Owen and Adams (1996), Legitimacy Theory and Stakeholder Theory are both derived from a broader theory which has been called *Political Economy Theory*. The other theory considered in this chapter—Institutional Theory—can also be linked to Political Economy Theory. The 'political economy' itself has been defined by Gray, Owen and Adams (p. 47) as 'the social, political and economic framework within which human life takes place'.

---

2   Social responsibility disclosures are considered more fully in Chapter 9. However, at this stage they can be defined as disclosures that provide information about the interaction of an organisation with its physical and social environment, inclusive of community involvement, the natural environment, human resources, energy and product safety (Gray & Bebbington, 2001; Gray, Owen & Adams, 1996).

The perspective embraced is that *society*, *politics* and *economics* are inseparable, and economic issues cannot meaningfully be investigated in the absence of considerations about the political, social and institutional framework in which the economic activity takes place. It is argued that by considering the political economy a researcher is able to consider broader (societal) issues that impact on how an organisation operates and what information it elects to disclose. According to Guthrie and Parker (1990, p. 166):

> The political economy perspective perceives accounting reports as social, political, and economic documents. They serve as a tool for constructing, sustaining, and legitimising economic and political arrangements, institutions, and ideological themes which contribute to the corporation's private interests. Disclosures have the capacity to transmit social, political, and economic meanings for a pluralistic set of report recipients.

Guthrie and Parker (1990, p. 166) further state that corporate reports cannot be considered as neutral, unbiased (or representationally faithful) documents, as many professional accounting bodies might suggest, but, rather, that corporate reports are 'a product of the interchange between the corporation and its environment and attempt to mediate and accommodate a variety of sectional interests'.[3] This view is consistent with Burchell et al. (1980, p. 6), who suggest that accounting can 'not be seen as a mere assembly of calculative routines, it functions as a cohesive and influential mechanism for economic and social management'.

Political Economy Theory has been divided (perhaps somewhat simplistically, but nevertheless usefully) into two broad streams which Gray, Owen and Adams (1996, p. 47) have labelled 'classical' and 'bourgeois' political economy. Classical Political Economy Theory is related to the works of philosophers such as Karl Marx, and explicitly places 'sectional (class) interests, structural conflict, inequity, and the role of the State at the heart of the analysis' (Gray, Owen & Adams, 1996, p. 47). This can be contrasted with 'bourgeois' Political Economy Theory which, according to Gray, Kouhy and Lavers (1995, p. 53), largely ignores these elements and, as a result, is content to perceive the world as essentially pluralistic.[4]

Classical Political Economy Theory tends to perceive accounting reports and disclosures as a means of maintaining the favoured position (for example, the wealth and power) of those who control scarce resources (capital), and as a means of undermining the position of those without scarce capital. It focuses on the structural conflicts within society.[5]

---

3   As would be appreciated, various professional accounting bodies throughout the world have released documents (normally as part of a conceptual framework project) indicating that financial reporting should embrace the attributes of neutrality and representational faithfulness. Proponents of political economy theories would argue that there are a multitude of political and social issues that make such a perspective unrealistic.

4   A pluralistic perspective assumes (typically implicitly) that many classes of stakeholders have the power to influence various decisions by corporations, government and other entities. Within this perspective, accounting is not considered to be put in place to favour specific interests (sometimes referred to as 'elites'). By using 'society' as the topic of focus rather than subgroups within society, theories such as Legitimacy Theory, which is derived from the bourgeois branch of Political Economy Theory, ignore 'struggles and inequities within society' (Puxty, 1991).

5   For example, in considering the practice of social responsibility reporting, classical political economists would typically argue that the growth of environmental disclosure by companies since the late 1980s can be seen as an attempt to act as if in response to environmental groups while actually attempting to wrest the initiative and control of the environment agenda from these groups in order to permit capital to carry on doing what it does best—making money from capital (Gray, Owen & Adams, 1996, p. 47).

According to Cooper and Sherer (1984), the study of accounting should recognise *power* and *conflict* in society, and consequently should focus on the effects of accounting reports on the distribution of income, wealth and power in society. This is consistent with Lowe and Tinker (1977) who argue that the majority of accounting research is based on a pluralist conception of society (which, as mentioned earlier, assumes that no one group dominates all others). According to Lowe and Tinker, this pluralistic view assumes (incorrectly, they argue) that power is widely diffused and that society is composed of many individuals whose preferences are to predominate in social choices, and with no individual able consistently to influence that society (or the accounting function therein). Researchers such as Lowe and Tinker (1977) and Cooper and Sherer (1984) oppose such a view and provide a counter-perspective that the pluralist view ignores a great deal of evidence that suggests that the majority of people in society are controlled by a small but 'well-defined elite'—an elite that uses accounting (as well as other mechanisms) as a means of maintaining their position of dominance. The works of authors who take this view are further considered in a discussion on critical accounting perspectives in Chapter 12. Such researchers tend to be extremely critical of current accounting and reporting techniques.

According to Gray, Owen and Adams (1996), and as briefly noted above, bourgeois political economy, on the other hand, does not explicitly consider structural conflicts and class struggles; rather, it 'tends to be concerned with interactions between groups in an essentially pluralistic world (for example, the negotiation between a company and an environmental pressure group, or between a local authority and the State)'. It is this branch of Political Economy Theory from which Legitimacy Theory and Stakeholder Theory derive. Neither theory questions or studies the various class structures (and possible struggles) within society.[6] However, Institutional Theory can be applied within either a classical or a bourgeois conception of political economy. We now turn our attention to Legitimacy Theory.

LEGITIMACY THEORY

Legitimacy Theory asserts that organisations continually seek to ensure that they are perceived as operating within the bounds and norms of their respective societies—that is, they attempt to ensure that their activities are perceived by outside parties as being 'legitimate'. These bounds and norms are not considered to be fixed, but change over time, thereby requiring organisations to be responsive to the ethical (or moral) environment in which they operate. Lindblom (1994) distinguishes between *legitimacy*, which is considered to be a status or condition, and *legitimation*, which she considers to be the process that leads to an organisation being adjudged legitimate. According to Lindblom (p. 2), legitimacy is:

> ... a condition or status which exists when an entity's value system is congruent with the value system of the larger social system of which the entity is a part. When a disparity,

---

6   Positive Accounting Theory, the focus of Chapter 7, also does not consider issues associated with inequities within society or the role of accounting in sustaining these inequities.

actual or potential, exists between the two value systems, there is a threat to the entity's legitimacy.

Legitimacy is a relative concept; it is relative to the social system in which the entity operates and is *time* and *place* specific. As Suchman (1995, p. 574) states:

Legitimacy is a generalised perception or assumption that the actions of an entity are desirable, proper, or appropriate *within* some socially constructed system of norms, values, beliefs, and definitions.

Within Legitimacy Theory, 'legitimacy' is considered to be a resource on which an organisation is dependent for survival (Dowling & Pfeffer, 1975; O'Donovan, 2002). It is something that is conferred upon the organisation by society, and it is something that is desired or sought by the organisation. However, unlike many other 'resources', it is a 'resource' that the organisation is considered to be able to affect or manipulate through various disclosure-related strategies (Woodward, Edwards & Birkin, 1996).

Consistent with resource dependence theory (see Pfeffer & Salancik, 1978), Legitimacy Theory would suggest that whenever managers consider that the supply of the particular resource—legitimacy—is vital to organisational survival, they will pursue strategies to ensure the continued supply of that resource. As will be seen shortly, strategies aimed at gaining, maintaining or repairing legitimacy (often referred to as 'legitimation strategies') may include targeted disclosures, or perhaps controlling or collaborating with other parties who in themselves are perceived by society to be legitimate and therefore able to provide 'legitimacy by association' (Oliver, 1991; Deegan & Blomquist, 2006).

For an organisation seeking to be perceived as legitimate, it is not the actual conduct of the organisation that is important; it is what society collectively knows or perceives about the organisation's conduct that shapes legitimacy. Information disclosure is vital to establishing corporate legitimacy. As Suchman (1995, p. 574) states:

An organisation may diverge dramatically from societal norms yet retain legitimacy because the divergence goes unnoticed. Legitimacy is socially constructed in that it reflects a congruence between the behaviours of the legitimated entity and the shared (or assumed shared) beliefs of some social group; thus legitimacy is dependent on a collective audience, yet independent of particular observers.

Consistent with the view that 'legitimacy' is based on *perceptions*, Nasi et al. (1997, p. 300) state:

A corporation is legitimate when it is judged to be 'just and worthy of support' (Dowling and Pfeffer, 1975). Legitimacy therefore is not an abstract measure of the 'rightness' of the corporation but rather a measure of societal perceptions of the adequacy of corporate behaviour (Suchman, 1995). It is a measure of the attitude of society toward a corporation and its activities, and it is a matter of degree ranging from highly legitimate to highly illegitimate. It is also important to point out that legitimacy is a social construct based on cultural norms for corporate behaviour. Therefore, the demands placed on corporations change over time, and different communities often have different ideas about what constitutes legitimate corporate behaviour.

LEGITIMACY, PUBLIC EXPECTATIONS AND THE SOCIAL CONTRACT

Legitimacy Theory relies on the notion that there is a 'social contract' between the organisation in question and the society in which it operates. The 'social contract' is not easy to define, but the concept is used to represent the multitude of implicit and explicit expectations that society has about how the organisation should conduct its operations. It can be argued that traditionally profit maximisation was perceived to be the optimal measure of corporate performance (Abbott & Monsen, 1979; Heard & Bolce, 1981; Patten, 1991, 1992; Ramanathan, 1976). Under this notion, a firm's profits were viewed as an all-inclusive measure of organisational legitimacy (Ramanathan, 1976). However, public expectations have undergone significant change in recent decades. Heard and Bolce (1981) note the expansion of the advocacy movement in the United States during the 1960s and 1970s, and the significant increase in legislation related to social issues, including the environment and employees' health and safety, which was enacted in the United States within the same period. With heightened social expectations it is anticipated that successful business corporations will react and attend to the human, environmental and other social consequences of their activities (Heard & Bolce, 1981).

It has been argued that society increasingly expects business to 'make outlays to repair or prevent damage to the physical environment, to ensure the health and safety of consumers, employees, and those who reside in the communities where products are manufactured and wastes are dumped' (Tinker & Neimark, 1987, p. 84). Consequently, companies with a poor social and environmental performance record may increasingly find it difficult to obtain the necessary resources and support to continue operations within a community that values a clean environment. Perhaps this was not the case a number of decades ago.

It is assumed within Legitimacy Theory that society allows the organisation to continue operations to the extent that it generally meets society's expectations—that is, to the extent that it complies with the social contract. Legitimacy Theory emphasises that the organisation must appear to consider the rights of the public at large, not merely those of its investors. Failure to comply with societal expectations (that is, comply with the terms of the 'social contract') may lead to sanctions being imposed by society, for example in the form of legal restrictions imposed on an organisation's operations, limited resources (for example, financial capital and labour) being provided and/or reduced demand for its products (sometimes through organised consumer boycotts).

Consistent with Legitimacy Theory, organisations are not considered to have any inherent right to resources. Rather, the right to access resources must be earned. Legitimacy (from society's perspective) and the right to operate go hand in hand. As Mathews (1993, p. 26) states:

> The social contract would exist between corporations (usually limited companies) and individual members of society. Society (as a collection of individuals) provides corporations with their legal standing and attributes and the authority to own and use natural resources and to hire employees. Organisations draw on community resources and output both goods and services and waste products to the general environment. The organisation has no inherent rights to these benefits, and in order to allow their existence, society would expect the benefits to exceed the costs to society.

Accounting Headline 8.1 provides a copy of a newspaper article in which an executive of one of Australia's largest banks concedes that his organisation broke the 'social contract'. It is

Australian, 20 May 1999, p. 1

Westpac chief admits banks failed in the bush

SID HARRIS

The rush by banks to shut branches in rural areas over the past decade was a 'mistake' and broke 'the social contract' with the community, a Westpac executive Michael Hawker said yesterday.

Mr Hawker, group executive for Business and Consumer Banking, said that in the face of intense competition following deregulation, banks had lost sight of the needs and fears of a number of their customers.

He told a National Farmers Federation conference in Longreach that many of the rural closures should have been handled more sensitively. 'I think what we are saying is what we did was probably not the most appropriate thing to do', he said.

'I think everyone in the community would say there's been a lot of dramatic change and I think we have made a number of mistakes. There is no doubt about that.'

Between 1990 and 1998, 1306 banks shut their doors across Australia—406 of them in country areas—while 1345 agencies also shut, 1071 outside major cities.

Mr Hawker said advances in technology meant 'in-store' banking—which provides basic teller transactions and a phone service at a sponsoring business—could spare rural communities from loss of services. Westpac initiated a $300 million review and refurbishment program last November for its 969 branches, which will see an estimated 150 convert to in-store operations.

interesting to note that the notion of a social contract is something that is increasingly being referred to by managers (and further evidence of this will be seen later in the chapter).

The idea of a 'social contract' is not new, having been discussed by philosophers such as Thomas Hobbes (1588–1679), John Locke (1632–1704) and Jean-Jacques Rousseau (1712–1778). Shocker and Sethi (1974, p. 67) provide a good overview of the concept of a social contract:

Any social institution—and business is no exception—operates in society via a social contract, expressed or implied, whereby its survival and growth are based on:

1. the delivery of some socially desirable ends to society in general, and
2. the distribution of economic, social, or political benefits to groups from which it derives its power.

In a dynamic society, neither the sources of institutional power nor the needs for its services are permanent. Therefore, an institution must constantly meet the twin tests of legitimacy and relevance by demonstrating that society requires its services and that the groups benefiting from its rewards have society's approval.

It is emphasised that the social contract is a theoretical construct, and hence an individual cannot simply go and find a copy of the social contract 'negotiated' between an organisation and the society in which it operates. Different managers will have different perceptions about how society expects the organisation to behave across the various attributes of its activities (that is, they will have different perspectives of the contract)—and this in itself can explain, at least in part, why some managers will elect to do things differently from other managers. If a manager undertakes certain actions that are subsequently found to be unacceptable to the community (for example, sourcing clothing from Asian sweatshops—an issue that recently outraged many people within the community), Legitimacy Theory would explain this in terms of the manager misinterpreting the terms of the social contract and this misinterpretation may subsequently have an adverse impact on the organisation's survival. Consider the implications for Nike, GAP and other clothing and footwear manufacturers when the media ran campaigns about their association with various abusive sweatshops.

The social contract is considered to be made up of numerous terms (or clauses), some explicit and some implicit. Gray, Owen and Adams (1996) suggest that legal requirements provide the explicit terms of the contract, while other non-legislated societal expectations embody the implicit terms of the contract. That is, there is an imperfect correlation between the law and societal norms (as reflected by the social contract), and, according to Dowling and Pfeffer (1975), there are three broad reasons for the difference. First, even though laws are reflective of societal norms and values, legal systems are slow to adapt to changes in the norms and values in society. Second, legal systems often strive for consistency, whereas societal norms and expectations can be contradictory. Third, it is suggested that, while society may not be accepting of certain behaviours, it may not be willing or structured enough to have those behavioural restrictions codified within law. It is in relation to the composition of the implicit terms of the 'contract' that managers' perceptions can be expected to vary greatly.

As indicated by David Morgan, CEO of Westpac, one of Australia's largest banks, and in Deegan and Rankin (1996, p. 54) and Deegan (2002, p. 293), in accordance with Legitimacy Theory if an organisation cannot justify its continued operation then in a sense the community may revoke its 'contract' to continue its operations. Again, this may occur through consumers reducing or eliminating the demand for the products of the business, factor suppliers eliminating the supply of labour and financial capital to the business, and/or constituents lobbying government for increased taxes, fines or laws to prohibit actions that do not conform with the expectations of the community. As shown in Accounting Headline 8.2, David Morgan specifically mentions the 'social contract' Westpac has with the community, and emphasises how compliance with the social contract is essential in securing the support of various sections of the community, including employees, customers, suppliers and investors. He emphasises that taking community expectations into account and embracing corporate social responsibility are in the interests of business—something that is commonly referred to as 'enlightened self-interest'.

Given the potential costs associated with conducting operations deemed to be outside the terms of the 'social contract', Dowling and Pfeffer (1975) state that organisations will take various actions to ensure that their operations are perceived to be legitimate. That is, they will attempt to establish congruence between 'the social values associated with or implied by their activities and the norms of acceptable behaviour in the larger social system of which they are a part' (Dowling & Pfeffer, 1975, p. 122). Trying to ensure that a company is aware of changing community expectations and responds accordingly requires managers to have particular 'skill sets'. This is reflected in the following comments made in an article in the Melbourne *Age*, entitled 'Corporate coaches emerge to make some difference', (27 July 2006, p. 10):

Former BHP Billiton chief executive John Prescott once told an audience of business people and business critics that winning a community licence to operate and the notion of legitimacy in public opinion were essential to business survival. 'To maintain this legitimacy, and to ensure a positive environment in which to operate, requires skills and approaches which are as important as the financial, technical and marketing capabilities we in business have traditionally valued,' he said.

Valuing values at the heart of the enterprise is how you create sustainable profit

David Morgan is the CEO of Westpac. *Age*, 18 August 2005

Progressive management is predicated on it, and the ethos of corporate responsibility delivers tangible benefits to companies, writes DAVID MORGAN.

There can be no question that the primary obligation of corporations is to maximise long-term returns for shareholders. So where does the concept of corporate social responsibility fit into this equation? Is it just a diversion from core business?

On the contrary. Corporate social responsibility is central to sustainable profit creation. Leaders who successfully manage social, ethical, environmental and other non-financial drivers help ensure a stable, resilient company that is better placed to deliver sustainable shareholder value.

Put simply, a company needs employees who want to work for it; customers who want to buy its products or services; suppliers who want to supply to it; and, of course, investors who want to invest in it long term.

For Westpac, corporate responsibility is about acting in an ethical, trustworthy and responsible manner. We accept our responsibility to manage the societal and environmental impacts of our business. We seek to honour the implicit social contract we have with the communities we serve.

Progressive management is increasingly predicated on this rational, responsible approach. That's why corporate responsibility isn't isolated from Westpac's core activities. It is not an add-on. It is at the heart of our strategy—embedded in our business model.

By creating a place where people want to work, we have improved employee retention and we are better able to attract quality staff—a critical issue for a service business facing profound demographic changes and a shrinking workforce in the coming decades. Motivated employees strongly and positively influence customer satisfaction. Customers feel good about doing business with a responsible and ethical institution. And the community lends its support to companies playing a positive local role.

These are some of the tangible benefits of the corporate responsibility ethos. We've also seen real bottom-line savings from our environmental initiatives. We have materially lowered our use—and the cost—of utilities and paper, which has delivered significant reductions in greenhouse gas emissions. In fact, since joining the Federal Government's Greenhouse Challenge program in 1996, we have slashed our greenhouse gas emissions by 32 per cent.

We are now working with our suppliers to ensure that they are aware of the specific environmental, social and ethical risks and opportunities relevant to their business, and are equipped to address them.

We have come a long way since this journey began. But the finish line is continually moving as we learn more about the opportunities to create financial, social and environmental capital and how to capture it.

Westpac was a founding global signatory, and the only Australian signatory, to the Equator Principles, a risk assessment framework designed to introduce best practice standards for the assessment of social and environmental risk in project financing.

One key challenge is that mainstream financial markets have yet to fully factor corporate social responsibility into investment and valuation decisions. So there is still some way to go before these value drivers are fully taken into account and valued appropriately.

We will continue to play a leading role in this debate, because it is the right thing to do—and because it makes good business sense.

LEGITIMACY AND CHANGING SOCIAL EXPECTATIONS

As community expectations change, organisations must also adapt and change. That is, if society's expectations about performance change, an organisation will need to show that what it is doing is also changing (or perhaps it will need explicitly to communicate and justify why its operations have not changed). This is consistent with a statement made in the BHP Billiton *Sustainability Report* (2008), where it is stated (p. 15):

> By anticipating and understanding trends in society—new regulations, heightened societal expectations and improved scientific knowledge—and assessing these against our business models, our ability to proactively plan for the longer term is improved.

In relation to the dynamics associated with changing community expectations, Lindblom (1994, p. 3) states:

> Legitimacy is dynamic in that the relevant publics continuously evaluate corporate output, methods, and goals against an ever evolving expectation. The legitimacy gap will fluctuate without any changes in action on the part of the corporation. Indeed, as expectations of the relevant publics change the corporation must make changes or the legitimacy gap will grow as the level of conflict increases and the levels of positive and passive support decreases.

The term 'legitimacy gap'—as used in the above quote—is a term that has been used by many researchers to describe the situation where there appears to be a lack of correspondence between how society believes an organisation *should act* and how it is perceived that the organisation *has acted*. In relation to how legitimacy gaps arise, Sethi (1978) describes two major sources of the gaps. First, societal expectations might change, and this will lead to a gap arising even though the organisation is operating in the same manner as it always has. As an example of this source of a legitimacy gap, Nasi et al. (1997, p. 301) state:

> For American tobacco companies in the 1970s, for example, the increasing awareness of the health consequences of smoking resulted in a significant and widening legitimacy gap (Miles and Cameron, 1982). The tobacco companies had not changed their activities, and their image was much the same as it had been, yet they suddenly faced a significantly different evaluation of their role in society; they faced a significant and widening legitimacy gap.

As already emphasised, community expectations are not static; rather, they change across time, thereby requiring the organisation to be responsive to current and future changes to the environment in which they operate. While organisations might change towards community expectations, if the momentum of their change is slower than the changing expectations of society, then legitimacy gaps will arise.

Legitimacy itself can be threatened even when an organisation's performance is not deviating from society's expectations of appropriate performance. This might be because the organisation has failed to make disclosures that show it is complying with society's expectations, which in themselves might be changing across time. That is, legitimacy is assumed to be influenced by disclosures of information, and not simply by (undisclosed) changes in corporate actions. As noted above, if society's expectations about performance change, then arguably an organisation will need to show that what it is doing is also changing (or perhaps it will need explicitly to communicate and justify why its operations have not changed).

The second major source of a legitimacy gap, according to Sethi (1977), occurs when previously unknown information becomes known about the organisation—perhaps through disclosure being made within the news media. In relation to this possibility, Nasi et al. (1997, p. 301) make an interesting reference to 'organisational shadows'. They state:

> The potential body of information about the corporation that is unavailable to the public—the corporate shadow (Bowles, 1991)—stands as a constant potential threat to a corporation's legitimacy. When part of the organisational shadow is revealed, either accidentally or through the activities of an activist group or a journalist, a legitimacy gap may be created.

In relation to the above source of a legitimacy gap, consider how society reacted to media revelations about certain sportswear companies' use of sweatshops in Asia (for example, Nike), revelations about the pollution being caused by mining companies' tailings dams in remote environments (for example, BHP Billiton's operations in Papua New Guinea), or revelations about how the products of particular companies affect consumer health (for example, the reaction to the investigation into McDonald's as told in the movie *Supersize Me*). All these revelations had significant cost implications for the companies involved—and to solve the legitimacy problems the organisations typically relied on various disclosure strategies.

The notion of a legitimacy gap has been depicted diagrammatically by O'Donovan (2002) (see Figure 8.2). In explaining the diagram, O'Donovan states:

> The area marked X [in Figure 8.2] represents congruence between corporate activity and society's expectations of the corporation and its activities, based on social values and norms. Areas Y and Z represent incongruence between a corporation's actions and society's perceptions of what these actions should be. These areas represent 'illegitimacy' or legitimacy gaps (Sethi, 1978). The aim of the corporation is to be legitimate, to ensure area X is as large as possible, thereby reducing the legitimacy gap. A number of legitimation tactics and disclosure approaches may be adopted to reduce the legitimacy gap.

Much of the work that has been undertaken within the social and environmental accounting area, and which has embraced Legitimacy Theory, has typically addressed actions undertaken by organisations to *regain* their legitimacy after some form of legitimacy-threatening event

Figure 8.2 Issues/events and corporate legitimacy

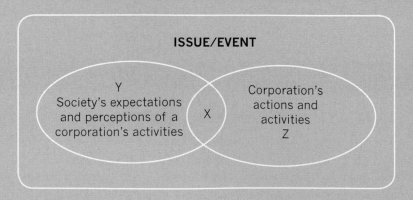

Source: G. O'Donovan (2002), 'Environmental disclosures in the annual report: extending the applicability and predictive power of legitimacy theory', *Accounting, Auditing and Accountability Journal*, 15(3).

occurs. But as authors such as Suchman (1995) and O'Donovan (2002) indicate, legitimation strategies might be used to either *gain*, *maintain* or *repair* legitimacy. According to O'Donovan (2002, p. 349):

> Legitimation techniques/tactics chosen will differ depending upon whether the organisation is trying to gain or extend legitimacy, to maintain its current level of legitimacy, or to repair or to defend its lost or threatened legitimacy.

While researchers have proposed that legitimation tactics might differ depending on whether the entity is trying to *gain*, *maintain* or *repair* legitimacy, the theoretical development in this area remains weak. Although the literature provides some general commentary, there is a lack of guidance about the relative effectiveness of legitimation strategies with regard to either gaining, maintaining or regaining legitimacy. In terms of the general commentary provided within the literature, gaining legitimacy occurs when an organisation moves into a new area of operations in which it has no past reputation. In such a situation, the organisation suffers from the 'liability of newness' (Ashforth & Gibbs, 1990) and it needs to proactively engage in activities to win acceptance.

The task of *maintaining* legitimacy is typically considered easier than *gaining* or *repairing* legitimacy (O'Donovan, 2002; Ashforth & Gibbs, 1990). One of the 'tricks' in maintaining legitimacy is to be able to anticipate changing community perceptions. According to Suchman (1995, p. 594), strategies for maintaining legitimacy fall into two groups—forecasting future changes and protecting past accomplishments. In relation to monitoring or forecasting changing community perceptions, Suchman (1995, p. 595) states:

> Managers must guard against becoming so enamoured with their own legitimating myths that they lose sight of external developments that might bring those myths into question. With advanced warning, managers can engage in pre-emptive conformity, selection, or manipulation, keeping the organization and its environment in close alignment; without such warning, managers will find themselves constantly struggling to regain lost ground. In general, perceptual strategies involve monitoring the cultural environment and assimilating elements of that environment into organizational decision processes, usually by employing boundary-spanning personnel as bridges across which the organization can learn audience values, beliefs, and reaction.

In relation to protecting past (legitimacy-enhancing) accomplishments, Suchman (1995, p. 595) states:

> In addition to guarding against unforeseen challenges, organizations may seek to buttress the legitimacy they have already acquired. In particular, organizations can enhance their security by converting legitimacy from episodic to continual forms. To a large extent this boils down to (a) policing internal operations to prevent miscues, (b) curtailing highly visible legitimation efforts in favour of more subtle techniques, and (c) developing a defensive stockpile of supportive beliefs, attitudes and accounts.

In relation to *maintaining* legitimacy, the greater the extent to which the organisation trades on its level of legitimacy, the more crucial it will be for that organisation to ensure that it does not deviate from the high standards that it has established. For example, compare an armaments manufacturer with, say, the Body Shop (a shop that has developed a reputation for sound social and environmental practices). The products of armaments manufacturers are designed to kill, so such an organisation arguably has less to worry about in terms of its legitimacy than the Body Shop. The Body Shop trades on its reputation for caring about the environment, society and the welfare of animals. If an organisation within the supply chain of the Body Shop—and without the knowledge of the Body Shop—undertook activities that were somehow related to animal testing or with particular environmental damage and these activities were discovered by the media, this could be extremely costly to the organisation. It has a lot of *investment in legitimacy* to lose.

In considering *repairing* legitimacy, Suchman (1995, p. 597) suggests that related legitimation techniques tend to be reactive responses to often unforeseen crises. In many respects, *repairing* and *gaining* legitimacy are similar. As O'Donovan (2002, p. 350) states:

> Repairing legitimacy has been related to different levels of crisis management (Davidson, 1991; Elsbach and Sutton, 1992). The task of repairing legitimacy is, in some ways, similar to gaining legitimacy. If a crisis is evolving proactive strategies may need to be adopted, as has been the case for the tobacco industry during the past two decades (Pava and Krausz. 1997). Generally, however, the main difference is that strategies for repairing legitimacy are reactive, usually to an unforseen and immediate crisis, whereas techniques to gain legitimacy are usually *ex ante*, proactive and not normally related to crisis.

In the discussion that follows, the strategies that can be used by corporate management in an effort to *gain, maintain* or *regain* legitimacy are considered. As already indicated, the theoretical development has not developed sufficiently to link specific legitimation techniques with efforts to either gain, maintain or regain legitimacy. Most of the proposed legitimation techniques appear to relate to regaining legitimacy in the light of particular crises—something that has been the focus of many researchers working within the social and environmental accounting area (and who embrace Legitimacy Theory). Nevertheless, all legitimation strategies rely on disclosure.

Dowling and Pfeffer (1975, p. 127) outline the means by which an organisation may, perhaps when confronted with legitimacy-threatening events, legitimate its activities:

- The organisation can adapt its output, goals and methods of operation to conform to prevailing definitions of legitimacy.
- The organisation can attempt, through communication, to alter the definition of social legitimacy so that it conforms to the organisation's present practices, output and values.
- The organisation can attempt, through communication, to become identified with symbols, values or institutions that have a strong base of legitimacy.

Consistent with Dowling and Pfeffer's strategy of 'communication', Lindblom (1994) proposes that an organisation can adopt a number of strategies where it perceives that its legitimacy is in question because its actions (or operations) are at variance with society's expectations and values. Lindblom identifies four courses of action (there is some overlap with Dowling and Pfeffer) that an organisation can take to obtain, maintain, or repair legitimacy in these circumstances. The organisation can:

1. seek to educate and inform its 'relevant publics' about (actual) changes in the organisation's performance and activities which bring the activities and performance more into line with society's values and expectations;

2. seek to change the perceptions that 'relevant publics' have of the organisation's performance and activities—but not change the organisation's actual behaviour (while using disclosures in corporate reports to indicate falsely that the performance and activities have changed);

3. seek to manipulate perception by deflecting attention from the issue of concern onto other related issues through an appeal to, for example, emotive symbols, thus seeking to demonstrate how the organisation has fulfilled social expectations in other areas of its activities; or

4. seek to change external expectations of its performance, possibly by demonstrating that specific societal expectations are unreasonable.

USE OF ACCOUNTING REPORTS IN LEGITIMATION STRATEGIES

According to Lindblom, and Dowling and Pfeffer, the public disclosure of information in such places as annual reports can be used by an organisation to implement each of their suggested strategies. Certainly, this is a perspective that many researchers of social responsibility reporting have adopted, as discussed shortly. For example, a firm may provide information to counter or offset negative news that is publicly available, or it may simply provide information to inform the interested parties about attributes of the organisation that were previously unknown. In addition, organisations may draw attention to their strengths, for instance environmental or community awards won or safety initiatives that have been implemented, while neglecting or down-playing information concerning negative implications of their activities, such as pollution or workplace accidents.

In considering the various proposed legitimising techniques, we can see that the techniques might be symbolic (and not actually reflect any real change in activities) or they might be substantive (and reflect actual change in corporate activities). As Ashforth and Gibbs (1990) indicate, the use of substantive management techniques might 'involve real, material change in organisational goals, structures, and processes or socially institutionalized practices' (p. 178). By contrast, symbolic management techniques of legitimation involve the portrayal of corporate behaviour in a manner to 'appear consistent with social values and expectations', but the actual operating policies of the organisation may not change (Ashforth & Gibbs, 1990, p. 180). For example, companies may publish policies on various issues including the environment but not enforce or set in place mechanisms for the full adoption of such policies. Other techniques relating to symbolic management techniques include offering excuses for behaviour or apologies (Ashforth & Gibbs, 1990).

According to Ashsforth and Gibbs, it is not necessary for corporations to use either substantive or symbolic management techniques exclusively, and they may adopt a mix of substantive and/or symbolic legitimating techniques which they apply with varying levels of intensity. As an example of the potential use of 'legitimising symbols', consider research reported by Deegan and Blomquist (2006).

Deegan and Blomquist investigated the development of the Australian Minerals Industry Code for Environmental Management by the Mineral Council of Australia. Many Australian mining companies signed up to this code of conduct. The code had among its many requirements a reporting requirement that required signatories to the code to prepare and release a publicly available environmental report within two years of signing the code. Concerned about the quality of reporting being undertaken within the minerals industry, WWF-Australia (formerly known as the World Wide Fund for Nature) undertook an exercise in which it assessed the quality of the reports being released by the signatories of the code. WWF assessed the reports using particular reporting criteria that WWF had developed. WWF's results were reported in a document it released entitled 'Mining Environmental Reports: Ore or Overburden?'. In explaining how the establishment of the code and the subsequent involvement of WWF might have contributed to the legitimacy of the minerals industry, Deegan and Blomquist referred to the work of Richardson and Dowling (1986). Richardson and Dowling refer to 'legitimating symbols' and 'procedural legitimation'—with the two being linked to one another. According to Richardson and Dowling (1986, p. 102):

> Procedural legitimation represents a process of negotiation through which the values of a community and their connotative link to particular social relations and artifacts is created and institutionalized, as legitimating symbols. In the process, both value standards and social structures are subject to change.

In discussing their results, Deegan and Blomquist (2006) state:

> The legitimating symbol in this case was the Australian Minerals Industry Code for Environmental Management. As Richardson and Dowling emphasise, legitimating symbols are open to 'challenge and change' and they can only sustain their existence through the support and affirmation of those parties that are perceived by the community as having high 'value standards' (a process of procedural legitimation involving a third party). WWF would arguably be perceived as having high 'value standards' and hence, their participation in the process would add to the legitimacy of the Code and increase the community perception that the Code had some form of 'higher order reality' that was independent of the creating body (the Mineral Council of Australia). Indeed, the comments made by the interviewees [from the Australian Minerals Council who were involved with the development of the Code] were consistent with the view that the WWF's involvement assisted the social standing of the Code. By reviewing the reporting policies of Code signatories, the WWF was effectively treating the Code as a 'value standard' which it was 'sanctioning' (Giddens, 1976)—something that would appear to be beneficial to the industry. While data was not collected from non-signatories at the time, it is conceivable that WWF's 'sanctioning' of the Code might have encouraged other organisations to subsequently become signatories. Certainly, the membership numbers increased subsequent to WWF's involvement (though obviously many factors could have contributed to this increase).

Consistent with the positions taken both by Dowling and Pfeffer and by Lindblom, Hurst (1970) suggests that one of the major functions of accounting, and subsequently accounting reports, is to legitimate the existence of the corporation. Such views highlight the strategic nature of financial statements and other related disclosures.

CORPORATE VIEWS ON THE IMPORTANCE OF THE SOCIAL CONTRACT

The view within Legitimacy Theory that organisations will be penalised if they do not operate in a manner consistent with community expectations (that is, in accordance with the social contract, or, as it is sometimes called, the 'community licence to operate') is a view being embraced publicly by corporate managers internationally. This is reflected, for example, in a recent statement made by a senior executive of Westpac, one of Australia's largest banks, in the *Westpac 2007 Stakeholder Impact Report*. Reflecting on the recent actions of Australian banks, and how such actions negatively impacted on the bank's legitimacy, the executive stated (p. 35):

> Ten years ago I saw first hand the cost of ignoring the community's expectations. Get this wrong and you quickly realise that reputation, social licence to operate and regulatory risk are not just abstract concepts. It has taken a long time to get the community back on side. These days we endeavour to be as open as possible, and to pay close attention to what people expect from business and from us in particular.

The 2000 *Corporate Social Responsibility Report* of the Anglo-Swedish-based pharmaceutical multinational AstraZeneca contained the following statement (p. 4):

> The objective of social sustainability is to provide a better quality of life for all members of society. In order to make our contribution to this objective we need to understand the changing expectations of society. Our social objectives can be more clearly identified by considering all of our stakeholders—employees, customers, shareholders and the wider community—and the impact, both positive and negative, that our operations could have on them.

In AstraZeneca's 2003 *Corporate Responsibility Summary Report* (p. 1), the chief executive (Sir Tom McKillop) continued this theme when he stated:

> Our reputation is built on the trust and confidence of all our stakeholders and is one of AstraZeneca's most valuable assets. Along with our commitment to competitiveness and performance, we will continue to be led by our core values to achieve sustainable success ... Stakeholder expectations are constantly evolving and we continuously monitor our internal and external environment for issues relating to our business that affect or concern society today ... Corporate responsibility (CR) is not an optional extra—it must be integral to all that we do. Our strategy to include considerations of corporate responsibility across all our activities is beginning to take effect.

Consistent with Legitimacy Theory, these statements reflect the view that organisations must adapt to community expectations if they are to be successful. This view is also reflected in the BHP Billiton *Sustainability Report 2008*, where it is stated (p. 15):

> Our bottom line performance is dependent on ensuring access to resources and securing and maintaining our licence to operate and grow ... Access to resources is crucial to the sustainability of our business. Fundamental to achieving access to resources is effectively addressing heightened political and societal expectations related to the environmental and social aspects of business.

The 2008 *Annual Report* of BHP Billiton also makes reference to the importance of complying with community expectations (as reflected in the 'licence to operate'). As page 11 states:

> Despite our best efforts and best intentions, there remains a risk that health, safety and/or environmental incidents or accidents may occur that may negatively impact our reputation or licence to operate.

Page 56 of the *Annual Report* further states:

> Our social licence to operate depends on our ability to operate all aspects of our business responsibly, including our ability to work effectively with our host communities. Regular, open and honest dialogue is the key to building strong relationships. Our community relations professionals are charged with developing and nurturing relationships with people impacted by, and interested in, our operations so we can understand their concerns, hopes and aspirations.

These statements illustrate that the notions embodied within Legitimacy Theory are reflective of the public positions being taken by corporate executives. They appear to consider that meeting the expectations of the community in which their organisations operate can protect or enhance profitability, while failure to do so can be detrimental to the organisations' ongoing operations and survival.

EMPIRICAL TESTS OF LEGITIMACY THEORY

In recent years Legitimacy Theory has been used by numerous accounting researchers who have elected to study social and environmental reporting practices.[7] A number of papers have identified specific types of social responsibility disclosures that have appeared within annual reports. The researchers have attempted to explain these disclosures on the basis that they form part of the portfolio of strategies undertaken by accountants and their managers to bring legitimacy to, or maintain the legitimacy of, their respective organisations. A number of such papers are now considered.

An early study that sought to link Legitimacy Theory to corporate social disclosure policies was conducted by Hogner (1982). This longitudinal study examined corporate social reporting in the annual reports of the US Steel Corporation over a period of eighty years, beginning in 1901, the data being analysed for year-to-year variation. Hogner showed that the extent of social disclosures varied from year to year and he speculated that the variation could represent a response to society's changing expectations of corporate behaviour.

Patten (1992) focused on the change in the extent of environmental disclosures made by North American oil companies, including Exxon Oil Company, both before and after the *Exxon Valdez* incident in Alaska in 1989—which was one of the largest oil spills in history and had a significant affect on many creatures and the environments in which they lived. He argued that if the Alaskan oil spill resulted in a threat to the legitimacy of the petroleum industry, and not just to Exxon, then Legitimacy Theory would suggest that companies operating within that industry would respond by increasing the amount of environmental disclosures in their annual reports. Patten's results indicate that there were increased environmental disclosures by the petroleum companies for the post-1989 period, consistent with a legitimation perspective. This disclosure reaction took place across the industry, even though the incident was directly related to only one oil company. He stated (p. 475):

> ... it appears that at least for environmental disclosures, threats to a firm's legitimacy do entice the firm to include more social responsibility information in its annual report.

---

7   However, it needs to be appreciated that Legitimacy Theory could be utilised as a basis for explaining various types of disclosures other than those relating to social and environmental performance issues. For whatever reason, social and environmental accounting researchers have tended to embrace Legitimacy Theory more so than other accounting researchers.

In an Australian study, Deegan and Rankin (1996) used Legitimacy Theory to try to explain systematic changes in corporate annual report environmental disclosure policies around the time of proven environmental prosecutions. The authors examined the environmental disclosure practices of a sample of Australian firms that were successfully prosecuted by environmental protection authorities (EPAs) for breaches of various environmental protection laws during the period 1990–93 (any prosecutions by these agencies were reported in the EPAs' annual reports, which were publicly available). The annual reports of a final sample of twenty firms, prosecuted a total of seventy-eight times, were reviewed to ascertain the extent of the environmental disclosures. These annual reports were matched by industry and size to the annual reports of a control group of twenty firms that had not been prosecuted.

Of the twenty prosecuted firms, eighteen provided environmental information in their annual report, but the disclosures were predominantly of a positive nature, providing 'good news' about the organisations' performance, and the disclosures were of a qualitative nature. Only two organisations made any mention of the prosecutions. Deegan and Rankin found that prosecuted firms disclosed significantly more environmental information (of a favourable nature) in the year of prosecution than in any other year of the sample period. Consistent with the view that companies increase disclosure to offset any effects of EPA prosecutions, the EPA-prosecuted firms also disclosed more environmental information relative to non-prosecuted firms. The authors concluded that the public disclosure of proven environmental prosecutions had an impact on the disclosure policies of the firms involved.

With the results of Patten (1992) and Deegan and Rankin (1996) in mind, consider Accounting Headline 8.3, which relates to BHP Billiton Ltd and documents concerns about the deaths of several mine workers. Read the article and then consider how Legitimacy Theory could be used to predict how companies in the industry might react to such publicity. Do you think that BHP Billiton would be deemed to have breached its 'social contract', and, if so, do you think that BHP Billiton might use its annual report in an attempt to reinstate its legitimacy? Do you think that the comments made by the chief executive could act to help the company reinstate its legitimacy?

In another study that embraced Legitimacy Theory, Deegan and Gordon (1996) reviewed annual report environmental disclosures made by a sample of companies from 1980 to 1991. They investigated the objectivity of corporate environmental disclosure practices and trends in environmental disclosures over time. They also sought to determine if environmental disclosures were related to concerns held by environmental groups about particular industries' environmental performance. The results derived by the Deegan and Gordon study indicated, among other findings, that during the period covered by the study: (1) increases in corporate environmental disclosures over time were positively associated with increases in the levels of environmental group membership; (2) corporate environmental disclosures were overwhelmingly self-laudatory; and (3) there was a positive correlation between the environmental sensitivity of the industry to which the corporation belonged and the level of corporate environmental disclosure.[8] These results were deemed to be consistent with Legitimacy Theory.

Gray, Kouhy and Lavers (1995) performed a longitudinal review of UK corporate social and environmental disclosures for the period 1979–91. In discussing the trends in corporate

---

8   Environmental sensitivity was determined by use of a questionnaire sent to environmental lobby groups in which office-bearers were required to rate industries (on a 0 to 5 scale) on the basis of whether the industry had been made the focus of action as a result of its environmental performance/implications.

Sydney Morning Herald, 6 September 2008, p. 43

Fourth BHP worker dies in five weeks

JAMIE FREED

BHP Billiton has temporarily halted its iron ore operations in Western Australia after reporting the third death of a worker in the division within five weeks.

Employees yesterday received an extra safety briefing in lieu of performing their normal activities after a 19-year-old contractor at its Yandi mine was killed in a vehicle accident on Thursday.

Since July 30, BHP has reported four deaths at its global operations. Three were at its WA iron ore operations—two of them contractors at the Yandi mine—and one was at a coalmine in South Africa.

In the previous financial year, BHP reported 11 fatalities, five of which occurred in a helicopter crash in Angola in November. It had reported three deaths a year in the three preceding years, during which Chip Goodyear was chief executive.

The deteriorating safety record since Marius Kloppers took the top job in October has not escaped his notice.

'In this new financial year it is essential that we take action to deliver on our most fundamental commitment to ensuring that each of us goes home safely at the end of each day,' he told staff in a memo in July. 'This is at the very core of our objectives for the coming year. Neither production nor financial results must ever come before safety.'

In a deeply emotional moment at BHP's annual meeting in November, Mr Kloppers said he had been 'personally devastated' by the helicopter crash in Angola.

Among the dead was BHP's chief operating officer in Angola, David Hopwood, a long-time friend of Mr Kloppers.

BHP's takeover target Rio Tinto has not been immune from deaths this calendar year. It lost 10 employees and contractors in a helicopter crash near its La Granja copper project in Peru and another employee at a talc operation in France.

Before this year, Rio had generally experienced fewer fatalities at its operations than BHP. It lost three employees a year at its managed operations in 2006 and 2007 and two in 2005.

The last death at Rio's Australian operations was in 2004, and not in the iron ore division.

BHP tends to use more contractors at its Pilbara operations than Rio. The two who died at Yandi recently were employed by contractor HWE Mining, which operates the mine on behalf of BHP.

Bonuses to divisional heads at Rio and BHP are in part based on safety records. Rio makes clear each year which divisional heads met, exceeded or missed their safety targets, but BHP does not.

environmental disclosure policies, they made use of Legitimacy Theory, with specific reference to the strategies suggested by Lindblom (1994) that were considered earlier in the chapter. After considering the extent and types of corporate disclosures, they stated (p. 65):

> The tone, orientation and focus of the environmental disclosures accord closely with Lindblom's first, second and third legitimation strategies. A significant minority of companies found it necessary to 'change their actual performance' with respect to environmental interactions (Lindblom's first strategy) and use corporate social reporting to inform their 'relevant publics' about this. Similarly, companies' environmental disclosure has also been an attempt, first, to change perceptions of environmental performance—to alter perceptions of whether certain industries were 'dirty' and 'irresponsible' (Lindblom's second strategy) and, second, as Lindblom notes, to distract attention from the central environmental issues (the third legitimation strategy). Increasingly, companies are being required to demonstrate a satisfactory performance within the environmental domain. Corporate social reporting would appear to be one of the mechanisms by which the organisations satisfy (and manipulate) that requirement.

In relation to trends found in regard to health and safety disclosures Gray, Kouhy and Lavers (p. 65) stated:

> We are persuaded that companies were increasingly under pressure from various 'relevant publics' to improve their performance in the area of health and safety and employed corporate social reporting to manage this 'legitimacy gap'. That is, while the disclosure did not, as such, demonstrate improved health and safety records (lack of previous information makes such assessment impossible), it did paint a picture of increasing concern being given by companies to the matter of protecting and training their workforce. This disclosure then helped add to the image of a competent and concerned organisation which took its responsibilities in this field seriously. As such, health and safety disclosure appears to be a strong illustration of Lindblom's second legitimation strategy—'changing perceptions'.

Deegan, Rankin and Voght (2000) also used Legitimacy Theory to explain how the social disclosures included within the annual reports of companies in selected industries changed around the time of major social incidents or disasters that could be directly related to their particular industry. The results of this study were consistent with Legitimacy Theory and showed that companies did appear to change their disclosure policies following major company- and industry-related social incidents. The authors argued that 'the results highlight the strategic nature of voluntary social disclosures and are consistent with a view that management considers that annual report social disclosures are a useful device to reduce the effects upon a corporation of events that are perceived to be unfavourable to a corporation's image' (p. 127).

Deegan, Rankin and Tobin (2002) undertook a further longitudinal study examining disclosures on social and environmental issues in the annual reports of BHP (now BHP Billiton), a large Australian company, over the period 1983–97. This study demonstrated positive correlations between media attention for certain social and environmental issues (which was taken as a proxy for social concerns with these issues) and the volume of disclosures on these issues.

Applying Legitimacy Theory to financial (as opposed to social and environmental) disclosure practices, in a US study the choice of an accounting framework was deemed to be related to a desire to increase the legitimacy of an organisation. Carpenter and Feroz (1992) argued that the New York State's (government) decision to adopt generally accepted accounting procedures (GAAP) (as opposed to a method of accounting based on cash flows rather than accruals) was 'an attempt to regain legitimacy for the State's financial management practices' (p. 613). According to Carpenter and Feroz, New York State was in a financial crisis in 1975, with the result that many parties began to question the adequacy of the financial reporting practices of all the associated government units. To regain legitimacy, New York State elected to implement GAAP (which incorporates accruals-based accounting). As Carpenter and Feroz (pp. 635, 637) state:

> The state of New York needed a symbol of legitimacy to demonstrate to the public and the credit markets that the state's finances were well managed. GAAP, as an institutionalized legitimated practice, serves this purpose ... We argue that New York's decision to adopt GAAP was an attempt to regain legitimacy for the state's financial management practices. Challenges to the state's financial management practices, led by the state comptroller, contributed to confusion and concern in the municipal securities market. The confusion resulted in a lowered credit rating. To restore the credit rating, a symbol of legitimacy in financial management practices was needed.

It is debatable whether GAAP was the solution for the state's financial management problem. Indeed, there is strong evidence that GAAP did not solve the state's financial management problems.

New York needed a symbol of legitimacy that could be easily recognised by the public. In the realm of financial reporting, 'GAAP' is the recognised symbol of legitimacy.

According to Carpenter and Feroz, few people would be likely to oppose a system that was 'generally accepted'—general acceptance provides an impression of legitimacy. As they state (p. 632):

> In discussing whether to use the term 'GAAP' instead of 'accrual' in promoting the accounting conversion efforts, panel members argued that no one could oppose a system that is generally accepted. The name implies that any other accounting principles are not accepted in the accounting profession. GAAP is also seemingly apolitical.

As emphasised in this chapter, Legitimacy Theory proposes a relationship between corporate disclosures (and other corporate strategies) and community expectations, the view being that management reacts to community concerns and makes the necessary changes. But we are left with a question—how does management determine community expectations? There is evidence that management might rely on sources such as the media to determine community expectations. For example, Brown and Deegan (1998) investigated the relationship between the print media coverage given to various industries' environmental effects and the levels of annual report environmental disclosures made by a sample of firms within those industries. The basis of the argument was that the media can be particularly effective in driving the community's concern about the environmental performance of particular organisations, and where such concern is raised organisations will respond by increasing the extent of disclosure of environmental information within the annual report.

Brown and Deegan used the extent of media coverage given to a particular issue as a measure (or proxy) of community concern. They made explicit reference to Media Agenda Setting Theory. Media Agenda Setting Theory proposes a relationship between the relative emphasis given by the media to various topics and the degree of salience these topics have for the general public (Ader, 1995, p. 300).[9] In terms of causality, increased media attention is believed to lead to increased community concern for a particular issue. The media are not seen as mirroring public priorities; rather, they are seen as shaping them.[10] That is, Media Agenda Setting Theory posits that the media shapes public awareness, with the media agenda preceding public concern for particular issues (McCombs & Shaw, 1972). The view taken is that members of the public need the media to tell them how important an issue within the 'real world' is, as, for many issues, individuals do not learn this from available real-world cues. Neuman (1990) identifies a distinction between 'obtrusive' and 'unobtrusive' issues. He notes, for example, that inflation is seen as a 'classic example' of an obtrusive issue because the public would become aware of it every time they went to the supermarket and they do not need the media to report the official statistics to realise that this

9   For an explanation of Media Agenda Setting Theory, see McCombs and Shaw (1972), Zucker (1978), Eyal, Winter & DeGeorge (1981), Blood (1981), Mayer (1980), McCombs (1981) and Ader (1995).

10   An extreme but somewhat interesting view of the media's power of influence is provided by White (1973, p. 23). In relation to the United States, he states that 'the power of the press in America is a primordial one. It sets the agenda of public discussion; and this sweeping political power is unrestrained by any law. It determines what people will talk and think about—an authority that in other nations is reserved for tyrants, priests, parties and mandarins.'

issue affects their lives. Unobtrusive issues, on the other hand, would include foreign events (such as polluting activities undertaken at offshore locations, or workplace practices in remote factories) that cannot be experienced or known by the public without the media functioning as a conduit (Zucker, 1978; Neuman, 1990). It is argued that the media's agenda-setting effect is most apparent in relation to unobtrusive events. Using a joint consideration of Media Agenda Setting Theory and Legitimacy Theory, the arguments provided in Brown and Deegan (1998) can be summarised as:

1. Management uses the annual report as a tool to legitimise the ongoing operations of the organisation (from Legitimacy Theory).
2. Community concerns with the environmental performance of a specific firm (or, indeed, any aspect of corporate performance) in an industry will also impact on the disclosure strategies of firms across that industry (consistent with Patten (1992), who adopted Legitimacy Theory).
3. The media are able to influence community perceptions about issues such as the environment (from Media Agenda Setting Theory).
4. If management responds to community concerns, and if it is accepted that community concerns are influenced by media attention given to particular social and environmental issues, then we should find a relationship between the extent of disclosure of social and environmental issues within the annual report and the media attention given to those issues.

The results in Brown and Deegan (1998) indicate that, for the majority of the industries studied, higher levels of media attention (as determined by a review of a number of print media newspapers and journals) are significantly associated with higher levels of annual report environmental disclosures.

O'Donovan (1999) also considered the role of the media in shaping community expectations, and how corporate management responds to potentially damaging media attention. O'Donovan provides the results of interviews with senior executives from three large Australian companies (Amcor Ltd, BHP Billiton Ltd and ICI Australia Ltd). The executives confirmed that, from their perspective, the media does shape community expectations, and that corporate disclosure is one way to correct 'misperceptions held or presented by the media'. O'Donovan reproduced a number of statements made by the executives who were interviewed. These quotes included:

> If there was something that was given prominent press coverage, yes (news reports influence disclosure decisions). This year and last year we mentioned the ground water survey at Botany Bay as it attracted press coverage and was important to Sydney residents (Company C–Interviewee No. 1).
>
> The environmental issues that are covered in the annual report really try to address matters of current concern as depicted in the media. Shareholders then get an understanding on where our company stands on issues such as recycling, forestry, chlorine and greenhouse gases (Company A–Interviewee No. 2).

Within the context of companies that source their products from developing countries, Islam and Deegan (2008a) undertook a review of the social and environmental disclosure practices of two leading multinational sportswear and clothing companies, Nike and Hennès & Mauritz. Islam and Deegan found a direct relationship between the extent of global news media coverage of a critical nature being given to particular social issues relating to the industry, and the extent of social disclosure. In particular, they found that, once the news media started running a campaign that exposed poor working conditions and the use of child labour in developing countries, it appeared that the multinational companies then responded by making various disclosures identifying initiatives that were being undertaken to ensure that the companies did not source their products from factories that had abusive or unsafe working conditions or used child labour. Islam and Deegan found the evidence to be consistent with the view that the news media influenced the expectations of western consumers (consistent with Media Agenda Setting Theory), thereby causing a legitimacy problem for the companies. The companies then responded to the legitimacy crisis by providing disclosures within their annual report that particularly focused on the highlighted issue. Islam and Deegan showed that, prior to the time at which the news media started running stories about the labour conditions in developing countries (media attention to these issues appeared to begin in the early 1990s), there was a general absence of disclosures being made by the companies. This was despite the fact that evidence suggests that poor working conditions and the use of child labour existed in developing countries for many years prior to the newspapers beginning coverage of the issues. Islam and Deegan speculate that had the Western news media not run stories exposing the working conditions in developing countries—which created a legitimacy gap for the multinational companies—the multinational companies would have not embraced initiatives to improve working conditions, nor provided disclosures about the initiatives being undertaken in relation to working conditions.

In considering the proposed relationship between media attention, corporate legitimacy and corporate disclosure policies (or strategies), it is interesting to consider Accounting Headline 8.4, which provides information about how a high-profile radio announcer is able to influence the community to support particular organisations. It is alleged within the article that, in return for corporate sponsorship, the radio announcers would moderate their previous attacks on organisations. The article refers to earlier investigations that related to payments by banks to radio broadcasters which had the alleged effect of reducing the criticisms being directed towards the banking industry. The article also discusses an investigation in 2003 by the Australian Broadcasting Tribunal (ABT) into sponsorship deals between the radio station and the corporations Telstra and NRMA. Read the article and decide whether you think that what is being said is consistent with some of the arguments presented in this chapter. Do you think that the organisations involved might use the broadcaster in an attempt to win community support for their organisations, and would you consider that such a strategy would complement or be a substitute for disclosures within an annual report? Further, do you think that the revelations about the banks and Telstra's and the NRMA's sponsorship deals could damage the organisations' legitimacy?

A range of other studies have investigated managerial attitudes towards the role of corporate reporting in legitimation strategies. While Legitimacy Theory has been supported in many studies, there are some studies in which Legitimacy Theory has not been supported.[11] For example, Wilmshurst and Frost (2000) conducted a questionnaire survey among a sample of chief financial officers (CFOs) which asked the executives to rank the importance of various factors in environmental disclosure decisions. Wilmshurst and Frost then analysed environmental disclosures within the annual reports of the companies for whom their sample of CFOs worked, and found

---

11 As emphasised in Chapter 1, empirical testing of particular theories cannot always be expected to support those theories. There can be various reasons for this, including errors in measurement caused by the researchers, inappropriate definition and measurement of variables, biased representations being received from those being interviewed and so forth. Further, even if the researchers have undertaken their research in an appropriate and rigorous manner, theories about human behaviour cannot always be expected to provide perfect predictions of that behaviour—hence previously 'successful' theories might not be supported in some studies.

Australian, 11 December 2003

Laws, 2UE in the dock again over corporate sponsorship

ERROL SIMPER

Lots of things got said and written in March 2001 when Tony Bell's Southern Cross group surprised some in paying $90 million for the Sydney radio station 2UE. But of all the things that were said there may have been nothing more imprudent than Bell's own assertion that the cash-for-comment inquiry, which had consumed 2UE for the two previous years, had simply been a media 'beat-up'.

Bell, SC's managing director, may be about to find out if it was quite such a beat-up as he imagined. Just three years after the biggest scandal in Australian commercial broadcasting history—the Australian Broadcasting Authority's cash-for-comment probe concluded 2UE and its high-profile presenters, John Laws and Alan Jones, had breached the Broadcasting Services Act five times and commercial radio's registered code of practice on 90 occasions—the station's conduct will now be referred to the federal director of public prosecutions. Nobody has yet found 2UE guilty of anything but, in theory, it could cost Bell the 2UE licence. In practical terms, it could cost him fines of more than $1 million.

The emotion most industry insiders concede to at last week's ABT claims that Laws has breached sponsorship disclosure regulations a further 19 times over his more recent sponsorship arrangements with Telstra and the NRMA, is astonishment.

It's an understandable emotion. Because the authority's August 2000 cash-for-comment report didn't spare Laws or, for that matter, Jones, who has since moved to the rival 2GB. Put simply, the authority found payments from corporate entities to specific presenters had a direct influence on what they said on air about those companies. Placing strict sponsorship disclosure obligations on 2UE, the authority said paid agreements between Laws and the Australian Bankers' Association, the Road Transport Forum, Registered Clubs and Sydney's Star City Casino had illustrated 'a causal link between the existence of an agreement and the on-air conduct of Mr Laws'.

Hence the astonishment. Surely a seasoned campaigner such as Richard John Sinclair Laws, 68, wouldn't go out there and do it all over again? Well, Laws's conscience appears to be clear. He told the *Australian's* Jane Schulze in the immediate wake of the latest ABA finding: 'Most of the 19 complaints are because I have said they are sponsors of ours [2UE's] rather than sponsors of mine, or because I said they were sponsors and not major sponsors. To me that doesn't seem to make much difference.'

But several media lawyers and academics disagree strongly with Laws's view that it 'doesn't make much difference'. Many believe that indicating a company 'sponsors' a radio station could, and probably would be, taken by many listeners to mean the company was an advertiser. But a sponsor of an individual presenter might, in view of the cash-for-comment inquiry findings, ring very different bells. It might also lead to a question: Why would a company want to pay both

a station, for advertising, as well as a presenter? Perhaps nothing provides a more comprehensive answer than the leaked letter—revealed via ABC television's Media Watch by its then presenter, Richard Ackland—which precipitated the cash-for-comment investigation. Outlining an agreement for the Australian Bankers' Association to pay $1.35 million to 2UE (of which $500,000 was earmarked for Laws himself) the association's then chief executive, Tony Aveling, wrote: 'The objective [in paying out the $1.35 million] is to reduce the negative comments about banks by John Laws from the present average of four a week to nil, concurrently to receive positive comments from Mr Laws [augmenting paid advertising] and, by doing so, to shift Australians' perceptions of—and attitudes toward—banks.'

No one is here suggesting Laws has had such a blatant agreement with Telstra or NRMA. Yet the letter clearly demonstrates the corporate mindset: if they're paid handsomely enough, on-air presenters will cease to be commentators. They'll effectively become propagandists for a corporate paymaster.

Telstra's willingness to pay Laws more than $100,000 a year for his 'personal endorsement' was revealed, amid a bit of legal huffing and puffing, in September 2002 by the *Australian's* Geoff Elliott. Telstra moved after Laws had attacked the federal Government as 'obsessed' with Telstra's privatisation, the desirability of which Laws seemed, at the time, to question.

(p. 22) 'the influences of the competitor response to environmental issues and customer concerns to have predictive power'. This provided 'limited support for the applicability of Legitimacy Theory'.

O'Dwyer (2002) interviewed twenty-nine senior executives from twenty-seven large Irish companies and found that managerial motives for engaging in corporate social and environmental reporting were only sometimes consistent with a Legitimacy Theory explanation. This was despite many managers perceiving clear threats to their organisations' legitimacy in the eyes of a range of powerful stakeholders. O'Dwyer states (p. 416) that detailed and close questioning revealed:

> ... an overwhelming perception of CSD [corporate social disclosure] as an unsuccessful legitimation mechanism. Therefore, while CSD is sometimes perceived as being employed as part of a legitimacy process, its employment in this manner is ultimately viewed as failing to aid in securing a state of legitimacy for organisations. Furthermore, despite the predominant view [among senior managers] that CSD is incapable of facilitating the achievement of a state of legitimacy, research into the CSD practices [of the companies interviewed] subsequent to the interviews ... reveals that many of the interviewees' companies continue to engage in some form of CSD. In conjunction with the interviewees' perspectives, this questions the pervasive explanatory power of Legitimacy Theory with respect to the motives for CSD when considered in the Irish context.

Conversely, in a different interview-based study which discussed a range of hypothetical situations with a sample of six managers, O'Donovan (2002) found support for Legitimacy Theory.

While a great deal of legitimising activity might be at a corporate level, some will also be taken at an industry level, thereby attempting to bring legitimacy to the industry in general. For example, Deegan and Blomquist (2006)—referred to earlier in the chapter—provided evidence that the Australian minerals industry developed its industry-wide environmental management code so as to bring legitimacy to the industry generally. For example, one of the senior executives of the Australian Minerals Council who was involved with the development of the code stated:

> It [the Code] was really developed in response to, I guess at the time, general concern about the performance of Australian mining companies overseas primarily but also within Australia, because we'd had things like Ok Tedi and the North Parks bird kill.[12] I think there was a tailings spill as well, so just general concern and a recognition from the Minerals Council that those concerns were probably at least in part legitimate, and that the industry did need to improve its approach to environmental management, and the Code was a response to that.

Before concluding the discussion of Legitimacy Theory, it needs to be appreciated that if a company makes disclosures because of concerns about its legitimacy then the disclosures are effectively being motivated by survival or profitability considerations rather than by a desire to demonstrate greater accountability. That is, there is much evidence to suggest that many corporate disclosures are a 'legitimation device and not an accountability mechanism' (Gray & Bebbington, 2000, p. 16). As Deegan, Rankin and Tobin (2002) state in relation to corporate social and environmental disclosure:

---

12 Briefly, reference to Ok Tedi refers to the ongoing operations, with which BHP Ltd (which subsequently became BHP Billiton Ltd) was associated, that caused significant environmental damage to rivers within Papua New Guinea over many years due to releases from tailings dams associated with mining activities. The damage received much adverse publicity within Australia, and elsewhere, over a number of years.

Legitimising disclosures are linked to corporate survival. In jurisdictions such as Australia, where there are limited regulatory requirements to provide social and environmental information, management appear to provide information when they are coerced into doing so. Conversely, where there is limited concern, there will be limited disclosures. The evidence in this paper, and elsewhere, suggests that higher levels of disclosure will only occur when community concerns are aroused, or alternatively, until such time that specific regulation is introduced to eliminate managements' disclosure discretion. However, if corporate legitimising activities are successful then perhaps public pressure for government to introduce disclosure legislation will be low and managers will be able to retain control of their social and environmental reporting practices.

DISTINGUISHING LEGITIMACY THEORY FROM POSITIVE ACCOUNTING THEORY

Some writers have suggested that the propositions generated by Legitimacy Theory (that annual report disclosure practices can be used in a strategic manner to manage an organisation's relations with the community in which it operates) are very similar to the propositions generated by the political cost hypothesis that is developed through Positive Accounting Theory (discussed in Chapter 7).[13] While there are some similarities, Legitimacy Theory relies on the central notion of an organisation's 'social contract' with society and predicts that management will adopt particular strategies (including reporting strategies) in a bid to assure the society that the organisation is complying with the society's values and norms (which are predicted to change over time). Unlike Positive Accounting Theory, Legitimacy Theory does not rely on the economics-based assumption that all action is driven by individual self-interest (tied to wealth maximisation) and it emphasises how the organisation is part of the social system in which it operates. Also, unlike Positive Accounting Theory, Legitimacy Theory makes no assumptions about the efficiency of markets such as the capital market and the market for managers.

STAKEHOLDER THEORY

We now turn to Stakeholder Theory. It has both an ethical (moral) or normative branch (which is also considered as prescriptive) and a positive (managerial) branch.[14] The ethical branch is considered first, followed by the positive (managerial) branch, which explicitly considers various groups (of stakeholders) that exist in society, and how the expectations of particular stakeholder

---

13 As Chapter 7 indicates, Positive Accounting Theory proposes that managers are motivated to undertake actions that will maximise their own wealth. To the extent that mechanisms have been put in place to align the interests of the managers with the goals of maximising the value of the organisation, the manager will adopt those accounting and disclosure methods that minimise the wealth transfers away from the organisation—wealth transfers that might be due to various political processes.

14 Stakeholder Theory itself is a confusing term. Many different researchers have stated that they have used Stakeholder Theory in their research, yet when we look at the research we see that different theories with different aims and assumptions have been employed—and all have been labelled 'Stakeholder Theory'. As Hasnas (1998, p. 26) states, 'stakeholder theory is somewhat of a troublesome label because it is used to refer to both an empirical theory of management and a normative theory of business ethics, often without clearly distinguishing between the two'. More correctly, perhaps, we can think of the term 'Stakeholder Theory' as an umbrella term that actually represents a number of alternative theories that address various issues associated with relationships with stakeholders, including considerations of the rights of stakeholders, the power of stakeholders or the effective management of stakeholders.

groups may have more (or less) impact on corporate strategies. This in turn has implications for how the stakeholders' expectations are considered or managed.

In the discussion that follows, we see that there are many similarities between Legitimacy Theory and Stakeholder Theory, and, as such, to treat them as two totally distinct theories would be incorrect. As Gray, Kouhy and Lavers (1995, p. 52) state:

> It seems to us that the essential problem in the literature arises from treating each as competing theories of reporting behaviour, when 'stakeholder theory' and 'legitimacy theory' are better seen as two (overlapping) perspectives of the issue which are set within a framework of assumptions about 'political economy'.

As Deegan (2002, p. 295) indicates, both theories conceptualise the organisation as part of a broader social system wherein the organisation impacts on, and is affected by, other groups within society. While Legitimacy Theory discusses the expectations of society in general (as encapsulated within the 'social contract'), Stakeholder Theory provides a more refined resolution by referring to particular groups within society (stakeholder groups). Essentially, Stakeholder Theory accepts that, because different stakeholder groups will have different views about how an organisation should conduct its operations, there will be various social contracts 'negotiated' with different stakeholder groups, rather than one contract with society in general. While implied within Legitimacy Theory, the managerial branch of Stakeholder Theory explicitly refers to issues of stakeholder power, and how stakeholders' relative power affects their ability to 'coerce' the organisation into complying with the stakeholders' expectations.

Hence, as already stated, this chapter treats Legitimacy Theory and Stakeholder Theory as largely overlapping theories that provide consistent but slightly different insights into the factors that motivate managerial behaviour (Gray, Kouhy & Lavers, 1995; O'Donovan, 2002). Differences between the theories largely relate to issues of resolution; Stakeholder Theory focuses on how an organisation interacts with particular stakeholders, while Legitimacy Theory considers interactions with 'society' as a whole. A consideration of both theories is deemed to provide a fuller explanation of management's actions. As Gray, Kouhy and Lavers (1995, p. 67) state in relation to social disclosure-related research:

> The different theoretical perspectives need not be seen as competitors for explanation but as sources of interpretation of different factors at different levels of resolution. In this sense, legitimacy theory and stakeholder theory enrich, rather than compete for, our understandings of corporate social disclosure practices.

It should be noted, however, that some researchers (for example, Nasi et al., 1997; Suchman, 1995) maintain that the theories are more discrete in nature than this chapter, and some others, assume. For example, Nasi et al. (p. 296) argue that although the perspectives 'are not precisely competing, each leads to a different general prediction regarding the likelihood and evolution of a corporate response in the face of a social issue'. They further state (p. 303) that 'although the perspectives agree on the need and reality of issues management activities, they disagree on the nature of the issues management and on managerial motivation for the issues management'.

THE ETHICAL BRANCH OF STAKEHOLDER THEORY

The moral or ethical (also referred to as the 'normative') perspective of Stakeholder Theory argues that all stakeholders have the right to be treated fairly by an organisation, and that issues of stakeholder power are not directly relevant. That is, the impact of the organisation on the life experiences of a stakeholder should be what determines the organisation's responsibilities to that stakeholder, rather than the extent of that stakeholder's (economic) power over the organisation. As Hasnas (1998, p. 32) states:

> When viewed as a normative (ethical) theory, the stakeholder theory asserts that, regardless of whether stakeholder management leads to improved financial performance, managers should manage the business for the benefit of all stakeholders. It views the firm not as a mechanism for increasing the stockholders' financial returns, but as a vehicle for coordinating stakeholder interests, and sees management as having a fiduciary relationship not only to the stockholders, but to all stakeholders. According to the normative stakeholder theory, management must give equal consideration to the interests of all stakeholders and, when these interests conflict, manage the business so as to attain the optimal balance among them. This of course implies that there will be times when management is obliged to at least partially sacrifice the interests of the stockholders to those of the other stakeholders. Hence, in its normative form, the stakeholder theory does imply that business has true social responsibilities.

Within the ethical branch of Stakeholder Theory there is a view that stakeholders have intrinsic rights (for example, to safe working conditions and fair pay), and that these rights should not be violated.[15] That is, each group of stakeholders merits consideration for its own sake and not merely because of its ability to further the interests of some other group, such as the shareholders (Donaldson & Preston, 1995, p. 66). As Stoney and Winstanley (2001, p. 608) explain, fundamental to the ethical branch of Stakeholder Theory is a:

> concern for the ethical treatment of stakeholders which may require that the economic motive of organizations—to be profitable—be tempered to take account of the moral role of organizations and their enormous social effects on people's lives.

Obviously, a normative discussion of stakeholder rights requires some definition of stakeholders. One definition of stakeholders that we can use is that provided by Freeman and Reed (1983, p. 91):

> Any identifiable group or individual who can affect the achievement of an organisation's objectives, or is affected by the achievement of an organisation's objectives.

Interestingly, this definition of stakeholders is very similar to the definition of 'key stakeholders' used by BHP Billiton. In the BHP Billiton *Sustainability Report* 2008 it is stated (p. 31):

> Key stakeholders are generally identified as people who are adversely or positively impacted by our operations, those who have an interest in what we do, or those who have an influence on what we do.

---

15 This perspective can be contrasted with that provided in Friedman (1962). He states: 'few trends could so thoroughly undermine the very foundation of our free society as the acceptance by corporate officials of a social responsibility other than to make as much money for their stockholders as possible. This is a fundamentally subversive doctrine' (p. 133).

Clearly, many people (or organisations) can be classified as stakeholders if the above definitions are applied (for example, shareholders, creditors, government, media, employees, employees' families, local communities, local charities, future generations and so on). With this in mind, Clarkson (1995) sought to divide stakeholders into primary and secondary stakeholders. A primary stakeholder was defined as 'one without whose continuing participation the corporation cannot survive as a going concern' (p. 106). Secondary stakeholders were defined as 'those who influence or affect, or are influenced or affected by, the corporation, but they are not engaged in transactions with the corporation and are not essential for its survival' (p. 107). According to Clarkson, primary stakeholders are the ones that must primarily be considered by management, because for the organisation to succeed in the long run it must be run for the benefit of all primary stakeholders. Clarkson's definition of primary stakeholders would be similar to the definition of stakeholders applied by many researchers working within a managerial perspective of Stakeholder Theory, but this focus on primary stakeholders would be challenged by proponents of the ethical branch of Stakeholder Theory–who would argue that all stakeholders have a right to be considered by management.

The broader ethical (and normative) perspective that all stakeholders (both primary and secondary) have certain minimum rights that must not be violated can be extended to a notion that all stakeholders also have a right to be provided with information about how the organisation is affecting them (perhaps through pollution, community sponsorship, provision of employment safety initiatives, and so on), even if they choose not to use the information, and even if they cannot directly have an impact on the survival of the organisation (see, for example, O'Dwyer, 2005).

In regards to the notion of rights to information, consider Gray, Owen and Adams' (1996) perspective of accountability as used within their 'accountability model'. They define accountability (1996, p. 38) as:

> The duty to provide an account (by no means necessarily a financial account) or reckoning of those actions for which one is held responsible.

According to Gray, Owen and Adams, accountability involves two responsibilities or duties:

1. the responsibility to undertake certain actions (or to refrain from taking actions); and
2. the responsibility to provide an account of those actions.

Under their accountability model, reporting is assumed to be responsibility-driven rather than demand-driven. The view being projected is that people in society have a right to be informed about certain facets of the organisation's operations.[16] By considering rights, it is argued that the model avoids the problem of considering users' needs and how such needs are established (Gray, Owen & Maunders, 1991). Applying the accountability model to corporate social reporting, Gray, Owen and Maunders (p. 15) argue that:

---

16 Within the model they refer to society as the 'principal' and the organisation (that owes the accountability) as the 'agent'. However, according to Gray, Owen and Maunders (1991, p. 17), their 'principal—agent model must be distinguished from "agency theory" or "economic principal—agent theory" as employed in, for example, Jensen and Meckling (1976), Ronen (1979), Fellingham and Newman (1979), Jensen (1983, 1993), Watts and Zimmerman (1986). Economic agency theory is grounded in neo-classical economics and takes its assumptions from it. Most significant among these are the assumptions about the single-minded greed of the principal and agent who are actively seeking to gain at the other's expense. The principal—agent model we are using makes no such assumptions and adopts no assumptions from economics, but rather owes its genesis to jurisprudence (Macpherson, 1973)'.

... the role of corporate social reporting is to provide society-at-large (the principal) with information (accountability?) about the extent to which the organisation (the agent) has met the responsibilities imposed upon it (has it played by the rules of the game?).

That is, the role of a corporate report is to inform society about the extent to which actions for which an organisation is deemed to be responsible have been fulfilled. Under the accountability model, the argument is that the principal (society) can elect to be entirely passive with regard to its demand for information. Nevertheless the agent (the organisation) is still required to provide an account—the passive, non-demanding principal is merely electing not to use the information directly. Gray, Owen and Maunders state (p. 6) that 'if the principal chooses to ignore the account, this is his prerogative and matters not to the agent who, nevertheless, must account'.

Hurst (1970) also emphasises the importance of accountability. He states (p. 58) that 'an institution which wields practical power—which compels men's wills or behaviour—must be accountable for its purposes and its performance by criteria not in the control of the institution itself'. The need to demonstrate accountability has also been stressed by the Research and Policy Committee of the Committee for Economic Development (a US-based organisation). The committee states (1974, p. 21) that 'the great growth of corporations in size, market power, and impact on society has naturally brought with it a commensurate growth in responsibility; in a democratic society, power sooner or later begets equivalent accountability'.

Gray, Owen and Adams (1996) make use of the concept of the social contract to theorise about the responsibilities of business (against which there is a perceived accountability). Under their perspective they also perceive the law as providing the explicit terms of the social contract, while other non legislated societal expectations embody the implicit terms of the contract.

In considering the normative perspectives of how organisations should behave with respect to their stakeholders (relating to intrinsic rights, including rights to information), it should be noted that these perspectives pertain to how the respective researchers believe organisations should act, which is not necessarily going to be the same as how they actually do act.[17] Hence, the various perspectives cannot be validated or confirmed by empirical observation—as might be the case if the researchers were providing descriptive or predictive (positive) theories about organisational behaviour. As Donaldson and Preston (1995, p. 67) state:

In normative uses, the correspondence between the theory and the observed facts of corporate life is not a significant issue, nor is the association between stakeholder management and conventional performance measures a critical test. Instead a normative theory attempts to interpret the function of, and offer guidance about, the investor-owned corporation on the basis of some underlying moral or philosophical principles.

Although there are researchers who promote a perspective that all stakeholders should be considered as important in their own right, irrespective of the resources they individually control, this ethical or moral view is not necessarily embraced by all. For example, the Chamber of Commerce and Industry of Western Australia (2005) in its submission to the 2005 Australian

---

17 Nevertheless, Donaldson and Preston (1995) argue that observation suggests that corporate decisions are frequently made on the basis of ethical considerations, even when doing so could not enhance corporate profit or shareholder gain. According to Donaldson and Preston, such behaviour is deemed to be not only appropriate but desirable. They argue that corporate officials are not less morally obliged than any other citizens to take ethical considerations into account, and it would be unwise social policy to preclude them from doing so.

Government Inquiry on Corporate Social Responsibility stated:

> Stakeholder views and practices should be accommodated only so far as they improve or safeguard shareholder value.

In another submission to the same inquiry, the Business Council of Australia (2005) stated:

> The litmus test for any activity or responsibility is whether the performance of that activity or responsibility can reasonably be seen to be contributing to the growth of the shareholder value.

Rather than embracing the ethical branch of Stakeholder Theory, the parties making the above comments would appear to embrace a perspective consistent with the managerial branch of Stakeholder Theory.

THE MANAGERIAL BRANCH OF STAKEHOLDER THEORY

We now turn to perspectives of Stakeholder Theory that attempt to explain when corporate management will be likely to attend to the expectations of particular (typically powerful) stakeholders. According to Gray, Owen and Adams (1996), this alternative perspective tends to be more 'organisation centred'. Gray, Owen and Adams (1996, p. 45) state:

> Here (under this perspective), the stakeholders are identified by the organisation of concern, by reference to the extent to which the organisation believes the interplay with each group needs to be managed in order to further the interests of the organisation. (The interests of the organisation need not be restricted to conventional profit-seeking assumptions.) The more important the stakeholder to the organisation, the more effort will be exerted in managing the relationship. Information is a major element that can be employed by the organisation to manage (or manipulate) the stakeholder in order to gain their support and approval, or to distract their opposition and disapproval.

Unlike the ethical branch of Stakeholder Theory, such (organisation-centred) theories can and are often tested by way of empirical observation.

As mentioned earlier, within Legitimacy Theory the audience of interest is typically defined as the society. Within a descriptive managerial branch of Stakeholder Theory the organisation is also considered to be part of the wider social system, but this perspective of Stakeholder Theory specifically considers the different stakeholder groups within society and how they should best be managed if the organisation is to survive (hence we call it a 'managerial' perspective of Stakeholder Theory).[18] Like Legitimacy Theory, it is considered that the expectations of the various stakeholder groups will impact on the operating and disclosure policies of the organisation. The organisation will not respond to all stakeholders equally (from a practical perspective, they probably cannot), but rather will respond to those stakeholders that are deemed to be 'powerful' (Bailey, Harte & Sugden, 2000; Buhr, 2002). Nasi et al. (1997) build on this perspective to suggest that the most powerful stakeholders will be attended to first. This is consistent with Wallace (1995, p. 87), who

---

18 By comparison, Donaldson and Preston (1995) refer to the instrumental perspective of Stakeholder Theory in which the principal focus of interest is the proposition that corporations practising stakeholder management will be relatively successful in conventional performance terms. This is obviously similar to our 'managerial' perspective of Stakeholder Theory.

argues that 'the higher the group in the stakeholder hierarchy, the more clout they have and the more complex their requirements will be'.

A stakeholder's (for example, owner's, creditor's or regulator's) power to influence corporate management is viewed as a function of the stakeholder's degree of control over resources required by the organisation (Ullman, 1985). The more critical the stakeholder's resources are to the continued viability and success of the organisation, the greater the expectation that the stakeholder's demands will be addressed. A successful organisation is considered to be one that satisfies the demands (sometimes conflicting) of the various powerful stakeholder groups.[19] In this respect Ullman (1985, p. 2) states:

> ... our position is that organisations survive to the extent that they are effective. Their effectiveness derives from the management of demands, particularly the demands of interest groups upon which the organisation depends.

Power in itself will be stakeholder-organisation specific, but may be tied to such things as command of limited resources (finance, labour), access to influential media, ability to legislate against the company or ability to influence the consumption of the organisation's goods and services. The behaviour of various stakeholder groups is considered a constraint on the strategy that is developed by management to match corporate resources as best it can with its environment.

Some researchers have considered stakeholder power in conjunction with other stakeholder attributes. For example, Mitchell, Agle and Wood (1997) provide a framework to identify stakeholders according to the relative importance of each type of stakeholder in terms of an organisation meeting its objectives. They argue that there are three features of a stakeholder that need to be considered, these being power, legitimacy and urgency. *Power* refers to the extent that a stakeholder can exert its influence on the organisation. A stakeholder has *legitimacy* when its demands conform to the norms, values and beliefs of the wider community. *Urgency* is the extent to which stakeholder demands require immediate attention from a firm. The greater the extent to which organisations believe that stakeholders possess these three attributes, the greater their importance to an organisation. Building on this perspective, Parthiban, Bloom and Hillman (2007) also found that organisations are more likely to respond to the expectations of stakeholders with power, legitimacy and urgency.

Freeman (1984) discusses the dynamics of stakeholder influence on corporate decisions. A major role of corporate management is to assess the importance of meeting stakeholder demands in order to achieve the strategic objectives of the firm. Further, as Friedman and Miles (2002) also point out, the expectations and power relativities of the various stakeholder groups can change over time. Organisations must therefore continually adapt their operating and disclosure strategies. Roberts (1992, p. 598) states:

> A major role of corporate management is to assess the importance of meeting stakeholder demands in order to achieve the strategic objectives of the firm. As the level of stakeholder power increases, the importance of meeting stakeholder demands increases also.

---

19 In considering the managerial perspective of Stakeholder Theory, Hasnas (1998, p. 32) states: 'when viewed as an empirical theory of management designed to prescribe a method for improving a business's performance, the stakeholder theory does not imply that business has any social responsibilities.'

If we accept the view that a 'good' management is one that can successfully attend to various and sometimes conflicting demands of various (important) stakeholder groups, then we might, consistent with Evan and Freeman (1988), actually redefine the purpose of the firm. According to Evan and Freeman (1988), 'the very purpose of the firm is, in our view, to serve as a vehicle for coordinating stakeholders. It is through the firm that each stakeholder group makes itself better off through voluntary exchanges' (p. 82).

As indicated above, as the level of stakeholder power increases, the importance of meeting stakeholder demands increases. Some of this demand may relate to the provision of information about the activities of the organisation. According to a number of writers, for example Ullman (1985) and Friedman and Miles (2002), the greater the importance to the organisation of the respective stakeholder's resources/support, the greater the probability that the particular stakeholder's expectations will be incorporated into the organisation's operations. From this perspective, various activities undertaken by organisations, including public reporting, will be directly related to the expectations of particular stakeholder groups. Furthermore, organisations will have an incentive to disclose information about their various programs and initiatives to the respective stakeholder groups to indicate clearly that they are conforming with those stakeholders' expectations. Organisations must necessarily balance the expectations of the various stakeholder groups. Unerman and Bennett (2004) are among others who argue that as these expectations and power relativities can change over time, organisations must continually adapt their operating and reporting behaviours accordingly.

Within the managerial perspective of Stakeholder Theory, information (including financial accounting information and information about the organisation's social performance) 'is a major element that can be employed by the organisation to manage (or manipulate) the stakeholder in order to gain their support and approval, or to distract their opposition and disapproval' (Gray, Owen & Adams, 1996, p. 46). This is consistent with the legitimation strategies suggested by Lindblom (1994), as discussed earlier in the chapter. In relation to corporate social disclosures, Roberts (1992, p. 599) states:

> ... social responsibility activities are useful in developing and maintaining satisfactory relationships with stockholders, creditors, and political bodies. Developing a corporate reputation as being socially responsible through performing and disclosing social responsibility activities is part of a strategy for managing stakeholder relationships.[20]

EMPIRICAL TESTS OF STAKEHOLDER THEORY

Using Stakeholder Theory to test the ability of stakeholders to impact on corporate social responsibility disclosures, Roberts (1992) found that measures of stakeholder power and their related information needs could provide some explanation about levels and types of corporate social disclosures.

20 Again, we find that a large number of the accounting-related studies that use Stakeholder Theory (as with Legitimacy Theory) have researched issues associated with social and environmental disclosures. While these theories could be applied to financial disclosures, most researchers of financial accounting practices have, at least to date, tended to use other theories, such as Positive Accounting Theory. Issues associated with firms' capital structures have been studied from a Stakeholder Theory perspective by Barton, Hill and Sundaram (1989) and Cornell and Shapiro (1987).

Neu, Warsame and Pedwell (1998) also found support for the view that particular stakeholder groups can be more effective than others in demanding social responsibility disclosures. They reviewed the annual reports of a number of publicly traded Canadian companies operating in environmentally sensitive industries for the period 1982–91. A measure of correlation was sought between increases and decreases in environmental disclosure and the concerns held by particular stakeholder groups. The results indicated that the companies were more responsive to the demands or concerns of financial stakeholders and government regulators than to the concerns of environmentalists. They considered that these results supported a perspective that, where corporations face situations where stakeholders have conflicting interests or expectations, the corporations will elect to provide information of a legitimising nature to those stakeholders deemed to be more important to the survival of the organisation, while down-playing the needs or expectations of less 'important' stakeholders.

In another study that investigated how stakeholder power influences corporate disclosure decisions, Islam and Deegan (2008b) investigated the social and environmental disclosure practices of a major trade organisation operating within a developing country. Specifically, they investigated the social and reporting practices of the Bangladesh Garments and Manufacturing Enterprise Association (BGMEA). This organisation is authorised by the government in Bangladesh to provide export licences to garment manufacturers, thereby enabling local garment manufacturers to sell their products to foreign buyers, many of which are large multinational companies. Islam and Deegan interviewed senior executives from BGMEA. The executives indicated that the operating and disclosure policies of BGMEA and its member organisations were particularly influenced by the demands and expectations of multinational buying companies (such as Nike, Gap, Reebok, Hennes & Mauritz), the group they considered to be their most powerful stakeholders. The senior executives also stated that they believed that the demands and expectations of the multinational buying companies directly responded to the expectations of Western consumers, and that the expectations of Western consumers were influenced by the Western news media (consistent with Media Agenda Setting Theory, as discussed earlier). In this regard, the executives of BGMEA noted that, prior to the mid-1990s, multinational companies placed no requirements or restrictions on the Bangladesh manufacturing companies in relation to factory working conditions or the use of child labour. However, once the Western news media began running stories on the poor working conditions in 'sweatshop' factories and stories on the use of child labour, this caused concern for Western consumers, who started to boycott the products of the large multinational sportswear and clothing companies. The Western consumers were key stakeholders of the multinational companies. At this point the multinational companies started imposing operating and reporting requirements on suppliers in terms of their employee conditions and their use of child labour. Reflective of the changes in perceived pressures, and the resultant reactions of BMGEA and its members, one of the senior executives of BGMEA stated (Islam & Deegan, 2008b, p. 860):

> The 1990 multinational buyers only wanted product, no social compliances were required and no restriction was placed on the employment of child labour. Now multinational buying companies have changed their attitudes towards us, perhaps because of the pressures from western consumers. We had to change ourselves following buyers' requirements and to fit with global requirements and restrictions. Western consumers and human rights organisations pressured foreign buyers, and then foreign buyers pressured us.

Stakeholder Theory of the 'managerial' variety does not directly provide prescriptions about what information *should* be disclosed other than indicating that the provision of information, including information within an annual report, can, if thoughtfully considered, be useful to the continued operations of a business entity. Of course, if managers accept this view of the world, they would still be left with the difficult problem of determining who their most important (powerful) stakeholders were, and what their respective information demands were.[21]

As discussed, organisations typically have a multitude of stakeholders with differing expectations about how the organisation should operate. Read Accounting Headlines 8.5 and 8.6. Accounting Headline 8.5 is critical of banks in terms of the high levels of bank fees being charged on various accounts—with the fees amounting to $3 billion. A senior executive of the Australian Consumers' Association provides a view that the banks are 'gouging' customers and that banks are not being held accountable for their actions. Would the Australian Consumers' Association, in your view, be considered to be a powerful stakeholder, such that its concerns would be met by the banks reducing the level of their fees (adopting the managerial perspective of Stakeholder Theory)? How would this view be different if we were adopting a moral/ethical perspective of Stakeholder Theory? Accounting Headline 8.6 provides an example from the United Kingdom. It addresses the lack of accessibility of bank credit for lone-parent families and the impact this has in 'forcing' lone-parent families to use very high-interest non-bank forms of credit. As with Accounting Headline 8.5, would you consider lone parents or the charity One Parent Families to be powerful stakeholders, such that their concerns would be met by the banks (adopting the managerial perspective of Stakeholder Theory)? Again, how would this view be different if we were adopting a moral/ethical perspective of Stakeholder Theory?

The above discussion has separately considered the normative moral/ethical perspective of Stakeholder Theory and the managerial (power-based) perspective of Stakeholder Theory. By discussing the theories separately it could be construed that management might be either ethically/morally aware or solely focused on the survival of the organisation, whereas in practice there is likely to be a continuum of possible positions between these two absolute points. Considering the two perspectives separately will give a partial view only, as it is unlikely that the managers of any company will be at one or other of the absolute extremes of the continuum. Instead, the managers of many companies will arguably be driven by both ethical considerations and performance-based decisions—not just one or

---

21 Again it is emphasised that this will not always be an easy exercise. For example, and for the purpose of illustration (perhaps at an extreme), we may find that a company has elected to provide an elderly woman who lives in a modest house nearby with a report that details when coal dust can be expected to be released from the company's furnaces so that she can ensure that no washing is left out at this time. At face value such a person may not appear to be a powerful stakeholder and we as outsiders might question why the company provides such disclosures. However, we may find that the woman has a daughter who is a popular, high-profile radio personality who will readily complain on air, at some cost to the company in terms of community support, each time her mother's washing is covered with coal dust. Through her connections the elderly woman is a powerful stakeholder, and, to alleviate her problems, coal-dust release information is provided so that she can schedule her washing. In relation to this illustration, it should be noted that an ethical/moral view of stakeholder information rights would perhaps be that this person has a right to information regardless of the fact that her daughter works in the media.

Sydney Morning Herald, 21 May 2004

Banking fees rake in nearly $9 billion

MATT WADE

Households forked out a record $3 billion in bank fees last year, fuelled by an unprecedented credit-card binge.

The Reserve Bank's annual report on bank fees reveals that income from credit-card fees rose 38 per cent to $604 million almost a doubling in two years.

Deposit-keeping fees topped $1 billion for the first time, rising 15 per cent from 2002.

Banks now make nearly as much from credit-card fees as they do from home-lending fees.

'The continued rapid growth in credit-card spending, together with increases in annual membership fees and higher charges for overdrawn accounts, late payments and cash advances, contributed to banks' fee income from credit cards,' the Reserve Bank said.

The booming card fee income was in addition to credit-card interest-rate charges, which averaged more than 16 per cent.

Separate Reserve Bank figures yesterday showed total credit-card debt rose to a record $26.7 billion in March.

The RBA's fee report shows that last year total bank fees rose 12 per cent to $8.7 billion, $1 billion more than in 2002.

Households paid $1.08 billion in deposit-account-keeping fees in 2003, an average of more than $400 per household. 'Strong growth in fees from credit cards contributed most to the growth in 2003, with fee income from deposit accounts and housing loans also making substantial contributions,' the RBA said.

The average monthly bank account-servicing fee remained steady at $5.25 last year, after having risen by 162 per cent between 1995 and 2002.

The average fee for using another bank's ATM rose from $1.40 to $1.45, but the internet banking fee was steady at 25 cents.

Income from households grew more quickly but business still paid two-thirds of all banking fees—$5.6 billion—last year.

Yesterday consumer groups stepped up calls for greater regulation of bank fees.

The Australian Consumers' Association's finance policy officer, Catherine Wolthuizen, said the RBA figures showed banks were 'gouging' customers, especially with credit-card fees.

'This is another stark demonstration of how far the banks can go when a regulator won't hold them accountable,' she said.

The director of the Financial Services Consumer Policy Centre at the University of NSW, Chris Connolly, said bank fees were bound to force their way onto the election agenda.

'Consumers will look back over the past 10 years and say everyone has been too inactive about addressing bank fee increases,' he said.

Labor's financial services spokesman, Stephen Conroy, said the Howard Government's 'hands-off' approach had failed consumers.

'Fees on households have increased by 161 per cent since 1997,' Senator Conroy said. 'Over the same period inflation has averaged just 2.6 per cent.'

He said Labor would direct the Australian Competition and Consumer Commission to monitor bank fees and charges.

But the chief executive of the Australian Bankers' Association, David Bell, said the Reserve Bank's figures showed consumers were paying less for banking than they were in 1997.

'While households are paying more for fees on some products like transaction accounts, they are getting large savings from interest margin declines,' he said.

The RBA said falls in interest charges, especially for home loans, offset rising fee income, although bank customers who only had deposit accounts had missed out.

BANK FEES 2003

- Total bank fee income up 12 per cent to $8.7 billion.
- Total household fee income up 15 per cent to $3 billion.
- Credit card fee income up 38 per cent to $604 million.
- Deposit-account-keeping fee income up 15 per cent to $1.08 billion.
- Home loan fee income up 13 per cent to $680 million.
- Business fee income up 10 per cent to $5.6 billion.

the other. As Wicks (1996) argues, many people have embraced a conceptual framework in which ethical considerations and market considerations are seen as constituting a categorically and independent realism. Wicks argues that this view is unrealistic, since it implies that people cannot introduce 'moral imaginations when they act in the market

Give lone parents credit, banks told

PHILLIP INMAN

The Guardian, 11 January 2005, copyright Guardian News & Media Ltd 2005

Single parents struggling with debts are ill-served by the banking industry, which punishes them with high interest rates on loans or refuses to offer credit at all, pushing them into the arms of doorstep lenders, the charity One Parent Families said yesterday.

Despite large government subsidies through the tax credit system, which have improved the finances of single parents over the past four years, banks and other lenders continue to discriminate against them and force them to pay more for credit.

Almost half (48%) of single-parent families had been in arrears in the past year, compared with a quarter of two-parent families. Even those parents who choose to work often fail to rid themselves of short-term, costly debts. The incidence of debt among working lone parents is twice as high as among couples where one person is in work—14% compared to 7%, according to the report.

The charity said a 32-page report, *Personal Finance and One-Parent Families: The Facts,* revealed the wide-ranging problems faced by lone parents, who were more likely to use overdrafts, credit cards and personal loans than couples with children.

... banks had to do more to make basic bank accounts easier to open. Like other low-income groups, single parents will often be shy of opening a current account, fearing excessive surcharges for unapproved overdrafts or bounced cheques.

Most high-street banks have developed stripped-down current accounts—known as basic bank accounts—following demands by the Treasury that they support measures to end financial exclusion among poorer households. But low-income groups have criticised banks for doing little to promote them.

Ms Simpson said the Treasury should consider setting a target for the number of basic accounts to be opened by 2006. She said ministers should consider ways to persuade mainstream banks to lend small sums at low cost, attracting single parents away from doorstep lenders that charge between 50% and 190% interest on loan products.

world'. In terms of future research in Stakeholder Theory, Rowley (1998) provides some interesting advice. He states (p. 2):

> The blurring of normative and descriptive analysis is problematic for the field, however, dividing them into separate camps is equally hazardous. I believe that if our most challenging issues 10 years from now are to be different from today, we will need to collectively understand the complementary roles that normative and descriptive research play in our research questions. Like market and society we cannot think of one without the other.

Again, we are left with a view that particular theories (of accounting) can provide us with only a partial view, and hence it is sometimes useful to consider the insights provided by different theoretical perspectives. One additional systems-oriented theoretical perspective, which has only recently begun to be applied to an analysis of voluntary corporate reporting decisions, is Institutional Theory. Institutional Theory supports the determinant of legitimacy. This theory explains that organisations are faced with institutional pressures and, as a result of these pressures, organisations within a field tend to become similar in their forms and practices.

INSTITUTIONAL THEORY

Broadly speaking, Institutional Theory considers the forms organisations take and provides explanations for why organisations within a particular 'organisational field' tend to take on similar characteristics and form.[22] While a theory such as Legitimacy Theory discusses how particular disclosure strategies might be undertaken to gain, maintain or regain legitimacy, Institutional Theory explores how—at a broader level—particular organisational forms might be adopted in order to bring legitimacy to an organisation. According to Carpenter and Feroz (2001, p. 565):

> Institutional theory provides another lens through which to view economic resource dependency incentives for accounting rule choice. Institutional theory views organizations as operating within a social framework of norms, values, and taken-for-granted assumptions about what constitutes appropriate or acceptable economic behaviour (Oliver, 1997). According to Scott (1987), 'organizations conform [to institutional pressures for change] because they are rewarded for doing so through increased legitimacy, resources, and survival capabilities' (p. 498).

Institutional Theory has been developed within the management academic literature (more specifically, in organisational theory) since the late 1970s, by researchers such as Meyer and Rowan (1977), DiMaggio and Powell (1983), Powell and DiMaggio (1991) and Zucker (1977, 1987).

A major paper in the development of Institutional Theory was DiMaggio and Powell (1983). These authors investigated why there was such a high degree of similarity between organisations. Specifically, in undertaking their research they state (p. 148):

> We ask why there is such startling homogeneity of organizational forms and practices; and we seek to explain homogeneity, not variation. In the initial stages of their life cycle, organizational fields display considerable diversity in approach and form. Once a field becomes well established, however, there is an inexorable push towards homogenization.

According to DiMaggio and Powell, there are various forces operating within society that cause organisational forms to become similar. As they state (1983, p. 148):

> Once disparate organizations in the same line of businesses are structured into an actual field (as we shall argue, by competition, the state, or the professions), powerful forces emerge that lead them to become more similar to one another.

While Institutional Theory has become a major and powerful theoretical perspective within organisational analysis, it has also been adopted by some accounting researchers. Several management accounting researchers, such as Covaleski and Dirsmith (1988), Broadbent, Jacobs and Laughlin (2001) and Brignall and Modell (2000), have used Institutional Theory. It has also been used by some researchers who investigate aspects of audit, such as Rollins and Bremser (1997), and others who research aspects of the development and role of the accounting profession, such as Fogarty (1996). More directly related to financial accounting theory, Fogarty

---

22 DiMaggio and Powell (1983, p. 147) define an 'organisation field' as 'those organizations that, in the aggregate, constitute a recognized area of institutional life: key suppliers, resource and product consumers, regulatory agencies, and other organisations that produce similar services or products.

(1992) applied Institutional Theory to an analysis of the accounting standard-setting process. Dillard, Rigsby and Goodman (2004, p. 506) state that:

> Institutional theory is becoming one of the dominant theoretical perspectives in organization theory and is increasingly being applied in accounting research to study the practice of accounting in organizations.

A key reason why Institutional Theory is relevant to researchers who investigate voluntary corporate reporting practices is that it provides a complementary perspective, to both Stakeholder Theory and Legitimacy Theory, in understanding how organisations understand and respond to changing social and institutional pressures and expectations. Among other factors, it links organisational practices (such as accounting and corporate reporting) to the values of the society in which an organisation operates, and to a need to maintain organisational legitimacy. There is a view that organisational form and practices might tend towards some form of homogeneity—that is, the structure of the organisation (including the structure of its reporting systems) and the practices adopted by different organisations tend to become similar to conform to what society, or particular powerful groups, consider to be 'normal'. Organisations that deviate from being of a form that has become 'normal' or expected will potentially have problems in gaining or retaining legitimacy. As Dillard, Rigsby and Goodman (2004, p. 509) state:

> By designing a formal structure that adheres to the norms and behaviour expectations in the extant environment, an organization demonstrates that it is acting on collectively valued purposes in a proper and adequate manner.

Dillard, Rigsby and Goodman (p. 507) explain that Institutional Theory:

> ... concerns the development of the taken for granted assumptions, beliefs and values underlying organizational characteristics ... [with accounting-based studies] suggesting the importance of social culture and environment on the practice of accounting; the use of accounting practices as rationalizations in order to maintain appearances of legitimacy; and the possibilities of decoupling these rationalizing accounting practices from the actual technical and administrative processes.

Institutional Theory therefore provides an explanation of how mechanisms through which organisations may seek to align perceptions of their practices and characteristics with social and cultural values (in order to gain or retain legitimacy) become institutionalised in particular organisations. Such mechanisms could include those proposed by both Stakeholder Theory and Legitimacy Theory, but could conceivably also encompass a broader range of legitimating mechanisms. This is why these three theoretical perspectives should be seen as complementary rather than competing.

There are two main dimensions to Institutional Theory. The first of these is termed *isomorphism* while the second is termed *decoupling*. Both of these can be of central relevance to explaining voluntary corporate reporting practices.

Isomorphism is considered first. The term 'isomorphism' is used extensively within Institutional Theory, and DiMaggio and Powell (1983, p. 149) have defined it as 'a constraining process that forces one unit in a population to resemble other units that face the same set of environmental conditions'. That is, organisations that adopt structures or processes (such as reporting processes) that are at variance with other organisations might find that the differences attract criticism. Carpenter and Feroz (2001, p. 566) further state:

DiMaggio and Powell (1983) label the process by which organizations tend to adopt the same structures and practices as isomorphism, which they describe as a homogenization of organizations. Isomorphism is a process that causes one unit in a population to resemble other units in the population that face the same set of environmental conditions. Because of isomorphic processes, organizations will become increasingly homogeneous within given domains and conform to expectations of the wider institutional environment.

Dillard, Rigsby and Goodman (2004, p. 509) explain that 'Isomorphism refers to the adaptation of an institutional practice by an organisation'. As voluntary corporate reporting by an organisation is an institutional practice of that reporting organisation, the processes by which voluntary corporate reporting adapts and changes in that organisation are isomorphic processes.

DiMaggio and Powell (1983) set out three different isomorphic processes (processes whereby institutional practices such as voluntary corporate reporting adapt and change), referred to as *coercive isomorphism*, *mimetic isomorphism* and *normative isomorphism*. The first of these processes, *coercive isomorphism*, arises where organisations change their institutional practices because of pressure from those stakeholders upon whom the organisation is dependent (that is, this form of isomorphism is related to 'power'). According to DiMaggio and Powell (1983, p. 150):

Coercive isomorphism results from both formal and informal pressures exerted on organizations by other organizations upon which they are dependent and by cultural expectations in the society within which organizations function. Such pressures may be felt as force, as persuasive, or as invitations to join in collusion.

DiMaggio and Powell provide two general hypotheses that relate to coercive isomorphism:

Hypothesis 1: The greater the dependence of an organisation on another organisation, the more similar it will become to that organisation in structure, climate and behavioural focus.

Hypothesis 2: The greater the centralisation of organisation A's resource supply, the greater the extent to which organisation A will change isomorphically to resemble the organisations on which it depends for resources.

Coercive isomorphism is related to the managerial branch of Stakeholder Theory (discussed earlier), whereby a company will, for example, use 'voluntary' corporate reporting disclosures to address the economic, social, environmental and ethical values and concerns of those stakeholders who have the most power over the company. The company is therefore coerced (in this case usually informally) by its influential (or powerful) stakeholders into adopting particular voluntary reporting practices.

The idea of coercive isomorphism has been applied to various practices adopted by organisations. For example, applying coercive isomorphism to government's selection of accounting procedures, Carpenter and Feroz (2001, p. 571) state:

Other organizations that can provide resources, such as the credit markets, can exercise power over government entities. This power can be used to dictate the use of certain institutional rules—such as GAAP.

A company could be coerced into adapting its existing voluntary corporate reporting practices (including the issues on which it reports) to bring them into line with the expectations and demands of its powerful stakeholders (while possibly ignoring the expectations of less powerful stakeholders). Because these powerful stakeholders might have similar expectations of other organisations as well, there will tend to be conformity in the practices being adopted by different organisations—institutional practices will tend towards some form of uniformity. In relation to the ability to create change, Tuttle and Dillard (2007 p. 393) state:

> Change is imposed by an external source such as a powerful constituent (e.g., customer, supplier, competitor), government regulation, certification body, politically powerful referent groups, or a powerful stakeholder. The primary motivator is conformance to the demands of powerful constituents and stems from a desire for legitimacy as reflected in the political influences exerted by other members of the organisational field. These influences may be formal or informal and may include persuasion as well as invitations to collude. If the influencing group has sufficient power, change may be mandated.

In the mid-1990s there was a great deal of concern by Western consumers that multinational clothing companies were sourcing their products from developing countries where local supply factories were using child labour (Islam & Deegan, 2008b). As a result of pressure (coercive pressure) from consumers, the Western news media and various lobby groups, most organisations put in place processes to help in ensuring that supply factories did not use child labour.

It has also been argued that funding bodies such as the World Bank, which often lends funds for projects being undertaken in developing countries, has the power to coerce borrowers to adopt accounting and reporting rules that comply with its requirements. In this way, those entities that receive funding from the World Bank tend to adopt the same reporting practices—a case of coercive isomorphism. As Neu and Ocampo (2007, p. 367) state:

> These organizations [such as the World Bank] operate in a variety of different institutional fields thereby 'spanning' fields. They also possess the economic capital necessary both to enter distant fields and to facilitate the diffusion of specific practices. The economic capital of the World Bank and International Monetary Fund, as evidenced by their lending activities, provides them with the ability to encourage coercive isomorphism (DiMaggio & Powell, 1983) thereby changing the day-to-day practices of previously autonomous fields ... Contained within the loan agreements are requirements that borrower countries adopt and utilize specific accounting practices such as budgeting, auditing and financial reporting practices. In this way, the lending agreements facilitate the diffusion of accounting/financial practices across heterogeneous fields.

The second isomorphic process specified by DiMaggio and Powell (1983) is *mimetic isomorphism*. This involves organisations seeking to emulate (or copy) or improve upon the institutional practices of other organisations, often for reasons of competitive advantage in terms of legitimacy. In explaining mimetic isomorphism, DiMaggio and Powell (1983, p. 151) state:

> Uncertainty is a powerful force that encourages imitation. When organizational technologies are poorly understood, when goals are ambiguous, or when the environment creates symbolic uncertainty, organizations may model themselves on other organizations.

According to DiMaggio and Powell, when an organisation encounters uncertainty it might elect to model itself on other organisations. In providing an example of modelling (mimetic isomorphism), they state (p. 151):

One of the most dramatic instances of modelling was the effort of Japan's modernizers in the late nineteenth century to model new governmental initiatives on apparently successful western prototypes. Thus, the imperial government sent its officers to study the courts, Army, and police in France, the Navy and postal system in Great Britain, and banking and art education in the United States. American corporations are now returning the compliment by implementing (their perceptions of) Japanese models to cope with thorny productivity and personnel problems in their own firms. The rapid proliferation of quality circles and quality-of-work-life issues in American firms is, at least in part, an attempt to model Japanese and European successes. These developments also have a ritual aspect; companies adopt these 'innovations' to enhance their legitimacy, to demonstrate that they are at least trying to improve working conditions.

DiMaggio and Powell (1983) provide two general hypotheses that relate to mimetic isomorphism:

Hypothesis 3: The more uncertain the relationship between means and ends, the greater the extent to which an organisation will model itself after organisations it perceives to be successful.

Hypothesis 4: The more ambiguous the goals of an organisation, the greater the extent to which the organisation will model itself after organisations that it perceives to be successful.

Applying the idea of mimetic isomorphism to corporate social reporting, Unerman and Bennett (2004) explain:

Some institutional theory studies ... have demonstrated a tendency for a number of organisations within a particular sector to adopt similar new policies and procedures as those adopted by other leading organisations in their sector. This process, referred to as 'mimetic isomorphism', is explained as being the result of attempts by managers of each organisation to maintain or enhance external stakeholders' perceptions of the legitimacy of their organisation, because any organisation which failed (at a minimum) to follow innovative practices and procedures adopted by other organisations in the same sector would risk losing legitimacy in relation to the rest of the sector (Broadbent, Jacobs & Laughlin, 2001; Scott, 1995). Drawing on these observations, in the absence of any legislative intervention prescribing detailed mechanisms of debate, a key motivating force for many managers to introduce mechanisms allowing for greater equity in the determination of corporate responsibilities would therefore be their desire to maintain, or enhance, their own competitive advantage. They would strive to achieve this by implementing stakeholder dialogue mechanisms which their economically powerful stakeholders were likely to perceive as more effective than those used by their competitors. It is unlikely that these managers would readily embrace mechanisms designed to facilitate widespread participation in the determination of corporate responsibilities unless their economically powerful stakeholders expected the interests of economically marginalised stakeholders to be taken into account in this manner, and these managers are only likely to implement the minimum procedures that they feel their economically powerful stakeholders would consider acceptable.

The above argument links pressures for mimetic isomorphism with pressures underlying coercive isomorphism. Unerman and Bennett (2004) maintain that without coercive pressure from stakeholders it is unlikely that there would be pressure to mimic or surpass the social reporting practices (institutional practices) of other companies.

The final isomorphic process explained by DiMaggio and Powell (1983) is *normative isomorphism*. This relates to the pressures arising from group norms to adopt particular institutional practices. In the case of corporate reporting, the professional expectation that accountants will comply with accounting standards acts as a form of normative isomorphism for the organisations for whom accountants work to produce accounting reports (an institutional practice) that are shaped by accounting standards. In terms of voluntary reporting practices, normative isomorphic pressures could arise through less formal group influences from a range of both formal and informal groups to which managers belong—such as the culture and working practices developed within their workplace. These could produce collective managerial views in favour of or against certain types of reporting practices, such as collective managerial views on the desirability or necessity of providing a range of stakeholders with social and environmental information through the medium of corporate reports. DiMaggio and Powell provide two general hypotheses that relate to normative isomorphism:

Hypothesis 5: The greater the reliance on academic credentials in choosing managerial and staff personnel, the greater the extent to which an organisation will become like other organisations in its field.

Hypothesis 6: The greater the participation of organisational managers in trade and professional associations, the more likely the organisation will be, or will become, like other organisations in its field.

These two hypotheses stress that particular groups with particular training will tend to adopt similar practices (including reporting practices), otherwise they will appear to be out of line with their 'group'—which in itself might lead to formal or informal sanctions being imposed by 'the group' on those parties that deviate from the accepted or expected behaviour. As another example of normative isomorphism, Palmer, Jennings and Zhou (1993) found that chief executive officers (CEOs) who attended elite business schools were likely to adopt an approach to organising a business known as the multi-divisional form (MDF) of organisation (the organisation being separately organised into different product divisions). The multi-divisional form of organisation was taught as part of conventional wisdom in elite business schools. This emphasis was passed on to students who subsequently became CEOs. The actions of these similarly trained executives resulted in organisational similarity within specific types of organisational fields.

Having described the three forms of isomorphic processes (coercive, mimetic and normative isomorphism), it is interesting to note that such processes are not necessarily expected to make the organisations more efficient. As DiMaggio and Powell (1983, p. 153) state:

It is important to note that each of the institutional isomorphic processes can be expected to proceed in the absence of evidence that they increase internal organizational efficiency. To the extent that organizational effectiveness is enhanced, the reason will often be that organizations are rewarded for being similar to other organizations in their fields. This similarity can make it easier for organizations to transact with other organizations, to attract career-minded staff, to be acknowledged as legitimate and reputable, and to fit into administrative categories that define eligibility for public and private grants and contracts. None of this, however, insures that conformist organizations do what they do more efficiently that do their more deviant peers.

Related to the above point, Carpenter and Feroz (2001, p. 569) state:

Institutional theory assumes that organizations adopt structures and management practices that are considered legitimate by other organizations in their fields, regardless of their actual usefulness. Legitimated structures or practices can be transmitted to organizations in a field, through tradition (organization imprinting at founding), through imitation, by coercion, and through normative pressures ... Institutional theory is based on the premise that organizations respond to pressure from their institutional environments and adopt structures and/or procedures that are socially accepted as being the appropriate organizational choice ... Institutional techniques are not based on efficiency but are used to establish an organization as appropriate, rational, and modern ... By designing a formal structure that adheres to the prescription of myths in the institutional environment, an organization demonstrates that it is acting in a proper and adequate manner. Meyer and Rowan (1977) maintain that myths of generally accepted procedures—such as generally accepted accounting procedures (GAAP)—provide a defence against the perception of irrationality and enhanced continued moral and/or financial support from external resource providers.

Although three types of isomorphism have been described above, in practice it will not necessarily be easy to differentiate between the three. As Carpenter and Feroz (2001, p. 573) state:

DiMaggio and Powell (1983) point out that it may not always be possible to distinguish between the three forms of isomorphic pressure, and in fact, two or more isomorphic pressures may be operating simultaneously making it nearly impossible to determine which form of institutional pressure was more potent in all cases.

In applying the various notions of isomorphism embraced within Institutional Theory to accounting, the decision to disclose particular items of information may be more about 'show' (or 'form') than about 'substance'. As Carpenter and Feroz (2001, p. 570) state in relation to accounting practices adopted by government:

One manifestation of organizations in need of institutional legitimacy is the collecting and displaying of huge amounts of information that have no immediate relevance for actual decisions. Hence those state governments that have adopted GAAP, yet do not use GAAP information in making financial management decisions (e.g. budgetary decisions), may have adopted GAAP for purposes of institutional legitimacy.

Carpenter and Feroz (2001) used Institutional Theory to explain four US state governments' decisions to switch from a method of accounting based on recording cash flows to methods of accounting based on GAAP. In describing the results of their analysis, they state (p. 588):

Our evidence shows that an early decision to adopt GAAP can be understood in terms of coercive isomorphic pressures from credit markets, while late adopters seem to be associated with the combined influences of normative and mimetic institutional pressures ... The evidence presented in the case studies suggests that severe, prolonged financial stress may be an important condition affecting the potency of isomorphic pressures leading to an early decision to adopt GAAP for external financial reporting.

They further explain (p. 592):

All states were subject to normative isomorphic pressures from the accounting profession, coercive isomorphic pressures from the credit markets, and from the federal government to adopt GAAP from 1975 through 1984. Coercive isomorphic institutional pressures were significantly increased in 1984 with the passage of the *Single Audit Act* (SAA) and the formation of the Government Accounting Standards Board (GASB). Since it is likely that both normative and coercive isomorphic pressures act in concert to move state governments to GAAP adoption, it may be impossible to empirically distinguish the two forms of isomorphic pressure ... We note that all state governments were subject to potent institutional pressure to adopt GAAP after 1973. These institutional pressures were created by the federal government, professional accounting associations, and representatives of the credit markets. Thus state governments were subjected to at least two forms of isomorphic pressures: normative and coercive ... We predict that all state governments in the USA will eventually bow to institutional pressures for change and adopt GAAP for external financial reporting. Our prediction is based on insights from institutional theory, coupled with insight on the potency of the institutional pressures for change identified in our four case studies.

We will now turn our attention to the other dimension of Institutional Theory (other than isomorphism)—'decoupling'. Decoupling implies that while managers might perceive a need for their organisation to be seen to be adopting certain institutional practices, and might even institute formal processes aimed at implementing these practices, actual organisational practices can be very different from these formally sanctioned and publicly pronounced processes and practices. Thus, the actual practices can be decoupled from the institutionalised (apparent) practices. In terms of voluntary corporate reporting practices, this decoupling can be linked to some of the insights from Legitimacy Theory, whereby social and environmental disclosures can be used to construct an organisational image that might be very different from the actual organisational social and environmental performance. Thus, the organisational image constructed through corporate reports might be one of social and environmental responsibility when the actual managerial imperative is maximisation of profitability or shareholder value. As Dillard, Rigsby and Goodman (2004, p. 510) put it:

Decoupling refers to the situation in which the formal organizational structure or practice is separate and distinct from actual organizational practice. In other words, the practice is not integrated into the organization's managerial and operational processes [it is decoupled]. Formal structure has much more to do with the presentation of an organizational-self than with the actual operations of the organization (Curruthers, 1996). Ideally, organizations pursue economic efficiency and attempt to develop alignment between organizational hierarchies and activities. However, an organization in a highly institutionalized environment may face conflicts and inconsistencies between the demands for efficiency and the need to conform to 'ceremonial rules and myths' of the institutional context (Meyer and Rowan, 1977). In essence, institutionalized, rationalized elements are incorporated into the organization's formal management systems because they maintain appearances and thus confer legitimacy whether or not they directly facilitate economic efficiency.

In concluding this overview of Institutional Theory, some of the above points can be summarised by stating that there will be various forces that cause organisations to take on particular forms or adopt particular reporting practices. While theories such as Legitimacy Theory and Stakeholder Theory explain why managers might embrace specific strategies (such as making particular disclosures to offset the legitimacy-threatening impacts of particular events), Institutional Theory tends to take a broader macro view to explain why organisations take on particular forms or particular reporting practices. Institutional Theory also provides an argument that, while organisations might put in place particular processes, such processes might be more for 'show' than for influencing corporate conduct. In the discussion of Legitimacy Theory we saw how managers might undertake particular activities—such as disclosure activities—to alter perceptions of legitimacy. By contrast, researchers who adopt Institutional Theory typically embrace a view that managers are expected to conform with norms that are largely imposed on them. Nevertheless, it needs to be appreciated that there is much overlap between Institutional Theory, Legitimacy Theory and Stakeholder Theory.

CHAPTER SUMMARY

This chapter provides a number of perspectives about why management elects to make particular disclosures. Specifically, it reviews Legitimacy Theory, Stakeholder Theory and the newly emergent (in a financial reporting context) Institutional Theory—three theories that can be classified as systems-oriented theories. Systems-oriented theories see the organisation as being part of a broader social system.

Legitimacy Theory, Stakeholder Theory and Institutional Theory are all linked to Political Economy Theory, wherein the political economy constitutes the social, political and economic framework within which human life takes place and social, political and economic issues are considered as inseparable. Political Economy Theory can be classified as either classical or bourgeois. Bourgeois Political Economy Theory ignores various tensions within society and accepts the world as essentially pluralistic with no particular class dominating another. Legitimacy Theory and Stakeholder Theory adopt the bourgeois perspective. Institutional Theory can adopt either the bourgeois or classical perspective.

Legitimacy Theory relies on the notion of a social contract, which is an implied contract representing the norms and expectations of the community in which an organisation operates. An organisation is deemed to be legitimate to the extent that it complies with the terms of the social contract. Legitimacy and the right to operate are considered to go hand in hand. Accounting disclosures are considered to represent one way in which an organisation can legitimise its ongoing operations. Where legitimacy is threatened, disclosures are one strategy to restore legitimacy. In practice, policies to maintain or restore corporate legitimacy are sometimes articulated in terms of reputation risk management.

Two different categories of Stakeholder Theory have been reviewed, the ethical (or normative) branch and the managerial branch. The ethical branch of Stakeholder Theory discusses issues associated with rights to information, rights that should be met regardless of the power of the stakeholders involved. Within the ethical branch, disclosures are considered to be responsibility-driven. The managerial branch of Stakeholder Theory, on the other hand, predits that organisations will tend to satisfy the information demands of those stakeholders who are important to the organisation's ongoing survival. Whether particular stakeholders receive information will be dependent on how powerful they are perceived to be, with power often considered in terms of the scarcity of the resources controlled by the respective stakeholders. The disclosure of information is considered to represent an important strategy in managing stakeholders.

Institutional Theory provides a complementary, and partially overlapping, perspective to both Legitimacy Theory and Stakeholder Theory. It explains that managers will be subject to pressures to change, or adopt, certain voluntary corporate reporting practices. These pressures can be coercive, mimetic or normative, and the resulting institutional image can sometimes be more apparent than real.

QUESTIONS

8.1 Explain the notion of a social contract, and what relevance the social contract has with respect to the legitimacy of an organisation.

8.2 What is organisational legitimacy and why might it be considered to be a 'resource'?

8.3 Explain why organisational legitimacy is place- and time-specific.

8.4 What does the notion of legitimacy and social contract have to do with corporate disclosure policies?

8.5 How would corporate management determine the terms of the social contract (if this is indeed possible) and what would be the implications for a firm if it breached the terms of the contract?

8.6 If an organisation's management considered that the organisation might not have operated in accordance with community expectations (it broke the terms of the social contract), consistent with Legitimacy Theory, what actions would you expect management to undertake in the subsequent period?

8.7 If an organisation was involved in a major accident or incident, would you expect it to use vehicles such as an annual report to try to explain the incident? If so, explain how and why it would use the annual report in this way.

8.8 What is a 'legitimacy gap' and why could such a gap suddenly occur?

8.9 What is the difference between legitimising strategies that are 'symbolic' and those that are 'substantive'? Is one type more effective than the other?

8.10 Consistent with the material provided in this chapter, would you expect management to make disclosures in relation to real-world events, or, alternatively, in relation to how it believed the community perceived the real-world events? Why?

8.11 Legitimacy Theory, Stakeholder Theory and Institutional Theory are considered to be systems-oriented theories. What does this mean?

8.12 This chapter divided Stakeholder Theory into the ethical branch and the managerial branch. Explain the differences between the two branches in terms of the alternative perspectives about when information will, or should, be produced by an organisation.

8.13 Under the managerial perspective of Stakeholder Theory, when would we expect an organisation to meet the information demands of a particular stakeholder group?

8.14 Read Accounting Headline 8.6 on p. 356, an article that relates to claimed financial exclusion of some sectors of society. After reading the article:

(a) Apply the managerial perspective of Stakeholder Theory to explain whether management would care about the concerns of the charity One Parent Families.

(b) If we applied an ethical perspective of Stakeholder Theory, should management care?

(c) If society considered that the banks' policies were unreasonable, would you expect the banks to use their annual reports to defend their position (legitimacy)?

8.15 Read Accounting Headline 8.7 and, using Legitimacy Theory as the basis of your argument, explain why a company such as McDonald's would not want a radio station to make adverse comments about it. If the station does make adverse statements, how might McDonald's react from a corporate disclosure perspective?

Accounting Headline 8.7 The potential influence of the media on an organisation's perceived legitimacy

Australian, 22 July 1999, p. 1

Lay off Big Macs, radio boss tells staff

AMANDA MEADE

Top management at radio 2UE ordered the station's broadcaster not to make derogatory comments about McDonald's on air or the station would lose its $170,000 advertising account with the fast-food chain, according to a leaked internal memo.

The memo from program director John Brennan in February reveals for the first time that the practice of tailoring editorial comment to suit 2UE's advertisers is an integral part of the top-rating radio station's culture.

'It's going to be a tough year for revenue and we need all the help we can get from everyone concerned,' the management memo says.

'It is obviously imperative that no derogatory comments about McDonald's are made by any broadcaster on the station. Any such comment would see an immediate cancellation of the contract.'

The memo will be investigated by the Australian Broadcasting Authority's inquiry into the radio station next month.

Mr Brennan's directive appears to contravene the Commercial Radio Code of Practice, under which a radio station must promote accuracy and fairness in news and current affairs programs. The code may be reviewed by the ABA in separate public hearings and may result in moves away from self-regulation.

The memo contradicts public statements by 2UE chief John Conde this week about the role of station management in the scandal involving John Laws and the now-defunct $1.2 million deal with the Australian Bankers' Association.

The banks' deal with Laws also involved refraining from negative comments about the client on air.

McDonald's spokesman John Blyth said the company was unaware the 2UE directive had been issued and would never make its advertising contracts conditional on editorial comment.

The memo was addressed to Alan Jones, John Laws, John Stanley, Mike Carlton, Peter Bosly, Ray Hadley, Stan Zemanek and eight other on-air presenters.

Senior management was also party to the directive.

In a letter to the *Australian* yesterday, Mr Conde confirmed Mr Brennan wrote the memo, which had 'reflected (his) exuberance'. He said Mr Brennan had promptly clarified the memo, telling staff he only intended to avoid any announcer 'sending up' the McDonald's ads. 'It was made plain 2UE was not seeking to curtail editorial comment.'

In a separate statement, Mr Conde said 2UE and its affiliates were to receive $707,000 from the bank deal. Laws says his share was $300,000.

8.16 Read Accounting Headline 8.8 and, with the material of this chapter in mind, explain why (or perhaps, why not) the community needs to be protected from the media.

A democratic duty not to abuse power

DAVID FLINT

Australian, 22 July 1999, p. 2

The Australian Broadcasting Authority Inquiry, which began yesterday, goes to the integrity of commercial broadcasting.

The media play a central role in our democracy, which has a healthy suspicion of concentrations of power. And the media is one of the most important checks and balances against abuse of power. There is, in effect, a compact between society and the media. In return for its considerable freedom, the media has a duty to be responsible.

Being responsible means that news, as far as possible, is true. It means that news and opinion must be distinguished. And it means that opinion be bona fide. Any blurring between advertising, news and opinion—advertorials—should be identifiable.

It is a well-established principle that the press must not be subject to government regulation because it would be too dangerous to do this. This is another example of the checks and balances necessary to preserve freedom. This does not, of course, mean the press is immune from the law.

The electronic media is fundamentally different. It is (still) a scarce public resource. Without regulation there would be anarchy, so licensing is essential.

The question for any democratic society is how to regulate the electronic media so it, too, can fulfill its role of informing the people on matters of public interest, fairly and accurately. In this, Australia has been remarkably innovative. We devised a mixed system, an independent public broadcaster, along with commercial broadcasting. The virtues of this only began to dawn on the Europeans decades later. This mixed model, now expanded to include SBS and community broadcasting, is important. It ensures greater diversity than, say, in a free market. Under this it is far more likely that the people will be informed fairly and accurately on matters of public interest.

Until 1992, commercial broadcasting was subject to a high degree of regulation. But this was too often paralysed because of the complexities of the law. Who benefited? Certainly not the public. Under the 1992 legislation greater autonomy was given to commercial broadcasting. But this was not intended to be the degree of self-regulation the print media enjoys.

Rather, it was to be a system of co-regulation. Codes of practice would be developed with public consultation. A breach of a code would not be a breach of the law or of any of the conditions in a licence. And only complaints the broadcaster could not resolve would come to the broadcasting authority. The strategy was to encourage good behaviour by example, transparency and persuasion. Hence the jibe the ABA is a 'toothless tiger'.

But if there is convincing evidence a code has failed to provide the community safeguards that society expects and the law requires, a more direct regulatory response can be designed to target a station, a network or even a whole broadcasting sector.

It would be premature to suggest this is going to happen. What the ABA has before it are allegations. Only through the discovery of documents and sworn evidence can the ABA determine the true state of affairs and take appropriate action.

Professor David Flint is Australian Broadcasting Authority chairman.

8.17 Would you expect management to worry about attitudinal surveys, such as the one described in Accounting Headline 8.9? Explain your answer, as well as explaining how such surveys might impact on the disclosure policies of an organisation.

8.18 Read Accounting Headline 8.10 and explain whether you think the banks would or should respond to the concerns of the Australian Consumers' Association and/or the concerns of the Finance Sector Union. What theories did you rely on (if any) to inform your judgement?

The Chronicle, 27 November 1998, p. 22

Health rates as top social issue

CANBERRA: Health has taken over from crime as the most important social issue seen to be facing Australia, figures showed yesterday.

The survey of people's views of environmental issues found the environment rated fifth in importance—even though three in four Australians had at least one environmental concern.

The Australian Bureau of Statistics (ABS) figures showed 29% of respondents believed health was the most important social issue.

This was followed by crime (24%), education and unemployment (both 16%), and environmental problems (16%).

In 1996, crime was seen as the most important social issue, followed by health, education, unemployment, then the environment.

In the latest survey, dated March 1998, health was the most important issue to older people and least important to people aged 35–44.

In general, younger people were more concerned about long-term environmental problems although 18–24 year olds, as well as 45-54 year olds, were most concerned about unemployment.

But the survey said 71% of Australians were concerned with at least one specific environmental problem.

The figure was up from 68% in 1996 but down from 75% in 1992.

People living in the ACT were most concerned while Tasmanians were the least concerned about environmental problems.

Air pollution continued to be the problem of greatest worry for Australians, with 32% reporting it as their major concern.

Herald-Sun 22, August 2002, p. 5

Bank to slash extra 1000 jobs

NICOLA WEBBER

The Commonwealth Bank will slash another 1000 jobs despite its annual profit jumping 11 per cent to $2.6 billion.

But the bank has vowed not to shut any more branches—even those already marked for closure.

Stunned union officials yesterday described the latest job cuts as scandalous. They said workers were worried about their future, unsure about which jobs would go and from where.

Consumer advocates claimed customers would bear the brunt of the cuts and urged the Federal Government to act.

Finance Sector Union national secretary Tony Beck said staff were already reeling from job losses and branch closures.

'It is unbelievable,' Mr Beck said. 'They have just shed 500 jobs, all from the retail network. Now we get this punch with another 1000 jobs.'

The Commonwealth Bank yesterday said it would cut 1000 staff by eliminating duplication, inefficiencies and some back-office processing. It said 1550 jobs would go, while another 550 jobs would be created, with redundancies and other changes tipped to cost $120 million.

The bank announced a net profit of $2.655 billion for the past financial year. At the same time, customers paid more than $1.8 billion in fees, commissions and other charges.

Income from lending fees rose 3 per cent to $618 million, mainly because of the boom in housing. And income from commission and other fees jumped 6 per cent to $1.242 billion.

The Australian Consumers' Association is urging the Federal Government to protect consumers from excessive fees.

It also wants a social charter set up laying out minimum standards of access and affordability to banking.

ACA finance policy officer Catherine Wolthuizen yesterday said there was a double whammy of record profits and job cuts.

'When does it stop?' Ms Wolthuizen said. 'A job shedding of that scale, given how close to the bone cuts have gone, there isn't much fat left to trim.

'How much profit is enough for greedy banks like the Commonwealth and how much further will it flout consumer and community demands before the Government acts?'

8.19 Explain the concepts *coercive isomorphism, mimetic isomorphism* and *normative isomorphism*. How can these concepts be used to explain voluntary corporate reporting practices?

8.20 Larrinaga-Gonzalez (2007, p. 151) wrote:

> The results of KPMG surveys of corporate social reporting reveal that while, in 1993, 13 per cent of the top 100 companies in 10 countries published a separate report about their environmental and social impacts, this figure almost tripled to 33 per cent (for 16 countries) in the 2005 survey. At the same time casual observation leads to the conclusion that in the 1990s 'environmental' and/or 'health and safety' reports dominated the reporting scene. More recently, however, most companies publish an 'environmental and social' or 'sustainability' report. In particular, from the 2002 survey to the 2005 survey, the percentage of separate reports (for the global top 250 companies) that correspond to the label 'sustainability' and 'social and environmental' have increased from 24 per cent to 85 per cent, with a corresponding decline (from 73 per cent to 13 per cent) for environmental, health and safety reports.

You are to use Institutional Theory to explain these large-scale shifts in both report production and the names being given to the reports.

8.21 To what extent do Stakeholder, Legitimacy and Institutional Theories provide competing, mutually exclusive, explanations of voluntary corporate reporting practices?

8.22 In July 2005 many newspaper articles discussed how the fast-food 'giant' McDonald's in Australia was reducing its use of Australian farm produce (particularly potatoes) in favour of cheaper overseas imports. A review of McDonald's Australia's website (September 2005) revealed a media release entitled 'Setting the record straight on recent media coverage'. It was presented in a question and answer format. The questions McDonald's posed to itself were:

- Is McDonald's planning to dump Australian farmers?
- I hear McDonald's is going to import beef and orange juice.
- Is it true that McDonald's doesn't treat its farmers fairly?
  The answers provided to each of these questions indicate that the various concerns were unfounded.

(a) Explain McDonald's reaction in terms of both Legitimacy Theory and Media Agenda Setting Theory.

(b) Do you think that McDonald's would be considered to have a great deal of 'legitimacy' to protect through such disclosures?

8.23 In an article entitled 'Profits before health, again: Tobacco products dominate supermarkets' top 10 in big boost to bottom line' (*Pharmacy News*, 28 February 2008, p. 12) it was reported:

> A cigarette brand—Winfield, manufactured by British American Tobacco Australia—is the number one product sold in supermarkets.
>
> I hope that as health professionals, you find this information as abhorrent as I do. It makes a complete mockery of the fact that the two leading supermarkets, Woolworths and Coles, have for a long time tried to get their hands on the pharmacy market.

Based on this information, one can only conclude that profit and greed are priorities set at a higher level than health outcomes. I urge the pharmacists of Australia to become passionate about this issue, as we are quickly becoming one of the few businesses in the retail environment for whom health priorities actually mean something ... The supermarkets have the ability, however, with their huge investment in marketing spin, to convince the Australian public that their priority is elsewhere, with the use of such marketing slogans as 'the fresh food people'.

Explain from both a Legitimacy Theory perspective and a Stakeholder Theory perspective how, or whether, Australian supermarkets might react to such publicity.

8.24 An article entitled 'The killing fields' appeared in the *Sunday Morning Post* (Hong Kong) on 7 August 2005. The article refers to practices used to produce furs from racoon dogs, foxes, spotted mountain cats and rabbits. Within the four-page article, the following comments are made:

Wu Zhenyu, 55, describes the trade that draws him 2,000 km from his home in Liaoning to a town where he spends two months at a time selling furs. 'We wait until the coldest part of winter, when their fur is at its thickest, to kill the foxes,' he says. You kill them, the important thing is to make sure you don't damage the fur. Some farmers kill them by electrocution, but many others beat the fox to death with a bamboo stick.' Asked if he thinks beating the animals is cruel, he laughs and shrugs. 'People murder each other all the time. Isn't that cruel?' ... For fur lovers it is a cut-price paradise. For animal welfare groups alarmed at China's rapidly expanding fur trade, it is a nightmare ... Buoyed by the revival of fur in the fashion industry in recent years, the Chinese mainland is, according to estimates by business experts, manufacturing up to 80 per cent of the fur coats sold around the world ... China is the fastest growing fur exporter in the world, but it is not just the scale of the fur trade on the mainland that concerns animal welfare groups such as Peta (People for Ethical Treatment of Animals) and Animals Asia, they are also alarmed at the lack of regulations and the cruelty the trade involves ... Female foxes are confined in small, stinking coops with litters of cubs and fed twice a day on bowls of grey slop. Nearby, racoon dogs and silver foxes show signs of severe distress, ramming their heads and trunks repeatedly against the crude wire than encloses them from birth until about four months old, when they are killed for their fur. In one cage a young fox stands protectively over the body of a month-old cub lying lifeless, its paws covered in flies dangling through the bottom of the cage ... Buy a jacket labelled 'Made in Italy' and its rabbit fur lining may have started as an 18 yuan pelt in Chongfu ... 'Our fur goes everywhere in the world', says Tan, tucking into a bowl of steamed rabbit meat, a bountiful dish in Guanhu thanks to him. 'We can't keep up with this demand. We are very happy about this' ... Peta and other animal welfare groups hope the approach of the 2008 Beijing Olympics will turn the eyes of the world on every aspect of Chinese life and encourage the government to introduce effective legislation to ensure animals are humanely treated. In the first campaign of its kind in China, Peta this year launched a Pamela Anderson poster offensive in Shanghai's underground train stations to try to dissuade wealthy women from wearing fur. The campaign showed the *Baywatch* star, one of the best-known western female faces on the mainland, baring a naked back to the camera with the slogan: 'Give fur the cold shoulder.' ... 'A lot of cruelty is effectively being outsourced to China. We shouldn't go down the path to encourage it or to make it less cruel. We should try to end it,' Smillie (education director for Hong Kong-based Animals Asia) says. 'Why should we regulate it and give them a slightly bigger cage or better access to water? The animals don't have a semblance of a normal life. Even if you bring in regulations, who is going to check on them?'

(a) After reading the extract, and adopting a Legitimacy Theory perspective, answer the following:

   (i) Explain why it might be possible that 'cruel' animal practices would be tolerated in some countries but not in others.

   (ii) How might European garment retailers respond if it becomes widely known that their fur garments are produced from a supply chain that includes farms with high levels of animal cruelty? In your answer, consider the past experiences of companies like Nike, and the legitimising mechanisms they used when negative issues associated with their supply chain came to light.

(b) From a Stakeholder Theory perspective explain whether the animal welfare groups in China are likely to affect the practices of the fur traders.

(c) Consider Media Agenda Setting Theory to explain whether you think that the prominent four-page article appearing in the major Hong Kong newspaper would impact on the views of Hong Kong residents?

REFERENCES

Abbott, W. & R. Monsen (1979), 'On the measurement of corporate social responsibility: self-reported disclosures as a method of measuring corporate social involvement', *Academy of Management Journal*, 22(3), pp. 501–15.

Ader, C. (1995), 'A longitudinal study of agenda setting for the issue of environmental pollution', *Journalism and Mass Communication Quarterly*, 72(3), pp. 300–11.

Ashforth, B. & B. Gibbs (1990), 'The double edge of legitimization', *Organization Science*, 1, pp. 177–94.

Bailey, D., G. Harte & R. Sugden (2000), 'Corporate disclosure and the deregulation of international investment', *Accounting, Auditing and Accountability Journal*, 13(2), pp. 197–218.

Barton, S., N. Hill & S. Sundaram (1989), 'An empirical test of stakeholder theory predictions of capital structure', *Financial Management* (Spring), pp. 36–44.

Blood, R. W. (1981), '*Unobtrusive issues and the agenda-setting role of the press*', unpublished Doctoral dissertation, Syracuse University, New York.

Brignall, S. & S. Modell (2000), 'An institutional perspective on performance measurement and management in the "New Public Sector"', *Management Accounting Research*, 11(3), pp. 281–306.

Broadbent, J., K. Jacobs & R. Laughlin (2001), 'Organisational resistance strategies to unwanted accounting and finance changes: the case of general medical practice in the UK', *Accounting, Auditing and Accountability Journal*, 14(5), pp. 565–86.

Brown, N. & C. Deegan (1998), 'The public disclosure of environmental performance information—a dual test of media agenda setting theory and legitimacy theory', *Accounting and Business Research*, 29(1), pp. 21–41.

Buhr, N. (2002), 'A structuration view on the initiation of environmental reports', *Critical Perspectives on Accounting*, 13(1), pp. 17–38.

Burchell, S., C. Clubb, A. Hopwood, J. Hughes & J. Naphapiet (1980), 'The roles of accounting in organisations and society', *Accounting, Organization and Society*, 5(1), pp. 5–28.

Business Council of Australia (2005), *Submission to the Parliamentary Joint Committee on Corporations and Financial Services, Inquiry into Corporate Responsibility and Triple Bottom Line Reporting*, Melbourne: BCA.

Carpenter, V. & E. Feroz (1992), 'GAAP as a symbol of legitimacy: New York State's decision to adopt generally accepted accounting principles', *Accounting, Organizations and Society*, 17(7), pp. 613–43.

Carpenter, V. & E. Feroz (2001), 'Institutional theory and accounting rule choice: an analysis of four US state governments' decisions to adopt generally accepted accounting principles', *Accounting, Organizations and Society*, 26, pp. 565–96.

Chamber of Commerce and Industry Western Australia (2005), *The Social Responsibilities of Business*, Perth: CCIWA.

Clarkson, M. (1995), 'A stakeholder framework for analyzing and evaluating corporate social performance', *Academy of Management Review*, 20(1), pp. 92–118.

Committee for Economic Development (1974), *Measuring Business Social Performance: The Corporate Social Audit*, New York: Committee for Economic Development.

Cooper, D. J. & M. J. Sherer (1984), 'The value of corporate accounting reports—arguments for a political economy of accounting', *Accounting, Organizations and Society*, 9(3/4), pp. 207–32.

Cornell, B. & A. Shapiro (1987), 'Corporate stakeholders and corporate finance', *Financial Management*, (Spring), pp. 5–14.

Covaleski, M. A. & M. W. Dirsmith (1988), 'An institutional perspective on the rise, social transformation, and fall of a university budget category', *Administrative Science Quarterly*, 33, pp. 562–87.

David, P., M. Bloom & A. Hillman (2007), 'Investor activism, manager responsiveness, and corporate social performance', *Strategic Management Journal*, 28, pp. 91–100.

Deegan, C. (2002), 'The legitimising effect of social and environmental disclosures—a theoretical foundation', *Accounting, Auditing and Accountability Journal*, 15(3), pp. 282–311.

Deegan. C. & C. Blomquist (2006), 'Stakeholder influence on corporate reporting: an exploration of the interaction between WWF-Australia and the Australian Minerals Industry', *Accounting, Organizations and Society*, 31, pp. 343–72.

Deegan, C. & B. Gordon (1996), 'A study of the environmental disclosure practices of Australian corporations', *Accounting and Business Research*, 26(3), pp. 187–99.

Deegan, C. & M. Rankin (1996), 'Do Australian companies report environmental news objectively? An analysis of environmental disclosures by firms prosecuted successfully by the Environmental Protection Authority', *Accounting, Auditing and Accountability Journal*, 9(2), pp. 52–69.

Deegan, C., M. Rankin & J. Tobin (2002), 'An examination of the corporate social and environmental disclosures of BHP from 1983–1997', *Accounting, Auditing and Accountability Journal*, 15(3), pp. 312–43.

Deegan, C., M. Rankin & P. Voght (2000), 'Firms disclosure reactions to major social incidents: Australian evidence', *Accounting Forum*, 24(1), pp. 101–30.

Dillard, J. F., J. T. Rigsby & C. Goodman (2004), 'The making and remaking of organization context: duality and the institutionalization process', *Accounting, Auditing and Accountability Journal*, 17(4), pp. 506–42.

DiMaggio, P. J. & W. W. Powell (1983), 'The iron cage revisited: institutional isomorphism and collective rationality in organizational fields', *American Sociological Review*, 48, pp. 146–60.

Donaldson, T. & L. Preston (1995), 'The stakeholder theory of the corporation—concepts, evidence, and implications', *Academy of Management Review*, 20(1), pp. 65–92.

Dowling, J. & J. Pfeffer (1975), 'Organisational legitimacy: social values and organisational behavior', *Pacific Sociological Review*, 18(1), pp. 122–36.

Evan, W. & R. Freeman (1988), 'A stakeholder theory of the modern corporation: Kantian capitalism', in T. Beauchamp & N. Bowie (eds), *Ethical Theory and Business*, Englewood Cliffs, NJ: Prentice Hall, pp. 75–93.

Eyal, C. H., J. P. Winter & W. F. DeGeorge (1981), 'The concept of time frame in agenda setting', in G. C. Wilhoit (ed.), *Mass Communication Yearbook*, Beverly Hills, CA: Sage Publications.

Fellingham, J. & D. Newman (1979), 'Monitoring decisions in an agency setting', *Journal of Business Finance and Accounting*, 6(2), pp. 203–22.

Fogarty, T. J. (1992), 'Financial accounting standard setting as an institutionalized action field: constraints, opportunities and dilemmas', *Journal of Accounting and Public Policy*, 11(4), pp. 331–55.

Fogarty, T. J. (1996), 'The imagery and reality of peer review in the US: insights from institutional theory', *Accounting, Organizations and Society*, 18, pp. 243–67.

Freeman, R. (1984), *Strategic Management: A Stakeholder Approach*, Marshall, MA: Pitman.

Freeman, R. & D. Reed (1983), 'Stockholders and stakeholders: a new perspective on corporate governance', *Californian Management Review*, 25(2), pp. 88–106.

Friedman, A. & S. Miles (2002), 'Developing stakeholder theory', *Journal of Management Studies*, 39(1), pp. 1–21.

Friedman, M. (1962), *Capitalism and Freedom*, Chicago: University of Chicago Press.

Gray, R. & J. Bebbington (2000), 'Environmental accounting, managerialism and sustainability', *Advances in Environmental Accounting and Management*, 1, pp. 1–44.

Gray, R. & J. Bebbington (2001), *Accounting for the Environment*, London: Sage Publications.

Gray, R., R. Kouhy & S. Lavers (1995), 'Corporate social and environmental reporting: a review of the literature and a longitudinal study of UK disclosure', *Accounting, Auditing and Accountability Journal*, 8(2), pp. 47–77.

Gray, R., D. Owen & C. Adams (1996), *Accounting and Accountability: Changes and Challenges in Corporate Social and Environmental Reporting*, London: Prentice Hall.

Gray, R., D. Owen & K. T. Maunders (1991), 'Accountability, corporate social reporting and the external social audits', *Advances in Public Interest Accounting*, 4, pp. 1–21.

Guthrie, J. & L. Parker (1990), 'Corporate social disclosure practice: a comparative international analysis', *Advances in Public Interest Accounting*, 3, pp. 159–75.

Hasnas, J. (1998), 'The normative theories of business ethics: a guide for the perplexed', *Business Ethics Quarterly*, 8(1), pp. 19–42.

Heard, J. & W. Bolce (1981), 'The political significance of corporate social reporting in the United States of America', *Accounting, Organizations and Society*, 6(3), pp. 247–54.

Hogner, R. H. (1982), 'Corporate social reporting: eight decades of development at US steel', *Research in Corporate Performance and Policy*, 4, pp. 243–50.

Hurst, J. W. (1970), *The Legitimacy of the Business Corporation in the Law of the United States 1780–1970*, Charlottesville: University Press of Virginia.

Islam, M. & C. Deegan (2008a), '*Media pressures and corporate disclosure of social responsibility performance: a study of two global clothing and sports retail companies*', Accounting and Finance Association of Australia and New Zealand Annual Conference, Sydney, July.

Islam, M. A. & C. Deegan (2008b), 'Motivations for an organisation within a developing country to report social responsibility information: evidence from Bangladesh', *Accounting, Auditing and Accountability Journal*, 21(6), pp. 850–74.

Jensen, M. C. (1983), 'Organisation theory and methodology', *The Accounting Review*, 58 (April), pp. 319–39.

Jensen, M. C. (1993), 'The modern industrial revolution: exit and failure of internal control systems', *Journal of Finance*, pp. 831–80.

Jensen, M. C. & W. H. Meckling (1976), 'Theory of the firm: managerial behavior, agency costs and ownership structure', *Journal of Financial Economics*, 3 (October), pp. 305–60.

Larrinaga-Gonzalez, C. (2007), 'Sustainability reporting: insights from neoinstitutional theory', in J. Unerman, J. Bebbington & B. O'Dwyer (eds), *Sustainability, Accounting and Accountability*, London: Routledge.

Lindblom, C. K. (1994), '*The implications of organisational legitimacy for corporate social performance and disclosure*', Critical Perspectives on Accounting conference, New York.

Lowe, E. A. & A. Tinker (1977), 'Sighting the accounting problematic: towards an intellectual emancipation of accounting', *Journal of Business Finance and Accounting*, 4(3), pp. 263–76.

McCombs, M. (1981), 'The agenda-setting approach', in D. Nimmo & K. Sanders (eds), *Handbook of Political Communication*, Beverly Hills, California: Sage Publicatons.

McCombs, M. & D. Shaw (1972), 'The agenda setting function of mass media', *Public Opinion Quarterly*, (36), pp. 176–87.

Macpherson, C. B. (1973), *Democratic Theory: Essays in Retrieval*, Oxford: Oxford University Press.

Mathews, M. R. (1993), *Socially Responsible Accounting*, London: Chapman & Hall.

Mayer, H. (1980), 'Power and the press', *Murdoch University News*, 7(8).

Meyer, J. W. & B. Rowan (1977), 'Institutionalised organizations: formal structure as myth and ceremony', *American Journal of Sociology*, 83, pp. 340–63.

Mitchell, R., B. Agle & D. Wood (1997), 'Toward a theory of stakeholder identification and salience: defining the principle of who and what really count', *Academy of Management Review*, 22(4), pp. 853–86.

Nasi, J., S. Nasi, N. Phillips & S. Zyglidopoulos (1997), 'The evolution of corporate social responsiveness—an exploratory study of Finnish and Canadian forestry companies', *Business and Society*, 38(3), pp. 296–321.

Ness, K. & A. Mirza (1991), 'Corporate social disclosure: a note on a test of agency theory', *British Accounting Review*, 23, pp. 211–17.

Neu, D., H. Warsame & K. Pedwell (1998), 'Managing public impressions: environmental disclosures in annual reports', *Accounting, Organizations and Society*, 25(3), pp. 265–82.

Neu, D. & E. Ocampo (2007), 'Doing missionary work: the World Bank and the diffusion of financial practices', *Critical Perspectives on Accounting*, 18, pp. 363–89.

Neuman, W. R. (1990), 'The threshold of public attention', *Public Opinion Quarterly*, Summer, 49, pp. 159–76.

O'Donovan, G. (1999), 'Managing legitimacy through increased corporate environmental reporting: an exploratory study', *Interdisciplinary Environmental Review*, 1(1), pp. 63–99.

O'Donovan, G. (2002), 'Environmental disclosures in the annual report: extending the applicability and predictive power of legitimacy theory', *Accounting, Auditing and Accountability Journal*, 15(3), pp. 344–71.

O'Dwyer, B. (2002), 'Managerial perceptions of corporate social disclosure: an Irish story', *Accounting, Auditing and Accountability Journal*, 15(3), pp. 406–36.

O'Dwyer, B. (2005), 'Stakeholder democracy: challenges and contributions from social accounting', *Business Ethics: A European Review*, 14(1), pp. 28–41.

O'Leary, T. (1985), 'Observations on corporate financial reporting in the name of politics', *Accounting, Organizations and Society*, 10(1), pp. 87–102.

Oliver, C. (1991) 'Strategic responses to institutional processes', *Academy of Management Review*, 16(1), pp. 145–79.

Palmer D., P. D. Jennings & Z. Zhou (1993), 'Politics and institutional change: late adoption of the multidivisional form by large U.S. corporations', *Administrative Sciences Quarterly*, 38(1), pp. 100–31.

Patten, D. M. (1991), 'Exposure, legitimacy and social disclosure', *Journal of Accounting and Public Policy*, 10, pp. 297–308.

Patten, D. M. (1992), 'Intra-industry environmental disclosures in response to the Alaskan oil spill: a note on legitimacy theory', *Accounting, Organizations and Society*, 15(5), pp. 471–75.

Pfeffer, J. & G. Salancik (1978), *The External Control of Organizations: A Resource Dependence Perspective*, New York: Harper & Row.

Powell, W. W. & P. J. DiMaggio (eds) (1991), *The New Institutionalism in Organizational Analysis*, Chicago, Illinois: University of Chicago Press.

Puxty, A. (1991), 'Social accountability and universal pragmatics', *Advances in Public Interest Accounting*, 4, pp. 35–46.

Ramanathan, K. V. (1976), 'Toward a theory of corporate social accounting', *The Accounting Review*, 21(3), pp. 516–28.

Richardson, A. J. & J. B. Dowling (1986), 'An integrative theory of organizational legitimation', *Scandinavian Journal of Management Studies*, November, pp. 91–109.

Roberts, R. (1992), 'Determinants of corporate social responsibility disclosure: an application of stakeholder theory', *Accounting, Organizations and Society*, 17(6), pp. 595–612.

Rollins, T. P. & W. G. Bremser (1997), 'The SEC's enforcement actions against auditors: an auditor reputation and institutional theory perspective', *Critical Perspectives on Accounting*, 8(3), pp. 191–206.

Ronen, J. (1979), 'The dual role of accounting: a financial economic perspective', in J. L. Bicksler (ed.), *Handbook of Financial Economics*, North Holland.

Rowley, T. (1998), 'A normative justification for stakeholder theory', *Business and Society*, 37(1), pp. 105–7.

Scott, W. R. (1995), *Institutions and Organisations,* Thousand Oaks, CA: Sage Publications.

Sethi, S.P. (1977), 'Dimensions of corporate social performance: an analytical framework', in A. B. Carroll (ed.), *Managing Corporate Social Responsibility,* Boston, MA: Little, Brown.

Sethi, S. P. (1978), 'Advocacy advertising— the American experience', *California Management Review,* 11, pp. 55–67.

Shocker, A. D. & S. P. Sethi (1974), 'An approach to incorporating social preferences in developing corporate action strategies', in S. P. Sethi (ed.), *The Unstable Ground: Corporate Social Policy in a Dynamic Society,* California: Melville, pp. 67–80.

Stoney, C. & D. Winstanley (2001), 'Stakeholding: confusion or utopia: mapping the conceptual terrain', *Journal of Management Studies,* 38(5), pp. 603–26.

Suchman, M. C. (1995), 'Managing legitimacy: strategic and institutional approaches', *Academy of Management Review,* 20(3), pp. 571–610.

Swift, T. (2001), 'Trust, reputation and corporate accountability to stakeholders', *Business Ethics: A European Review,* 10(1), pp. 16–26.

Tinker, A. & M. Neimark (1987), 'The role of annual reports in gender and class contradictions at General Motors: 1917–1976', *Accounting, Organisations and Society,* 12(1), pp. 71–88.

Tuttle, B. & J. Dillard (2007), 'Beyond competition: institutional isomorphism in U.S. accounting research', *Accounting Horizons,* 21(4), pp. 387–409.

Ullman, A. (1985), 'Data in search of a theory: a critical examination of the relationships among social performance, social disclosure,

and economic performance of US firms', *Academy of Management Review,* 10(3), pp. 540–57.

Unerman, J. & M. Bennett (2004), 'Increased stakeholder dialogue and the internet: towards greater corporate accountability or reinforcing capitalist hegemony?', *Accounting, Organizations and Society,* 29(7), pp. 685–707.

Wallace, G. (1995), 'Balancing conflicting stakeholder requirements', *Journal for Quality and Participation,* 18(2), pp. 84–98.

Watts, R. L. & J. L. Zimmerman (1986), *Positive Accounting Theory,* Englewood Cliffs, NJ: Prentice Hall.

White, T. (1973), *The Making of the President 1972,* New York: Bantam Press.

Wicks, A. (1996), 'Overcoming the separation thesis: the need for a reconsideration of business and business research', *Business and Society,* 35(1), pp. 89–118.

Wilmshurst, T. & G. Frost (2000), 'Corporate environmental reporting: a test of legitimacy theory', *Accounting, Auditing and Accountability Journal,* 13(1), pp. 10–26.

Woodward, D. G., P. Edwards & F. Birkin (1996), 'Organizational legitimacy and stakeholder information provision', *British Journal of Management,* 7, pp. 329–47.

Zucker, H. G. (1977), 'The role of institutionalization in cultural persistence', *American Sociological Review,* 42, pp. 726–43.

Zucker, H. G. (1978), 'The variable nature of news media influence', in B. D. Rubin (ed.), *Communication Yearbook No. 2,* New Jersey, pp. 225–45.

Zucker, H. G. (1987), 'Institutional theories of organizations', *Annual Review of Sociology,* 13, pp. 443–64.

EXTENDED SYSTEMS OF ACCOUNTING—THE INCORPORATION OF SOCIAL AND ENVIRONMENTAL FACTORS WITHIN EXTERNAL REPORTING

LEARNING OBJECTIVES

On completing this chapter readers should:

- be aware of various perspectives about the responsibilities of business;
- be able to provide an explanation of the relationship between organisational responsibility and organisational accountability;
- be aware of the relationship between accounting and accountability;
- be aware of various theoretical perspectives that can explain why organisations might voluntarily elect to provide publicly available information about their social and environmental performance;
- be aware of the theoretical underpinnings of some recent initiatives in social and environmental accounting;
- be able to explain the concept of sustainable development and be able to explain how organisations are reporting their progress towards the goal of sustainable development;
- be able to identify some of the limitations of traditional financial accounting in enabling users of reports to assess a reporting entity's social and environmental performance.

OPENING ISSUES

1. Many companies throughout the world publish reports that discuss their economic, environmental and social performance. There are also numerous instances of companies publicly stating their commitment to sustainable development. For example, in the first two pages of *Responsible Energy: The Shell Sustainability Report 2007*, Shell (the large multinational oil company) states:

Welcome to *The Shell Sustainability Report*. It describes our efforts in 2007 to live up to our commitment to contribute to sustainable development. For us that means helping meet the world's growing energy needs in economically, environmentally and socially responsible ways. This includes both running our operations responsibly today and helping to build a responsible energy system for tomorrow ... We first made our commitment to contribute to sustainable development a decade ago, including it in the Shell General Business Principles in 1997. Since then, its importance to us has grown further ... For us, contributing to sustainable development means helping meet the world's growing energy needs in economically, environmentally and socially responsible ways. In short, helping secure a responsible energy future ... Meeting this commitment requires us to consciously balance short- and long-term interests; integrate economic, environmental and social considerations into business decisions; and regularly engage with our many stakeholders. This mindset is also about being determined to tackle seemingly insurmountable environmental and social problems through creativity and perseverance ... We remain committed to contributing to sustainable development because it is aligned with our values. It makes us a more competitive and profitable company. It brings us closer to our customers, employees and neighbours, reduces our operating and financial risk, promotes efficiency improvements in our operations and creates profitable new business opportunities for the future.

Moves towards sustainable development require organisations explicitly to consider various facets of their economic, social and environmental performance. But why would companies such as Shell embrace sustainability as a corporate goal rather than simply aiming for increased and continued profitability? Furthermore, if an entity embraces 'sustainability reporting' (perhaps through releasing a stand-alone sustainability report), what does this imply about the perceived accountability of business?

2. Many professional accounting bodies throughout the world are actively sponsoring research that looks at various social and environmental reporting issues. For example, in 2004 the Institute of Chartered Accountants in England and Wales produced a report entitled *Sustainability: The Role of Accountants* (ICAEW, 2004). Another accounting body based in the United Kingdom—the Association of Chartered Certified Accountants—has run an environmental reporting award since 1991 (and subsequently a sustainability reporting award, which runs in numerous countries, including Australia and New Zealand). Such activity leads us to question whether social and environmental reporting issues are really within the domain of professional accounting bodies? If not, who should be responsible for formulating social and environmental reporting guidelines?

3. What sort of social and environmental information do you think organisations should disclose (a normative question), and to whom should they make the disclosures (who are the relevant stakeholders)? Do you think your views about organisations' accountabilities would be the same as those of your fellow readers? Just how subjective do you consider such assessments to be?

INTRODUCTION

The first seven chapters of this book predominantly focus on issues related to the role of externally published financial accounting information in providing information about the economic/financial performance of an entity. Given the title of this book—*Financial Accounting Theory*—a focus on financial accounting would be anticipated. As would be appreciated from a study of financial accounting, in most countries financial accounting is heavily regulated according to applicable corporations laws, stock exchange requirements and accounting standards. By contrast, however, there is a relative absence of regulatory requirements relating to the public disclosure of information about the social and environmental performance of an entity—the topic of attention in this chapter. For example, within Australia, our many accounting standards focus on various issues associated with financial performance but none have social or environmental performance as their focus. This does not appear likely to change in the near future. Similarly, the requirements incorporated within the *Corporations Act* and the Australian Stock Exchange listing requirements fixate on financial performance, with very little consideration being given to performance of a non-financial nature—such as social and environmental performance. This is despite the growing concerns about issues such as climate change and the very real contribution that large corporations make to this problem (and the capacity they have to help devise solutions). Nevertheless, for a number of years many organisations within Australia and throughout the world have been voluntarily providing public disclosures about the social and environmental impact of their operations.

Chapter 8 examined some issues related to accountability for the broader (non-financial) aspects of an organisation's activities, by exploring theories that explain voluntary (unregulated) reporting practices. This chapter will develop our theoretical understanding of these issues, by examining aspects of the rapidly growing body of research that investigates the social and environmental reporting practices being adopted by an increasingly large number of organisations. These social and environmental reporting practices are often referred to as 'corporate social responsibility reporting' or 'sustainability reporting', with the latter covering aspects of (the more traditional) financial/economic performance or sustainability in addition to social and environmental sustainability. Social and environmental reporting typically involves the provision, to a range of stakeholders, of information about the performance of an entity with regard to its interaction with its physical and social environment, inclusive of information about an entity's support of employees, local and overseas communities, safety record and use of natural resources. Corporate social responsibility itself has been defined in a variety of ways. An accepted definition would be consistent with the definition provided by the Commission of European Communities (2001, p. 6), which defines corporate social responsibility as:

> a concept whereby companies integrate social and environmental concerns in their business operations and in their interaction with their stakeholders on a voluntary basis. Being socially responsible means not only fulfilling legal expectations, but also going beyond compliance and investing 'more' into human capital, the environment and the relations with stakeholders.

Because the area of corporate social responsibility reporting (or 'social and environmental reporting', as it will also be referred to) is relatively new and continually evolving (and also generally unregulated), it is a very exciting area for accountants to be involved in. We are starting to see new 'breeds' of accountants—environmental accountants and social accountants—who work alongside 'traditional' financial accountants. While there is a general lack of regulation requiring corporations to provide an account of their social and environmental impacts and performance, many large companies voluntarily provide reasonably comprehensive accounts of their performance in these areas.[1]

---

1   To gain an insight into the many and varied organisations that are producing social and environmental reports, we can refer to various websites. Within Australia, the Department of Environment, Water, Heritage and the Arts has developed a site that provides links to many Australian social and environmental reports. This site is located at http://www.environment.gov.au/settlements/industry/corporate/reporting/. At an international level, CorporateRegister.com provides a link to corporations throughout the world that are producing social and environmental reports. Its website is located at www.CorporateRegister.com.

BRIEF OVERVIEW OF HISTORY OF SOCIAL AND ENVIRONMENTAL REPORTING

The public disclosure of information about the social and environmental impact of operations has become widespread among companies in many countries since the early 1990s, when a number of large companies made considerable advances in reporting aspects of their environmental impact. Subsequently, from about the mid-1990s, reporting about aspects of the social impact of organisations' operations became an increasingly popular practice (ICAEW, 2004). Development of these practices in the early and mid-1990s tended to take the form of disclosures within the annual report (accompanying the annual financial statements) about the environmental (and subsequently social) policies, practices and/or impact of the reporting organisation. As these reporting practices became more widespread, and social and environmental disclosures made by some organisations became more extensive, some of the 'leading edge' reporting organisations began separating their detailed social and environmental disclosures from the annual report and financial statements, by publishing a separate stand-alone social and environmental report (while still providing a summary of these disclosures in their annual reports). These separate, stand-alone reports were produced by some corporations from the early 1990s. However, they have become more common since the late 1990s and have become standard practice among many large multinational companies in several industrial sectors and several countries. As an example, within the Australian context large organisations that release separate, stand-alone reports that address social and environmental aspects of their performance include:

- BHP Billiton, whose latest report (at the time of writing), *Resourcing the Future: BHP Sustainability Report 2008*, is available at http://www.bhpbilliton.com.au/bb/sustainableDevelopment.jsp.
- Westpac Banking Corporation, whose two reports released in 2008—the *Environmental, Social and Governance Performance Report* and the *Stakeholder Impact Report*—are available at http://www.westpac.com.au/internet/publish.nsf/Content/WICR+Sustainability+Reports.
- Boral Ltd, who latest report, *Boral Ltd Sustainability Report 2008*, is available at http://www.boral.com.au/common/CI_CommunitySustainability.asp?nodes=&AUD=CommunitySustainability&site=CI.
- Wesfarmer Ltd, whose latest report, *Sustainability07*, is available at http://www.wesfarmers.com.au/wesfarmer%5Fsusrep/.
- VicSuper, whose latest report, *VicSuper Sustainability Report*, is available at http://www.vicsuper.com.au/www/html/964-sustainability.asp?intSiteID=1.

Since the late 1990s, many corporations have made increasing use of the Internet to disseminate information about aspects of their social and environmental policies and performance. The Internet has also been used by a number of organisations to engage in dialogue with a variety of stakeholders about various social and environmental issues.

Although social and environmental reporting practices have only become widespread since the early to mid-1990s, this does not tell the whole story of the development of these practices. Some studies have found and analysed voluntary non-financial disclosures in a variety of different forms of corporate reports for periods commencing long before the 1990s, and have demonstrated that forms of social and environmental reporting have existed for many decades.

For example, Guthrie and Parker (1989) examined social disclosures in the Australian company Broken Hill Proprietary for a 100-year period from 1885; Unerman (2000a, b) found evidence of social disclosures in a variety of reports produced annually by the Anglo-Dutch oil company Shell dating back to 1897, with these disclosures becoming more prevalent from the 1950s; Hogner (1982) found evidence of social reporting practices at US Steel dating back to 1905; Tinker and Neimark (1987, 1988) and Neimark (1992) analysed social-type disclosures in the annual reports of the US company General Motors from 1916; and Adams and Harte (1998) analysed forms of social reporting in UK banks and retailers from 1935. There have also been several studies examining social and environmental disclosures in company reports from the 1960s and 1970s, such as Buhr (1998) and Campbell (2000). Thus the development of social and environmental reporting from the early 1990s might more accurately be considered a development of non-financial reporting practices rather than a completely new phenomenon.

So far, the chapter has used the terminology 'social and environmental reporting' and 'sustainability reporting', but another related term that has gained prominence is 'triple bottom line reporting'. Triple bottom line reporting has been defined by Elkington (1997) as reporting that provides information about the economic, environmental and social performance of an entity. The large multinational company Shell was responsible for popularising the term, as it was the first organisation in the 1990s to release what it referred to as a 'triple bottom line report'. The notion of reporting against the three components (or 'bottom lines') of economic, environmental and social performance is directly tied to the concept and goal of sustainable development—something that from the beginning of the 1990s has become visible within the agenda of many countries and large corporations. There are various definitions of sustainable development, but the one most commonly cited is 'development that meets the needs of the present world without compromising the ability of future generations to meet their own needs' (World Commission on Environment and Development, 1987).

Triple bottom line reporting, if properly implemented, is often perceived as providing information that enables report readers to assess how sustainable an organisation's or a community's operations are. The perspective taken is that for an organisation (or a community) to be sustainable (a long-run perspective) it must be financially secure (as evidenced through such measures as profitability); it must minimise (or ideally eliminate) its negative environmental impacts; and it must act in conformity with societal expectations or else lose its 'community licence to operate' (a concept that was discussed in Chapter 8). These three factors are obviously highly interrelated. Because corporations are increasingly referring to 'sustainability' as part of their business agendas, we will now briefly consider this term in more depth.

DEVELOPING NOTIONS OF SUSTAINABILITY

Since the 1970s there has been much discussion in various forums about the implications of continued economic development for the environment and, relatedly, for humankind. Sustainable development is not something that will be easily achieved, and many consider that, at least at this stage, it is nothing more than an ideal.

A significant step in placing sustainability on the agenda of governments and businesses worldwide was a report initiated by the General Assembly of the United Nations. The report, entitled *Our Common Future*, was presented in 1987 by the World Commission of Environment and Development chaired by Gro Harlem Brundtland, the then Norwegian prime minister. This important document subsequently became known as the *Brundtland Report*. The brief of the report was to produce a global agenda for change in order to combat or alleviate the ongoing pressures on the global environment—pressures that were clearly unsustainable. It was generally accepted that business organisations must change the way they do business and they must learn to question traditionally held business goals and principles (perhaps with encouragement from governments). As already indicated, the *Brundtland Report* defined sustainable development as:

> ... development that meets the needs of the present world without compromising the ability of future generations to meet their own needs.

The *Brundtland Report* clearly identified that equity issues, and particularly issues associated with intergenerational equity, are central to the sustainability agenda. That is, globally we must ensure that our generation's consumption patterns do not negatively impact on future generations' quality of life. Specifically, we should be in a position to say that the planet that we leave our children is in as good a shape as the planet we inherited (and preferably in better shape). The move towards sustainability implies that something other than short-term self-interest should drive decision making (this is a normative position). It implies that wealth creation for current generations should not be held as the all-consuming pursuit, and that consumption and personal wealth creation by us (now), while perhaps being considered as economically 'rational' (using the definition often applied in the economics literature), is not necessarily rational from a global and intergenerational perspective.[2]

There is evidence from a number of sources that for many years the ecological impacts of human (including business) activities have exceeded the earth's capacity to absorb these impacts (see, for example, Venetoulis, Chazan & Gaudet, 2004). This evidence demonstrates that our current levels of consumption (and other activities) are achieved at the expense of a degraded biosphere in which our children, grandchildren and great-grandchildren will have to live. If we continue to 'consume' the world's environmental resources at this level, a time is likely to come where the biosphere will have been degraded to the extent that it can no longer support human life in anywhere near the numbers it currently supports—clearly an unsustainable position for nature, society and business profitability. As indicated in Accounting Headline 9.1, this view has now become the dominant view among the worldwide scientific community.

Also implicit in the definition of sustainability is a requirement that intra-generational equity issues be addressed—that is, the needs of all 'of the present world' inhabitants need to be met, which requires strategies to alleviate the poverty and starvation that currently besets the peoples of various countries. While from a moral perspective efforts should clearly be undertaken with a view to eradicating poverty and starvation (again, this is a normative assertion), from a broader perspective communities cannot be expected to focus on local or global environmental issues

---

2   Hence, the quest towards sustainable development ultimately relies on people not being driven solely by their own self-interest, and not putting wealth creation above all else. If we believe the assumptions embraced by Positive Accounting theorists, as described in Chapter 7, that all action is driven by self-interest, there would be little hope that people would ever consider the needs of future generations. Let's hope the assumptions of PAT theorists are not always right—or else this planet is in very big trouble!

It's climate change, as forecast

A year of climatic disasters is now persuading politicians to accept the warnings of 20 years ago, writes GEOFF STRONG.

Age, 31 October 2005, p. 13

If war is said to be a means of teaching Americans geography, what then is needed to teach them and fossil-fuel profligate sidekicks like ourselves about global warming? After the US has faced death and massive economic loss from two large hurricanes, and after Wilma gave the area another kicking last week, it seems the message is starting to register.

In one of the greatest of shocks, in Australia federal Environment Minister Ian Campbell has conceded the debate is over: humans have to accept their actions are warming the planet and the consequences will probably be disastrous.

But why have we taken so long to take the problem seriously and do something about it? Scientists who know about the greenhouse effect have been, by any reasonable standard, certain for two decades.

One of the problems appears to be that the scientific definition of certainty sounds like equivocation to the ordinary public, particularly to their elected and often scientifically ignorant representatives.

It is nearly 20 years since I wrote my first report about greenhouse gas global warming for the now defunct *National Times*. I remember asking scientists how certain they were of their predictions and I got an answer often repeated over the subsequent years: 'Well, we are not 100 per cent certain, but we think the consequences will be ...'

In science-speak, that means they could have been 95 to 99 per cent certain but were leaving the 1 per cent margin for error in case somebody ripped them apart in a scientific paper.

The world's greatest gamblers, the insurance industry, didn't need that level of certainty. It had been banking on scenarios being right since at least 1995.

In March that year, the world's biggest re-insurer, Munich Re of Germany, stunned the industry by saying manmade warming was increasing natural disasters. The head of the company's geoscientific research group, Dr Gerhard Berz, said: 'Today there can be no doubt the growing number and intensity of windstorms, thunderstorms and floods all over the world are attributable to the rapid increase of air and sea temperatures.'

Despite many years of research using supercomputers to model climate, the list of consequences climate change scientists rattled off in 1986 have turned out to be pretty well on target: temperature changes, extreme events and predictions on hydrology, snow cover and ecology are holding up and some changes are now being observed.

The boffins at our own CSIRO division of atmospheric research at Aspendale even got the timing right of when the impact would first be showing against background noise. They said it would appear after 2000 and it has.

I have gone back to some of the scientists interviewed then, such as the former head of the division, Dr Graeme Pearman, and scientific adviser Dr Willem Bouma. Pearman said the present level of carbon dioxide in the atmosphere had not been higher in 20 million years. 'What we didn't know 20 years ago was how long CO_2 lasts when it is in the atmosphere. We now know the residence time is 80 years.'

What's more, we have a world of more than 6 billion people, population pressure the planet has never before had to endure.

Bouma says that, in hindsight, perhaps scientists should have worded their predictions differently and conveyed more certainty to the public because two decades have been lost. By appearing uncertain, they might have protected their backsides, but allowed a whole army of vested interest groups such as the fossil-fuel lobby and right-wing think tanks to attempt to lever apart the argument and create 20 years of delay.

The think tank apparatchiks who hate government involvement in anything except deregulation paint climate scientists as creating fear to carve out well-paid government-funded careers.

The flaws in this argument: first, no one really wanted to see it happen and, second, anyone who could disprove it would win the Nobel prize.

Journalists who wrote what scientists believed were pilloried too. I was taken to the press council in 1999 by a reader for writing about global warming a decade on. My alleged crime was I hadn't given oxygen to those who didn't believe.

The complaint was dismissed.

A problem is global warming's complexity. This makes it a blessing that someone who is able to simplify science, such as Tim Flannery, has become a convert.

We can make a difference. One of the simplest and least painful ways would be to make it mandatory for all new houses to have solar hot-water systems. Hot water is 25 per cent of household energy use and solar systems reduce this by 80 per cent. Any extra capital cost is paid back by reduced energy bills.

The value of such measures is emphasised with the National Climate Centre saying Victoria is likely to be hotter than average causing a blow-out in greenhouse unfriendly air-conditioner use this summer.

As the hurricanes demonstrated, the earth's atmosphere is capable of destroying the structures and

(continued)

institutions humans have so carefully crafted into civilisation. The rapid initial breakdown of law and order in New Orleans after Katrina should be proof of its fragility. I think the battle with the weather in future will make our war against jihadist terrorism pale into insignificance.

When I wrote that first report, one of the primary concerns was about sea levels rising and the *National Times* editors ran a cartoon of the Opera House being swamped. Now climatologists concede sea level rises were one area they initially over-estimated and are likely to be at the lower end of predictions.

The Opera House will probably be safe. Pity about Bangladesh, Tuvalu and Kiribati.

(necessary for sustainability) if they are in desperate need of money. (If they are starving, can they really be expected to keep their forests intact when such forests provide a means of 'free' heating and income?) Decisions by particular impoverished nations, such as to remove large tracts of rainforest, can have huge global implications. Any vision of sustainability clearly needs to address poverty on a global scale.[3]

A further significant event that followed the *Brundtland Report* was the 1992 Earth Summit in Rio de Janeiro, which was attended by government representatives from around the world as well as numerous social and environmental experts and non-government organisations. The Earth Summit again placed the issue of sustainable development at the forefront of international politics and business. Globally, the summit attracted considerable media attention. An important outcome was Agenda 21, which was deemed to be an action plan for the twenty-first century and which placed sustainability as the core consideration for ongoing national and global development.

In the same year as the Earth Summit (1992), the European Union (EU) released a document entitled *Towards Sustainability* as part of its Fifth Action Programme. One of the suggestions of the program was for the accounting profession to take a role in implementing costing systems that internalise many environmental costs. As discussed later in the chapter, traditional financial accounting typically ignores social and environmental costs and benefits. Specifically, the EU called for a 'redefinition of accounting concepts, rules, conventions and methodology so as to ensure that the consumption and use of environmental resources are accounted for as part of the full cost of production and reflected in market prices' (European Commission, 1992, Vol. II, Section 7.4, p. 67). The rationale for the EU's proposal was that if the prices reflected the 'full costs' of production, including environmental costs, such costs would flow through the various production and consumption cycles, and as a result of the higher costs there would be an inclination towards more sustainable consumption patterns.[4] To date, accounting professions throughout the world have effectively ignored the calls made by the EU in 1992.

---

3   As another example of this, the severe landslide in the Philippines in February 2006 which claimed hundreds of victims was in part due to the removal of trees through illegal logging.

4   There is an ethical issue here in that the higher priced goods (those with a high 'environmental price') will thereafter be available only to the wealthy.

In 2002 a follow-up to the Rio de Janeiro Earth Summit was held in Johannesburg. One of the outcomes of this Earth Summit was the launch of a revised set of guidelines for the process of reporting the social and environmental impact of an organisation's operations. These guidelines are known as the Sustainability Reporting Guidelines and were developed by a broad range of organisations under the auspices of the Global Reporting Initiative (GRI). These guidelines and the Global Reporting Initiative are discussed in depth later in the chapter.

Since the important early developments of notions of sustainability in the late 1980s and early 1990s, many governments, industry and professional associations and non-government organisations have released various documents addressing the need for shifts towards sustainable development. Indeed, sustainability appears to have become a central part of the language of government and business worldwide, and the definition provided within the *Brundtland Report* has attracted widespread acceptance. As an example, consider the following comments by the chief executive officer of Nokia in Nokia's 2004 *Environmental Report* (p. 4):

> With leadership comes great responsibility. As the leading company in our industry, Nokia also strives to be a leader in environmental performance. Future generations are relying on us to protect and preserve the natural environment. We believe that everyone must do their part.
>
> Nokia promotes sustainable development by managing its operations in a responsible way. We take environmental aspects into account throughout the life cycles of all our products. Energy efficiency continues to be one of the key focus areas in continuously improving environmental performance. We have consistently reduced the energy intensity of our products while the total use of materials in mobile devices has been reduced to a fraction of what it was a few years ago.

A more detailed explanation about a particular organisation's commitment to sustainability is given in the following extract from the UK Co-operative Financial Services Group's *Sustainability Report 2007/08* (p. 4):

> Co-operative Financial Services (CFS) recognises the need to develop its business in a sustainable manner—i.e. business development that meets the needs of the present without compromising the ability of future generations to meet their own needs ... alongside 'profitability', which is absolutely vital to CFS' continued existence, 'balance' [between the needs of different stakeholders] is a key component of our pursuit of sustainability.
>
> We recognise that there are physical limits to the resources of the Earth (both in terms of generating materials and absorbing wastes), and that any business activity that exceeds these limits is, by definition, unsustainable in the long-term and will need to be reconstituted. Nature cannot withstand a progressive build-up of waste derived from the Earth's crust, nor can it withstand a progressive build-up of society's waste, particularly substances that it cannot degrade into harmless materials. In addition, the productive area of nature should not be diminished in terms of quality (diversity) or quantity (volume) and must be enabled to grow. These we recognise as the minimum conditions for ecological sustainability.

Again, what the above quotes show is that sustainability is something that is on the minds of business on a global scale and students of business and accounting need to be aware of it.

Adopting perspectives provided by several of the theories explored in Chapter 8, it can be further argued that if sustainability becomes part of the expectations held by society (that is, it becomes part of the 'social contract'), it must become a business goal. As the concept of sustainable development continues to become part of various communities' expectations, communities will expect to be provided with information about how organisations, governments and other entities have performed against the central requirements of sustainability.

SUSTAINABILITY AND THE 'TRIPLE BOTTOM LINE'

As noted earlier, many organisations conceive of sustainability as comprising three strands: economic, social and environmental. This model is often referred to as the 'triple bottom line' approach to sustainability. Indeed, the Sustainability Reporting Guidelines developed by the Global Reporting Initiative (to be discussed later in the chapter) divides its suggested performance indicators into economic, environmental and social indicators (with social indicators being further subdivided into labour practices, human rights, society and product responsibility classifications). The financial performance, or profit, of a business is often colloquially referred to as the business's 'bottom line', so a focus solely on economic performance can be considered as a focus predominantly on the single bottom line (figure) of financial profitability. The triple bottom line broadens this performance evaluation of an organisation, from a narrow focus on the single bottom line of financial profit to an evaluation of the three 'bottom lines' of economic, social and environmental performance.

These three aspects of sustainability tend to converge over long time horizons. In the short term, it is possible to generate profits while negatively impacting on society and the environment. In the medium term, given that businesses operate within society, negative impacts on society caused by some business activities might lead to a breakdown in social functions that are necessary to continued business profitability. The argument here is that most businesses rely on the effective functioning of many social systems—such as physical infrastructure (transport systems, utilities and so on), well-ordered markets and a respect for property rights (law and order). If any of these systems breaks down, future profitability will be threatened.

Although businesses might evolve to address, and thereby profit from, breakdowns in some social systems, these are unlikely to address all the problems arising for many businesses from large-scale social breakdown, and they will add financial costs to businesses that have to buy the additional services from the market. For example, if a narrow focus on profit maximisation by businesses contributed to increased unemployment and poverty in many sections of society, and if this led to a breakdown in law and order, then although some businesses could profit from supplying additional private security services to those with wealth who were threatened by the breakdown in law and order, many other businesses could suffer a negative economic outcome, as their activities/markets might be negatively affected and they might have to pay for additional security services.

This scenario is just one of many possible outcomes from a business focus on profit maximisation, and many people would argue that other scenarios are more likely to occur. Nevertheless, it highlights one way in which a narrow focus on short-term profit maximisation could contribute to a breakdown in social systems.[5] As this scenario demonstrates, in the medium

5   Some people would argue that an example of largely unrestrained profit maximisation leading to a breakdown in many social systems occurred in Russia during the 1990s—in the period of 'cowboy capitalism' following the collapse of the Soviet Union, when a small proportion of the population became very wealthy while vast numbers had little to eat.

term if a narrow focus on profit maximisation leads to a breakdown in social systems, this might be neither socially nor financially/economically sustainable.

In the long term the argument for equating economic, social and environmental sustainability is reasonably straightforward. This argument is that the economy (including business activities) and all social systems operate within the natural environment. As outlined earlier in the chapter, if business (and other human) activities contribute to the destruction of the biosphere, there will be no humans left to run businesses, buy the products of businesses or operate social systems. In an extreme scenario, destruction of the environment leads to destruction of the human race, following which there would clearly be no profits and no social systems. Thus, in the long term, environmental sustainability is necessary for both social and economic sustainability, so attention to 'bottom line' performance (or minimising impact) in respect of the environment is necessary to ensure a sustainable social and economic bottom line.

The implication of these arguments is similar to the implication of the intergenerational requirement of sustainability (discussed earlier)—it might be necessary to sacrifice some short-term economic profitability to ensure long-term sustainable economic profits within a sustainable social and ecological system.

Dillard, Brown and Marshall (2005, p. 81) explain that, in practice, an obstacle to the triple bottom line approach to sustainability is that 'social systems have come to dominate and exploit natural systems'—in particular economics-based (profit-based) social systems are dominant. They argue that moves towards sustainability will therefore require an explicit reversal of this socially constructed dominance of the economic over the ecological. We can only ponder whether such a reversal can occur. Based on your own assumptions about what drives human behaviour, what do you think?

STAGES OF SUSTAINABILITY REPORTING

Having established that social and environmental reporting (sustainability reporting or triple bottom line reporting) is not a new phenomenon, and having discussed the concept of sustainable development, we will now turn our attention to various assessments or decisions that need to be made in the process of reporting aspects of an organisation's social and environmental performance. Such decisions relate to the following issues:

- *Why* would an entity decide to disclose publicly information about its social and environmental performance?
- *Who* are the stakeholders to which the social and environmental disclosures will be directed?
- *What* types of social and environmental disclosures will be made?
- What should be the *format* of the disclosures?

The first issue—*why would an entity decide to disclose information?*—relates to management's *motivations* to report. For example, an organisation would need to consider whether it is reporting because it believes it has an *accountability* to various stakeholders, or whether, perhaps, it is reporting because it wants to win the support of *powerful stakeholders*. That is, the broad objectives driving any particular organisation to undertake sustainability reporting can range from an ethically motivated desire to ensure that the organisation benefits, or does not have a negative impact on, society and the natural environment, through to an economically focused motive to use social and environmental reporting to protect or enhance shareholder value. Aspects of this range of motives were discussed in Chapter 8, when the ethical/moral (or normative) and the managerial branches of Stakeholder Theory were explored. This chapter adds to these perspectives by introducing additional research studies that address the broad objectives (or motives) and seek to explain *why* organisations engage in social and environmental reporting.

Once it is determined *why* an entity decides to report, this decision will in turn inform the decision as to *whom* the information will be directed at (the second dot-point above). Referring back to the discussion in Chapter 8 of the ethical/moral and the managerial branches of Stakeholder Theory, it should be clear that, if a corporation's social and environmental reporting is motivated exclusively by managerial reasoning and strategising, the stakeholders to whom that corporation's social and environmental reporting is directed might be narrowly defined as those who hold and exercise the greatest economic power over the corporation. Conversely, social and environmental reporting motivated by ethical/moral reasoning (the ethical branch of Stakeholder Theory) will seek to address the information needs of a broader range of stakeholders. Specifically, a broader 'ethical' approach to reporting would direct the reports towards those stakeholders most affected by the operations of the organisation.

Once the organisation has determined which stakeholders are the target recipients of the reports, they can then consider the information demands of these particular stakeholders. This will then determine *what* types of information will be disclosed (the third dot-point above) and *what* issues the social and environmental reporting should address. Identifying *what* issues an entity is held responsible and accountable for involves dialogue between the organisation and its identified target stakeholders. Several research studies have addressed aspects of this process of communication with stakeholders.

Once an organisation has identified the objectives of the reporting process (*why* report), the stakeholders to be addressed by the reporting process (*who* the report is intended for) and the information requirements of these stakeholders (for *what* issues the entity is held responsible and accountable by its stakeholders—or what issues the report should cover), the final stage in the social and environmental reporting process is the production of a report (or more than one form of report) that addresses these issues (or stakeholders' information needs). This is a very broad stage which involves many more detailed stages regarding *how* the report(s) should be compiled. In this stage, several elements of the social and environmental reporting process diverge considerably from the financial reporting processes embodied in financial accounting conceptual frameworks, although some issues (such as reliability of information) are important in both.

In the following pages of this chapter, the examination of sustainability reporting will be structured in accordance with the *why-to whom-for what-how* stages of social and environmental reporting explained above. It begins with a detailed exploration of the motives (or objectives, or the *why* question) for organisations in general, and business corporations specifically, to engage in corporate social responsibility and sustainability reporting.

OBJECTIVES OF THE SOCIAL AND ENVIRONMENTAL REPORTING PROCESS—THE *WHY* STAGE

Social and environmental reporting—the topic of this chapter—is predominantly a voluntary process given the general lack of regulation in the area. Even with the lack of regulation, many organisations publicly release information about their social and environmental performance. This leads to the obvious question of why they choose to do it. What motivates them to release this information voluntarily? Answers to such questions are directly tied to our beliefs about what drives individual behaviour. The author of this book (Deegan) has been asked on a number of occasions to help organisations produce a social and environmental report. A necessary first step is to ask the organisation to consider 'why' it is reporting. The answer to this question will then help put the 'to whom–for what–how' stages in context.

As seen in previous chapters, different researchers will have differing views about why companies adopt particular operating and reporting strategies. For example:

1. Chapter 8 considered Legitimacy Theory and the associated notion of a 'social contract'. Adopting this perspective, we could argue that an entity would undertake certain social activities (and provide an account thereof) if management perceived that the particular activities were expected by the communities in which it operates. That is, it is part of the social contract, or, as companies often state, part of their licence to operate. As a practical example, BHP Billiton, in its 2008 *Sustainability Report*, had a page dedicated to the 'business case' for sustainable development.[6] One of the cases for sustainable development the company noted was provided under the heading 'Gaining and maintaining our licence to operate and grow'.[7] Under this heading the report stated:

   Access to resources is crucial to the sustainability of our business. Fundamental to achieving access to resources is effectively addressing heightened political and societal expectations related to the environment and social aspects of our business.

   This view is consistent with the premises of Legitimacy Theory. Failure to undertake those activities that are expected by society may, according to Legitimacy Theory, result in the entity no longer being considered legitimate (it is perceived as breaching its social contract) and this in turn will impact on the support it receives from the community, and

---

6   The 'business case' is often used to explain why companies embrace corporate social responsibility (CSR) activities. The Business Council of Australia (2005, p. 6) states that its 'member companies are actively engaged in CSR activities because there is a business case for them to do so'. This would imply that if there was not a business case then the members would not embrace the idea of corporate social responsibility. Arguably, quests towards sustainability and urgent moves to address climate change should ideally not be justified on the basis of a 'business case'.

7   This business case has also been identified, using the same words, in a number of previous BHP *Sustainability Reports*. Although not provided in 2008, BHP Billiton has typically provided a glossary of key definitions, in which the 'licence to operate' has been defined as 'securing and maintaining the trust and confidence of the community and regulators in order to set up and conduct business'.

hence its survival.[8] Success is contingent upon complying with the social contract. Within Legitimacy Theory, organisational legitimacy is considered to be a valuable resource which can be influenced by the disclosure policies used by the organisation. In discussing the 'community licence to operate' (which is generally considered to be the same as the 'social contract'), the Business Council of Australia (2005, p. 34) states:

> Poor corporate behaviour can threaten a company's licence to operate through the community demanding greater regulatory restrictions being placed on the company, increasing its cost base and limiting its future prospects. Ultimately, this can lead to prohibitions on the company selling certain products or accessing valuable resources. The converse is that companies with strong CSR reputations will gain quicker access to resources and be subject to less regulation than their competitors.

It is interesting to see that the Business Council of Australia considers that complying with the community licence to operate (or the social contract) will be beneficial because it might in turn mean that the organisation would be subject to lower levels of regulation.

2. Chapter 8 also considered Stakeholder Theory. One version of Stakeholder Theory (the managerial/positive version and *not* the ethical/normative version) predicts that management is more likely to focus on meeting the expectations of powerful stakeholders. Powerful stakeholders are those who control resources that are both scarce and essential to the achievement of the organisation's (or its managers') objectives. For most businesses, powerful stakeholders will be those who have the greatest potential to influence the firm's ability to generate maximum financial returns (or profits)—in other words, those stakeholders with the most economic power and influence over the firm. Under this managerial stakeholder perspective, management would be expected to embrace those economic, social and environmental activities expected by the powerful stakeholders, and to provide an account of those activities to these stakeholders. Chapter 8 also described an ethical branch of Stakeholder Theory. This branch adopts a normative position and prescribes that an organisation should consider the rights of all parties affected by the operation of the entity regardless of the power they can exercise. Under this perspective, the definition of stakeholders would be broader and would be consistent with the definition provided by Freeman (1984). Freeman defines a stakeholder as 'any group or individual who can affect *or is affected by* the achievement of the firm's objectives' (emphasis added).[9] Hence, the answer to the 'why report' question is directly a function of whether management embraces ethical or managerial reasoning.

---

8   As indicated in Chapter 8, the social contract is a concept used within Legitimacy Theory to represent the multitude of implicit and explicit expectations that society has about how an organisation should conduct its business. It is assumed that society allows an organisation to continue operations to the extent that it generally meets society's expectations. These expectations will change over time and different individuals (including the organisation's managers) will have different perspectives about what these expectations actually encompass at a given point in time. Hence, to all intents and purposes it is not possible to provide any form of accurate depiction of what specifically the terms of the social contract are; nevertheless, it is arguably a useful construct to describe the relationship between an organisation and the society in which it operates.

9   In its 2008 *Sustainability Report*, BHP Billiton defines its stakeholders as 'people who are adversely or positively impacted by our operations, those who have an interest in what we do, or those who have an influence on what we do'. Such a definition would be consistent with the definition of stakeholders that somebody working in the ethical branch of Stakeholder Theory would adopt (for example, Freeman, 1984), as it includes a consideration of the effects of BHP on others, rather than defining stakeholders solely on the basis of the effects they could have on BHP Billiton.

3. Chapter 8 further considered the accountability model developed by Gray, Owen and Adams (1996). Under this normative model, which has much in common with the ethical branch of Stakeholder Theory, organisations have many responsibilities (at a minimum, as required by law but expanded by society's expectations that have not also been codified within the law), and with every organisational responsibility comes a set of rights for stakeholders, including rights to information from the organisation to demonstrate its accountability in relation to the stakeholders' expectations. Obviously, determining responsibilities is not a straightforward exercise—different people will have different perspectives of the responsibilities of business, and hence the accountability of business. The accountability model is related to the ethical branch of Stakeholder Theory.

4. Institutional Theory was also considered in Chapter 8. This perspective assumes that the managers of an organisation will develop or adopt new practices (such as corporate social responsibility and/or social and environmental reporting) because of a variety of institutional pressures, such as other organisations developing new practices in these areas and managers being concerned that, if they do not emulate these organisations, they will risk disapproval from some of their economically powerful stakeholders.

5. Chapter 7 considered Positive Accounting Theory, which predicts that all people are driven by self-interest.[10] As such, this theory predicts that particular social and environmental activities, and their related disclosure, would occur only if they had positive wealth implications for the management involved.

Hence, there could be various motivations for managers to decide to disclose information—inclusive of information about social and environmental performance. The various theoretical perspectives on the broad reasons why organisations might engage in voluntary social and environmental reporting practices are not mutually exclusive. Furthermore, as emphasised throughout this book, the acceptance of particular theories to explain particular actions is, at least in part, tied to one's own value system.

While the discussion of possible motivations to report is tied to particular theories, it is interesting to consider some factors that industry believes motivates corporations to be socially responsible and to provide an account of their social and environmental performance. In a submission made in late 2005 to an Australian government inquiry on corporate social responsibility, the Business Council of Australia identified a number of 'existing drivers towards greater corporate social responsibility'. These were identified as:

■ employee recruitment, motivation and retention;
■ learning and innovation;
■ reputation management;
■ risk profile and risk management;
■ competitiveness and market positioning;
■ operational efficiency;
■ investor relations and access to capital; and
■ licence to operate.

---

10 As such, and as already indicated, it is probably not a theory that provides a great deal of hope in terms of moves towards sustainable development—moves which, if we accept the *Brundtland Report* definition of sustainability discussed earlier in the chapter, would require current generations to consider forgoing consumption and wealth generation to ensure that future generations' needs are met. Sacrificing current consumption and wealth creation for the benefit of future generations and Positive Accounting Theory's central assumption of self-interest could be deemed to be mutually inconsistent.

The purpose of the 2005 Australian government inquiry was to consider the merit of introducing greater regulatory requirements in relation to corporate social responsibility and the associated reporting. Interested parties were requested to make submissions to the inquiry and more than 100 submissions were received, many of which came from corporations and industry bodies. Most corporations and business associations—such as the Business Council of Australia—were opposed to the introduction of additional legislation. This opposition to legislation could be explained in terms of some of the theories of regulation discussed in Chapter 3.[11]

If we consider the 'drivers' identified by the Business Council of Australia—which it argued were sufficient for companies to do the 'right thing' even in the absence of regulation—we can see that they are all tied to maximising the value of business, rather than necessarily doing the 'right thing' by the stakeholders with whom they interact (that is, the motivations are tied to managerial reasoning rather than broader ethical considerations). Indeed, throughout its submission to government, the Business Council of Australia continually refers to the imperative to maximise shareholder value. Taking this imperative to its extreme, the council stated in its submission that:

> The litmus test for any activity or responsibility is whether the performance of that activity or responsibility can reasonably be seen to be contributing to the growth of shareholder value.

Such views place shareholders at the top of the 'pecking order' of all stakeholders. Again, we can question whether a fixation on maximising the wealth of one group of stakeholders (investors) will provide long-term solutions to real and evolving problems such as climate change—arguably not. Hence, if we were to ask the Business Council of Australia 'why' companies should report, it would probably reply that it is in the shareholders' interests to do so. Similarly, embracing this perspective, the council would probably argue that its members should only address climate change issues if doing so will have positive implications for shareholder value. Indeed, business organisations often justify corporate social responsibility activities in terms of the positive benefits the activities will have for the owners of the business—that is, the shareholders. The Business Council of Australia (2005, p. 11) states, 'Broader considerations, such as the community and environment, are essential to contribute to and protect value in the long-term and accordingly the potential shareholder wealth that can be achieved over time'. The idea that doing the 'right thing' by the community and the environment will provide benefits to the owners (shareholders) is often referred to as 'enlightened self-interest'. For example, in relation to one of the business cases for corporate social responsibility (employee recruitment, motivation and retention), the Business Council of Australia (2005, p. 16) states:

> The reputation of a company affects its desirability as a potential workplace. It is *in the company's strategic interests* to attract and retain the most highly skilled and expert employees, and this can be encouraged by maintaining an ethical and attractive reputation (emphasis added).

---

11 The Business Council of Australia (2005, p. 6) states that 'given the difficulty defining corporate social responsibility (CSR), as well as the fact that CSR activities are already broadly being pursued in Australia by large corporations, mandating CSR through legislative intervention runs the risk of stifling the innovative and creative approaches to CSR that are being adopted by Australian companies'. If we think about the Business Council's statement, we may decide that it is very hard to determine the logic of this argument, as it is not clear why if government set minimum standards for CSR activities this would stifle what companies could do. As many corporations do now, they could simply do more than is required by the legislation. The legislation would simply establish a lower limit for what companies must do in relation to their social and environmental responsibilities.

Accounting Headlines 9.2 and 9.3 provide examples of situations where corporations have exhibited enlightened self-interest—situations where embracing certain social and environmental performance standards has led to benefits for a corporation and its owners.

Any consideration of what motivates managers to report particular information cannot be considered in the absence of a consideration of the accountabilities of business. As indicated within the accountability model proposed by Gray, Owen and Adams (1996)—as described in Chapter 8 and briefly referred to above—whether the senior managers of an organisation elect to disclose particular information (that is, whether they will provide an account), will at least in part be linked to their own perceptions about whether they believe they are accountable for particular

Accounting Headline 9.2 Arguments suggesting that corporations will be motivated to raise their social and environmental performance even in the absence of regulation

Responsibility seen as issue no longer

TIM SHEEHY

Age, 27 October 2005, p. 3

There is no compelling case for tighter regulation to make Australian companies more socially responsible.

Existing laws requiring directors to act in the best interests of the company as a whole already allow companies to take account of the impact of their decisions on stakeholders other than shareholders, such as employees, customers, suppliers, investors and the broader community.

Companies with a high-performance culture already embrace corporate responsibility simply because it's good for business.

It is becoming increasingly obvious that companies that ignore the long-term social and environmental impact of their activities and refuse to participate in ongoing dialogue with their stakeholders are putting their long-term future at risk.

In short, Chartered Secretaries Australia (CSA) does not support any moves to legislate corporate responsibility duties for directors.

One of the great benefits of increased shareholder participation is the recognition that a short-sighted focus on profits alone is not a sustainable approach to business. In contrast, pursuing a bona fide corporate responsibility policy can open up value-corporate opportunities, build customer trust and promote innovation—all of which gives a company a competitive advantage and builds a strong, positive brand in the long run.

Many Australian companies already have corporate responsibility initiatives in place.

For example, National Australia Bank participates in the Carbon Disclosure Project, a global assessment by 85 institutional investors on the extent to which the *Financial Times* 500 most valuable companies are taking carbon risk and climate change risk into consideration as part of their core business.

Like NAB, BHP Billiton undertakes a range of corporate responsibility activities throughout the world and reports comprehensively on these activities in an annual sustainability report.

Nor is good corporate responsibility restricted to large publicly listed companies. Zurich Financial Services Australia Limited, in partnership with United Way, runs a program that supports and encourages employees to engage with the community by donating their time and money. Zurich also recently launched a national Green Office initiative to encourage its office to be more environmentally responsible.

And Flinders Ports Pty Ltd sponsors the South Australian Maritime Museum and funds the education program 'A Day at the Port' through the South Australian Investigator Science Centre.

These are just a few examples of what is fast becoming sound business practice in corporate Australia. The reality is good corporate responsibility is happening without regulatory intervention. Many companies today are already living and breathing the values of corporate responsibility through active engagement in their communities.

Tim Sheehy is chief executive of Chartered Secretaries Australia.

Australian Financial Review, 31 March 2005, p. 19

Social responsibility pays, says AMP

CHRIS WRIGHT

Share prices of companies that act in a socially responsible way outperform those that fail to do so by more than 3 per cent a year, according to a research report.

AMP Capital Investors, which runs the AMP Capital Sustainable Australian Share Fund, analysed the impact of corporate social responsibility, a company's behaviour towards stakeholders, employees and the environment on share price performance over four- and 10-year periods.

After removing the effects of sector, size and momentum, AMP concluded that stocks with a high corporate social responsibility rating outperformed those with a low rating by 4.8 per cent annually over four years and 3 per cent over 10. Data on industry sustainability, the impact of social, economic and technological trends on the long-term viability of an industry, was not statistically significant.

Australia's ethical or socially responsible investment (SRI) funds, which have $4.6 billion under management, according to the Ethical Investment Association, face a constant battle to persuade investors their techniques do not limit performance.

There are two sides to the debate. The negative stance is that any fund that limits the stocks it can invest in also limits its ability to outperform competitors.

Others argue that any company that implements sustainable practices towards its staff, shareholders and the environment must be stronger over the long run.

While the AMP study supports the argument that ethically well-run stocks do well, the more relevant question is whether ethical funds can stand comparison with mainstream competitors. AMP claims its fund is top-quartile even when compared with mainstream managers over one to three years. However, Mercer Investment Consulting says the median SRI Manager modestly underperformed the median Australian share fund over every time frame to February 28.

---

types of performance. That is, the act of providing particular accounts (that is, accounting) is directly tied to perceptions about the responsibilities and associated accountabilities of business.

A NARROW VIEW OF BUSINESS RESPONSIBILITIES

Moves by many companies throughout the world to implement reporting mechanisms that provide information about the social and environmental performance of their entities imply that the managements of these organisations consider that they have an accountability not only for their economic performance but also for their social and environmental performance. While this is a view held by many individuals, it is not necessarily a view that is accepted universally. For example, if we were to adopt a fairly extreme view that corporations do not have social or moral responsibilities beyond simply generating profits for the benefits of owners, we might not see the need to produce social and environmental accounts, except to the extent that such accounts would enhance corporate profitability. For example, consider the views of the famous economist Milton Friedman. In his widely cited book *Capitalism and Freedom*, Friedman (1962) rejects the view that corporate managers have any moral obligations beyond maximising their profits. In relation to the view that organisations have social responsibilities, he notes (p. 133) that such a view:

... shows a fundamental misconception of the character and nature of a free economy. In such an economy, there is one and only one social responsibility of business, to use its resources and engage in activities designed to increase its profits as long as it stays within the rules of the game, which is to say, engages in open and free competition, without deception or fraud.[12,13]

Arguably, Milton Friedman would not have been a strong advocate for social and environmental reporting, unless of course it could be linked to enhancing business profitability. Accounting Headline 9.4 raises a number of issues in relation to the responsibilities of business entities, and the relationship between corporate social responsibility and the 'bottom line'. The article also

Age, 11 July 2007, p. 2

Accounting Headline 9.4 Views about the social responsibility of business

Business of earning a social reputation

LEON GETTLER

Nearly 40 years after economist Milton Friedman wrote that the 'social responsibility of business is to increase its profits', business chiefs are saying they want to play a leadership role in tackling sociopolitical issues such as education, health care and foreign policy.

A study by consulting firm McKinsey found that almost half of US executives want to play a bigger role. Still, only one in seven consider themselves to be playing that role now, citing reasons such as lack of time, fear of negative publicity or negative repercussions for themselves and their company and a lack of desire to engage with politicians.

The study coincides with three studies—from the United Nations,

Goldman Sachs and McKinsey again—put to a meeting of the UN Global Compact last week highlighting the links between corporate responsibility and the bottom line.

According to Goldman Sachs, companies that perform well on governance, social responsibility and environment have performed better than the general sharemarket over the past couple of years.

But the reports highlighted the difficulties companies face embedding these issues into their strategies and operations.

Instead, what they seem to do is lump corporate responsibility into a single, corporate sub-site.

Clearly, there has been a change since the days of Friedman. Social issues are not necessarily peripheral

to the business of business and they can be fundamental. Ignore the wrong ones and you risk having your reputation trashed or having laws brought in. It's also important because business makes an enormous contribution to society. Think of jobs, innovation, research, and social connections. And yet business struggles with the issue.

So, is this a role for companies and business leaders? Should business leaders be doing more to tackle social issues, or should that be left to governments and the rest of society? Is the business of business just business, or is it more? Are you more likely to invest in, or work for a boss that takes these issues more seriously?

---

12 According to Clarkson (1995, p. 103), 'Friedman chose to interpret social issues and social responsibilities to mean non-business issues and non-business responsibilities. He, like so many neo-classical economists, separated business from society, which enabled him to maintain that "the business of business is business". By placing the two abstractions of business and society into separate compartments, Friedman was able to deny the necessity, or even the validity, of the concept of corporate social responsibility, decrying it as a fundamentally subversive doctrine.'

13 In contrast to Milton Friedman, Anita Roddick, founder of the Body Shop made the following statement in the introduction to her book *Business as Unusual: The Journey of Anita Roddick and the Body Shop* (2007): 'In terms of power and influence, you can forget the church, forget politics. There is no more powerful institution in society than business, which is why I believe it is now more important than ever before for business to assume a moral leadership. The business of business should not be about money, it should be about responsibility. It should be about public good, not private greed.'

reflects some differences in opinion about corporate social responsibilities relative to the views of Friedman.

Somewhat surprisingly, many students of accounting complete their accounting qualifications without ever considering issues associated with the accountability of business. But the practice of accounting, which, at a fairly simplistic level, can be defined as the provision of information about the performance of an entity to a particular stakeholder group, cannot be divorced from a consideration of the extent of an entity's responsibility and accountability. That is, an organisation will provide an account of those things for which it is deemed to be accountable. One cannot be considered without the other (so we should be left wondering how a study of accounting can be undertaken without a detailed consideration of the concept of corporate accountabilities).

If accountants were to accept that an entity has a responsibility for its social and environmental performance and is accountable for it, they would see it as a duty to provide an account of an organisation's social and environmental performance. If they did not accept this, they would not be motivated to provide such an account. For example, if they adopt a perspective that the dominant accountability of a corporation is to its shareholders in terms of its financial performance, they might believe that corporations only need to provide an account of their financial performance. There will be no motivation to provide social and environmental performance information to a broader group of stakeholders. Indeed, this is a view which arguably has been embraced by many regulators in the past who have fixated on putting in place extensive regulations in relation to financial accounting but have tended to ignore the regulation of social and environmental accounting. Such regulators would seem to question the relevance of social and environmental accountability. This narrow approach to accountability, in which prime attention appears to be given to the needs and expectations of shareholders and other individuals with a financial stake in the organisation (rather than stakeholders generally), is commonly referred to as a 'shareholder primacy' view of corporate reporting. Such an approach to regulating external reporting is (unfortunately) found in many countries. Likewise, if students who study 'accounting' at university are simply taught about how to account for organisations from a financial perspective, without consideration of social or environmental performance, those in charge of the programs must themselves be embracing a perspective that the major responsibility and accountability of a business organisation is restricted to its financial performance. Is this a reasonable assumption to make?

The shareholder primacy approach generally adopted within Australia and many other countries is increasingly being challenged. At this stage, however, government has tended to leave corporations, their industry bodies and 'the market' to determine the extent of corporate social and environmental disclosure. This is evidenced by the very limited disclosure requirements pertaining to non-financial performance issues associated with social and environmental matters. In this regard, Frank Cicutto, former chief executive officer of National Australia Bank, stated (as quoted in the *Journal of Banking and Financial Services*, December 2002, p. 17):

> In recent decades the efficient use of shareholder funds has been carefully protected by the creation of ASIC and the continuing development of the ASX listing rules. In a regulatory sense the focus of legislative change has been around accountability to investors rather than to the community.

Further related to the issues of responsibilities and accountabilities is the question of whether the responsibility of business is restricted to current generations, or should the implications for future generations be factored into current management decisions? As mentioned earlier, sustainable development has been defined as 'development that meets the needs of the present world without compromising the ability of future generations to meet their own needs'. If sustainability is embraced, then, as this definition indicates, our current production patterns should not be such that they compromise the ability of future generations to satisfy their needs. Such a view is being publicly acknowledged throughout the world by many organisations. For example, consider the following statement by the British telecommunications multinational BT Group in its 2004 *Social and Environmental Report* (p. 25):

> The concept of sustainable development has increasingly come to represent a new kind of world—where economic growth delivers a more just and inclusive society, at the same time as preserving the natural environment and the world's non-renewable resources for future generations.

Such quotes reflect the public positions being promoted by many organisations. Whether these public positions actually dominate decision making within the firm is another issue—we clearly cannot be sure. Accounting Headline 9.5 provides a counter-perspective in which it is argued that corporations are not doing enough in relation to their corporate social responsibilities and associated accountabilities. Read the article and consider whether you are inclined to agree with the perspective.

Accounting Headline 9.5 An insight into the social responsibilities of business

Courier-Mail, 20 September 2008, p. 3

Firms failing social duty

COLIN BRINSDEN

It was the buzz phrase among corporations at the turn of the century, but many Australian businesses appear not to be pulling their weight when it comes to their social responsibility.

The concept of Corporate Social Responsibility (CSR) is that, while businesses are focused on profits and jobs, they should also be aware of the impact they are having on the environment and the community.

A study by consultant firm Grant Thornton found that only 52 per cent of the country's top 300-listed companies in the latest profit reporting season published information on their environmental performance or policies. Only 28 per cent provided details on action to reduce greenhouse gases.

Grant Thornton director of business risk services Peter Moloney says the results are disappointing.

'We actually think that companies that don't get this right will get left behind,' Mr Moloney says.

'If you can't demonstrate you have good CSR credentials, you can't demonstrate you are taking them seriously and you are less likely to get the business.

'And if you look at the shareholder groups, they are clearly asking for more information in that area at the moment.'

The study also found that a mere 36 per cent of companies divulged their human resources policies—including maternity leave and diversity, while only 47 per cent reported on their community activities and initiatives.

In Australia, there is no requirement for companies to produce their CSR obligations, but in Britain there are a number of requirements that have to be fulfilled.

'Some of the larger (Australian) companies actually get it and are providing that sort of information, but the smaller ones are definitely not getting it,' Moloney said.

'It's obviously time for there to be more guidance.'

Many companies were talking about climate change, but he was not confident that they were approaching it in a structured manner.

'Everyone knows, but have they got a program in place to deal with it? The answer is probably no.'

Returning to the restricted view of corporate responsibility which fixates on the interests of shareholders and maximising corporate profitability (the shareholder primacy perspective that many corporate executives seem to be embracing), there are some people who argue that this rather self-interested position will actually benefit everybody within society. They argue that if the actions of all individuals (and businesses) are motivated solely by a self-interested desire to maximise personal wealth, this will benefit all in society because (through the resulting economic growth) the wealth generated by the successful individuals will 'trickle down' to the less successful. With this view, they argue, the conditions of all in society will be improved if all people in society actively pursue their own self-interest, with this being a morally desirable outcome. Indeed, this 'trickle down' theory is commonly repeated as a key moral justification for the capitalist system. The main problem with this moral justification for a narrow and exclusive focus on maximising shareholder wealth (or shareholder value) is that there is little, if any, evidence to show that it occurs. As Gray (2005, pp. 6–7) states:

> It is disturbing ... to discover that there is no direct evidence to support this precarious construction. The view relies, for its empirical support, on the generalised argument that, for example, we are all better off than we have ever been; that we are all getting better off all the time; and that this increase in well-being has coincided with the triumph of international capitalism. Such arguments are, at best, contestable. While for many in the West this statement has a superficial veracity, it ignores the growing gap between rich and poor ...

A considerable amount of economic evidence shows that not only is there lack of support for the existence of a generalised 'trickle down' effect but the reverse may have occurred. Hence many people question whether the social and environmental responsibilities of corporations should be left largely unregulated. Hutton (1996, p. 172) provides evidence that in the largely free-market economic conditions of the United Kingdom in the 1980s, the real (inflation-adjusted) incomes of the wealthiest one-tenth of the population rose by more than 50 per cent, while the poorest 15 per cent of the population experienced a real-term fall in their incomes.

Despite an apparent lack of empirical support for this 'moral' position underlying a narrow focus on shareholder value, we could be excused for thinking that many individuals working within the contemporary financial press hold the same view as Milton Friedman. The financial press continues to praise companies for increased profitability and to criticise companies that are subject to falling profitability. They often do this with little or no regard for any social costs or social benefits being generated by the operations of the particular entities—costs and benefits not directly incorporated within reported profit. Further, even though Friedman advocated his views approximately fifty years ago, these views still tend to resonate with some (but not all!) business leaders and organisations. For example, the Chamber of Commerce and Industry of Western Australia (2005) stated:

> Regulating to encourage decision makers to have regard for stakeholders beyond this [current requirement to manage the organisation in the 'best interests of the corporation'] is not in the public interest, and it is not the role of business. Stakeholder views and practices should be accommodated only so far as they improve or safeguard shareholder value.

Accounting Headline 9.6 provides a further insight into the differing opinions about the social responsibilities of business. The article provides the opinion of one of the financially richest individuals on the planet, Bill Gates, and it contrasts his views with those espoused by Friedman.

A BROADER VIEW OF BUSINESS RESPONSIBILITIES

Returning to the earlier view (Friedman, 1962) that the maximisation of profits (or shareholder value) should be management's top priority, it should be noted that there is (as you might expect) a contrary view embraced by many researchers working in the area of corporate social reporting.

Accounting Headline 9.6 Further views about the social responsibilities of business

Herald-Sun, 29 January 2008, p. 30

Copping flak over corporate socialism

LEELA DE KRETSER

With the world's financial markets in freefall, the United States economy grinding to a halt and a French trader forcing his bank to bring out the begging bowls, who would've thought a five-minute speech about corporate socialism could cause an uproar in the press?

But that's exactly what Microsoft genius Bill Gates faces at home after suggesting to his fellow billionaires at Davos [where the World Economic Forum holds its annual meeting; see www.weforum.org] that the free market is failing the world's poor—and that it's time to introduce a little bit of creative capitalism.

According to the one-time richest man on the planet, it's possible for a business to make profits and also improve the lives of others who don't necessarily benefit from market forces.

But—and with all good speeches the 'but' often contains the main point—Gates said profits are not always possible when business tries to serve the very poor.

In such cases, there needs to be another incentive, and that incentive is recognition.

Many of us may not find the concept of companies being socially responsible all that shocking, but you wouldn't have known it reading blogs and newspapers this week.

Gates was basically accused of burning the bible—otherwise known as The Social Responsibility of Business is to Increase Profits by Milton Friedman—by suggesting that corporations should consider philanthropy for philanthropy's sake.

Gates' desire for companies to dedicate their top people to poverty could prove disastrous for the corporate sector, screamed Peter Foster in the *Financial Post*.

Foster and his band of free-market-worshipping buddies accused Gates of taking the power of philanthropy out of the hands of the people who deserve it most—shareholders and employees.

Espousing the views of the great Friedman, these commentators argue that the best way for corporations to contribute to society is to increase their bottom lines, and therefore increase the amount of money going into shareholders' pockets and to employees in the form of wages.

Let these individuals—and not a bumbling middle manager or a bureaucratic machine—be the ones to decide how to donate money to the poorest people, Foster said.

According to this view, a corporation's only justifiable expense on philanthropy should be to increase its public relations value.

Many of these columnists used as an example the large amounts of money individual Americans donate to charities every year.

CNET's Declan McCullagh points out that while the US Government only gave $900 million for tsunami relief, individuals donated about $2 billion.

In total, he says, about $260 billion from American pockets goes to 1.4 billion charities every year.

The problem with this argument is that it doesn't take into account that individual donors in the US aren't equipped with the ability to target the money where it's needed most in the world.

The United States contributes only 0.34 per cent of its national income to foreign aid, well behind the United Nation's target of 0.7 per cent and leaders such as the Dutch, who give 2.44 per cent of their national income to the poorest countries in the world.

Those arguing against creative capitalism also fail to see the benefits that people like Gates, through his charities, have already brought to business.

Perhaps they need to think back to 1999 when major riots marred the WTO meeting in Seattle and contrast that with the relative peace of Davos.

This is that organisations, public or private, earn their right to operate within the community. This right, which was considered in Chapter 8, is provided by the society in which they exist, and not solely by those parties with a direct financial interest (such as the shareholders who directly benefit from increasing profits) or by government. That is, business organisations themselves are artificial entities that society chooses to create (Donaldson, 1982). Donaldson notes that if society chooses to create organisations, they can also choose either not to create them or to create different entities. The view held is that organisations do not have an inherent right to resources. As Mathews (1993, p. 26) states:

> Society (as a collection of individuals) provides corporations with their legal standing and attributes and the authority to own and use natural resources and to hire employees. Organisations draw on community resources and output both goods and services and waste products in the general environment. The organisation has no inherent rights to these benefits and, in order to allow their existence, society would expect the benefits to exceed the costs to society.

Consequently, the corporation receives its permission to operate from society, and is ultimately accountable to society for how it operates and what it does (Benston, 1982).

If society (and not just shareholders) considers that increasing profits is the overriding duty of businesses, then this factor alone may be sufficient (as Friedman argues) to ensure the businesses' survival. However, if society has greater expectations (such as that a business must provide goods or services that are safe, that it must not exploit its employees, that it must not exploit its physical environment, and so on), then it is arguable whether a business that is preoccupied with profitability alone could maintain an existence. Supporting this reasoning, a report based on a survey of chief executives from the Global Fortune 500 (the world's largest companies by revenue), which was published by the Judge Institute of Management at the University of Cambridge (Brady, 2003, p. 5), showed that:

> Despite recent financial scandals (Enron, WorldCom etc.), [chief executives] predict that in the near future social credibility will be as important as financial credibility, and environmental credibility will only be marginally less important.

The survey also found (p. 12) that chief executives:

> Appear to believe that six key elements will contribute most towards the preservation of a positive corporate reputation. Conversely, any neglect of these key elements could result in the formation of a negative reputation. Notably, these six key elements include both environmental and social credibility (rated as being individually important).

Furthermore, a study by Ernst & Young (2002) which involved interviews conducted with senior executives at 147 of the Global 1000 companies found (p. 5) that:

> Companies are increasingly acknowledging that corporate ethical, environmental and social behaviour can have a material impact on business value. The great majority of companies (79 percent) forecast the importance of this issue to rise over the next five years as companies across a range of industry sectors recognise its relevance to their business. Research has found that a company's reputation in respect to issues pertaining to CSR is a factor in purchasing decisions for 70 percent of all consumers.

Some senior executives have gone further than this, and have released statements indicating that they do not consider that the pursuit of profits alone is an acceptable strategy. As the chief executive officer of Dutch multinational logistics company TPG (the owner of, among other companies, the courier company TNT) stated in his introduction to TPG's *Corporate Sustainability Report 2004* (p. 2):

> ... For us, sustainability is our ongoing search for opportunities to actively do good things and then report on our progress.
>
> More than anything else, we want TPG to be a well-respected and trusted entity that demonstrates accountability not only to customers and shareholders, but also to our employees and the world at large. Over the last two years we have integrated our sustainability initiatives and approaches to ensure that our policies and practices effectively reflect our vision.

More common, however, and consistent with the studies from the University of Cambridge (Brady, 2003) and Ernst & Young (2002), are senior executives who justify their reasons for engaging in corporate social responsibility initiatives by reference to the necessity of these initiatives for long-term (sustainable) profits. As O'Dwyer (2003) points out, these justifications are often explained in terms of win–win outcomes, where it is claimed that what is beneficial for society and the environment is also beneficial for shareholder financial returns. For example, the chief executive's foreword to British Airways' *Social and Environmental Report 2003/04* includes the following statement (p. 1):

> ... we have recognised that our sustainability as a business depends not only on improving financial performance but also on continuing to manage responsibly. Without the loyalty and support of our customers and employees, and the trust of the communities in which we operate, we will not prosper and succeed over the longer term. Our social and environmental performance is critical to earning this loyalty, support and trust.

This section has addressed the *why* stage of social and environmental reporting, which is the initial stage where companies consider arguments in favour of engaging in corporate social responsibility and sustainability reporting. Consistent with some of the insights developed in Chapter 8, these motivations can range from a desire to maximise financial returns for shareholders and/or managers by using social and environmental reporting as a tool to maintain and enhance the support of economically powerful stakeholders, through to a desire to discharge duties of accountability for the social and environmental impact the organisation (potentially) has on a wide range of stakeholders. Different managers will be driven by different motivations to report. The section explored notions of sustainability to explain that shareholder interests of profit maximisation tend to converge with interests of social and environmental sustainability over longer time horizons. Thus, in the long term, companies aiming for sustainable financial profits need to ensure that they (and other businesses) are also socially and environmentally sustainable. This can make it difficult in practice to discern the true motives for why a company's executives develop and implement corporate social responsibility programs and policies, and engage in social and environmental reporting, where the reasons for sustainability are explained in terms both of a need to avoid negative impacts on society and the environment and as being necessary to ensure future profitability.

For example, the introduction to the environment section of Tesco's *Corporate Responsibility Report 2005* (p. 42) stated:

> We believe in sustainable growth—it is responsible, it is what our customers want and it makes sound business sense. If we take decisions that are unsustainable, we may harm the world we all live in. Similarly, if we fail to minimise our environmental impacts, we will be inefficient and increase our costs.

Having considered several perspectives on *why* organisations might be motivated to report on their social and environmental impacts, we will now turn to the second broad stage of the sustainability reporting process—identifying the stakeholders whose information needs are to be addressed.[14]

IDENTIFYING STAKEHOLDERS—THE *WHO* STAGE

The range of stakeholders whose needs and expectations are considered by an organisation when it is determining its corporate social responsibility policies, and when compiling its social and environmental reports, will be directly related to its motives for adopting these policies and practices. For an organisation whose managers are motivated exclusively by the maximisation of shareholder value, and who therefore might use social and environmental reporting only to win or maintain the approval of economically powerful stakeholders, the stakeholders to be addressed by social and environmental reporting might be restricted to the economically powerful stakeholders.

Economically powerful stakeholders can vary over time for an organisation. For example, for a company that requires a large number of semi-skilled employees and sells its products in reasonably competitive markets, consumers may have considerable economic power in times of economic recession but may lose some of this power in times of economic boom (when consumer demand grows faster than supply). Conversely, the semi-skilled workforce may become more economically powerful during an economic boom if unemployment falls and a general shortage of semi-skilled workers arises. In this case, the economically powerful stakeholders whose views the company will seek to address, in accordance with the managerial branch of Stakeholder Theory, may shift from the company's consumers to its employees.

In contrast to the narrow focus on economically powerful stakeholders provided by the managerial branch of Stakeholder Theory, a much wider range of stakeholders will be considered if the ethical branch of Stakeholder Theory is followed. Organisations whose corporate social responsibility and whose sustainability reporting are motivated by broader ethical considerations of reducing the negative impact (or maximising the positive impact) that the organisation has on every person and entity affected by the organisation's operations might consider as stakeholders to whom the organisation is accountable all humans from current and future generations on whom their operations could have an impact (no matter how remote these people are from the

---

14 Stakeholders have been defined in various ways. For our purposes we broadly define stakeholders as parties affected by, or having an effect upon, the organisation in question. This is also consistent with definitions provided by Freeman (1984) and Gray, Owen and Adams (1996).

organisation), all animals living today and in the future on whom the organisation's operations could impact, and any other elements of nature potentially affected by the organisation's operations. What is being emphasised is that the question about *who* the social and environmental reports will be targeted at will ultimately be dependent on managers' views about their responsibilities and accountabilities. Again, views will vary from manager to manager.

In looking at how some organisations define their stakeholders, consider a comment made by the Business Council of Australia (2005, p. 22). In discussing one of the 'business cases' for companies to embrace corporate social responsibility, the Business Council refers to 'reputation management':

> Business success is highly dependent on reputation within the community. The breadth of stakeholders which influence business today means reputation is increasingly important. Reputation can affect, amongst other things, whether customers purchase products, whether investors will give up funds and whether employees will commit to the corporation. Understanding the expectations and pressures from stakeholders and responding effectively is crucial to the success of a business's reputation and the control of possible risks.

It is clear that the Business Council of Australia is relatively fixated on the interests of those stakeholders who have the power to influence corporations, rather than considering the needs of those stakeholders who might be *affected by* the operations of the corporations. That is, the Business Council does not appear to consider stakeholders in a way that would be suggested by the ethical branch of Stakeholder Theory.

The theoretical position that ethically motivated organisations should take account of the views and needs of all stakeholders (present and future) on whom their operations might potentially impact represents a philosophical ideal rather than a practical and attainable aim. In practice, the operations of many organisations are likely to have some form of impact on many people, animals and other elements of nature, and to try to take account of all of these potential effects, and to seek to communicate to all those potentially affected, would be an impossible task.

This impossibility arises partly because in our highly complex and interrelated world many activities have the potential to lead to numerous unintended and unforeseeable consequences (Beck, 1992, 1999). Where these future consequences of current actions are unforeseeable, it is difficult to conceive of how an organisation could take them into account when determining the stakeholders affected (now and in the future) by its current operations, and thereby the stakeholders to whom the organisation is accountable today. This impossibility also partly arises because, when it comes to the communication element of accountability (which, after all, is what this chapter is about), it is not possible to communicate effectively today with many non-human elements of nature or with future generations.

Thus, even when an organisation's corporate social responsibility and social and environmental reporting are motivated by ethical rather than managerial reasoning, the organisation will always need to identify a subset from all of the stakeholders who might be affected by its operations. The social and environmental needs and expectations of this subset of stakeholders will then determine the social and environmental responsibilities and accountability of the organisation, and the social and environmental reporting that addresses these accountability duties.

Some theorists, such as Gray et al. (1997) and Unerman and Bennett (2004), argue that an ethical approach to identifying, from a large number of stakeholders, those stakeholders to whom an organisation is responsible and accountable requires consideration of the views of those stakeholders on whom an organisation's operations have the most impact. These will not always be those stakeholders who are closest to the organisation's operations in economic (or even in physical/geographical) terms. This approach would require organisations to prioritise the views and interests of those stakeholders on whose lives their operations were likely to have the largest impact.

The practical implications of this theoretical approach to stakeholder prioritisation (in accordance with the ethical branch of Stakeholder Theory) is that organisations whose corporate social responsibility and social and environmental reporting are motivated by a desire to minimise the negative social and environmental impact of their operations will prioritise stakeholders' needs according to the extent of the impacts that the organisation's operations are likely to have on any stakeholder's life. In determining its policies and practices, the organisation will then seek to minimise its negative impacts on as many of these stakeholders as possible—addressing the needs and expectations of those stakeholders on whom its operations have a potentially larger impact before the needs and expectations of stakeholders on whom its operations are likely to have a lesser impact. However, O'Dwyer (2005) demonstrates how problematic this process of stakeholder prioritisation can be in practice, as stakeholders who some would regard as highly dependent on the organisation may, for reasons of expediency, be omitted from the prioritised subset of stakeholders defined and determined by the organisation's managers.

As an example of how some organisations are defining their stakeholders in practice, in the *Sustainability Report 2007/08* of the Co-operative Financial Services (CFS) group in the United Kingdom (which includes the Co-operative Bank), the organisation defines its main stakeholders rather broadly as members, customers, employees, suppliers, the wider society and the co-operative movement, and it explains how each of these groups is defined. In its earlier 2003 *Sustainability Report* it explicitly explained why the identified stakeholders did not include the environment (p. 13):

> Unlike some organisations, CFS does not define 'The Environment' as a separate Partner. The relationship between business and the 'Natural World' is essentially non-negotiable (in contrast to the relationship with suppliers, staff, etc.). The activities of CFS and its Partners are ultimately governed by nature's limited capacity to generate resources and assimilate waste. For this reason, CFS assesses the degree to which value is delivered to each Partner in an ecologically sustainable (and socially responsible) manner.

Broader evidence regarding how organisations are defining, and prioritising, their stakeholders is provided by Owen, Shaw and Cooper (2005). As part of a UK survey investigating managerial attitudes towards the provision of social and environmental information, they asked managers to rate the importance of a variety of different stakeholder groups as recipients of stand-alone sustainability reports on a scale of 0 (not important) to 5 (very important). According to the managers who were surveyed, shareholders were considered to be the most important audience for this information (mean importance of 3.95 out of 5), followed by employees (3.83), environmental pressure groups (3.68), governmental regulators (3.58), local communities (3.48), customers (3.20), non-equity investors (2.80) and suppliers (2.65). This managerial ranking of important stakeholders can vary between different countries. For example, Adams (2002) shows that views regarding which stakeholders are the most important varied between a sample of UK managers and German managers.

In practice, whichever approach to stakeholder prioritisation is taken by an organisation—whether prioritising stakeholders on the basis of those stakeholders most able to exert an influence on the organisation's profits (or shareholder value), prioritising stakeholders on the basis of those whose lives are most affected by the organisation's activities, or adoption of a position somewhere on the continuum between these extreme positions—once the organisation has identified the stakeholders whose social and environmental needs and expectations it will address, it then has to identify what the information needs and expectations of these stakeholders are. This takes us to the third stage of the *why–who–for what–how* process of social and environmental reporting.

IDENTIFYING STAKEHOLDER INFORMATION NEEDS AND EXPECTATIONS—THE '*WHAT* DO WE REPORT?' STAGE

A useful starting point to begin addressing the question 'For what social and environmental issues do stakeholders wish to hold organisations responsible and accountable?' is to identify whether there is actually any demand among stakeholders for social and environmental information.[15]

STAKEHOLDER DEMANDS FOR AND REACTIONS TO SOCIAL AND ENVIRONMENTAL INFORMATION

Obviously, for any form of public reporting to be useful in shaping community perceptions (one of the goals of corporate disclosure, according to Legitimacy Theory) there needs to be an external demand for, or a reaction to, the particular information being disclosed. As Deegan and Rankin (1997) point out, the ability to shape perceptions through annual report or social and environmental report disclosures (as would be suggested by Legitimacy Theory, which was discussed in Chapter 8) is possible only if members of society actually use the reported information. Deegan and Rankin (1997) examined the issue of whether people actually use or rely on the environmental performance information provided within annual reports. They solicited, by way of a questionnaire survey, the views of shareholders, stockbrokers and research analysts, accounting academics, representatives of financial institutions, and a number of organisations performing a general review or oversight function regarding:

- the materiality of environmental issues to certain groups in society who use annual reports to gain information;
- whether environmental information is sought from annual reports; and
- how important environmental information is to the decision-making process compared with other social responsibility information and information about the organisation's financial performance and position.

---

15 However, it needs to be appreciated that unless particular stakeholders know that particular information exists, or know how they might use the information, they might not show any demand for it. To explain this point by analogy, and as indicated in Chapter 5, a person required to dig a hole in soil might demand a screwdriver if he or she had never been exposed to a shovel. According to Gray, Owen and Maunders (1991, p. 15), even if particular stakeholders do not read particular accounts, the entity nevertheless has a responsibility to provide an account.

Deegan and Rankin (1997) found, at statistically significant levels, that shareholders and individuals within organisations with a review or oversight function—these included consumer associations, employee groups, industry associations and environmental groups—considered that environmental information was material to the particular decisions they undertook. In addition, shareholders, accounting academics and individuals from organisations with a review or oversight function were found to seek environmental information from the annual report to assist in making their various decisions. The annual report was perceived by the total group of respondents to be significantly more important (in the mid-1990s) than any other source of information concerning an organisation's interaction with the environment.[16] This study shows that various stakeholder groups within society *do* demand information about the social and environmental performance of organisations and thus, at a very broad level, there are issues for which stakeholders hold organisations responsible and accountable.

Another approach to determining whether people demand or react to certain disclosures is to review share price reactions to particular disclosures. The underlying theory used in many of these studies is derived from capital markets research and the use of the Efficient Markets Hypothesis, which proposes that the information content of news announcements, if relevant to the marketplace, will be immediately and unbiasedly impounded within share prices (capital markets research is explained in Chapter 10). That is, if an item of information about an organisation can be associated with a change in the share price of that organisation, it is assumed that the information is of importance to investors and they have reacted to the disclosure of the information (with the reaction being reflected by the change in share price). Share price reaction studies are considered in more depth in Chapter 10.

As an example of a share price study, Ingram (1978) and Anderson and Frankle (1980) found that the share market does react to social disclosure, with Ingram concluding that the reaction is a function of, among other things, the industry to which the organisation belongs and the types of social disclosures being made.

Belkaoui (1976) and Jaggi and Freedman (1982) studied investors' reactions to pollution disclosures. Belkaoui observed a positive share market reaction to firms that provided evidence of responsible pollution control procedures compared with firms that could not demonstrate responsibility. He concluded that the results verified the existence of an 'ethical investor', that is, an investor who responds to demonstrations of social concern and invests in corporations that are socially responsible.

Jaggi and Freedman (1982) studied the market impact of pollution disclosures made by firms operating within highly polluting industries. Consistent with Belkaoui's results, Jaggi and Freedman observed a positive share market reaction to those firms that could demonstrate greater pollution controls.

What needs to be appreciated is that the above discussion illustrates that there are alternative ways to determine whether people use particular information. One way is to ask people, perhaps through a questionnaire as in the Deegan and Rankin study, while another is to infer that people used the information by simply looking at a share price reaction around the time particular information is released by an organisation.

---

16 However, since the mid-1990s many companies have started releasing very detailed stand-alone sustainability reports, often hundreds of pages in length. As such, if the Deegan and Rankin study was undertaken now, it is likely that the annual report would not be seen as the most important source of information about an entity's social and environmental performance.

The above studies examined the market's reaction to disclosures made by the organisations themselves. In contrast, Shane and Spicer (1983) undertook a study that investigated the market's response to environmental performance information emanating from a source outside the firm, specifically that produced by the Council on Economic Priorities, an organisation based in New York that provides independent ranking on organisations' social and environmental performance. Shane and Spicer found that organisations identified by the Council on Economic Priorities as having poor pollution-control performance rankings were more likely to have significant negative security returns on the day the rankings were publicly released compared with organisations with higher pollution-control performance rankings. Shane and Spicer considered that the results were consistent with an assumption that the information released by the Council on Economic Priorities permitted investors to discriminate between organisations with different pollution-control performance records.

Similarly, Lorraine, Collison and Power (2004) examined share price reaction in the United Kingdom to 'publicity about fines for environmental pollution as well as commendations about good environmental achievements' (p. 7) over a five and a half year period. They found that, while there was little market reaction on the day fines or commendations were announced publicly, there was a significant impact on share prices within a week of these announcements.

Examining market reactions to negative environmental performance information from sources both inside and outside the firm, Freedman and Patten (2004) found that, where corporations (in the United States) published information in their annual reports about high levels of pollution emissions from their factories, the share price reaction was lower than for companies that were known to emit high levels of pollution but did not report this in their annual reports.

From the limited evidence provided above, it would appear that investors do react to an organisation's social responsibility disclosures, and therefore the broad answer to the *accountable for what* question is *accountable for some level of social responsibility practices and/or impacts*.

Furthermore, in recent years, banking and insurance institutions have become a key user of social and environmental information, particularly about organisations' environmental performance. In some countries, banks will not provide funds to organisations unless information about their environmental policies and performance is provided. The reason for this, in part, would be that an organisation that has demonstrated poor environmental performance is considered to be a higher risk in terms of compliance with environmental laws and in terms of potential costs associated with rectifying environmental damage caused. Further, in some industries it is possible that collateral provided for loans (such as land) might be contaminated because of poor environmental management systems. Some analysts also evaluate the social and environmental performance of corporations as part of their investment analysis.

Another increasing source of demand for corporate social and environmental information is the growing ethical investment market, and fund managers are also using their power to demand that corporations provide social and environmental performance information. According to Greene (2002):

Funds managers are beginning to use their financial clout to impose environmental requirements on companies. Morley Fund Management, a major London-based asset manager, recently announced it would begin requiring large UK companies to publish environment reports. Morley is the asset manager of CGNU plc, the UK's largest insurer and the world's sixth largest insurance group. It manages assets equivalent to 2.5% of the

UK stock market. With this kind of market influence, Morley's policy changes are sure to be felt by a significant number of companies.

Due to supply chain pressures, many organisations are also now demanding that suppliers provide them with details of their social and environmental performance prior to entering supply arrangements. Supply chain considerations have in the past negatively impacted on a number of organisations, with a corporation like Nike being a prime example.

Hence, while reference has been made here to only a very small proportion of the studies of demand for environmental performance information, it is clear that there *is* a demand. For reasons discussed at the beginning of the section, this demand indicates that many stakeholders do hold organisations responsible and accountable for some social and/or environmental issues. But identifying that stakeholders do use, and therefore that there is a demand for, social and environmental information, does not tell us precisely *for what* issues the stakeholders of a particular organisation will hold that organisation responsible and accountable. To identify these issues at the level of an individual organisation requires the organisation to enter into some form of dialogue with its stakeholders.

IDENTIFYING INFORMATION NEEDS THROUGH DIALOGUE WITH STAKEHOLDERS

As seen earlier, managers motivated to engage in corporate social responsibility (and sustainability reporting) for strategic managerial economic reasons (following the managerial branch of Stakeholder Theory) will tend to identify relevant stakeholders as being those who are able to exert the most influence over their company's ability to generate profits (or maximise shareholder value). Such managers will seek to convince these economically powerful stakeholders that their organisation's policies and actions accord with the social, environmental, economic and ethical views and expectations of these stakeholders, with social and environmental reporting being one of the mechanisms that may be used to convince these stakeholders. For social and environmental reporting to be effectively used to convince these stakeholders that the organisation has operated in accordance with their expectations, the organisation will need to know and understand these expectations—which will define what information is provided in the organisation's social and environmental reports.

Conversely, following the ethical branch of Stakeholder Theory, managers who seek to minimise their organisation's negative impact on a wide range of stakeholders will need to know and understand how their organisation is likely to impact on the lives of a range of stakeholders. The attitudes and experiences of these stakeholders regarding actual and potential organisational impacts are an important element of developing this knowledge and understanding. With an awareness of these views and expectations, managers can then focus their social responsibility policies and actions accordingly, and direct their social and environmental reporting towards providing an account to these stakeholders regarding how the organisation has acted in relation to these responsibilities. Furthermore, ethical reasoning indicates that people should be allowed to participate in making decisions on matters that are likely to affect their lives. Therefore, where managers are motivated by broader ethical considerations, they will actively encourage all those stakeholders who are (or might be) affected by the organisation's activities to participate in decision making regarding these activities. To be able to participate in this manner, a wide range of stakeholders will need information about the effects the organisation has (or is likely to have) on them, and managers will need to provide this information. In this situation, the answer to the *accountable for what* question is clearly *accountable to all stakeholders for the impact that the organisation's actions have (or may have) on these stakeholders.*

In these cases, and for any position on the continuum between these cases, managers need to understand their relevant stakeholders' views, needs and expectations to determine 'for what' economic, social and environmental issues they will provide an account. Ascertaining these views, needs and expectations is likely to be more straightforward where corporate social responsibility has been motivated by a strategic economic desire to maintain or increase the support of economically powerful (or influential) stakeholders, as many of these stakeholders will often be close to, and therefore relatively easily identifiable by, the organisation. For many commercial organisations, these powerful stakeholders will often be located in developed nations (or will be part of wealthy elites in developing nations) and will be accessible through commercial mass media such as television/radio, newspaper articles and the Internet.

However, for organisations whose social responsibility and social and environmental reporting are motivated by ethical reasoning to minimise the organisation's impact on those most affected by its operations (and to allow these stakeholders to participate in decisions on issues that significantly affect their lives), ascertaining these stakeholders' views, needs and expectations is likely to be more problematic. First, there is likely to be a broader range of stakeholders whose views need to be ascertained. Second, while many of the stakeholders who are significantly affected by an organisation's activities (such as employees) might be close to the organisation, many others (such as those affected indirectly but substantially by environmental damage caused by the organisation's operations, or workers of subcontractors in remote parts of the world) are likely to be remote from the organisation itself. Third, as demonstrated by O'Dwyer (2005), some of the stakeholders who are considerably affected by an organisation's operations might feel constrained by concerns about the consequences of 'upsetting' the organisation if they express their 'true' feelings, in which case the organisation can be regarded as being in a position of power which prevents open and honest dialogue with some stakeholders. Fourth, Adams (2004, p. 736) reports that there is often a 'lack of stakeholder awareness of, and even concern for, corporate impacts', and this can reduce the capacity of some stakeholders to engage in dialogue with the organisation. Finally, if, following the reasoning discussed earlier in the chapter, we include future generations, non-humans and nature within our definition of stakeholders who are potentially significantly negatively affected by an organisation's current operations, it is difficult to conceive of how an organisation could engage in dialogue effectively with these stakeholders to ascertain directly their views, needs and expectations regarding current organisational policies and practices.[17]

To overcome some (but not all) of these difficulties, organisations need to use a variety of channels of communication to engage in active (and not just reactive) dialogue with their stakeholders. For example, some companies have made use of the interactive communication facilities of the Internet to solicit the views of anyone worldwide regarding the social, environmental, ethical and economic responsibilities that should be applied to their organisation. However, as Unerman and Bennett (2004) have contended, because access to the Internet is not available to all those potentially affected by an organisation's activities (particularly in many

---

17   These views are, however, often 'represented' by a variety of campaign groups.

developing nations), Internet-based communication with stakeholders needs to be supplemented with other channels of communication that, between them, are accessible (and likely to be accessed by) a large proportion of the stakeholders on whom an organisation's operations might have an impact.

Such communications can include, for example, face-to-face meetings with a variety of stakeholders, questionnaire surveys, opinion polls, focus groups and invitations to write to the company about specific issues. O'Dwyer (2005, p. 286) indicates that, whatever channels of communication are used to engage stakeholders in dialogue, to be effective these communication channels need to be adapted to the 'cultural differences encountered' between different groups of stakeholders. Another approach to discovering stakeholder expectations—and which relates to the above discussion—is to undertake a 'social audit'. Social audits are referred to later in the chapter.

NEGOTIATING A CONSENSUS AMONG COMPETING STAKEHOLDER NEEDS AND EXPECTATIONS

In practice, many organisations are faced with a variety of values and expectations held by different stakeholders, and often these values and expectations will be incompatible with each other—so the organisation will not be able to meet all of the expectations. As indicated by the managerial branch of Stakeholder Theory, where an organisation is motivated to engage in these practices for strategic economic reasons (for example, to maximise shareholder value), managers will usually choose to address the social, environmental and economic values and expectations of their most economically powerful stakeholders. As Gray, Owen and Adams (1996, p. 45) state:

> Here (under this perspective), the stakeholders are identified by the organisation of concern, by reference to the extent to which the organisation believes the interplay with each group needs to be managed in order to further the interests of the organisation. (The interests of the organisation need not be restricted to conventional profit-seeking assumptions.) The more important the stakeholder to the organisation, the more effort will be exerted in managing the relationship. Information is a major element that can be employed by the organisation to manage (or manipulate) the stakeholder in order to gain their support and approval, or to distract their opposition and disapproval.

Conversely, where, following the ethical branch of Stakeholder Theory, an organisation's social responsibility and sustainability reporting is motivated by a desire to address the interests of those stakeholders on whom the organisation has the largest impact, it will need to identify and select the interests of those stakeholders on whom the organisation's activities have the largest negative impact. Given that there may be incompatible views among different stakeholders regarding the nature and extent of an organisation's impacts, and regarding the priority among different stakeholders' interests, in practice the process of arriving at a consensus set of social, environmental and economic responsibilities is highly problematic.

While in theory it makes sense for organisations to provide information to meet the specific needs of the respective stakeholders—meaning a 'one size fits all' approach might not be appropriate—many organisations do nevertheless use reporting guidelines generated by particular organisations such as the Global Reporting Initiative (GRI) to guide them on what to disclose. The rationale for adopting such guidelines as the basis for determining what to disclose would be based on a belief that organisations such as the GRI have done extensive research to determine the information needs of a cross-section of stakeholders. But in providing the basis for a general purpose sustainability report, such reporting guidelines will not necessarily meet the specific needs of particular stakeholders. This is similar to the position in financial reporting wherein conceptual frameworks and accounting standards are used to produce general purpose financial statements that are considered to meet most of the information needs of readers. For specific information needs, the stakeholders might request the organisation to produce special purpose financial reports.

In summarising this section on 'what do we report', such decisions will directly be affected by whether managers decide to provide information to a broad group of stakeholders or, alternatively, whether they restrict their consideration to a narrow (and perhaps powerful) group of stakeholders. What appears to be clear is that there is a demand for social and environmental information. To determine the types of information required, organisations can undertake various strategies to find out what information different categories of stakeholders require. In practice, not all demands for information can be met.

The next section moves on from the discussion of theoretical perspectives regarding mechanisms that organisations can use to determine 'for what' issues their stakeholders hold them responsible and accountable to consider some theoretical perspectives regarding how social and environmental reports can be constructed to meet this 'set' of prioritised (or consensus) stakeholder expectations

THEORETICAL PERSPECTIVES ON SOME SOCIAL AND ENVIRONMENTAL REPORTING PROCEDURES—THE *HOW* STAGE

Because there is a general lack of regulation in the area of social and environmental reporting, as well as an absence of an accepted conceptual framework for social and environmental reporting, there is much variation in how this reporting is being done in practice. Some reporting approaches represent quite radical changes from how financial accounting has traditionally been practised. This section starts by analysing whether the rules and procedures of financial accounting alone could provide suitable mechanisms for capturing and reporting the social and environmental impacts of organisations. If financial accounting practices are unable to capture and report on these social and environmental impacts effectively, it is necessary to develop other (or additional) social and environmental reporting mechanisms. One very broad mechanism that has been proposed as a method for reporting the social and environmental (in addition to the economic) performance and impact of organisations is *triple bottom line reporting*, and the key features and some drawbacks of triple bottom line reporting are discussed further in this section. The discussion then focuses on one of the more influential (and more detailed) sustainability reporting guidelines (the Global Reporting Initiative), which can be regarded as a form of conceptual framework for social and environmental reporting. The section concludes with a brief discussion about how to account for the social and environmental externalities caused by business entities.

SOME POSSIBLE LIMITATIONS OF TRADITIONAL FINANCIAL ACCOUNTING IN CAPTURING AND REPORTING SOCIAL AND ENVIRONMENTAL PERFORMANCE

Most of us would be familiar with financial accounting given that if we have been studying 'accounting' the emphasis has probably been on 'financial accounting'. Hence, in beginning our discussion of 'how' to report social and environmental information, we will consider the potential role of financial accounting systems in providing such information. Financial accounting is often criticised on the basis that it ignores many of the social and environmental externalities caused by the reporting entity. Hence, its suitability for assisting in the disclosure of social and environmental information is questioned. Gray (2005, p. 3) has more profound criticisms of the relationship between financial accounting and sustainability. He argues that:

> Few ideas could be more destructive to the notion of a sustainable planet than a system of economic organisation designed to maximise those things which financial reporting measures [for example, increasing sales, profits, growth, and so on]. Few notions could be more fundamentally antagonistic to financial reporting and all its cosmetic adjustments than a planet wishing to seek sustainability.

The following are some of the reasons why traditional financial accounting may not be able to reflect the social and environmental impact of organisations effectively:

1. As conceptual frameworks such as the *IASB Framework for the Preparation and Presentation of Financial Statements* emphasise, financial accounting focuses on the information needs of those parties involved in making resource allocation decisions. That is, the focus tends to be restricted to stakeholders with a financial interest in the entity, and the information that is provided consequently tends to be primarily of a financial or an economic nature. This means that people who are affected in a way that is not financial are denied access to information. Companies can, of course, elect to voluntarily provide social and environmental information.

2. Following on from this, one of the cornerstones of financial accounting is the notion of 'materiality', which has tended to preclude the reporting of social and environmental information, given the difficulty associated with quantifying social and environmental costs. 'Materiality' is an issue involving a great deal of professional judgement. Paragraph 9 of Accounting Standard AASB 1031[18] 'Materiality' states that information is material if its omission, misstatement or non-disclosure has the potential, individually or collectively to (a) influence the economic decisions of users taken on the basis of the financial report, or (b) affect the discharge of accountability by the management or governing body of the entity. Because decisions about materiality depend greatly on individual professional judgement, numerous professional accounting bodies throughout the world have provided some guidelines on materiality. For example, in Australia the guidelines provided in AASB 1031 indicate that if an amount is more than 10 per cent of the total equity or the appropriate total for the respective class of assets or liabilities, or is 10 per cent of the

---

18 This standard was developed within Australia and had no international equivalent. It will ultimately be replaced by an International Financial Reporting Standard (IFRS).

operating profit or loss, then the item is material. If something is not judged to be *material*, it does not need to be disclosed in the financial reports. Unfortunately, this has often meant that if something cannot be quantified (as is the case for many social and environmental externalities) it is generally not considered to be material and therefore does not warrant separate disclosure. This obviously implies that *materiality* may not be a relevant criterion for the disclosure of social and environmental performance data. Social and environmental performance is quite different from financial performance. Yet many accountants have been conditioned through their education and training to adopt the materiality criterion to decide whether any information should be disclosed. In a review of British companies, Gray et al. (1998) indicate that companies frequently provide little or no information about environmental expenses (however defined) because individually the expenditure is not considered to be material.

3. As highlighted in Gray, Owen and Adams (1996), another issue that arises in financial accounting is that reporting entities frequently discount liabilities, particularly those that will not be settled for many years, to their present value. This tends to make future expenditure less significant in the present period. For example, if our current activities are creating a need for future environmental expenditure of a remedial nature, but that work will not be undertaken for many years, then as a result of discounting we will recognise little or no cost now (which does appear to be at odds with the sustainability agenda). For example, if we were anticipating that our activities would necessitate a clean-up bill of $100 million in thirty years' time to remove some contamination, and if we accept that our normal earnings rate is, say, 10 per cent, then the current expenses to be recognised in our financial statements under generally accepted accounting principles would be $5.73 million. While discounting makes good economic sense, Gray, Owen and Adams (1996) argue that it does tend to make the clean-up somewhat trivial (and therefore not that important) at the current time, perhaps thereby providing little current discouragement for an entity contemplating undertaking activities that will damage the environment but which will not be remediated for many years.

4. Financial accounting adopts the 'entity assumption', which requires the organisation to be treated as an entity distinct from its owners, other organisations and other stakeholders. If a transaction or event does not directly impact on the entity, the transaction or event is to be ignored for accounting purposes. This means that the externalities caused by reporting entities will typically be ignored, thereby meaning that performance measures (such as profitability) are incomplete from a broader societal (as opposed to a 'discrete entity') perspective. Consider Accounting Headline 9.7, which discusses the introduction of a new range of cigarettes. It is generally accepted that cigarettes cause many health problems, yet externalities such as the medical costs being incurred by individuals and governments to treat tobacco-related illnesses are ignored by the entity when calculating profit figures. Hence, making particular cigarettes more attractive will potentially increase accounting profits for the company producing the cigarettes as it might encourage additional people to start smoking. However, this increased demand will inevitably create various social costs, reflected by treatment costs incurred within hospitals. However, consistent with the entity principle, these costs will not be recognised by the companies making the cigarettes. Arguably, any moves towards accounting for sustainability would require a modification to, or a move away from, the entity assumption such that the costs borne by other parties outside the organisation, as a

West Australian, 4 June 2004, p.7
Reproduced courtesy The West Australian.

Sweet-tasting cigarettes spark uproar

CATHY O'LEARY

A major anti-smoking lobby group has condemned tests by a major tobacco company to design chocolate- and wine-flavoured cigarettes, saying it is an attempt to increase their appeal to teenagers.

British American Tobacco, whose brands include Kent, Dunhill and Rothmans, is conducting scientific trials on animals in Canada using cigarettes flavoured with sweeteners such as maple syrup, vanilla and wine, according to London newspaper *The Independent*.

The trials, outlined in the journal *Food and Chemical Toxicology*, showed how 482 ingredients were tested.

The newspaper said the company had admitted commissioning the work to see if cigarettes with added ingredients had different effects on health to cigarettes without additives.

The study was conducted over 90 days on three groups of rats at a laboratory.

It follows a move last month by an American cigarette manufacturer to test-market cigarettes with names such as Mandarin Mint and Cherry Cheesecake.

Health experts have likened the US and British trials to the push by the alcohol industry to introduce 'alcopops' to increase the appeal to teenagers.

The Australian Council on Smoking and Health condemned the move yesterday and called on the Federal Government to keep strict controls on all the additives, including flavourings, used in cigarettes sold in Australia.

Stephen Hall, director of ACOSH, said it was not the first time that cigarette manufacturers had tested new additives in their products.

'There is a truckload of information that tobacco companies have been manipulating the product for many years and this has been done for a raft of reasons, but underlying those changes has been the motive of profit and the flow-on benefit to the company balance sheet,' he said.

'The fact that companies are adding chocolate and other sweets to tobacco is very disturbing and reinforces the need for Australia to have laws that regulate the manufacture of cigarettes and permit government to monitor all chemicals that are added to the product for whatever reason.

'As well as monitoring toxicity this could be used to prevent anything being added that could make tobacco more attractive or easier to use.'

result of consuming the outputs of the entity, would be factored into profit calculations, rather than being ignored as is currently the case.[19]

5. A related area in which our traditional financial accounting system generates a rather strange outcome is the treatment of tradable pollution permits. In an increasing number of countries certain organisations are provided with permits, often free of charge, that allow the holder to release a pre-specified amount of a particular pollutant. If the original recipient of the permit is not going to emit as much as the licence allows, then that party is allowed to sell the permit to another party.[20] As such, what is being seen in some jurisdictions is that particular organisations are treating tradable pollution permits as

---

19 As another example, many companies make significant contributions to climate change and therefore to problems confronting current and future generations. Traditionally, such 'costs' have been ignored entirely when calculating corporate profits. However, moves to introduce 'carbon taxes' will act to internalise at least some of these costs.

20 As an example, details of the EU emissions trading scheme, which became operational on 1 January 2005, can be found at www.europa.eu.int/comm/environment/climat/emission.htm.

assets. This may make sense from an 'economic' perspective, but it is questionable whether something that will allow an organisation to pollute is an asset from a broader 'societal' perspective.

6. In financial accounting and reporting, expenses are defined in such a way as to exclude the recognition of any impacts on resources that are not controlled by the entity (such as the environment) unless fines or other cash flows result. For example, under the International Accounting Standards Board's conceptual framework (the IASB Framework, as discussed in Chapter 6), expenses for financial reporting purposes are defined as:

> ... decreases in economic benefits during the accounting period in the form of outflows or depletions of assets or incurrences of liabilities that result in decreases in equity, other than those relating to distributions to equity participants [paragraph 70b].

An understanding of expenses therefore requires an understanding of assets. Assets are defined as resources *controlled* by the entity as a result of past events and from which future economic benefits are expected to flow to the entity' (paragraph 49a, emphasis added). The recognition of assets therefore relies on control, and hence environmental resources such as air and water, which are shared and therefore not controlled by the organisation, cannot be considered as 'assets' of that organisation. Thus their use, or abuse, is not considered as an expense. This is an important limitation of financial accounting and one that must be emphasised. As indicated in Deegan (1996), and using a rather extreme example, under traditional financial accounting if an entity were to destroy the quality of water in its local environs, thereby killing all local sea creatures and coastal vegetation, then, to the extent that no fines or other related cash flows were incurred, reported profits would not be directly affected.[21] No externalities would be recognised, and the reported assets/profits of the organisation would not be affected. Adopting conventional financial reporting practices, the performance of such an organisation could, depending on the financial transactions undertaken, be portrayed as being very successful. In this respect, Gray and Bebbington (1992, p. 6) provide the following opinion of traditional financial accounting:

> ... there is something profoundly wrong about a system of measurement, a system that makes things visible and which guides corporate and national decisions, that can signal success in the midst of desecration and destruction.[22]

7. Another point, considered more fully in Chapter 12, is that 'profits' as calculated by applying accounting standards provide a measure of possible future returns (dividends) to one stakeholder group—shareholders. In commending organisations for high profits, we are, perhaps, putting the interests of the investors (the owners) above the interests of other stakeholders. It is not uncommon to see a report in the financial press that a particular company generated a sound profit *despite* increased wage costs. In such a context there is an implication that returns to

---

21 To prove this to yourself, ask yourself what accounts you would debit and credit if your company inadvertently released toxic water into the local river system thereby killing thousands of endangered species of plants and animals while at the same time no fines or penalties were imposed for the reckless action.

22 Motivated by their concern about the limitations of traditional financial accounting, Gray and Bebbington have sought to develop alternative methods of accounting—methods that embrace the sustainability agenda. See, for example, Gray and Bebbington, 2001.

one stakeholder (employees) are somehow bad, but gains to other stakeholders (the owners of capital) are good. As Collison (2003, p. 7) states:

Financial description of the factors of production in the business media, and even in textbooks, makes clear that profit is an output to be maximised while recompense to labour is a cost to be minimised. Furthermore, a high cost of capital may be described as an exogenous constraint on business, rather than as an indication of the size of resource flows to providers of capital. *Financial Times* contributors are fond of words like 'ominous' to describe real wage rises: such words are not used to describe profit increases.

As discussed in Chapter 12, some accounting researchers, referred to as 'critical theorists', would consider that our whole system of accounting acts to support the interests of those with power (often proxied by financial wealth) and to undermine others (such as employees). Promoting performance indicators such as 'profits' will, it is argued, maintain the 'favoured' position of those in command of financial resources.

Consider Accounting Headline 9.8, which provides details of how an organisation 'axed' jobs in an endeavour to cut 'costs'. In the same way as our traditional systems of financial accounting ignore social costs, such media articles ignore the social costs that arise as a result of 'axing' employees and thereby making them unemployed. Putting people out of work might increase the profits of the entity, but the hardship this causes and the social security payments thereafter paid by government will not be reflected in the financial statements of the entity.

Accounting Headline 9.8 An illustration of activities that concurrently increase profits and 'social costs'

Bank defends profit in wake of job cuts

Cairns Post, 11 August 2005, p. 43

The Commonwealth Bank of Australia was yesterday forced to defend its record on job losses as it announced a massive $4 billion annual profit.

Outgoing chief executive David Murray hit back at union criticism as he unveiled CBA's 55 per cent jump in net profit to $3.99 billion—a record for the bank and one of the biggest profits in Australian corporate history.

The Finance Sector Union said the massive profit came at the expense of staff satisfaction and masked the 20,000 jobs that had been lost during Mr Murray's 13-year tenure.

'We know from our own research that one in three staff say they live in fear of losing their job and the majority wouldn't recommend CBA as a good place to work,' FSU national assistant secretary Sharron Caddie said.

'They are not signposts of happy and engaged employees.'

But Mr Murray said the union should stop criticising CBA's staff.

'What I would like the union to do is to stop criticising our people who come to work every day and do their best to serve customers,' he said. 'It doesn't help the employment prospects of our people. It doesn't help attract customers.

'And the sentiments they express are just not backed by the information that I get talking to people every day who are increasingly enthusiastic.'

Mr Murray said both staff and customer satisfaction had been boosted by the bank's three-year 'Which new Bank' transformation program, which involves the overhaul of its customer service computer system, refurbishment of branches and retraining of staff.

In total 3700 jobs will have been cut by the time the program wraps up next June with Mr Murray yesterday hinting that there could be more restructuring.

8. There is also the issue of 'measurability'. For an item to be recorded for financial accounting purposes it must be measurable with reasonable accuracy. As paragraph 83 of the *IASB Framework for the Preparation and Presentation of Financial Statements* states:

An item that meets the definition of an element should be recognised if:

(a) it is probable that any future economic benefit associated with the item will flow to or from the entity; and

(b) the item has a cost or value that can be measured with reliability.

Trying to place a value on the externalities caused by an entity often relies on various estimates and 'guesstimates', thereby typically precluding their recognition from the financial accounts on the basis of the potential inaccuracy of the measurement.

The above limitations are consistent with a view that financial accounting and reporting does not seem to possess suitable mechanisms for capturing and reporting on the social and environmental impacts of organisations. Hence, in discussing 'how' to report social and environmental information we could justifiably have concerns about doing it through existing financial reporting systems. Financial accounting and reporting alone is therefore unsuitable as a mechanism to provide an account of these social and environmental impacts and to meet stakeholders' information needs and expectations. Consequently, other mechanisms need to be employed to provide a suitable social and environmental account to these stakeholders. One broad mechanism that has been discussed widely in the business world as a way to provide a desirable balance of information about the social and environmental performance of organisations, in addition to the economic, is *triple bottom line reporting*.

TRIPLE BOTTOM LINE REPORTING

As previously indicated, *triple bottom line reporting* is based on the triple bottom line approach to business sustainability discussed earlier in the chapter, where a balance is sought between economic, social and environmental sustainability. Advocates of triple bottom line reporting argue that, if properly implemented, it should provide information to enable others to assess how sustainable an organisation's or a community's operations are. Hence, perhaps triple bottom line reporting provides a solution to the question of 'how' we should report. The perspective taken is that for an organisation (or a community) to be sustainable (a long-run perspective) it must be financially secure (as evidenced by such measures as profitability), it must minimise (or ideally eliminate) its negative environmental impacts, and it must act in conformity with societal expectations. Triple bottom line reporting therefore provides a very broad answer to the question of *how* an organisation should report on its social, environmental and economic impacts (or performance).

Brown, Dillard and Marshall (2005) demonstrate that, while there has been much discussion of triple bottom line reporting, there have been few concrete proposals to realise this reporting model. They highlight several problems with implementing the triple bottom line reporting model in practice. First, although the use of the 'bottom line' metaphor has been useful in capturing the attention of managers for issues of social and environmental impact, the metaphor is severely restricting, as the term 'bottom line' conveys the impression of something that can be measured in a single number. The economic profit figure is the summation, in a common currency,[23] of all the income and expenses figures over a period of time. Brown, Dillard and Marshall (2005) demonstrate that it is highly problematic, and probably impossible in practice, to reduce all environmental impacts, or all social impacts, to a common currency. Indeed, most reports that have claimed to be based on a triple bottom line approach have tended to report on social and environmental impacts using a combination of narrative reports and a number of different metrics. If neither social nor environmental factors can be reduced to a single currency, then it is not possible to equate trade-offs between these factors. A trade-off between 'maximising' economic performance, social performance and environmental performance appears to be a key element (or requirement) of the triple bottom line.

Second, the economic bottom line is commonly understood among managers as being a metric that should be maximised. Brown, Dillard and Marshall (2005) argue that it is difficult to apply this objective of maximisation to nature. While there could be agreement on maximising a factor such as biodiversity, there is no commonly accepted understanding of what this might mean, and how it could be measured. Even more problematic is knowing which social metric should be maximised. Thus, attempting to equate the notion (and management) of the social and environmental bottom lines with the more conventional economic bottom line is not possible in practice. Therefore, attempting to report on, or manage, all three bottom lines in a common manner is not appropriate.

Third, if it is not possible to adopt metrics that treat each of the bottom lines equally, then the notion of three separate bottom lines might give the impression that the economic, social and environmental are not interconnected. For reasons explained earlier in the chapter, this would be a fundamental misconception, and from a social and environmental sustainability viewpoint could be highly damaging. Brown, Dillard and Marshall (2005) believe that, due to these problems in the triple bottom line concept, management and reporting on the triple bottom line is likely to result in a focus on the economic bottom line to the detriment of social and environmental sustainability.

It therefore appears that the process of triple bottom line reporting is, at present, not very helpful in providing guidance to organisations regarding the details of how to produce a sustainability report that will address the specific information needs of their stakeholders. Perhaps what is required is a conceptual framework for social and environmental reporting. The Global Reporting Initiative (GRI), which is discussed in the next subsection, could possibly be considered to be an example of a move towards a conceptual framework for social and environmental reporting. However, before considering the GRI we will consider a measure of performance often used at a national level—the GDP. While criticisms abound (some provided above) about how businesses calculate their financial performance in accordance with generally accepted accounting practice, criticisms can also be made about how countries calculate their economic success. For example, the performance of governments (and thus of nations) is often related to the outputs of their systems of national accounts, a well-known output being gross domestic product, or GDP. With such a system, the greater the levels of production, the better the numbers. Obviously, such a metric does not consider issues of resource efficiencies or the equities associated with how the resources are distributed. Current methods of calculating GDP provide some strange outcomes. For example, if we build more jails (perhaps reflective

23 This notion of economic profit being a summation of economic factors in a common currency does, however, need to allow for the effects of changing prices—which is discussed in Chapter 5.

of a breakdown in society) this will have positive implications for GDP, as would the sale of harmful tobacco products to Third World nations. Sustainability requires a reduced reliance upon indicators such as GDP. Criticisms of GDP abound internationally. For example, consider Accounting Headline 9.9, which provides a view about the 'deficiency' of measures like GDP.

Australian Financial Review, 15 August 2005, p. 22

Accounting Headline 9.9 Perceived deficiencies in GDP as a measure of national success

Measure our welfare

ADAM McHUGH

Australia should adjust GDP to fight the climate change enemy, Adam McHugh writes.

Economic policy should be driven by a concern for human welfare. So it is unfortunate that our modern fixation with GDP in full growth as a proxy for human improvement is so deficient, as climate change has revealed.

Most economists acknowledge that GDP is a defective indicator of welfare. We know, for example, that a car accident or an oil spill increases GDP but obviously decreases welfare. So why have we used such a measure?

The answer is that GDP was developed around the time when our enemies were fascism and communism. It was therefore a sensible measure of industrial militarisation. But even though these foes are now long defeated, the same old war-cry continues: produce, produce, produce and all your enemies shall be vanquished.

Unfortunately, our newly recognised enemy is itself a factor of production. Much of the GDP growth this century has come about due to massive exploitation of fossil fuels.

We are completely reliant on the black stuff and desperate for it to keep flowing. But we are also quite certain that the burning of hydrocarbons is now resulting in increasing global temperatures, and this new enemy is looming as one of the greatest threats to human welfare ever faced.

Change is often motivated by need. One extreme of economic and climatic modelling reveals the real possibility of global cataclysm, the extinction of our species, a climatic disaster so terrible that adaptation would be impossible no matter how much net present wealth is hoarded and no matter how high the interest rate at which it is invested.

However, even the opposite extreme, a relatively small per-capita welfare loss for all future generations, has to be seen in aggregate terms, if avoidable, as a complete economic failure.

So how do you defeat an enemy like global climate change? Some will stick to the same old thinking: increase your GDP and the problem will be dissolved away by human preferences.

They will point to the mysterious Kuznets curve (an upside down U) which suggests that environmental degradation will eventually decrease with increased income. In the language of economics the environment is a luxury that richer people will demand more of.

So the solution is the same for the climate change enemy as it was for fascism and communism: just increase your GDP and the market will provide the solution.

Of course, it is true that people with higher incomes will demand environmental quality; it is a normal good in that sense. But the Kuznets curve does not explain how the market will provide for environmental quality.

Consider China, where as incomes rise a million cars are being added to the road each year, along with an associated increase in the tonnage of atmospheric carbon dioxide. Are these motorists demanding higher environmental quality as they get richer? Probably. But environmental quality is a difficult good to find on the shelves of the bright new shopping malls that are popping up all around that country. They just can't buy it.

Yet China, despite its previously dire environmental record under communism, is at least attempting to provide for sound economic measurement of environmental quality. It is producing an experimental GDP figure that accounts for environmental damage and resource depletion. In this sense China, by recognising a broader basket of goods, is quite clearly ahead of others in measuring the welfare of its population.

The primary function of economic policy is to recognise when the market fails to provide the right allocation of goods. As always the goal ought to be to maximise welfare.

Surely then, Australia's national accounting system should reflect this goal. An adjustment is in order, to which end we need some focus on the costs side of the ledger, where currently there is none.

With any enemy, intelligence is the key in a successful policy of pre-emption. Climate change is no different. Environmental goods are only deliverable if policy makers can be informed by sound scientific measurement through an adjusted GDP.

There have been various experiments worldwide that have sought to 'Green GDP', which would monetarise various environmental effects for inclusion within traditionally calculated GDP. However, these experiments have been subject to various criticisms, many related to the lack of an accepted methodology. *The Economist* (18 April 1998, p. 77) highlighted the problems involved in placing a monetary valuation on certain environmental resources:

> Some assets, such as timber, may have a market value, but that value does not encompass the trees' role in harbouring rare beetles, say, or their sheer beauty. Methods for valuing such benefits are controversial. To get round these problems, the UN guidelines suggest measuring the cost of repairing environmental damage. But some kinds of damage, such as extinction, are beyond costing, and others are hard to estimate.

A US organisation, named Redefining Progress, is promoting various approaches to adjusting GDP to give a 'truer' measure of national performance. According to its website:

> Redefining Progress created the Genuine Progress Indicator (GPI) in 1995 as an alternative to the gross domestic product (GDP). The GPI enables policymakers at the national, state, regional, or local level to measure how well their citizens are doing both economically and socially. Economists, policymakers, reporters, and the public rely on the GDP as a shorthand indicator of progress; but the GDP is merely a sum of national spending with no distinctions between transactions that add to well-being and those that diminish it. GPI starts with the same accounting framework as the GDP but then makes some crucial distinctions. It adds in the economic contributions of households and volunteer work, but subtracts factors such as crime, pollution, and family breakdown. The GPI is one of the first alternatives to the GDP to be vetted by the scientific community and used regularly by governmental and non-governmental organizations worldwide. Redefining Progress advocates for the adoption of the GPI as a tool for sustainable development and planning. On a yearly basis, Redefining Progress updates the U.S. Genuine Progress Indicator to document a more truthful picture of economic and social progress. Our latest update, which plots GPI accounts from 1950 to 2004, shows that economic growth has been stagnant since the 1970s.

The Redefining Progress website can be found at www.rprogress.org.

THE GLOBAL REPORTING INITIATIVE—A CONCEPTUAL FRAMEWORK FOR SOCIAL AND ENVIRONMENTAL REPORTING?

Despite (or perhaps because of) the deficiencies in the ability of traditional financial reporting (and triple bottom line reporting) to capture and reflect the social and environmental impacts of organisational activities, many organisations have developed a variety of practices that seek to report on these broader impacts. The inclusion of particular items for disclosure tends to be based on particular managers' perceptions of the information needs of particular stakeholder groups (Solomon & Lewis, 2002), while much reliance also tends to be placed on reviewing particular corporate examples of what is acknowledged as best reporting practice (as perhaps evidenced by an entity winning a reporting award for its disclosures).

As an attempt to codify best reporting practice, several bodies have been active in developing social and environmental reporting guidelines. At an international level, one source of reporting guidance that has taken a dominant position in the social and environmental (and sustainability) reporting domain is the Global Reporting Initiative's Sustainability Reporting Guidelines (commonly referred to as the *GRI Guidelines*).[24] These guidelines are generally accepted as representing current 'best practice'. The first version of the GRI Guidelines was released in 2000 (following the release of draft guidelines in 1999). A second version of the guidelines (often referred to as G2) was released in 2002. The third generation of the guidelines (referred to as G3) was released in 2006 and was developed as a result of multi-stakeholder collaboration that occurred during 2004 and 2005. It provides forty-nine 'core indicators' and thirty 'additional indicators' that can be used by reporting organisations. According to GRI (2006, p. 24):

> Core Indicators have been developed through GRI's multi-stakeholder processes, which are intended to identify generally applicable Indicators and are assumed to be material for most organizations. An organization should report on Core Indicators unless they are deemed not material on the basis of the GRI Reporting Principles. Additional Indicators represent emerging practice or address topics that may be material for some organizations, but are not material for others.[25]

The sustainability performance indicators (both 'core' and 'additional') are organised under the categories of economic performance, environmental performance and social performance (with the social indicators being further subdivided into labour practices and decent work performance indicators, investment and procurement practices, social performance indicators, and product responsibility performance indicators). Under each category there is required to be a 'Disclosure on Management Approach' (which covers such things as policies, responsibilities and goals). This disclosure is then followed by the indicators (which, as already mentioned, are divided into the 'core' and 'additional' indicators).

While the GRI guidelines are argued by many to have brought about improvements to sustainability reporting, it must be acknowledged that, not being mandatory, many companies are selective about which indicators they choose to use in their reporting. Such companies might still indicate that they are using the GRI Guidelines and therefore gain the 'legitimacy' that is associated with using the guidelines. As SustainAbility Ltd and United Nations Environmental Programme (2002, p. 17) note:

> The GRI Guidelines themselves allow companies partially off the hook. A company can be GRI compliant whilst looking at the least impactful aspect of their business. Consider the case of McDonald's whose inaugural GRI-based report, released in 2002, makes only passing mention of agriculture issues, where an enormous proportion of McDonald's impact lies ... Alan Willis, one former GRI Steering Committee member and Verification Working Group participant urges: 'GRI needs to be increasingly vigilant of company abuse of the guidelines or process—claiming their reporting is "In Accordance" when it's not; [when it's] incomplete, inaccurate, misleading or inappropriate'.

---

24 See www.globalreporting.org for details of the GRI and the sustainability reporting guidelines. According to the website of the GRI (accessed in late 2008): 'To date, more than 1,500 companies, including many of the world's leading brands, have declared their voluntary adoption of the Guidelines worldwide. Consequently the G3 Guidelines have become the *de facto* global standard for reporting. GRI is a collaborating centre of the United Nations Environment Programme.'

25 The guidelines provide a number of external factors (such as issues raised by stakeholders, and local, national and international regulations) and internal factors (such as major risks to the organisation, organisational values, goals and targets) that need to be considered in determining the 'materiality' of an item.

The GRI provides a number of categories for disclosing sustainability performance information, together with related performance indicators. The key categories and subcategories of the draft G3 Guidelines, together with details of the 'indicator aspects' covered within the respective categories, are provided in Exhibit 9.1.[26]

Exhibit 9.1 An overview of the categories of indicators used within the GRI Sustainability Reporting Guidelines

A. Economic performance

The economic dimension of sustainability concerns the organisation's impacts on the economic conditions of its stakeholders and on economic systems at the local, national and global levels.

Economic performance indicators[27]

- Aspect: Economic Performance (four core indicators)
- Aspect: Market Presence (two core and one additional indicator)
- Aspect: Indirect Economic Impacts (one core and one additional indicator)

B. Environmental performance

The environmental dimension of sustainability concerns the organisation's impacts on living and non-living natural systems, including ecosystems, land, air and water. The structure of environmental indicators covers input (material, energy, water) and output (emissions, effluents, waste) related performance. In addition the indicators cover performance related to biodiversity, environmental compliance and other relevant information such as environmental expenditure and the impacts of products and services.

Environmental performance indicators

- Aspect: Materials (two core indicators)
- Aspect: Energy (two core and three additional indicators)
- Aspect: Water (one core and two additional indicators)
- Aspect: Biodiversity (two core and three additional indicators)
- Aspect: Emissions, Effluents and Waste (seven core and three additional indicators)
- Aspect: Products and services (two core indicators)
- Aspect: Compliance (one core indicator)
- Aspect: Transport (one additional indicator)
- Aspect: Overall (one additional indicator)

C. Social performance

The social dimension of sustainability concerns an organisation's impacts on the social systems within which it operates. The GRI social performance indicators identify key performance aspects surrounding labour practices, human rights and broader issues affecting consumers, community and other stakeholders in society. (Unlike economic and environmental performance, the G3 Guidelines divide social performance into four subgroups of performance indicators.)

---

26 Indicators provide a measure to enable evaluation and subsequent decision making with regard to the particular aspect being measured. Within the G3 Guidelines an 'indicator aspect' is defined as 'The general types of information that are related to a specific indicator category (e.g., energy use, child labor, customers)'.

27 Interested readers should go to the GRI Guidelines (www.globalreporting.org) to review the details of the specific indicators pertaining to each aspect.

Social performance indicators

C.1 Social performance: labor practices and decent work performance indicators

- Aspect: Employment (two core and one additional indicator)
- Aspect: Labour/Management Relations (two core indicators)
- Aspect: Occupational Health and Safety (two core and two additional indicators)
- Aspect: Training and Education (one core and two additional indicators)
- Aspect: Diversity and Opportunity (two core additional indicators)

C.2 Social performance: human rights performance indicators

- Aspect: Investment and Procurement Practices (two core and one additional indicator)
- Aspect: Non-discrimination (one core indicator)
- Aspect: Freedom of Association and Collective Bargaining (one core indicator)
- Aspect: Child Labour (one core indicator)
- Aspect: Forced and Compulsory Labour (one core indicator)
- Aspect: Security Practices (one additional indicator)
- Aspect: Indigenous Rights (one additional indicator)

C.3 Social performance: society performance indicators

- Aspect: Community (one core indicator)
- Aspect: Corruption (three core indicators)
- Aspect: Public Policy (one core and one additional indicator)
- Aspect: Anti-Competitive Behaviour (one additional indicator)
- Aspect: Compliance (one core indicator)

C.4 Social performance: product responsibility performance indicators

- Aspect: Customer Health and Safety (one core and one additional indicator)
- Aspect: Products and Service Labeling (one core and two additional indicators)
- Aspect: Marketing Communications (one core and one additional indicator)
- Aspect: Customer Privacy (one additional indicator)
- Aspect: Compliance (one core indicator)

Adapted from Global Reporting Initiative (2006).

The multi-stakeholder GRI was established in 1997. According to the GRI website (as accessed late 2008):

> The Global Reporting Intitiative (GRI) refers to the 30,000 strong multi-stakeholder network that collaborates to advance sustainability reporting. The Global Reporting Initiative (GRI) has pioneered the development of the world's most widely used sustainability reporting framework and is committed to its continuous improvement and application worldwide. This framework sets out the principles and indicators that organizations can use to measure and report their economic, environmental, and social performance.
>
> The cornerstone of the framework is the Sustainability Reporting Guidelines. The third version of the Guidelines—known as the G3 Guidelines—was published in 2006, and is a free public good. Other components of the framework include Sector Supplements (unique indicators for industry sectors) and Protocols (detailed reporting guidance) and National Annexes (unique country-level information).

Sustainability reports based on the GRI Framework can be used to benchmark organizational performance with respect to laws, norms, codes, performance standards and voluntary initiatives; demonstrate organizational commitment to sustainable development; and compare organizational performance over time. GRI promotes and develops this standardized approach to reporting to stimulate demand for sustainability information—which will benefit reporting organizations and those who use report information alike.

The GRI was originally convened by the US-based organisation Coalition for Environmentally Responsible Economies (a non-profit, non-government organisation based in Boston) in partnership with the United Nations Environment Programme (whose website is at www.unep.org), with subsequent inputs from the Association of Chartered Certified Accountants (United Kingdom), Tellus Institute, World Business Council for Sustainable Development, World Resources Institute, Canadian Institute of Chartered Accountants, Institute of Social and Ethical Accountability (United Kingdom), Council on Economic Priorities (United States), and other organisations and corporate bodies from around the world. Given its representation, the initiative is clearly 'global' in nature.

According to the Global Reporting Initiative (2006, p. 3):

The GRI Reporting Framework is intended to serve as a generally accepted framework for reporting on an organization's economic, environmental, and social performance. It is designed for use by organizations of any size, sector, or location, and takes into account the practical considerations faced by a diverse range of organizations—from small enterprises to those with extensive and geographically dispersed operations. The GRI Framework describes the general and sector-specific content that has been agreed by a wide range of stakeholders around the world to be generally applicable for reporting an organization's sustainability performance.

The guidelines consist of principles for defining report content and ensuring the quality of reported information as well as standard disclosures comprising performance indicators and other disclosure items. The guidelines also include guidance on specific technical issues in reporting. The 2006 guidelines (G3) comprise two main parts:

■ Part 1—Defining report content, quality and boundary
■ Part 2—Standard disclosures.

The guidelines also include an introduction which provides an overview of sustainability reporting and addresses such issues as the purpose of preparing a sustainability report. The guidelines also provide an overview of issues associated with having the report reviewed by an independent third party. In relation to defining report content (which is included within Part 1), reference is made to a number of reporting principles:

(a) **Materiality** The information in a report should cover topics and indicators that reflect the organization's significant economic, environmental, and social impacts, or that would substantively influence the assessments and decisions of stakeholders.
(b) **Stakeholder Inclusiveness** The reporting organization should identify its stakeholders and explain in the report how it has responded to their reasonable expectations and interests.

(c) **Sustainability Context** The reporting organization should present the organization's performance in the wider context of sustainability.

(d) **Completeness** Coverage of the material topics and indicators, and definition of the report boundary should be sufficient to reflect significant economic, environmental, and social impacts and enable stakeholders to assess the reporting organization's performance in the reporting period.

In relation to the 'quality of reported material', reference is made to a number of 'reporting principles for defining quality':

(a) **Balance** The report should reflect positive and negative aspects of the organization's performance to enable a reasoned assessment of overall performance.

(b) **Comparability** Issues and information should be selected, compiled and reported consistently. Reported information should be presented in a manner that enables stakeholders to analyze changes in the organization's performance over time, and could support analysis relative to other organizations.

(c) **Accuracy** The reported information should be accurate and sufficiently detailed for stakeholders to assess the reporting organization's performance.

(d) **Timeliness** Reporting occurs on a regular schedule and information is available for stakeholders to make informed decisions.

(e) **Clarity** Information should be made available in a manner that is understandable and accessible to stakeholders using the report.

(f) **Reliability** Information and processes used in the preparation of a report should be gathered, recorded, compiled, analyzed and disclosed in a way that could be subject to examination and that establishes the quality and materiality of the information.

As we can see, the principles and qualitative characteristics are very similar to the qualitative characteristics that are typically promoted in relation to financial reporting. It is interesting to consider whether sustainability reporting should have similar attributes to financial reporting. What do you think?

In relation to Part 2 of the guidelines—to do with 'standard disclosures'—there are three different types of disclosures contained in the section:

■ *Strategy and profile*: Disclosures that set the overall context for understanding organisational performance, such as the organisation's strategy, profile and governance.

■ *Management approach*: Disclosures that cover how an organisation addresses a given set of topics in order to provide a context for understanding performance in a specific area.

■ *Performance indicators*: Indicators that elicit comparable information on the economic, environmental and social performance of the organisation (summaries of the various indicators have been detailed earlier).

Again, interested readers are encouraged to go to the GRI's website to review the entire guidelines for themselves. The guidelines are expected to evolve continually over time. Clearly they have evolved to provide extensive guidance on the issue of 'how' to report.

Apart from the GRI, a number of other organisations have also released reporting guidelines:

■ Department of Environment and Heritage (2003), *Triple Bottom Line Reporting in Australia—A Guide to Reporting Against Environmental Indicators*.

- Group of 100 (2003), *Sustainability: A Guide to Triple Bottom Line Reporting*.
- Association of British Insurers (2002), *Disclosure Guidelines on Socially Responsible Investment*.
- Business in the Community (UK) (2001), *Winning with Integrity: A Guide to Social Responsibility*.
- Environmental Task Force of the European Federation of Accountants (1999), *FEE Discussion Paper: Towards a Generally Accepted Framework for Environmental Reporting*.
- European Chemical Industry Council (1998), *Responsible Care: Health, Safety and Environmental Reporting Guidelines*.
- Global Environmental Management Initiative (USA) (1994), *Environment Reporting in a Total Quality Management Framework*.
- Institute of Chartered Accountants in England and Wales (1996), *Environmental Issues in Financial Reporting*.
- Public Environmental Reporting Initiative (USA) (1992), *The PERI Guidelines*.
- UK Government's Advisory Committee on Business and the Environment (UK) (1997), *Environmental Reporting and the Financial Sector—An Approach to Good Practice*.
- United Nations Environment Programme (and SustainAbility) (1996), *Engaging Stakeholders— Second International Progress Report on Company Environmental Reporting*.

Summarising this section about 'how' to report, there are a number of limitations with financial accounting practices that tend to preclude financial accounting as a means of producing information about the social and environmental performance of reporting entities. Given these limitations, alternative processes have been suggested. Triple bottom line reporting has been advocated by various people as a sound means of providing information about an entity's economic, social and environmental performance. However, as noted, there is some hesitation that the concept of a 'bottom line' can realistically be applied to social and environmental performance. Another alternative to reporting is the development of structured guidelines, such as the Global Reporting Initiative's Sustainability Reporting Guidelines. Before concluding the discussion about 'how' to report, another proposed approach to accounting for social and environmental performance will be considered. This approach—which has not been widely embraced—requires an entity to calculate a cost for the social and environmental externalities it creates.

ACCOUNTING FOR EXTERNALITIES

Reporting guidance such as that provided by the GRI provides numerous sustainability-related key performance indicators (KPIs) but does not consider the issue of trying to 'cost' the externalities caused by businesses. For example, the GRI does not provide guidance about placing a cost on such things as the pollution being generated by an organisation, or any adverse health effects caused by the products or processes of a reporting entity. As explained earlier, generally accepted financial accounting practices also ignore the social and environmental externalities generated by a reporting entity. However, a very limited number of organisations have attempted to put a cost on the environmental externalities and benefits caused by their operations.[28] These costs and benefits are then usually taken from (or added to) traditionally calculated profits to come up with some measure of 'real profit'. This is an interesting approach which represents a departure from generally accepted accounting principles, and is based on many estimates and 'guesstimates'. Again, however, it needs to be emphasised that there are only a very limited number of companies worldwide that place a cost on externalities. For example, the Dutch computer consultancy organisation BSO/Origin has provided some environmental accounts in which a notional value is placed on the environmental costs imposed by the organisation on society. (The last set of accounts prepared by BSO/Origin addressing 'environmental costs' was released in 1995.) This value is then deducted from profits determined using conventional financial accounting to provide a measure of 'net value added'. Obviously, quantifying environmental effects/impacts in financial terms requires many assumptions. As BSO/Origin stated in its 1994 environmental report:

> This is the fifth year that BSO/Origin has presented an environmental account as well as a financial report. This is done on the basis of the 'extracted value' concept, the burden a product places on the ecosystem from the moment of its manufacture until the moment of its decomposition. This burden is expressed in terms of the costs which would have been incurred either to undo the detrimental effect to the point where the natural ecosystem could neutralise it, or to develop a responsible alternative. The entries are based on absolute data as supplied by the cells, educated guesstimates and extrapolations. The purpose is not to provide precise calculations accurate to the last decimal point, but to fulfil the principle of complete accounting, in which extracted as well as value added is included.

By including environmental costs and benefits in their profit calculations, organisations may be contributing to ongoing debates questioning the validity of profitability calculations that omit important social costs such as damage done to the environment. A number of companies are now experimenting with methods designed to determine the notional costs of the externalities being generated by their activities. Companies that have adopted some form of 'full-cost' accounting currently include Baxter International Inc. (USA), IBM (UK), Interface Europe, Anglian Water (UK), Wessex Water (UK) and Landcare Ltd (NZ).

The approaches adopted by some of these organisations include determining a notional 'sustainable cost'. This is explained by Gray and Bebbington (1992, p. 15) as follows:

> ... sustainable cost can be defined as the amount an organisation must spend to put the biosphere at the end of the accounting period back into the state (or its equivalent) it was in at the beginning of the accounting period. Such a figure would be a notional one, and disclosed as a charge to a company's profit and loss account. Thus we would be presented with a broad estimate of the extent to which the accounting profits had been generated from a sustainable source ... our estimates suggest that the sustainable cost calculations would produce the sort of answer which would demonstrate that no Western company had made a profit of any kind in the last 50 years or so.

---

28 An externality can be defined as 'an impact that an entity has on parties external to the organisation' (Deegan, 2005, p. 1186). From an accounting perspective, an 'externality' is not recognised in the financial statements. In part, this is because of the 'entity principle' embraced within financial accounting.

According to Bebbington and Gray (2001, p. 567), the sustainable cost calculation involves two elements:

(i) a consideration of the costs required to ensure that inputs to the organisation have no adverse environmental impacts in their production. These are costs which arise in addition to those costs already internalised in the most environmentally sound products and services which are currently available; and

(ii) the costs required to remedy any environmental impacts which arise even if the organisation's inputs had a zero environmental impact.

One company to embrace the 'sustainability cost' calculation is Interface Europe. In discussing how the 2000 financial reports of Interface Europe (a leading producer of floor coverings) embrace the 'sustainability cost' calculation, *Environmental Accounting and Auditing Reporter* (September 2000, p. 6) made the following comments:

The environmental impacts disclosed in the accounts have been valued where possible on the basis of their avoidance or restoration costs. That is, on the basis of what Interface would need to spend in order to either avoid the impacts in the first place or to restore the environmental damage caused by the activities and operations if they are unavoidable. Costs, as far as possible, are based on 'real' or market based prices.

The emissions associated with Interface's significant use of electricity, for example, have been valued based on an estimated premium for the company to switch to electricity generated from renewable, and hence (more or less) carbon neutral energy sources. Carbon emissions from transport and gas consumption have been valued based on the market price to sequester carbon and a significant proportion of non carbon dioxide transport related emissions have been valued on the cost of converting the company's car fleet to liquid petroleum gas (LPG). Whilst emissions of carbon dioxide remain about the same or slightly higher with LPG, other emissions are reduced substantially.

The total valuation is based on what it would cost to reduce emissions or impacts to a 'sustainable level'. Although we don't really know what a sustainable level may be for each of the impacts/emissions, a pragmatic approach based on current scientific understanding and opinion has been used. In the case of carbon, a sustainability standard of zero has been adopted. For non carbon transport related emissions, for example, the sustainability standard has been based on reducing emissions by at least 50% to meet health based guidelines for air quality. The sustainability cost therefore represents the financial cost of closing the sustainability gap of the company's operations.

Other interesting approaches to presenting information about the social and environmental performance include approaches adopted by the US organisation Baxter Inc. and by the New Zealand organisation Watercare Services. Baxter International Inc. is an organisation that produces, develops and distributes medical products and technologies. It has revenues in excess of US$5 billion. In the mid-1990s Baxter decided to develop what it labelled its Environment Financial Statement (EFS). According to Bennett and James (1998, p. 295):

the purpose of the EFS was to collect together in a single report, annually, the total of the financial costs and benefits that could be attributed not only to the environmental programme itself but to the environmentally beneficial activities across the corporation. Its aim was to demonstrate that, contrary to the preconception of many, the environment need not be only a burden on business performance but could make a positive contribution.

Baxter's approach represents a departure from 'normal' financial accounting practice in that it explicitly records information about savings—something that financial reports typically do not identify—but it is still a relatively conservative approach to accounting. It ignores any externalities caused by the business and only considers those costs and benefits that directly relate to actual cash flows. Exhibit 9.2 provides details of Baxter's 2007 EFS. In the EFS, 'Income' refers to actual monies received in the report year; 'Savings' refers to reduction in costs between report year and prior year (an increase in actual costs is negative savings); and 'Cost Avoidance' refers to

Exhibit 9.2 Environmental Financial Statement as shown in the *2007 Environmental, Health and Safety Performance Report* of Baxter International

Baxter 2007 Environmental Financial Statement

Estimated Environmental Costs, Income, and Savings and Cost Avoidance Worldwide (dollars in millions)[1]

Environmental Costs	2007	2006	2005
Basic Program			
Corporate Environmental—General and Shared Business Unit Costs[2]	1.6	1.4	1.5
Auditors' and Attorneys' Fees	0.4	0.4	0.4
Energy Professionals and Energy Reduction Programs	1.0	1.0	1.0
Corporate Environmental—Information Technology	0.3	0.3	0.3
Business Unit/Regional/Facility Environmental Professionals and Programs	7.4	7.2	6.8
Pollution Controls—Operations and Maintenance	3.1	3.2	2.9
Pollution Controls—Depreciation	0.9	0.8	0.7
Basic Program Total	**14.7**	**14.3**	**13.6**
Remediation, Waste and Other Response Costs			
(Proactive environmental action will minimize these costs.)			
Attorneys' Fees for Cleanup Claims and Notices of Violations	0.1	0.1	0.1
Settlements of Government Claims	0	0	0
Waste Disposal	10.0	7.1	6.1
Carbon Offsets[3]	0.1	0.0	0.0
Environmental Fees for Packaging[4]	0.9	0.9	1.1
Environmental Fees for Electronic Goods and Batteries	0.1	0.1	0.0
Remediation/Cleanup—On-site	0.5	0.1	0.1
Remediation/Cleanup—Off-site	0.0	0.3	0.0
Total Remediation, Waste and Other Response Costs	**11.7**	**8.6**	**7.4**
Total Environmental Costs	**26.4**	**22.9**	**21.0**

(continued)

Exhibit 9.2 *(continued)*

Environmental Income, Savings and Cost Avoidance

(see Detail on Income, Savings and Cost Avoidance from 2007 Activities online)

From Initiatives in Stated Year

Regulated Waste Disposal	(0.7)	0.3	(0.1)
Regulated Materials[5]	(2.7)	0.8	(0.3)
Non-hazardous Waste Disposal	(0.8)	0.0	0.3
Non-hazardous Materials	(0.8)	(2.5)	5.7
Recycling Income	4.8	4.7	4.3
Energy Conservation	4.1	3.3	6.8
Packaging Cost Reductions	2.9	1.7	2.4
Water Conservation	0.6	0.6	0.0
From Initiatives in Stated Year Total[6]	4.4	7.2	16.7
As a Percentage of the Costs of Basic Program	30%	51%	123%
Cost Avoidance from Initiatives Started in the Six Years Prior to and Realized in Stated Year[7]	78.2	83.8	78.7
Total Environmental Income, Savings and Cost Avoidance in Stated Year	**$82.6**	**$91.0**	**$95.4**

Detail on Income, Savings and Cost Avoidance from 2007
(dollars in millions)

	Income and Savings	Cost Avoidance	Total Financial Benefits
Regulated Waste Disposal Cost Reduction	$(0.6)	$(0.1)	$(0.7)
Regulated Waste Materials Cost Reduction	(3.1)	(0.4)	(2.7)
Non-hazardous Waste Disposal Cost Reduction	(2.3)	1.5	(0.8)
Non-hazardous Waste Materials Cost Reduction	(4.1)	3.3	(0.8)
Recycling Income	4.8	0.0	4.8
Energy Consumption Cost Reduction	(3.6)	7.7	4.1
Water Consumption Cost Reduction	(0.3)	0.9	0.6
Total	**$(9.2)**	**$13.7**	**$4.4**

Cost Avoidance Detail from Efforts Initiated in the Six Years Prior to Report Year
(dollars in millions)

	2007	2006	2005
Regulated Waste Disposal	$0.8	$1.5	$1.0
Regulated Waste Materials	2.7	6.0	3.9
Non-hazardous Waste Disposal	3.3	3.4	2.8
Non-hazardous Waste Materials	18.8	21.5	25.1
Energy Consumption	48.1	47.1	42.8
Water Consumption	4.5	4.3	3.1
Total	**$78.2**	**$83.8**	**$78.7**

[1]Total cost numbers are rounded to reflect an appropriate degree of data accuracy.

[2]Corporate environmental costs comprise environmental costs related to operating corporate environmental programs that report into manufacturing and legal groups. While corporate EHS and certain business unit EHS groups integrated in the third quarter of 2003, business unit program costs remain in the Business Unit/Regional/Facility Environmental Professionals and Programs line, as those environmental costs more directly support facility programs.

[3]Cost of carbon offsets includes expenses associated with purchasing renewable energy, carbon credits purchased through the Chicago Climate Exchange (CCX) and the annual CCX membership fee.

[4]Following completion of the packaging reduction goal in 2005, Baxter no longer tracks program costs or financial savings associated with packaging reduction initiatives at the corporate level.

[5]Reflects change (positive for decrease and negative for increase) for purchases of raw materials due to changes in material use efficiency and associated generation of waste.

[6]In calculating savings and cost avoidance for waste-reduction activities, it is assumed that production and distribution grew proportionately with the cost of goods sold, adjusted for changes in inventory and inflation. Baxter uses a three-year rolling average of the annual percentage change in growth to determine the financial values for each stated year. For 2007, the three-year rolling average was 3 percent; for 2006, 2 percent; for 2005, 5 percent; and for 2004, 10 percent. This rolling average helps avoid distortions due to acquisitions/divestitures and delayed environmental effects from production changes.

[7]To be conservative, the accumulation of reported cost avoidance is terminated after seven years, the approximate duration of many facility conservation and process-improvement projects.

Undetermined Costs and Savings

The following undetermined costs are not included in the environmental financial statement (EFS):

- Environmentally driven materials research and other research and development. These are typically offset by increased sales and other non-environmental benefits not reported in the EFS;
- Capital costs of modifying processes other than adding pollution controls. These are typically offset by increased production rates, efficiencies and other non-environmental benefits not reported in the EFS;
- Cost of substitutes for ozone-depleting substances and other hazardous materials. This cost is estimated to be relatively minor; and
- Time spent by non-environmental employees on environmental activities. Environmental training and responsibilities are a part of every employee's job.

Baxter's proactive program produces savings and other benefits that are not easily measurable. Examples include the following:

- Reduced liability exposure resulting from the removal of all known single-wall underground storage tanks, waste site evaluations and other risk-management programs;
- Reduced regulatory burden due to Baxter sites reducing waste generation below certain thresholds (training, recordkeeping, reporting and administrative costs);
- Avoidance of costs for environmental problems that did not occur due to Baxter's proactive efforts.
- Ability for employees to focus on higher value tasks due to the reduction of waste, spills and other environmental problems; and
- Increased goodwill, reputation, brand value and any increased sales and employee morale.

additional costs other than the report year's savings that were not incurred but would have been incurred if the waste-reduction activity had not taken place.

In principle, all the figures presented in Baxter's EFS would be available from the organisation's main accounting system. For example, where electricity costs have fallen as a result of decreasing use pursuant to specific energy-reduction initiatives, this reduction in cost is shown as a saving. No consideration is given to the fact that the electricity consumption is still resulting in the emission of harmful greenhouse gases. As such, the approach is rather uncontroversial from an accounting perspective. What it attempts to demonstrate is that by explicitly considering the environment actual cost savings can be made. Without such an analysis these savings may be unknown and more emphasis may be placed on the cost of putting in place recycling initiatives, cleaner production techniques and so on. By considering only the costs and savings incurred by the organisation, and by excluding recognition of externalities (impacts of greenhouse emissions and so on), Baxter is still applying the usual 'entity assumption' when producing its EFS.

Watercare Services Sustainability Accounting Analysis, as it appeared in Watercare Services' 2008 annual report, is reproduced in Exhibit 9.3. Its approach also represents a departure from conventional financial accounting treatment. Watercare identified additional costs that it would need to incur if it were to meet the social and environmental standards that it believes are appropriate. Conventional accounting would not record information about unincurred costs.

Exhibit 9.3   Watercare Services Sustainability Accounting Analysis

Watercare Services
Sustainability Accounting Analysis

	2005/06 $ million	2006/07 $ million	2007/08 $ million
Total expenditure including that necessary to meet the statutory and legal obligations	142.1	157.7	163.2
Additional expenditure to meet the standards expected of Watercare			
1. wastewater treatment plant midge control	0.3	0.6	0.6
2. odour control	0.7	0.1	0.1
3. wastewater overflow clean-up	0.1	0.1	0.1
4. wastewater pump station 'failsafe' maintenance	0.9	0.7	0.9
Subtotal	2.0	1.5	1.7
Costs forming the basis of water and wastewater charges— per audited financial statements	**144.1**	**159.2**	**165.70**
Annualised cost of the additional activities that could improve the environmental standards			
5. CO_2 emission reduction	0.7	0.7	0.7
6. compensation flows below water supply dams	17.7	179	18.2
7. odour emission elimination	3.2	3.3	3.4
8. wastewater overflow minimisation	58.4	58.6	62.4
9. visual enhancement	3.7	3.9	4.6
10. biosolids re-use	15.4	15.4	16.3
11. Partial (30Ml/d) wastewater reuse for industry, forestry and agriculture	5.3	5.4	5.6
12. Partial (100Ml/d) wastewater recharge to catchments used for water extraction	63.4	63.5	65.9
13. Partial (170Ml/d) wastewater reuse to potable water	90.1	90.2	93.0
Subtotal	**257.9**	**418.1**	**435.8**
Cost base required to deliver sustainable performance	**402.0**	**418.1**	**435.8**

Exhibit 9.3 *(continued)*

Notes

1. Wastewater treatment plant midge control

   The treated effluent in the transfer channel and inter-tidal storage basin is now so clean that it is a fertile breeding ground for midges, a considerable social nuisance. In 2007/08 spraying and decanting were used to reduce the midge habitat at a cost of $600,000.

2. Odour control

   In the past year, the operating and maintenance costs of facilities to minimise odours in the reticulation network and at the wastewater treatment plant were approximately $100,000.

3. Wastewater overflow clean-up

   The wastewater reticulation network overflows in heavy storms and, as the result of system failure or third party damage, Watercare employees clean and disinfect overflow sites, which costs approximately $100,000 per year.

4. Wastewater pump station 'failsafe' maintenance

   Watercare spends a considerable amount of its maintenance budget (approximately 67 per cent) on planned maintenance, which is necessary to minimise the occurrence of pump station failures and consequential environmental damage. This safeguard cost approximately $900,000 this year.

5. CO_2 emissions

   Watercare's total greenhouse gas emissions were 27.820 tonnes for the year. If this is 'charged' at $25 per tonne it equates to $745,500.

6. Compensation flows from water supply dams

   The water supply dams cut off most of the flows from the streams below the dams. To promote the stream ecosystems, Watercare could release larger compensation flows. This would reduce the yield of the water supply system and require the construction of a new water source at $115 million and operation and maintenance costs of $10 million per year. The annual costs, including interest but excluding depreciation, would be $18.2 million.

7. Odour emission elimination

   Reducing the system's odours to minimal levels at all site boundaries, primarily by constructing new biofilters, would involve $40 million in capital cost and $500,000 per year in operating and maintenance costs. The annual costs, including interest but excluding depreciation, would be $3.4 million.

8. Wastewater overflow minimisation

   Watercare has estimated that eliminating all wet-weather overflows except in extreme storms could be achieved through installing storage tunnels and tanks in the network. The estimated capital cost of this is $800 million (which includes a further wastewater treatment plant upgrade) with a $5 million annual operating and maintenance cost. The annual cost, including interest but excluding depreciation, would be $62.4 million.

9. Visual enhancement

   Watercare estimates that the cost of camouflaging, removing or replacing 'unattractive' assets would be approximately $50 million and $1 million a year in operating and maintenance costs. The annual cost, including interest but excluding depreciation, would be $4.6 million.

10. Biosolids re-use

    Watercare estimates that the cost of developing a long-term use for biosolids would be approximately $200 million and $2 million a year in maintenance and operating costs. The annual cost, including interest but excluding depreciation, would be $16.3 million.

11. Partial wastewater recharge to catchments used for water extraction

    Part (100Ml/d) of the treated wastewater could be further treated and piped to recharge catchments which have had the water extracted from them. This is estimated to cost $500 million and $30 million a year in operation and maintenance costs. The annual cost, including interest but excluding depreciation would be $65.9 million.

(continued)

Clearly, there is great diversity in how organisations account for their social and environmental impacts. This diversity is to be expected given the lack of regulation in this area of reporting. The chapter concludes by considering social audits. Social audits provide data that are then typically used in an entity's social and environmental reports. A social audit relies on engaging a multitude of stakeholder groups.

SOCIAL AUDIT

The importance of organisations complying with community expectations has been discussed in this chapter and in Chapter 8. As argued, if an organisation does not comply with community expectations (often referred to as breaching the 'social contract') or the expectations of particularly powerful stakeholders, this can have negative implications for the survival of the organisation. One way of seeing whether the organisation's performance is conforming with the expectations of various stakeholder groups is to undertake what is referred to as a 'social audit'.

According to Elkington (1997, p. 88), the purpose of social auditing is for an organisation to assess its performance in relation to society's requirements and expectations. This is often done by directly soliciting the views of various stakeholder groups. Obviously, different management teams will be interested in the views of different stakeholder groups. Managers that take a broader ethical perspective to identifying their stakeholders will typically seek the opinions and views of a broader cross-section of stakeholders. Social audits allow a company to examine its social impacts and to establish whether it is meeting its own social objectives. The results of a social audit often form the basis of an entity's publicly released social accounts (thereby increasing the apparent transparency of the organisation), and the outcomes of social audits can be considered as an important part of the ongoing dialogue with various stakeholder groups. The Body Shop provides an insight into its social audit. According to the Body Shop *Social Performance Report 2007* (pp. 2, 3):

Our social audit program is one way we can listen to all our stakeholders and evaluate how well they feel we are fulfilling and demonstrating our values every day. Importantly, through this process we also gather feedback and ideas that contribute to positive organizational change and our plans for the future ... Our social performance data is collected through a bi-annual stakeholder survey process. We ask our stakeholders to share their thoughts on how well they believe we fulfill and demonstrate our company goals and values based on their experience. We evaluate the numbers and written comments to identify opportunities for organizational improvement. Feedback and comments are an important part of the survey process because they help us understand the sources of stakeholder satisfaction and dissatisfaction with our values ... Our social audit process is externally verified and includes an independent assurance statement.

In discussing who was involved in the social audit, the Body Shop *Social Performance Report 2007* stated (p. 4):

In 2006, over a period of four months from March to June, more than 17,000 stakeholders participated in our social audit program. The key stakeholder groups were our staff (all businesses), The Body Shop customers, The Body Shop At Home consultants, Children's Centre families, suppliers and community organisations. The largest group of participants were our customers, followed by our staff. There was lower participation within the supplier and community organization stakeholder groups.

In relation to employees, the Body Shop social audit asked the employees a number of questions on each of the following issues:

- Company values and ethos
- Care, honesty and respect
- Equal employment opportunity
- Pride and trust
- Communication
- Pay, benefits and recognition
- Career development
- Commitment to environmental issues.

In relation to the employees' perspective of 'company values and ethos', the Body Shop reported the following findings:

Social indicator	% of agreement
'I trust The Adidem Group is actively working to achieve integration of our three company goals'	84.5
'I trust The Adidem Group takes steps to balance the needs of its employees, customers, and other people'	84.1
'I trust The Adidem Group to stick to the principles it has stated'	82.2
'staff mostly share company values'	84.1

In relation to areas requiring improvement, the Body Shop made the following comments about 'career development':

> While 78.2% agreed the recruitment process for new staff was fair and transparent, only 61.5% felt the same way about the process for internal selection and promotion. Staff were generally satisfied with the appraisal process and the two-way communication. They were less satisfied with opportunities gained from the appraisal process for development and regular follow up to check progress towards goal achievement. 86.7% said they felt they were trained appropriately for their position. However, only 68% were satisfied with the link between learning opportunities and future career paths.

The Body Shop report provided a great deal more information than has been reproduced above, in relation to both employees and other stakeholder groups. What we have tried to demonstrate here is the types of information an organisation might report in respect of how particular stakeholder groups perceive it is operating. Information such as this allows an organisation to determine whether particular stakeholder groups seem to believe that an organisation is complying with its 'social contract'.

Again, many people might question whether the results reported in Exhibits 9.2 (from Baxter International) and 9.3 (from Watercare Services), and the data from the Body Shop *Social Performance Report 2007*, represent 'accounting' results? As explained in this chapter, and in Chapter 8, it really gets back to the issue of 'accountability'. The concept of 'accounting' cannot really be considered independently of the concept of 'accountability'. If the managers of organisations, such as some of those discussed in this chapter, accept that they have a responsibility (accountability) in relation to the financial, social and environmental aspects of their organisations' performance, they will choose to provide a financial account (that is, financial reports), a social account and an environmental account (all of which might be provided within a sustainability report, or provided separately). That is, their 'accounting systems' will embrace a broad perspective of 'accountability' rather than restricting the analysis to financial accounting.

Returning to the issue of social audits, the use of questionnaires is a common approach to determining stakeholders' concerns and expectations. Such reviews provide details of where improvements are necessary from the perspective of the stakeholders. In undertaking a review of an organisation's actual social performance and, importantly, the stakeholders' expectations about performance, there is a view that it is preferable to anticipate potential stakeholder backlash before a given activity is undertaken. This is a view that has been publicly endorsed by the management of the Royal Dutch/Shell Group for over a decade, as reflected in the newspaper article reproduced as Accounting Headline 9.10.

Reflective of the interest in social accounting and social auditing, a social accounting standard was released in 1998 by the organisation known as Social Accountability International, which until recently was known as the Council on Economic Priorities Accreditation Agency (Social Accountability International is a non-profit affiliate of the Council on Economic Priorities).[29] The standard, entitled

---

29 The website of Social Accountability International states: 'Our mission is to promote human rights for workers around the world as a standards organization, ethical supply chain resource, and programs developer. SAI promotes workers' rights primarily through our voluntary SA8000 system. Based on the International Labor Organization (ILO) standards and UN Human Rights Conventions, SA8000 is widely accepted as the most viable and comprehensive international ethical workplace management system available. SAI works with an array of stakeholders who are instrumental in the ever-continuing effort to improve and implement the SA8000 system.

Financial Times, 17 March 1997

Human rights and environmental activists to participate in projects

Shell to consult pressure groups

ROBERT CORZINE

Royal Dutch/Shell, the largest international oil company, is to invite environmental and human rights groups to participate in some of its more sensitive projects in the developing world.

In a radical departure from past practice, the Anglo-Dutch oil group says the early involvement of the non-governmental organisations in sensitive projects, especially in Africa and Latin America, will become standard practice.

Managers at the company are believed to have reassessed the way it operates after international criticism of its record on human rights and environmental issues.

In 1995 Shell faced wide-spread condemnation of its activities in Nigeria following the execution of minority rights activist Ken Saro Wiwa and an outcry in Europe over its plan—later dropped—to dump the obsolete Brent Spar oil installation in the Atlantic Ocean.

'We learned from those two events that we have not been listening enough,' said Mr John Jennings, chairman of Shell Transport and Trading, the group's UK arm.

Shell hopes the new approach will identify environmental or social issues with the potential to flare up into serious problems.

Shell also plans to ask pressure groups to monitor and audit the implementation of sensitive projects. It says it will publish the results of the monitoring even if they are not flattering to the company.

'We should use the increased scrutiny of NGOs as a tool to strengthen our performance,' said Mr Jennings. Shell intends to use a wide range of pressure groups, 'including those who wish you were not there'.

SA8000 ('SA' stands for 'Social Accountability') focuses on issues associated with human rights, health and safety, and equal opportunities.

SA8000 requires the audit of site performance against the principles of the UN Declaration of Human Rights, the International Labour Organization conventions and the UN Convention on the Rights of the Child. According to the website of Social Accountability International, the requirements necessary to comply with SA8000 can be summarised as:

1. Child Labor: No workers under the age of 15; minimum lowered to 14 for countries operating under the ILO Convention 138 developing-country exception; remediation of any child found to be working

2. Forced Labor: No forced labor, including prison or debt bondage labor; no lodging of deposits or identity papers by employers or outside recruiters

3. Health and Safety: Provide a safe and healthy work environment; take steps to prevent injuries; regular health and safety worker training; system to detect threats to health and safety; access to bathrooms and potable water

4. Freedom of Association and Right to Collective Bargaining: Respect the right to form and join trade unions and bargain collectively; where law prohibits these freedoms, facilitate parallel means of association and bargaining

5. Discrimination: No discrimination based on race, caste, origin, religion, disability, gender, sexual orientation, union or political affiliation, or age; no sexual harassment

6. Discipline: No corporal punishment, mental or physical coercion or verbal abuse

7. Working Hours: Comply with the applicable law but, in any event, no more than 48 hours per week with at least one day off for every seven day period; voluntary overtime paid at a premium rate and not to exceed 12 hours per week on a regular basis; overtime may be mandatory if part of a collective bargaining agreement

8. Compensation: Wages paid for a standard work week must meet the legal and industry standards and be sufficient to meet the basic need of workers and their families; no disciplinary deductions

9. Management Systems: Facilities seeking to gain and maintain certification must go beyond simple compliance to integrate the standard into their management systems and practices.

Social Accountability International's approach can be contrasted with the approach adopted by the Body Shop. The Body Shop tends to structure its social audit to issues that are developed 'in house' rather than considering issues specified by an external body such as those responsible for the development of SA8000. Developing an organisation-specific social audit, as the Body Shop has done, can be time-consuming and relatively expensive—but it does allow an organisation to tailor its approach so that it is effective in determining stakeholder expectations. Standardised approaches, such as SA8000, in a sense adopt a 'one size fits all' approach to social audits. However, such approaches provide an efficient approach for organisations that elect not to develop their own social audit methodologies.

In relation to SA8000 requirements, there are strict procedures laid down to ensure that those carrying out the audit (who must receive special training to qualify) will get to learn of local opinion and operations. Auditors are to consult trade unions, workers and local non-government organisations. People living close to a site have the right to appeal against an SA8000 award if they disagree with it. Arguably, the impetus for the development of SA8000 were controversies such as those that involved Nike (use of cheap labour in Indonesia—see Accounting Headline 9.12) and Shell (human rights issues in Nigeria, as noted in Accounting Headline 9.10). If an organisation can have its operations (particularly those being undertaken in developing countries) certified to SA8000 standards by an independent party, it is conceivable that its legitimacy from the perspective of its stakeholders will be enhanced relative to that of its competitors. This in itself should generate business benefits (and of course, more importantly, it should generate real benefits for the employees involved).

Apart from SA8000, in late 1999 the Institute of Social and Ethical Accountability (ISEA) launched a standard, labelled AA1000, which is concerned with processes relating to setting up and operating social and ethical accounting and auditing systems. The guidelines, which are voluntary, emphasise the need to define clearly social and ethical goals and targets and to report levels of achievement in meeting the targets. The importance of involving stakeholders in the process is heavily emphasised. As *Environmental Accounting and Auditing Reporter* (January 2000, p. 2) states:

> The process set out in AA1000 guides an organisation through the definition of goals and targets, the measurement of progress against these targets, the auditing and reporting on performance, and feedback mechanisms. The involvement of stakeholder groups is crucial to each stage of the process, building trust in the organisation and the ethical claims it

makes. Whilst the process remains the same for each organisation, the goals and targets set will be specific to the needs of their stakeholders, covering a range of issues from employee rights through to conditions in supply chains.

AA1000 also provides guidance in relation in developing programs to train social and ethical accountants and auditors, which possibly signals the genesis of a new subset of the accounting profession. In reflecting on the benefits to companies from complying with AA1000, Simon Zadek, representative of ISEA states (as quoted in *Environmental Accounting and Auditing Reporter*, January 2000, p. 2):

> There is an increasing body of evidence that organisations which listen to their stakeholders are more likely to be successful in the long term. AA1000's continuous cycle of consultation with stakeholders is designed to encourage transparency, clear goal-setting and the building of trust in relationships with people. Organisations which adhere to its principles and processes will be able to draw strength from association with this quality standard and, ultimately, can expect to achieve competitive advantage. Companies like Railtrack and Monsanto must wish, in retrospect, they had invested in these kinds of processes to help avoid billions being wiped off their market values.[30]

Once activities such as social audits are undertaken, they can act as a catalyst for organisations, and, importantly, for senior management to embrace new values. A 'sustainable organisation' needs to ensure that it complies with community expectations. As such, activities such as social audits make good business sense. As noted in the quote from Simon Zadek, failure to comply with community expectations can have major implications for the ongoing survival of the organisation (regardless of how efficiently they are using the financial resources or the environment). As WMC Ltd stated in its *Environmental Progress Report* back in 1997, 'the greater the community's confidence in a company, the more secure its longer-term viability'. It also appears that some organisations are undertaking social audits as a means of gaining (or regaining) some legitimacy from the perspective of their stakeholders. Undertaking a social audit, particularly if the audit is undertaken by a credible, independent party, should act to increase the perceived transparency of the organisation. A newspaper article, reproduced as Accounting Headline 9.11, supports this view in relation to the activities of Camelot—the organisation responsible for running lotteries in the United Kingdom. Camelot was seeking another term to run the lotteries, but had been the subject of much public criticism about how it was using the substantial funds that it was attracting. The organisation elected to undertake a social audit to highlight the positive aspects of its operations and to help it achieve its aim of having the government renew is licence to run lotteries.

With the power of the media to beam information about an organisation's international operations into our lounge rooms, an organisation must consider not only the expectations of the local community it which it operates (whether gained through the process of a social audit, or otherwise) but its stakeholders worldwide—many of which will focus on social issues.[31] Organisations must be able to indicate that they are not exploiting particular communities

---

30 ISEA's website is http://www.accountability21.net.

31 In the 1997 Health Safety and Environmental Report of Shell International, the chairperson refers to the world in which we live as a 'CNN world'—a world in which global news networks will very quickly let us know about corporate misdemeanours, no matter where they occur.

Camelot puts itself on trial

Lottery firm's social audit aims to counter critics, writes ROGER CROWE.

Camelot, the National Lottery Operator, has decided to conduct a social audit in an effort to rescue its reputation before bidding for a new licence in 2001.

The exercise will aim to give an independent seal of approval to the way the lottery has been run, countering accusations that Camelot has made too much money, failed customers and charities and abused its monopoly position.

It follows Camelot's appointment in July of the campaigner Sue Slipman to the new post of director of social responsibility. Ms Slipman will be responsible for the audit until next month. She has described it as 'a challenging project'.

The £250,000 audit will report the views of six groups including staff, retailers and the general public, on how the lottery company is carrying out its responsibilities.

The decision to follow companies such as Body Shop and Shell in seeking external scrutiny of its social role was taken by the board in June.

Companies such as BP and BT, as well as some of the international accountancy firms, have focused on social auditing as a means of justifying controversial actions and protecting reputations.

PricewaterhouseCoopers (PWC), the international audit and consultancy firm, is preparing to launch a Reputation Assurance Service which aims to help multinationals assess their social and environmental impact. Glen Peters, the firm's director of futures, said that managing a company's reputation will be one of the greatest challenges of the next decade. He expects 1,000 companies in the US and Europe to embrace the notion of wider accountability over the next five years.

Six large companies have been testing the PWC system, which will be launched in January. They are using the approach to examine their responsibilities to five groups—shareholders, employees, customers, society in general, and 'partners', including suppliers.

Mr Peters said big businesses were interested in such an exercise because of the need to back up promises such as 'the customer is number one' and 'employees are our most valuable asset'.

'Reputation is going to be a business's most important asset,' he said. 'Businesses will need to adopt a systematic approach to protecting their reputations.'

Camelot has adopted a social audit after facing a furore over bonuses for directors and accusations of misconduct against its technical supplier, GTech.

The lottery operator has commissioned the New Economics Foundation (NEF) to manage the audit. The NEF pioneered the concept in Britain, initially with Traidcraft, the Third World crafts importer, then the cosmetics chain, Body Shop.

Adrian Henriques, head of social audit at NEF, said: 'social auditing is becoming part of the mainstream. It is about determining what impact a company has on society and how society affects the company.'

Richard Brown, director of government relations at Camelot, said it was crucial that an external agency such as the NEF was involved to counter accusations that this was merely a public relations exercise. 'NEF will ensure that all stakeholder groups are involved in ongoing dialogue which is externally verified.'

Mr Brown said the decision to undertake the audit was not driven solely by the campaign to win a second licence term for the lottery. 'It is responding to changing values of the 1990s,' he said. 'But it is also an important way of telling people there are plenty of things we can be proud of.'

He suggested the row over directors' bonuses might have been avoided if Camelot had been carrying out a social audit from the start, because the board would have understood how controversial the pay packages were.

Mr Brown dismissed worries about the link with GTech, which was originally a partner in the lottery consortium but is now merely a supplier.

'If people have concerns about GTech, we would like to know about it.'

One unusual feature of the Camelot audit will be the establishment of a permanent 'stakeholder council' which will oversee the process and continue to monitor action or issues arising from it.

The audit will take about 18 months to complete and is not expected to be published until 2000, when applications for the new lottery licence will be submitted.

or subgroups—even though they might be complying with local laws. For example, consider the implications for Nike when it became apparent to others that the organisation was selling sportswear that was being produced in Indonesia by individuals being paid less than $10 a week (at the same time it was paying Michael Jordan many millions of dollars to endorse the same products), or the implications for BHP Billiton when it became apparent to the world how much environmental damage was being caused in Papua New Guinea as a result of operations that BHP Billiton was associated with. Other examples include Shell's operations in Nigeria, in which it was deemed by many parties that Shell was appearing to be supportive of an oppressive regime, and Disney's use of cheap labour in Haiti. In relation to Disney's operations in Haiti, a newspaper article in a leading UK newspaper, the *Independent* (10 October 1997), had the headline 'No glamour for Disney's sweatshop toilers'. The article discussed the 'huge profits' being earned by Disney at the same time as it was sourcing products from 'sweatshops' that were paying 17 pence an hour and providing substandard working conditions. Accounting Headline 9.12 is also reflective of the media coverage that was given to some of the social performance issues discussed. Consistent with Media Agenda Setting Theory (see Chapter 8), it is reasonable to assume that such negative media coverage would have impacted on the public's perceptions about the legitimacy of the companies involved. Consistent with Lindblom (1994), an organisation that suffers a potential 'legitimacy crisis' may undertake certain actions in an attempt to improve its image in the eyes of its stakeholders, including educating and informing its stakeholders about changes in the organisation's performance and activities, or perhaps by attempting to change external expectations about an entity's performance (Lindblom's work was considered in Chapter 8). As noted earlier, social auditing and social reporting can be useful in this regard and it is interesting that many organisations that have been challenged about their social conduct (with extensive negative media attention) have subsequently put in place social reporting and auditing mechanisms. Nike now gives great publicity to its social audits.

When reading Accounting Headline 9.12, consider whether the attitudes attributed to the management of Nike are consistent with the goal of sustainability, which has been publicly embraced by many corporations.

Undertaking social audits on a periodic basis is becoming accepted as a necessary part of a well-functioning governance system. For example, Nike now ensures that supply chains pay appropriate wage rates and provide appropriate conditions for employees. Had a social audit been undertaken previously, Nike could have insisted on this earlier and its name would not have been so badly tarnished by the bad publicity it was receiving in the news media.

An organisation's operations can have many social impacts. A social audit (and related report) can obviously not cover all such impacts. Some prioritisation is necessary and this prioritisation will be dependent on professional judgements. Consideration must be given to stakeholder needs, selection of appropriate performance indicators to satisfy information needs and so on—issues that were covered earlier in the chapter. Ideally, management should explain the reasons for selecting particular social areas for subsequent review.

CHAPTER SUMMARY

This chapter has reviewed various issues associated with corporate social and environmental reporting. Since the early 1990s many organisations throughout the world have been providing an increasing amount of information about their social and environmental performance in a variety of reports. Concerns associated with sustainability (which relates to economic, social and

Nike work at 16p an hour? Just do it

In the West trainers are equated with liberty, but in Asia the shoe is on the other foot, reports ROCASTA SHAKESPEARE.

Observer, 3 December 1995. Copyright Gardian, News and Media Limited, 1995.

Sweating in the 90-degree heat, 22-year-old Eni dabs paint on to the soles of freshly moulded Reebok, Nike and Adidas trainers as they pass along a production line in Jakarta's Eltri factory. Presses thump and hiss, glue stinks and rubber burns as machines drum 23,000 stitches into each leather upper. But the Nike advertisement posted to the wall above her head implores 'Just Do It'.

'If we make a mistake they call us dogs and prostitutes and sometimes they hit us,' says Eni ... Eni and her fellow workers on Line Four are paid 16 pence an hour. A pair of Reebok Instapump Fury Graphite costs £99.99.

Tomorrow Christian Aid will launch a campaign called 'The Globe-Trotting Sports Shoe' to highlight conditions in sport shoe factories in China, the Philippines and Thailand which, together with Indonesia, employ more than 75,000 workers. In an industry that spends millions of pounds on advertising campaigns and takes millions in profits, the labour costs are minute. For example, labour costs for a pair of Nike Air Pegasus shoes that retail for $70 are $1.66 (£1.07).

The Indonesian Government admits that its minimum wage of 4,600 rupiahs (£1.30) a day is fixed below the poverty line to encourage foreign investment. By that criterion, the policy has been a huge success. Nike started using subcontractors in Indonesia in the late 1980s when Korean wages increased. Top names such as Adidas, Puma, Converse, LA Gear and Fila followed and more than 25,000 workers—85 per cent of them women—are now employed in the shoe factories around Jakarta.

In Indonesia, free trade unions are illegal and attempts to organise one can end in violence or murder. Working conditions can be dangerous and hours long. Work begins at 7.30 am and can continue for up to 18 hours. While compulsory overtime is illegal, enforcement is lax. 'We are often forced to work until midnight or later if the factory has a high quota or deadline, like Christmas, to meet,' says 20-year-old Lely, who works at the Pratama Abadi Indus factory outside Jakarta. 'If we refuse to do overtime we are fired.'

A complaint of any kind can result in sacking. Sadisah, 24, was fired in 1992 along with 23 fellow workers after striking to demand compliance with statutory labour laws at the Eltri factory. She now works at the Nikomas factory in Serang, a Jakarta suburb.

Dusty Kidd, Nike's head of communications, said: 'We can't dictate to governments how they run their labour laws.' He points out that in a country where the population is increasing at the rate of 2.5 million per year, with 40 per cent unemployment, it is better to work in a shoe factory than not to have a job at all.

Philip Knight, Nike's founder, says he wants Nike to be thought of as a company with 'a soul that recognises the value of human beings'.

Reebok intends to stay in Indonesia. Its founder, Paul Fireman, says: 'Rather than impose US culture on other countries, we work to make every country its own headquarters—sort of a 'when in Rome do as the Romans' philosophy'.

Such a statement amazes Rahman, 20, a hot press operator at Jakarta's Nasa shoe factory. 'We need protection from our government. We don't need foreign companies to come to Indonesia to take advantage of Suharto's denial of human rights.' ...

The scene is about as far as you can get from the fit and aggressive image projected by the sports shoe companies in the West. Here, they spend millions signing up sports stars and then more millions on buying advertising space. In 1994, Reebok spent $70 million on US advertising alone; Nike spent £187 million. More than £6.5 million has been spent on advertising in Britain.

'To you in England these shoes have an image of freedom and individuality,' Sadisah says. 'To us they mean oppression.' ...

Nike's profits last year were $299 million while those of Reebok's were $254 million. It is not known how much of a shoe's price goes for profit or marketing, but neither can be insignificant in a market where image is everything. The endorsement deals are huge, with the likes of American star Michael Jordan being paid $20 million.

Peter Madden of Christian Aid says the irony is that companies which claim to be masters of the latest technology say they have no control of the factories. 'These companies are developing the most complex design specifications yet they are not able to regulate what goes on in the factories.'

environmental performance issues) have increased since the early 1990s and the evolution of corporate social and environmental performance reporting appears to be related to these concerns, as developments in reporting are probably a reflection of changing community expectations about the performance and responsibilities of business. In examining various theoretical issues associated with social and environmental reporting, the discussion was structured to follow the *why–who–for what–how* stages of the sustainability reporting process.

In the *why* stage, various aspects of the motivations for organisations to engage in corporate social responsibility and social and environmental reporting were explored. When a firm voluntarily discloses information publicly about its social and environmental performance, this may imply that the managers are acknowledging that they are accountable to a broad group of stakeholders in relation to not only their financial performance but also their social and environmental performance. However, as this chapter indicates, not all people consider that managers have social responsibilities to a broad group of stakeholders. Some researchers believe that the prime responsibility of managers is to shareholders alone and, within these confines, to maximising shareholder (financial) value. However, this narrow perspective of corporate responsibility seems to be becoming less widely accepted, as concepts of an interrelated triple bottom line of social, environmental and economic sustainability become more widely accepted.

For the *who* (or *to whom*) stage, the chapter examined the range of stakeholders that different organisations are likely to wish to address in their social and environmental (or sustainability) reporting strategies. This range of stakeholders is likely to be directly related to an organisation's motives for engaging in social and environmental reporting. It will be very broad for organisations that operate in a manner consistent with the ethical branch of Stakeholder Theory. Conversely, organisations following the managerial branch of Stakeholder Theory will tend to focus on the demands and expectations of a narrower range of stakeholders—those with the most power over the organisation.

The chapter then explored some theoretical perspectives regarding the mechanisms that organisations may use to identify *what* information these stakeholders need, or *for what* issues these stakeholders believe the organisation is socially and environmentally responsible and accountable. It first drew on several studies that demonstrated that stakeholders *do* appear to make use of information about the social and environmental performance of organisations, and thus it can be concluded that stakeholders *do* want some social and environmental performance information. An analysis was undertaken of theoretical perspectives on processes of stakeholder dialogue, which can be used by organisations to develop an understanding of what social and environmental information is likely to be demanded by their stakeholders. It was seen that there were difficulties involved in seeking to reach an acceptable consensus view among a wide range of stakeholders regarding the social, environmental and economic responsibilities of an organisation—and the consequent accountability duties related to these responsibilities.

Finally, in the *how* stage, theoretical perspectives on some of the processes involved in the production of social and environmental reports were reviewed, including the limitations of conventional financial reporting for capturing and reflecting the social and environmental impact of an organisation's policies and practices, the potential and drawbacks of the triple bottom line reporting model, key aspects of the Global Reporting Initiative, and some issues related to social auditing. Evidence shows that the practice of social accounting and social auditing, which was promoted in the 1970s, has re-emerged as a major issue in corporate accountability and reporting in the twenty-first century.

QUESTIONS

9.1 What has the environment to do with accounting?

9.2 What is accountability and what is its relationship to:

(a) accounting?

(b) an organisation's responsibilities?

9.3 What is sustainable development?

9.4 Do conventional financial accounting practices and definitions encourage or assist corporations to adopt sustainable business practices? Explain your answer.

9.5 Are 'economic rationality' (as defined by economists) and 'sustainability' mutually inconsistent?

9.6 Would advocates of Positive Accounting Theory (as explained in Chapter 7) believe that organisations will embrace sustainable development in the way described by *The Brundtland Report?* Explain your view.

9.7 What is an externality, and why do financial accounting practices typically ignore externalities?

9.8 What is a social audit and why would a profit-seeking entity bother with one?

9.9 Why do you think the European Union called for a 'redefinition of accounting concepts, rules, conventions and methodology so as to ensure that the consumption and use of environmental resources are accounted for as part of the full cost of production and reflected in market prices' (European Commission, 1992, Vol. II, Section 7.4, p. 67)?

9.10 What is triple bottom line reporting, and what has it to do with sustainable development?

9.11 Do you think that triple bottom line reporting can actually lead to separate 'bottom lines' for the social, environmental and economic performance of an entity? Explain your view.

9.12 Of what relevance to the accounting profession is sustainable development?

9.13 Why do you think that the accounting profession has generally not released any accounting standards pertaining to the disclosure of environmental information?

9.14 Evidence shows that business entities and business associations typically make submissions to government which argue in favour of maintaining the voluntary status of social and environmental performance reporting. That is, they typically oppose the introduction of legislation to require them to report information about their social and environmental performance. Why do you think this is the case?

9.15 Collison (2003, p. 861) states: 'Attention to the interests of shareholders above all other groups is implicit in much of what is taught to accounting and finance students. The very construction of a profit and loss account ... is a continual, and usually unstated, reminder that the interests of only one group of stakeholders should be maximised. Indeed it may be very difficult for accounting and finance students to even conceive of another way in which affairs could be ordered ... even at the algebraic level, let alone the moral.'

(a) Do you agree or disagree with Collison, and why?

(b) If 'profit' maximisation is biased towards maximising the interests of only one stakeholder group, would you expect that over time there will be less emphasis on profits and more emphasis on other performance indicators? Why? What might be some of the alternative measures of performance?

(c) Would Collison's comments provide a justification for moves towards profit measures that incorporate 'full costs' (that is, that consider the externalities of business)?

9.16 If a particular social or environmental incident occurs that involves an organisation and that generates negative media attention, how would you expect the organisation to react from a disclosure perspective?

9.17 How would the following theories (addressed in Chapters 7 and 8) explain corporate social responsibility reporting?

(a) Positive Accounting Theory

(b) Legitimacy Theory

(c) Stakeholder Theory

(d) Institutional Theory

9.18 In publicly released reports a number of organisations are referring to their 'public licence to operate'. What do you think they mean by this, and is there a theoretical perspective that can explain what this term means?

9.19 What is 'enlightened self-interest'?

9.20 Some people argue that fixating on maximising corporate profits and increasing shareholder value will ultimately lead to benefits for all people within society (perhaps through a 'trickle-down effect'). Evaluate this view.

9.21 Read the following statement from the Business Council of Australia (2005) and then explain whether such a perspective ties in well with the very real need for corporations to embrace sustainable development for the good of the planet. On the basis of such a statement, to which stakeholder groups would corporations be primarily accountable according to the Business Council?

'The litmus test for any activity or responsibility is whether the performance of that activity or responsibility can reasonably be seen to be contributing to the growth of shareholder value.'

9.22 Consider how the concept of sustainable development, as it applies to business entities, compares with the accountant's notion of a 'going concern'. Do you believe that they are similar, or are they quite different?

9.23 Is gross domestic product (GDP) a 'good measure' of national performance? Explain your views.

9.24 If a major Australian mining company reports record profits, is this profit figure misleading if the same company has polluted various river systems and has emitted various toxic substances into the air, but has not placed a cost on these externalities?

9.25 Review the approaches to reporting embraced by Baxter International and Watercare Services, as shown in this chapter, and identify some strengths and limitations of the respective reporting approaches.

9.26 In 1995, the Institute of Chartered Accountants in Australia (ICAA) established an Environmental Accounting Task Force (which subsequently became the Triple Bottom Line Issues Group, which ultimately was discontinued). The task force released a number of documents, one being *The Impact of Environmental Matters on the Accountancy Profession* (released in January 1998). Within this document the ICAA Environmental Accounting Task Force raised a number of environmental reporting issues that it believed require consideration. These included:

(a) Are standards or guidelines needed to assist companies to meet the information needs of stakeholders in respect of the disclosure of environmental information?

(b) Do environmental impacts, whether quantifiable in monetary terms or not, warrant some form of disclosure to the extent the environmental implications are deemed 'significant' rather than material within the meaning of accounting standards?

(c) Does the provision of environmental performance information and advising on control aspects of environmental management systems fall within the core skills of accountants?

(d) Are the definitions of 'assets' and 'liabilities' in the conceptual framework appropriate to environmental accounting. If not, how should they be expanded? Specifically: Should the definition of an asset based on 'control' apply? Should it be amended to recognise specifically the environment as an entity, thereby allowing liabilities to be recognised without the intervention of a third party?

(e) Is the concept of materiality relevant to environmental reports?

(f) Should reporting of environmental issues according to traditional accounting concepts be progressed while the difficulties of monetary measurement are researched further?

(g) Should general or industry-specific approaches be adopted to advance issues associated with environmental performance evaluation, reporting and auditing?

Attempt to provide your own views on these issues.

9.27 Read Accounting Headline 9.13 and consider the implications (externalities) associated with the promotion of tobacco use by cigarette companies. If the allegations made against the tobacco companies were true, what would be the implications for these companies' reported results if:

(a) conventional financial accounting practices were employed?

(b) some form of 'full cost' accounting, which took account of externalities, was adopted?

9.28 Read Accounting Headline 9.14 and discuss how the BBC will account for the job losses it creates. Do you think it is a limitation of financial accounting that the BBC can show an increase in profits when such an increase is as a result of negatively impacting on a particular group of stakeholders? Explain your view.

9.29 Read Accounting Headline 9.15 which discusses the health effects caused by tobacco, and then:

(a) Explain how or why tobacco companies can report accounting profits even though the consequences of their activities are believed to be causing significant social and economic impacts within society.

(b) Suggest an approach to accounting that would require tobacco-producing organisations to internalise the social and economic impacts that their products create for society. Your suggestion can represent a departure from existing or traditional accounting practices.

Financial Times, 22 September 2004, p. 8

Tobacco industry deliberately misled smokers on health risks, court told

DEMETRI SEVAST OPULO

The tobacco industry engaged in a massive 50-year fraud to deceive consumers about the risks from smoking, the US Justice Department said yesterday at the start of a landmark trial. In opening arguments, government lawyers said that tobacco companies deliberately misled the public about the harmful effects of smoking while privately acknowledging the dangers.

The government wants the tobacco companies to forfeit $280bn (€228bn, £156bn) of past profits. It claims the industry marketed cigarettes to young people, manipulated nicotine levels in cigarettes and funded studies that cast doubt on whether smoking causes lung cancer and other diseases.

The industry denies fraud and says it has already changed many of the marketing practices the government criticises.

Government lawyers produced internal company documents suggesting tobacco executives understood the risks of smoking but continued to say publicly that there was insufficient evidence to reach that conclusion. Frank Marine, a government lawyer, provided details of a 1953 meeting of top industry executives which, he argued, represented the first step in 'one of the most elaborate public relations schemes in history'.

The companies argue the meeting was not secret because they had told the government it would take place. The government counters that the companies hid its true intention, which it alleges was to form an industry-wide alliance to obscure the issue of the dangers of smoking.

The suit is being brought under the 1970 *Racketeer-Influenced and Corrupt Organizations (Rico) Act*, which was designed to crack down on organised crime. The defendants—Philip Morris, RJ Reynolds, Brown & Williamson, Lorillard, Liggett and British American Tobacco—have challenged the government's legal authority to seek a $280bn penalty. An appeals court is expected to decide that issue in November.

The industry is also opposing restrictions on cigarette marketing sought by the government, saying they mirror those imposed by the 1998 Master Settlement Agreement. Under that deal, tobacco companies agreed to pay $264bn to settle claims with the 50 US states.

The companies are expected to argue there was no concerted effort to mislead consumers. The industry cites, for example, the requirement that packets of cigarettes carry health warnings since 1966—two years after the US surgeon-general concluded that smoking caused cancer—as evidence that it could not have deceived consumers.

Australian, 23 March 2005

Thousands to lose jobs in BBC bid to save $860m

AFP

LONDON: One in seven jobs will be slashed at the British Broadcasting Corporation as the world's biggest public broadcaster sheds 3780 staff in a cost-cutting drive.

The BBC, which employs more than 27,000 people in Britain and around the world, said it would slash 2050 posts, after 1730 job losses confirmed earlier this month, in what it termed its 'toughest period' in memory.

The cuts would bring savings of pound stg 355 million ($860 million) a year to reinvest in programs— pound stg 35 million more than first targeted by the BBC in December. The figure amounts to 880 more job cuts than the 2900 the BBC announced when it disclosed a massive reorganisation and modernisation overhaul in December.

Among the redundancies announced yesterday would be

(continued)

420 posts in news, 66 in sport, 150 in drama, entertainment and children's programs, 735 in the regions, 58 in new media and 424 in factual and learning.

BBC director Mark Thompson told staff the cuts were 'a difficult and painful process, but necessary'. 'This is all money we plan to spend on programs and content, both to improve the services we deliver to audiences right now and to build strong BBC services in the future,' he said. 'We are going through the toughest period any of us can remember.' The broadcaster said the elimination of 3780 jobs amounted to 19 per cent of the workforce in Britain, or almost 14 per cent of the corporation's staff worldwide.

The BBC—which draws most of its pound stg 2.8 billion annual revenue from a yearly licence fee of pound stg 121 levied on all British homes with a television set—suffered a deficit of pound stg 249 million in the fiscal year 2003–04. Planned changes will mean the news departments will need to do some things differently and in many areas will have less money to spend, an internal memo said.

Despite the cuts, about pound stg 1 million will be spent next year on creating an investigations unit in Manchester, northwest England, and a new fund to enhance the coverage of major stories.

Journalists who will be leaving because of the cuts were told they had done nothing wrong.

'All of you have contributed to our success over the years. However, in a rapidly moving media industry, change is inevitable, though none of us underestimate how painful it can be,' the memo said.

Union leaders will meet later this week to decide how to respond to the cuts, but have already warned they will ballot staff for industrial action if there are any compulsory redundancies.

Luke Crawley, an official with the broadcasting workers' union Bectu, was shocked by the announcement. 'This is the worst day in the BBC's history,' he said.

Time to stop killing customers to make a profit

KEVIN PURSE

Advertiser, 13 June 2008, p. 18

In 2003, the Federal Government backed long-standing calls by trade unions and public-health advocates for a comprehensive ban on the production, importation and use of asbestos. As a result, Australia is now one of more than 40 countries worldwide to have prohibited the use of asbestos.

Despite this decision, up to 40,000 Australians are expected to die from past asbestos exposure by 2020. Appalling as this figure is, it is dramatically overshadowed by the death toll from tobacco-related causes. Smoking continues to be Australia's largest cause of preventable disease, costing more than $31 billion annually and resulting in 15,050 deaths each year.

Tobacco smoke is the world's most lethal consumer product, containing more than 4000 chemicals, including more than 60 that cause cancer. In addition to cancers of the lung, stomach, cervix, bladder and mouth, tobacco products cause fatal diseases such as chronic heart disease, stroke, emphysema and other health problems. These include asthma and reduced fertility in both men and women.

Like their counterparts in the asbestos industry, tobacco companies conspired long and hard to keep these facts from the public. In the US, it was not until 1997, during congressional hearings, that tobacco industry executives finally acknowledged the deadly effects of

their products. A similar charade was played out in Australia. Until the late 1990s, the industry was still claiming there was no proof that smoking caused lung cancer and heart disease.

Nor was it prepared to fess up to the fact that nicotine is addictive—in fact, one of the most highly addictive substances known. The tobacco industry has been aware of the addictive nature of nicotine for decades.

Similarly, the industry has known for more than 40 years that cigarette smoking causes lung cancer. As late as 2006, it was still denying links with passive smoking. Despite stalling tactics based on denial and deception, the tobacco industry has been subjected

(continued)

to increasing regulation. By international standards, Australia has a good track record in tobacco control.

Restrictions on advertising, packaging and labelling requirements for tobacco products, smoking bans in workplaces and other public places as well as programs to assist smokers quit have all contributed to an overall decline in smoking rates.

However, despite these improvements, the death toll from tobacco products is still far too high. The major limitation of current regulatory controls is that their focus is on reducing demand for tobacco. A more systematic approach is required. This means dealing with the problem at its source—the supply of tobacco products. As has been the case with asbestos, we need to consider a comprehensive ban on the commercial production, sale and importation of tobacco products.

A tobacco ban would not be easy to achieve. There would almost certainly be a massive lobbying and PR blitz from the tobacco corporations, as there was with the asbestos industry.

Another concern is the likely emergence of a black market, which fortunately Australia is much better placed to deal with than most other countries by virtue of its geography and sophisticated Customs service.

There would also need to be greater assistance for people who want to quit their tobacco habit and a substantial increase in anti-smoking awareness campaigns, particularly for young people.

However, the bottom line is that an industry that kills customers to make a profit has no place in a civilised society.

Dr Kevin Purse is a Research Fellow with the Hawke Research Institute at the University of South Australia.

9.30 Read Accounting Headline 9.16 and then answer these questions.

(a) How would a brewery company account for the social costs created by alcohol abuse?

(b) Should a brewery company account for the social costs created by alcohol abuse?

(c) Would GDP be positively or negatively affected by costs that arise from alcohol abuse? (Such costs might include those that arise from alcohol-related accidents, alcohol-related crime and so forth)?

Accounting Headline 9.16 Another example of where counting profits ignores the social impacts of a corporation's products

Interstate growth cheers SA's Coopers

CHRIS MILNE

Australian Financial Review, 6 January 2005, p. 13

Coopers Brewery expects more profit growth this year, helped by markedly lower malt costs, after a 5.3 per cent increase in full-year net profit to $9.48 million.

The Adelaide-based, unlisted public company's performance was driven by a 29 per cent increase in interstate sales. Revenue rose from $83.7 million to $92.6 million in the year to June 30.

Its national sales volumes rose 16.9 per cent in an overall domestic market that slipped 1 per cent over the year, as Australia's third-largest brewer continued to outpoint its larger rivals.

Managing director Tim Cooper said sales in the first half of this financial year were about 20 per cent ahead of the previous first half.

He said Coopers was benefiting from lower malt costs, as barley prices dropped from about $675 a tonne in 2003–04 to about $500 a tonne this financial year.

'The very high price of barley took more than $2 million off our bottom line,' Dr Cooper said.

'It was a very encouraging result in the circumstances and this year's result should be quite a bit better.'

The strong growth in sales beyond its South Australian base where sales grew 10.5 per cent had resulted largely from the 75 per cent investment in the Premium Brands joint venture with American

(continued)

Beverage Distributors, which began trading in March 2003 and had enhanced national distribution.

Higher export sales, up 14.2 per cent, had been gained in Britain, the United States and New Zealand, although they accounted for only about 2 per cent of total revenues.

However, Coopers did not have everything its own way, with its business in home brewing kits suffering a 12.8 per cent fall in sales volumes as Foster's CUB unit and Lion Nathan entered the mature market.

Dr Cooper said the home-brew market had been in 'gradual decline' since the mid-1990s but still accounted for about 20 per cent of revenue.

'The entry of Lion Nathan in 2003 and then CUB last year did hurt us but we're holding our own,' he said.

9.31 An article appearing in the *Independent* newspaper (UK, 18 April 2005, p. 20) entitled 'The ethical revolution sweeping through the world's sweatshops' identified how organisations such as Nike and Gap had put in place various mechanisms to help ensure improvement in the conditions of factory workers. In relation to the responses of Nike and Gap:

(a) Why do you think that companies like Nike and Gap responded to the community concerns?

(b) Is this a case of enlightened self-interest or a case of a company embracing a form of responsibility to the stakeholders affected by its operations?

9.32 Read Accounting Headline 9.17 and then, drawing on material covered in this chapter, identify some ways in which you think corporations would respond to such allegations.

Accounting Headline 9.17 Illustrations of some negative impacts of business

Irish Independent, 1 December 2004 © 2004
Independent Newspapers Ireland Ltd

Think before you spend ...

Here are some of the products *The Rough Guide to Ethical Shopping* believes we should think about before buying:

Beverages: Maxwell House. One of the thousands of familiar brands—Bird's, Jacobs, Ritz and Toblerone are others—owned by tobacco giant Philip Morris of Marlboro cigarette fame, which recently changed its name to Altria.

It denies to this day that smoking is addictive, was fined for failing to disclose political donations and was one of George Bush's largest corporate campaign contributors.

Clothing: Nike trainers. Nike is said to have petitioned the Indonesian government for exemption from the minimum wage and has been accused of lying about labour conditions at its contractor factories.

According to Sweatshop Watch, an average Nike worker would need to put in 72,000 years of work to receive what Tiger Woods gets for one five-year contract to publicise the brand.

Food: Tiger prawns. Hugely popular nowadays in restaurants and supermarkets, tiger prawns are mostly raised in man-made pools in Bangladesh and the Philippines.

It takes 50,000 litres of water to produce a kilogram of prawn meat, and the chemical additives to promote rapid growth ends up polluting the surrounding farming land.

People are routinely displaced to make way for these farms. Rape and murder have been reported in some cases.

Sport: Snooker cues. Thousands of snooker cues are made every year using wood from the Indonesian ramin tree. The ramin, which is also used for furniture and window blinds, is a rare and endangered tree listed under the Convention on International Trade in Endangered Species, but continues to be logged illegally at an alarming rate.

REFERENCES

Accounting Standards Steering Committee (1975), *The Corporate Report*, London: Institute of Chartered Accountants in England and Wales.

Adams, C. A. (2002), 'Internal organisational factors influencing corporate social and ethical reporting', *Accounting, Auditing and Accountability Journal*, 15(2), pp. 223–50.

Adams, C. A. (2004), 'The ethical, social and environmental reporting—performance portrayal gap', *Accounting, Auditing and Accountability Journal*, 17(5), pp. 731–57.

Adams, C. A. & G. Harte (1998), 'The changing portrayal of the employment of women in British banks' and retail companies' corporate annual reports', *Accounting, Organizations and Society*, 23(8), pp. 781–812.

Anderson, J. C. & A. W. Frankle (1980), 'Voluntary social reporting: an Iso-beta portfolio analysis', *The Accounting Review*, 55(3), pp. 467–79.

Bebbington, J. & R. Gray (2001), 'An account of sustainability: failure, success and a reconceptualisation', *Critical Perspectives on Accounting*, 12(5), pp. 557–605.

Beck, U. (1992), *Risk Society: Towards a New Modernity*, London: SAGE Publications.

Beck, U. (1999), *World Risk Society*, Cambridge: Polity Press.

Belkaoui, A. R. (1976), 'The impact of the disclosure of environmental effects of organizational behavior on the market', *Financial Management* (Winter), pp. 26–31.

Bennett, M. & P. James (1998), *The Green Bottom Line: Environmental Accounting for Management—Current Practice and Future Trends*, Greenleaf Publishing.

Benston, G. J. (1982), 'Accounting and corporate accountability', *Accounting, Organizations and Society*, 6(2), pp. 87–105.

Brady, A. (2003), *Forecasting the Impact of Sustainability Issues on the Reputation of Large Multinational Corporations*, Cambridge: Judge Institute of Management, University of Cambridge.

Brown, D., J. F. Dillard & R. S. Marshall (2005), 'Triple bottom line: a business metaphor for a social construct', paper presented at Critical Perspectives on Accounting conference, Baruch College, City University of New York, 28–30 May.

Buhr, N. (1998), 'Environmental performance, legislation and annual report disclosure: the case of acid rain and Falconbridge', *Accounting, Auditing and Accountability Journal*, 11(2), pp. 163–90.

Business Council of Australia (2005), *Submission to the Parliamentary Joint Committee on Corporations and Financial Services—Inquiry into Corporate Responsibility and Triple Bottom Line Reporting*, Melbourne: BCA.

Campbell, D. J. (2000), 'Legitimacy theory or managerial construction? Corporate social disclosure in Marks and Spencer Plc corporate reports, 1969–1997', *Accounting Forum*, 24(1), pp. 80–100.

Chamber of Commerce and Industry of Western Australia (2005), *The Social Responsibilities of Business: A Submission to the 2005 Inquiry into Corporate Responsibility*, Perth: CCIWA.

Clarkson, M. (1995), 'A stakeholder framework for analyzing and evaluating corporate social performance', *Academy of Management Review*, 20(1), pp. 92–118.

Collison, D. J. (2003), 'Corporate propaganda: its implications for accounting and accountability', *Accounting, Auditing and Accountability Journal*, 16(5), pp. 853–86.

Commission of European Communities (2001), *Promoting a European Framework for*

Corporate Social Responsibility, Green Paper, Brussels: Commission of European Communities.

Deegan, C. (1996), 'A review of mandated environmental reporting requirements for Australian corporations together with an analysis of contemporary Australian and overseas environmental reporting practices', *Environmental and Planning Law Journal*, 13(2), pp. 120–32.

Deegan, C. (2005), *Australian Financial Accounting*, 4th edn, Sydney: McGraw-Hill.

Deegan, C. & M. Rankin (1997), 'The materiality of environmental information to users of accounting reports', *Accounting, Auditing and Accountability Journal*, 10(4), pp. 562–83.

Dillard, J. F., D. Brown & R. S. Marshall (2005), 'An environmentally enlightened accounting', *Accounting Forum*, 29(1), pp. 77–101.

Donaldson, T. (1982), *Corporations and Morality*, Englewood Cliffs, NJ: Prentice-Hall.

Elkington, J. (1997), *Cannibals with Forks: The Triple Bottom Line of 21st Century Business*, Oxford: Capstone.

Environmental Accounting and Auditing Reporter (2000), 'First standard for building corporate accountability and trust', 5(1).

Ernst & Young (2002), *Corporate Social Responsibility: A Survey of Global Companies*, Melbourne: Ernst & Young.

European Commission (1992), *Towards Sustainability: A Community Programme of Policy and Action in Relation to the Environment and Sustainable Development*, Brussels: European Commission.

Freedman, M. & D. M. Patten (2004), 'Evidence on the pernicious effect of financial report environmental disclosure', *Accounting Forum*, 28(1), pp. 27–41.

Freeman, R. (1984), *Strategic Management: A Stakeholder Approach*, Marshall, MA: Pitman.

Friedman, M. (1962), *Capitalism and Freedom*, Chicago: University of Chicago Press.

Global Reporting Initiative (1999), 'GRI Vision and Mission Statements', www .globalreporting.org/about/mission.asp, accessed 11 July 2005.

Global Reporting Initiative (2002), *Sustainability Reporting Guidelines*, Boston, MA: Global Reporting Initiative.

Global Reporting Initiative (2006), *Sustainability Reporting Guidelines: Version 3*, Amsterdam: GRI.

Gray, R. (1992), 'Accounting and environmentalism: an exploration of the challenge of gently accounting for accountability, transparency and sustainability', *Accounting, Organizations and Society*, 17(5), pp. 399–426.

Gray, R. (2005), 'Social, environmental and sustainability reporting and organisational value creation? Whose value? Whose creation?', paper presented at European Accounting Association annual congress, Symposium on New Models of Business Reporting, Gothenburg, 18–20 May.

Gray, R. & J. Bebbington (1992), 'Can the grey men go green?', discussion paper, Centre for Social and Environmental Accounting Research, University of Dundee.

Gray, R. & J. Bebbington (2001), *Accounting for the Environment*, London: Sage Publications.

Gray, R., J. Bebbington, D. Collison, R. Kouhy, B. Lyon, C. Reid, A. Russell & L. Stevenson (1998), *The Valuation of Assets and Liabilities: Environmental Law and the Impact of the Environmental Agenda for Business*, Edinburgh: Institute of Chartered Accountants in Scotland.

Gray, R., C. Dey, D. Owen, R. Evans & S. Zadek (1997), 'Struggling with the praxis of social accounting: stakeholders, accountability, audits and procedures', *Accounting, Auditing and Accountability Journal*, 10(3), pp. 325–64.

Gray, R., D. Owen & C. Adams (1996), *Accounting and Accountability: Changes and Challenges in Corporate Social and Environmental Reporting*, London: Prentice Hall.

Gray, R., D. Owen & K. T. Maunders (1991), 'Accountability, corporate social reporting and the external social audits', *Advances in Public Interest Accounting*, 4, pp. 1–21.

Greene, D. (2002), *Socially Responsible Investment in Australia 2002: Benchmarking Survey Conducted for the Ethical Investment Association*, Sydney: Ethical Investment Association.

Guthrie, J. & L. D. Parker (1989), 'Corporate social reporting: a rebuttal of legitimacy theory', *Accounting and Business Research*, 19(76), pp. 343–52.

Habermas, J. (1992), *Moral Consciousness and Communicative Action*, Cambridge: Polity Press.

Hogner, R. H. (1982), 'Corporate social reporting: eight decades of development at US Steel', *Research in Corporate Performance and Policy*, 4, pp. 243–50.

Hutton, W. (1996), *The State We're In*, London: Vintage.

ICAEW (2004), *Sustainability: The Role of Accountants*, London: Institute of Chartered Accountants in England and Wales.

Ingram, R. W. (1978), 'Investigation of the information content of certain social responsibility disclosures', *Journal of Accounting Research*, 16(2), pp. 270–85.

ISEA (2003), *Assurance Standard AA1000*, London: Institute of Social and Ethical Accountability.

ISEA (2005a), 'AA1000 Series: Assurance Standard', www.accountability.org.uk/aa1000/default.asp? pageid=52, accessed 11 June 2005.

ISEA (2005b), 'Accountability: AA1000 Series', www.accountability.org.uk/aa1000/default.asp, accessed 8 June 2005.

Jaggi, B. & M. Freedman (1982), 'An analysis of the information content of pollution disclosures', *Financial Review*, 19(5), pp. 142–52.

Lindblom, C. K. (1994), 'The implications of organisational legitimacy for corporate social performance and disclosure', paper presented at the Critical Perspectives on Accounting conference, New York.

Lorraine, N. H. J., D. J. Collison & D. M. Power (2004), 'An analysis of the stock market impact of environmental performance information', *Accounting Forum*, 28(1), pp. 7–26.

Mathews, M. R. (1993), *Socially Responsible Accounting*, London: Chapman & Hall.

Neimark, M. K. (1992), *The Hidden Dimensions of Annual Reports: Sixty Years of Social Conflict at General Motors*, New York, NY: Markus Wiener Publishing.

O'Dwyer, B. (2003), 'Conceptions of corporate social responsibility: the nature of managerial capture', *Accounting, Auditing and Accountability Journal*, 16(4), pp. 523–57.

O'Dwyer, B. (2005), 'The construction of a social account: a case study in an overseas aid agency', *Accounting, Organizations and Society*, 30(3), pp. 279–96.

Owen, D., K. Shaw & S. Cooper (2005), *The Operating and Financial Review: A Catalyst for Improved Corporate Social and Environmental Disclosure?*, London: ACCA.

Shane, P. & B. Spicer (1983), 'Market response to environmental information produced outside the firm', *The Accounting Review*, 58(3), pp. 521–38.

Solomon, A. & L. Lewis (2002), 'Incentives and disincentives for corporate environmental disclosure', *Business Strategy and the Environment*, 11(3), pp. 154–69.

Solomon, J. F. & A. Solomon (2006), 'Private social, ethical and environmental disclosure', *Accounting, Auditing and Accountability Journal*, 19(4), pp. 564–91.

SustainAbility Ltd and United Nations Environmental Programme (2002), *Trust Us: The Global Reporters 2002 Survey of Global Sustainability Reporting*, London: SustainAbility Ltd/UNEP.

Tinker, A. & M. Neimark (1987), 'The role of annual reports in gender and class contradictions at General Motors: 1917–1976', *Accounting, Organisations and Society*, 12(1), pp. 71–88.

Tinker, A. & M. Neimark (1988), 'The struggle over meaning in accounting and corporate research: a comparative evaluation of conservative and critical historiography', *Accounting, Auditing and Accountability Journal*, 1(1), pp. 55–74.

Unerman, J. (2000a), 'An investigation into the development of accounting for social, environmental and ethical accountability: A century of corporate social disclosures at Shell', unpublished PhD thesis, Sheffield University Management School, University of Sheffield.

Unerman, J. (2000b), 'Reflections on quantification in corporate social reporting content analysis', *Accounting, Auditing and Accountability Journal*, 13(5), pp. 667–80.

Unerman, J. & M. Bennett (2004), 'Increased stakeholder dialogue and the internet: towards greater corporate accountability or reinforcing capitalist hegemony?', *Accounting, Organizations and Society*, 29(7), pp. 685–707.

Venetoulis, J., D. Chazan & C. Gaudet (2004), *Ecological Footprint of Nations*, Oakland, CA: Redefining Progress.

World Commission on Environment and Development (1987), *Our Common Future (The Brundtland Report)*, Oxford: Oxford University Press.

CHAPTER 10

REACTIONS OF CAPITAL MARKETS TO FINANCIAL REPORTING

LEARNING OBJECTIVES

On completing this chapter readers should:

- understand the role of capital markets research in assessing the information content of accounting disclosures;
- understand the assumptions of market efficiency typically adopted in capital markets research;
- understand the difference between capital markets research that looks at the information content of accounting disclosures, and capital markets research that uses share price data as a benchmark for evaluating accounting disclosures;
- be able to explain why unexpected accounting earnings and abnormal share price returns are expected to be related;
- be able to outline the major results of capital markets research into financial accounting and disclosure.

OPENING ISSUES

Assume that there are five companies from the same industry with the same reporting date, 31 December. All five companies are to make earnings announcements for the financial year (the announcements being made in February), but the earnings announcements are spread over two weeks, with no two companies announcing their earnings on the same date.

- Would you expect the earnings announcements made by each company to impact on its share price and, if so, why?
- If it is found that the share prices of some entities change more around the date of the earnings announcement than others, what might have caused this price–effect differential?
- Would you expect the share prices of larger companies or smaller companies to be relatively more affected by an earnings announcement?
- Once the first company in the sample of five makes its earnings announcement, would you expect this announcement to impact on the prices of shares in the other four companies? Why?

INTRODUCTION

Some of the previous chapters have considered various normative prescriptions pertaining to how accounting *should* be undertaken. For example, Chapter 5 discussed theories that had been developed to prescribe how accounting should be undertaken in times of rising prices (for example, general price level accounting, current cost accounting and Continuously Contemporary Accounting). Chapter 6 considered the role of conceptual frameworks in providing prescription (such frameworks can tell us what the objective of accounting is; what qualitative characteristics accounting information should possess; how elements of accounting should be defined and recognised; and how assets and liabilities should be measured). Chapter 9 provided an insight into various approaches adopted to disclose information about an organisation's social and environmental performance (which has indeed become a rapidly growing area of accounting research in recent years).

While these chapters provided a great deal of prescription, they tended not to provide any theoretical arguments as to the *motivations* for managers to make the disclosures. This void was filled by Chapters 7 and 8, which provided different theoretical perspectives about what drives management to make the disclosures. Chapter 7 discussed Positive Accounting Theory and it indicated that, where management had a choice in selecting a particular approach to accounting, both *efficiency* arguments and *opportunistic* arguments could be advanced to explain and predict management's accounting choices. Chapter 8 provided alternative explanations of management's behaviour. It showed that the choice of a particular accounting method might be made to restore the *legitimacy* of an organisation (from Legitimacy Theory), or because such disclosure was necessary to retain the support of powerful stakeholders (from Stakeholder Theory), or because the accounting method had been adopted by other organisations (from Institutional Theory).

While this material provided a perspective of what motivates managers to disclose particular accounting information, it did not consider the further issue of how individuals, or groups of individuals in aggregate, react to accounting disclosures. This chapter and Chapter 11 provide material that addresses this issue. That is, the focus has changed to research and theories that describe how individuals, or groups of individuals, react to accounting disclosures (rather than what motivated preparers to make the disclosures).

This chapter and Chapter 11 examine the impact of financial accounting and disclosure decisions on the users of financial reports. Specifically, the chapters look at research that focuses on the impact of alternative accounting and disclosure choices on the investment decisions of financial statement users such as sharemarket investors, financial analysts, bank lending officers and auditors.

Reported profit depends on many financial accounting decisions. Managers have much scope in selecting between alternative accounting methods and accounting assumptions. For example, they will choose between expensing particular costs and capitalising them; they will choose between straight-line depreciation and reducing-balance depreciation; they will exercise discretion in relation to accounting estimates such as the useful life of assets to be depreciated; and so on. Further, decisions must be made in relation to how much information to disclose, the medium for disclosure, and, in some circumstances, whether to recognise particular items in the financial statements or merely disclose them in the footnotes to the financial statements.

Financial reporting decisions impact on the information subsequently provided to the users of financial statements. This in turn may have implications for the decisions that users make. There are two ways to assess the impacts of financial reporting decisions: (1) determine the impact of the information on the decisions of individual information users (behavioural research), and (2) determine what impact the release of information has on share price (capital markets research). This chapter looks at capital markets research (which considers reactions at an aggregate or market level). Chapter 11 reviews behavioural research undertaken at the individual level.

AN OVERVIEW OF CAPITAL MARKETS RESEARCH

Capital markets research explores the role of accounting and other financial information in equity markets. That is, it investigates how the disclosure of particular information influences the aggregate trading activities taken by individuals participating within capital markets. According to Kothari (2001, p. 108):

> A large fraction of published research in leading academic accounting journals examines the relation between financial statement information and capital markets, referred to as capital markets research.

Capital markets research often involves examining statistical relations between financial information and share prices or returns. Reactions of investors are evidenced by their capital market transactions. Favourable reactions to information are presumed to be evidenced by a price increase in the particular security, whereas unfavourable reactions to information are evidenced by a price decrease. No price change around the time of the release of information implies no reaction to the information (the information release does not provide anything that is new).

Conclusions about the market's reaction to particular information releases or events are generally based on evidence from a large number of companies, with data sometimes spanning several years. This type of research is often used to examine equity market reactions to announcements of company information, and to assess the relevance of alternative accounting and disclosure choices for investors. If security prices change around the time of the release of particular information, and assuming that the information and not some other event caused the price change, it is considered that the information was relevant and useful for investment decision making. That is, investors reacted to the information.

In contrast to behavioural research (considered in Chapter 11), which analyses individual responses to financial reporting, capital markets research assesses the aggregate effect of financial reporting, particularly the reporting of accounting earnings, on investors.[1] By analysing share price reactions to financial information releases, the sum of individual investor decisions is captured in aggregate. But when considering such research, a possible question that comes to

---

1   Capital markets research is also used to investigate the response of investors to other types of information besides financial accounting information. For example, capital markets research could be used to investigate how share prices react to particular government announcements, or how share prices react to companies winning particular awards. Nevertheless, a great deal of capital markets research focuses on share price reaction to the disclosure of financial information and this will be the main focus of this chapter.

mind is: why have so many research studies been undertaken that focus on the market's response to accounting earnings announcements? Brown (1994, p. 24) provides one answer:

> Four reasons are that, according to the Financial Accounting Standards Board, information about earnings and its components is the primary purpose of financial reporting; earnings are oriented towards the interests of shareholders who are an important group of financial statement users; earnings is the number most analysed and forecast by security analysts; and reliable data on earnings were readily available.

Another important difference between capital market and behavioural research is that capital markets research considers only investors, while behavioural research is often used to examine decision making by other types of financial statement users, such as bank managers, loan officers or auditors.

Capital markets research relies on the underlying assumption that equity markets are efficient. Market efficiency is defined in accordance with the Efficient Market Hypothesis (EMH) as a market that adjusts rapidly to fully impound information into share prices when the information is released (Fama et al., 1969). Capital markets research in accounting typically assumes that equity markets are *semi-strong-form efficient*. That is, that all publicly available information, including that available in financial statements and other financial disclosures, is rapidly and fully impounded into share prices in an unbiased manner as it is released. Relevant information is not ignored by the market. But why does the capital market react so quickly to information? According to Lee (2001, p. 236):

> Why do we believe markets are efficient? The answer boils down to a visceral faith in the mechanism of arbitrage. We believe markets are efficient because we believe arbitrage forces are constantly at work. If a particular piece of value-relevant information is not incorporated in price, there will be powerful economic incentives to uncover it, and to trade on it. As a result of these arbitrage forces, price will adjust until it fully reflects the information. Individual agents within the economy may behave irrationally, but we expect arbitrage forces to keep prices in line. Faith in the efficacy of this mechanism is a cornerstone of modern financial economics.[2]

Semi-strong-form efficiency is the most relevant for capital markets research in accounting, since it relates to the use of *publicly available* information. Again, predictions based on the assumption that markets are 'semi-strong form' efficient are based on the view that markets respond rapidly to publicly available information. Other hypotheses about market efficiency are the *weak-form efficiency* perspective and the *strong-form efficiency* perspective. The weak form of market efficiency assumes that existing security prices simply reflect information about past prices and trading volumes. The strong form of market efficiency assumes that security prices, on average, reflect all information known to anyone at that point in time (including information not publicly available). According to Watts and Zimmerman (1986, p. 19) the available evidence is generally consistent with the semi-strong form of the EMH.[3] That is, the share market reacts rapidly to impound within the share prices publicly available information that is considered to be relevant for determining the value of such shares.

---

2   The *Macquarie Dictionary* defines arbitrage as 'the simultaneous purchase and sale of the same securities, commodities or moneys in different markets to profit from unequal prices'.

3   Brown (1994, p. 14) notes that 'few if any investors would seriously accept the strong form, although many would accept the semi-strong form as their working hypothesis'.

The view that markets are efficient does not imply that share prices will always provide an accurate prediction of the value of future cash flows. Market predictions are sometimes proved in hindsight to be wrong, thus necessitating subsequent adjustments. As Hendriksen and Van Breda (1992, p. 177) state:

> It needs to be stressed that market efficiency does not imply clairvoyance on the part of the market. All it implies is that the market reflects the best guesses of all its participants, based on the knowledge available at the time. New information appears all the time that proves the market was incorrect. In fact, by definition, the market will not react until it learns something that it did not know the day before. One cannot prove the market inefficient, therefore, by looking back, using the benefits of hindsight and pointing to places where the market was incorrect. Market efficiency simply asserts that prices are appropriately set based on current knowledge; practical evidence shows that with hindsight the market is always incorrect.

The assumption of market efficiency is central to capital markets research.[4] But why is the assumption of information efficiency so important for capital markets research in accounting? Simply put, unless such an assumption of efficiency is accepted, it is hard to justify efforts to link security price movements to information releases. A great deal of capital markets research considers the relationship between share prices and information releases. The reason for looking at this relationship is that share prices in an efficient market are deemed to be based on expectations about future earnings. If particular information leads to a price change, the assumption is that the information was useful and caused investors to revise their expectations about the future earnings of the organisation in question. That is, share prices and returns are used as benchmarks against which the usefulness of financial information is assessed. If we do not assume market efficiency, there is an inability to explain how or why share prices change around the date of information releases. If share markets are not semi-strong-form efficient, they do not provide accurate benchmarks against which to assess alternative financial reporting choices. Overall, market inefficiency would render capital market research results to be at best less convincing, and at worst extremely unreliable, depending on the extent of inefficiency present.

Assumptions about market efficiency in turn have implications for accounting. If markets are efficient, they will use information from various sources when predicting future earnings, and hence when determining current share prices. If accounting information does not impact on share prices, then, assuming semi-strong-form efficiency, it would be deemed not to provide any information over and above that currently available. At the extreme, accounting's survival would be threatened.[5]

While the acceptance of market efficiencies is central to much capital markets research, there is some research that suggests that markets might not impound information as quickly as many

---

4   Given this is a central assumption of the research, if particular researchers did not accept this central assumption about market efficiency then they would be inclined to disregard many of the results being generated by capital markets research. As emphasised throughout this book, and from a logical perspective, before we are prepared to accept particular theories or particular research we must consider and evaluate the assumptions being made within the research.

5   Once we relax notions of efficiency, and once we consider broader issues about corporate accountability to stakeholders other than investors, threats to accounting's survival tend to dissipate.

IAG boss falls on his sword

NICK LENAGHAN

Extract from the *Geelong Advertiser*, 27 May 2008, p. 22

Shareholder anger over rejection of QBE offer forces Hawker's resignation.

Insurance Australia Group Ltd chief executive Michael Hawker has resigned amid mounting shareholder anger over the insurer's rejection of QBE Insurance Group Ltd's $8.7 billion takeover bid.

Mr Hawker, who will be replaced immediately by chief operating officer Michael Wilkins, said he had lost the confidence of a number of shareholders.

'I believe we are currently undervalued and our underlying performance is improving, however, I also believe I have lost the confidence of a number of our shareholders, which is not tenable for the company,' Mr Hawker said.

'Given ultimate accountability sits with me, I have offered my resignation to the board.'

IAG's shares tumbled after QBE eventually pulled its offer off the table last week but they rallied yesterday after the resignation was announced.

The shares rose seven cents, or 1.76 per cent, to $4.05.

researchers have assumed (see Frankel & Lee, 1998). Nevertheless, most researchers working within the capital markets research area still assume that relevant information is impounded very quickly into share prices.[6] Issues related to potential market inefficiencies will be discussed towards the end of the chapter.

Within an 'efficient market', share prices will react to new information to the extent that the information has implications for reassessing the future cash flows of an organisation. While the focus here is on the market's reaction to financial accounting information, information of a non-financial nature is also of relevance to capital markets if that information has implications for expectations about a firm's future cash flows. For example, consider Accounting Headline 10.1, which is an extract from a newspaper article that discussed how a senior executive's resignation appeared to have an immediate impact in creating an increase in the company's share price. Share price changes often are reported to occur around the time of the departure or appointment of a senior executive. What do you think the market is indicating if share prices increase when an executive's resignation is announced?

As indicated, share prices are predicted to react to various types of information, some of which will be of an accounting nature, while some will relate to other corporate matters. Various capital market researchers investigate how the capital market reacts to different events and different types of information. Again, an efficient capital market is predicted to respond to all types of information to the extent that it is of relevance in predicting future cash flows associated with a firm's securities. As one such example, Clarkson, Joyce and Tutticci (2006) investigated

---

6   According to Kothari (2001, p. 109), the view that markets do not react rapidly has had the effect of 'spurring research on fundamental analysis'. According to Kothari, 'fundamental analysis entails the use of information in current and past financial statements, in conjunction with industry and macroeconomic data, to arrive at a firm's intrinsic value. A difference between the current price and the intrinsic value is an indication of the expected rewards for investing in the security.' Rewards from fundamental analysis would diminish in an efficient market.

whether takeover rumours on a particular Internet discussion site created a share price reaction within the Australian context.[7] The authors identified the time when takeover rumours were posted to the Hotcopper Internet discussion site (a site which, according to the authors, is one of the most visited Australian 'business and finance' websites), and they then investigated whether there appeared to be an associated share price change. In looking for a market reaction, they looked at intraday return and trading volume data ('intraday' data is data that is collected at various points of time within a particular day). The authors reviewed ten-minute trading intervals surrounding the time of the positing of the rumours. In justifying the use of the narrow (ten-minute) observation periods, the authors state:

> By examining intraday return and trading volume data, we are better able to isolate the effects of the rumour posting, if any. Although an analysis of daily return and trading volume data surrounding the rumour posting day has the potential to provide insights into the market reaction to the posting, competing explanations also exist. For example, the market reaction might simply be to information released through other media that could not reasonably be screened during the sample construction process. Alternatively, if posters are merely reacting to increases in share price and/or trading volume, the observed market activity, although correlated with the IDS rumour, would not be in response to its posting. It is far less likely that reactions observed in the 10 min posting interval would be vulnerable to these or other competing explanations.

According to Clarkson, Joyce and Tutticci (2006), their results indicate a price increase and an increased trading volume around the time the takeover rumours were posted. This is deemed to indicate that such information is of relevance to investors, and is being used despite the fact that it is based on rumour. As already indicated, the basis of capital markets research is that the market is expected to quickly respond to relevant information from various sources. In discussing the implications of their finding, Clarkson, Joyce and Tutticci refer to concerns held by regulators that some individuals ('posters') have been posting information to particular Internet sites to 'pump up' share prices before they subsequently sell the shares at a profit. The authors state (p. 33):

> Litigation by the Australian Securities and Investment Commission (ASIC) and the US Securities and Exchange Commission (SEC) of posters deemed to have inappropriately used Internet Discussion Sites, including 'pump and dump' strategies, indicates a belief by regulatory bodies that rumour posted on these sites affects firm value. Our findings provide formal support for the regulators' view of Internet Discussion Sites as a source of information for the market.

Reflective of the concerns of regulators in relation to rumours, and in particular the spreading of 'false rumours', Accounting Headline 10.2 provides some extracts from a newspaper article that appeared in the *New York Times* on 14 July 2008. The article examined investigations being undertaken by the Securities and Exchange Commission in the United States in relation to the spreading of rumours and its impact on share prices.[8]

---

7   For the purposes of their research, any information not capable of objective verification was classified as a rumour.

8   The 'short sellers' referred to in the extract are individuals or organisations that sell a security before they actually own it. They can gain by selling at a particular price and then acquiring it at a lower price. They then transfer the security to the new owner and make a gain in the overall transaction.

Extract from the *New York Times*, 14 July 2008, p. C1

S.E.C. warns Wall Street: Stop spreading the false rumors

STEPHANIE CLIFFORD AND JENNY ANDERSON

The Securities and Exchange Commission announced on Sunday that it and other regulators would begin examining rumor-spreading intended to manipulate securities prices.

The timing of the announcement, made before the markets opened in Asia, was meant to warn broker-dealers, hedge funds and investment advisers to quell any spreading of rumors before trading started Monday ... The examinations are expected to begin Monday and will focus on what policies firms have in place to prevent the passing of false information. The intent is to stop malicious rumors without hampering the natural exchange of information in the marketplace.

Since the almost overnight collapse of Bear Stearns earlier this year, top-level Wall Street executives have been pleading with regulators to investigate what they see as efforts by short sellers to plant false information and profit from it.

Lehman Brothers, for example, faced rumors last week that two major clients had stopped doing business with the firm. Lehman's stock dived almost 20 percent before recovering somewhat as both clients denied the rumors.

Following the theme that an efficient market will react to various types of relevant information, it might also be anticipated that any concerns raised by external auditors as a result of undertaking their audit work would also have the potential to create share price changes. This would particularly be the case if the audit opinion signalled to investors that there were uncertainties about the future profitability, and hence, about the future cash flows of an organisation. In this regard Herbohn, Ragunathan and Garsden (2007) considered the share price reaction of a number of Australian companies around the time the companies received a going concern modification (GCM) of their audit report. A GCM in the form of a qualification is issued when the auditor is satisfied that it is highly improbable that the entity will continue as a going concern. According to the authors, a GCM of an audit report is a significantly unambiguous 'bad news' event for stock-market participants and an adverse stock-market reaction is to be expected (p. 465). The authors study share price movements in the twelve months leading to, and the twelve months following, a company receiving its first GCM. They also study share price reactions around the event date, which is defined as the day of the release of the annual report that includes the audit qualification. The authors found no evidence of a market reaction to a first-time GCM announcement around the event date. The lack of a share price reaction to the audit report is explained by the authors on the basis that, in an efficient market, investors would have been preconditioned to expect that the organisations to receive the GCMs were suffering financial difficulties. The audit report would act to confirm market expectations, rather than to cause a revision to expectations (a revision to market expectations about future cash flows would have caused a price change). In explaining their results, the authors stated (p. 489):

> The underlying research question of this paper is what is the value added from the audit report. Prima facie, our results that show a significant negative market reaction in the pre-event period rather than the post-event period are consistent with the audit report fulfilling an attestation function rather than signalling additional information to the market. Additionally,

in the 12 months prior to the GCM announcement, the sample of GCM firms underperforms a matched sample of firms in similar financial distress that have unmodified audit opinions for the same period. We contend that these results are consistent with investors viewing a GCM as having information content because it confirms a deteriorating financial condition. That is, a GCM is an independent confirmation by an auditor that, at the very least, there is significant uncertainty that a firm is able to pay its debts as and when they fall due. Furthermore, once issued a GCM increases the financial pressures on a firm through bank credit freezes, possible debt defaults and worsening relations with suppliers. Therefore, receipt of a GCM confirms the likelihood of tightening of debt constraints for the firm.

A question raised by our results is why does the negative market reaction for GCM firms occur in the 12 months prior to the GCM announcement and not persist in the 12 months post-announcement as documented on the LSE by Taffler et al. (2004)? One explanation is that the Australian market is well informed because of the continuous disclosure regime in place. The announcement of a GCM is not an isolated or sudden event. Rather, it is a culmination of multiple events over time. The majority of these events are likely to be price-sensitive and, therefore, are required to be disclosed immediately to the market under the continuous disclosure regime of the Australian Stock Exchange. Therefore, it seems likely that the underperformance of our sample firms in the 12 months pre-GCM announcement is a result of a conditioning of market expectations from the price-sensitive disclosures made to the ASX. Because the market is fully informed at the time of the GCM announcement, there is no significant adverse market reaction that persists in the 12 months post-GCM.

Hence, Herbohn, Ragunathan and Garsden (2007) were able to use assumptions about the efficiency of the market to explain how the market would have anticipated the news provided by the auditor (as a result of the 'continuous disclosure regime' in Australia), and hence, as the audit report was in accordance with expectations, no significant share price movement would occur.

Some of the above events relate to specific firms (for example, a particular firm receiving a particular form of audit report), but share prices will also react to market-wide events. For example, within the United States the introduction of the *Sarbanes–Oxley Act* of 2002 had potential cash-flow implications for a very large number of organisations.[9] Zhang (2007) used capital markets research to investigate reactions to the introduction of the Act. In considering the implications of the Act, Zhang (p. 75) stated:

By requiring more oversight, imposing greater penalties for managerial misconduct, and dealing with potential conflicts of interest, the Act aims to prevent deceptive accounting and management misbehaviour. However, despite the claimed benefits of this Act, the business community has expressed substantial concerns about its costs. Whereas the out-of-pocket compliance costs are generally considered significant (Solomon and Bryan-Low, 2004), they are likely swamped by the opportunity costs SOX imposed on business. Executives complain that complying with the rules diverts their attention from doing business (Solomon and Bryan-Low, 2004). Furthermore, the Act exposes managers and directors to greater

---

9   US Congress passed the *Sarbanes–Oxley Act* in July 2002 in response to a number of high-profile corporate scandals that came to light in 2001, most notably scandals associated with the major US company Enron. The Act was named after two people who were largely involved in its development, Senator Paul Sarbanes and Congressman Michael Oxley. The Act imposed additional disclosure requirements as well as requiring significant changes in corporate governance policies.

litigation risks and stiffer penalties. CEOs allegedly will take less risky actions, consequently changing their business strategies and potentially reducing firm value (Ribstein, 2002).

Whereas US corporations had to comply with the Act, non-US companies that traded their securities within the United States did not have to comply with the Act. Zhang (2007) examined the abnormal returns earned on the shares of US companies around the time of significant Sarbanes–Oxley (SOX) legislative events relative to returns earned on the shares of foreign firms listed in the United States. Zhang found that the introduction of the Act appeared to be associated with negative share price reactions for US firms relative to foreign firms that did not comply with the Act. While the negative share price reaction could be interpreted as a negative consequence of introducing the Act, Zhang does note (p. 77) that focusing on share price reactions alone does not take into consideration various social benefits that might arise as a result of introducing the Act—benefits that would be shared by individuals who are not investors:

> This study does not explore the social welfare implication of the Act. An investigation of changes in security prices provides evidence for the private benefits and costs of regulations, but social benefits and costs may not be fully reflected in stock prices.

What the preceding discussion has highlighted is the variety of events than can influence share prices. It also reflects the variety of issues or events that capital markets researchers explore as part of their research. As emphasised, a share price reaction to the release of financial information or other information is taken to indicate that the announcement has 'information content'. The absence of share price movement indicates either that the information is irrelevant or that it confirms market expectations. In relation to accounting information, a high association between financial information and share prices or returns over an extended period of time indicates that the information provided by the accounting system reflects information that is being used by the capital market (and this information will come from a multitude of sources). Each of these roles for accounting information in equity markets is explored in the following sections. While the 'information content' of many types of financial information can be assessed using capital markets research, the bulk of this work has focused on earnings as the primary measure of the financial accounting system. For example, one issue that has been the subject of many research papers is whether corporate earnings announcements cause a movement in share price. This focus is reflected in the following discussion.

THE INFORMATION CONTENT OF EARNINGS

Many research papers have investigated capital market reactions to corporate earnings announcements. That is, when a company announces its earnings for the year (or half-year), what is the impact, if any, on its share price? These studies, which look at the changes in share prices around a particular event, such as the release of accounting information, are often referred to as 'events studies'.[10] According to Kothari (2001, p. 116):

---

10 The studies considered earlier, such as the study by Clarkson, Joyce and Tutticci (2006) (on Internet discussion sites) and by Zhang (2007) (on the *Sarbanes–Oxley Act*), would also be considered to be 'event studies' because they investigated share price reactions around particular events.

In an event study, one infers whether an event, such as an earnings announcement, conveys new information to market participants as reflected in changes in the level or variability of security prices or trading volume over a short time period around the event (see Collins and Kothari, 1989, p. 144; Watts and Zimmerman, 1986, Chapter 3). If the level or variability of prices changes around the event date, then the conclusion is that the accounting event conveys new information about the amount, timing, and/or uncertainty of future cash flows that revised the market's previous expectations. The degree of confidence in this conclusion critically hinges on whether the events are dispersed in calendar time and whether there are any confounding events (e.g., a simultaneous dividend and earnings announcement which in themselves could have been responsible for causing revised estimates about the firm's future cash flows thereby creating revisions in share prices) co-occurring with the event of interest to the researcher. As noted earlier, the maintained hypothesis in an event study is that capital markets are informationally efficient in the sense that security prices are quick to reflect the newly arrived information. Because event studies test for the arrival of information through an accounting event, they are also referred to as tests of information content in the capital markets literature in accounting. Besides Ball and Brown (1968) and Beaver (1968), other examples of event studies include Foster (1977), Wilson (1986), Ball and Kothari (1991), Amir and Lev (1996), Vincent (1999), and many more.

Assuming that capital markets are semi-strong-form efficient (they react swiftly and in an unbiased manner to *publicly available* information), a movement in share price is considered to indicate that the new information in the public earnings announcement has been incorporated into the security's price through the activities of investors in the market. The information was useful in reassessing the future cash flows of the entity.

A number of studies have shown information about earnings to be linked to changes in the price of securities. But, why would we expect accounting earnings and share prices to be related? Modern finance theory proposes that a share price can be determined as the sum of expected future cash flows from dividends, discounted to their present value using a rate of return commensurate with the company's level of risk. Further, dividends are a function of accounting earnings, since they can generally only be paid out of past and current earnings. It follows therefore that, if cash flows are related to (a function of) accounting earnings, the price of a share in company i, which we can denote as P_i, can be viewed as the sum of expected future earnings per share $(\bar{E})$, discounted to their present value using a risk-adjusted discount rate (k_i).[11] That is, for company i today:

$$P_i = \sum_{t=1}^{\infty} \bar{E}_t / (1 + k_i)^t \qquad \text{(Equation 1)}$$

Equation 1 shows that a relation exists between share price and expected future earnings. In general, after adjusting for risk, companies with higher expected future earnings will have higher share prices. These expectations are formed, at least in part, on the basis of historical earnings for the company. However, all currently available information (for example, media releases, analysts' reports, production statistics, market surveys, market rumours, impending legislation) is

---

11 The risk-adjusted discount rate chosen should be commensurate with the level of uncertainty associated with the expected earnings stream.

Extract from the *Australian*, 15 August 2008, p. 31

Faring well amid a volatile environment

LISA MACNAMARA

The Australian Securities Exchange has emerged from one of the most financially turbulent times in history with a record profit, exceeding market expectations and triggering strong buying of its stock.

The ASX yesterday announced a 17 per cent lift in net profit to $366 million, driven mainly by the exchange's equity business, which attracted record volumes of trade that jumped 87 per cent for the year. The profit figure was above analysts' forecasts of $361 million.

'They tend to do fairly well in volatile environments because they get reasonable transaction volumes,' Citigroup analyst Mike Younger said yesterday.

'Their derivative business has certainly fallen quite a lot in volume, but in terms of the equities business, we all look at the value of equities being traded, and that has fallen.

'The actual number of trades is up over 60 per cent even in the last three months.'

Cash market revenue from trading, clearing and settlement of equities made up almost a third of the overall earnings, jumping by 21.2 per cent to $188.8 million, while turnover rose by 22 per cent to a record $1.6 trillion for the year. Overall revenue jumped 13.1 per cent to $624.38 million, up from $552.7 million with a final dividend of 93.9c, up from 91.5c a year ago.

The results, which also found a 2.3 per cent jump in listings revenue to $120.2 million, helped send the ASX share price 2.5 per cent higher yesterday to close at $35.66.

considered when predicting future earnings. Any revisions to expectations about future earnings per share, including those resulting from new information contained in announcements of current earnings, will be reflected in a change in share price.

Revisions to expectations about future earnings per share will result only from new information, since under the maintained assumption of a semi-strong-form-efficient market, price is assumed to reflect already all *publicly known* information, including expectations about current earnings. Therefore, only the unexpected component of current earnings announcements constitutes new information. That is, unexpected earnings, rather than total earnings, are expected to be associated with a change in share price. For example, if CMR Company announces annual earnings of $11 million when only $10.5 million had been expected, unexpected earnings are equal to $0.5 million. Any share price reaction will be to these unexpected earnings rather than to the total annual earnings of $11 million, since investors had already anticipated most of this. Accounting Headlines 10.3 to 10.5 provide extracts of articles that discuss unexpected profit results and how these unexpected results impacted on share prices. Again, it is emphasised that if reported profits were in accord with market expectations then we would not expect share prices to adjust.

A change in share price results in a return to investors (R_{it}), since returns are a function of capital gains or losses, in addition to dividends received (D_{it}). Thus, for an investment in firm i for one holding period $(t-1$ to $t)$, the return would be:[12]

$$R_{it} = \frac{(P_{it} - P_{it-1}) + D_{it}}{P_{it-1}}$$ (Equation 2)

12 Where price at the end of the holding period (P_{it}) is adjusted for any capitalisation changes such as rights issues or bonus issues.

Extract from the *Herald Sun*, 10 May 2008, p. 93

Accounting Headline 10.4 Another example of a market response to an unexpected profit announcement

NAB weathers storm

GEORGE LEKAKIS

National Australia Bank's share price soared yesterday after the country's largest bank revealed that its British subsidiaries were weathering the financial storm in the UK banking market.

But the group bottom line was damaged by the rampaging Australian dollar, which crimped the earnings contribution of the British businesses.

Chief executive John Stewart unveiled a higher-than-expected group interim result of $2.68 billion, up 26 per cent on the 2007 first-half performance.

The announcement triggered a sharp rally in the share price, which closed up $1.24 or 4 per cent at $32.24 on high turnover.

Extract from the *Age*, 15 February 2008, p. 3

Accounting Headline 10.5 A further example of a market response to an unexpected profit announcement

AMP full-year leaves investors unimpressed

STUART WASHINGTON

AMP joined the companies bruised in the reporting season when its 8% profit growth did not meet expectations, sending the share price falling by as much as 4%.

The $985 million full-year net profit, up from $915 million in 2006, narrowly missed analysts' forecasts, fuelling concerns about AMP's performance in a more hostile equities market.

In his first profit announcement as chief executive, Craig Dunn cast AMP as a business that had avoided subprime icebergs and was positioned to perform well. Mr Dunn took over from Andrew Mohl on January 1.

'While AMP is not immune to investment market volatility, the company's transformation in recent years from a traditional life insurance company to a modern wealth management business means we are well placed to withstand these conditions,' Mr Dunn said.

He said operating earnings from businesses, such as AMP's financial planners, now outstripped its traditional reliance on investment income by five to one.

AMP shares recovered during the day to close 3¢ down at $7.75, failing to make up the 6% fall during Wednesday's sell-off of financial services companies caught out by Commonwealth Bank's cautious outlook.

The length of time over which returns are calculated (the return period) depends on the particular research focus but is generally not less than one day (although shorter intraday returns could be used) or longer than one year. In return periods where no dividend is paid, returns can simply be calculated as a percentage change in share price. This is generally the case when returns are calculated on a daily (or shorter) basis. For example, if CMR Company's share price moved from $5.42 to $5.56 during the day when earnings were announced, the daily return (R_{CMR}) is equal to ($5.56 − $5.42)/$5.42, or 2.6%.

Given that returns are a function of changes in share prices (from Equation 2), and share price can be expressed as a function of expected future earnings (from Equation 1), returns are related to changes in expected future earnings. This relation is often referred to as the earnings/return relation. For CMR Company, the unexpected announcement of an additional $0.5 million of earnings has resulted in a return to investors of approximately 2.6%, as indicated in the above calculation. This positive return indicates that investors expect future earnings to be higher than originally expected.

Of course, not all share returns are due to investors trading on information about individual companies. Share prices tend to change on a daily basis due to things that affect the whole market, or sectors of it. These can be called 'systematic changes'. For example, the publication of new (and unexpected) statistics about factors likely to affect the whole economy to some extent—such as rates of inflation, new legislation that will impact on the activities of investors or companies, levels of unemployment, or the general level of consumer or business confidence—and daily returns for individual companies largely reflect this.

The market model (see Fama 1976 for details about its early development), which is derived from the capital asset pricing model (CAPM), is used to separate out firm-specific share price movements from market-wide movements.[13] The CAPM explains how a market should decide the appropriate return on a share, given its riskiness. It predicts a linear relationship between expected returns and systematic risk, where systematic risk is the riskiness of an asset when it is held as part of a thoroughly diversified portfolio. Systematic risk is the non-diversifiable or unavoidable risk that investors are compensated for through increased returns. The market model is expressed as:

$$R_{it} = \alpha_{it} + \beta_{it}R_{mt} + \mu_{it} \qquad \text{(Equation 3)}$$

where R_{it} is the return for company i during period t, calculated in accordance with Equation 2; R_{mt} is the return for the entire market during period t (as would be approximated by the average return generated from a very large diversified portfolio of securities); and β_{it} is company i's level of systematic risk, which indicates how sensitive the returns of firm i's securities are relative to market-wide (systematic) movements.[14] Again, market-wide movements will potentially account for a significant proportion of the change in a company's share prices. α_{it} is a constant specific to firm i, while μ_{it} is an error term that provides an indication of how the return on a security relates or moves with respect to specific events, such as the release of new accounting information. It is μ_{it} that capital markets researchers are typically interested in identifying, as it is considered to reflect the reaction of the company's shares to the new information being disclosed. It reflects the difference between what the market return was expected to be (based on the model) and what it actually was following a particular event, such as the release of accounting earnings data.

For the market model, it is assumed that the variations in returns on individual securities are largely due to market-wide factors. As a portfolio of investments increases in diversity, the non-systematic risk of the diversified portfolio (measured by $\alpha_{it} + \mu_{it}$) tends to disappear, thereby leaving only returns that are due to market-wide movements (that is, $\beta_{it}R_{mt}$). The market model

---

13 For further information on the development of the CAPM, reference can be made to Sharpe (1964) or Lintner (1965).

14 For example, if the returns of firm i's securities are expected to fluctuate in period t at the same rate as a very large diversified portfolio of securities, then beta (β_{it}) would be approximately 1. If the returns of the individual firm are twice as sensitive or volatile as general market movements (indicating that the returns on the undiversified security are more risky than the returns on a very large diversified portfolio), then the beta would be approximately 2, and so on.

makes a number of assumptions, including that investors are risk averse and that investors have homogeneous expectations (they think alike).

Equation 3 shows that total or actual returns can be divided into normal (or expected) returns, given market-wide price movements ($\alpha_{it} + \beta_{it}R_{mt}$), and abnormal (or unexpected) returns due to firm-specific share price movements (μ_{it}).[15] Normal returns are expected to vary from company to company, depending on their level of systematic risk in relation to the market, while abnormal returns are expected to vary from company to company depending on whether there is new information about the company that causes investors to revise expectations about future earnings. According to Kothari (2001, p. 115):

> The risk-related variation in returns is generally not of interest to researchers who focus on firm-specific accounting information and its relation to the firm-specific component of the stock return. Therefore, the Capital Asset Pricing Model (CAPM), along with the efficient market hypothesis, greatly facilitated the estimation of the firm-specific return component. The use of the firm-specific component alone enhances the power of the tests of information content of accounting reports (Brown and Warner, 1980, 1985).

The market model is used to control for share price movements due to market-wide events, allowing the researcher to focus on share price movements due to firm-specific news. For example, part of the 2.6 per cent return earned by CMR Company on announcing its annual earnings may be due to an overall rise in the market on the announcement day. A researcher analysing the impact of the earnings announcement would control for the impact of this rise in the market by deducting it from CMR Company's return. Assuming $\alpha_{CMR} = 0$, $\beta_{CMR} = 1$ and $R_m = 1\%$, this calculation would leave an abnormal return (μ_{CMR}) of 1.6 per cent.[16] It is abnormal returns, or firm-specific share price movements, that are analysed by researchers to determine the information effects of company announcements.

Capital markets research into the earnings/return relation analyses firm-specific price movements (abnormal returns) at the time of earnings announcements. These abnormal returns are used as an indicator of the information content of the announcement. That is, how much, if any, new information has been released to the capital markets. If there is no share price reaction, it is assumed that the announcement contained no new information. That is, the information was already known or anticipated by market participants or, alternatively, was deemed to be irrelevant.

RESULTS OF CAPITAL MARKETS RESEARCH INTO FINANCIAL REPORTING

Capital markets research has been a major focus of financial accounting research over the past forty years. The research has investigated the information content of corporate earnings announcements as well as many other accounting and disclosure items. Results of this research

---

15   Normal returns can also be thought of as the level of return to investors that is expected simply as a reward for investing and bearing risk. Abnormal returns are the realised rate of return, less the expected normal rate of return (calculated by reference to the market model).

16   When returns are calculated on a daily basis, the assumption that $\alpha = 0$ and $\beta_{it} = 1$ is not unrealistic.

are useful for both practising accountants and finance professionals such as security analysts. Knowledge of these results is considered to be particularly useful in relation to making financial reporting decisions. It is often argued that more informed choices between accounting and disclosure alternatives can be made if the expected impacts on share prices are anticipated when making financial reporting decisions. A summary comprising some of the more important capital markets research results follows.

HISTORICAL COST INCOME IS USED BY INVESTORS

Ball and Brown (1968), in the first major capital markets research publication in accounting, investigated the usefulness of accounting earnings under a historical cost model. Prior to their research, there was a widely held view that historical cost accounting methods resulted in 'meaningless' information that was not useful for investors and other users of financial statements.[17] Ball and Brown saw the need for empirical evidence about whether accounting earnings, calculated using historical cost accounting principles, provide useful information to investors. They stated (p. 159):

> If, as the evidence indicates, security prices do in fact adjust rapidly to new information as it becomes available, then changes in security prices will reflect the flow of information to the market. An observed revision of stock prices associated with the release of the income report would thus provide evidence that the information reflected in income numbers is useful.[18]

Using data for 261 US companies, Ball and Brown tested whether firms with unexpected increases in accounting earnings had positive abnormal returns, and firms with unexpected decreases in accounting earnings had negative abnormal returns (on average). Unexpected earnings were calculated (quite simplistically) as the difference between current earnings and the previous year's earnings. That is, Ball and Brown assumed that this year's earnings were expected to be the same as last year's earnings. Monthly share price data were used, with the market model being used to calculate abnormal returns for each company. Cumulative abnormal returns (CARs) were then calculated for each of (1) the full sample of companies, (2) firms with unexpected increases in earnings (favourable announcements), and (3) firms with unexpected decreases in earnings (unfavourable announcements), by summing the average abnormal returns for each of these groups over time.

Ball and Brown found evidence to suggest that the information contained in the annual report is used in investment decision making, despite the limitations of the historical cost accounting system. This result is evidenced by the CARs during the month of the earnings announcements (month 0). As can be seen from Figure 10.1, firms with unexpected increases in earnings (favourable announcements), represented by the top line in the chart, had positive abnormal returns during the announcement month (on average), while firms with unexpected

---

17 For example, see Chambers (1965) and Sterling (1975).

18 However, just because the market reacts to information, which might reflect that the information was used to revise expectations about future cash flows (that is, the information was useful and led to changes in share prices), this does not necessarily mean that other forms of accounting not based on historical costs might not have been more useful for revising expectations about future cash flows.

decreases in earnings (unfavourable announcements), represented by the bottom line in the chart, had negative abnormal returns. Since Ball and Brown's early study, this research has been replicated many times using more sophisticated data and research methods. The results appear to confirm the usefulness of historical cost income to investors. This is not to say that the historical cost accounting system is the 'most useful', since a present value or current cost accounting system may be more useful, but it gives some credence to the continued use of historical costs.

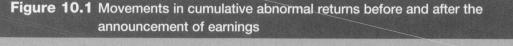

Figure 10.1 Movements in cumulative abnormal returns before and after the announcement of earnings

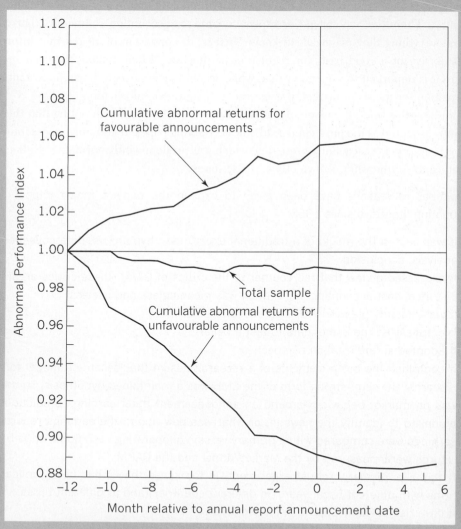

Source: R. Ball & P. Brown (1968), 'An empirical evaluation of accounting income numbers', *Journal of Accounting Research*, 6(2), pp. 159–78.

PRIOR TO AN EARNINGS RELEASE, INVESTORS OBTAIN MUCH OF THE INFORMATION THEY NEED FROM OTHER SOURCES

In addition to confirming the usefulness of the historical cost accounting model, Ball and Brown (1968) found that most of the information contained in earnings announcements (85–90 per cent) is anticipated by investors. The gradual slope in the lines (which represent the cumulative abnormal returns) prior to the earnings announcements (which were made at time 0) in Figure 10.1 provide evidence of this. Anticipation of earnings changes by investors indicates that investors obtain much of the information useful for investment decision making from sources other than annual earnings announcements (perhaps from media releases, analysts' releases, information about the industry's production and sales trends, and so on). This is not surprising given that alternative sources of information such as conference calls to analysts and press releases are generally more timely than the annual report, which tends to be issued several weeks after year end (the reporting date) and less frequently than many alternative sources of information. Therefore, we can never expect to produce accounting statements that will tell investors everything they may want to know. That is, the provision of *all* relevant information to investors is not a good basis for regulation or practice. When making financial reporting decisions, it is important to remember that, while accounting appears to be an important source of information for the share market, it is not the only source of information.

In finishing this brief discussion of Ball and Brown (1968), it is worth noting that this paper is generally accepted as the most cited academic accounting paper. It certainly represented quite a change from previous accounting research, which was predominantly normative. Reflecting on the significance of the work, Brown (1994, p. 24) states:

A number of reasons have been given to explain the paper's major impact on the accounting literature since 1968:

■ It was cast in the mould of a traditional experiment: hypothesis, data collection, data analysis, conclusion.

■ It expressed a view that ran counter to the critics of GAAP (these critics arguing that historical cost accounting information was meaningless and useless).

■ It was an early plea for 'empirical research'.

■ It emphasised the use of data to test a belief.

■ It adopted an information perspective.

■ It contained the basic elements of a research design that became a model for future research: the semi-strong form of the EMH was a maintained hypothesis, so the focus was on market behaviour around an announcement date; earnings predictions were modelled to identify the news in, or what was new about, the earnings report; GAAP earnings were compared with a primary version of operating cash flows; and abnormal returns were measured by the Market Model and the CAPM.

■ It was a particularly robust experiment, in the sense that it has been replicated for firms with different fiscal years, in different countries, and at different times.

■ It gave rise to many papers in related areas.

As Chapter 7 indicates, Watts and Zimmerman (1986) credit the development of Positive Accounting Theory, at least in part, to the early experimental approach adopted by Ball and Brown.

Studies of markets' reactions to particular accounting disclosures—such as Ball and Brown's—have been used to make recommendations to accounting standard-setters. Relying on the maintained assumption that capital markets are efficient, researchers have been known to argue against standard-setters requiring particular information if research has shown that share prices did not react when the particular information was disclosed. As Kothari (2001, p. 119) states:

> The early evidence of earnings' association with security returns and evidence of capital market efficiency in finance and economics led some accounting researchers to draw standard-setting implications. For example, Beaver (1972) in the Report of the American Accounting Association Committee on Research Methodology in Accounting, suggests that the association of accounting numbers with security returns can be used to rank order alternative accounting methods as a means of determining the accounting method that should become a standard. The report states that the 'method which is more highly associated with security prices ought to be the method reported in the financial statements' (p. 428), subject to considerations of competing sources of information and costs.

THE INFORMATION CONTENT OF EARNINGS ANNOUNCEMENTS DEPENDS ON THE EXTENT OF ALTERNATIVE SOURCES OF INFORMATION

Research indicates that the information content of earnings varies between countries and between companies within a country. For example, Brown (1970) found that, when compared with US markets, the Australian market had slower share price adjustments during the year, with larger adjustments at the earnings announcement date. This result implied that annual reports were a more important source of information for the Australian capital markets than they were for US capital markets because there were fewer alternative sources of information for Australian companies. The difference in the extent of alternative sources of information was partly due to Australian regulations that required only semi-annual rather than quarterly reporting, and partly also a function of differences in average firm sizes between the two countries. Small firms tend to have fewer alternative sources of information than larger firms, and are less likely to be followed by security analysts. This difference causes differences in the usefulness of earnings announcements, with these being more useful for smaller Australian firms than larger Australian firms.

Therefore, the extent of alternative sources of information should be considered when making financial reporting decisions. (The issue of size is returned to later in the chapter.)

THE CAPITAL MARKET IMPACT OF UNEXPECTED CHANGES IN EARNINGS DEPENDS ON WHETHER THE CHANGE IS EXPECTED TO BE PERMANENT OR TEMPORARY

Following Ball and Brown's finding that the *direction* of unexpected earnings changes is positively related to the *direction* of abnormal share price returns, further research was conducted into the relation between the *magnitude* of the unexpected change in earnings, or earnings per share, and the *magnitude* of the abnormal returns. This relationship is often referred to as the *earnings response coefficient*. The results show that this is not a one-to-one relationship. Indeed, some research has shown that the average abnormal return associated with a 1 per cent unexpected change in earnings is only 0.1 to 0.15 per cent (Beaver, Lambert & Morse, 1980). This relationship varies, depending on whether the change in earnings is expected to be permanent or temporary. Permanent increases are expected to result in increased dividends, and therefore increased future cash flows, and this implies a change in the value of the company. On the other hand, temporary increases are discounted or ignored, since they are not expected to have the same impact on expected future dividends (Easton & Zmijewski, 1989). While some earnings changes such as those due to one-off restructuring charges are obviously temporary, it is more difficult to determine whether other earnings changes are likely to persist.

EARNINGS PERSISTENCE DEPENDS ON THE RELATIVE MAGNITUDES OF CASH AND ACCRUALS COMPONENTS OF CURRENT EARNINGS

The accrual system of accounting differs from the cash basis of accounting owing to differences in when cash flows are recognised in the financial statements. Under the accrual system, some items are recognised before the cash flows are received or paid (for example, credit sales and purchases), while others are recognised on a periodic basis (for example, the cost of a fixed asset is recognised over its useful life through periodic depreciation charges). Therefore, the accrual process involves adjusting the timing of when the cash inflows and outflows of a firm are recognised to achieve a matching of revenues and expenses. Earnings, the summary performance measure of the accrual system, has fewer timing and mismatching problems than performance measures based on unadjusted cash flows (for example, cash flows from operations). However, application of the accrual system can be a subjective rather than an objective process and, depending on the choices made, many different earnings figures can be achieved. For example, if the reducing-balance method of depreciation is chosen over the straight-line method, reported profits will initially be lower, owing to a greater depreciation expense. However, reported earnings will be higher in the later years of the asset's life due to lower depreciation expense. Sloan (1996) undertook a study to see if share prices behave as if investors simply 'fixate' on reported earnings without considering how those numbers have actually been determined (that is, without considering the methods of accounting that have been employed). According to Sloan (1996, p. 291):

> A meaningful test of whether stock prices fully reflect available information requires the specification of an alternative 'naive' expectation model, against which to test the null of market efficiency. The naive model employed in this study is that investors 'fixate' on earnings and fail to distinguish between the accrual and cash flow component of current earnings. This naive earnings expectation model is consistent with the functional fixation hypothesis, which has received empirical support in capital market, behavioral and experimental research.[19]

Sloan provides evidence that firms with large accruals relative to their actual cash flows are unlikely to have persistently high earnings, since the accruals reverse over time, reducing future earnings. However, share prices are found to act as if investors simply 'fixate' on reported earnings, thereby failing to take account of the relative magnitudes of the cash and accrual components of current earnings (fixation implying a degree of market inefficiency). In concluding his paper, Sloan (p. 314) states:

> This paper investigates whether stock prices reflect information about future earnings contained in the accrual and cash flow components of current earnings. The persistence

---

19 According to Watts and Zimmerman (1986, p. 160), 'the hypothesis of functional fixation maintains that individual investors interpret earnings numbers in the same way, regardless of the accounting procedures used to calculate them. If all investors acted in this way, there would be a mechanical relation between earnings and stock prices, and the stock market would not discriminate between efficient and less efficient firms.'

of earnings performance is shown to depend on the relative magnitudes of the cash and accrual components of earnings. However, stock prices act as if investors fail to identify correctly the different properties of these two components of earnings.

Hence, while earnings can be managed up through various discretionary accruals, this cannot be done indefinitely, and earnings will eventually be lower as the accruals subsequently reverse. Likewise, while it may be possible to increase share price through reporting higher earnings, this effect will be reversed when lower earnings are reported in the future. Although the lower earnings are due to the reversal of accruals, evidence indicates that the market fixates on the lower reported earnings, and share prices therefore fall as the accruals subsequently reverse. Notions questioning market efficiency, such as the functional fixation perspective, have been hotly contested in the accounting literature.

THE EARNINGS ANNOUNCEMENTS OF OTHER FIRMS IN THE SAME INDUSTRY HAVE INFORMATION CONTENT

When a company announces its annual earnings, this generally results in abnormal returns not only for the company concerned, but also for other companies in the same industry (Foster, 1981). That is, there is information content for similar firms as well as for the announcing firm. This phenomenon, known as 'information transfer', reduces the surprise (unknown) element in earnings announcements of other firms in the industry that choose to announce their earnings later. The direction of the capital market reaction is related to whether the news contained in the announcement reflects a change in conditions for the entire industry or changes in relative market share within the industry. Because information is gained from the announcements of similar firms, information releases about sales and earnings changes result in price reactions for other firms in an industry, as well as the firm making the announcement (Freeman & Tse, 1992). Therefore, in forming expectations about how information releases, such as earnings announcements, might affect share prices, it is important to consider the timing of information releases relative to those of similar firms, since information about a company can be gained from the information releases of similar companies.

Firth (1976) investigated the 'information transfer' issue. He sought to 'investigate the impact of a company's results being publicly announced on the share price behaviour of competing firms' (p. 298). His results indicated that when 'good news' was released about accounting earnings, the share prices of the non-announcing firms in the same industry reacted quickly (the same day) by showing a statistically significant increase. Interestingly, there seemed to be no abnormal returns in the days before the announcement (limited anticipation) or the days after the announcement. That is, most of the adjustment appeared to occur fairly immediately. Similar results were found with respect to 'bad news' earnings announcements. The share prices of non-disclosing firms in the industry tended to fall on the day of the 'bad news' earnings announcement.

If the announcement of earnings by one company impacts on the share prices of other companies in the same industry, there would be an expectation that if a number of companies are about to release earnings information then, all other things being equal, the largest share price reactions might be generated by the entity that makes the first release. By the time the last entity releases its earnings announcements for a particular year end, it could be expected that a great deal of this information would already have been impounded in share prices and hence

Australian Financial Review, 12 August 2005, p. 73

An indication of what's in the pipeline

Results by one of the four majors offer clues as to what's in store for the others, says ERIC JOHNSTON.

Investors yesterday switched their focus to other major banks as the Commonwealth Bank of Australia's record profit this week put to rest fears of a sharp slowdown in lending, deep margin compression or a collapse in loan quality.

As the only major bank with a fiscal year to June 30, Commonwealth Bank gives investors an insight into the health of the sector before its rivals with a September 30 year-end begin handing down profits from late October.

'We expect that the ... reporting seasons are likely to be fairly robust for the banks, with earnings certainty looking fairly solid across the sector,' Goldman Sachs JBWere said.

Shares in Commonwealth Bank's three biggest rivals ended higher yesterday. Westpac closed up 1.1 per cent at $19.80, ANZ jumped 0.9 per cent to $21.96, and National Australia Bank was also up 0.9 per cent at $31.24.

NAB is widely regarded among analysts as a turnaround story, but with its shares trading at almost 15 times forecast 2005 earnings, it is seen as expensive. Both ANZ and Westpac are trading at a discount to the sector.

After charging to record highs in the lead-up to this week's record $4 billion profit and recommendation downgrades from several brokers, Commonwealth Bank shares drifted lower yesterday, closing down 0.4 per cent at $38.50.

Despite intense competition, Commonwealth Bank reported solid loan growth on Wednesday, with second-half housing up 14 per cent on the first half, although gains were also helped by improved market share.

Significantly, higher-margin business lending also delivered 14 per cent growth over the first half.

'The credit environment appears quite reasonable. Obviously, there's been some softening on the domestic mortgage front, but business lending is certainly picking up the slack,' Investors Mutual senior portfolio manager Monik Kotecha said.

Analysts had been fearing an interest-rate increase earlier this year may have brought about a hard landing for the nation's housing market. But with the Reserve Bank of Australia this week suggesting the threat of further rate rises have subsided in the near team, bankers expect this will further underpin confidence in the lending market.

Another focal point was Commonwealth Bank's flat overall margins. While deposit markets remain fierce, the threat of competitive pressures on lending may have been overplayed. Commonwealth Bank's margins shed eight basis points over fiscal 2005, but grew a point in the second half.

As a lender with exposure to almost all sectors of the economy, Commonwealth Bank said credit quality remained strong and was expected to remain robust into 2006.

'There wasn't anything untoward in the results that could reflect badly on any other banks,' a Melbourne-based fund manager said.

the last announcement would have relatively little impact on share prices. This expectation was confirmed by Clinch and Sinclair (1987). In summarising their findings they stated (p. 105):

> The directional association between daily price changes for announcing and non-announcing firms and the magnitude of the price change diminishes for subsequent announcing firms in the same industry over the reporting period.

The view that announcements by one company can impact on the share prices of another company is reflected in Accounting Headline 10.6. The newspaper article shows that when one bank—the Commonwealth Bank of Australia—released its record profit figures, this seemed to cause positive share price reactions in the shares of other banks.

While the above discussion has discussed the industry implications of corporate earnings or profit announcements, other studies have also shown that there can be industry share price implications that flow from other events that impact on specific organisations within the industry.

Blacconiere and Patten (1994) examined the market reaction to Union Carbide's chemical leak in India in 1984. In December 1984, methyl isocyanate (MIC) gas leaked from the Union Carbide India Limited (UCIL) plant in Bhopal killing approximately 3,800 people and causing several thousand other individuals to experience permanent or partial disabilities. Using a sample of forty-seven US firms, Blacconiere and Patten observed a significant impact on the share prices of Union Carbide directly following the disaster (as might be expected). They also found a significant intra-industry market reaction to the event. However, firms with more extensive environmental disclosures in their annual reports before the disaster (with the disclosures covering such issues as emergency response policies) experienced a smaller negative share price reaction than those with less extensive disclosures.

EARNINGS FORECASTS HAVE INFORMATION CONTENT

Announcements of earnings forecasts by both management and security analysts are associated with share returns. That is, not only do announcements of actual earnings appear to cause share prices to change but announcements of expected earnings also appear to cause price changes. Similar to earnings announcements, earnings forecasts are associated with market returns in terms of both direction and magnitude (Imhoff & Lobo, 1984; Penman, 1980). These results are not surprising, since earnings forecasts are expected to contain new information that can be used in the prediction of future earnings. Forecasts of expected future earnings appear to be an effective way of communicating information to the share market. Also, bad news forecasts about lower than anticipated future earnings may be useful for avoiding potential shareholder lawsuits (Skinner, 1997).

Earnings forecasts have also been explored in terms of the 'information transfer' phenomenon discussed earlier. Baginski (1987) generated results that showed that the share prices of firms within the same industry that did not provide an earnings forecast were positively correlated with the change in earnings expectation indicated by earnings forecasts released by managers of other firms within the same industry.

Accounting Headline 10.7 provides an example of where it appears that a profit forecast led to an increase in share price, consistent with some of the research results reported above. However, what must be remembered in research that looks at market reactions around particular events is that it is possible that share prices might actually be reacting to other unknown (by the researcher) contemporaneous events.

THERE ARE BENEFITS ASSOCIATED WITH THE VOLUNTARY DISCLOSURE OF INFORMATION

The disclosure of additional information, over and above that required by accounting regulations, has benefits in the capital markets. Voluntary disclosures include those contained within the annual report, as well as those made via other media such as press releases and conference calls to security analysts as well as various voluntary disclosures made on corporate websites. For example, Lang and Lundholm (1996) show that firms with more informative disclosure policies have a larger analyst following and more accurate analyst earnings forecasts. They suggest that potential benefits to disclosure include increased investor following and reduced information asymmetry. Further, Botosan (1997) shows that increased voluntary disclosure within the annual report is associated with reduced costs of equity capital, particularly for firms with low analyst following. For these low-analyst firms, disclosure of forecast information and key non-financial

Downgrade slams Vita

KERRIE SINCLAIR

Courier-Mail, 11 June 2008, p. 56

Vita Group has shed 30 per cent of its market value in two days after the Fone Zone mobile phone chain owner issued a profit warning and any Apple iPhone hopes were lost.

The Brisbane-based group's share price yesterday fell to a new all-time low, down 6 cents to 37 cents, against a 2006 all-time high of $1.39. Its market value fell to $52.3 million, against an all-time peak of $196.3 million.

It followed a 17 per cent stock price fall on Friday after Australia's biggest provider of Telstra mobile products and services cut its profit forecast and said it would shut some underperforming Fone Zone stores.

A company official also said on Friday it was unlikely to catch a wave from sales of Apple's iPhone because Telstra was not a carrier.

statistics is particularly important, while for firms with a high analyst following, disclosure of historical summary information is beneficial. Therefore, the potential benefits of increased disclosure should perhaps not be ignored when deciding the extent of voluntary disclosure.

RECOGNITION IS PERCEIVED DIFFERENTLY TO MERE FOOTNOTE DISCLOSURE

Recognising an item by recording it in the financial statements and including its numerical amount in the financial statement's totals is perceived differently to merely disclosing the amount in footnotes to the financial statements. For example, Aboody (1996) finds that where firms in the US oil and gas industry recognise a write-down in their financial statements the negative pricing effect is significant, whereas when firms in the same industry merely disclose such a write-down in footnotes the pricing effect is not significant. In other words, the market perceives recognised write-downs to be more indicative of a value decrement than disclosed write-downs. Further, Cotter and Zimmer (1999) show that mere disclosure of current values of land and buildings indicates that the amount is less certain when compared with current values that are recognised in the statement of financial position (balance sheet) via an asset revaluation. These results indicate that investors place greater reliance on recognised amounts than on disclosed amounts. Therefore, while it is not necessary to recognise information in the statement of financial position for it to be useful, since merely disclosing the information in the footnotes conveys the information to investors, disclosed information is perceived to be less reliable than recognised information.

SIZE

There is evidence that the relationship between earnings announcements and share price movements is inversely related to the size of an entity. That is, earnings announcements have been found generally to have a greater impact on the share prices of smaller firms relative to larger firms. This is explained on the basis that with larger firms there is generally more information available in the marketplace and therefore greater likelihood that projections about earnings have already been impounded in the share price. The earnings announcement for larger firms would have a relatively limited unexpected component. For example, research has shown that the relationship between the information content in earnings announcements and changes in share prices tends to be more significant for smaller firms. That is, in general, larger firms' earnings announcements have relatively less information content (for example, Collins, Kothari & Rayburn, 1987; Freeman, 1987). This is consistent with the EMH and is explained by the fact that larger firms tend to have more information being circulated about them as well as attracting more attention from such parties as security analysts. Hence, on average, earnings announcements for larger firms tend to be more anticipated, provide less surprise, and are already impounded in the share price prior to the earnings announcement.

Grant (1980) also explored this issue. He investigated the information content of earnings announcements of securities traded on the New York Stock Exchange, as well as securities traded on what is known as the 'over-the-counter' market (OTC). Firms traded on the OTC are typically smaller than firms traded on the New York Stock Exchange. Consistent with the perceived size effect, the prices of securities traded on the OTC were more responsive to earnings announcements than were the prices of securities traded on the New York Stock Exchange.

UNEXPECTED CHANGES IN ACCOUNTING EARNINGS CREATED BY UNEXPECTED INCREASES IN REVENUES RATHER THAN UNEXPECTED REDUCTIONS IN EXPENSES

Where there is an unexpected increase in earnings (profits), this could be due to an increase in revenues, a reduction in expenses, or a combination of both. In this regard, would it make a difference to the share price reaction if an unexpected increase in earnings was due to a revenue increase rather than a reduction in expenses, or vice versa? Jegadeesh and Livnat (2006) explored this issue. They state (p. 148):

> We examine the incremental information conveyed by revenues reported during preliminary earnings announcements. Several factors motivate our analysis of the information content of revenues. Earnings, by definition, is revenues minus aggregate expenses. If earnings surprises are accompanied by revenue surprises of similar magnitude in the same direction, then the earnings surprises are driven by revenue growth rather than by a reduction in expenses. We expect earnings growth driven by revenue growth to exhibit a different level of persistence compared with earnings growth driven by expense reduction.

Jegadeesh and Livnat's results indicate that the market does tend to react more to unexpected earnings when these 'surprises' are due to increases in revenues. These results are generally consistent with those provided by Ertimur, Livnat and Martikainen (2003), who found that market prices react significantly to unexpected revenue increases on earnings announcement dates after controlling for unexpected earnings announcements.

DO CURRENT SHARE PRICES ANTICIPATE FUTURE ACCOUNTING EARNINGS ANNOUNCEMENTS?

The previous discussion has provided evidence that accounting earnings announcements, because of their potential information content, can have some impact on share prices. That is, prices change in relation to information as it becomes available. However, the impact of 'new' information seems to be more significant for smaller firms. As we saw, this is explained on the basis that there tends to be more information available for larger firms (for example, through analysts paying particular attention to the larger firms). Hence, as firm size increases, the general perspective taken is that share prices incorporate information from a wider number of sources (including, perhaps, numerous forecasts of the larger entity's earnings) and therefore there is relatively less unexpected information when earnings are ultimately announced. For large firms, we might actually be able to argue that share prices *anticipate* future earnings announcements with some degree of accuracy. As Brown (1994, p. 105) states, if we take the perspective that share prices anticipate earnings announcements, we are effectively 'looking back the other way' from traditional perspectives that assume that earnings or profit announcements actually drive share price changes.

A more recent focus taken by some capital markets researchers is on how well accounting information, such as annual profits, captures information that is relevant to investors. This is a different focus from research considered previously in the chapter. Rather than determining whether earnings/profit announcements *provide* information to investors, this alternative form of research seeks to determine whether earnings announcements *reflect* information that has already been used by investors in decision making. That is, this research views market prices, and hence returns, as leading accounting earnings, while 'information content' research (the previous focus of the chapter) views earnings as leading (or driving) market returns. Both perspectives have merit, since the earnings announcement is likely to contain some information about a firm's activities that was not previously known to investors, as well as information that investors have already determined (or anticipated) from alternative sources.

In considering why share prices convey information about future accounting earnings, Brown (1994, p. 106) argues:

> In a world of rational expectations, events that affect future distributions to shareholders will be reflected in today's share price, whereas accounting standards often require that the recognition of those events be deferred until some future accounting period.

Share prices and returns ('returns' being changes in share prices plus dividends) are considered by some researchers to provide useful benchmarks for determining whether accounting information is relevant for investor decision making. Share prices are deemed to represent a benchmark measure of *firm value* (per share), while share returns represent a benchmark measure of *firm performance* (per share). These benchmarks are in turn used to compare the usefulness of alternative accounting and disclosure methods. For example, this methodology is used to answer questions such as: are cash flows from operations a better measure of a firm's performance than earnings calculated using the accruals system? Each of these accounting measures of performance is compared with the market benchmark measure of performance (returns) to determine which accounting measure best *reflects* the market's assessment of company performance. This type of capital markets research also assumes that the market is efficient, and acknowledges that financial statements are not the only source of information available to the markets, such that security prices reflect information that is generally available from a multitude of sources. In particular, it assumes that investors and financial analysts actively seek out relevant information when making investment decisions or recommendations, rather than awaiting the release of the annual report. Further, this area of the research allows researchers to consider questions about balance sheet (statement of financial position) measures. For example, are disclosures about current values of assets value-relevant? That is, are they associated with, or linked to, the current market value of the company? Again, there is an assumption that market values reflect all publicly available information, including, but not limited to, information contained in financial statements.

This area of the research is based on a theoretical framework that is derived from the premise that market values and book values are both measures of a firm's value (stock of wealth), even though book value measures wealth with some error. That is, at any point in time, the market value of a company's equity (MV_{it}) is equal to the book value of shareholders' equity (BV_{it}) plus some error (ε_{it}):

$$MV_{it} = BV_{it} + \varepsilon_{it} \qquad \text{(Equation 4)}$$

This error is due to the conservative nature of the accounting system. Book value is generally expected to be lower than market value for a number of reasons. First, not all assets and liabilities are recognised in the financial statements. For example, human resources, customer satisfaction levels and internally generated intangible assets including goodwill are not recognised in the statement of financial position, nor are their values amortised to the income statement (or as it has become known in recent years, the statement of comprehensive income). Nevertheless, while such assets are not recognised for accounting purposes, the expectation is that an efficient market will consider such assets when determining the appropriate market price for the firm's securities.[20] Second, some assets are recognised at less than their full value. For example, fixed assets that have not been revalued to fair value and inventory are generally recorded at less than their expected sale prices.

If markets are assumed to be efficient, the market value of the firm's shares provides a benchmark measure against which alternative measures of book value can be assessed. As will be seen shortly, there is a great deal of research that evaluates the output of the accounting system on the basis of how the accounting information relates to or compares with current market prices of the firm's securities.[21]

If market value (based on the number of securities issued and their respective market values) and book value of a company are considered as 'stocks' of wealth, then changes in each of these measures of wealth between two points in time can be considered as 'flows' of wealth. Just as market and book measures of stocks of wealth equate, with error, market and book measures of flows of wealth (changes in value) can be equated, albeit with some degree of error:

$$\Delta MV_{it} = \Delta BV_{it} + \varepsilon'_{it} \qquad \text{(Equation 5)}$$

---

20 As another example, the appointment of a very reputable managing director would be value-relevant because it is an action that could be expected to lead to improved company performance, cash flows and hence share value. However, such an appointment would not generally be reflected in the financial statements themselves. The disparity between the value of net assets as represented in the statement of financial position (balance sheet) and the market value of the firm's securities will tend to be greater for those organisations with operations that are more dependent on intangible assets (such as human capital) relative to those organisations that rely more heavily on tangible assets (such as property and equipment).

21 This research assumes, perhaps somewhat simplistically, that the market has it 'right' in its determination of the firm's value. Thereafter, accounting figures are compared with the market's 'benchmark'. Clearly, the benchmark figure of valuation might overvalue or undervalue the entity relative to the value that would be placed on it if all private and public information was known and 'appropriately' used. As noted earlier in the chapter, market predictions are sometimes, in hindsight, proved to be wrong, thus necessitating subsequent adjustments.

Change in market value (ΔMV_{it}) is simply the difference in the market capitalisation of a company between two points in time ($t - 1$ to t). On a 'per share' basis, it can be expressed as the change in the price of one share.

$$\Delta MV_{it}/\text{no. of shares} = P_{it} - P_{it-1} \qquad \text{(Equation 6)}$$

Change in book value (ΔBV_{it}) is the difference between opening and closing total shareholders' equity. However, if we assume that there have been no additional capital contributions during the period, ΔBV_{it} can also be measured by considering the change in retained earnings for the period. On a per share basis, this is measured as earnings per share (E_{it}) less dividends paid per share (D_{it}):

$$\Delta BV_{it}/\text{no. of shares} = E_{it} - D_{it} \qquad \text{(Equation 7)}$$

This formula is based on the concept of 'clean surplus' earnings, which assumes that all increases in book value pass through the income statement (or, as would be the case now, the statement of comprehensive income). Clean surplus earnings does not always hold in practice, since items such as asset revaluation increments are credited directly to owners' equity (through a credit to revaluation surplus). However, the assumption of clean surplus is useful for simplifying our analysis. Substituting Equations 6 and 7 into Equation 5 gives:

$$P_{it} - P_{it-1} = E_{it} - D_{it} + \varepsilon'_{it} \qquad \text{(Equation 8)}$$

That is, there is a theoretical relationship between change in price and change in retained earnings for the period. With a small amount of manipulation, this equation can be expressed to relate returns to earnings (the return/earnings relation). First, adding dividends to both sides of the equation, and dividing through by beginning of period price, gives:

$$\frac{(P_{it} - P_{it-1}) + D_{it}}{P_{it-1}} = E_{it}/P_{it-1} + \varepsilon''_{it} \qquad \text{(Equation 9)}$$

Since the left-hand side of the equation, $((P_{it} - P_{it-1}) + D_{it})/P_{it-1}$, is equal to returns (Equation 2), we are left with an equation relating returns to earnings:

$$R_{it} = E_{it}/P_{it-1} + \varepsilon''_{it} \qquad \text{(Equation 10)}$$

Equation 10 shows that we should expect returns (R_{it}) and earnings per share divided by beginning of period price (E_{it}/P_{it-1}) to be related.

In short, this perspective says that, if market value is related to book value, returns should be related to accounting earnings per share, divided by price at the beginning of the accounting period. This analysis provides an underlying reason why we should expect returns to be related to earnings over time. However, it is interesting to note that it is *total earnings per share* rather than *unexpected earnings per share* that this theoretical framework proposes should be associated with returns. This is in contrast to research that assesses the 'information content' of earnings announcements by analysing the association between unexpected earnings per share and abnormal returns at the time of the announcement. It will be seen that there have been a number of studies that evaluate reported earnings (which is an accounting number) on the basis of how closely the movements in reported earnings (or earnings per share) relate to changes in share prices.[22]

Beaver, Lambert and Morse (1980) were the authors of an early paper that sought to investigate how efficiently data about share prices enable a researcher to estimate future accounting earnings. Accepting that share price is the capitalised value of future earnings, they regressed the annual percentage change in share price on the percentage change in annual earnings per share. Consistent with Equation 10, they found that share prices and related returns were related to accounting earnings, but they also found that share prices in year t were positively associated with accounting earnings in year $t + 1$ (share prices led accounting earnings). It was accepted that share price movements provided an indication of future movements in accounting earnings. Because of various information sources, prices appeared to anticipate future accounting earnings. These findings were also supported in a later study by Beaver, Lambert and Ryan (1987), who regressed changes in security prices on the percentage changes in earnings.

An earlier discussion showed that research indicates that share prices of large firms do not adjust as much to earnings announcements as do the share prices of small firms. This was explained on the basis that there is more information available and analysed in relation to large firms, and hence information about earnings is already impounded in the share price. That is, 'for larger firms, there is a broader and richer information set, and there are more market traders and more analysts seeking information' (Brown, 1994, p. 110).

If we adopt the position taken in this section of the chapter that share prices can actually anticipate earnings announcements ('looking back the other way'), as indicated in Beaver, Lambert and Morse (1980) and Beaver, Lambert and Ryan (1987), then perhaps share prices anticipate accounting earnings more efficiently in the case of larger firms. Collins, Kothari and Rayburn (1987) found evidence to support this view—*size does matter*, with the share prices being a better indicator of future earnings in large companies.

As noted above, there have been a number of studies using share market valuations as a basis for evaluating accounting information. In Equation 10 we indicated that, theoretically, market returns should be related to earnings. Dechow (1994) investigates how well accounting earnings reflect market returns. She also considers whether another measure of performance, based on cash flows, relates better to returns than earnings based on the accrual accounting system, and states (p. 12):

> This paper assumes that stock markets are efficient in the sense that stock prices unbiasedly reflect all publicly available information concerning firms' expected future cash flows. Therefore, stock price performance is used as a benchmark to assess whether earnings or realised cash flows better summarise this information.

According to Dechow, earnings are predicted to be a more useful measure of firm performance than cash flows because they are predicted to have fewer timing and matching problems. In her conclusions, she states (p. 35):

> This paper hypothesizes that one role of accounting accruals is to provide a measure of short-term performance that more closely reflects expected cash flows than do realized

---

22 Again, this research assumes, perhaps somewhat simplistically, that the market has determined the 'right' valuation of the organisation.

cash flows. The results are consistent with this prediction. First, over short measurement intervals earnings are more strongly associated with stock returns than realized cash flows. In addition, the ability of realized cash flows to measure firm performance improves relative to earnings as the measurement interval is lengthened. Second, earnings have a higher association with stock returns than do realized cash flows in firms experiencing large changes in their working capital requirements and their investment and financing activities. Under these conditions, realized cash flows have more severe timing and matching problems and are less able to reflect firm performance.

Using the market value of a firm's securities as a benchmark, a number of studies have also attempted to determine which asset valuation approaches provide accounting figures that best reflect the valuation the market places on the firm. The perspective taken is that book values that relate more closely to market values (determined through a review of share prices) provide more relevant information than other accounting valuation approaches. Barth, Beaver and Landsman (1996) undertook a study that investigated whether fair value estimates of a bank's financial instruments (as required in the United States at the time) seem to provide a better explanation of bank share prices relative to values determined on the basis of historical cost accounting. Their findings indicate that the disclosures required by the US accounting standard SFAS No. 107 'provide significant explanatory power for bank share prices beyond that provided by book values' (p. 535), thereby providing evidence that such values are the values that are relevant to investors.

Easton, Eddey and Harris (1993) investigate whether revaluations of assets result in an alignment between information reflected in annual reports and information implicit in share prices and returns. Again, share price data are used as the 'benchmark' against which accounting data are assessed. According to Easton, Eddey and Harris (p. 16):

> Prices are used to assess the extent to which the financial statements, including asset revaluations, reflect the state of the firm at a point in time, while returns are used to assess the summary of change in financial state that is provided in the financial statements.

They found that the revaluation of assets generally resulted in better alignment of market and book values. In concluding their paper, they state (p. 36):

> Our analyses support the conclusion that book values including asset revaluation reserves are more aligned with the market value of the firm than book values excluding asset revaluation. That is, asset revaluation reserves as reported under Australian GAAP help to provide a better summary of the current state of the firm. Thus, allowing or requiring firms to revalue assets upward should be carefully considered by organizations such as the UK Accounting Standards Board, the Japanese Ministry of Finance, and the International Accounting Standards Committee as they debate the merits of various proposed changes in asset revaluation practice.

Consistent with a view that market prices already seem to reflect the current values of an entity's assets, as indicated in the research discussed above, it is interesting to note that asset revaluations do not appear to provide information to investors over and above historical cost accounting information. That is, some studies have indicated that the provision of current cost data in financial statements does not have information content (Brown & Finn, 1980). These results suggest that investors are able to estimate current value information prior to it being disclosed in the financial statements. Therefore, while the provision of current value information does not provide new information to investors, it appears to reflect the information used by investors in making their investment decisions.

RELAXING ASSUMPTIONS ABOUT MARKET EFFICIENCY

The research discussed so far in this chapter has relied on a fundamental assumption that capital markets are efficient—which basically means that relevant publicly available information is quickly (or instantaneously) impounded within share prices. According to Kothari (2001, p. 114):

> Building on past theoretical and empirical work, Fama (1965) introduced, and subsequently made major contributions to the conceptual refinement and empirical testing of, the efficient markets hypothesis. Fama (p. 4) notes that 'In an efficient market, on the average, competition' among rational, profit maximising participants 'will cause the full effects of new information on intrinsic values to be reflected "instantaneously" in actual prices'. The maintained hypothesis of market efficiency opened the doors for positive capital markets research in accounting. Ball and Brown (1968, p. 160) assert that capital market efficiency provides 'justification for selecting the behaviour of security prices as an operational test of usefulness' of information in financial statements. Beaver (1968) offers a similar argument. Unlike previous normative research on accounting theories and optimal accounting policies, positive capital markets research began using changes in security prices as an objective, external outcome to infer whether information in accounting reports is useful to market participants.

However, in recent years there has been a deal of research that has questioned assumptions of market efficiency. As Kothari (2001, p. 107) states:

> The mounting evidence of apparent market inefficiency documented in the financial economics and accounting literature has fueled accounting researchers' interest in fundamental analysis, valuation, and tests of market efficiency. Evidence of market inefficiency has created an entirely new area of research examining long-horizon stock-price performance following accounting events. This is in sharp contrast to the boom in short window event studies and studies of economic consequences of standard setting of the 1970s and 1980s. Future work on tests of market efficiency with respect to accounting information will be fruitful if it recognizes that (i) deficient research design choices can create the false appearance of market inefficiency; and (ii) advocates of market inefficiency should propose robust hypotheses and tests to differentiate their behavioral-finance theories from the efficient market hypothesis that does not rely on irrational behavior.

A deal of the research that challenges market efficiencies does so on the basis that it appears that the capital market's response to information takes longer than previously believed. As already indicated, much previous research was predicated on the view that capital markets react—through changes in share prices—almost instantaneously to relevant information. According to Kothari (2001, p. 130):

> If the market fails to correctly appreciate the implications of a current earnings surprise in revising its expectations of future earnings, the price change associated with earnings change will be too small. There is a large body of evidence that suggests that the stock market under-reacts to earnings information and recognizes the full impact of the earnings information only gradually over time. Smaller-than-predicted values of earnings response coefficients are consistent with capital market inefficiency.

Where share prices are found to take time to react to particular information—such as a corporate earnings announcement—this is referred to in the literature as 'drift'. As Kothari (2001, p. 193) states:

> Post-earnings-announcement drift is the predictability of abnormal returns following earnings announcements. Since the drift is of the same sign as the earnings change, it suggests the market under-reacts to information in earnings announcements. Ball and Brown (1968) first observed the drift. It has been more precisely documented in many subsequent studies. The drift lasts up to a year and the magnitude is both statistically and economically significant for the extreme good and bad earnings news portfolios. A disproportionate fraction of the drift is concentrated in the three-day periods surrounding future quarterly earnings announcements, as opposed to exhibiting a gradually drifting abnormal return behavior. Because of this characteristic and because almost all of the drift appears within one year, I characterize the drift as a short-window phenomenon, rather than a long-horizon performance anomaly. The profession has subjected the drift anomaly to a battery of tests, but a rational, economic explanation for the drift remains elusive.

If we relax assumptions about the speed with which the capital market reacts to information (that is, if we accept that the market does not react instantaneously and there is 'drift'), this leads to opportunities for some capital market participants to make gains in periods when share prices do not fully reflect the available information. Lee (2001, p. 238) states:

> Is it possible for mispricing to exist in equilibrium? Certainly. In fact, it strikes me as self-evident that arbitrage cannot exist in the absence of mispricing. Arbitrageurs are creatures of the very gap created by mispricing. Therefore, either both exist in equilibrium, or neither will. Arbitrage cannot take place without some amount of mispricing. If by some mystical force prices always adjust instantly to the right value, we would have no arbitrageurs. Therefore, if we believe that arbitrage is an equilibrium phenomenon, we must necessarily believe that some amount of mispricing is also an equilibrium phenomenon.

If further evidence continues to surface that capital markets do not always behave in accordance with the EMH, should we reject the research that has embraced the EMH as a fundamental assumption? In this regard we can return to earlier chapters of this book in which it was emphasised that theories are abstractions of reality. Capital markets are made of individuals and as such it would not (or perhaps, should not) be surprising to find that the market does not always act in the same predictable manner. Nevertheless, the EMH has helped provide some useful predictions and no doubt will continue to be relied on by many researchers for a considerable period of time. As Lee (2001, p. 238) states:

> A common assertion is that even if the EMH is not strictly true, it is sufficient to serve as a starting point for research purposes. Like Newtonian physics, it is more than good enough for everyday usage. Unfortunately, it is becoming increasingly more difficult to accommodate what we know about the behavior of prices and returns within this traditional framework.

At the present time there is a deal of research into capital markets that does not rely on market efficiencies. The consideration of 'other forces' that shape share prices and returns might eventually lead to a revolution in thought (Kuhn, 1962)—but it will arguably take a long time. As stated in Chapter 1, Kuhn (1962) explained how knowledge, or science, develops: scientific progress is not evolutionary; rather, it is revolutionary. His view is that knowledge advances when one theory is replaced by another as particular researchers attack the credibility of an existing paradigm and advance an alternative, promoted as being superior, thereby potentially bringing the existing paradigm into 'crisis'. As knowledge develops, the new paradigm may be replaced by a further research perspective, or a prior paradigm may be resurrected. In discussing the process of how researchers switch from one research perspective (or paradigm) to another, Kuhn likens it to one of 'religious conversion'.[23] Whether the EMH will ever be abandoned in favour of a different perspective is an interesting issue to consider.

CHAPTER SUMMARY

Capital markets research has investigated a number of issues. Central to the research are assumptions about the efficiency of the capital market. The chapter looked at 'information content' studies, in which researchers investigated share market reactions to the releases of information, often specifically the release of accounting information. The view taken was that the accounting disclosures often revealed new information, and in a market that was deemed to be informationally efficient with regard to acting on new information, share prices react to this information.

The chapter also considered studies that investigated whether accounting disclosures reflected, or perhaps confirmed, information already impounded in share prices. The perspective taken was that in an informationally efficient capital market, market prices of shares will reflect information from a multitude of sources. Some researchers would argue that, if the accounting information does not reflect the information already impounded in share prices, accounting data that do not relate to share prices, and changes therein, are somewhat deficient. The idea is that market prices reflect information from many sources and if the accumulated data provide a particular signal the accounting disclosures should provide similar signals. This approach implies

---

23 Kuhn's 'revolutionary' perspective about the development of knowledge is in itself a theory about how knowledge developes, and, as with financial accounting theories, there are alternative views of how knowledge develops and advances. Although a review of the various perspectives of the development of science is beyond the scope of this book, interested readers are referred to Popper (1959), Lakatos and Musgrove (1974), Feyerabend (1975) and Chalmers (1982).

that the market has it 'right' when determining share prices and hence returns. In practice, the market cannot be expected always to get it 'right'.

Because much knowledge about the performance of an entity will be gained from sources other than accounting, it is perhaps reasonable to expect that accounting information should relate (not perfectly) to expectations held by capital market participants, as reflected in share prices. However, because there will arguably always be some unexpected information released when accounting results are made public, we might expect that not all accounting disclosures will be of a confirmatory nature. Some information in the accounting releases will be new and, in a market that is assumed to be informationally efficient, some share price revisions are to be expected.

Many share price studies have investigated the market's reaction to particular disclosures. Often, if no reaction is found, it is deemed that the information is not useful and therefore entities should not go to the trouble and expense involved in making such disclosures. This form of argument has been used to criticise accounting regulators for mandating particular disclosure requirements. What must be recognised, however, is that capital markets research investigates the aggregate reaction of one group of stakeholders, the investors. While the share market is an important user of accounting information, provision of information to the share market is not the only function of the accounting system. Accounting information is also used for monitoring purposes (Jensen & Meckling, 1976; Watts & Zimmerman, 1990), and hence financial statements play an important role in relation to the contracting process (see Chapter 7). Financial statements provide a relatively low cost way of measuring managers' performance and monitoring compliance with accounting-based contractual terms, thereby helping to reduce agency costs. Further, financial statement information can be used to satisfy people's 'rights to know', that is, to fulfil the duty of accountability (see Chapter 8 for an overview of the notion of accountability). Therefore, while investors are important users of financial statements, it would be foolish to focus solely on the investor-information role of financial reporting, to the exclusion of considerations about the monitoring/accountability role. Arguably organisations have an accountability to a broader group of stakeholders than just shareholders.

QUESTIONS

10.1 What is the role of capital markets research?

10.2 What assumptions about market efficiency are typically adopted in capital markets research? What do we mean by 'market efficiency'?

10.3 If some research is undertaken that provides evidence that capital markets do not always behave in accordance with the Efficient Markets Hypothesis, does this invalidate research that adopts an assumption that capital markets are efficient?

10.4 What would be the implications for capital markets research if it was generally accepted that capital markets were not efficient in assimilating information?

10.5 If an organisation releases its earnings figures for the year and there is no share price reaction, how might capital market researchers explain this finding?

10.6 How would a researcher undertaking capital markets research typically justify that a particular item of information has 'value' to investors?

10.7 Evaluate the following statement: If an item of accounting information is released by a corporation and there is no apparent change in the share price of the company, the information is not relevant to the market and therefore there is no point in disclosing such information again.

10.8 What, if any, effect would the size of an entity have on the likelihood that the capital market will react to the disclosure of accounting information?

10.9 if an organisation's operations rely heavily on the specialised expertise of its management team, would you expect there to be a higher or a lower correspondence between the net assets recognised in the statement of financial position (balance sheet), and the total market value of the organisation's securities, relative to an organisation that relies more on tangible assets (for example, commonly used plant and machinery) to generate its income?

10.10 Would you expect an earnings announcement by one firm within an industry to impact on the share prices of other firms in the industry? Why?

10.11 The following is an extract from a newspaper article entitled 'Westpac chief in $3bn parting shot' (by George Lekakis in the *Advertiser*, 2 November 2007, p. 72):

OUTGOING Westpac chief David Morgan yesterday delivered his final annual result for the group—a bumper bottom line harvest of $3.45 billion.

Net profit was up 12.4 per cent for the year following spectacular growth in fee income businesses, particularly funds management and institutional banking.

Dr Morgan, who makes way for incoming managing director Gail Kelly in February, described the 2007 earnings performance as 'one of the best" in his nine years at the group's helm.

'I think we've got enormous growth ahead of us,' he said. 'I've never seen momentum in the company as we have now.'

Investors responded positively to the profit announcement, driving up the share price by 52c to a record close of $31.06.

Using the material provided in this chapter, provide an explanation of why the capital market responded as positively as it did to Westpac's profit announcement.

10.12 The following is an extract from a newspaper article entitled 'Record profit In pipeline for Exxon as oil price soars' (by Steven Mufson, *Canberra Times*, 3 February 2008, p. 27):

BUOYED by soaring crude oil prices, Exxon Mobil has announced that it set new records for US quarterly and annual corporate profits in 2007, and Chevron, America's second-largest oil company, also reported big gains in earnings.

Exxon broke the record it previously had set for profits by a US corporation, earning $40.6 billion ($A45 billion) last year. In the fourth quarter alone, it earned $A13 billion, or $A2.35 a share, up 14 per cent from the fourth quarter of 2006. Exxon's net income for the year came to $A5.1 million an hour.

Chevron said its profit rose 29 per cent to $A5.4 billion, or $A2.57 a share. Profits of the world's five biggest oil companies have tripled since 2002.

Exxon Mobil's vice-president for public affairs, Kenneth Cohen, said the earnings reflected the company's 'long-term, disciplined approach' and investments made a decade ago when oil prices were dismally low. With mounting exploration costs and increasingly remote oil prospects, Mr Cohen said the large revenues were needed to meet 'the massive scale of the energy challenge before us'. But in Congress, the earnings were seen as outsized. The chairman of the Joint Economic Committee, Democrat senator Charles Schumer, issued a statement saying, 'Congratulations to ExxonMobil and Chevron for reminding Americans why they cringe every time they pull into a gas station and for reminding the US why it needs to act swiftly to break our dependence on foreign oil and roll back unnecessary tax incentives for oil companies.'

You are to provide a prediction as to whether the news about the record profits of Exxon would have created a change in the company's share price. What factors would have an impact on the nature of any potential share price reaction?

10.13 Researchers such as Chambers and Sterling have made numerous claims that historical cost information is meaningless and useless. Are the results of capital markets research consistent with this perspective?

10.14 Some recent capital markets research investigates whether accounting information reflects the valuations that have already been made by the market (as reflected in share prices). In a sense, it assumes that the market has it 'right' and that a 'good' accounting approach is one that provides accounting numbers that relate to, or confirm, the market prices/returns. If we assume that the market has it 'right', what exactly is the role of financial accounting?

10.15 Review Accounting Headline 10.6 (a newspaper article entitled 'An indication of what's in the pipeline') and explain the reason for the change in the prices of the Commonwealth Bank's shares. Also, what might have caused the price changes in the shares in the other banks?

10.16 This chapter has emphasised that the capital market appears to respond to information from many sources, including but not limited to accounting. As an illustration of how non-accounting information appears to affect share prices, consider an article by Stephen Romei that appeared in the *Australian* on 8 December 1999 (p. 1). The article, entitled 'Aussies the real thing, Coke hopes', discussed how Douglas Daft was to 'take the helm of the Atlanta-based global beverages empire in April following the resignation of chairman and chief, Douglas Ivester'. According to the article, 'The news went down like a flat Coke with investors, with Coca-Cola shares falling 6 percent to $US64, knocking about $US 10 billion off the company's market value. While Mr Daft is considered a star performer inside Coca-Cola, he is not well known on Wall Street'. Why do you think the market reacted in the way it did to the announcement, and do you think that the announcement implies market efficiency or inefficiency?

10.17 Read Accounting Headline 10.8 and then consider why we might expect, or not expect, the market to react to radio announcements made by Alan Jones. Would a market reaction imply anything about the efficiency of the capital market?

Jones helps himself to high-rise share of development deal

Australian, 18 November 1999, p. 1

AMANDA MEADE

Broadcaster Alan Jones has been paid $250,000 a year since 1997 by major developer the Walker Corporation to promote its interests on Radio 2UE.

And if the company's share price rises, the breakfast show host receives a maximum bonus of $200,000.

But last year, Jones was so impressed by his own efforts on behalf of Walker, he wrote to his agent, Harry M. Miller, suggesting they ask for more money because the company was doing so well.

'I notice the press release from the Walker Corporation talking about the net profit before taxation of $18.6 million, an increase of 107%,' Jones wrote in February last year.

'They are boasting about all of that. Are we being paid enough!! Let's face it, they wouldn't be in the public place without moi! Tell me what you think?'

But yesterday, after being recalled to give evidence to the broadcasting inquiry for the second time, Jones claimed the memo was written in jest.

The Walker deal, which Jones has not yet terminated despite an order from 2UE chairman John Conde, includes an incentive fee.

The first time the share price hits $1.55 after the first anniversary of the July 1997 contract Walker had to pay him $100,000. The incentive rose to $200,000 by the second and third anniversaries, provided there was a further rise in the share price.

The Australian Broadcasting Authority inquiry heard it was significant because it provided almost exclusively for Jones to provide on-air support.

But Jones offered the same defence he has for all his seven personal endorsement contracts that are in breach of 2UE's rules—he has never actually given them any free plugs on air.

Counsel assisting the inquiry, Julian Burnside QC, remarked: 'The curious thing is that what you have done, you weren't obliged to do, and what you were obliged to do, you haven't done.'

Jones was asked by reporters if he had any investment in the Walker Corporations' finger wharf apartments at Woolloomooloo.

'I have,' he said. 'I think it's a good development, but it's a bit slow. Yes I have, I have been impressed with the quality and finish of the product.'

A year after signing with Walker, Jones agreed a similar deal with another developer, Walsh Bay Finance, which was redeveloping the historic wharves in the Rocks.

David Mann, the Walsh Bay executive who arranged the deal, which runs until December 15, 2001, told the inquiry he approached Jones to 'minimise the negative publicity' the project was receiving.

Mr Burnside: 'Did he start broadcasting favourable comments about the Walsh Bay redevelopment?'

Mr Mann: 'Yes.'

These favourable comments appeared almost immediately after Jones signed the June 1, 1998 $200,000-a-year contract. On June 2, he broadcast the first of four substantial editorials praising the 'magnificent' development.

Mr Burnside said he had recalled Jones in relation to the two development companies because the contracts 'stand in marked contrast' to evidence already given by the broadcaster.

'The Walker Corporation agreement seems to provide for nothing except on-air conduct apart from going to four functions a year,' Mr Burnside said.

He said if there was 'any doubt' the contract was concerned with on-air conduct, the panel should consider the four broadcasts that followed the signing of the deal.

The first of Jones' laudatory editorials came on the day the *Daily Telegraph's* columnist, Piers Akerman, also praised the Walsh Bay project. The inquiry heard Akerman was also lobbied and provided with briefing notes by the developers.

Akerman said last night he had never been offered, nor taken, money for a story, although he had discussed the Walsh Bay project over lunch with an old friend, who was also a Transfield executive.

After the column was published, on June 2, Transfield had offered a case of Grange Hermitage wine, which Akerman said he declined.

10.18 Read Accounting Headline 10.9 and, relying on some of the capital markets studies considered in this chapter, explain why the share prices of the pharmaceutical companies might have reacted in the way they did.

10.19 Read Accounting Headline 10.10 and then explain how a capital markets researcher would differentiate between the component of the share price change of UAL that related to market-wide movements and the component that related to the write down of the organisation's intangible assets.

Accounting Headline 10.9 Market reactions to drug marketing ruling

Drug company shares bounce in 'relief rally' as FDA clears Vioxx

RACHEL STEVENSON

Independent, 22 February 2005, p. 34

SHARES in the pharmaceutical sector received a shot in the arm yesterday after an American drug authority panel ruled that controversial painkillers could stay on sale.

AstraZeneca, GlaxoSmithKline and Shire Pharmaceuticals all saw their share prices soar following a Food and Drug Administration (FDA) advisory panel recommendation on Friday that Vioxx, Merck's controversial painkiller, can return to shelves and drugs of the same class can stay on sale.

The FDA said Vioxx, which was pulled from the market in September on concerns it doubled the risk of heart attacks and strokes, was safe to market, albeit with heightened safety warnings, because the benefits of the drug outweighed the risks. Pfizer's rival painkillers, Celebrex and Bextra, which have also been under threat because of elevated risks of heart problems, were also given clearance to stay on sale.

GlaxoSmithKline, which is developing a painkiller in the same class as Vioxx, saw its shares rise 4.4 per cent, closing 54p up at 1,295p. It is due to meet with FDA officials to discuss developments on its drug shortly.

AstraZeneca also rose more than 4 per cent to close at 2,162 and Shire bounced up 3.4 per cent to 581p. Shire saw its shares tumble 16 per cent last week after its key hyperactivity and attention deficit disorder drug was withdrawn in Canada after fears for its safety. The three companies were yesterday's highest risers in the FTSE 100.

There had been fears that the FDA would introduce much tighter safety regulations, causing many more drug withdrawals and a slower rate of approvals on new treatments. Adrian Howd, an analyst at ABN Amro, said: 'This was a relief rally after the FDA showed some common sense with regard to drug safety. All drugs carry risks and some side effects will always be found … but the FDA appears to have seen the balance between safety and the rewards from drugs.'

The panel found that the key component of the drugs, called Cox-2 inhibitors, did increase risks of heart problems and should carry the strongest possible warnings, but the drugs would help patients who have struggled to find other treatments that work.

Extract from *Wall Street Journal*, 12 July 2008, p. B5

Corporate news: UAL to record up to $2.7 billion in charges

SUSAN CAREY

Shares of United Airlines parent UAL Corp. fell 13% Friday to hit a 52-week low after the carrier said it plans to take second-quarter noncash charges of as much as $2.7 billion, mostly to reflect a write-down to zero of the value of its intangible assets, or goodwill.

Its stock slump came as the larger market plummeted on oil and mortgage worries.

Chicago-based UAL, the second-largest U.S. airline by traffic after AMR Corp.'s American Airlines, said the write down is the result of record-high fuel prices hammering its financial results and its market capitalization.

As of Friday, UAL, which generates about $20 billion in annual revenue, had an equity value of $433 million, less than the retail price of two jumbo jets. Its stock has plunged 93% in the past year, more than most of its big U.S. rivals, although the entire sector has been rocked by the rapid run-up in fuel prices.

UAL shares fell 54 cents to $3.63 in 4 pm composite trading on the Nasdaq Stock Market, hitting a 52-week low of $3.47 in intraday trading.

REFERENCES

Aboody, D. (1996), 'Recognition versus disclosure in the oil and gas industry', *Journal of Accounting Research*, (Supplement), pp. 21–32.

Baginski, S. P. (1987), 'Intra-industry information transfers associated with management forecasts of earnings', *Journal of Accounting Research*, 25(2), pp. 196–216.

Ball, R. & P. Brown (1968), 'An empirical evaluation of accounting income numbers', *Journal of Accounting Research*, 6(2), pp. 159–78.

Barth, M., W. Beaver & W. Landsman (1996), 'Value-relevance of banks fair value disclosures under SFAS 107', *The Accounting Review*, 71(4), pp. 513–37.

Beaver, W. H., R. Lambert & D. Morse (1980), 'The information content of security prices', *Journal of Accounting and Economics*, 2(1), pp. 3–38.

Beaver, W. H., R. A. Lambert & S. G. Ryan (1987), 'The information content of security prices: a second look', *Journal of Accounting and Economics*, 9(2), pp. 139–57.

Blacconiere, W. & D. Patten (1994), 'Environmental disclosures, regulatory costs, and changes in firm value', *Journal of Accounting and Economics*, 18, pp. 357–77.

Botosan, C. A. (1997), 'Disclosure level and the cost of equity capital', *The Accounting Review*, 72(3), pp. 323–50.

Brown, P. (1970), 'The impact of the annual net profit report on the stock market', *Australian Accountant* (July), pp. 273–83.

Brown, P. (1994), *Capital Markets-Based Research in Accounting: An Introduction*. Coopers and Lybrand Research Methodology Monograph No. 2, Melbourne: Coopers and Lybrand.

Brown, P. & F. Finn (1980), 'Asset revaluations and stock prices: alternative explanations of a study by Sharpe and Walker', in R. Ball (ed.), *Share Markets and Portfolio Theory*, St Lucia: University of Queensland Press.

Chambers, R. (1965), 'Why bother with postulates?', *Journal of Accounting Research*, 1(1).

Chalmers, A. F. (1982), *What Is This Thing Called Science?*, 2nd edn, St Lucia: University of Queensland Press.

Clarkson, P., D. Joyce & I. Tutticci (2006), 'Market reaction to takeover rumour in Internet discussion sites', *Accounting and Finance*, 46(1), pp. 31–52.

Clinch, G. J. & N. A. Sinclair (1987), 'Intra-industry information releases: a recursive systems approach', *Journal of Accounting and Economics*, 9(1), pp. 89–106.

Collins, D., S. Kothari & J. Rayburn (1987), 'Firm size and information content of prices with respect to earnings', *Journal of Accounting and Economics*, 9(2), pp. 111–38.

Cotter, J. & I. Zimmer (1999), 'Why do some firms recognize whereas others merely disclose asset revaluations?', unpublished working paper, Universities of Queensland and Southern Queensland.

Dechow, P. (1994), 'Accounting earnings and cash flows as measures of firm performance: the role of accounting accruals', *Journal of Accounting and Economics*, 18, pp. 3–24.

Easton, P. D., P. Eddey & T. S. Harris (1993), 'An investigation of revaluations of tangible long-lived assets', *Journal of Accounting Research*, 31 (Supplement), pp. 1–38.

Easton, P. D. & M. E. Zmijewski (1989), 'Cross-sectional variation in the stock market response to accounting earnings announcements', *Journal of Accounting and Economics*, 11(2), pp. 117–41.

Ertimur, Y., J. Livnat & M. Martikainen (2003), 'Differential market reactions to revenue and expense surprises', *Review of Accounting Studies*, 8(2–3), 185–211.

Fama, E. F. (1976), *Foundations of Finance*, New York: Basic Books.

Fama, E. F., L. Fisher, M. C. Jensen & R. Roll (1969), 'The adjustment of stock prices to new information', *International Economic Review*, 10(1), pp. 1–21.

Feyerabend, P. (1975), *Against Method: Outline of an Anarchic Theory of Knowledge*, London: New Left Books.

Firth, M. (1976), 'The impact of earnings announcements on the share price behavior of similar type firms', *Economic Journal*, 96, pp. 296–306.

Foster, G. J. (1981), 'Intra-industry information transfers associated with earnings releases', *Journal of Accounting and Economics*, 3(4), pp. 201–32.

Frankel, R. & C. Lee (1998), 'Accounting valuation, market expectation, and cross-sectional stock returns', *Journal of Accounting and Economics*, 25, pp. 283–319.

Freeman, R. N. (1987), 'The association between accounting earnings and security returns for large and small firms', *Journal of Accounting and Economics*, 9(2), pp. 195–228.

Freeman, R. & S. Tse (1992), 'Intercompany information transfers', *Journal of Accounting and Economics* (June/September), pp. 509–23.

Grant, E. B. (1980), 'Market implications of differential amounts of interim information', *Journal of Accounting Research*, 18(1), pp. 255–68.

Hendriksen, E. S. & M. F. Van Breda (1992), *Accounting Theory*, 5th edn, Homewood: Irwin.

Herbohn, K., V. Ragunathan & R. Garsden (2007), 'The horse has bolted: revisiting the market reaction to going concern modifications of audit reports', *Accounting and Finance*, 47(3), pp. 473–93.

Imhoff, E. A. & G. J. Lobo (1984), 'Information content of analysts forecast revisions', *Journal of Accounting Research*, 22(2), pp. 541–54.

Jegadeesh, N. & J. Livnat (2006), 'Revenue surprises and stock returns', *Journal of Accounting and Economics,* 41(1–2), pp. 147–71.

Jensen, M. C. & W. H. Meckling (1976), 'Theory of the firm: managerial behavior, agency costs and ownership structure', *Journal of Financial Economics,* 3 (October), pp. 305–60.

Kothari, S. P. (2001), 'Capital markets research in accounting', *Journal of Accounting and Economics*, 31, pp. 105–231.

Kuhn, T. S. (1962), *The Structure of Scientific Revolutions*, Illinois: University of Chicago Press.

Lakatos, I. & A. Musgrove (1974), *Criticism and the Growth of Knowledge*, Cambridge: Cambridge University Press.

Lang, M. H. & R. J. Lundholm (1996), 'Corporate disclosure policy and analyst behavior', *The Accounting Review*, 71(4), pp. 467–92.

Lee, C. M. C. (2001), 'Market efficiency and accounting research: a discussion of "capital market research in accounting" by S.P. Kothari', *Journal of Accounting and Economics*, 31, pp. 233–53.

Lintner, J. (1965), 'The valuation of risk assets and the selection of risky investments in stock portfolios and capital budgets', *Review of Economics and Statistics*, 47, pp. 13–37.

Penman, S. H. (1980), 'An empirical investigation of the voluntary disclosure of corporate earnings forecasts', *Journal of Accounting Research*, 18(1), pp. 132–60.

Popper, K. R. (1959), *The Logic of Scientific Discovery*, London: Hutchinson.

Sharpe, W. F. (1964), 'Capital asset prices: a review of market equilibrium under conditions of risk', *Journal of Finance*, 19, pp. 425–42.

Skinner, D. J. (1997), 'Earnings disclosures and stockholder lawsuits', *Journal of Accounting and Economics*, 23, pp. 249–282.

Sloan, R. G. (1996), 'Do stock prices fully reflect information in accruals and cash flows about future earnings?', *The Accounting Review*, 71(3), pp. 289–316.

Sterling, R. (1975), 'Towards a science of accounting', *Financial Analysts Journal*.

Watts, R. L. & J. L. Zimmerman (1986), *Positive Accounting Theory*, Englewood Cliffs, NJ: Prentice Hall.

Watts, R. L. & J. L. Zimmerman (1990), 'Positive accounting theory: a ten year perspective', *The Accounting Review*, 65(1), pp. 259–85.

Zhang, I. X. (2007), 'Economic consequences of the Sarbanes—Oxley Act of 2002', *Journal of Accounting and Economics*, 44(1), pp. 74–115.

CHAPTER 11

REACTIONS OF INDIVIDUALS TO FINANCIAL REPORTING: AN EXAMINATION OF BEHAVIOURAL RESEARCH

LEARNING OBJECTIVES

On completing this chapter readers should understand:

- how behavioural research differs from capital markets research;
- how different accounting-related variables can be manipulated in behavioural research;
- how the results of behavioural research can be of relevance to corporations and the accounting profession for anticipating individual reactions to accounting disclosures;
- how the results of behavioural research can form the basis for developing ways to use accounting-related data more efficiently;
- the limitations of behavioural research.

OPENING ISSUES

The accounting profession often considers introducing new regulations relating to the disclosure of new items of information, or specifically requiring information to be disclosed in a particular format. A concern that often arises is how or whether various categories of financial statement users will react to the new disclosures that are potentially going to be mandated, particularly given that new disclosure requirements typically impose costs on those entities required to make the disclosures. How can behavioural research be used to assist the concerns of accounting regulators about financial statement users' reactions to the proposed requirements?

INTRODUCTION

Chapter 10 discussed capital markets research, which considers the *aggregate behaviour* of investors in the capital market. This aggregate behaviour is typically observed by looking at movements in share prices around the time of particular events, such as when earnings announcements are made. Capital markets research does not consider how items of information are actually processed or used by the market participants; it simply looks for a share price reaction.

This chapter considers decision making at the *individual level*. The research, referred to as behavioural research, involves performing studies to see how a variety of financial statement user groups (not just investors, as is the case in capital markets research) react to a variety of accounting information, often presented in different forms and in different contexts. According to Birnberg and Shields (1989, p. 24):

> Behavioural Accounting Research applies theories and methodologies from the behavioural sciences to examine the interface between accounting information and processes and human (including organizational) behaviour.

In previous chapters, theories that seek to explain or predict particular actions, such as the manager's choice of accounting methods, were discussed. Chapter 7, for example, discussed Positive Accounting Theory and agency theory. Economics-based theories such as these make assumptions about what motivates human actions (for example, a quest to maximise personal wealth), and such motivations are attributed to all individuals. By contrast, behavioural research studies individuals' actions and choices and typically does not make broad-based assumptions about how all individuals behave, or about their motivations. Further, behavioural research is typically grounded in organisational theory, and theories from psychology and sociology rather than from economics. However, like theories such as Positive Accounting Theory, Legitimacy Theory and Institutional Theory (discussed in Chapters 7 and 8), behavioural research can be thought of as 'positive research', because it seeks to explain particular actions or behaviours (in contrast to 'normative research', which prescribes how certain activities *should* be undertaken).

By generating knowledge about how different categories of financial statement users (investors, research analysts, auditors, bankers, loan officers and so on) react to particular accounting disclosures, corporations, the accounting profession and regulators (such as the International Accounting Standards Board) will be better placed to *anticipate* how different individuals will react to particular information.

Apart from the anticipatory implications associated with behavioural research, the results of analysis of the decision making processes of individuals can also provide the basis for developing procedures to improve future decision making.

The field of behavioural research can be subdivided into a number of different 'schools'. According to Birnberg and Shields (1989), behavioural research in accounting can be classified into five main branches (or 'schools'):

1. Managerial control. This research considers such issues as the role of budgets in affecting the level of managerial performance and behaviour, the impact of leadership style on managerial performance, the role of feedback on managerial performance, and the impact of different incentives on managerial performance.

2. Accounting information processing. This research considers how users of financial reports process accounting information—often referred to as the human information processing (HIP) branch of behavioural research. This research frequently involves the use of the 'lens model'—something that is discussed in this chapter. The lens model allows the researcher to assess the effects of multiple cues (items of information, for example) on decisions without the need for a prohibitively large number of subjects in a between subjects design (a between subjects design is an experimental design in which each subject is randomly assigned to only one of the treatment conditions).

3. Accounting information system design. This branch of research relates behavioural issues to the design of information systems.

4. Auditing process research. This branch of research often uses the lens model. It delves into the decision–making processes of auditors and covers such issues as what cues an auditor would use in formulating an opinion about financial statements.

5. Organisational sociology. This branch of research investigates changes that may occur in an organisation's accounting system over time, and links changes in accounting systems to particular events.

Not all of these branches of behavioural accounting research are discussed in this chapter. Rather, the chapter concentrates on those areas that are related to individual behaviour with respect to financial accounting (not managerial accounting) information. Thus, the focus is on accounting information processing (human information processing) and auditing process research.

AN OVERVIEW OF BEHAVIOURAL RESEARCH

Chapter 10 considered research that investigated the aggregate reaction of the capital market to various accounting disclosures. This chapter turns to a different approach to research, which considers how *individuals* react to various accounting disclosures. Research that considers how individuals react or behave when provided with particular items of information can be classified *behavioural research*. According to Libby (1975, p. 2), research that attempts to describe individual behaviour is often grounded in a branch of psychology called *behavioural decision theory*, which has its roots in cognitive psychology, economics and statistics. According to Libby (1975, p. 2):

> The goal of much of this work is to describe actual decision behavior, evaluate its quality, and develop and test theories of the underlying psychological processes which produce the behavior. In addition, these descriptions reveal flaws in the behavior and often suggest remedies for these deficiencies.

Behavioural research was first embraced by accounting researchers in the 1960s (Maines, 1995) but became particularly popular in the 1970s when embraced by researchers such as Ashton and Libby. In reflecting on the evolution of behavioural research, Dyckman (1998, p. 1) states:

> While research in behavior is anything but new, it was not until the twentieth century that researchers investigated the behavior of individuals in business organizations. Research into the behavioral impact of what occurs in accounting is an even more recent

phenomenon, traceable perhaps back to the early sixties although the groundwork for much of the early efforts had been laid earlier.

Behavioural research has been used to investigate a variety of decision making processes, such as the valuation of market shares by individual analysts, the lending decisions of loan officers, the assessment of bankruptcy by bankers or auditors, and the assessment of risk by auditors. According to Birnberg and Shields (1989, p. 25):

> The method of systematic observation in behavioural accounting research usually involves the systematic observation of people either in the laboratory or field as opposed to archival data on human behaviour or computer simulation of behaviour.[1] The theories which are used to identify important variables for a study or to explain the behaviours observed are drawn from the behavioural sciences. Thus, behavioural studies can be differentiated from Efficient Markets Research because the latter relies exclusively on archival data and focuses on market forces not individual or group behaviour.

Some of the published behavioural accounting research studies have been undertaken in a laboratory setting, where a group of individuals are assigned a number of simple or complex tasks (which may or may not be reflective of 'real-life' tasks), while other research has been conducted in the individual's own workplace.[2] Behavioural research can have a number of aims. Some research has been undertaken to understand underlying decision making processes, while other research has been conducted to improve decision making. Some research manipulates the amount and types of information provided to particular subjects to assess how such differences impact on any final decisions, while other research provides all subjects with the same information and attempts to derive a model to explain how decisions by a particular category of decision makers appear to be made (for example, decisions by auditors, stockbrokers, bankers or lending officers).

THE BRUNSWIK LENS MODEL

In explaining behavioural research, a number of researchers have found it useful to relate their work to a model developed by Brunswik (1952), the Brunswik Lens Model. Libby (1981, p. 6) provides a simplistic representation of the Lens Model. See Figure 11.1.

According to Birnberg and Shields (1989, p. 45):

> The suggestion that the lens model be adapted to behavioural accounting research from the psychological literature was outlined in the report of the Committee on Accounting Valuation Basis (1972) in a section initially authored by Nick Gonedes. Ashton (1974) discussed the lens model and asked what kinds of phenomena could be examined by the lens model.

---

1   Where data are generated by the researcher, perhaps through an experiment, the data are often labelled 'primary data'. Data that are already available independent of the researcher, from sources such as publicly assessable archives, is referred to as 'secondary data'. Share price data, the subject of Chapter 10, are secondary data.

2   A laboratory setting would constitute a setting different from where the subjects would normally undertake their work and where the researcher is relatively more able to control certain variables relating to the decision-making task than would otherwise be possible.

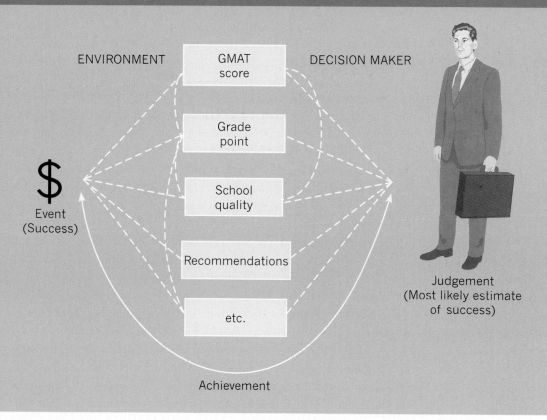

Figure 11.1 A simple diagrammatic representation of the Brunswik Lens Model (after Libby, 1981, p. 5)

ENVIRONMENT   GMAT score   DECISION MAKER

Grade point

School quality

$ Event (Success)

Recommendations

etc.

Achievement

Judgement (Most likely estimate of success)

Libby (1975) was the first to utilise the lens model to look at a user oriented issue, the prediction of corporate failure by loan officers. He developed a model of loan officers' behaviour and examined both the predictability and the stability of their judgements. Libby (1975) served to demonstrate the richness of the lens model and to demonstrate the greater insight into user behaviour available using the lens model compared to the earlier stimulus-response studies. As one might expect, Libby's study led to a series of subsequent studies using the lens model to examine the use of accounting data. The lens model made it possible for the experimenter to examine the patterns of cue utilization by the subjects and in that way begin to investigate what previously had been viewed as a 'black box'.

Libby (1981, p. 5) illustrates the application of the Brunswik Lens Model to the decision by graduate schools to admit students. As indicated in Figure 11.1, the criterion event is the students' future success, denoted by '$' (on the left-hand side of the model). Given that this event will take place in the future, the decisions made by admissions officers within particular schools must be based on a number of factors or environmental 'cues' (pieces of information), which can be probabilistically related to the particular event under consideration (in this case, student success). A number of cues (in this case, items of information) can be used, for example GMAT scores, grade point averages in prior studies, quality of the undergraduate school attended, recommendations or references from various people, whether the individual participates in extracurricular activities and answers to particular subjective questions.[3] As Libby indicates, none of these individual cues, or combinations of cues, can be expected to provide a perfect indication of the future success of the student, but some may be linked, with some degree of probability, to success. In effect, perspectives about the environment (the issue in question in this case being student success) are generated (observed) through a 'lens' of imperfect cues. The relationships between these imperfect cues and the judgement about success are represented by broken lines.[4]

There would also be an expectation that some of the cues will be interrelated. For example, the GMAT score might be expected to be correlated with grade point averages, as well as quality of school attended. Such interrelationships are represented by the broken lines linking the various cues, as indicated in Figure 11.1. To determine the weighting (or importance) of the various cues (independent variables) to the criterion event of success (the dependent variable which could simplistically be categorised as either success or failure in this case), as well as the correlations between the cues, various advanced statistical modelling approaches are applied. One model might be developed that provides a linear representation of the assessors' weightings of the various cues. This then provides a model of how the assessors actually went about their job of assessing applications. Knowledge of this model may be useful to a number of parties. For example, intending students would know what factors (cues) are particularly important to the assessors and hence the students may then know what factors to concentrate on. From the assessors' perspective it might be interesting for them to see how as a group they appear to be making their judgements. This might not be obvious until such a model is developed.

A model could also be developed that looks at the relationship between the actual outcome (student success or failure) and the various items of information available. That is, a model could be developed by looking in the reverse direction from the event (the left-hand side) back to the cues (that is, not involving individuals making judgements). Obviously, such analysis could only be undertaken when a measure of actual success or failure can be obtained.

Libby (1981) provides an insight into the general applicability of the Lens Model to various decision making scenarios. As he states (p. 6):

> This structure is very general and can be applied to almost any decision making scheme. Again, consider a simplified commercial lending decision in which the principal task of the loan officer is to predict loan default. Loan default–non default is mainly a function of the future cash flows which will be available to the customer to service the debt. The customer provides a number of cues, some of which are probabilistically related to future cash flows. These include indicators of liquidity, leverage, and profitability drawn from financial statements, management evaluations resulting from interviews, plant visits, discussions with other knowledgeable parties, and outside credit ratings. No individual cue or combinations of cues is a perfect predictor of future cash flows, and there is overlap in the information (e.g., credit ratings are closely associated with profitability and liquidity measures). In making this judgement, the loan officer combines these cues into a prediction

---

3   As we show later, in an accounting study such as the prediction of bankruptcy the 'cues' might be information about various accounting ratios.

4   Libby (1981, p. 5) notes also that relative reliance on various cues is likely to change over time as a result of fatigue, special circumstances, learning and so on.

of future cash flows. Even if the banker's judgemental policy is highly stable over time, some inconsistencies are likely to arise, which will result in a probabilistic relationship between the cues and the final judgement. At the end of the term of each loan, the officer's prediction of cash flows can be compared with the actual event, and any resulting losses can be computed to measure achievement. While this example is highly simplified, it illustrates the generality of the framework and its importance for accountants. The model's principal concern with information-processing achievements in an uncertain world coincides with accountants' interest in improving the decisions made by users of accounting information and their more recent attention to the quality of their own decisions.

In applying the Lens Model it is common for researchers to model mathematically both the left-hand and right-hand sides of the lens. For example, on the right-hand side of the model we are interested in providing a model (typically linear) of how the individual uses cues to make an ultimate decision about the issue under investigation. This is often the major goal of much behavioural research. This can be undertaken by considering how each particular cue individually relates to the ultimate decision (univariate analysis), or how the entire set of cues relates to the ultimate decision or judgement (multivariate analysis). If statistical regression is undertaken as part of the multivariate analysis, the decision maker's response might be summarised or modelled as follows:[5]

$$\hat{Y}_s = a_s + B_{1s}X_1 + B_{2s}X_2 + \cdots B_{ks}X_k \qquad \text{(Equation 1)}$$

where:

$\hat{Y}_s$ is the model's prediction of the judgement (for example, that the student succeeds or fails) based on the individual's judgements or predictions;

$X_1, X_2, \ldots X_k$ represent the set of cues (for example, the GMAT score, grade point average) for cue number 1 through to cue number k;

$B_1, B_2, \ldots B_k$ represent the weighting in the model given to each of the cues, based on the responses of the subjects.

If a cue contributes nothing to the prediction, it will be given a zero weighting. Conversely, if a particular item of information (cue) is relatively important in making a particular decision or judgment, it will have a greater weighting. Because the model will need to be generated from many observations and because models such as the above assume that individual cues contribute to the decision in a linear manner, it is clear that the model will not explain or predict with total accuracy the actual judgements made by particular individuals. But as we would appreciate, it is not expected to—it is a model of individual behaviour. As Libby states (1981, p. 22):

It is important to note that the algebraic models resulting from these studies simply indicate the functional relationship between the cues and the judgement. These, like all models, are abstractions and do not purport to represent 'real' mental processes.

Some researchers also model the left-hand side of the Lens Model (often referred to as the 'environmental' side), which looks at the relationship between the actual phenomenon under

5   Only a brief overview of this modelling is provided here. For further insight, interested readers are referred to Libby (1981, pp. 19–21) and Trotman (1996, pp. 33–36).

consideration and the particular cues provided. Without relying on judgements provided by individuals, this equation can be used to predict a particular environmental event.[6] The model can be represented as follows:

$$\hat{Y}_e = a_e + B_{1e}X_1 + B_{2e}X_2 + \cdots B_{ke}X_k \qquad \text{(Equation 2)}$$

where:

$\hat{Y}_e$ is the model's prediction of the environmental event under consideration (for example, student succeeds or fails);

$X_1, X_2, \ldots X_k$ represent the set of cues (for example, the GMAT score, grade point average) for cue number 1 through to cue number k;

$B_1, B_2, \ldots B_k$ represent the weighting in the model given to each of the cues, based on the modelling of the relationship between the actual event and the available cues.

Researchers often compare the results of the model derived from studying the decision-making processes of individuals (Equation 1) with the results of the model provided by considering the relationship of the actual environmental event and the various cues (Equation 2). As we will see below, other issues focused on by researchers include how different individuals or groups weight particular cues, the consistency (or stability) of the weighting, what issues associated with the presentation format of the cues might influence factor usage and weighting, and so on.

Because the Lens Model generates an explanation that is in the form of an equation (see above), there is an implicit assumption that all relevant factors are considered simultaneously, rather than sequentially. In reality, individuals might not consider information simultaneously, but would consider particular information cues before moving on to other items of information.[7]

The Lens Model can be used to categorise a great deal of the behavioural research that has been undertaken over the last twenty to thirty years. The Lens Model explicitly considers *inputs* (uses of various cues), the *decision process* and *outputs* (ultimate decisions). Libby (1981, p. 8) provides a summary of the type of issues that can be considered when undertaking research about how individuals process information when making a decision. These issues include:

At the *input* level (that is, issues pertaining to the cues):

- scaling characteristics of individual cues (for example, whether the presentation of the cues as nominal, ordinal, discrete, continuous, deterministic or probabilistic influences whether the cues are used in making a decision);
- method of presentation (for example, does the presentational format appear to impact on the use of the cue(s));
- context (for example, do perceived rewards, social setting and so on seem to impact on the use of the various cues).

---

6   For example, Altman (1968) developed a bankruptcy prediction model by forming equations that related a particular environmental event (bankruptcy) with particular financial variables (derived from financial statements). Representative of modelling the left-hand side of the 'lens', no use was made of decisions of individual judges or experts.

7   Later in the chapter, protocol analysis is considered, which requires subjects of an experiment to 'think aloud' about how they make decisions. This research method would help to identify the sequence of how individuals process information.

At the level of *processing* the information:

- characteristics of the person making the judgement (for example, whether the demographics, attitudes of the judge or the level of prior experience or interest impact on the decision that is made);
- characteristics of the decision rule (for example, how the individuals weight the cues, whether the judgements are stable over time, whether the judges use any simplifying heuristics when presented with potentially complex data).

At the *output* or decision level:

- qualities of the judgement (whether the response is accurate, quick or reliable, whether it incorporates particular biases, whether the judgements are consistent over time, whether there is consensus between the various judges);
- self-insight (whether the judge is aware of how he/she appears to weight various factors, etc.). The results of the research may provide individuals with insights about their decision-making processes that they were previously unaware of.

THE USE OF PARTICULAR INFORMATION ITEMS AND THE IMPLICATIONS OF DIFFERENT FORMS OF PRESENTATION

At the input level, the issue of how and whether particular cues (information items) are used in decision making is particularly relevant to the accounting profession. If it is shown that users of financial statements do not use particular information items (cues), it could be deemed that such information is not *material* and hence does not require disclosure or associated disclosure regulation. Alternatively, it could indicate that users of financial statements do not know how to use particular information, which might indicate some needs for education. The accounting profession would also be particularly interested in whether the form of disclosure (for example, whether an item is provided in the statement of financial position, in a supplementary financial statement or in a footnote) impacts on users' decisions. We now consider a limited number of papers that have considered such issues.[8]

In relation to the use of particular items of accounting information, Pankoff and Virgil (1970) investigated financial analysts' predictions of financial returns on particular shares. They found that the analysts acquired earnings and sales information (often through purchasing such information) more often than other types of information. In another study of financial analysts' information demands (cue usage) Mear and Firth (1987) also found that analysts believed that sales growth and profitability were particularly important for estimating returns on particular securities.

From time to time accounting professions throughout the world consider whether they should require reporting entities to provide additional information as a supplement to existing

---

8   The overview of research provided in this chapter is certainly not comprehensive. Rather, the intention is to provide an insight into some of the different research that has been undertaken in the area. For those readers desiring a more comprehensive insight, reference could be made to Libby (1981), Ashton (1982), Ashton and Ashton (1995) and Trotman (1996).

financial information. One particular instance of this was the accounting profession's move in the 1980s to require supplementary current cost (inflation-adjusted) financial information to be disclosed in corporate annual reports. Clearly, research can be useful in providing an insight into how and whether current cost information would actually be used by readers of annual reports.[9] Such research includes that undertaken by Heintz (1973) and McIntyre (1973). These studies examined how three forms of disclosure impacted on investment decisions. Subjects were provided with either historical cost information (only), current cost information (only), or both current cost and historical cost information. The results generally questioned the provision of current cost information, as the subjects did not appear to alter their decisions as a result of being provided with current cost information. Such results obviously challenged the accounting profession's move to require supplementary current cost information.[10]

Behavioural research has also been undertaken in human resource accounting, an area that has been typically neglected by the accounting profession. In related research, both Elias (1972) and Hendricks (1976) found that the disclosure of information on costs incurred in relation to recruiting, training and personnel development had an impact on subjects' decisions about acquiring shares in particular sample companies. It could be imagined that such results, particularly if replicated across a number of studies, would potentially act as a stimulus for the accounting profession to put such issues on their agenda for consideration. In the absence of this type of research, the accounting profession might be ignorant of the fact that people would actually use such information if it were provided.

In relation to the *format of presentation*, some studies have found that different presentation formats seem to impact on users' decisions. For example, some researchers have investigated how the presentation of particular graphics, such as the inclusion of bar charts, line graphs, pie charts and tables, impact on the decisions of different user groups (Davis, 1989; DeSanctis & Jarvenpaa, 1989). In a famous piece of research, Moriarity (1979) examined whether the accuracy of subjects' (students and accounting practitioners) judgements pertaining to potential bankruptcy of merchandising firms was affected by whether they were given a number of financial ratios or were provided with a series of schematic faces (referred to as 'Chernoff' faces; see Chernoff & Rizvi, 1975), where the faces themselves were constructed on the basis of the various ratios. Depending on the ratios, different facial features were provided (mouth shape, angle of the eyebrow, nose length and so on represented changes in ratios). The findings of the research indicated that the students and accountants using the faces outperformed those using ratios in predicting bankruptcy. Further, the subjects using the faces were able to outperform models of bankruptcy that had been developed by other researchers (for example, Altman, 1968).

---

9   Also, behavioural research relating to reactions to particular disclosures can be done in advance of an accounting requirement being introduced. On the basis of the behavioural research findings, accounting regulators might determine that there is no point in progressing a particular issue past its initial stages of development. This can be contrasted with capital markets research which relies on historical share price data—data that capture how the market actually reacted to the implementation or formal proposal of the particular requirement.

10 Chapter 7 discussed research that investigated the incentives for managers to lobby in support of and/or potentially to adopt general price level accounting (which, like current cost accounting, adjusts historical cost accounting information to take account of rising prices). Specifically, it considered Watts and Zimmerman (1978). This research applied economic-based theory to explain lobbying positions of individuals. It did not directly involve any human subjects in the experimentation. Other research has considered how capital markets react to current cost information by investigating share price changes around the time of the information disclosure (for example, Lobo & Song, 1989). What is being emphasised here is that there is a variety of approaches that can be taken to investigate particular phenomena.

The potential implications of this research are interesting. On the basis of the results, companies perhaps should provide numerous cartoon-like faces in their annual reports if they want to assist people in their decision-making processes (perhaps the accounting profession might release an accounting standard on drawing faces?). However, to date, the disclosure of faces in annual reports is not an approach adopted by corporate management.

Another disclosure issue that has been addressed is whether subjects will make different decisions depending on whether particular information is incorporated within the financial statements themselves or included in footnotes only. One study that investigated this issue was by Wilkins and Zimmer (1983). They studied the decisions of bank lending officers and how their decisions were influenced by whether information about leases was incorporated in the financial statements or simply provided in the footnotes. They found that from the lending officers' perspective the format of disclosure did not affect their assessment of the entity's ability to repay a debt. Again, such evidence should be of potential interest to the accounting profession when deciding whether to mandate adoption of particular accounting methods within the financial statements or simply within the footnotes to those accounts.[11]

Research has also investigated whether the disclosure of segmental information will impact on the decisions of particular individuals. For example, Stallman (1969) found that providing information about industry segments reduced the subjects' reliance on past share prices when making choices to select particular securities. Doupnik and Rolfe (1989) found that subjects were more confident in making assessments about future prices of an entity's shares when they were also provided with information about geographical performance.

Another issue often addressed in behavioural research is the issue of 'information overload'. It has been found that increasing the amount of information (cues) provided to individuals can improve the quality of decision making to a point, beyond which the introduction of additional cues can actually lead to a reduction in the quality of the decisions being made (Snowball, 1980).

Chapter 9 addressed an area of reporting that is attracting attention, sustainability (social and environmental) reporting. Because of the growing importance of information about the social and environmental performance of organisations, it could be anticipated that accounting researchers will explore how various information cues influence environmentally and socially related activities. In this regard, consider research undertaken by Wood and Ross (2006). These authors explored how particular 'environmental social controls' can affect managers' capital investment decisions with respect to investing in less-polluting plant and equipment. The environmental social controls that were examined for their impact on capital investment decisions were:

- mandatory disclosure, meaning environmental disclosure required by law and accounting standards;
- regulatory costs, meaning direct payments on pollutant emissions, clean-up costs and/or regulatory compliance;

---

11 Consistent with a great deal of behavioural research, the results of Wilkins and Zimmer were contradicted by other research. For example, Sami and Schwartz (1992) provided evidence that loan officers' judgements about an entity's ability to repay a debt were influenced by whether information about pension liabilities was included in the financial statements or in the footnotes. However, because this research relates to pension liabilities, it is not clear whether the results contradict a general notion that users can equate information provided by way of footnote disclosure with information provided by financial statement disclosure, or whether the differences in the respective studies' results were due to the fact that one study considered pension liabilities while the other study considered lease liabilities.

- subsidisation, meaning depreciation allowances that provide higher tax benefits;
- stakeholder opinion, meaning how the investment will be perceived by various non-government stakeholder groups such as shareholders, creditors and customers.

In their experiment, which was undertaken using corporate financial managers, the four 'environmental social controls' (mandatory disclosure, regulatory costs, depreciation allowances and stakeholder opinion) were varied to gauge their influence on the managers' capital investment in less-polluting plant and machinery. The results of the study indicated that stakeholder opinion was the most influential factor in management decisions to invest in 'environmentally friendly' plant and equipment, followed by subsidisation. Regulatory costs ranked third, while mandatory disclosure was quite lowly rated and was ranked fourth. In discussing the results, Wood and Ross (2006, p. 691) state:

> Stakeholder opinion is a very important social control, with approximately 40 per cent of the combined weight of the environmental social controls. This suggests that managers are much more responsive to stakeholder opinion than they are to regulatory costs, subsidy or mandatory disclosure.

In considering the implications of their study for government action, Wood and Ross (p. 692) state:

> Subsidisation, the 'carrot' among social controls, was found to be an influential factor, with a weighting of 27 per cent. This was second only to stakeholder opinion. The relatively high level responsiveness of managers to change in the level of subsidy suggests that managers would be very responsive to increased subsidisation. This finding adds support to the suggestion in the published literature (Lockhart, 1997; EPA (South Australia), 2001) that subsidies can be very effective as an incentive for environmental improvement. The experiment adds support to the conclusion that there is room for increased use of subsidisation. Some (or all) of the cost to government might be offset by increased tax receipts from higher profits made by firms, savings in the cost of 'policing' of small firms, and reduction in environmental damage.

While the above examples of behavioural research provide only a small snapshot of the total research that is available, they nevertheless provide an insight into how researchers can manipulate various items (or cues) to see how this impacts on particular decisions. The results of such research are valuable for understanding and potentially improving particular decision-making processes.

DECISION-MAKING PROCESSES AND THE USE OF HEURISTICS

In relation to research that considers the processes involved in making a judgement (the middle part of the Lens Model), a number of studies have considered issues associated with how the various cues (information items) are weighted. Schultz and Gustavson (1978) used actuaries as subjects (who were deemed to be experts) to develop a model to measure the litigation risk of accounting firms. They found that cues deemed to be important (relatively more weighted) were the number of accountants employed within the firm, the extent to which the work of the accountants was rotated among themselves, the size and financial condition of the clients and the percentage of 'write-up' work performed.[12]

Another issue that has been considered is *consistency*. For example, do the individuals make the same judgements over time? Ashton (1974) investigated this issue. Ashton used sixty-three practising auditors in a study that required the auditors to assess the internal control system associated with an organisation's payroll. In undertaking the assessment, the subjects were required to do the task twice, the second time being between six and thirteen weeks after the first time. The findings indicated that the subjects were very consistent in their weightings over time and that the weightings between the various subjects were quite consistent. Further, the cue that was weighted the most was 'separation of duties'.

When considering how individuals make decisions, researchers have also found evidence that decision makers often appear to employ simplifying heuristics when making a decision.[13] Tversky and Kahneman (1974) identified three main heuristics often employed in decision making: representativeness, anchoring and adjustment, and availability.

According to Maines (1995, p. 83), individuals who use the *representativeness heuristic* assess the likelihood of items belonging to a category by considering how similar the item is to the typical member of this category. For example, the probability that a certain person is an accountant would be assessed by how closely he or she resembles the image of a typical accountant. The fact that there may be few or many accountants is ignored. An implication of this bias is that individuals typically ignore the base rate of the population in question. In some cases this bias has the effect of overstating the number of cases placed within a particular category. For example, in bankruptcy prediction studies, this bias may lead to an overstatement in the prediction of bankrupt firms as the base rate of real bankrupt firms is typically quite low.

The *anchoring and adjustment heuristic* indicates that individuals often make an initial judgement or estimate (perhaps based on past experience or through partial computation of the various factors involved) and then only partially adjust their view as a result of access to additional information. That is, they 'anchor' on a particular view and then will not move sufficiently in the light of additional information or changing circumstances. Joyce and Biddle (1981) undertook research that sought to provide evidence of this heuristic being used by auditors when they assess internal control systems. They found that new information (obtained through various substantive testing) was used by auditors to revise their assessments about the quality of internal controls, and that no evidence could be found of anchoring and adjustment. However, results of anchoring and adjustment were found when Kinney and Ueker (1982) investigated similar tasks. Other research to support the use of this heuristic is provided in Biggs and Wild (1985) and Butler (1986).

The *availability heuristic* relates to whether recollections of related occurrences and events can easily come to mind. That is, the probability judgements regarding the occurrence of an event are influenced by the ease with which the particular type of event can be recalled (Maines, 1995, p. 100). For example, in assessing the likelihood of a plane crash, a subject might overstate the

---

12 Another approach to gathering such information would simply be to send out questionnaires asking respondents to rank the importance of various items of information in terms of the various decisions they make. Of course, this would be much simpler than a process involving the actual modelling of decision making, which typically occurs in Lens Model–type research.

13 A heuristic can be defined as a simplifying 'rule of thumb'. That is, rather than fully considering all the potentially relevant factors, a simplifying rule may be employed which takes a lot less time but nevertheless generates a fairly acceptable (and cost-effective) prediction or solution.

probability as a result of remembering a number of highly publicised crashes. The actual base rates of such an occurrence are ignored. In a study of this heuristic, Moser (1989) found that when subjects were required to make an assessment about whether the earnings of a company would increase, their assessments were influenced by the order of the information provided to them.

A number of heuristics, or rules of thumb, that might be employed in decision making have been briefly considered. But, *so what?* Why would it be useful to know about such heuristics? First, if the heuristic results in inappropriate decisions being made (for example, lending funds to organisations that are not creditworthy, or accepting that internal controls are functioning soundly when they are not), this behavioural tendency should be highlighted so that remedial action (perhaps training) can be undertaken.[14] Second, perhaps the heuristic employed by particular experts are efficient relative to costly data gathering and processing. If this is the case, perhaps novices should be encouraged to adopt the rule of thumb.

Just as decision making undertaken by individuals within an organisation might show particular biases, such as those described above, so might the decision making of investors. As one particular example, investors might have a tendency to hold loss-making shares for too long when things are not going well, or they may have a tendency to sell 'winning' shares too early and thereby miss out on larger gains. Behavioural research could be used to investigate such investor tendencies (and many others). For example, Krishnan and Booker (2002) investigated the existence of a 'disposition effect' in relation to investor choices.[15] They state (p. 130):

> Prior research in finance and economics has documented the presence of a 'disposition effect', that is, the tendency for investors to sell winning stock too early and hold losing stocks too long. The disposition effect is an application of prospect theory (Kahneman and Tversky 1979) to investments and predicts that investors are risk-averse in gains and risk-seeking in losses. Hence, they will sell a winning stock so as to cash in on their sure gains and hold on to a losing stock in order to avoid a sure loss. Empirical support for the disposition effect has been found in financial markets (Shefrin and Statman 1985; Ferris et al. 1988; Odean 1998) and experimental markets (Weber and Camerer 1998). We examine if executive subjects commit the disposition error and then examine whether the availability of an analyst summary recommendation report reduces the occurrence of the disposition error. We also examine if the reduction in the disposition error is a function of the strength of supporting arguments in the analysts' summary recommendation report.

For the purposes of Krishnan and Booker's research an 'analysts' summary recommendation' is a report that contains the average recommendation of several analysts to either buy (if the future prospects seem favourable), hold (if the future prospects seem marginally favourable) or sell (if the future prospects seem unfavourable), and some supporting arguments. The investor

---

14 For example, Kida (1984) provides evidence that auditors when undertaking particular tasks often initially formulate a hypothesis to explain a certain event (for example, the reduction in bad debt write-offs) and then seek information to confirm this hypothesis (hypothesis-confirming strategies). Clearly, such information gathering is not objective and could expose the auditors to certain risks. Knowledge of this behavioural tendency would therefore be useful.

15 In their study they actually used MBA students as surrogates for investors. They justified using MBA students as the subjects of their experiment because the MBA students were deemed likely to have had prior investing experience and would have read analyst reports.

evaluates the report and decides to buy, hold or sell the stock. The researchers vary the strength of the recommendations given to different subjects and the researchers predict that the strength of the supporting arguments provided with the analysts' report will mitigate the disposition effect by motivating investors to act in a manner consistent with the analysts' recommendations (that is, to sell losing stocks and hold winning stocks). In explaining how they conducted their behavioural experiment, Krishnan and Booker (2002, p. 136) state:

In the first experiment, we examine subjects' likelihood to sell or hold a stock on which they have a paper gain or loss position, when presented with a simple favorable or unfavorable future scenario in the absence of analysts' recommendations. This experiment provides a benchmark to measure the extent of the disposition error. In the second experiment, we present information about a stock with expected values identical to the stock in Experiment 1, in the form of a summary analyst recommendation report. One-half of the subjects in Experiment 2 receive a 'weak' form of analysts' recommendations, i.e., with no supporting information, while the second half of the subjects receive a 'strong' form of analysts' recommendations, i.e., with supporting information.[16] The second experiment allows us to examine whether the presence of an analysts' summary recommendation report has any influence on subjects' decisions. It also allows us to examine whether the strength of the analysts' summary recommendation report has any effect on subjects' decisions.

In relation to the results of their study, Krishnan and Booker (2002, p. 131) state:

Our results indicate that information presented in the form of a summary report of analysts' recommendations reduces the disposition error for winning stocks. That is, when subjects receive information about the future prospects of a stock, and the information is not presented in the form of a summary analyst recommendation report, subjects commit the disposition error and sell winning stocks too early and hold losers too long. However, when information about a stock with identical expected values is presented in the form of a summary analyst report, the disposition error is reduced for the winning stocks but not for losing stocks. Our findings also suggest that the strength of information disclosed in analysts' recommendations affects the tendency for subjects to sell winners too soon and hold losers too long. A strong form of the summary analyst report (i.e., with supporting information used by the analysts to arrive at the stock judgment) further reduced the disposition error for winning stocks. For losing stocks, a weak-summary recommendation report did not reduce the dispositional tendency to hold. However, a strong summary recommendation report significantly reduced the tendency to hold. It appears that individuals have a much greater desire to avoid losses and that this 'loss aversion' is adequately mitigated only by a strong analyst summary recommendation report. Our study demonstrates that summary analysts' reports are not only valuable for their information content, but also as instruments that reduce judgment errors and that this error-reduction property is enhanced by greater detail and strength of arguments in the summary analysts' report.

---

16 Strength of the recommendation was manipulated via an additional paragraph that provided either supporting information for the recommendation (strong) or no details for the recommendation (weak).

In reflecting on the implications of their study, Krishnan and Booker (2002, p. 150) state:

This study contributes to the literature on investors' use of analyst recommendations in several ways. First, it shows that subjects' acting in the absence of summary analyst recommendations expressed likelihood to sell winning stocks too early and hold losing stock for too long. These 'noise traders' with common judgmental biases can affect stock prices (De Long et al. 1989). Second, it finds that the mere presence of summary analyst recommendations reduces the level of the disposition error for winning stocks. Thus, even the use of a weak analyst recommendation may reduce the irrational behavior of selling winning stocks too early. Third, we show that subjects pay attention to and appeared persuaded by supporting arguments to the analyst recommendation. Thus, the availability of strong analyst recommendations with supplementary information reduces the likelihood to sell winning stock too early and hold losers too long. The implications of our findings may extend beyond the current setting to error reduction properties of accounting disclosures in general.

Accounting Headline 11.1 is a newspaper article that discusses some of the common ways people act in relation to buying and selling securities. The information in the article was based on findings generated through behavioural research, and the findings question some common assumptions made in much of the economics literature (for example, that individuals are risk averse). The article also refers to heuristics such as 'anchoring' and how this can distort our decision-making processes. The article concludes with the view that if we can predict how people will behave, even if it appears to be irrational, we can use that knowledge to our own financial benefit.

ISSUES OF DECISION ACCURACY

When looking at the actual *output* of the decision-making process (the decision or judgement), some research has considered how *accurate* the predictions are relative to the actual environmental outcomes. For example, Libby (1975) investigated the accuracy with which loan officers predict business failure. The results showed that loan officers were able to predict bankruptcies fairly regularly, with their various answers also being relatively consistent.

In a similar study, Zimmer (1980) investigated how accurate bankers and accounting students were in predicting bankruptcy when provided with a number of accounting-related cues. The results showed that bankruptcies were typically correctly predicted. Also, a composite model of bankruptcy prediction generated from pooling all the bankers' responses typically outperformed the judgements of individuals.[17] A particularly interesting finding was that the students with limited experience performed nearly as well as the bankers.

Research has also considered the potential improvements to decision making that might result from combining the decisions of multiple decision makers. As noted above, Zimmer (1980) found

---

17 As the composite model out-predicted the individuals, there could be a case to make the model available to the lending officers, particularly the inexperienced bankers. The model could provide a low-cost approach to screening loan applications at the initial stages of the application.

Road to wealth may lie in marching out of step

ROSS GITTINS

Sydney Morning Herald, 30 September 2006, p. 38

If the price of a share you owned fell below what you'd paid for it, would that make you more likely or less likely to want to sell it?

One company's profits have been buoyant in recent times, whereas another company hasn't been doing at all well. Which company's shares would you be more inclined to buy?

If in answer to the first question you said you'd be less likely to want to sell a share that had fallen below what you paid for it, congratulations—you're normal.

Unfortunately, you're also sadly misguided. That fact should have no bearing on your decisions about whether to sell the share.

Why not? Because what you paid for a share is in the past. There's nothing you can do to change it, so you should ignore it. It's what economists call a 'sunk cost' and what accountants call 'irrelevant information'.

The point is that the only thing you can hope to influence is the future, so that's what you should focus on. And the question you should ask yourself is this: do I know of any other share (or other investment) that offers a better prospect of gain than the share I've got my money in now?

If so, sell the old one and buy the new one. If not, stick with the old one. If there isn't a lot in it, sit tight—because you pay brokerage fees every time you change horses.

But why do so many investors find it so hard to live by that simple rule? Why do we find it so hard to ignore what we paid for our T2 Telstra shares, for instance?

Well, as we're reminded in an interesting little booklet from JP Morgan Asset Management, *A Primer in Behavioural Finance Theory*, these are the sort of ques-

tions that specialists in 'behavioural finance' seek to answer.

The two American psychologists who pioneered this school of thought, Daniel Kahneman and Amos Tversky, discovered almost 30 years ago that losses create much more distress among investors (and ordinary consumers) than the happiness created by equivalent gains.

Whereas conventional economists believe people are 'risk averse', it's more accurate to say most people are 'loss averse'. They're highly reluctant to crystallise a paper loss by selling up and, in fact, often are willing to take more risks to avoid losses than to realise gains.

The behavioural finance specialist Professor Terrance Odean examined data on the whole of the Taiwanese sharemarket and found that, similar to previous studies, people were four times more likely to sell a winner than a loser.

He also looked at investors who repurchased shares they'd previously owned and found they were much more likely to repurchase a stock they sold for a gain than for a loss.

Our obsession with the price we paid for shares is a specific instance of a wider behavioural bias psychologists call 'anchoring'—we make decisions based on a single fact or figure that should have little bearing on the decision.

Salespeople often exploit our tendency to focus on figures of limited relevance. Car salespeople, for example, may anchor their prospective buyers to a vehicle's sticker price.

Bargaining with the buyer and slowly lowering that price makes the buyer think they're getting a good deal. But the sticker price

may have been deliberately set too high.

The JP Morgan booklet says even experienced investment analysts can be guilty of anchoring. When faced with new information that contradicts their forecast, they tend to dismiss it as a short-term phenomenon.

This is in direct contradiction to conventional finance theory—the 'efficient market hypothesis'—which holds that all new information is almost instantly incorporated into the market and reflected in share prices.

OK, let's turn to the second question: more inclined to buy the share of a buoyantly profitable company or one that hasn't been doing so well?

Of course you'd buy the one that had been doing well. And, simply because so many other people act that way, it's a pretty good bet you'd be rewarded by seeing the price of the share keep rising after you'd bought it.

The efficient market hypothesis holds that, because all new information is immediately incorporated into a share's price, and because we don't know whether the next bit of information to come along will be good or bad, it's impossible to predict whether the next move in a share's price will be up or down.

But the behavioural finance people had disproved that contention, demonstrating that if a share price has been rising, it's more likely to rise further than to fall back. Similarly, if it's been falling, it's more likely to keep falling.

In other words, share prices tend to develop momentum. And the market contains a lot of 'momentum

(continued)

traders' who follow a policy of buying shares whose price is rising and selling shares whose price is falling.

But going along for the ride will benefit you only in the short term. Longer term, it's quite likely that a share whose price has risen a long way because everyone's been piling into it may by now be overvalued.

Similarly, a share whose price has fallen a long way may by now be undervalued—and so represents good buying.

Studies show that shares with a low P/E (ratio of price to earnings) tend to outperform those with a high P/E. (They get a low P/E by being undervalued and a high P/E by being overvalued.)

And then you have that familiar statutory warning—'past performance is no guarantee of future performance'—we all keep forgetting to heed.

Just because a company's had a good run of profits lately doesn't mean the good run's likely to continue.

And just because another company's had a bad run lately doesn't mean the bad run's likely to continue.

Indeed, there's a statistical phenomenon called 'reversion to the mean' which says an exceptionally good run is more likely to be followed by a weak performance, while an exceptionally bad run is more likely to be followed by a strong performance.

Why? Because, in the end, most things tend to average out.

JP Morgan's point about behavioural finance is that, because so many investors act irrationally, but in systematic and hence predictable ways, there ought to be ways for the better-informed investor to make a quid out of second-guessing them.

that the composite model developed by combining the judgements of the different subjects was able to outperform judgements and models derived from individual subjects. Such findings are also presented in Libby (1976). Further, evidence indicates that decision makers working together in an interactive team can also outperform individuals working alone. Chalos (1985) found this result when reviewing the bankruptcy predictions of interacting loan officers relative to predictions provided by loan officers working independently. Such results were subsequently explained by Chalos and Pickard (1985) as being due to the greater consistency in decision making that happens when groups, as opposed to individuals, are involved in making decisions. Again, these findings have implications for how organisations might make decisions in practice. Perhaps when major loans are being made, and assuming that these results are perceived as being reliable, banks should consider requiring approvals to be based on committee decisions.

PROTOCOL ANALYSIS

Another approach to researching the decision-making processes at the individual level is research undertaken using *verbal protocol analysis*. This form of analysis usually requires subjects to think aloud (that is, to verbalise their thought processes) while they are making decisions or judgements. The subjects' comments are taped and then transcribed for further coding and analysis.[18] This form of research has tended to be more popular in auditing than in other financial

---

18 This form of data collection can sometimes lead to many hundreds of pages of typed quotes which can tend to become quite unmanageable. There are a number of computer packages available to organise transcribed data into a more manageable form. One such package is NUD*IST, which stands for non-numerical, unstructured, data indexing, searching and theorising. Another package is NVivo. (NVivo is not an acronym, but is based around the term 'in vivo', which means it is done in real life.)

accounting areas. One of the first studies using this method was undertaken by Biggs and Mock (1983), who reviewed judgements being made by auditors when assessing internal controls. Other auditing-based studies to use verbal protocol analysis include Biggs, Mock and Watkins (1989) and Bedard and Biggs (1991).

According to Trotman (1996), there are a number of advantages and disadvantages in the use of protocol analysis. In relation to possible advantages, he states (p. 56):

> One of the main advantages of verbal protocol analysis is the ability to examine the process by which judgements are made. Understanding how judgements are made is an important start in improving those judgements. Second, verbal protocols are particularly useful in examining information search. The sequence in which information is obtained can be traced and the amount of time a subject devotes to particular cues can be determined. Third, verbal protocol can be useful in theory development. For example, Biggs, Mock and Watkins (1989) suggest the need to 'begin gathering data about how auditors make analytical review judgements in realistic settings and attempt to build a new theory from the results' (p. 16).

In relation to some of the potential disadvantages or limitations that arise from using verbal protocol analysis, Trotman states (p. 56):

> Consistent with all other methods of studying auditor judgements, verbal protocol studies have a number of limitations. First, it has been noted that the process of verbalising can have an effect on the auditors' decision process (Boritz, 1986). Second, there is an incompleteness argument (Klersy and Mock, 1989) which suggests that a considerable portion of the information utilised by the subjects may not be verbalised. Third, some have described the process as epiphenomenal, that is, subjects provide verbalisations which parallel but are independent of the actual thought process. Fourth, there has been some criticism of the coding methods. For example, Libby (1981) notes that the choice of coding categories, the choice of phrases that serve as the unit of analysis, and the assignment of each phrase to categories are highly subjective. Libby suggests the need for comparisons using competing coding schemes. Finally, there are significant difficulties in communicating the results to the reader, given the large quantity of data and possibly large individual variations in decision processes.

Trotman has provided a number of limitations in relation to protocol analysis which, as he indicates, can also be applied to behavioural research in general. This discussion on behavioural research concludes by considering some of these limitations further (following a brief consideration of 'culture').

THE RELEVANCE OF DIFFERENCES IN CULTURE

The issue of 'culture' was considered in Chapter 4, where it was seen that culture can influence the accounting information being demanded and produced in different countries. It was argued that efforts to standardise financial accounting internationally ignore research that suggests that different cultures have different financial information demands and expectations. Some cultures, for example, are considered to be more secretive than others, some cultures seek greater uncertainty avoidance than others, and so forth. These differences at a national level were then related back to the international differences in accounting practices that existed prior to the international adoption of International Financial Reporting Standards issued by the IASB (Gray, 1988). Culture has also been suggested as a factor in influencing organisational structures, legal systems and so on. Given a view that differences in culture influence the cognitive functioning of individuals (Triandis, Malpass & Davidson, 1971), it is reasonable to argue that an individual's use of particular cues (information items) will in part be dependent on the cultural background of the individual. Hence, although issues of culture have not been considered in this chapter so far, it is reasonable to expect that studies that investigate decision-making processes in particular countries will not necessarily be generalisable to other countries—particularly if the respective countries have significantly different cultural attributes. Determining the validity of a particular decision-making model across different cultures would be an important area for future accounting research. At this point in time there is little behavioural accounting research that explores how the usage of cues in particular decisions is affected by specific cultural attributes.

LIMITATIONS OF BEHAVIOURAL RESEARCH

First, as indicated in some of the material presented in this chapter, many of the studies that review similar issues generate conflicting results. This clearly has implications for whether the research can confidently provide guidance in particular areas. Unfortunately, it is often difficult or impossible to determine what causes the inconsistencies in the various results, because typically a number of variables differ between the studies (the issue of concern, the realism of the setting, the experience and background of the subjects, the incentives provided and so on). Further, within the studies, differences in judgements between the subjects are frequently not explored to any extent, meaning that some unknown but potentially important decision-making factor remains unknown.

Another perceived limitation relates to the settings in which the research is undertaken. These settings are quite often very different from real-world settings, with obvious implications for the generalisability of the findings. In the 'real world' there would typically be real incentives to make particular decisions and real and ongoing implications from them, and this usually cannot be replicated in a laboratory setting.[19] Further, there will be no real accountability for the decisions being made.

---

19 Interestingly, at one meeting of professional accountants held in Sydney some time ago (attended by the author) some researchers made use of the assembled attendees to undertake an experiment related to interactive judgements and their impact on bankruptcy prediction tasks. In an attempt to provide an 'incentive' (perhaps in an effort to increase the 'realism' of the task) at the commencement of the task the subjects were told that each member of the 'winning team' was to be provided with a bottle of fine Scotch whisky. Clearly this is an imperfect incentive and might actually introduce other unwanted factors into the analysis. For example, people with a 'drinking problem' might find this a tremendous incentive and really try hard to win. Others might be fairly indifferent, whereas others, perhaps with a religious objection to alcohol, might actually make judgements that guarantee that they and their team mates will not 'win'. What this indicates is that when offering incentives to increase the realism of a task, great care needs to be taken in selecting appropriate incentives.

Related to this point is the realism of the cues provided to the subjects. It is very difficult to replicate the various cues that would typically be available in the workplace. Also, knowing that the results of a particular judgement are being carefully scrutinised could clearly be expected to have an effect on the decision-making processes being employed.

A number of studies use students as surrogates for auditors, investors, lending officers and so on. This has also been seen as a limitation, because such people may have had limited training in the area and may not have had the same background experiences as the parties for whom they are acting as proxies. (There has been some research that shows that students do make judgements comparable to those of particular experts; however, such findings are not universal.)

A final criticism is the typically small number of subjects used in experiments and, again, whether results based on relatively small samples can be expected to apply to the larger population.

What still appears to be lacking in this area of research is a theory as to why people rely on particular items of information, adopt simplifying heuristics in some situations, and so on. For example, much of the research tells us that some decision makers were consistent in their judgements while others were not, or that particular groups seemed to adopt a particular heuristic. But it is still not certain why they did this. Perhaps theory will develop in this area. It is perhaps not surprising that behavioural accounting research is not grounded in a particular underlying theory. Unlike capital markets researchers (Chapter 10) and Positive Accounting theorists (Chapter 7), who have theories that are generated from particular fields of economics, behavioural accounting researchers embrace a variety of theoretical backgrounds, from psychology, sociology and so on.

CHAPTER SUMMARY

This chapter considered how individuals use information to make decisions. More specifically, it considered how individuals use accounting information to make a variety of judgements. Research pertaining to individual decision making (behavioural research) has shed a great deal of light on how various groups of individuals such as auditors, lending officers and bankers make decisions. Financial statement users often employ simplifying heuristics when making particular judgements. The perspective taken is that if it is known how individuals appear to make decisions it can be anticipated how they will react to particular accounting disclosures and forms of disclosures. This could be particularly relevant to the accounting profession and accounting regulators when contemplating the introduction of a new accounting requirement. Knowledge of how financial statement users make decisions could also provide the basis for making suggestions about how decision making could be improved. (For example, it might be found that certain financial statement users are inappropriately adopting particular heuristics, possibly unknowingly, that could lead to potentially costly implications.)

QUESTIONS

11.1 Contrast behavioural research with capital markets research.

11.2 How and why would the accounting profession use the results of behavioural research in accounting?

11.3 Why would the management of individual reporting entities be interested in the results of behavioural research in accounting?

11.4 Briefly explain the Brunswik Lens Model and its relevance to explaining the various facets of the decision-making process.

11.5 What is a 'heuristic' and why could it be beneficial for a group of financial statement users to be informed that they are applying a particular heuristic?

11.6 What is the point of modelling the decision-making processes of different financial statement user groups (that is, for example, identifying how they appear to weight particular cues when making judgements)?

11.7 If the results of behavioural research indicate that a particular accounting-related information item (cue) is not used by individuals when making decisions, should this be grounds for the accounting profession to conclude that such information is not material and therefore does not warrant the related development of mandatory disclosure requirements? Explain your answer.

11.8 There have been a number of behavioural studies in financial accounting and auditing that have generated conflicting results. What are some possible reasons for the disparity in results?

11.9 What is 'protocol analysis' and what are some of its strengths and weaknesses?

11.10 What are some general strengths and limitations of behavioural research?

11.11 How 'generalisable' are the results derived from behavioural accounting research?

11.12 The International Accounting Standards Board (IASB) in conjunction with the Financial Accounting Standards Board (FASB) are going through a process of revising the conceptual framework (the *Framework for the Preparation and Presentation of Financial Statements*). This process is expected to take a number of years to complete. As part of that work they are addressing 'measurement' issues. Could the IASB and the FASB use techniques from behavioural accounting research in revising the conceptual framework and, if so, how?

REFERENCES

Altman, E. I. (1968), 'Financial ratios, discriminant analysis and the prediction of corporate bankruptcy', *Journal of Finance*, 23(4), pp. 589–609.

Ashton, A. H. & R. H. Ashton (eds) (1995), *Judgement and Decision Making Research in Accounting and Auditing*, Cambridge: Cambridge University Press.

Ashton, R. H. (1974), 'An experimental study of internal control judgements', *Journal of Accounting Research*, 12, pp. 143–57.

Ashton, R. H. (1982), *Human Information Processing in Accounting: American Accounting Association Studies in Accounting Research No. 17*, Florida: American Accounting Association.

Bedard, J. C. & S. F. Biggs (1991), 'Pattern recognition, hypothesis generation, and auditor performance in an analytical review task', *The Accounting Review*, 66(3), pp. 622–42.

Biggs, S. F. & T. J. Mock, T. J. (1983), 'An investigation of auditor decision processes in the evaluation of internal controls and audit scope decisions', *Journal of Accounting Research*, 21(1), pp. 234–55.

Biggs, S. F. & T. J. Mock & P. R. Watkins (1989), *Analytical Review Procedures and Processes in Auditing: Audit Research Monograph No. 14*, Canadian Certified Accountants' Research Foundation.

Biggs, S. F. & J. J. Wild (1985), 'An investigation of auditor judgement in analytical review', *The Accounting Review*, 60(4), pp. 607–33.

Birnberg, J. & J. Shields (1989), 'Three decades of behavioural accounting research: a search for order', *Behavioural Research in Accounting*, 1, pp. 23–74.

Boritz, J. E. (1986), 'The effect of research on audit planning and review judgements', *Journal of Accounting Research*, 24(2), pp. 335–48.

Brunswik, E. (1952), *The Conceptual Framework of Psychology*, Chicago: University of Chicago Press.

Butler, S. (1986), 'Anchoring in the judgmental evaluation of audit samples', *The Accounting Review*, 61(1), pp. 101–11.

Chalos, P. (1985), 'Financial distress: a comparative study of individual, model and committee assessments', *Journal of Accounting Research*, 23, pp. 527–43.

Chalos, P. & S. Pickard (1985), 'Information choice and cue use: an experiment in group information processing', *Journal of Applied Psychology*, 70, pp. 634–41.

Chernoff, H. & M. Rizvi (1975), 'Effect of classification error on random permutations of features in representing multivariate data by faces', *Journal of the American Statistical Association*, 70, pp. 548–54.

Davis, L. (1989), 'Report format and the decision makers task: an experimental investigation', *Accounting, Organizations and Society*, 14, pp. 495–508.

DeSanctis, G. & S. Jarvenpaa (1989), 'Graphical presentation of accounting data for financial forecasting: an experimental investigation', *Accounting, Organizations and Society*, 14, pp. 509–25.

Doupnik, T. & R. Rolfe (1989), *The Relevance of Aggregation of Geographic Area Data in the Assessment of Foreign Investment Risk: Advances in Accounting*, Vol. 7, Greenwich CT: JAI Press.

Dyckman, T. R. (1998), 'The ascendancy of the behavioral paradigm in accounting: the last 20 years', *Behavioral Research in Accounting*, 10, pp. 1–10.

Elias, N. (1972), 'The effects of human asset statements on the investment decision: an experiment', *Journal of Accounting Research*, 10, pp. 215–33.

Gray, S. J. (1988), 'Towards a theory of cultural influence on the development of accounting systems internationally', *ABACUS*, 24(1), pp. 1–15.

Heintz, J. A. (1973), 'Price-level restated financial statements and investment decision making', *The Accounting Review*, 48, pp. 679–89.

Hendricks, J. (1976), 'The impact of human resource accounting information on stock investment decisions: an empirical study', *The Accounting Review*, 51, pp. 292–305.

Hofstede, G. (1983), 'Dimensions of national cultures in fifty countries and three regions', in J. B. Derogowski, S. Dziuraweic & R. Annis (eds), *Expiscations in Cross-Cultural Psychology*, Swets and Zeitlinger.

Joyce, E. J. & G. C. Biddle (1981), 'Anchoring and adjustment in probabilistic inference in auditing', *Journal of Accounting Research*, 19, pp. 120–45.

Kida, T. (1984), 'The impact of hypothesis testing strategies on auditors' use of judgement data', *Journal of Accounting Research,* 22, pp. 332–40.

Kinney, W. R. & W. C. Ueker (1982), 'Mitigating the consequences of anchoring in auditor judgements', *The Accounting Review,* 57, pp. 55–69.

Klersy, G. F. & T. J. Mock (1989), 'Verbal protocol research in auditing', *Accounting, Organizations and Society,* 14(2), pp. 133–51.

Krishnan, R. & D. Booker (2002), 'Investors' use of analysts' recommendation', *Behavioral Research in Accounting,* 14, pp. 130–56.

Libby, R. (1975), 'Accounting ratios and the prediction of failure: some behavioral evidence', *Journal of Accounting Research,* 13(1), pp. 150–61.

Libby, R. (1976), 'Man versus model of man: the need for a non-linear model', *Organizational Behavior and Human Performance,* 16, pp. 13–26.

Libby, R. (1981), *Accounting and Human Information Processing: Theory and Applications,* Englewood Cliffs, NJ: Prentice Hall.

Lobo, G. & I. Song (1989), 'The incremental information in SFAS 33 income disclosures over historical cost income and its cash and accrual components', *The Accounting Review,* 64(2), pp. 329–43.

Maines, L. A. (1995), 'Judgment and decision making research in financial accounting: a review and analysis', in R. H. Ashton & A. H. Ashton (eds), *Judgment and Decision Making Research in Accounting and Auditing,* Cambridge: Cambridge Press.

McIntyre, E. (1973), 'Current cost financial statements and common stock investment decisions', *The Accounting Review,* 48, pp. 575–85.

Mear, R. & M. Firth (1987), 'Assessing the accuracy of financial analyst security return predictions', *Accounting, Organizations and Society,* 12, pp. 331–40.

Moriarity, S. (1979), 'Communicating financial information through multidimensional graphics', *Journal of Accounting Research,* 17, pp. 205–24.

Moser, D. (1989), 'The effects of output interference, availability, and accounting information on investors' predictive judgements', *The Accounting Review,* 64(3), pp. 433–44.

Pankoff, L. & R. Virgil (1970), 'Some preliminary findings from a laboratory experiment on the usefulness of financial accounting information to security analysts', *Journal of Accounting Research,* 8, pp. 1–48.

Sami, H. & B. Schwartz (1992), 'Alternative pension liability disclosure and the effect on credit evaluation: an experiment', *Behavioral Research in Accounting,* 4, pp. 49–62.

Schultz, J. J. & S. G. Gustavson (1978), 'Actuaries' perceptions of variables affecting the independent auditors legal liability', *The Accounting Review,* 53, pp. 626–41.

Snowball, D., (1980), 'Some effects of accounting expertise and information load: an empirical study', *Accounting, Organizations and Society,* pp. 323–28.

Stallman, J. (1969), 'Toward experimental criteria for judging disclosure improvements', *Journal of Accounting Research,* 7, pp. 29–43.

Triandis, H., R. Malpass & A. Davidson (1971), 'Cross-cultural psychology', in B. J. Siegel (ed.), *Biennial Review of Anthropology 1971,* California: Stanford University Press, 1972.

Trotman, K. T. (1996), *Research Methods for Judgement and Decision Making Studies in Auditing: Coopers and Lybrand Research Methodology Monograph No. 3,* Melbourne: Coopers and Lybrand.

Tversky, A. & D. Kahneman (1974), 'Judgment under uncertainty: heuristics and biases', *Science*, 185, pp. 1124–31.

Watts, R. & J. Zimmerman (1978), 'Towards a positive theory of the determination of accounting standards', *The Accounting Review*, 53(1), pp. 112–34.

Wilkins, T. & I. Zimmer (1983), 'The effect of leasing and different methods of accounting for leases on credit evaluation', *The Accounting Review*, 63, pp. 747–64.

Wood, D. & D. Ross (2006), 'Environmental social controls and capital investments: Australian evidence', *Accounting and Finance*, 46, pp. 677–95.

Zimmer, I. (1980), 'A lens study of the prediction of corporate failure by bank loan officers', *Journal of Accounting Research*, 18(2), pp. 629–36.

CHAPTER 12

CRITICAL PERSPECTIVES OF ACCOUNTING

LEARNING OBJECTIVES

On completing this chapter readers should:

- have gained an insight into particular perspectives that challenge conventional opinions about the role of accounting within society;
- understand the basis of arguments that suggest that financial accounting tends to support the positions of individuals who hold power, wealth and social status, while undermining the positions of others;
- understand that the disclosure (or non-disclosure) of information can be construed to be an important strategy to promote and legitimise particular social orders, and maintain the power and wealth of elites.

OPENING ISSUES

As we saw in Chapter 6, conceptual framework projects promote approaches to financial accounting that are built on qualitative characteristics such as *neutrality* and *representational faithfulness*. How do arguments regarding the unequal distribution of power between different social groups, as espoused by critical accounting theorists, challenge the assumptions of the neutrality and objectivity of financial reports?

INTRODUCTION

Previous chapters explored numerous issues, including how accounting may be used to assist in decision making (Chapters 5 and 6), to reduce agency and political costs (Chapter 7), to maintain or assist in bringing legitimacy to an organisation (Chapter 8), and to satisfy the information demands of particular stakeholders (Chapter 8). How the practice of accounting could be modified to take into account some social and environmental aspects of an organisation's operations has also been explored (Chapter 9), along with how accounting disclosures might impact on share prices (Chapter 10). This chapter provides an overview of an alternative perspective about the role of accounting. This perspective, which is often called the *critical perspective*, explicitly considers how the practice of accounting tends to support particular economic and social structures, and reinforces unequal distributions of power and wealth across society. In doing so, this form of accounting research rejects the view that accounting provides an objective and unbiased account of particular transactions and events.

The view promoted by researchers operating from a critical perspective is that accounting, far from being a practice that provides a neutral or unbiased representation of underlying economic facts, actually provides the means of maintaining the powerful positions of some sectors of the community (those currently in *power* and with *wealth*) while holding back the position and interests of those without wealth. These theorists challenge any perspectives that suggest that various *rights* and *privileges* are spread throughout society[1]—instead they argue that most rights, opportunities and associated power reside in a small (but perhaps well-defined) group (often referred to as an 'elite').

This chapter considers various (critical) arguments about the role of the state (government), the role of accounting research and the role of accounting practice in sustaining particular social orders that are already in place—social orders that some researchers argue function on the basis of inequities, where some individuals (with capital, or wealth) prosper at the expense of those without capital and where accounting is therefore regarded as one of the tools used by those with (more) capital to help subjugate (undermine) those without (or with considerably less) capital. It will be seen that researchers adopting a critical perspective often do not provide direct solutions to particular inequities; rather, they seek to highlight the inequities that they perceive exist in society, and the role that, they argue, accounting plays in sustaining and legitimising the inequities. Because the theoretical perspectives investigated in this chapter make calls for changes that will have broad impacts across society, they are quite different from the other theories addressed in this book.

---

1   The assumption that there is a spread of rights and privileges across different groups within society is commonly referred to as 'pluralism'.

THE CRITICAL PERSPECTIVE DEFINED

Under the heading (or umbrella) of *critical accounting theory*, there are several different specific perspectives on critical accounting. Therefore, a single critical perspective is not easy to define. In broad terms, 'critical accounting theory' is used to refer to an approach to accounting research that goes beyond questioning whether particular methods of accounting should be employed, and instead focuses on the role of accounting in sustaining the privileged positions of those in control of particular resources (capital) while undermining or restraining the voice of those without capital. According to Roslender (2006, p. 250):

> Critical Theory is intimately wedded to change. More specifically it is concerned with the promotion of a better society, one in which the prevailing social arrangements serve the interests of the mass of people, whose 'potentialities' are perceived to be constrained by those arrangements already in place ... Critical Theory seeks to provide a form of knowledge that is questioning of the prevailing social arrangements, i.e. an alternative knowledge. More than this, however, the resulting knowledge will serve as an input into a process of reflection by society's members on the nature of their involvement within the prevailing social arrangements and how this might be changed, for their benefit. Critical Theory is not concerned with the provision of insights for their own sake but for the purpose of informing the transformation of 'what is' into what those who experience it wish it to be, through a process of interaction and reflection. Or put another way, Critical Theory aims to promote self-awareness of both 'what is' and 'what might be', and how the former might be transformed to install the latter.

Roslender (2006, p. 264) further states that from a critical perspective:

> Simply interpreting or understanding what we chose to study is not enough. The purpose of the exercise is to turn this learning to the advantage of society, i.e. the promotion of a better society. The presupposition is that there are many things about the existing social arrangements that merit changing. 'Traditional' theory does not subscribe to this axiom. It is this quality that distinguishes 'critical' theory from traditional theory. This is not to imply that all of those scholars who elect to embrace other ways of seeing are committed to the reproduction of the existing social arrangements, rather that they do not avail themselves of a way of seeing, Critical Theory, that explicitly links understanding and change to the enactment of the philosophy of praxis (a philosophy in which 'theory' informs 'practice' and vice versa). Viewed in a slightly different way, Critical Theory makes no pretence of being objective. Those who embrace a Critical Theory perspective do so because they recognise and value its partiality.

Tony Tinker (2005, p. 101), who is one of the founders of the critical accounting movement, has also offered a useful definition of critical accounting research. He sees it as encompassing:

> all forms of social praxis that are evaluative, and aim to engender progressive change within the conceptual, institutional, practical, and political territories of accounting.

A key element of this definition is the notion of 'social praxis', as distinct from the investigation (for example, in other branches of accounting theory and research) of social (accounting) practice.[2] *Praxis* within critical accounting research envisages a broad understanding of both 'theory' and 'practice' and is generally understood to refer to the assumption that there is a two-way (and possibly circular) relationship between theories and practices, whereby theory influences social practices (that is, the theoretical views and assumptions we have about practice actually impacts practice) while social practices also influence theory. That is, theory informs (or provides a foundation for) existing practice and also existing practice informs theory.[3] One implication of this relationship between theory and practice is that when social conditions (and practices) change, theories based on these conditions need also to change. This should not be a new concept to you, as many parts of this book have discussed accounting theories that evolved to suit (or reflect) business practices.

The other key implication of the two-way relationship between theory and practice embodied in the term *praxis*, and possibly the more important implication from the perspective of critical accounting, is that development of different theoretical perspectives can bring about (needed) changes in social practices and structures (such as the distribution of wealth and power). For example, if we develop theories that question the wealth distribution impacts of unregulated markets, or question the operations of capital markets in terms of providing sustainable outcomes, and if our arguments gain acceptance with various parties within society, then this might have implications for how such markets are regulated. Our theories will impact on practice. Similarly, if we have well-developed theories that question the objectivity of financial accounting, and if we are able to generate sufficient support for the theory, then ultimately this could create the necessary impetus for changes in the way financial accounting is practised. For example, perhaps the compelling nature of our newly developed theories might act to reduce society's focus on corporate financial performance (which critical theorists believe particularly promotes the interests of investors and senior managers); instead, our new theory might encourage a new business philosophy in which measures of corporate performance reflect efforts made towards benefiting a diverse group of stakeholders and the environment; that is, the theory could ultimately lead to reforms in how business and society operate (which again links to the notion of 'social praxis', in which theory informs practice, and vice versa).

What is different about the relationship between theory and practice as embodied in the term *praxis* (as used in critical accounting research) is the explicit notion of a two-way relationship. All of the theoretical perspectives studied earlier tend to rely on a one-way relationship whereby either theory determines practice or practice determines theory.

What is also different is the focal point of changes in practice implied in the term *praxis*. While the normative theories examined earlier sought to develop and then implement specific

---

2 The *Oxford English Dictionary* (2nd edition, 1989) contains several definitions of the word 'praxis', including 'The practice or exercise of a technical subject or art, as distinct from the theory of it' and 'Habitual action, accepted practice, custom'. However, as will become clear from the discussion in the next few paragraphs, the word 'praxis' in most critical accounting research is used in a very specific manner which accords with the following definition from the *Oxford English Dictionary*: 'A term used ... to denote the willed action by which a theory or philosophy (esp. a Marxist one) becomes a social actuality'.

3 For example, if we believe in, and promote, a theory of economics that says that markets operate most efficiently when left unregulated, this will influence market-based practices. Regulators may use the research to further support efforts to reduce market regulation. Conversely, if we observe markets and find that those markets that operate efficiently are unregulated, this will influence the theories we develop. Hence, theories might impact practice, or existing practice might impact theories.

accounting practices which particular normative researchers argued were (in some way) superior to existing practices, the focus of the changes in practice embodied in the term *praxis* are usually at the broader level of society rather than specific technical accounting practices within that society. More specifically, a critical accounting understanding and use of the term *praxis* is usually informed by a Marxist-inspired approach, 'whose central concern [is] to study and influence the role of free creative activity in changing and shaping ethical, social, political, and economic life along humanistic socialist lines' (De George, 1995, p. 713), and this is why we argue that the role of theory in changing social practices is probably more important to many critical accounting scholars than the role of changed social practices in altering theories. Tinker (2005, p. 101) argues that this approach to critical accounting both 'promises a rich synthesis of new forms of praxis' and requires that critical accounting scholars 'who participate [in critical accounting research] must do so from committed, partisan, passionate, and sometimes militant positions'.

INSIGHTS INTO THE PARTISAN NATURE OF ACCOUNTING

It has been argued earlier that all research is likely to be influenced to some extent by the (possibly subconscious) biases of the researchers involved, but this explicit promotion of partisan research in critical accounting studies might upset and worry researchers who adopt other approaches.[4] However, it could be considered simply more honest in that it is making explicit that all research in social sciences relies on the subjective (and therefore biased) interpretations of the researchers involved. Within critical accounting research, these explicit biases usually range from moderate socialism to more extreme anti-capitalist positions, which could be regarded as threatening by accounting researchers (and students and practitioners) who have prospered under the capitalist system. This point will be returned to later in the chapter.

Researchers within the critical accounting area, critical accounting theorists, therefore seek to highlight, through critical analysis, the key role of accounting in society. The perspective they provide challenges the view that accounting can be construed as being objective or neutral, and these researchers often seek to provide evidence to support this view. Accounting is seen as a means of constructing or legitimising particular social structures. As Hopper et al. (1995, p. 528) state:

> ... in communicating reality accountants simultaneously construct it (Hines, 1988) and accounting is a social practice within political struggles and not merely a market practice guided by equilibrium in an efficient market.

This view is supported by Baker and Bettner (1997, p. 305), who state:

> Critical researchers have convincingly and repeatedly argued that accounting does not produce an objective representation of economic 'reality', but rather provides a highly contested and partisan representation of the economic and social world. As such, the underlying substance of accounting cannot be obtained through an ever more sophisticated elaboration of quantitative methods. Accounting's essence can be best captured through an understanding of its impacts on individuals, organisations and societies. Hence it is important for accounting research to adopt a critical perspective.

---

4   According to the *Oxford English Dictionary*, a partisan approach is one taken 'by an adherent or supporter of a person, party, or cause'. Therefore, if critical theorists had a particular view (or theory) about how society should function to achieve certain ends or causes, then, in accord with a partisan approach, this will impact on the practices they support or oppose.

As noted at the beginning of this section, the term 'critical accounting' is a very broad term that captures a variety of different perspectives about accounting. However, what these perspectives have in common is that they seek to highlight, oppose and change the perceived role of accounting in supporting the privileged position of some people in society. As Hopper et al. (1995, p. 535) state:

> Critical theory is an umbrella term for a wide variety of theoretical approaches perhaps more united in what they oppose than what they agree upon.

Consistent with the above perspective of critical theory, Reiter (1995, p. 53) states:

> In the critical world, there is no single established theory or approach, and little consensus on how to proceed, aside from an absolute horror of modernity and neo-classical economics.

A MARXIST CRITIQUE OF ACCOUNTING

One of the main branches, and probably the founding branch, of critical accounting theory is grounded (as indicated above in discussing the term 'social praxis') in a Marxist-informed critique of capitalism. Within this Marxist critique, owners of capital are regarded as having (unfairly) accumulated their wealth by the historical exploitation and expropriation (over several centuries) of the value created by workers (or labour); workers are seen as feeling alienated both from society and from the products they produce, as their lives are largely controlled by external and impersonal markets rather than by their own free choices.[5] Capitalism is also regarded as being fundamentally structurally flawed. To give an example of one such structural flaw, a key Marxist argument is that one effective way for individual businesses to increase profits (or economic returns to capital) over a long period of history has been to increase the level of mechanisation in a factory or office process, and thereby replace the productive capacity of some workers (labour)—who have to be paid and cannot work 24 hours a day—with the productive capacity of additional machinery (capital—which ultimately has been paid for by accumulating the value created by labour and expropriated over the years by capital). The costs of usage of this machinery (such as depreciation, repairs and the opportunity cost of capital invested in the machinery) were historically often considerably lower than the cost of the labour displaced by the machinery, and the machinery could also be 'worked' for long periods with minimal stoppage (rest) periods. While such mechanisation might have been in the economic interests of the owners of one business, Marxists argued that there was a fundamental contradiction in the drive of all owners of all businesses to increase the returns to capital through ever greater mechanisation. This fundamental flaw in the structure of the capitalist system is that, for capital to earn returns, not only do costs need to be minimised but also revenues need to be maximised. While the actions of one or two factory owners in replacing some labour with capital might not affect the market for their goods, and therefore makes economic sense for these business owners individually, Marxists historically argued that if all business owners acted in this way then the total amount paid to labour overall would decline and the total buying capacity in the consumer markets overall would

---

5   In this Marxist perspective on workers' feelings of alienation, 'the market-place … purports to be a sphere of individual freedom, but is in fact a sphere of collective slavery to inhuman and destructive forces' (Wood, 1995, p. 525).

also decline. At some point, the reduction in resources available to consumers to purchase the end products of the production process would, it was argued, be greater than the increase in productive capacity from mechanisation and would therefore lead to a reduction (or collapse) in demand, and thereby threaten the overall prosperity of capital.

Marxist theorists argue that as the capitalist system operates in a manner that alienates workers (and the working class), and is riddled with inherent structural contradictions (such as the one discussed), it is fundamentally unstable. This inherent instability will, it is argued, manifest itself in different symptoms in different eras, such as unemployment, inflation and economic depression. While action might be taken by governments and businesses to address the negative symptoms (or outcomes) of the instability of capitalism that manifest themselves in a particular era, Marxists regard this as treating a symptom (such as policies against unemployment in one era, anti-inflation policies in another era) rather than addressing the common cause of all these symptoms—the structural instability of the capitalist system itself. Furthermore, 'successfully' treating the current negative symptom of the inherent instability of capitalism will not, it is argued, prevent the inevitability of new symptoms (whose precise nature is unforeseen and largely unforeseeable) arising in future periods. Policies to address these symptoms are therefore regarded as acting at a relatively superficial level and, rather like pharmaceutical products that treat the symptoms rather than the underlying causes of a disease, will do little in the long term to cure what Marxists regard as the deeper malaise of capitalism.

Many of these symptoms, and/or the social unrest caused by these symptoms, are regarded by Marxist scholars as threatening to undermine the power and wealth of capital (to quote Marx: 'capitalism produces its own gravediggers' (Marx & Engels, 1967, p. 94, as cited in Tinker, 2005, p. 122)). Therefore, the privileges, power and wealth of capital are regarded by Marxists as being unstable, and owners of capital will take action to defend their privileges, power and wealth.

Critical accounting theorists regard accounting as a powerful tool in both enhancing the power and wealth of capital and helping to protect this power and wealth from threats arising from the structural instability of capitalism. As, following Tinker's (2005) arguments outlined earlier, many critical accounting researchers tend to be opponents of many aspects of the capitalist system and of accounting, they seek to expose the role of accounting in supporting unequal distributions of power and wealth across society, and some seek to subvert this role of accounting. This aim also tends to be shared by several of the critical accounting researchers who do not adopt a pure Marxist perspective.

As Gray, Owen and Adams (1996, p. 63) state, a major concern of the critical (or 'radical' theorists) is that:

> ... the very way in which society is ordered, the distribution of wealth, the power of corporations, the language of economics and business and so on, are so fundamentally flawed that nothing less than radical structural change has any hope of emancipating human and non-human life. The social, economic and political systems are seen as being fundamentally inimical.

Given that the practice of accounting is in the hands of reporting entities, such as large corporations, and accounting regulation is in the hands of government and associated regulatory bodies (which are viewed as being linked to, or under substantial influence from, large corporations and therefore as having a vested interest in maintaining the status quo), accounting information will, it is argued, never act to do anything but support our current social system, complete with all its perceived problems and inequities. Moore (1991) also suggests that the low level of consideration or use of critical accounting theory by US accounting academics could be due to the universities' reliance on business funding—funding that does not tend to support research of a 'critical' nature.

CRITICAL ACCOUNTING RESEARCH VERSUS SOCIAL AND ENVIRONMENTAL ACCOUNTING RESEARCH

One of the key areas in which our current social system is perceived by large numbers of people (and not just Marxist scholars) to produce many problems and inequities is in the area of the social and environmental impact of business. Many of the issues in this area, and their relationship to accounting theory and practice, are discussed in Chapter 8 and 9. Here, we consider how critical accounting research differs from and/or complements social and environmental accounting research, as it might be considered that both are seeking substantial changes in social practices.

The critical perspective adopted by many critical accounting researchers is grounded in Political Economy Theory, which was also considered in Chapter 8. More specifically, critical accounting research tends to be grounded in 'classical' Political Economy Theory. As Chapter 8 indicates, the 'political economy' has been defined by Gray, Owen and Adams (1996, p. 47) as the 'social, political and economic framework within which human life takes place'. The view is that society, politics and economics are inseparable, and economic issues cannot meaningfully be investigated in the absence of considerations about the political, social and institutional framework in which economic activity takes place. Relating these arguments specifically to accounting, Guthrie and Parker (1990, p. 166) state:

> The political economy perspective perceives accounting reports as social, political, and economic documents. They serve as a tool for constructing, sustaining and legitimising economic and political arrangements, institutions and ideological themes which contribute to the organisation's private interests.

As Chapter 8 also indicates, Political Economy Theory has been divided into two broad streams that Gray, Owen and Adams (1996, p. 47) and others have classified as 'classical' and 'bourgeois' political economy. The 'bourgeois' political economy perspective does not explore structural inequities, sectional interests, class struggles and the like.[6] It accepts the way society is currently structured as 'a given'. Many critical theorists consider that research which simply accepts the existing nature and structure of society without challenge effectively supports that (undesirable) society (Hopper & Powell, 1985). By accepting a pluralist conception of society it thereby tends to ignore the struggles and inequities within society (Puxty, 1991). Prominent critical researchers such as Tinker, Puxty, Lehman, Hopper and Cooper have therefore often considered it necessary to challenge the work of researchers who they regard as researching within the bourgeois stream of political economy, such as Gray, Owen, Maunders, Mathews and

---

6 Legitimacy Theory and Stakeholder Theory, which are both examined in Chapter 8, are embedded within a 'bourgeois' political economy perspective.

Parker (these researchers, plus a number of others, have researched numerous issues associated with corporate social responsibility reporting); individuals who have for many years been promoting the need for organisations to be more accountable for their social and environmental performance (that is, to provide more information in relation to whether the corporations are meeting community expectations in relation to their social and environmental performance). As Gray, Owen and Adams (1996, p. 63) state, critical theorists believe that:

> Because corporate social reporting (CSR) will be controlled by the reporting corporations and a State which has a vested interest in keeping things more or less as they are, CSR has little radical content. Furthermore, CSR may do more harm than good because it gives the impression of concern and change but, in fact, will do no more than allow the system to 'capture' the radical elements of, for example, socialism, environmentalism or feminism and thus emasculate them.

Critical theorists argue that any such emasculation (undermining or weakening) of these movements, which seek to protect and advance the interests of groups or entities often regarded as negatively affected by capitalism, will have the effect of protecting the capitalist system from 'threats' these movements pose to the power and wealth of capital.[7]

Thus, while calls for greater disclosure of social responsibility information would seem to be a move in the right direction, some critical theorists argue that such efforts are wasted unless they are accompanied by fundamental changes in how society is structured. They would argue that the disclosure of corporate social responsibility information acts to legitimise, and not challenge, those providing the information. Cooper and Sherer (1984), for example, argue that attempts to resolve technical issues (such as how to account for environmental externalities) without consideration of inequities in the existing social and political environment may result in an imperfect and incomplete resolution, owing to the acceptance of current institutions and practices—which are seen to be part of the problem itself.

Reflecting on some of the views of critical theorists about the deficiencies of social and environmental accounting research, Owen, Gray and Bebbington (1997, p. 181) note:

> Early radical critique of the social accounting movement emanated from a socialist, largely Marxist, perspective. For writers such as Tinker et al. (1991) and Puxty (1986, 1991) society is characterised by social conflict. In Tinker et al.'s (1991) analysis, the social accounting movement, particularly as represented in the work of Gray et al. (1988, 1987), fails to examine the basic contradictions and antinomies of the social system under investigation and is therefore, at best, irrelevant, and, at worst, malign, in implicitly adopting a stance of 'political quietism' that simply benefits the already powerful (i.e. the capitalist class). Thus, for example, Puxty writing in 1986 suggested the irrelevance of social accounting, in noting that 'more radical critics of capitalist society have been more concerned with the broader issues of accountancy and accountants within that society than particular (almost parochial) issues such as social accounting which appears to be … rearranging the deck chairs on the Titanic' (p. 107).

---

7 Included in the *Oxford English Dictionary*'s (2nd edn, 1989) definition of emasculation is: 'The depriving of force, vigour … making weak'.

However, by 1991, Puxty had taken his critique a stage further in arguing that by leaving basic social structures intact, social accounting can even lead to legitimation 'since the powerful can point to their existence as evidence of their openness in listening to criticism, it paves the way for ... the extension of power' (p. 37).

As accounting is deemed to sustain particular social structures, the introduction of new forms of accounting (for example, experimental methods relating to accounting for social costs) will only help sustain that social system. Reflecting on the critical theorists' perception of the ongoing research being undertaken to explore how to account for the social and environmental implications of business, Gray, Owen and Adams (1996, p. 63) state that some critical theorists consider that by undertaking such research:

> ... one is using the very process (current economics and accounting) that caused the problem (environmental crisis) to try to solve the problem. This is known as the process of 'juridification' and it is well established that one is unlikely to solve a problem by applying more of the thing which caused the problem.

Although the above discussion indicates substantial disagreements (or even antagonisms) from some critical accounting researchers towards social and environmental accounting research, in recent years several social and environmental accounting researchers have made attempts to address the concerns expressed by these critical accounting researchers.[8] For example, works by Bailey, Harte and Sugden (2000), Lehman (1999, 2001), O'Dwyer (2005) and Unerman and Bennett (2004) are just some of the social and environmental accounting research studies that have touched on issues and implications of differential power between organisations and different groups of stakeholders in accountability relationships. Furthermore, one of the foremost (if not *the* foremost) social and environmental accounting researcher, Rob Gray, recently wrote a joint paper (Tinker & Gray, 2003) with one of the foremost critical accounting scholars, Tony Tinker (who, as can be seen from the above discussion, was a longstanding critic of aspects of Rob Gray's work), in which it was recognised that many academically driven environmental and sustainability initiatives—including those in the area of social and environmental accountability—had been 'captured' by the corporate world and subverted to serve the needs of (and deflect some of the threats to) continued capital accumulation by rich and powerful companies—while enabling these corporations to continue operating in an environmentally and socially damaging manner.

Having briefly explored the relationship between critical accounting research and social and environmental accounting research, we now turn to an examination of the impact of critical accounting research on accounting and business practices and on so-called 'mainstream' accounting research, including a discussion of some possible reasons for the marginalisation that many critical accounting scholars believe they experience.

8 However, there does not seem to have been much of a reciprocal movement by some critical accounting researchers towards recognising the potential impact that some social and environmental accounting research may have had in reducing a variety of negative social and environmental externalities of some businesses. This lack of movement by some critical accounting researchers is implied, for example, in a statement by Tony Tinker (2005, p. 124, footnote 18) that, in selecting areas of accounting research for one of his latest critiques based on a Marxist approach to critical accounting, 'Environmental research is another candidate, however as far as "the canon" is concerned I have little to add to the 1991 critique (Tinker et al., 1991)'.

POSSIBLE IMPACT OF CRITICAL ACCOUNTING RESEARCH ON SOCIAL PRACTICE

As previously stated, the critical perspective tends to be grounded in a 'classical' political economy perspective, and as such explicitly considers structural conflict, inequity and the role of the state at the heart of the analysis.

By adopting a research (and, arguably, ideological) perspective that is grounded in classical Political Economy Theory, critical accounting researchers can highlight particular issues that might not otherwise be addressed. According to Cooper and Sherer (1984, p. 208):

> Social welfare is likely to be improved if accounting practices are recognised as being consistently partial; that the strategic outcomes of accounting practices consistently (if not invariably) favour specific interests in society and disadvantage others. Therefore, we are arguing that there already exists an established, if implicit, conceptual framework for accounting practice. A political economy of accounting emphasises the infrastructure, the fundamental relations between classes in society. It recognises the institutional environment which supports the existing system of corporate reporting and subjects to critical scrutiny those issues (such as assumed importance of shareholders and securities markets) that are frequently taken for granted in current accounting research.

While a substantial amount of critical research is informed by the work of philosophers such as Karl Marx, not all critical accounting research is based on a pure Marxist critique of capitalism. For example, reference is made by Owen, Gray and Bebbington (1997) to critical researchers who are identified as 'deep ecologists' and 'radical feminists'. The 'deep ecologists' question the trade-off between economic performance and ecological damage—they question the morality of systems that justify the extinction of species on the basis of associated 'economic benefits'. According to Gray, Owen and Adams (1996, p. 61):

> The essence of these views is that the very foundation—even the existence—of our economic (and social) system is an anathema. Put at its simplest, our economic system can, and does, contemplate trade-offs between, for example, the habitat of threatened species and economic imperatives. To a deep ecologist it is inconceivable that a trade-off could have any form of moral justification. Such a view therefore challenges virtually every aspect of taken for granted ways of human existence, especially in the developed Western nations.

The 'radical feminists', on the other hand, believe that accounting maintains and reinforces masculine traits such as the need for success and competition, and that accounting acts to reduce the relevance of issues such as cooperation, respect, compassion and so forth. The masculine versus feminine dichotomy was also discussed in Chapter 4 when various societal values were considered in the context of international accounting and how a country's ranking in terms of 'masculinity' or 'femininity' in turn influenced the national accounting practices being adopted. According to Hofstede (1984):

> Masculinity stands for a preference in society for achievement, heroism, assertiveness, and material success. Its opposite, Femininity, stands for a preference for relationships, modesty, caring for the weak, and the quality of life.

Researchers working with the feminist literature argue for the need for accounting to be less 'masculine' and more 'feminine' in orientation. According to Reiter (1995, p. 35):

Feminist theory has many voices, and the considerable volume of feminist criticism published to date represents many different viewpoints. In the late 1980s, accounting scholars began exploring the idea that feminist theory could be used to critique accounting.

In relation to economic theory, on which much accounting theory is developed, Reiter (1995, p. 40) states:

Economic theories tend to value the characteristics associated with masculine stereotypes such as abstraction, mind, efficiency, equilibrium, rationality, pursuit of self-interest, and autonomy. The opposite characteristics of concretism, body, randomness, humanity, mutuality and connectedness, which are associated with feminine stereotypes, are missing from economic theory.

In explaining how the incorporation of feminist values in economic theory could potentially lead to a more promising theory, Reiter (1995, p. 47) states:

Folbre and Hartmann (1988) explain that 'a growing body of interdisciplinary feminist research complements the efforts many economists are making to develop a more complete theory of economic interests, one that can encompass concepts like cooperation, loyalty and reciprocity' (p. 197). Nelson (1992) suggests that incorporation of positive feminine qualities such as flexibility, intuition, humanism and connectedness of individuals and the concept that individual choice is influenced by societal and cultural factors would lead to increased richness and applicability of economic theory. She also argues that the exclusive focus of neo-classical economics on problems of exchange is also a denial of the feminine quality of need ... The view of economic behaviour incorporated in financial economic theories such as agency theory concentrated on conflict and discipline rather than on productive activity and mutuality of interests. A single goal (profit maximisation) benefiting a single group (shareholders) is promoted rather than a multiplicity of goals benefiting all parties. Suppose in contrast that we concerned ourselves with modes of co-operation between shareholders and managers to promote development of quality products and services and the skills to thrive in the complex international markets of the twenty-first century? A different set of concepts and metaphors would be appropriate, and a different view of the roles of capital markets and accounting information would be needed.

In adopting positions, and/or pursuing outcomes, that are at variance with the dominant capitalist ideology (whether motivated by a pure Marxist position or, as is the case with many critical accounting researchers, motivated by other philosophical positions such as the deep ecologists or the radical feminists) critical theorists provide arguments that are often driven by a desire to create a climate for change in social structures. By arguing for a change in the status quo it has been argued that 'critical researchers' are often marginalised to a greater extent than researchers adopting other theoretical or ideological perspectives (Baker & Bettner, 1997). Another possible basis of some of this 'marginalisation' is that critical theorists often do not provide solutions to what they see as perceived problems (Sikka & Willmott, 2005). That is, they are often 'critical' without providing direct guidance on how the perceived problems can be solved.[9] For example, Owen, Gray and Bebbington (1997) argue that critical analysis alone is perhaps not enough. As they state (p. 183):

> Restricting one's activities to critique, rather than actively seeking to reform practice, we would suggest, poses a minimal threat to current orthodoxy. Thus Neu and Cooper (1997) are led to observe that: 'while critical accounting scholars have illuminated the partisan functioning of accounting, we have been less successful in transforming accounting (and social) practices' (p. 1).

Further, Sikka and Willmott (2005, p. 142) state that:

> Marxist traditions must continuously be renewed through lived experiences and opposition to institutions of oppression and exploitation in an effort to enable human beings to live less brutalised and destructive lives. But how are the agents of such change to be galvanized? While there is a role for scholarship and related forms of rarefied intellectual engagement with radical ideas, this activity should not displace principled involvement in the mundane world of practical affairs.

Accountants are often trained to provide information to solve particular (predominantly economic) problems; hence, 'culturally' many accountants might be conditioned against criticism that does not provide a solution. Reflecting on the 'attitudes and orientations' of accountants, Cooper and Sherer (1984, p. 222) state:

> A critical approach to accounting, however, starts from the premise that problems in accounting are potentially reflections of problems in and of society and accordingly that the latter should be critically analysed. Thus if a major problem in accounting is identified, say as its overwhelming orientation to investors, then a critical perspective would suggest that this problem is a reflection of society's orientation and to change accounting practice requires both social awareness (e.g. identification of alternative 'accounts' and the roles of accounting in society) and ultimately social change.
>
> Whether critical theory can in practice be applied to accounting research depends on whether researchers can free themselves from the attitudes and orientations which result from their social and educational training and which are reinforced by the beliefs of the accounting profession and the business community. For this socialisation process has produced accounting researchers who may exhibit subconscious bias in the definition of the problem set of accounting and the choice of theories to analyse and solve these problems. The criterion of critical awareness involves recognising the contested nature of the problem set and theories and demystifying the ideological character of those theories.

9　From a research perspective it has also been argued that critical theorists have been marginalised because they do not tend to use mathematical modelling and statistical analysis—both of which have become (to many researchers, as well as to a number of editors of accounting journals) part of accepted accounting research. As Hopper et al. (1995, p. 532) state: 'Critical researchers emphasise the social embeddedness of accounting practice, consequently, they tend to neglect mathematical modelling, preferring detailed historical and ethnological studies of structures and processes which help identify societal linkages to show that accounting is not merely a technically rational service activity but plays a vital role in effecting wealth transfers at micro-organisational and macro-societal levels (Chua, 1986).'

Critical theorists are often strong in their condemnation of accountants, and this in itself could provide a basis for some of the marginalisation that many believe they experience. Consider the statement of Tinker, Lehman and Neimark (1991, p. 37):

> The enduring nature of this 'Radical Critique' is attributable to the persistence of the underlying social antagonisms, to which it attempts to speak, and the complicity of accountants, which it seeks to elucidate.

More specifically, Sikka and Willmott (2005, p. 138) explain that some of the critical accounting studies in which they have been involved have:

> ... shown that [some accountancy professional associations] have a long history of opposing reforms which arguably would have advanced the accountability of major corporations (Puxty, et al., 1994); that accounting technologies play a major part in the exploitation of workers (Sikka, et al., 1999); and that the accountancy industry is engaged in a ruthless exploitation of citizens (Cousins, et al., 2000). We have also sought to mobilise opinion by holding a mirror to the accountancy trade associations and argue that their claims of ethics, integrity etc are little more than rhetorical garnishes, and that neither their policies nor their actions come anywhere near their self-representations (Cousins, et al., 2000, Mitchell, et al., 1994, Puxty, et al., 1994, Willmott, 1990).

In reflecting on the quote from Sikka and Wilmott (2005), reference can be made to a 2005/2006 Australian government inquiry by the Parliament of Australia Joint Committee on Corporations and Financial Services into corporate social responsibility. Within the terms of reference of the inquiry, the government solicited views about whether corporate social responsibilities and associated reporting should be regulated. Sikka and Willmott claimed that some accounting professional associations 'have a long history of opposing reforms which arguably would have advanced the accountability of major corporations', so it is interesting to note that all three major accounting professional bodies within Australia (the Institute of Chartered Accountants in Australia, the National Institute of Accountants, and CPA Australia) made submissions which stated that they were opposed to mandating corporate social responsibility disclosures. They referred to such factors as the effectiveness of self-regulation and the disciplining mechanisms of the capital market as providing the basis for ensuring that companies move towards doing 'the right thing'. Referring to its own research, CPA Australia (2005, p. 6) stated: 'While there is strong public (88%) and shareholder (86%) support for Government to mandate the reporting of companies' social and environmental reporting this is not reflected in the views of business leaders (53%). CPA Australia believes this reflects a valid business concern that mandatory reporting would not enhance the value of the information provided and introduce an unnecessary layer of regulation.' To a critical theorist such comments would coincide with their views that accounting practices—and the accounting profession itself—operates to support the views of 'business'. CPA Australia further stated (p. 9) that 'A proactive approach towards voluntarism from business negates the risk of attracting excessive and inflexible regulations'. Again, from a 'critical perspective' such comments indicate that the accounting profession primarily promotes a position that favours business entities rather than promoting broader accountability to stakeholders other than corporate shareholders.

In further considering the quote from Sikka and Willmott, accountants are being informed by the critical theorists that they are complicit in relation to 'social antagonisms', 'exploitation of workers' or 'a ruthless exploitation of citizens'. This is not something that is likely to be seen in a favourable light by many accountants and accounting researchers. It is confronting. However, although accountants might elect not to agree with what a number of the critical theorists are saying (perhaps because of profound ideological differences), it is nevertheless useful, perhaps, for accountants to put themselves under scrutiny from a broader societal perspective. The critical theorists (both Marxists and non-Marxists) encourage such scrutiny.

A review of the academic literature shows that a number of critical theorists have been vocal critics of research that has adopted Positive Accounting Theory as its theoretical basis, as well as being critical of related capital markets research (this issue is looked at more closely later in the chapter). Positive Accounting Theory focuses on conflicts between what might be construed as 'powerful' groupings within society (for example, owners, managers, debtholders) and does not consider conflicts between these powerful groups and parties that have less ability to impact on the wealth of such powerful parties. Many critical theorists have also been particularly critical of the anti-regulation stance often advocated by Positive Accounting theorists because such a stance further advances the interests of those with power or wealth (for example, owners of corporations, because lack of regulation enables the power and wealth of capital to be exercised largely unhindered by anything other than market forces—which operate to the benefit of many powerful businesses) while undermining the interests of those who might need some form of regulatory protection. Critical theorists would also argue that in assessing the usefulness of accounting information we really need to look beyond capital market (share price) reactions. The capital market response is driven (obviously) by those with capital. Capital market studies ignore 'other voices'.

We now turn from an examination of the role and possible impact of critical accounting theorists to a consideration, informed by critical accounting theory, of perspectives about the role of the state, accounting research and, ultimately, accounting practice in supporting current social structures (and inequalities). Again, as has been emphasised throughout this book, the views that are presented are those of a subset of the research community. There will be other 'subsets' of the research community that challenge such views.

THE ROLE OF THE STATE IN SUPPORTING EXISTING SOCIAL STRUCTURES

Researchers working within the critical perspective typically see the state (government) as being a vehicle of support for the holders of capital (for example, shareholders), as well as for the capitalist system as a whole. Under this perspective the government will undertake various actions from time to time to enhance the legitimacy of the social system, and thereby protect and advance the power and wealth of those who own capital, even though it might appear (to less critical eyes) that the government was acting in the interests of particular disadvantaged groups. For instance, a government might impose mandatory disclosure requirements for corporations in terms of the disclosure of information about how the corporations attend to the needs of certain minorities or the disabled. Arnold (1990) would argue, however, that such disclosures (which, on average, really do not cause excessive inconvenience for companies) are really implemented to pacify the challenges, for example by or on behalf of particular minorities, that may be made against the capitalist system in which corporations are given many rights and powers. Relating this perspective to the development of various securities acts throughout the world, Merino and Neimark (1982, p. 49) contend that 'the securities acts were designed to maintain the ideological, social, and economic status quo while restoring confidence in the existing system and its institutions'. Within the Australian context, it is interesting to note that a chief executive officer of one of Australia's largest companies conceded that corporate regulations overwhelmingly support the interests of the owners of capital (shareholders) rather than stakeholders generally. Frank Cicutto, then chief executive officer of National Australia Bank, stated:[10]

> In recent decades the efficient use of shareholder funds has been carefully protected by the creation of the Australian Securities and Investments Commission (ASIC) and the continuing development of the Australian Stock Exchange (ASX) listing rules. In a regulatory sense the focus of legislative change has been around accountability to investors rather than to the community.

It is generally accepted that to make informed decisions an individual or groups of individuals must have access to information. Restricting the flow of information, or the availability of specific types of information, can restrict the ability of other parties to make informed choices. Hence, restricting available information is one strategy that can be employed to assist in the maintenance of particular organisations and social structures. Puxty (1986, p. 87) promotes this view by arguing that:

> ... financial information is legislated by the governing body of society (the state) which is closely linked to the interests of the dominant power group in society (Miliband, 1969, 1983, Offe and Ronge, 1978) and regulated either by agencies of that state or by institutions such as exist within societies like the United Kingdom, United States, and Australia that are linked to the needs of the dominant power group in partnership with the state apparatus (albeit a partnership that is potentially fraught with conflict).

Hence we are left with a view that government does not operate in the public interest but in the interests of those groups that are already well off and powerful.[11]

Apart from the state and the accounting profession, researchers and research institutions have also been implicated as assisting in the promotion of particular (inequitable) social structures. Some of the arguments that have been advanced to support this view are now considered.

THE ROLE OF ACCOUNTING RESEARCH IN SUPPORTING EXISTING SOCIAL STRUCTURES

Rather than thinking of accounting researchers as being relatively inert with respect to their impact on parties outside their discipline, numerous critical theorists see many accounting

---

10 As quoted in the *Journal of Banking and Financial Services*, December 2002, p. 17.

11 Contrast this with the view provided by public interest theory—a theory of regulation described in Chapter 3 and in which it is argued that government puts in place rules and regulations for the benefit of society generally.

researchers as providing research results and perspectives that help to legitimise and maintain particular political ideologies. Again, this is a different perspective from what most accountants and accounting students would be used to.

ACCOUNTING RESEARCH AND SUPPORT FOR DEREGULATION OF ACCOUNTING

As an example, in the late 1970s and in the 1980s there were moves by particular governments around the world towards deregulation. This was particularly the case in the United States and the United Kingdom. Around this time, researchers working within the Positive Accounting framework, and researchers who embraced the Efficient Market Hypothesis, came to prominence.[12] These researchers typically took an anti-regulation stance, a stance that matched the views of the government of the time. Coincidentally, perhaps, such research, which supported calls for deregulation, tended to attract considerable government-sourced research funding.[13] As Hopper et al. (1995, p. 518) state:

> Academic debates do not exist in a vacuum. It is not enough for a paradigm to be intellectually convincing for its acceptance, it must also be congruent with prevailing powerful beliefs within society more generally. The history of ideas is littered with research that was mocked but which subsequently became the dominant paradigm when other social concerns, ideologies and beliefs became prevalent. The story of PAT can be told in such terms. Its rise was not just due to its addressal of academic threats and concerns at the time of its inception but it was also in tandem with and connected to the right wing political ideologies dominant in the 1980s.

Mouck (1992) also adopts a position that argues that the rise of Positive Accounting Theory (PAT) was made possible because it was consistent with the political views of those in power (that is, the state):

> … the credibility of Watts and Zimmerman's rhetoric of revolt against government regulation of corporate accountability was conditioned, to a large extent, by the widespread, ultra-conservative movement toward deregulation that was taking place in society at large … I would argue that accountants have been willing to accept the PAT story, which is built on Chicago's version of laissez faire economics, because the rhetoric of the story was very much attuned to the Reagan era revolt against government interference in economic affairs.

Consistent with the development of PAT, in the late 1970s a great deal of accounting research sought to highlight the economic consequences of new accounting regulation. This perspective (which was considered in Chapters 2 and 3) argues that the implementation of new accounting regulations can have many unwanted economic implications, and hence before a new requirement such as an accounting standard is mandated careful consideration is warranted. Economic

---

12 According to Tinker, Merino and Neimark (1982), researchers within the Positive Accounting and Efficient Markets paradigms adopted 'a neoconservative ideological bias that encourages us to take the "free" market and implicit institutional apparatus as given'. PAT and the Efficient Markets Hypothesis were discussed in Chapters 7 and 10 respectively.

13 Consistent with this perspective, in 1979 Milton Friedman, a leading advocate of deregulation, became a senior adviser to US President Reagan.

consequences analysis often provided a rationale for not implementing accounting regulation. Critical researchers have argued that it was the economic implications for shareholders (for example, through changes in share prices) and managers (for example, through reductions in salary or loss of employment) that were the focus of attention by those who researched the economic consequences of accounting regulation. As Cooper and Sherer (1984, pp. 215, 217) argue:

> It seems unfortunate, however, that the 'rise of economic consequences' (Zeff, 1978) seems to have been motivated, at least in the United States, by a desire of large corporations to counter attempts to change the existing reporting systems and levels of disclosure. To date, it would seem that accounting researchers have generally reiterated the complaints of investors and businessmen about the consequences of changes in required accounting practice. Studies using ECA (economic consequences analysis) have almost invariably evaluated the consequences of accounting reports solely in terms of the behaviors and interest of the shareholder and/or corporate manager class (Selto and Neumann, 1981).
>
> More fundamentally, studies adopting the ECA approach have focused their attention on a very limited subset of the total economy, namely, the impact on the shareholder or manager class. The effects of accounting reports directly on other users, e.g. governments and unions, and indirectly on 'non-users', e.g. consumers, employees, and taxpayers, have been ignored. The basis of such a decision can, at best, be that any such effects are either secondary and/or lacking in economic significance. Thus, these studies have made an implicit value statement that the needs of the shareholder and manager class are of primary importance and the concentration on those needs is sufficient for an understanding of the role of accounting reports in society. Unless the insignificance of the effects on other users and 'non-users' is demonstrated rather than merely assumed, the conclusion from this research cannot be generalised for the economy as a whole and these studies are insufficient for making accounting prescriptions intended to improve overall social welfare.

Apart from indicating that economic consequences research focused predominantly on the economic implications for managers and shareholders, Cooper and Sherer (1984) also note that major studies that adopted this paradigm were funded by the US Securities and Exchange Commission and the US Financial Accounting Standards Board. It was considered that the interests of these bodies were aligned with the 'shareholder and manager class', rather than society as a whole.

In a similar vein, Thompson (1978) and Burchell et al. (1980) suggest that the research efforts into inflation accounting in the 1960s and 1970s were not actually motivated by the rate of inflation per se. Instead, they argue that the research had been motivated by a desire to alleviate the shifts in real wealth away from owners (in the form of lower real profits and dividends) and towards higher wages.

If research gains prominence because it supports the particular political beliefs of those in power, we might assume that as the views of those in 'power' change so will the focus of research. During the 1990s many governments around the world tended to move away from deregulation. Reflecting on this, Hopper et al. (1995, p. 540) noted:

> The environment is continually being reconstituted within changing economic and political conditions. Accordingly, the ability of PAT to resonate with the prevailing discursive climate

may be subject to challenge … Following the removal of the Republican government in the USA, this particular period and form of conservative reform may have ended. In the USA President Clinton is [was] adopting a more interventionist strategy and in the UK, the Major regime claims [claimed] to espouse an alternative 'caring society', albeit with market forces, in contrast to the harsher face of Thatcherism. In the 1990s a new set of values may be emerging which do not emphasise so greatly the efficiency and effectiveness of unregulated markets, for example, ecology, health care in the USA, gender issues. The ability of PAT to resonate with this changed environment may be brought into question; for example, the consecutive failure of some business enterprises and the stock market crash of 1987 augmented the call for more regulation.

A CRITICAL ACCOUNTING INTERPRETATION OF INCREASED ACCOUNTING REGULATION POST-ENRON

Despite the election of what many consider to be a highly pro-business and anti-regulation (former) Republican president (George W. Bush) and government in the United States at the beginning of the twenty-first century, and the re-election of this president and government at the end of 2004, few governments (including the US government) have reversed the 1990s trend against the deregulation of accounting. Although the Bush government initially made moves towards greater deregulation of accounting, this policy direction was reversed following public revelations about the large-scale accounting failures (or abuses) at Enron, WorldCom and several other large US corporations in 2001 and 2002, and the apparent complicity of Enron's auditor (Andersen) in some of these failed and damaging accounting practices. Despite any existing governmental desire there may have been to empower large corporations further by deregulating accounting practices, Unerman and O'Dwyer (2004) argue that these highly publicised accounting failures led to a considerable reduction in the trust placed by many investors and workers in both accounting practices and, more importantly, the reliability of capital markets as a medium for investment. One reaction of many governments throughout the world to these corporate and accounting failures was to increase the regulation of accounting and corporate governance, in an attempt to rebuild trust in the reliability of accounting information and in the capital markets, which are supposedly dependent on the claimed reliability of this accounting information. From a critical perspective, this increase in regulation would be regarded as serving the needs of large corporations (rather than protecting investors), as it was aimed at sustaining investor trust in the capital markets on which large corporations rely.

The damaging impact of accounting failures at Enron, followed by highly publicised accounting failures over a relatively short period of time at several other large corporations—in North America, Australia and Europe (for example, Parmalat in Italy, Ahold in the Netherlands, Addeco in Switzerland and One. Tel and HIH in Australia)—could be regarded by critical accounting scholars as just another symptom of the inherent instability of the capitalist system (as discussed earlier). These researchers would tend to argue that any actions taken to prevent a reoccurrence of this latest symptom of the structural conflicts inherent in capitalism (accounting failures) misses the point that it is the capitalist system itself which is flawed, and the only way to prevent other (different) failures emerging in the future is to replace the capitalist system with a different system in which the weak (employees, the environment, many sections of society) are not exploited by the powerful (large corporations and the governments they support). Several researchers have indeed examined the early twenty-first century accounting failures at Enron (and other large corporations), and/or the regulatory reaction to these failures, from a variety of critical perspectives (see, for example, Arnold and De Lange, 2004; Baker, 2003; Briloff, 2004; Craig and Amernic, 2004; Froud et al., 2004; Fuerman, 2004; O'Connell, 2004; and Williams, 2004).

A CRITICAL ACCOUNTING VIEW ON THE ACTIVE ROLE OF ACADEMIC AND NON-ACADEMIC DISCOURSE IN PROTECTING CAPITALISM

In another area, some critical theorists have implicated the editors of accounting journals in ensuring that accounting research does not challenge the interests of dominant groups in society, arguing that these editors will reject research that does not have 'complementarity with themes prevailing in the social milieu' (Mouck, 1992). In relation to the role of accounting journals, Tinker, Lehman and Neimark (1991, p. 44) state:

> Accounting literature represents the world in a manner conducive to the changing needs of capital accumulation. Journals such as *Accounting Review* adjudicate in secondary conflicts by filtering research, scholarship (and untenured scholars) in a manner conducive to this primary purpose. The hostility of this journal to even the tamest 'deviants' is well known.[14]

Other research in critical accounting demonstrates that it is not just academic discourse which is biased in a manner designed to support the interests of capitalism. For example, Collison (2003) characterises as propaganda many of the justifications that are given by organisations operating in the corporate sector in support of existing business and accounting practices, where subjective values (biased in the direction of furthering the power and wealth of capital) are portrayed as objective facts. He argues (p. 853):

> The effect of this use of propaganda ... is to buttress the hegemony of discourse ... in which the contestable values that are often implicit in the practices and terminology of accounting and finance are treated as though they are uncontentious ... [and that propaganda is] a tool that can be used by powerful interests, often covertly, to support and proselytise a prevailing ideology.

Developing this theme of accounting being used as a tool to 'objectify' subjective views, our analysis moves to the critical theorists' perceptions of the role of accounting practice in supporting existing social structures.

---

14 In recent years, however, it does appear that more research of a critical nature is being published within some leading accounting journals. One journal that has been in existence for a number of years (for many years edited by David Cooper and Tony Tinker) and that publishes various 'critical' papers is *Critical Perspectives on Accounting*. According to the journal (as per its Instructions to Authors'), it 'aims to provide a forum for a growing number of accounting researchers and practitioners who realize that conventional theory and practice is ill-suited to the challenges of the modern environment, and that accounting practices and corporate behaviour are inextricably connected with many allocative, social and ecological problems of our era. From such concerns, a new literature is emerging that seeks to reformulate corporate, social and political activity, and the theoretical and practical means by which we apprehend and affect that activity.'

THE ROLE OF ACCOUNTING PRACTICE IN SUPPORTING EXISTING SOCIAL STRUCTURES

The qualitative attributes of *objectivity*, *neutrality* and *representational faithfulness* are promoted in various conceptual framework projects throughout the world as being 'ideals' to which external financial statements should aspire. There is a view promoted by the profession that accounting can and should provide an objective representation of the underlying economic facts.[15]

However, a number of critical theorists see a different role for conceptual frameworks: a role that involves legitimising the accounting profession, as well as the financial statements produced by reporting entities. Hines (1991, p. 328) states:

> Conceptual Frameworks (CFs) presume, legitimise and reproduce the assumptions of an objective world and as such they play a part in constituting the social world ... CFs provide social legitimacy to the accounting profession. Since the objectivity assumption is the central premise of our society ... a fundamental form of social power accrues to those who are able to trade on the objectivity assumption. Legitimacy is achieved by tapping into this central proposition because accounts generated around this proposition are perceived as 'normal'. It is perhaps not surprising or anomalous then that CF projects continue to be undertaken which rely on information qualities such as 'representational faithfulness', 'neutrality', 'reliability', etc., which presume a concrete, objective world, even though past CFs have not succeeded in generating Accounting Standards which achieve these qualities. The very talk, predicated on the assumption of an objective world to which accountants have privileged access via their 'measurement expertise', serves to construct a perceived legitimacy for the profession's power and autonomy.

THE ROLE OF ACCOUNTING STATEMENTS IN CREATING A SELECTIVE 'REALITY'

Hines (1988) argues that accountants impose their own views about which performance characteristics are important and thereby require emphasis (for example, 'profits'). Accountants also decide which attributes of organisation performance are not important, and therefore are not worthy of measurement or disclosure. Through the practice of accounting, attention will be directed to the particular measures the (apparently objective) accountant has emphasised and in turn these measures will become a means of differentiating 'good' organisations from 'bad' organisations. For example, if 'profits' are promoted as an objective measure of organisational performance, then people will focus on profits as calculated by the accountant, and a profitable company will be deemed to be a good company and a loss-making company will be deemed to be a bad company. This is despite the fact that 'profits', as determined by the accountant, will ignore many social and environmental externalities caused by the business (as discussed

---

15 This is consistent with the argument provided by Solomons (1978) that to increase the usefulness of accounting reports they should be as objective as cartography. That is, just as an area can be objectively 'mapped', so can the financial position and performance of an organisation.

in Chapter 9). For example, if the organisation emits pollution but there are no costs or fines attached to the emissions, no costs will be recognised despite the damage to the environment and society that is potentially being caused by the emissions. Hines argues that in communicating reality accountants simultaneously construct reality. Hence, for example, the failure to account for the effects of pollution emissions means that to many people such emissions are non-existent. They do not appear in the accounts of the company's performance. If the accountant put a cost on such emissions, they would become 'real', and the organisation would become accountable. Accounting provides a selective visibility for particular issues within an organisation that dictates which financial issues are 'significant' (Carpenter & Feroz, 1992). Cooper, Hayes and Wolf (1981, p. 182) also adopt this perspective in stating:

> Accounting systems encourage imitation and coercion by defining the problematic (by choosing which variables are measured and reported) and they help to fashion solutions (by choosing which variables are to be treated as controllable). Of course, the way accounting systems are used is highly significant, but nevertheless the structure and elements of accounting systems help to create the appropriate and acceptable ways of acting, organising and talking about issues in organisations. Accounting systems are a significant component of the power system in an organisation.

In exploring the role of accounting reports in 'constructing' particular 'realities', Macintosh and Baker (2002) and Macintosh (2001) draw on developments in literary theory, and argue that accounting reports can be viewed as a form of literary text/document. They demonstrate that in literary theory the 'expressive realism' notion that a text is an objective reflection of an underlying reality (that a novel, for example, 'acts like a mirror to reflect reality' (Macintosh & Baker, 2002, p. 189)) has long been regarded as highly problematic, and they draw on these criticisms from literary theory to demonstrate how similar assumptions of accounting reports objectively reflecting an external economic reality are equally problematic (p. 192):

> ... the common sense view of accounting assumes that the financial reality of an enterprise is 'out-there' prior to its capture in accounting reports. The proper way of ascertaining this reality is thought to be with objective and verifiable measurement processes. This realist correspondence view of the accounting assumes the financial reality of a corporation exists independently of accountants, auditors, and accounting reports. Yet accounting runs up against the same problem that undermined expressive realism [in literary theory]. Different equally qualified professional accountants come up with different financial statements for identical transactions and events.

Macintosh (2001) and Macintosh and Baker (2002) then use different paradigms in literary theory to analyse and explain the subjectivity of accounting reports, and the partial views of reality constructed by these reports. They argue that any accounting report will tend to present selective and biased information in a manner designed to lead to the construction of a single view of the underlying reality, with this view being the one that most favours management and providers of capital. These academics then argue, based on poststructuralist literary theory, for accounting reports to change so they contain a sufficient variety of information to enable different users of accounts to see a variety of sometimes contradictory views of the reality underlying the business, rather than accounting information being selectively presented in an objectified manner to 'force' a single partisan view of the business.

2. THE POWER OF ACCOUNTANTS THROUGH A FALSE IMAGE OF NEUTRALITY

For those people who have not previously considered accountants in the same light as do the critical theorists, there may be some form of bewilderment. How can accountants have so much power? In part, some arguments for this issue have been provided in the discussion above. The accounting profession is portrayed (through such vehicles as conceptual frameworks) as being objective and neutral—that is, free from any form of bias. Such characteristics (if true) are apparently beyond reproach. In fact, accountants are perceived as so objective and neutral that they have a reputation for being very dull. But if we are to believe the critical theorists, this 'dullness' is a façade that perhaps hides a great deal of social power.[16] As Carpenter and Feroz (1992, p. 618) state:

> ... accounting may be viewed as a means of legitimising the current social and political structure of the organisation. Hopwood (1983) further suggests that the legitimising force of accounting derives in part from the apparently dull, unobtrusive, and routine nature of accounting procedures, which generate an aura of objectivity and legitimacy in the eyes of financial statement users. Far from being dull and routine, accounting and accountants can and do take sides in social conflicts.

Tinker, Merino and Niemark (1982, p. 184), argue:

> This image of the accountant—often as a disinterested, innocuous 'historian'—stems from a desire to deny the responsibility that accountants bear for shaping subjective expectations which, in turn, affect decisions about resource allocation and the distribution of income between and within social classes. The attachment to historical facts provides a veneer of pseudo-objectivity that allows accountants to claim that they merely record—not partake in—social conflicts.

Research that investigated the economic consequences of accounting requirements was discussed earlier in the chapter (as well as in Chapter 3). Once a profession starts considering the economic consequences of particular accounting standards, it is difficult to perceive that the accounting standards, and therefore accounting, would really be considered as truly objective and neutral.

3. A CRITICAL ACCOUNTING PERSPECTIVE OF ACCOUNTING AND LEGITIMATION

Moving onto another aspect of how critical accounting researchers believe that accounting practices 'silently' and 'stealthily' reinforce capitalist power, among the other theoretical perspectives considered earlier is Legitimacy Theory (discussed in Chapter 8). Organisations often use documents such as annual reports to legitimise the ongoing existence of the entity. While these disclosures can be explained in terms of a desire by the corporation to appear to be acting in terms of the 'social contract' (which may or may not be the case), some critical theorists see the legitimation motive as potentially quite harmful, particularly if it legitimises

---

16 We are again back to the position that was introduced in Chapter 2—accountants are indeed very powerful individuals.

activities that are not in the interests of particular classes within society. As Puxty (1991, p. 39) states:

> I do not accept that I see legitimation as innocuous. It seems to me that the legitimation can be very harmful indeed, insofar as it acts as a barrier to enlightenment and hence progress.

In considering the use of social and environmental disclosures to legitimise corporate behaviour, Deegan, Rankin and Tobin (2002, p. 334) state:

> Legitimising disclosures mean that the organisation is responding to particular concerns that have arisen in relation to their operations. The implication is that unless concerns are aroused (and importantly, the managers perceive the existence of such concerns) then unregulated disclosures could be quite minimal. Disclosure decisions driven by the desire to be legitimate are not the same as disclosure policies driven by a management view that the community has a right-to-know about certain aspects of an organisation's operations. One motivation relates to survival, whereas the other motivation relates to responsibility.

Deegan, Rankin and Tobin (2002, p. 335) further state:

> Legitimising disclosures are linked to corporate survival. In jurisdictions where there are limited regulatory requirements to provide social and environmental information, management appear to provide information when they are coerced into doing so. Conversely, where there is limited concern, there will be limited disclosures. The evidence suggests that higher levels of disclosure will only occur when community concerns are aroused, or alternatively, until such time that specific regulation is introduced to eliminate managements' disclosure discretion. However, if corporate legitimising activities are successful then perhaps public pressure for government to introduce disclosure legislation will be low and managers will be able to retain control of their social and environmental reporting practices.

Consistent with the above discussion, Guthrie and Parker (1990, p. 166) believe that the political economy perspective adopted by critical theorists emphasises the role of accounting reports in maintaining (or legitimising) particular social arrangements:

> The political economy perspective perceives accounting reports as social, political, and economic documents. They serve as a tool for constructing, sustaining, and legitimising economic and political arrangements, institutions, and ideological themes which contribute to the corporation's private interests.

THE ROLE OF ACCOUNTING IN LEGITIMISING THE CAPITALIST SYSTEM

Given the role of accounting reports in 'constructing, sustaining, and legitimising economic and political arrangements, institutions, and ideological themes which contribute to the corporation's private interests' (Guthrie & Parker, 1990, p. 166), the classical political economy perspective views one of the key roles of accounting reports as being to legitimise the capitalist system as a whole, and to protect this system from threats arising as a result of the outcomes of the structural conflict inherent in the capitalist system (as discussed earlier in the chapter). This, for example, is part of the reason why many critical accounting scholars are opposed to much research into corporate social reporting practices, as highlighted earlier in the chapter.

A major critical accounting empirical study, examining the role that disclosures in annual reports played in protecting (and legitimising) the capitalist system as a whole from the outcomes of social conflict, analysed the annual reports of the US-based car multinational General Motors over the period 1917 to 1976. This empirical material was analysed in a series of papers (Neimark, 1983; Neimark & Tinker, 1986; Tinker, Lehman & Neimark, 1991; Tinker & Neimark, 1987; Tinker & Neimark, 1988) which demonstrated that the focus of voluntary, discursive material in the annual reports tended to change to address the changing challenges to capitalism arising from the structural instability of capitalism. For example, in times when the (claimed) symptoms of this structural instability were weaknesses in overall consumer demand, the annual reports focused on giving the impression that increased consumption—such as regularly buying a new car—was an ideal social norm. At other times, when the symptoms of the structural instability of capitalism was labour militancy, the focus of the core messages in the annual report switched to a demonstration that workers were better off if they acted in cooperation rather than in conflict with managers.

The argument in these studies seems to be that while successful articulation of these management viewpoints might benefit General Motors economically, through maintaining the support of economically powerful stakeholders, they also benefited the capitalist system as a whole because, for example, developing a norm of consumption in times of weakened overall economic demand should result in greater demand for the products of many businesses. If other businesses also used their annual reports, in conjunction with messages in other media such as advertising and newspaper articles, at this point in history to help reinforce a consistent message about the social desirability of consumption, this would help protect and advance the power and wealth of many businesses by increasing overall consumer demand. As Tinker, Lehman and Neimark (1991, p. 39) state:

> The General Motors studies ... focus on the various ways the company uses its annual reports as an ideological weapon, and the social circumstances that govern one use rather than another ... [they uncover] the conflictual and antagonistic situations that embroiled GM over that period, and the way the firm's reports were used to modify and ameliorate these conflicts ... This is not to argue that annual reports have a dramatic impact on business and political decision making. Rather, like other ideological materials (party political statements, advertising, public relations 'fluff', religious dogma) it is the repetition of the mundane and particularly the censoring of other points of view that make these reports most effective.

CHAPTER SUMMARY

This chapter provides an overview of research that has been undertaken by people who have been classified as working within the critical perspective of accounting. These researchers are very critical of current accounting practices. They argue that existing financial accounting practices support the current economic and social structures—structures that unfairly benefit some people at the expense of others. The view that financial accounting practices are neutral and objective (as promoted in various conceptual framework projects) is challenged.

The critical perspective of accounting covers many different specific perspectives, and this chapter has explored only a few of the major ones. However, at a broad level, much critical accounting research is grounded in classical Political Economy Theory, in which conflict, inequity and the role of the State are central to the analysis. While the research positions of many critical accounting scholars are informed by a Marxist critique of capitalism, there are many other critical accounting researchers whose critiques of the role of accounting in sustaining inequities in society are not based on Marxist philosophy. A common theme among most Marxist (and some non-Marxist) critical accounting theorists is a call for fundamental changes in how society is structured, as, without this restructuring, they believe that any changes or modifications to accounting practices will have no effect in making society more equitable for all. Critical theorists also argue that governments (the State) tend to put in place mechanisms and regulations to support existing social structures. Many accounting researchers are also believed to be supporters of particular political ideologies, with the results of their research being influential in supporting those people with privileged access to scarce capital.

Although this chapter is relatively brief, the aim has been to provide an insight into a point of view that traditionally has not received a great deal of attention in accounting education or in accounting journals. Perhaps, as the critical theorists would argue, this lack of attention is due to the fact that this branch of the accounting literature challenges so many of the views and values held not only by accountants but by many others within society. The literature can indeed be quite confronting. It does, however, provide a different perspective on the role of accountants, and one that we should not immediately dismiss. If the literature causes us to be critical of our own position as accountants within society, well and good. As a concluding quote, reflect on the following statement by Baker and Bettner (1997, p. 293):

> Accounting's capacity to create and control social reality translates into empowerment for those who use it. Such power resides in organisations and institutions, where it is used to instill values, sustain legitimising myths, mask conflict and promote self-perpetuating social orders. Throughout society, the influence of accounting permeates fundamental issues concerning wealth distribution, social justice, political ideology and environmental degradation. Contrary to public opinion, accounting is not a static reflection of economic reality, but rather is a highly partisan activity.

QUESTIONS

12.1 What is a critical perspective of accounting?

12.2 What are some of the fundamental differences between the research undertaken by critical theorists, relative to the work undertaken by other accounting researchers?

12.3 From a critical perspective, what is the role of a conceptual framework project?

12.4 From a critical perspective, can financial statements ever be considered objective or neutral? Explain your answer.

12.5 If it is accepted that there are many inequities within society, would critical theorists argue that introducing more accounting, or improved methods of accounting, would or could help, or would they argue that such a strategy will only compound existing problems? Explain your answer. Do you agree with the position taken by the critical theorists? Why?

12.6 Critical theorists would challenge the work of authors whose work is grounded within Positive Accounting Theory. What is the basis of their opposition?

12.7 Critical theorists would challenge the work of authors whose work is grounded within Legitimacy Theory. What is the basis of their opposition?

12.8 If accounting is deemed to be complicit in sustaining social inequities, how would critical theorists argue that accounting can be 'fixed'?

12.9 Tinker, Merino and Neimark (1982) argue that 'the social allegiances and biases of accounting are rarely apparent; usually, they are 'masked' pretensions of objectivity and independence'. Explain the basis of this argument.

12.10 Cooper and Sherer (1984) argue that 'accounting researchers should be explicit about the normative elements of any framework adopted by them. All research is normative in the sense that it contains the researcher's value judgements about how society should be organised. However, very few accounting researchers make their value judgements explicit'. Do you agree or disagree with this claim? Why?

12.11 Explain the importance in critical accounting theory of assumptions regarding the distribution of power in society. How do these assumptions differ from those adopted in other theoretical perspectives?

12.12 CPA Australia (2005) made a submission to the Australian government inquiry into corporate social responsibility in which it stated (p. 6):

> While there is strong public (88%) and shareholder (86%) support for Government to mandate the reporting of companies' social and environmental reporting this is not reflected in the views of business leaders (53%). CPA Australia believes this reflects a valid business concern that mandatory reporting would not enhance the value of the information provided and introduce an unnecessary layer of regulation.

Evaluate this statement from a 'critical' perspective.

12.13 Why might critical theorists be opposed to academic research that attempts to assist corporations to put a cost on their social and environmental impacts?

12.14 Evaluate the following quote from the Business Council of Australia (2005) from a 'critical perspective':

> Given the difficulty defining corporate social responsibility (CSR), as well as the fact that CSR activities are already broadly being pursued in Australia by large corporations, mandating CSR through legislative intervention runs the risk of stifling the innovative and creative approaches to CSR that are being adopted by Australian companies.

REFERENCES

Arnold, B. & P. De Lange (2004), 'Enron: an examination of agency problems', *Critical Perspectives on Accounting*, 15(6–7), pp. 751–65.

Arnold, P. (1990), 'The state and political theory in corporate social disclosure research: a response to Guthrie and Parker', *Advances in Public Interest Accounting*, 3, pp. 177–81.

Bailey, D., G. Harte & R. Sugden (2000), 'Corporate disclosure and the deregulation of international investment', *Accounting, Auditing and Accountability Journal*, 13(2), pp. 197–218.

Baker, C. & M. Bettner (1997), 'Interpretive and critical research in accounting: a commentary on its absence from mainstream accounting research', *Critical Perspectives on Accounting*, 8(1), pp. 293–310.

Baker, R. C. (2003), 'Investigating Enron as a public private partnership', *Accounting, Auditing and Accountability Journal*, 16(3), pp. 446–66.

Briloff, A. (2004), 'Accounting scholars in the groves of academe In Pari Delicto', *Critical Perspectives on Accounting*, 15(6–7), pp. 787–96.

Burchell, S., C. Clubb, A. Hopwood, J. Hughes & J. Naphapiet (1980), 'The roles of accounting in organisations and society', *Accounting, Organizations and Society*, 5(1), pp. 5–28.

Business Council of Australia (2005), *Submission to the Parliamentary Joint Committee on Corporations and Financial Services—Inquiry into Corporate Responsibility and Triple Bottom Line Reporting*, Melbourne: BCA.

Carpenter, V. & E. Feroz (1992), 'GAAP as a symbol of legitimacy: New York State's decision to adopt generally accepted accounting principles', *Accounting,*

Organizations and Society, 17(7), pp. 613–43.

Chua, W. F., (1986), 'Radical developments in accounting thought', *The Accounting Review*, LXI(4).

Collison, D. J. (2003), 'Corporate propaganda: its implications for accounting and accountability', *Accounting, Auditing and Accountability Journal*, 16(5), pp. 853–86.

Cooper, D., D. Hayes & F. Wolf (1981), 'Accounting in organized anarchies', *Accounting, Organizations and Society*, 6, pp. 175–91.

Cooper, D. J. & M. J. Sherer (1984), 'The value of corporate accounting reports—arguments for a political economy of accounting', *Accounting, Organizations and Society*, 9(3/4), pp. 207–32.

Cousins, J., A. Mitchell, P. Sikka, C. Cooper & P. Arnold (2000), *Insolvent Abuse: Regulating the Insolvency Industry*, Basildon: Association for Accountancy and Business Affairs.

CPA Australia (2005), *Submission to the Parliamentary Joint Committee on Corporations and Financial Services—Inquiry into Corporate Responsibility*, Melbourne: CPA Australia.

Craig, R. J. & J. H. Amernic (2004), 'Enron discourse: the rhetoric of a resilient capitalism', *Critical Perspectives on Accounting*, 15(6–7), pp. 813–52.

De George, R. (1995), 'Praxis', in T. Honderich (ed.), *The Oxford Companion to Philosophy*, Oxford: Oxford University Press, p. 713.

Deegan, C., M. Rankin & J. Tobin (2002), 'An examination of the corporate social and environmental disclosures of BHP from 1983–1997', *Accounting, Auditing and Accountability Journal*, 15(3), pp. 312–43.

Froud, J., S. Johal, V. Papazian & K. Williams (2004), 'The temptation of Houston: a case study of financialisation', *Critical Perspectives on Accounting*, 15(6–7), pp. 885–909.

Fuerman, R. D. (2004), 'Accountable accountants', *Critical Perspectives on Accounting*, 15(6–7), pp. 911–26.

Gray, R., D. Owen & C. Adams (1996), *Accounting and Accountability: Changes and Challenges in Corporate Social and Environmental Reporting*, London: Prentice Hall.

Gray, R., D. Owen & K. Maunders (1988), 'Corporate social reporting: emerging trends in accountability and the social contract', *Accounting, Auditing and Accountability Journal*, 1(1), pp. 6–20.

Gray, R., D. Owen & K. T. Maunders (1987), *Corporate Social Reporting: Accounting and Accountability*, Hemel Hempstead: Prentice Hall.

Guthrie, J. & L. Parker (1990), 'Corporate social disclosure practice: a comparative international analysis', *Advances in Public Interest Accounting*, 3, pp. 159–75.

Hines, R. (1988), 'Financial accounting: in communicating reality, we construct reality', *Accounting, Organizations and Society*, 13(3), pp. 251–62.

Hines, R. (1991), 'The FASB's conceptual framework, financial accounting and the maintenance of the social world', *Accounting, Organizations and Society*, 16(4), pp. 313–51.

Hofstede, G. (1983), 'Dimensions of national cultures in fifty countries and three regions', in J. B. Derogowski, S. Dziuraweic & R. Annis (eds), *Expiscations in Cross-Cultural Psychology*, Lisse Swets and Zeitlinger.

Hofstede, G. (1984), 'Cultural dimensions in management and planning', *Asia Pacific Journal of Management;* 1(2), pp. 81–98

Hopper, T., M. Annisette, N. Dastoor, S. Uddin & D. Wickramasinghe (1995), 'Some challenges and alternatives to positive accounting research', in S. Jones, C. Romano & J. Ratnatunga (eds), *Accounting Theory: A Contemporary Review*, Australia: Harcourt Brace & Company.

Hopper, T. & A. Powell (1985), 'Making sense of research into the organisational and social aspects of management accounting: a review of its underlying assumptions', *Journal of Management Studies*, pp. 429–65.

Hopwood, A. G. (1983), 'On trying to study accounting in the context in which it operates', *Accounting, Organizations and Society*, 8(2/3), pp. 287–305.

Lehman, G. (1999), 'Disclosing new worlds: a role for social and environmental accounting and auditing', *Accounting, Organizations and Society*, 24(3), pp. 217–42.

Lehman, G. (2001), 'Reclaiming the public sphere: problems and prospects for corporate social and environmental accounting', *Critical Perspectives on Accounting*, 12, pp. 713–33.

Macintosh, N. B. (2001), *Accounting, Accountants and Accountability*, London: Routledge.

Macintosh, N. B. & R. C. Baker (2002), 'A literary theory perspective on accounting: towards heteroglossic accounting reports', *Accounting, Auditing and Accountability Journal*, 15(2), pp. 184–222.

Marx, K. & F. Engels (1967), *The Communist Manifesto*, Harmondsworth: Penguin.

Merino, B. & M. Neimark (1982), 'Disclosure regulation and public policy: a socio-historical appraisal', *Journal of Accounting and Public Policy*, 1, pp. 33–57.

Miliband, R. (1969), *The State in Capitalist Society*, Weidenfeld & Nicolson.

Miliband, R. (1983), 'State power and class interest', *New Left Review* (March), pp. 57–68.

Mitchell, A., A. Puxty, P. Sikka and H. Willmott (1994), 'Ethical statements as smokescreens for sectional interests: the case of the UK accountancy profession', *Journal of Business Ethics*, 13(1), pp. 39–51.

Moore, D. (1991), 'Accounting on trial: the critical legal studies movement and its lessons for radical accounting', *Accounting, Organizations and Society*, 16(8), pp. 763–91.

Mouck, T. (1992), 'The rhetoric of science and the rhetoric of revolt in the story of positive accounting theory', *Accounting, Auditing and Accountability Journal*, pp. 35–56.

Neimark, M. (1983), 'The social constructions of annual reports: a radical approach to corporate control', unpublished Doctoral dissertation, New York University.

Neimark, M. & A. Tinker (1986), 'The social construction of management control systems', *Accounting, Organization and Society*, 11(3), pp. 369–96.

Neu, D. & D. Cooper (1997), 'Accounting interventions', paper presented at Fifth Interdisciplinary Perspectives on Accounting Conference, University of Manchester.

O'Connell, B. T. (2004), 'Enron Inc.: "He that filches from me my good name ... makes me poor indeed"', *Critical Perspectives on Accounting*, 15(6–7), p. 733.

O'Dwyer, B. (2005), 'The construction of a social account: a case study in an overseas aid agency', *Accounting, Organizations and Society*, 30(3), pp. 279–96.

Offe, C. & V. Ronge (1978), 'Theses on the theory of the state', in A. Giddens & D. Held (eds), *Class, Power and Conflict*, London: Edward Arnold, pp. 32–39.

Owen, D., R. Gray & J. Bebbington (1997), 'Green accounting: cosmetic irrelevance or radical agenda for change?', *Asia-Pacific Journal of Accounting*, 4(2), pp. 175–98.

Puxty, A. (1986), 'Social accounting as immanent legitimation: a critique of a

technist ideology', *Advances in Public Interest Accounting*, 4, pp. 95–112.

Puxty, A. (1991), 'Social accountability and universal pragmatics', *Advances in Public Interest Accounting*, 4, pp. 35–46.

Puxty, A., P. Sikka & H. Willmott (1994), '(Re)Forming the circle: education, ethics and accountancy practices', *Accounting Education*, 3(1), pp. 77–92.

Reiter, S. (1995), 'Theory and politics: lessons from feminist economics', *Accounting, Auditing and Accountability Journal*, 8(3), pp. 34–59.

Roslender, R. (2006), 'Critical theory', in Z. Hoque (ed.), *Methodological Issues in Accounting Research: Theories and Method*, London: Spiramus Press, pp. 247–70.

Selto, F. & B. Neumann (1981), 'A further guide to research on the economic consequences of accounting information', *Accounting and Business Research*, 11(44), pp. 317–22.

Sikka, P., B. Wearing & A. Nayak (1999), *No Accounting for Exploitation*, Basildon: Association for Accountancy and Business Affairs.

Sikka, P. & H. Willmott (2005), 'The withering of tolerance and communication in interdisciplinary accounting studies', *Accounting, Auditing and Accountability Journal*, 18(1), pp. 136–46.

Solomons, D. (1978), 'The politicization of accounting', *Journal of Accountancy*, 146(5), pp. 65–72.

Thompson, G. (1978), 'Capitalist profit calculation and inflation accounting', *Economy and Society*, pp. 395–429.

Tinker, A. & R. Gray (2003), 'Beyond a critique of pure reason: from policy to politics and praxis in environmental and social research', *Accounting, Auditing and Accountability Journal*, 16(5), pp. 727–61.

Tinker, A., C. Lehman & M. Neimark (1991), 'Falling down the hole in the middle of the road: political quietism in corporate social reporting', *Accounting, Auditing and Accountability Journal,* 4(1), pp. 28–54.

Tinker, A. & M. Neimark (1987), 'The role of annual reports in gender and class contradictions at General Motors: 1917–1976', *Accounting, Organizations and Society,* 12(1), pp. 71–88.

Tinker, A. & M. Neimark (1988), 'The struggle over meaning in accounting and corporate research: a comparative evaluation of conservative and critical historiography', *Accounting, Auditing and Accountability Journal,* 1(1), pp. 55–74.

Tinker, A. M., B. D Merino & M. D. Neimark (1982), 'The normative origins of positive theories: ideology and accounting thought', *Accounting, Organizations and Society,* 7(2), pp. 167–200.

Tinker, T. (2005), 'The withering of criticism: a review of professional, Foucauldian, ethnographic, and epistemic studies in accounting', *Accounting, Auditing and Accountability Journal,* 18(1), pp. 100–35.

Unerman, J. & M. Bennett (2004), 'Increased stakeholder dialogue and the internet: towards greater corporate accountability or reinforcing capitalist hegemony?', *Accounting, Organizations and Society,* 29(7), pp. 685–707.

Unerman, J. & B. O'Dwyer (2004), 'Enron, WorldCom, Andersen et al: A challenge to modernity', *Critical Perspectives on Accounting,* 15(6–7), pp. 971–93.

Williams, P. F. (2004), 'You reap what you sow: the ethical discourse of professional accounting', *Critical Perspectives on Accounting,* 15(6–7), p. 995.

Willmott, H. (1990), 'Serving the public interest', in D. J. Cooper & T. M. Hopper (eds), *Critical Accounts,* London: Macmillan.

Wood, A. (1995), 'Marx, Karl Heinrich', in T. Honderich (ed.), *The Oxford Companion to Philosophy* Oxford: Oxford University Press, pp. 523–26.

Zeff, S. A. (1978), 'The rise of economic consequences', *Journal of Accountancy,* 146(6), pp. 56–63.

INDEX

Page numbers in *italics* refer to figures

Coalition for Environmentally Responsible
    Economies 426
Coase, Ronald 268
Coca-Cola Amatil 84
coercive isomorphism 359, 360, 364, 366
collectivism 136–37, 137n, 139
Collett, P. 91
Collins, D. 487
Collison, D.J. 67–68, 68n, 409, 418, 546
Commission of European Communities 381
Committee for Economic Development (US) 349
Committee on Accounting Procedure (US) 39
Committee on Accounting Valuation Basis 504
common law 145–49
Commonwealth Bank of Australia (CBA) 48–49,
    297–98, 418, 471, 480
communication strategy 332–33, 405, 411–12
community licence to operate. *see* social contract
comparability 114–15, 230, 232, 427
Competition Commission (UK) 295
completeness 229, 427
comprehensive income 235
Conceptual Framework Project 4, 20–21,
    35n, 224
conceptual frameworks
    absence of 212, 216, 226, 246
    benefits of 244–46
    components of 212–13, *213*, 220–44,
        247–48
    criticisms of 246
    definitions 211–15
    development of, history of 215–20
    expenses and assets in 417
    legitimising role of 130–31, 246–48, 547
    as normative theories 21, 208–52
    see also entries for specific frameworks
conflict, in society 323
Connolly, Chris 355
Conroy, Stephen 355
conservatism 138–42, *141*, 230, 289–90
    see also neo-conservatism
consistency 230, 513
consolidated financial statements 275
constant dollar accounting. *see* current
    purchasing power accounting
constructive obligations 239
Consumer Price Index (CPI) 171–72
consumption 384, 393n
continental European model, of accounting 116,
    133, 133n, 142, 149, 150

Continuously Contemporary Accounting
    (CoCoA) 8n, 12, 190–96, 201, 203, 226,
    237, 257
contract(s) 265, 265n
    debt 290n, 290–92, 307
    nexus of 267–69
    social 325–28, 334–35, 345–46, 349, 365,
        388, 391, 549
contracting
    costs of 269, 269n
    owner-manager 277–88
control
    of reporting entities 237
    social 512
control mechanisms 267, 417
Convergence Project (FASB-IASB) 115, 121–24,
    210–12, 214, 219–20
    Exposure Draft 21, 35n, 90, 211, 224
Converse 444
Cooper, D.J. 323, 535, 537, 539, 544, 548
Cooper, K. 61n, 65
Cooper, S. 406
Co-operative Financial Services Group 387, 406
Coopers 112
Corporate Law Economic Reform Program
    (CLERP) 110, 119
CorporateRegister.com (website) 381n
The Corporate Report 218–19, 223–24, 227
Corporate Reporting: Its Future Evolution 219
corporate social responsibility (CSR)
    Australian inquiries into 68–70, 70n
    defined 381
corporate social responsibility reporting
        378–456
    in accounting theories 352n, 352–53
    argument for 36n, 445
    Australian government inquiry into 350,
        393–94, 540
    business case for 394–95
    business responsibilities and 396–401
    conservative view of 348n
    content of 407–13, 426–27
    critical theory and 534–36
    elements of 381
    environmental disclosure 300–301, 336–37, 344
    externalities in 428–36
    guidelines for 422–28
    history of 382–83, 445
    limitations of traditional accounting for 414–19
    motivations for 389–90

Elias, N. 510
elite 323, 528
Elkington, J. 383, 436
Elliot, R.K. 165, 166n, 196
Elliott, Geoff 343
Emanuel, D. 268, 281
emissions trading scheme 416n
emotional thinking 21–22
enforcement, of international standards 128–32
enlightened self-interest 69–70, 70n, 394–95
Enron
    accounting failures 6, 58, 121n
        accounting method and 108
        disclosure and 40, 61n, 64
        impact of 58, 72, 78, 467n, 545–46
        users' understanding of reports and 35
    creative accounting 45–46, 91, 151, 233
entity assumption 415, 434
environmental accountants 381
Environmental Accounting and Auditing Reporter
    430, 440, 441
environmental capital 169
environmental costs, of production 386, 429–30
Environmental Financial Statement (EFS)
    430–31, *431–33*
environmental performance of companies 325,
    330, 333–34, 336–37, 344n
environmental protection authorities (EPAs) 337
environmental reporting. *see* corporate social
    responsibility reporting
environmental resources, valuation of 422
Environmental Task Force on the European
    Federation of Accountants 428
Equator Principles 328
equitable obligations 239
equity 235, 240–41
equity investments, measurement of 200n
Ernst & Young 131, 402, 403
Ertimur, Y. 483
ethical branch, of Stakeholder Theory 345–50, 354,
    365, 390, 392, 393, 404, 405, 410, 412, 445
Ethical Investment Association 396
Ettredge, M. 295
European Chemical Industry Council 428
European Financial Reporting Advisory Group
    (EFRAG) 117
European Union (EU)
    emissions trading scheme 416n
    international standards adopted by 107, 115–18
    lobbying against IAS 89

    membership 115n
    regulation in 40, 43n, 50, 86
    Towards Sustainability 386
Evan, W. 352
Evans, Alan 273
event studies 468n
evidence
    of international differences in accounting 107–9
    theory evaluation using 18–24
ex ante perspective. *see* efficiency perspective
exit price accounting 190–96, 203
expectations gap 91, 91n
expected earnings 262, 481
expected returns 473, 473n
expenses 235, 241–42, 417
ex post perspective. *see* opportunistic perspective
*Exposure Draft of an Improved Conceptual
    Framework for Financial Reporting* 21, 35n,
    90, 211, 224
externalities 413, 414, 419, 428–36, 547–48
Exxon Oil Company 336

F

fair value model 129, 165n, 165–66, 166n, 200n,
    202, 210
falsificationism 17n, 17–18, 260
Fama, E. 261, 267, 269, 489
FASB. *see* Financial Accounting Standards Board
Federal Trade Commission (US) 295
feedback 229
Feltham, G. 65
Felton, S. 46, 46n, 47n
femininity 137, 140n, 537–38
Feroz, E. 339–40, 357, 358–59, 363, 549
Fields, T. 277, 296, 304–5
Fiji 111, 143–44, 148
Fila 444
Finance Sector Union 418
Financial Accounting Foundation (FAF) 123n,
    123–25
Financial Accounting Standards Board (US) 120
    accounting standards released by 43n
    APB replaced by 40, 120n
    conceptual framework 4, 210, 217–18, 235–36
    on deregulation 544
    Discussion Memorandum (1974) 197, 225n, 270–71
    Financial Accounting Standard 94 274n
    IASB Convergence Project 115, 121–23,
    210–12, 214, 219–20
        Exposure Draft 21, 35n, 90, 211, 224

Friedman, Milton 67–68, 256, 396–97, 397n, 400,
    401, 543n
Frost, G. 342
frozen GAAP 280, 291
full-cost accounting 429
functional fixation hypothesis 478, 478n
fundamental analysis 464n

G
gain and losses, in financial reporting 235–36,
    241–42
Garsden, R. 466, 467
Gates, Bill 401
2GB 343
GCM (going concern modification) 466–67
GDP (Gross Domestic Product) 420–21
generalisations, in social science 23–24
generally accepted accounting practice (GAAP)
    floating (rolling) 280n, 281, 291–92
    frozen 280, 291
    Institutional Theory and 363–64
    investor information and 476
    legitimacy and 339–40
Generally Accepted Accounting Procedures (US)
    106, 108, 120
General Motors 383, 551
general price level accounting 86, 175, 197, 270
    see also current purchasing power accounting
general price level adjustments (GPLAs) 270–71
general purchasing power accounting. *see* current
    purchasing power accounting
general purpose financial reports 221, 225–28
    conceptual frameworks for 122, 214n
    defined 34, 34n
Genuine Progress Indicator (GPI) 422
Gerboth, D.L. 89
Germany 126–27, 128, 152, 406
Gettler, Leon 397
G2 Guidelines 423
G3 Guidelines 423n, 423–24
Gibbs, B. 333
Gittins, Ross 517
Global Environment Management Initiative
    (US) 428
Global Fortune 500 402
Global Reporting Initiative (GRI) 387, 388, 412,
    420, 422–28, 423n, *424–25*, 445
global warming 385–86, 421
GMAT scores 505–6
going concern modification (GCM) 466–67

Goldberg, L. 37
Goldman Sachs JBWere 480
Gonedes, Nick 504
Goodman, C. 358, 359, 364
Goodyear, Chip 338
Gordon, B. 337
government 296–97, 300, 364, 528, 537,
    542–46
Government Accounting Standards Board
    (US) 364
GPI (Genuine Progress Indicator) 422
Grady, P. 9, 191n, 215
Grant, E.B. 483
Grant Thornton 399
Gray, Rob 8, 11n, 12, 16, 20, 47, 85, 166n, 169n,
    226, 245, 303, 320, 321, 327, 337, 339, 345,
    350, 393, 395, 400, 405, 407n, 412, 414, 415,
    417, 429, 533–35
Gray, S.J. 135–36, 138–43
Greene, D. 409
Green Paper on Law Reform (UK) 218
GRI (Global Reporting Initiative) 387, 388, 412,
    420, 422–28, 423n, *424–25*, 445
GRI Guidelines 423
Gross Domestic Product (GDP) 420–21
Group of 100 84, 428
Group of Seven 113
GTech 442
Gustavson, S.G. 512
Guthrie, J. 322, 383, 534, 550

H
Hagerman, R. 271
Haiti 443
Hakansson, N.H. 61n
Hall, Stephen 416
Hall, Wayne 82
Hamid, S. 137n, 144–45
Handel, W. 49–50, 234
harmonisation, in international accounting 106,
    109–10
Harris, K. 8, 10
Harris, T.S. 488
Harris Scarfe 6, 276
Harte, G. 383
Hartmann, H. 538
Hasnas, J. 345n, 351n
Hatfield, H.R. 37n, 39
Hawker, Michael 66, 326, 464
Healy, P. M. 281, 282n

Moonitz, M. 9, 201, 215
Moore, D. 534
Morgan, David 327–28
Moriarty, S. 510
Morley Fund Management 409–10
Morris, R. 87, 274
Morse, D. 487
Moser, D. 514
Most, K. 215n
Mouck, T. 546
movies, accountants portrayed in 47, 47n
Mueller, G.G. 133–34
Muir, Thomas 276
multi-divisional form (MDF) 362
multinational companies 110, 148–49, 342, 353, 360
   see also entries for specific companies
multivariate analysis 507
Munich Re 385
Murphy, K. 279
Murray, David 49, 298, 418
Myddelton, David 72

N

Nagar, V. 286
Nanda, D. 286
Nasi, J. 324, 329–30, 348, 350
National Australia Bank (NAB) 395, 398, 471, 480, 542
National Institute of Accountants 540
Neimark, M.D. 88, 306, 325, 383, 540, 542, 543n, 546, 549, 551
Nelson, J. 538
neo-conservatism 543n, 543–44
Ness, K. 300
net monetary assets 173, 175, 179–81
net realisable value 217
Neu, D. 353, 360, 539
Neuman, W. R. 340
neutrality 51, 58, 89, 93, 229–30, 232–35, 322n, 547, 549
New Economics Foundation (NEF) 442
newness, liability of 331
News Corporation Ltd 84, 108
New South Wales Corporate Affairs Commission 79n
New York Stock Exchange (NYSE) 38, 38n, 274n, 483
New York Times 465
New Zealand 198, 219, 300
nexus of contracts 267–69
Nigeria 443
Nike 330, 341, 410, 440, 442, 443, 444

Nobes, C. 107, 109, 110, 126, 126n, 128, 134, 146, 146n, 147, 151, 152, 153
Nokia 387
non-current assets 166, 183n, 184
non-disclosure tendency 286–87
non-monetary assets 172–75, 175, 189, 202
non-monetary liabilities 173
normal returns 473, 473n
normative isomorphism 359, 362, 366
normative research 10, 256, 260
normative theories 10n, 12, 164
   changing prices and 162–206
   conceptual frameworks as 21, 208–52
   criticism of 14–15, 164
   defined 4, 12
   empirical testing of, difficulty with 24
   logical evaluation of 19
   positive theories compared with 164n, 256, 257, 259–61
   relationship between practice and 530–31
   Stakeholder Theory as 347–50
   sustainability as a normative position 341
   see also entries for specific theories
North Parks 344
Norwalk Agreement 121n
NRMA 273, 342, 343
Nussbaumer, N. 217

O

objectivity 44, 51, 58, 78, 89, 93, 232–35, 547, 549
observation 7–8, 10, 15, 18, 19
Ocampo, E. 360
occupational health and safety 338, 439
Odean, Terrance 517
O'Donovan, G. 330, 331, 332, 341, 344
O'Dwyer, B. 7, 40, 91, 344, 403, 406, 411, 412, 545
off balance sheet funding 46
oil companies 273, 295–96, 300–301, 336, 379, 383
Ok Tedi 344, 344n
O'Leary, T. 320
One Parent Families 354, 356
One.Tel 6, 545
open-systems theories 318–77, *321*
   see also entries for specific theories
operating costs 60
opportunistic perspective 19, 45–46, 266n, 267, 274–77, 278, 287, 300n, 460